Y

Also available in Pan Books

WORLD COOKERY – Marguerite Patten
LEARNING TO COOK – Marguerite Patten
DEEP-FREEZE COOKERY – Marika Hanbury Tenison
THE CORDON BLEU BOOK OF
JAMS, PRESERVES AND PICKLES –
Rosemary Hume and Muriel Downes
SIX ROBERT CARRIER PARTY BOOKS
MISS READ'S COUNTRY COOKING

MRS BEETON'S
ALL ABOUT COOKERY

COMPLETE & UNABRIDGED

PAN BOOKS LTD : LONDON

First published 1961 by Ward Lock & Co. Ltd.
This edition published 1963 by Pan Books Ltd.,
33 Tothill Street, London, S.W.1

ISBN 0 330 43009 2

2nd Printing 1964
3rd Printing 1968
4th Printing 1968
5th Printing 1970
6th Printing 1972

PRINTED AND BOUND IN ENGLAND BY
HAZELL WATSON AND VINEY LTD
AYLESBURY, BUCKS

CONTENTS

	page
NUTRITION	11
THE KITCHEN	16
KITCHEN CRAFT	31
CARVING	55
HORS D'ŒUVRES	60
SOUPS	67
SAUCES, GRAVIES AND FORCEMEATS	91
FISH	113
MEAT	144
BEEF	147
LAMB AND MUTTON	162
PORK	173
VEAL	179
COLD MEAT DISHES AND POTTED MEATS	186
POULTRY	190
HARE AND RABBIT	205
VEGETABLES	209
SALADS AND SALAD DRESSINGS	237
HOT SWEETS	246
COLD SWEETS	278
ICES	300

DESSERT	305
BAKING	306
CAKE-MAKING	314
PASTRY-MAKING	338
SAVOURIES AND APPETIZERS	353
BREAKFAST AND SUPPER DISHES	360
CEREALS, RISOTTOS AND PASTA	366
RÉCHAUFFÉS	369
PRESERVES	376
BOTTLING	387
PICKLES, CHUTNEYS, SAUCES	392
DAIRY PRODUCE	397
PRESSURE COOKERY	411
BEVERAGES	412
COMMONWEALTH COOKERY	415
INDEX	419

ILLUSTRATIONS IN PHOTOGRAVURE

(between pages 216 and 217)

PLATE 1   Gas, electric and solid fuel cookers

2   Kitchen utensils

3   Cake tins, moulds, etc.

4   Dressing a crab

5   Making a raised pie

6   Making beefsteak pudding

7   Jointing a chicken

8 & 9   Dressing poultry

10   Dressing a hare

11   Jointing a hare or rabbit

12   Making short crust pastry

13   Making flaky pastry

14   Icing a cake

15   Making a flan case

16   Decorating tarts

ACKNOWLEDGEMENTS

The illustrations have always been a feature of earlier editions of this work and many photographs were taken by Ward Lock staff to illustrate this new edition. In addition we are indebted to the following firms and authorities for kindly supplying the plates indicated.

The Gas Council (plate 1, top right); Creda Domestic Appliances (plate 1, bottom right); Sofono, Federated Foundries Ltd. (plate 1, top left); Macfisheries Ltd. (plate 4); Tate and Lyle Ltd. (plate 14).

We should also like to thank the following firms for offering facilities to take photographs or for providing material for photographs: Staines Kitchen Equipment Co. Ltd., S.W.1; National Federation of Meat Traders' Associations; The Fatstock Marketing Corporation Ltd.

The following institutions and firms have also rendered valuable assistance: The Flour Advisory Bureau; Frigidaire Division of General Motors Limited; Kelvinator Ltd.; the White Fish Authority; the Superintendent, Billingsgate Fish Market; G.E.C.; Hotpoint Electric Appliance Co. Ltd.; the Coffee Publicity Association; Prestcold Refrigeration; the Gas Council; the British Electricity Development Association; Walls Ice Cream Ltd.

NUTRITION

A BALANCED DIET

ALL kinds of food should normally be included in the family menus, as with variety it is unlikely that any of the essential substances will be missed and the danger of monotonous meal planning will be avoided. The daily menus should contain a selection of foods from all sections of Table I (p. 13).

MENU SUGGESTIONS

Breakfast: The breakfast of porridge, other cereal dish, or fruit with cereal, followed by tomato, egg, bacon or fish, or a combination of any two of these and toast, butter and marmalade with tea or coffee, is an adequately balanced meal with which to start the day.

Main meal: The main meal of the day, whether midday or evening, should contain meat or fish or an equivalent source of protein served with potatoes and a second or even a third vegetable. This is usually followed by a second course planned to give extra energy with a light first course or to avoid heaviness after, for example, a meal of roast meat and Yorkshire pudding.

Third meal: The third meal should again, if possible, contain either meat, fish, cheese or egg. It is at most times of a simpler form than the main meal and it usually has a less defined pattern. This meal is often the opportunity for introducing fresh fruit or salad into the menu and for putting in a junket or similar dish which increases the milk consumption without offering too much liquid milk.

Snacks: The content of these snacks can make very important contributions when it is necessary to raise the nutritional value of the diet. Conversely it is often from these snacks that redundant food is obtained by those who find themselves more than adequately nourished. The snack meals should therefore be watched as carefully as the main meals by those who guard the family health.

Season: Although the general principles of menu planning always remain the same, it is known that a menu made out for summer differs in composition of actual foods from that made out for winter. This is because:

(*a*) foods which are in season are used, in order to reduce costs.

(*b*) in the cold weather the requirement for heat and energy is increased, with the result that heavier meals containing more carbohydrate and fat are needed.

Table II gives suggestions for a weekly menu in the winter. In the summer when it is hot, more salads and cold desserts replace some of the savoury dishes and the heavier baked desserts.

COOKING METHODS

In order that good food may be used to the best advantage it must be cooked well, and served attractively. This is of particular importance with an invalid, as usually the appetite needs to be tempted to encourage an adequate intake of food. The methods of cooking and serving food not only influence the flavour, colour and texture, but also the nutritive value.

SERVICE OF FOOD

Although the food may have been cooked carefully to contain the maximum amount of vitamins and minerals, if it is allowed to stand about for some time before it is eaten more than half the nutritive value is often lost. Unpleasant flavours and colours sometimes are developed in waiting about in a warm oven, or on a hot plate. It is best, therefore, to serve food as soon after it is cooked as is possible.

HYGIENE IN FOOD HANDLING

The yearly incidence of food poisoning is still too high. The three main sources of these food-poisoning bacteria are given below:

(a) The *human carrier*.

(b) The *animal carrier*.

(c) Certain foodstuffs may reach the kitchen already contaminated with small numbers of food-poisoning bacteria.

Canned goods freshly opened are safe, but if food is stored in opened tins or taken out of the tin for storage, then contamination may occur.

To cut down the risk of cross-contamination from one food to another in the kitchen, all surfaces and washing-up sinks should be capable of being easily cleaned. Plastic brushes with nylon bristles and the use of paper instead of cloths will minimize the spread of infection.

The main preventive measures are summarized below:

1. Wash the hands frequently, always after using the toilet, and always before handling food.
2. Do not touch food with the hands more than necessary.
3. Cover cuts, burns, spots with waterproof dressing.
4. Keep food stored in the cold if it is not eaten immediately after preparation.
5. Cook thoroughly all foods likely to harbour micro-organisms which cause food-poisoning (i.e. meat, meat preparations, ducks' eggs).
6. Protect food from flies, rats, mice and other animals and pests.
7. Clean all pots, pans, dishes, cutlery and glasses with a good detergent and rinse in very hot water; drain dry if possible.
8. Keep a patient's dishes separate from those of the remainder of the family. This is essential with infectious diseases, but even with non-infectious cases it is a wise precaution.

TABLE I

TABLE OF FOOD VALUES FOR A BALANCED DIET

BODY-BUILDING FOODS

Meat	Cheese
Offal	Milk
Poultry	Beans
Game	Peas
Fish	Nuts
Eggs	Wholemeal bread

ENERGY FOODS

Butter	Honey
Margarine	Jam
Lard	Sugar
Cooking fats	Dried peas
Bread	Haricot beans
Potatoes	Rice
Oatmeal	Sago
Biscuits	Macaroni
Cakes	Spaghetti

FOODS THAT GIVE CALCIUM

Cheese	Eggs
Milk	Green vegetables
Sardines	Bread—white
Herrings	Black treacle

FOODS THAT GIVE IRON

Lean meat	Bread—white
Liver	Wholemeal bread
Kidney	Black treacle
Eggs	Raisins
Watercress	Currants
Spinach	Dried Apricots
Oatmeal	

FOODS THAT CONTAIN VITAMIN A

Butter	Green vegetables
Margarine	Carrots
Eggs	Halibut liver oil
Milk	Cod-liver oil
Liver	

FOODS THAT CONTAIN VITAMIN D

Butter
Margarine
Eggs
Milk
Halibut liver oil
Cod-liver oil

FOODS THAT CONTAIN THE VITAMIN B GROUP

Liver	Milk
Meat	Cheese
Yeast	Oatmeal
Yeast extracts	Wholemeal bread
Eggs	

FOODS THAT CONTAIN VITAMIN C

Blackcurrants	Parsley
Rosehip syrup	Cauliflower
Oranges	Parsnips
Lemons	Swedes
Grapefruit	Tomatoes
Green vegetables	Potatoes
Watercress	Lettuce

The vitamin-containing foods are arranged roughly in order of their contribution to the diet.

TABLE II

Suggested Weekly Menu for the Main Meals of a Balanced Winter Diet

	Breakfast	Lunch	Dinner
Sunday	Boiled egg Toast Butter and marmalade Tea or coffee	Roast beef Yorkshire pudding Roast potatoes Gravy Brussels sprouts Egg jelly	Cream of mushroom soup Rolls Cheese and bacon savouries Raw fruit
Monday	Porridge Mince meat on toast Toast Butter and marmalade Tea or coffee	Savoury omelet Watercress and chicory Banana Brown bread and butter	Cold beef Mashed potatoes Carrots and parsnips Apple shortcake and custard
Tuesday	Porridge Bacon and egg Toast Butter and marmalade Tea or coffee	Sausage toad Junket and stewed prunes Cheese and biscuits	Steak pie Boiled potatoes Cabbage Turnips—white Steamed chocolate pudding and chocolate sauce

Wednesday	Porridge Bacon and tomato Toast Butter and marmalade Tea or coffee	Macaroni cheese Fruit salad Cheese and biscuits	Liver and bacon Brussels sprouts Mashed potatoes Gooseberry sponge
Thursday	Grapefruit Sausage and fried potatoes Toast Butter and marmalade Tea or coffee	Barley broth Fish soufflé Grilled tomatoes Apple, raw Cheese and biscuits	Grilled lamb chops Chipped potatoes Spinach Carrots Lemon meringue pie
Friday	Porridge Scrambled egg on toast Toast Butter and marmalade Tea or coffee	Cream of celery soup Curried vegetables Chutney, rice Rolls and butter	Fried fillet of cod Green peas Mashed potatoes Apple crumble
Saturday	Stewed apples and cornflakes Poached egg on toast Toast Butter and marmalade Tea or coffee	Meat rissoles Tomato sauce Mashed potato Raw fruit Cheese and biscuits	Fricassée of rabbit Jacket potatoes Swedes Pear upside-down

THE KITCHEN

PLANNING THE KITCHEN

IT is difficult to lay down hard-and-fast rules about how to plan kitchens that meet the ever-changing patterns of modern living. Social requirements as well as the design of domestic equipment are altering all the time, and if the kitchen is to remain the "hub of the house" it must adapt itself with them.

There are certain fundamental questions to which the planner must find the answers before beginning, and it is the interpretation of these answers that makes the difference between a well-planned, labour-saving kitchen and one that is a constant source of annoyance to its user. These questions are only three in number and are:

1. What part does the kitchen play in the life of the family?

There are three ways of living in the kitchen, depending on its physical limitations and the pattern of family life. It may be designed purely as a workroom, when all the other family activities go on in other rooms; it may be a room where the work is done and some or all of the family meals are taken; or it may be the real centre of the house, where the work is done, meals are taken, and where the family sit in their leisure moments.

2. What is going into the kitchen?

The equipment found in a kitchen varies with every individual family; ideally it should be tailored to the person who is going to use it, but this is often difficult if standard units are installed.

Sinks: Great advances have been made recently in the materials of which sinks are made: plastic and nylon ones are available, and there is an application of plastic on steel, all of which may supersede the vitreous-enamelled or plain steel or aluminium sinks, which have certain disadvantages. Most modern sinks are made in one with the draining board; where space is not restricted a double sink with a draining board at either end is ideal.

Worktables: These may be built-in to the other fitments or free-standing, according to the available space. The smooth, hard, washable tops of modern worktables are ideal for all kitchen purposes.

Refrigerators: In recent years a refrigerator has become a necessity in most households, and if one is not installed when the kitchen is designed, it is as well to leave a space where it can be incorporated later.

Larders: Nowadays the larder is often nothing more than a ventilated food cupboard; some kind of ventilated storage is still needed, however, even if the kitchen includes a refrigerator, as there are some foods which should not be refrigerated

Laundry equipment: Most households do at least some of the weekly wash at home, and provision must be made for such things as washing machines, drying cupboards, spin dryers, ironing and airing.

Storage: The amount of storage space depends very much on the individual needs of the family, but room must be found for dry goods, vegetables, bread, cooking utensils and cutlery, dining-room cutlery, glass and crockery, cleaning equipment, linen and miscellaneous articles.

Rubbish: Rubbish disposal must be considered early on; most people still rely on the small bin under the sink which feeds the big dustbin placed conveniently near the back door, but new methods are coming into use where the refuse is ground to sludge under the sink and washed away with the washing-up water, or is incinerated on the spot.

3. What will make the kitchen a pleasant place to work in?

The short answer to this can probably be summed up in the one word "surroundings", but this includes several sub-headings, all of which must be considered.

Ventilation: Good ventilation all the year round is important. A flued appliance in the room gives adequate air changes for comfort, but where no such appliance exists some form of extraction is necessary. This may take the form of airbricks, window ventilators or mechanical extraction.

Lighting: Both normal and artificial lighting must be carefully studied so that they are, if anything, more than adequate and the housewife is never in her own light as she works.

Finishes: Modern finishes are so varied that no definite advice on the kind to choose can be given. Walls and ceilings should be easy to clean and should not reflect glare, and if possible should be semi-porous to cut down condensation. Floors should be easy to clean, quiet and resilient.

Heating: Very often the kitchen is left unheated in the assumption that the cooking and laundry processes which are carried out there will provide the heat that is required. Many jobs that are done in the kitchen, however, do not generate heat, and unless there is

a solid-fuel cooker or boiler there, some other form of background heating should be considered.

Outlook: It is becoming generally recognized that the housewife who spends a large amount of her working day in one room suffers from boredom of which she may not consciously be aware. To prevent this, modern kitchens are being built with their windows looking either on to the garden or the road outside.

GETTING DOWN TO PLANNING

Although the planner who has found the answers to all these questions is well on the way to knowing what sort of design will eventually be produced, there is still the actual placing of the furniture and appliances to be considered. First consideration there will be the way in which the work should flow.

This should always follow a logical sequence. Briefly, food should come in to be stored, go from the storage centres to the preparation centres, be made up, cooked, served, eaten, the remains cleared away, washed up, and put away. In the domestic kitchen, therefore, the sequence is as follows:

Back door → larder and refrigerator → worktable → cooker → serving table → dining-room → sink → dustbin → cupboards.

It is obviously impossible in any but the largest domestic kitchens to follow this exactly, and the whole art of planning is to adapt the arrangement of the equipment to make the best of such things as the physical and structural limitations of the room.

DRAWING THE PLAN

First, all the fitments and appliances should be measured accurately, and then the room itself, taking into account all the projections and corners which might prevent the placing of the actual furniture when it is installed. Next an accurate scale drawing of the floor plan should be made; the angle through which the doors open should be indicated and the height of windows and other projections above floor level should be marked. After this the furniture and equipment may be drawn in, taking care that they are accurately scaled, and fixing the cooker, sink and worktable before anything else. Passageways of at least 30 in. in width should be left between pieces of equipment which are not side by side, and if the furniture is not built-in there should be room to clean between the various pieces. The openings of all cupboard doors should be shown, and there should be no inaccessible places, particularly where pieces of equipment meet at corners.

COOKING BY ELECTRICITY

Modern electric cookers are not only very attractive in appearance, but they also provide instant heat at the touch of a switch which can be controlled at will.

TYPES OF ELECTRIC COOKERS

Electric cookers are made in a variety of sizes, types and colours to suit every possible requirement. Practically all cookers (with the possible exception of small table models) are available today with Automatic Time-Switch Controls, although they can be obtained without, if required. Many cookers are supplied with glass doors.

Auto-Time Controls: These are in effect electric clocks which are connected to the controls so that the oven and sometimes the heated drawer may be switched ON and OFF, or just OFF at pre-determined times. Some timers can also control the hotplates and grill. They are very simple to use: after turning the dial from Manual to Automatic Control and setting the oven ther-

mostat to the required temperature, it is only necessary to set one dial for the length of the cooking period and the other for the delay period before the cooking is required to commence. The Auto-Control will then take over.

USING THE COOKER

Boiling Plates: Most cookers are supplied with plates of two sizes, the larger plate boiling more quickly than the smaller one. When plates are all the same size, sometimes one is designed to boil more rapidly than the others. Because the whole surface of an electric boiling plate becomes hot it is advisable, especially when speedy results are required, to use a pan which covers the whole surface of the plate.

The polished aluminium or vitreous-enamelled deflectors or spillage trays can be removed quite easily for cleaning purposes.

Grill: The grill pan is always supplied with an adjustable rack which provides several grilling positions and is capable of evenly grilling quite a quantity of food satisfactorily whether the grill is controlled by a three-heat, variable heat or just an ON/OFF switch. The grill-boiler type of plate does have the added advantage of being able to keep pans boiling or simmering on top of the plate whilst food is being grilled underneath, and when the reflector plate is placed underneath the grill to deflect the heat into the top, this plate can be used as a griddle or girdle plate to make various types of scones, etc.

Oven: The majority of electric ovens will reach a baking temperature in 15 minutes.

Although most ovens have heating elements fitted in either the sides or sides and bottom, the top of the oven is, of course, slightly hotter than the centre, and just below the centre is usually the coolest part.

It is always advisable to use baking-tins which do not quite fit across the whole width of the oven. A gap at each side of about one to two inches will enable the heat to circulate freely. Food may be placed on the floors of ovens having side heat only, and will cook quite satisfactorily. All ovens have a ventilator which is permanently open to allow any moisture from the food to escape.

CLEANING AND CARE

Electric cookers are very easy to clean. Before cleaning always turn the control switch OFF. It is usually only necessary to wipe over the cooker whilst still warm with a damp cloth immediately the cooking is finished.

Periodical thorough cleaning of cooker: Normally a damp cloth wrung out in warm soapy water should be sufficient, and harsh abrasives should not be used. If the cooker is badly stained, a mild abrasive paste can be applied to the vitreous-enamelled parts.

Hob: This is usually either hinged, or will lift off so that the under side can be wiped. The majority of boiling plates and grill-boilers are of the "plug-in" type and can be removed enabling the surrounding supports to be wiped over with a well-wrung cloth. Do NOT allow any water to get into the sockets from which the plates have been removed. The boiling plates and grill-boilers must NOT be immersed in water. The warming cupboard space (or spillage tray) can be easily wiped over before the plates are again plugged into position. Some boiling plates are raised above the level of the hob and a stainless bezel or rim provides a seal between the plate and the hob. It is only necessary in this instance to wipe the recessed spillage tray incorporated

into the hob. Neither the hob nor plates are removable.

Oven: After removing the roasting-tin and oven racks, the element guards should be removed. These may consist of side guards only or there may be a guard over the bottom element too.

Parts of the oven such as the back and the top (if the grill is not in the top of the oven) which are not removable, should be washed well before the guards are replaced.

The Warming Drawer: The warming drawer can often be removed to clean underneath when necessary. The drawer itself only requires wiping over with a damp cloth.

COOKING BY GAS

Gas is an infinitely flexible fuel; the modern gas cooker takes advantage of this, and of the simplicity with which the fuel can be controlled. Any degree of heat can be obtained by turning the tap.

Automatic ignition: Every new cooker that comes on the market has automatic ignition to the hotplate taps, and many extend this to cover every burner of the cooker. All ovens are vented towards the front, so that cooking vapours are dispersed into the air and not directed on to the wall behind the cooker as they used to be. This has made it possible for the cookers to be fitted flush against the wall, so as to bring the front level with the other kitchen fitments.

Safety taps which cannot be turned on accidentally are generally fitted on all cookers, and a thermostat is universal, except on very small cookers, which have a graduated tap to help the user to find the right temperature.

USING THE COOKER

Hotplate: The cooker may have four identical burners, or four of different sizes; the former are equally efficient as fast-boiling burners or as low-rated simmering ones, while the latter are specialists. Where a griddle plate is fitted it can be used to simmer several pots at the same time. Many burners are fitted with "arrest" stops; these enable the burner tap to be turned in one movement from "full on" to "very low" without danger of the gas being extinguished.

The gas hotplate will take every kind of appliance on the market; no special pans need be bought. The only "kitchen aid" that should not be used is the asbestos mat: this causes the enamel on the bars under it to overheat and become distorted, and its use is unnecessary on modern burners, which give very even heat distribution.

Grill: Gas grills heat over a wide area and their infra-red rays are the best way to cook the expensive cuts of meat. A grill pan and a wire or semi-solid grid are supplied with all cookers.

Oven: There are three distinct zones of heat in the gas oven. The centre corresponds with the thermostat setting, the top is about 10° F. higher, and the floor or baseplate (a cooking position that is too often disregarded) about thirty or forty degrees lower.

Most ovens are heated by a single back burner, but some have one at either side; both give equally even heat distribution. To make the best use of the oven the cake trays and meat tins that are supplied with it should always be put in with their longer sides parallel with the burners or burner. For best results no tins or trays larger than those supplied should be used, but when necessary two dishes may be put on the same shelf without any great loss of evenness of heat distribution. If this is done, the two dishes should be placed side by side in back-burner ovens, and one behind the other in side-burner ovens.

All themostats are numbered in the same sequence, and use the same marks for the same foods.

CLEANING AND CARE

The practical rule of wiping down the cooker after use while it is still warm would, if faithfully carried out, prevent the necessity for anything further or more strenuous. However, this is not always possible, and spillage and grease may become burnt on to some extent. Warm water and a detergent, with an impregnated steel-wool pad, or a gentle abrasive and fine steel wool, or a nylon sponge, are the only cleaning materials required for a cooker in this condition; if very bad staining has occurred, it may be necessary to resort to a caustic paste jelly.

Burners: These need washing occasionally in warm soapy water, and care must be taken to see that any clogged holes are cleared with a sharpened matchstick or an orange stick. When burners with aluminium heads become brown they should be rubbed with fine steel wool. All parts of the grill are removable for cleaning, although the frets, the parts that get hot, will probably only need brushing with a stiff brush to remove any charred particles. Caustic jelly and soda should never be used on aluminium trims.

Oven: Excess grease should be removed from the oven with newspaper before the residue is attacked with a steel-wool pad. The oven burner is removable for cleaning, and this should be done periodically.

COOKING WITH SOLID FUEL

The large coal ranges of the nineteenth century are fast disappearing and are being replaced by modern solid-fuel cookers designed on entirely new principles.

Heat-storage Cookers: There are today two well-known firms making cookers of this type in a variety of sizes. The cookers are self-contained, free-standing and "self-setting", i.e. they require only to be connected to a good brick flue. The outer parts are made of cast-iron or steel, coated with vitreous enamel to give a smooth, clean surface which only requires wiping down and, in general, the appearance of the cooker is most attractive. The cookers are heavily insulated, so that very little heat escapes into the kitchen and the hotplates are covered, when not in use, by insulated covers, or "bolsters". These cookers maintain a very high degree of internal heat with a very small consumption of fuel, by means of a specially designed fire-box and a "heat-storage unit" or thick metal block, in which the heat is stored. They are always ready for use, and will boil a kettle for early morning tea in a few minutes. Stoking is necessary only twice in twenty-four hours, and fuel consumption is extremely low, whether burning coke, "Phurnacite" or anthracite—except for one cooker, bituminous coal is not suitable. Two or four ovens are provided for roasting, baking, etc., and also slow cooking, and some models will also supply a certain amount of hot water, sufficient for two or three baths per day.

Free-standing Cookers: These are similar in appearance to the more expensive heat-storage type cookers, the main difference being that more manipulation by the cook is necessary in order to obtain the required cooking temperatures. They take a little longer to boil a kettle after the shut-down period during the night but, on the other hand, they are less selective in fuel, as it is possible to burn bituminous coal, coke, anthracite, various manufactured fuels and even peat or wood.

Combination Grates: The modern varieties of these cookers combine a side oven, and a hotplate with an open fire, usually with a back boiler to supply hot water. Combination grates are very suitable where it is desirable to have an open fire to sit by. The appearance is not unattractive, particularly in the modern types. Most models include a movable iron plate which can be pulled over the open fire to provide a very fast boiling surface and which also allows long-period burning when the grate is not in use. Coal, coke or processed fuels can be used for combination grates, but coal has on the whole been more widely used, mainly because a long-flame fuel is better suited for distributing the heat through the flueways around the oven and boiler. These grates are economical in providing four services (oven, hotplate, hot water and open-fire heating), but care must be taken to arrange the work of the house so that calls on all four services are not made simultaneously.

Back-to-back Grates: This type of appliance can be installed in houses where the layout of the rooms allows it. The principle involves an inset fire or slow-combustion stove in the living-room, providing space heating and hot water, and the oven and hotplate in the kitchen backing on to the living-room. Heat from the fire passes through a flueway to the cooking unit in the kitchen, before entering the chimney.

Oven-over-fire Grates: These appliances are a variant of the combination grate, and have been greatly improved in recent years. The oven is placed over an open fire, which can be covered to provide the fast hotplate. The oven is heated by the hot flue gases from the fire passing around the oven on their way to the chimney, and usually a back boiler provides the hot water.

MANAGEMENT AND CLEANING

All reputable makers now provide working instructions, which naturally differ slightly from one make to another. These instructions should be carefully followed, particular attention being paid to the points concerning overheating and ash removal. Overheating should be avoided. To clean the outside of the cooker, a wipe with a damp, soapy rag is all that is required and an occasional polish when cold with furniture cream. If milk or anything acid is spilt on the cooker, this should be wiped off immediately, otherwise the enamel will be stained. The inside of the oven should be cleaned at intervals with hot water and washing soda when the cooker is cold.

FUELS

Bituminous Coal can be used on most modern appliances. "Doubles" or "Trebles" are the best sizes, i.e. 1 in. to 3 in., for cookers. Slack should be put aside to use either to bank up the fire for long periods of slow burning, or to make briquettes. These can be made at home by mixing eight parts of sifted coal slack to one of cement. Mix well with a little water, press hard into containers, leave till set, turn out carefully. They can be used for banking and should not be poked.

Anthracite is an excellent fuel for modern cookers as, although difficult to ignite, once it is well alight it will give more heat than any other solid fuel and will burn for long periods without attention. Anthracite is a smokeless fuel and

does not produce soot.

Coke varies in size and quality, but coke of correct size is very suitable for modern solid-fuel cookers. Coke requires a deep firebox, and burns best if a deep, bright firebed is maintained by refuelling fairly frequently in small quantities when cooking is being done. It is not so convenient as anthracite for overnight burning, but most cookers will bank overnight quite satisfactorily by adjusting the dampers correctly and also by making sure that the fire is de-ashed before refuelling last thing at night.

Manufactured Fuels: There is a number of reliable manufactured fuels of various kinds on the market, most of which are very suitable for solid-fuel cookers, but, if in doubt, the advice of the coal merchant should be sought.

COOKING BY OIL

New advances in the design of kitchen apparatus have brought an old method of cooking up to date. There are now available combined oil cookers and water heaters which give continuous service both for cooking and for a supply of constant hot water. They will cater for families of from six to eight people, having two large ovens (hot and simmering) and a hotplate that will accommodate six saucepans. In action they are, therefore, like the solid-fuel appliances except that they use oil.

Over a period of 24 hours the average consumption of oil is approximately 1 pint per hour (varying from $\frac{1}{2}$ pint when idle to 2 pints at high). The burner operates for from three to four weeks before it requires cleaning and then it is quite a simple operation.

There are also available stoves with single or double burners for use with Propane gas, colloquially known as "Bottled Gas".

PRESSURE COOKING

When foods are cooked in liquid or steam in an ordinary pan, under normal atmospheric pressure, the temperature cannot rise above the boiling-point of the liquid. This is 212° F. (100° C.) for water, and only slightly higher for solutions containing salt, sugar and other dissolved solids. Thus, no matter how much the heat is increased, the food can never cook more quickly. If, however, all the air can be expelled and the steam sealed in, this will create pressure in the pan, and, as the pressure increases, so there will be a consequent rise in temperature. At 5 lb. above normal atmospheric pressure, water will boil at 229° F. (109° C.), at 10 lb. the temperature will be 240° F. (115·5° C.) and at 15 lb. pressure 252° F. (122° C.). This then, is the function of a pressure cooker—a pan from which all air can be expelled and in which the pressure can be built up to give a rise in temperature. Correctly used it will give quicker cooking, a saving of fuel and a higher retention of colour, flavour and food values.

For the housewife catering for a growing family, for the business-woman and others, it is important to realize that this quick-cooking method does not mean any loss in nutritive values.

Each pressure cooker consists of a cover and base together with a trivet. Inserts in the form of perforated separators or solid containers are available so that certain foods can be satisfactorily cooked together.

A separate safety plug must be fitted to every pressure cooker and each manufacturer has his own variation, though the principle remains the same. The safety plug will come into action should an excess pressure or too high a temperature, or both, be built up in the pan.

Cleaning a pressure cooker: Washing-up in the ordinary way is all that is required for the base and inserts. Soap and detergents are suitable, though soda should not be used, as it has a harmful effect on aluminium. Should the inside of the base, the trivet or the containers become discoloured, steel wool is recommended. The cover requires a little extra care. After each use, the steam vent should be examined, to make certain that it is not blocked—running water or a skewer will clear it easily.

It should seldom be necessary to remove the gasket. If it is obvious that food has boiled over it or into the rim of the cover, then it should be washed in warm, soapy water, the rim wiped and the gasket replaced, with as little handling as possible.

Neither the cover nor the base should be left standing in water. This will spoil their fine, high polish which can always be restored by the use of a metal polish.

When the pressure cooker is ready to put away, it should be stood with the lid upside down, tilted or in the cooker, but open. To close the cover and valve prevents the free circulation of air through the cooker.

Replacements: Most manufacturers recommend that both gasket and safety plug should be replaced at regular intervals—usually at least once a year.

REFRIGERATORS

From the health and hygiene angle alone, a refrigerator should be considered a necessity and not a luxury in every home today.

The important thing to remember when using a refrigerator is to cover all the food being stored. This prevents the transference of any strong smells from one type of food to another and prevents the drying out of any of the foodstuffs.

It must be remembered that a refrigerator will keep food fresh, but is not able to make stale or bad food fresh again.

Unless ice cream is being made or ice is required quickly, a refrigerator should not be run constantly at maximum setting, but should be set at "NORMAL." or at the setting recommended by the manufacturers for normal use.

Try to site the refrigerator in a convenient position in relation to the rest of the working equipment. The heat drawn from the interior of the refrigerator has to be expelled, so it is advisable not to put it in a larder or cupboard, unless they are airy and well ventilated. Site it in a cool place away from heat if possible, because if warm air enters the cabinet each time the door is opened, ice forms more rapidly on the evaporator and defrosting must be carried out more frequently.

DEFROSTING AND CLEANING

It is essential to keep the refrigerator clean. To do this, it should be washed out and defrosted each week. In order that the refrigerator may work as efficiently and economically as possible, the ice around the evaporator should not be allowed to become thicker than a quarter of an inch.

Particular attention must be paid to keeping the inside of the cabinet clean at all times and any spillage should be wiped up as soon as it has happened. Soap, abrasives or any cleaning materials having a scent or strong smell should not be used; a little bicarbonate of soda dissolved in warm water is all that is required for cleaning out the interior of the refrigerator.

To defrost, either turn the control to the "DEFROST" or minimum position or turn off the electricity or gas. Remove all food and leave the door open; the frost round the freezing unit will then thaw out and drip into the drip tray or chill drawer under the evaporator, which can then be emptied.

When frozen foods or ice cream are being stored the defrosting process must be as rapid as possible so that they do not have time to thaw out. They should be removed, wrapped in several thicknesses of newspaper and surrounded with ice cubes whilst the refrigerator is being cleaned and defrosted.

THE HOME FREEZER

Deep-freezers can help the housewife in many ways with her catering problems; chest type and upright models of freezers are now available for domestic use, and varying in size from 4 to 10 cu. ft. capacity.

In addition to freezing poultry, meat, fruit and vegetables, such things as sponge cakes, genoese pastries (decorated with butter cream), mince pies, etc., can be prepared in readiness for Christmas three or four weeks ahead if necessary, which can be a great convenience.

LABOUR-SAVING APPLIANCES

Coffee Percolators: Coffee percolators are available in a range of styles; some with auto-controls, which allow coffee to be percolated for the desired length of time to give the strength required and to keep it hot as long as necessary.

Another coffee-maker which is quite popular is the vacuum type which is made from heat-resisting glass, and this is used either on a separate boiling plate, or over a small spirit stove.

Toasters: The ordinary type of electric toaster will toast two slices of bread at once, toasting one side at a time. It will, however, automatically reverse the bread when the doors are opened without further handling of the bread. The automatic toaster will toast two slices of bread on both sides at the same time. It is possible to obtain automatically any degree of browning required with this type. When toasted it automatically "pops up" and the toaster is switched off as this occurs.

Warming Plates: Warming plates are attractively designed from metal or heat-resistant glass, and as they have insulated feet they can be used on a table or sideboard. They will keep plates and dishes, etc., hot until required for use.

Electric Food Mixers: There is quite a range of food mixers, from the electrically powered "egg whisk" which is held in the hand, to the large mixer which can perform many tasks in the kitchen.

To obtain the greatest possible convenience from any type of mixer, it is essential to keep it permanently in position on a table or working surface beside a power socket outlet.

Rotisseries: An electrically heated rotisserie has provided the perfect twentieth-century answer to the cooking of foodstuffs by means of a rotating spit, in this case under infra-red heat without any of the disadvantages and discomforts of earlier methods. The meat or poultry to be cooked is firmly skewered on the spit, which will then rotate slowly under the heat at the required temperature for as long as desired. The heat will automatically switch off and the spit will stop rotating at the end of the predetermined time.

Infra-red Grills: Food can be quickly and effectively cooked after contact grills have been thoroughly heated. The heat is automatically controlled and steaks and chops will cook in only one to two minutes, according to the thickness and degree of cooking required.

Garbage Disposal Units: Garbage disposal units can be incorporated into sink units, and provide an excellent method of quickly and satisfactorily emulsifying garbage to enable it to pass through the normal drainage system.

Washing-up Machines: These are designed to wash, rinse and dry any type of crockery and cutlery. Hot soapy water is usually sprayed with some force on to the crockery, etc., which is afterwards rinsed in very hot water and then allowed to stand for a few minutes, when everything will be found to be dry.

THE BASIC WELL-EQUIPPED KITCHEN

There is now an almost unlimited choice of kitchen utensils on the market, and the housewife's choice of what is included in her kitchen is governed largely by the amount of cupboard space available in the kitchen, and the amount of money she can afford to spend on utensils.

We list here the utensils a young couple setting up home would require. Much will depend, of course, on the couple's way of life, the amount of entertaining they do, and the amount of cooking done in the home.

Pots and Pans

1 pt. milk saucepan with pouring lip
3 saucepans with lids—6 in., 8 in., and 9 in. diameter
1 frying-pan
1 double saucepan
1 kettle
1 coffee percolator

Cooking Utensils

1 colander
1 casserole with lid
2 pie-dishes—1 and 1½ pt. sizes
3 pudding basins—small, medium and large
1 sieve
1 pastry board
1 rolling-pin
1 chopping board
1 mincer
1 strainer
1 funnel
1 measuring jug
2 7-in. sandwich tins
1 7-in. cake tin
1 bun tin to hold 12 buns
1 meat tin } unless supplied
1 baking-sheet } with cooker
2 wire cooling trays

Kitchen Cutlery

1 wooden spoon
1 whisk
1 grater
1 large cook's knife
1 small cook's knife
1 serrated knife
1 vegetable knife
1 fork
1 potato peeler
1 palette knife or spatula
1 wide flat lifter or slice
1 solid metal spoon
1 perforated metal spoon
1 can opener
1 bread knife
1 set measuring cups
1 set measuring spoons
1 pastry brush
1 pair kitchen scissors
1 corkscrew
Pastry cutters
Icing pipes
Lemon squeezer

General

1 flour bin
1 bread bin
1 egg timer
1 tin for cakes

1 bread board
1 pair scales
1 flour dredger
1 washing-up bowl
1 garbage bin
1 tea caddy

Tableware, Glass and Cutlery

6 dinner plates
6 sweet plates
6 side or tea plates
1 meat dish
2 vegetable dishes
6 bowls for fruit or cereals
1 large bowl
6 cups
6 saucers
1 teapot
1 milk jug
1 gravy boat
1 sugar bowl
1 cruet
6 glasses and 1 water jug
6 all-purpose wineglasses
1 hot-water jug
6 large knives
6 small knives
6 tablespoons
6 dessertspoons
6 soupspoons
6 large forks
6 small forks
6 teaspoons
1 carving knife and fork
1 steel
1 butter knife
1 butter dish
1 cheese dish
6 fish knives
6 fish forks

COOKING UTENSILS

There is such a wide variety of cooking utensils on the market today that it is impossible to give more than the most general advice on choice. The old axiom that it pays to buy the best still holds good; but the best is not always the most expensive; many of the lower-priced ranges of kitchen equipment are well designed and give excellent service

The materials used for cooking utensils today are mainly aluminium, stainless steel, mild steel finished with vitreous enamel, or heatproof glass. Many accessories to the cooking process, such as bowls, colanders, etc., are made from what is loosely called "plastic". This material has many good points, and reputable makes have a long life, providing that they are not allowed to come into contact with heat.

There are certain general points which should be considered when buying new equipment. Surfaces should be smooth, and there should be no sharp corners or protuberances either inside or out; the whole utensil should be well balanced whether full or empty; handles should be comfortable to hold, and should stay cool. The question of balance is extremely important. Good balance means good stability; utensils should always stand steady on a flat surface and should never tilt towards the handle even when they are empty.

Solid electric hotplates and the hobs of solid-fuel cookers need pans with machined bases so that good contact can be obtained and the heat will not be wasted; radiant electric hotplates and all gas hotplates will take any kind of pan, but utensils with re-entrant bases, where there is a rim below the actual base of the utensil, should be avoided, as they will waste heat.

Saucepans: Probably nearly 90% of modern saucepans are made from aluminium; this is light, durable and inexpensive.

The correct saucepan should be of medium weight, strong enough to withstand being knocked or dropped, and light enough to be easy to use. Large pans should always have a knob or boss opposite the handle, so that they may be carried comfortably in both hands when they are full. Any material used for handles should be heat-resisting, in case the pans are ever used in the oven. Lids should fit well, and be of the same thickness as the pan.

Special care should be taken when buying milk saucepans. Pouring lips should be deep, and should pour positively in a well-defined stream.

Frying-pans: Most frying-pans are made from aluminium, and the chief requirement for a good one is that it should be reasonably weighted so that heat is evenly distributed over the whole base. Very light pans tend to give local hot-spots, and may warp in use.

Kettles: The main requirement for a kettle is that it should boil quickly. This can be done on gas cookers either in a very thin kettle, which is cheap to replace when it burns out, which happens fairly frequently, or in a more expensive kettle with a specially finned base with an increased heating area, which will pay for itself in the economical way it uses fuel and has a long life. Solid-fuel cookers and the solid types of electric hotplates need machined-base kettles.

All kettles should be easy to fill, and must pour well down to the last drop. The lids must stay on even when the kettle is tilted, and handles must be far enough away from the body to prevent the hand coming in contact with it when the kettle is being held in the hand.

Casseroles and *Oven-ware:* Although some casseroles are still made in earthenware the majority are usually of steel or cast iron finished in vitreous enamel, or of heatproof glass. The metal ones can be used either in the oven or on the hotplate, but most of the glass ones are only suitable for the oven. Before using a glass utensil on the hotplate it is as well to check that it is intended to be used for that purpose.

THE STORE-CUPBOARD

Although the refrigerator has become a familiar part of the kitchen it has not, and never will, entirely replace the larder; some foods are best kept away from extreme cold.

The larder must be kept cool and airy, as far away as possible from heat and steam; it must be fly-proof, and easily kept clean, as hygiene is the most important consideration in food storage.

Other things which have to be stored are vegetables, which should be kept in wire containers or on racks so that the air can circulate round them, and soaps, detergents, and cleaning materials, which must be kept well away from the food, so that it will not be tainted from the scent they emit.

PERISHABLE FOODS

Under this heading come meat, fish, and dairy produce of all sorts, which are kept either in a refrigerator or in the larder. They should be covered with greaseproof paper or aluminium foil or put in polythene bags or plastic boxes. Meat and fish should not be stored raw for any length of time, and cooked left-overs should be put on clean plates and dishes and covered before storing. Milk is sometimes a problem in the summer if there is no refrigerator; the earthenware milk-cooler is probably the best answer to this. Milk should never be left in bright sunlight or a strong light, as this will quickly destroy most of its food value. Cheese keeps well in a polythene bag in a cool place; butter, margarine and lard also need to be kept cool and covered.

GROCERIES

Most groceries are sold in well-packed cartons and containers and may be stored in these until they are opened, after which some foods should be put into air-tight tins.

The following comments on some of the staple groceries may be helpful:

Coffee is either bought ready ground in a vacuum pack; or loose, when it should be put straight away into a tin or air-tight jar; or as beans, which are then ground in a mill as required. For the emergency cupboard a tin of instant coffee is a useful stand-by.

Tea keeps best in a tin or a caddy. The right blend to buy depends partly on personal taste and partly on the composition of the water in the locality; this can have a considerable effect on the flavour in some districts.

Sugar needs to be kept in a dry place away from steam or moisture.

Flour should be kept in a dry bin, and not in the packet, once it has been opened. Both plain and self-raising flours are desirable in a store-cupboard.

Rice comes in many varieties; Patna is best for curries, Italian for risottos and pilaffs, and Carolina for sweet dishes.

Salt must be kept very dry. Table salt can be used for cooking, but ideally block salt is better for this purpose.

Dried fruit is sold either already cleaned and ready for use, or, at a slightly cheaper price in its original state. Uncleaned fruit must be washed well, dried *slowly* and picked over before use; the methodical housewife will do this as soon as possible after purchase, before storing in suitable jars.

Breakfast cereals should be kept in a dry, warm place. If they become soft, they can be quickly crisped up again by placing them in a hot oven for a few minutes.

Canned foods are useful stand-bys in the store-cupboard.

Herbs can open up a whole new field of flavour if they are introduced into cooking. For those with gardens, fresh herbs are easily obtainable but the dried varieties can be used with good results.

Flavourings and *seasonings* should also be kept in small quantities in the store-cupboard. Salt, white pepper and mustard are found in every store-cupboard but there are others which might very well be added. Black peppercorns, which are ground in a mill as required; paprika, a delicately flavoured pepper; and cayenne, a strong one, are all good seasonings to have in reserve. Cloves, cinnamon, nutmeg and ginger; vanilla and other essences; Worcester sauce; tomato purée; malt, wine and chilli vinegars; olive oil and curry paste and powder are all useful additions to the store-cupboard of the imaginative cook.

STORE-CUPBOARD STAPLES

The following list is a reminder to those starting a store-cupboard. As the staples are used up they should be replaced so that the supply is always adequate to meet a sudden demand:

Baking-powder
Biscuits—plain and sweet
Breadcrumbs
Butter
Cereals
Cheese—whole and grated
Cocoa and chocolate
Coconut—desiccated
Coffee
Cornflour
Cream—canned
Curry powder
Custard powder
Dried fruit—sultanas, raisins, dates, currants, prunes
Flavouring essences
Flour
Fruit—canned
Fruit juice—canned
Gravy browning
Herbs
Jam
Jellies—packet
Lard and/or cooking fats
Lemon juice—canned or in plastic bottle
Macaroni and spaghetti
Margarine
Marmalade
Meat—canned
Meat—extract
Milk—evaporated and/or condensed
Mustard
Olive oil
Pepper
Rice
Salt
Sauces
Soup—canned or packet
Spices
Sugar
Syrup
Tea
Vanilla essence
Vegetable colourings
Vegetables—canned and/or dried
Vinegar

WASHING-UP

The most essential requirement for washing-up is a constant supply of hot water; this should be as hot as the hand can bear for the actual washing, and very hot indeed for rinsing, so that as well as sterilizing the articles the heat can help to dry them.

The various agents used for washing-up are largely a matter of personal choice; synthetic detergents are perhaps better for this than soap, because of their greater grease-removing properties.

Before commencing to wash, food should be scraped off plates, dishes and pans, and any very stubborn particles should be put to soak in lukewarm water. Cups, glasses, jugs and teapots should be emptied, and if the glasses have contained milk, they should be given an initial rinse in cold water. After this, everything should be stacked in an orderly way on the draining-board.

Washing, rinsing, and draining are continuous operations; the temperature of the wash and rinse waters must be maintained throughout and both waters should be changed if they become dirty. The articles should be washed and then transferred immediately to the rinse water, and then put straight on to the draining-board or into a drainer. The order in which the articles are washed is important: glasses, cutlery, crockery, and finally pots, pans and other utensils which have been used in the cooking operations.

If the rinse water is really hot, as it should be, most articles will be almost dry in a minute or so, and will need only a final polish with a clean soft cloth before they are put away. Cloths should be boiled regularly, and many people prefer to dry with soft kitchen paper, so that any possibility of germs being transferred to the clean utensils is eliminated.

A FEW HELPFUL HINTS

Glass: A polish with a soft cloth will bring up the lustre on glass very well, but if the glass is dull a little vinegar should be added to the rinse water. Stained decanters should be half filled with cold tea or with water and detergent, and well shaken; finally several good rinses must be given to remove any chance of a taste remaining.

Knives: These should never be completely immersed in hot water or the cement which holds the blade to the handle may become loosened, and the handles discoloured. Some people prefer to rinse them by immersing them in very hot water in a jug, in such a way that the handles are kept out of the water.

Cake-tins: Unless they are badly stained these should never be washed at all, as this will destroy the "seasoning" of the tin and cause the next cake to be cooked to stick to it. They should be rubbed clean with kitchen paper as soon as they have come out of the oven and the cake has been removed, while they are still hot, and until every crumb has been rubbed away.

Breakages: These can be kept to a minimum by having a plastic mat in the bottom of the sink, and by using a plastic rinsing bowl and drainer. Very delicate china should be washed separately, and should be rinsed at the same temperature as it is washed.

Care of the Sink: A sink basket is an essential part of the furniture of the sink; it should be put over the drain so that it will catch everything that is emptied into it. At least once a week some disinfectant or antiseptic should be poured gently into the waste, left for five minutes, and then flushed away with boiling water.

KITCHEN CRAFT

THE COOKING OF FOOD

THERE are two basic methods of cooking food:

(*a*) in water.

(*b*) in fat; either of which may be actually constituent in the food, or supplied as a cooking medium.

The water methods include boiling, poaching and stewing, where liquid is supplied as a cooking fluid in varying quantities, according to whether it is to be consumed or not, and heated to temperatures suitable for rendering the food palatable and digestible. Steaming is also a wet method as the food is cooked either by its own juices or by steam at ordinary atmospheric or compressed pressure, being served in a moist state whatever the process.

Cooking in fat aims at producing a crisp dry-surfaced food, and is therefore usually described as cooking by "dry" methods. "Dry" frying is used to describe the use of a hot pan to extract melted fat from those foods rich in fat, such as bacon rashers, pork chops and sausages. Shallow and Deep (French) frying merely denote the difference in the depth of fat, and therefore the essential difference in temperature between the two methods. Roasting and grilling make use of the natural fat in the food, though present-day adaptations of oven-roasting require extra fat on cut surfaces, as does grilling.

Cooking in fat gives a more highly flavoured surface to food and for this reason less tender cuts of meat are often cooked by mois-ture but browned in hot fat, as in braising, where the food is cooked by steaming and roasting.

Baking is a dry method of cooking food, usually in an enclosed container.

(*a*) COOKING IN WATER

BOILING

This means ebullition or "bubbling", and actual boiling is used only on rare occasions, such as for the deliberate evaporation of sugar syrups; meat stock when making a fumet, or glaze; chutneys and sauces. Also when cooking rice and Italian pasta to be served whole and well drained, when plenty of water should be used to allow for evaporation and absorption. Green vegetables should also be cooked as quickly as possible, but in only sufficient depth of water to provide steam, and with a lid firmly in place.

All foods should be put into water at 212° F., with perhaps the possible exception of old potatoes, which tend to cook too quickly on the outside. The use of hot water shortens cooking time, saves fuel and helps to impart stronger colour and flavour to food as heat coagulates the surface proteins of meat and fish and gelatinizes the surface starch of vegetables and cereals, so preventing early losses of extractives in the water. Conversely, when making soup, food should be cut up finely to expose as much surface as possible to the water which is used cold, and heated gently so that flavours may be drawn into the liquid. The rate of boiling must be adjusted to the structure of the food.

STEWING

This term is used when food is cooked slowly in a small quantity of water or liquor either in the oven or on top of the cooker. "Casserole" cookery involves the use of a sauce as the liquid, as it is not practical to thicken the contents of a casserole after cooking unless it is truly fireproof. Stewing is a very economical method of cooking as all the flavours are retained and the lengthy process renders the toughest food digestible. Thick pans or casseroles with tight lids are essential to prevent evaporation, and seasoning must be done at the beginning. Food which is to be stewed should be cut into pieces to expose more surface to the moderate heat of the liquor. Birds and rabbits should be jointed, meat cut *across* the fibres, fruit quartered or, if small, left whole. The consistency of the liquor at the completion of the stew should be just thick enough to coat the solid ingredients and so keep them moist in the serving dish, where they should be visible and not completely submerged in an excessive amount of liquid. Thickening is achieved by the use of blended flour, etc., or by the inclusion of potatoes which fall during cooking.

Approximate proportion: 1 lb. meat to ¾ pt. water.

A stew should never be boiled.

STEAMING

Here food is cooked in steam from boiling water or from the food itself, in which case it is enclosed in a container surrounded by steam or boiling water. For example, small pieces of food (fish) wrapped in buttered paper may be steamed between two plates over a pan of boiling water, as for invalids. Foods cooked in steam must be covered to protect them from condensing steam, which would make them sodden, and they will require longer cooking than if boiled; usually half as long again. Water providing the steam must be kept boiling and replenished with *boiling* water when necessary, especially for puddings, otherwise they will be heavy.

POACHING

The process of poaching is similar to that of boiling, except that the liquid must not bubble and the food is only just submerged, the temperature being just below boiling-point.

(b) COOKING IN FAT

ROASTING

Roasting and grilling are similar methods applied to large and small pieces of food respectively when a quick, fierce heat is used. These methods are suitable only for top-quality flesh foods, as these are composed of thin muscle-fibres and even-graining of fine fat, which is quickly released by heat.

The ideal weight of a joint for high-temperature roasting is approximately 4 lb. The oven must be hot when the food is put in. Joints which require to be cooked through, such as joints of pork, veal and mutton, will need a reduced temperature after the first hour. Tender joints of beef and lamb should be cooked quickly so that the interior is served pink.

The oven should be pre-heated to 450° F., Gas 8, and the joint should be placed on a trivet in a tin in the middle of the oven. The trivet is necessary to raise the joint from the fat and thus prevent spitting fat splashing the inside of the oven.

Joints lacking in fat, such as veal, and poultry, may be kept moist by occasional basting or barding.

SLOW ROASTING OR POT ROASTING

This method is used for joints of poor-quality meat, when the temperature should not exceed 360° F., Gas 4. The meat is cooked on a trivet in a roasting tin in the oven or on a trivet in a saucepan with a little fat and a very small quantity of liquid—either stock or water. It should be covered with a lid or aluminium foil to retain the steam. If the meat is cooked in a pan it may be browned first in hot fat to give it a good colour and flavour. If cooked in the oven, uncover the joint for the last ½ hour. As these joints are cooked at a lower temperature there is less evaporation and therefore more moisture is retained in the tissues of the meat and this helps to soften the coarser muscle-fibres. The inclusion of vegetables (onions) flavours the steam, and the use of strips of green bacon placed over the top of the joint will moisten the flesh, and help to brown the surface.

BRAISING

The method is the same as for slow roasting but the cover is removed half an hour before serving and the heat of the oven increased to allow the top to brown. Alternatively the meat may be fried to brown the surface before being placed in the cooking container. The meat is cooked on a bed of roughly sliced vegetables in a little stock. The layer of vegetables, chosen for flavour, should be sufficiently thick to support the joint above the level of the stock so that the meat is steamed. Bacon rinds, bones, mushroom trimmings and a bouquet garni are utilized for flavouring, especially immature meat such as veal. After dishing, a suitable accompanying sauce may quickly be produced from the strained vegetable liquor, diluted with water, thickened with blended flour or cornflour and made piquant with tomato purée, wine, cider, etc.

GRILLING (OR BROILING)

This involves the use of a well-heated radiant; charcoal imparts the finest flavour and is used extensively for portable grills and rotisseries. For indoors, the electrically operated infra-red grill and rotisserie is considered to be the best equipment yet designed to produce meat of the finest flavour by searing and crisping the outside while retaining all the juices inside. As the food being grilled is spitted, it is essential that it is carefully arranged on the spit so that turning is smooth. If not, the food will not cook evenly and the machine will be strained. Gas and electrically heated fixed grills must be pre-heated to an even, glowing heat before food is placed under them. Grill-cuts should be not less than 1 inch thick and should be seasoned and brushed with fat before being cooked. Both sides of the food are exposed to the heat to coagulate the surface protein and sear the flesh. This forms a seal on the outside which retains the juices. Further cooking may entail placing the food farther away from the heat to allow it to penetrate more slowly. Food must not be pierced after the seal has formed (two spoons should be used to turn the meat if tongs are not available). Delicate-skinned food, such as fish, may be grilled successfully if wrapped in thickly greased foil or parchment and placed in the bottom of the grill-pan. This prevents charring of the skin and retains all the juices.

FRYING

Frying resembles grilling in that

only small pieces of food are cooked and the process is quick. In fact, the "pan-broiling" of America is comparable to dry-frying, when the hot pan is used to draw fat from the food. Fats chosen for frying must be capable of being heated to a temperature of 400° F. approximately, without burning or disintegrating. Commercially prepared frying fats, clarified dripping and some vegetable oils are all suitable. ALL fats must be heated slowly so that the heat may spread throughout the depth of fat evenly, otherwise the fat at the bottom of the pan will burn before the frying temperature of the whole fat has been reached. ALL food must be dried before being placed in the hot fat, either by shaking in a towel, or by dusting with seasoned flour, oatmeal, etc., as for oily fish, or by coating with a suitable medium which will dry on contact with hot fat, such as egg and breadcrumbs, batter or pastry. Wet foods, like fish fillets, need to be dried with flour before being coated, otherwise the coating may be dislodged by the steam forming underneath it. The choice of coating depends on the nature of the food and the method of frying. All foods fried in deep fat should be coated unless they are of a starchy nature, such as potatoes and doughnuts, to prevent any flavour of them escaping into the fat, so making it unfit for further use. A pan of deep fat is considerably hotter than shallow fat and food is consequently cooked at a higher temperature. Immediate sealing should prevent adulteration of the fat so that it may be used for many differently flavoured foods at a time: e.g. fish, apple fritters, cutlets. A frying basket facilitates the removal of food from deep fat. It should be a very easy fit in the pan, and must be heated with the fat so that food does not stick to it when put in, and does not cool the fat by being cold when lowered into the pan. Never overload the basket; only sufficient food to cover the bottom should be fried at once to avoid cooling the fat too much. Draining after frying is essential, first over the pan, then on absorbent paper, before dishing on a dishpaper.

The temperature of the fat can be tested simply, by frying a cube of day-old bread. If it becomes golden brown in 1 minute, the fat is approximately 360° F., in ½ minute the fat is approximately 380° F. *N.B.* If a fat thermometer is used, it must be remembered that it must be heated gradually in the fat and cooled slowly after use.

Generally speaking, raw foods are fried at the lower temperature to ensure thorough cooking, and re-heated foods at the higher one, as they are merely heated and only the coating needs to be cooked.

All fat must be kept clean, otherwise food will taste of the impurities, as a little fat is always absorbed. Strain through a fine mesh after each use, and clarify occasionally.

Foods fried in shallow fat must be thin enough for complete cooking merely by being turned over during frying. Turn with spoons to avoid piercing the seal and drain well when lifting from the pan.

SAUTEING

Sautéing is a French term applied to the practice of shaking food in fat while it is frying. It may be used as a preliminary method of developing the flavour of vegetables for sauces and soups, or as a method of cooking complete in itself, as in the cooking of kidneys. A well-flavoured fat must be used, as it is absorbed: butter, chicken fat rendered down, etc. A lid is used to keep in the steam to assist with the cooking of raw food, but cooked food such as sliced potatoes is usually turned in the melted fat with a fork.

BAKING

Baking in an oven subjects food to the heat radiated from the walls and top, to convection currents of hot air, and to heat conducted along shelves, baking-sheets and tins, steel skewers, etc., which is a very dry heat. There are occasions when a water bath is included for the purpose of providing insulation against this, as in baked custard.

AUTOMATIC TIME-CONTROLLED MEALS

It is possible to obtain surprisingly good results by placing food in an oven and leaving the auto-controls to switch the oven ON and OFF. Generally speaking, dishes which require approximately the same temperature and the same length of time to cook are suitable. For example, when planning a breakfast menu which will include: bacon, sausages, tomatoes, mushrooms, kippers (whole or filleted), porridge (made from the quick-type rolled oats), the bacon should be rolled so that it will be cooked ready for serving with the other dishes. Alternatively, the bacon could be rolled around the chipolata sausages. The kippers and porridge should be placed in dishes with lids or covered well with aluminium foil.

Various types of casserole dishes, any root vegetables, stewed fruit and milk puddings always produce good results cooked by this method from cold. Pies, etc., made from shortcrust pastry; sponge and batter puddings are also a success. Cakes requiring a very short cooking time (e.g. buns and scones, Swiss rolls, etc.) are not very satisfactory when placed in a cold oven.

Victoria sandwich, fruit cakes and gingerbread, etc., which require a comparatively longer time to cook, are all quite successful. With the exception of the Victoria sandwich (which will take approximately 10 minutes longer than the cooking time given in the normal recipe) they will require cooking for the same length of time as when placed in an oven at the correct temperature. The auto-timer can be used merely to switch off the oven at the end of the cooking period, which is an added convenience.

PREPARATION TERMS

To bard: To place very thinly cut rashers of fat, green (or plain) bacon on the breasts of poultry and game to prevent them from drying up when roasting, the reason being that the legs take longer to cook. Very thinly cut rashers should be tied on with string and only removed just before completion of cooking, so that the poultry or game can brown. Certain joints of butcher's meats, such as veal and lean beef, are barded for roasting. This does not obviate basting from time to time.

To baste: To pour liquid or melted fat over food during cooking to keep the food moist.

To beat: To turn cake mixtures, batters, etc., over and over with a circular motion to mix in the maximum amount of air.

To blanch: Some foods are blanched to improve their colour, others to remove some strong, undesirable flavour, and nuts such as almonds are blanched to facilitate removal of their skins. In all cases, the method is the same: immerse the article to be blanched in a saucepan of cold water (without a lid) bring to the boil, then strain the water off.

To blend: To mix smoothly. When referring to thickening liquids with flour, it means mixing the flour to a smooth paste with a little cold liquid before adding the hot liquid.

To coat: To cover completely with a thin layer of sauce, icing, etc.

To cream: To mix fat and sugar with a wooden spoon or with the hand until light and fluffy and white in colour. To mix to the consistency of whipped cream.

To devil: To rub a highly-flavoured paste—mustard, cayenne pepper, etc.—into the legs of game, poultry, etc., before grilling.

To dice: To cut (food) into small cubes. A simple method is to slice the food first, cut the slices into strips, then holding the strips together, cut into dice by cutting across them.

To dredge: To sprinkle lightly with flour or sugar.

To fold in: This means the combining of an aerated ingredient with other ingredients so that the air entrapped is retained. Place the ingredient to be folded in, on top of the whisked mixture or other ingredients. With a spoon, cut a line vertically through the centre of the mixture, take the spoon round the half of the bowl, spoon up half the mixture and lay it lightly on the other half, thus trapping the dry ingredient between two layers of whisked mixture. Repeat this process until all the dry ingredient has been folded in.

To glaze: To brush over the tops of pies, galantines, etc., with some preparation to improve their appearance. Fruit pies and buns are usually brushed over with egg and water, or milk or sugar and water; meat with a glaze made of thickened clear stock.

To grate: To rub food into fine shreds on a grater. Food to be grated should be firm.

To knead: To work dough lightly until smooth, using the knuckles.

The dough should be brought from the outside into the centre each time.

To lard: To insert strips of fat bacon into the breasts of poultry, game or into pieces of meat, to prevent them drying up when roasting. The fat bacon should be cut into short pieces about 2 in. long and $\frac{1}{4}$ in. thick, chilled well to harden them and make them firm, then inserted into the bird or meat with a larding needle. The ends should be left protruding, but they can be trimmed with scissors if they look ragged or uneven.

To mask: To cover with a thin layer—of sauce, icing, etc.

To parboil: To partly boil. The food is boiled by the normal method, but for only half the normal time, and finished by some other cooking method.

To reduce: To boil (mixtures) quickly in an open pan to reduce the amount and thus strengthen the flavour and make a thicker consistency.

To rub in: To combine fat and flour for shortcrust pastry, plain cakes, etc. First cut the fat into small pieces with a knife, then using the tips of the fingers, rub the fat into the flour. When all the lumps of fat have been worked down the mixture should resemble breadcrumbs.

To scald: To heat a liquid to just below boiling-point; to pour boiling water on to an article of food.

To score: To make gashes or cut narrow grooves, to make incisions in the surface of food.

To sear: To brown or form a hard surface on meat to seal in the juices by exposing to fierce heat, after which the heat is reduced and cooking continued.

To sieve: To rub or pass through a sieve to reduce the food to a fine consistency and to introduce air into the food. Sieving some purées is not an easy process, but it may be facilitated by mostening the purée with any liquid ingredients included in the recipe.

To sift: This is the same as "to sieve".

To simmer: To cook at just below boiling-point; only an occasional bubble should rise to the surface when a liquid is simmering.

To steep: To soak in liquid, which may be hot or cold.

To tammy: To pass sauces or soups through a tammy cloth (a cloth made of fine wool) to produce a smooth, glossy finish.

CULINARY HINTS

To clarify Butter: Put the butter into a saucepan, heat it slowly, removing the scum as it rises, and when quite clear, pour it carefully into clean and dry jars, leaving the sediment behind.

Clarified butter, or as it is sometimes called, oiled or melted butter, is often served instead of sauce with fish, meat and vegetables; it is also used to moisten the surface of many things grilled or cooked "au gratin"; for oiling moulds and baking-tins; and for sealing potted meats.

To de-salt Butter: Put into a bowl and pour over boiling water. Leave until cold. The butter will then have risen to the top of the water and can be lifted off. The water will have washed out the salt.

To clarify Fat: To clean fat, put the fat in a saucepan and cover with cold water. Bring slowly to the boil, removing the scum as it rises. Strain into a bowl and leave to cool. When the fat has formed a solid cake, remove from bowl, and scrape off the impurities which will have settled at the bottom of the cake. Finally, put in a pan and heat *slowly* to drive off any water.

To clarify Margarine for greasing purposes: Heat the margarine in a saucepan until the sizzling sound has ceased—this means that the water has been driven off and the salt has fallen to the bottom of the pan. Carefully pour the fat which is left, through muslin into a bowl. The resulting clear oil is suitable for greasing purposes and should be kept liquid over a pan of warm water.

To render Fat or Suet: Cut the fat into small pieces, put into a saucepan and cover with cold water. Bring to the boil and continue boiling until nearly all the water has evaporated, then cook more slowly, stirring occasionally. When the fat is ready it should be clear, and any piece of skin shrivelled and light brown in colour. Allow to cool slightly before straining through a fine strainer into a clean basin.

Fat may also be rendered in the oven. Cut it into pieces, place in a roasting tin in a warm oven until the fat has melted, and any piece of skin shrivelled. Strain into a clean basin, pressing the pieces of skin and tissue against the strainer to extract all the fat.

Do not have the heat too fierce for either method or the fat will burn and be spoiled.

To make Baking Powder: Mix well together 2 oz. ground rice, 2 oz. bicarbonate of soda and 4½ oz. cream of tartar *or* 2 oz. tartaric acid, and pass them through a fine sieve. Keep in an air-tight tin.

To make Breadcrumbs: Fresh white breadcrumbs: Remove the crusts from some bread that is at least 1 day old and either rub the bread through a fine wire sieve, or grate it; or rub between the palms of the hand until fine crumbs are obtained; the crusts are not used. Note: Fresh crumbs will not keep.

Dried white breadcrumbs are fresh white breadcrumbs which have been dried slowly. They may be dried in a very cool oven, or left in a warm place until thoroughly dry. They will keep for several weeks if kept in an air-tight tin or jar.

Any crumbs left over from egging and crumbing should be dried in the oven, passed through a sieve, and kept in an air-tight tin or jar for future use.

Browned breadcrumbs or raspings: Put the crusts or any pieces of stale bread in a moderate oven (350° F., *Gas* 4) and bake them until golden and crisp. Then crush them with a rolling-pin or put them through the mincer. Store in an air-tight tin or jar. Use for coating croquettes, fish cakes, rissoles, or for covering au gratin dishes.

Fried Breadcrumbs: Put some fresh, fine white breadcrumbs in a frying-pan or baking-tin, with a little butter; season with salt and pepper, and either fry or bake until well browned. Drain well on kitchen paper and serve hot with roast game.

Egging and crumbing: Food is often given a protective coating of egg and breadcrumbs before frying.

An egg, slightly beaten, is often used, but better results may be obtained by adding 1 teasp. salad oil, 1 dessertsp. milk and a little salt and pepper. Mix these together in a deep plate. Lightly flour the food to dry it, dip each piece individually in the egg coating and then toss lightly in plenty of crumbs held in a piece of kitchen paper, pressing them on firmly with the hand or knife blade. Shake off the loose crumbs. Use fine crumbs as they will adhere more firmly than coarse ones.

White breadcrumbs should be used for coating uncooked food and browned breadcrumbs (raspings) for coating food which is already cooked and only requires heating.

To make Egg Wash: Lightly beat together ½ teasp. salt and 1 egg with a fork. Use for glazing.

To mix Mustard: Mustard is usually prepared for use by simply mixing it smoothly with cold water, and it is generally considered of the right consistency when sufficiently moist *to drop slowly* from the spoon. A milder flavoured mustard may be obtained by mixing with cream or milk instead of water.

A more pungent mustard may be obtained by mixing a little chilli vinegar and cayenne with the mustard; add a good pinch of sugar to soften the flavour.

Mustard should be mixed only in small quantities, as it quickly loses its flavour and fresh appearance.

To make Panada: Put ½ pt. water, 1 oz. butter and a good pinch of salt into a small pan. When boiling, gradually stir in 4 oz. sifted flour and work vigorously with a wooden spoon over heat until the panada leaves the sides of the pan clear. Spread on a plate, and when cool, use as directed.

Panada is used to bind together ingredients which possess no adhesive properties themselves.

To make Quenelles: Use 2 dessertspoons. Dip one spoon into boiling water, shake off the surplus water, then fill it with quenelle mixture. Press the mixture from the sides and shape it into an oval shape with a knife dipped in hot water. Dip the second spoon into hot water and scoop the mixture carefully from the first spoon into the second, and place the quenelle in the pan.

To prepare Rice for Curry: Put ½ lb. Patna rice in a saucepan with sufficient cold water to cover. Bring to the boil, then strain, and hold the strainer under running cold water until the rice is thoroughly washed. Have ready 3–4 pt. boiling salted water, put in the rice, and cook for 12–15 min., then turn into a colander. Rinse with hot water, cover with a clean dry cloth, and leave in a warm place until dry ($\frac{1}{2}$–$\frac{3}{4}$ hr.), stirring occasionally with a fork.

The above is the better method of boiling rice for curry, but if time is short the following method cuts out the first boiling. Drop the dry rice into sufficient fast boiling salted water to keep it moving in the pan, boil for 7–10 min. Drain and dry as above.

To whisk Egg White: All utensils must be perfectly clean and free from grease, and once the process has been started it must be carried through without a break. Separate the egg whites from the yolks so that the whites are perfectly clean and free from egg yolk. Put the whites into a basin with a pinch of salt, then whisk until they stand up in firm peaks.

To make Meringue: To make meringue, whisk the egg whites as above and when stiff add half the quantity of sugar given in the recipe, one tablespoon at a time, whisking stiffly between each addition. Take out the whisk and lightly fold in the rest of the sugar with a metal spoon, taking care not to break down the meringue. Use at once.

Meringue is usually put into a cool oven to colour slightly, to set the egg, and to slightly caramelize the sugar.

GARNISHES

With all the gadgets and equipment now on the market, preparing garnishes is a relatively simple matter. One important point to remember is that the garnish should be prepared beforehand so that it can be arranged before the dish gets cold—work quickly.

Almonds: To prepare almonds *see* p. 315.

To make almond acorns: Dip the rounded ends of 8 blanched almonds into raspberry jam so that half is covered with jam; then dip the jammed ends into chocolate nibs.

To make Celery Curls: Cut 2–3 pieces of celery about 2 in. long. Cut lengthwise in very fine shreds or shred by drawing the pieces lengthwise over a coarse grater. Put the shreds into very cold water (iced if possible) and leave for $\frac{1}{2}$ hr. Drain the curls well.

Croûtes and Croûtons: To make croûtes: Croûtes, used as bases for entrées, are usually cut to the size of the dish in which they are to be served. Cut them from stale bread, discard the crusts, and fry or toast.

To make croûtons: Small croûtons for garnish or savouries should be cut from slices of stale bread about $\frac{1}{2}$ in. thick, in round, oval, square, triangle or heart shapes. Fry in clarified fat (preferably butter) until lightly brown, drain well and keep hot and crisp until required. They can be toasted if liked.

To make croûtons to serve with soup, remove the crusts from stale bread and cut into $\frac{1}{4}$ in. dice, fry in hot butter or fat (deep or shallow) then drain on kitchen paper until quite free from grease. Alternatively butter a $\frac{1}{4}$ in. thick slice of bread, cut it into cubes, arrange on a tin butter-side down and bake in a moderate over (350° F., Gas 4) till crisp and golden.

Decorative Ice Cubes: If you have a refrigerator and wish to add interest to fruit or alcoholic drinks, colour the water for ice cubes with a little vegetable colouring, or make the cubes with diluted fruit juice. Alternatively, half-fill the ice trays with cold water; chill, and when nearly

frozen place a cherry, a piece of
angelica or shred of orange or
lemon rind in each section; chill;
almost fill with cold water, and
complete the freezing.

To make Glaze: Strictly speaking, glaze should be made by reducing 4 quarts of stock to about
¼ pt. As this is extravagant, gelatine is often used.

Demi-glaze is made by reducing
stock until it is slightly thick and
syrupy.

Imitation glaze economical: Add
1½ oz. gelatine to 1 pt. cold water;
at once warm it gently, stirring
with a metal spoon until dissolved.
Do not allow the solution to boil
but while hot add 1 level teasp.
meat extract, 1 level teasp. yeast
extract and sufficient gravy browning to colour.

Use the glaze hot for glazing
galantines, etc.

*Note: This glaze can only be
kept for a few days.*

To skin Hazelnuts and Peanuts:
Heat the nuts under a slow grill or
in a cool oven. Rub in a cloth to
remove papery skins.

*To make Lemon or Orange
Baskets:* Take a clean lemon or
orange and with a sharp stainless
steel knife remove almost a whole
quarter segment. Leaving a strip of
rind wide enough for the handle,
remove the corresponding segment. Remove the pulp from the
lower half.

To make Lemon Butterflies:
Wash and dry a lemon. Cut thin
slices from the widest part of the
lemon and remove the pips. Cut
the slices either in halves or quarters, depending on the width of
"wings" required. Cut through the
rind in the middle of each piece
and gently pull into 2 wings without breaking into 2 pieces. A piece
of parsley may be placed in the
centre to represent the butterfly's
body.

Parsley: To chop parsley: If
parsley is chopped by the following
method, it is bright green in colour, retains most of its Vitamin C
and is chopped quickly, without
leaving a stain on the chopping
board. (1) hold a bunch of parsley
by the stalks and plunge the leaves
into boiling water. Leave for 1
min. in the water. (2) Shake the
parsley well and wring it tightly
in the corner of a cloth. (3) Cut
off the stalks and chop the
parsley.

Pistachio Nuts: To prepare
pistachio nuts *see* p. 315.

*To make a Potato Border: White
border:* Allow 3 medium-sized
potatoes for a border. Boil or steam
the potatoes, then sieve them. Add
1 raw egg yolk, ½ oz. butter, season
to taste and beat well over heat.
When smooth and creamy, allow
to cool sufficiently to handle, then
shape mixture into a long, narrow
roll, using as little flour as possible.
Arrange the roll on the serving
dish in a ring or oval form, re-heat
in the oven and use. Alternatively
put the potato mixture into a
forcing bag and pipe a round or
oval-shaped border.

Brown border: Prepare a border
as directed above, place on a
greased baking-sheet, brush over
with beaten egg, bake until nicely
browned, then transfer to a hot
dish.

To make Radish Roses: Cut off
the roots of the radishes, make 4–6
cuts down almost to the base, taking care not to cut right through,
thus cutting the radishes in pieces.
Put into cold water, preferably
iced, and leave until the radishes
open like roses.

ASPIC JELLY

1 qt. jellied veal stock   1 oz.
gelatine   bouquet garni (parsley,
thyme, bay leaf)   2 sticks of celery
2 egg whites and shells   1 glass
sherry (optional)   ¼ pt. vinegar

Let the stock become quite cold, and remove every particle of fat. Put it into a stewpan with the gelatine, herbs, celery cut into large pieces, the egg whites previously slightly beaten and the shells previously washed and dried. Whisk over heat until nearly boiling, then add the wine and vinegar. Continue the whisking until quite boiling, then reduce the heat and simmer for about 10 min., strain till clear, and use as required.

ASPIC JELLY (from gelatine)

2 egg whites and shells 1 lemon
2 chicken or veal bouillon cubes
1 qt. water 2½ oz. gelatine ¼ pt. malt vinegar 1 tablesp. tarragon vinegar 1 onion 1 carrot 2–3 sticks of celery bouquet garni (parsley, thyme, bay leaf)
10 peppercorns 1 teasp. salt

Whisk the egg whites slightly, wash the shells; peel the lemon rind as thinly as possible, and strain the juice; crumble the cubes. Put them with the rest of the ingredients into a pan, whisk over heat until boiling, then simmer very gently for about 20 min. Strain through a jelly bag.

NOTE: This jelly is used principally for lining and garnishing moulds. If too stiff it may be diluted with a little water, or sherry, when additional flavour is desired.

ASPIC CREAM

1 gill double cream 1½ gills aspic jelly 1 teasp. lemon juice pinch of white pepper pinch of castor sugar

Put the cream into a basin, stir it with a whisk, and gradually add the aspic, which must be liquid. Add the lemon juice and seasoning and pass through a tammy cloth or fine strainer.

Use for masking entrées, chicken, etc.

TOMATO ASPIC

½ oz. gelatine 2 tablesp. water
½ pt. tomato pulp ½ gill aspic
1 tablesp. meat glaze

Soak the gelatine in the water. Put all the ingredients in a saucepan over heat, stir until boiling, season to taste with salt and a pinch of cayenne pepper. Strain through a cloth or fine sieve.

Use for masking and decorating purposes.

GLOSSARY OF CULINARY TERMS

À la carte (Fr.) A list of dishes with the prices attached to each dish.

À la mode de (Fr.) After the style or fashion of, e.g. à la Française French style: à la Reine Queen style; à la Russe Russian style, etc.

Albumine (Fr.) Albumen (Eng.) Egg white.

Anglaise, à l' (Fr.) English style.

Apéritif (Fr.) Drink taken before meals.

Appetissants (Fr.) Appetizers (Am.) Small tit-bits or savouries.

Aromates (Fr.) Aromatic herbs used for flavouring, such as thyme, bay leaves, tarragon, chervil, etc.

Aspic (Fr.) A savoury jelly used for garnishing, etc.

Au bleu (Fr.) Term applied to fish boiled in salted water, seasoned with vegetables, herbs, and white wine or vinegar.

Au four (Fr.) Baked in the oven.

Au gratin (Fr.) A term, derived from the French verb gratiner, to brown, applied to certain dishes prepared with sauce, garnish and breadcrumbs, baked brown in the oven or under the grill; and served in the dish in which they are baked. The term does not necessarily imply that cheese is an ingredient although it often is.

Au jus (Fr.) A term for dishes of meat dressed with their juice or gravy.

Au naturel (Fr.) Food served without cooking or cooked plainly and simply.

Bain-Marie (Fr.) The culinary water bath. It is a large open vessel, half filled with hot water, in which saucepans containing sauces, etc., are placed so that their contents are kept nearly at boiling-point without burning or reducing.

Barbecue (Fr.) Originally the method of cooking (roasting) an animal whole; to dress and roast whole; a social entertainment where the food is cooked outside in the open.

Bavaroise (Fr.) Bavarian cream. A term applied to creams, but incorrectly used, unless custard forms their base.

Bombay duck A small East Indian fish, which when salted and cured is eaten as a relish.

Bouchées (Fr.) Literally "A mouthful". Small patties of puff pastry (petits pâtés) with savoury or sweet fillings.

Bouillabaisse (Fr.) A kind of fish stew, very popular in France.

Canapés Small shapes of fried bread, toast or pastry on which savouries, etc., are served.

Caramel (Fr.) A colouring substance made by boiling sugar.

Carmine Crimson colouring used in confectionery, etc.

Carte du Jour (Fr.) The bill of fare for the day.

Casserole (Fr.) Originally a copper stewpan, now a fireproof earthenware or glass cooking dish with a lid, used especially for stews. The food is served in the dish.

Caviar (Fr.) *Caviare* (Eng.) The salted roe of the sturgeon or sterlet fish.

Cereals All grains such as rice, wheat, oats, oatmeal, barley and semolina.

Charlotte (Fr.) A corruption of the old English word Charlyt, "a dish of custard".

Chartreuse A mixture of fruit, or meat, or vegetables, served as an entrée. A French liqueur, there are two well-known kinds—yellow and green.

Chaudfroid (Fr.) A cold entrée, a sauce for masking cold fish, game, etc.

Chipolata (It.) Small Italian sausages. Also dishes which contain Italian sausages, or a kind of mixed minced meat with which they are served.

Chowder (Eng.) A dish of American origin, consisting of boiled pickled pork cut in slices, fried onions, slices of turbot or other fish, and mashed potatoes, all placed alternately in a stewpan, seasoned with spices and herbs, claret and ketchup, and simmered.

Clam A bivalve shell-fish, several kinds of which are edible, popular in N. America.

Cochenille (Fr.) Cochineal. A liquid pink colouring substance, used for colouring creams, sauces, icing, etc.

Cocottes Small fireproof cooking and serving dishes which hold one portion.

Compôte (Fr.) Fruit stewed with sugar. A stew of small birds.

Condé (Fr. Several soups, entrées and sweets, of which rice forms an essential part, are styled "à la Condé".

Cordon Bleu (Fr.) An ancient culinary distinction bestowed on skilful female cooks in France since the time of Louis XV. It consists of a rosette made of dark blue ribbon.

Court Bouillon (Fr.) Name given to a liquid in which fish is poached; a highly-seasoned fish stock and stew.

Crêpes (Fr.) Pancakes.

Croissants (Fr.) Crescent-shaped bread rolls.

Croquettes (Fr.) Savoury mince of fowl, meat, fish or potatoes mixed with a binding ingredient, and formed into various shapes. They are usually coated with egg and breadcrumbs and fried crisp.

Croustades (Fr.) Shapes of fried bread, rice or pastry, in which various mixtures are served.

Croûtes (Fr.) Blocks or shapes of fried bread on which salmis, whole birds, etc. are served.

Croûtons (Fr.) Sippets of fried bread or toast cut into dice shapes and fried, used for garnishing dishes.

Cuisine (Fr.) Kitchen, cookery.

Culinaire (Fr.) Anything connected with the kitchen or the art of cooking.

Curaçao (Fr.) A liqueur prepared from the yellow part of the rind of a peculiar kind of bitter orange. Used for flavouring jellies, ices, etc.

Dariole (Fr.) A small tin mould. A kind of small entrée mixture, composed of a compound of forcemeat or mince, baked or steamed in these small moulds.

Dragées (Fr.) A kind of sweetmeat made of fruits, small pieces of rinds or aromatic roots, or nuts, covered with a coating of sugar icing.

Dripping The fat obtained from cooked meat or from rendering down pieces of fat.

Eclair (Fr.) A French pastry made from choux pastry filled with cream or custard.

En casserole (Fr.) A dish cooked and served in an earthenware or glass casserole.

Entrée (Fr.) A course of dishes, or corner dish for the first course; the conventional term for hot or cold side dishes. Also defined as dishes generally served with a sauce.

Epigrammes (Fr.) Used as a culinary term for breast of lamb or mutton braised and divided into small portions, egged, crumbed and fried. Also defined as a dish of alternate cutlets of the neck and breast.

Escalopes (Fr.) Thin round steaks of veal called "collops", also thin slices of any kind of meat, usually egged, crumbed and fried. Fish, meat, etc., served in escallop shells.

Escargot (Fr.) The edible vineyard snail.

Farce (Fr.) Forcemeat or stuffing.

Farinaceous Consisting or made of meal or flour.

Filet (Fr.) Fillet. The under-cut of a loin of beef, mutton, veal, pork and game. Boned breasts of poultry, birds, and the boned sides of fish are also called fillets.

Fines herbes (Fr.) A combination of finely-chopped fresh herbs, such as parsley, tarragon, chervil and other kitchen herbs; mostly used in omelets and sauces.

Flan (Fr.) An open tart.

Flapjack A griddle cake.

Fleurons (Fr.) Small half-moon shapes of puff pastry, baked, used for garnishing.

Foie gras (Fr.) Fat goose liver.

Forcemeat Stuffing.

Frangipane A substitute for custards made of eggs, milk, some flour, with lemon peel, rum, brandy, vanilla, etc., to flavour.

Frappé (Fr.) Iced (champagne, etc.). *Frapper:* To place on ice; ice (used when cooling champagne).

Fricassée (Fr.) *Fricasséed* A white stew of chicken or veal.

Frosting (Am.) Icing.

Fumet (Fr.) The flavour or essence of game, fish, or any highly flavoured concentrated substance used to impart a rich flavour to certain dishes.

Galantine (Fr.) A dish of white meat, rolled, glazed and served cold. A fowl or breast of veal, boned and stuffed with farce, tongue, ham, etc.

Garnish The decorations added to a dish to improve its appearance.

Gâteau (Fr.) A cake, usually implies a richly decorated cake.

Gelatine A manufactured substance for giving solidity to liquids.

Glacé (Fr.) Frozen, iced or glazed; coated or masked with glaze.

Glaze (Eng.) Stock or gravy reduced to the thickness of jelly; used for glazing meats, etc., to improve their appearance. Well-made glaze adheres firmly to the meat. Used also for strengthening soups and sauces.

Gnocchi (It.) Dumplings; a light savoury dough, boiled and served with tomato sauce and grated Parmesan cheese. Also fancy-shaped pieces of semolina paste used for garnishing soups and savoury dishes.

Goulash Hungarian dish. A rich meat stew.

Gourmet (Fr.) An epicure; a judge of good living; one who values and enjoys good eating; a connoisseur of wine.

Hominy A farinaceous food made of maize.

Hors d'œuvre (Fr.) Small side dishes, served cold, generally before the soup, in order to create an appetite. Large hors d'œuvre may be served as a main course.

Icing or *Glacé* Covering for cakes, etc.

Isinglass Egg preservative.

Jardinière (Fr.) A garnish of mixed spring vegetables; vegetables stewed down in their own sauce.

Julienne (Fr.) Name of a vegetable clear soup named after the 18th-century French chef, Jean Julien; also a garnish consisting of fine strips of mixed vegetables.

Junket (Eng.) A dessert made of sweetened and flavoured curds.

Jus (Fr.) Juice, broth, gravy. The juice of cooked meats seasoned, but without any thickening.

Kebobs, Kabobs, Khubab Originally name of a dish served in India and Turkey, consisting of small slices of mutton run on skewers, and either grilled or braised; now term given to any savoury items, e.g. tomatoes, sausages, slices of kidney, etc., run on skewers and grilled.

Kedgeree, Kadgiori, Kitchri, or *Kegeree* An Indian dish of fish and rice often curried.

Liquor Any liquid or juice produced by cooking, as meat liquor.

Macédoine (Fr.) A mixture of various kinds of vegetables or fruits, cut in even-shaped dice. The name is also applied to a collection of fruit embedded in jelly and set in a mould, or a fruit salad flavoured with liqueurs and syrup.

Madère (Fr.) Madeira wine. A Spanish wine very often used in cooking.

Maître d'Hôtel, à la (Fr.) Hotel stewards' fashion. The name of a butter served on grilled meats. Dishes named Maître d'Hôtel are usually composed of food quickly and plainly prepared, parsley being the principal flavouring.

Marinade (Fr.) A mixture of oil, herbs, vinegar, etc., in which fish or meat is soused or pickled.

Mayonnaise (Fr.) A kind of salad of fish or poultry, with a thick cold sauce made of egg yolks, oil and vinegar. A salad sauce or dressing.

Menu (Fr.) The bill of fare. Literally, the word means minute detail of courses.

Minute, à la (Fr.) A surname given to dishes which are hurriedly prepared or anything cooked in the quickest possible way.

Mirepoix (Fr.) The foundation bed of mixed vegetables, herbs and bacon on which meat and vegetables are braised; also a mixture of diced carrots, onions, ham sautéed in fat then added to brown soups and sauces for flavouring.

Miroton (Fr.) Thin round slices of meat, about 2 in. in diameter, braised, stewed, and dished up in a circle.

Navarin (Fr.) A stew of mutton or lamb. A kind of haricot mutton.

Noisettes Neatly trimmed, round or oval shapes of lamb, mutton, or beef not less than ½ in. thick.

Okra Name of a vegetable extensively used in South America. Used as a vegetable and also for soup.

Papillotes (Fr.) Paper cases in which food is cooked and served.

Parson's nose. The extreme end portion of the carcass of a bird.

Pâté (Fr.) A pie, pastry; a savoury meat paste or a raised pie.

Pilaf, Pilloff, Pillau, Pilaw Fish or meat with savoury rice, i.e. rice flavoured with spices and cooked in stock.

Pimiento A red Spanish pepper pod used in salads, and as garnish.

Pizza (It.) Pie; a large flat tart spread with tomatoes, cheese and often meat, anchovies, etc.

Polenta (It.) A standard Italian dish made of Indian cornflour.

Pot-au-feu (Fr.) is an economical and wholesome beef broth. It is the standard dish of all classes in France, and the origin of beef stock.

Praline (Fr.) Burnt almond.

Pulses Term for peas, beans, lentils and split peas.

Pumpernickel (Ger.) Westphalian brown bread.

Purée (Fr.) A smooth pulp; mashed vegetables or fruit; thick soup. The name is also given to meat or fish which is cooked, pounded, then passed through a sieve.

Quenelles (Fr.) Forcemeat of different kinds, composed of fish, poultry or meat, eggs, etc., shaped in various forms—balls, ovals, etc., poached, and served as an entrée or garnish to soup, etc.

Ragoût (Fr.) A rich stew of meat, highly seasoned.

Ramequin (Fr.) *Ramakin* Cheese fritter; small fondues served in china or paper cases.

Raspings Very fine crumbs made from baked bread, used with beaten egg to coat foods for frying, and for au gratin dishes.

Ratafie or *Ratafia* A culinary essence; the essence of bitter almonds. A special kind of almond biscuit. The name is also given to a liqueur flavoured with almonds.

Réchauffé (Fr.) Warmed-up food, left-over food re-cooked or re-dressed.

Rennet The name given to the prepared inner membrane of a calf's, pig's, hare's or fowl's stomach; used for curdling or coagulating milk.

Rissoles (Fr.) A mixture of minced fish or meat, enclosed in pastry half-moon shapes, and fried in deep fat. The name is now given to meat mixtures which are shaped into rolls and coated with egg and breadcrumbs before frying.

Roe Fish eggs.

Roux (Fr.) A mixture of equal quantities of fat and flour cooked together and used for thickening soups and sauces. There are 3 kinds—"white", "blond" and "brown", depending on the length of time of the preliminary cooking.

Royal Name of an egg custard used for garnishing clear soups. Also the name applied to an icing (glacé royale) made with egg whites and icing sugar, and used for coating and decoration.

Saccharometer A device for measuring the amount of sugar in a solution.

Salami (It.) A kind of uncooked sausage that is smoked or air-dried and keeps indefinitely in a dry atmosphere.

Sally Luns or *Lunn* Name of a kind of teacake, slightly sweetened and raised with yeast.

Salmi or *Salmis* A hash made of half-roasted game.

Salpicon A mince of poultry or game with ham, tongue, and mushrooms, used for croquettes, rissoles, etc., or for filling bouchées, patty cases, etc.

Salsify or Salsifis An edible plant: sometimes called oyster-plant.

Sauerkraut (Ger.) *Choucroûte* (Fr.) A kind of pickled cabbage, cabbage preserved in brine. A national dish of Germany. Served hot with bacon or sausages.

Sauté-pan, Sautoire (Fr.) A shallow cooking-pan.

Sauterne (Fr.) A French white wine much used in cookery.

Savarin. A light pudding made from a yeast mixture.

Seasoned flour Flour mixed with salt and pepper usually in the proportion of 1 tablesp. flour, 1 teasp. salt and ½ teasp. pepper.

Sippets Bread cut into crescents and triangles, then fried, used as a garnish.

Skewer A metal or wooden pin used for fastening pieces of meat together, also used for trussing poultry.

Sorbet (Fr.) An iced Turkish drink. Also the name of a water ice with fruit or liqueur flavour, usually served in goblets.

Soufflé (Fr.) A light, fluffy, very lightly-baked or steamed pudding. Also applied to light sweet or savoury creams set with gelatine and served cold, similar to mousses.

Soy A dark-brown condiment sauce, originally made in Japan; there are many English relishes in which soy is employed as an ingredient.

Spaghetti (It.) An Italian paste made into long tubes, intermediate in size between macaroni and vermicelli.

Table d'Hôte (Fr.) A general title for a meal of several courses at a fixed price. Table at which meals at an hotel or restaurant are served; common table for guests.

Tamis (Fr.) *Tammy* (Eng.) Woollen canvas cloth which is used for straining soups and sauces.

Tepid Almost blood heat, the temperature of a mixture of 2 parts cold water and 1 part boiling water.

Terrapin South American freshwater and tidal turtle.

Timbale (Fr.) Literally "kettledrum". A kind of crusted hash baked in a mould.

Toddy A punch. The fundamental juice of various palms of the East Indies; a mixture of whisky, sugar and hot water.

Tournedos (Fr.) Small thin fillets of beef served as entrées.

Vermicelle (Fr.) *Vermicelli* (It.) Very fine strings of paste, made from a wheat flour dough, forced through cylinders or pipes till it takes a slender, worm-like form, when dried; used in soups, puddings, and (crushed) for coating.

Vol-au-vent (Fr.) A light round puff-pastry case, filled with delicately flavoured ragoûts of chicken, sweetbread, etc.

Zéphire (Fr.) Name of a small oval-shaped forcemeat dumpling, poached and served with a rich sauce; anything shaped in a Zéphire mould.

Zest The coloured, oily, outer skin of citrus fruits added to cookery for flavouring. It should be very finely cut, grated, or rubbed off with lumps of sugar.

SPICES AND FLAVOURINGS

Allspice: This is the popular name given to pimento or Jamaica pepper. It is called "allspice" because its smell and flavour very closely resembles that of a combination of cloves, cinnamon and nutmeg. It may be used whole or ground.

Capsicums: Several varieties of this plant are cultivated in the East and West Indies and in America. The red chilli is the pod of the capsicum, and chilli vinegar is made by infusing capsicum pods in vinegar until some of their pungency and strength is extracted. From the same source comes cayenne pepper, obtained from the pods and the seeds, which are well dried and then ground to a fine powder.

Cayenne: This is an acrid and stimulating spice. It is a powder prepared from several varieties of the capsicum.

Cinnamon: The cinnamon tree is a species of the laurel family. When the branches are three years old they are stripped of their outer bark, the inner bark is dried, caus-

ing it to shrivel up. The bark is sold in stick form and in powdered form.

Cloves: The clove contains about 20 per cent of volatile aromatic oil, to which is attributed its peculiar pungent flavour, its other parts being composed of woody fibre, water, gum and resin. They form a well-known spice, and are much used in cookery, both in sweet and savoury dishes.

Curry: Curry is composed of various condiments and spices, which include cardamom seed, coriander seed, cumin seed, dried cassia leaves, dried chillies, cayenne, ginger, mustard seed, turmeric, cinnamon, mace and cloves. It owes its peculiar smell and bright colour to the presence of turmeric, a variety of ginger largely cultivated in the East Indies. Thorough cooking is absolutely necessary to develop the full flavour of the various ingredients.

Garlic: This is a pungent, strong-scented bulb, composed of smaller bulbs called "cloves".

Ginger: Ginger is the tuber of a perennial plant called *Zingiber officinale*. It is sold in root or ground form. Ginger is much used in culinary operations; grated green ginger is considered by epicures to be an important item in a dish of curry.

Krona Pepper: This well-known condiment is bright red in colour, with a pleasant flavour, and is less pungent than cayenne. Consequently it may be regarded as an exceedingly useful combination of flavouring and seasoning ingredients.

Mace: Mace is the outer shell or husk of the nutmeg, and naturally resembles it in flavour. Its general qualities are the same as those of nutmeg, producing a pleasant aromatic odour. It is sold in "blade" or ground form.

Mustard: There are two varieties of mustard seeds: *Sinapis nigra* (the common), and *Sinapis alba* (the white). Commercial mustard is composed of the seeds of both varieties ground and mixed together. Mustard taken in small quantities is said to stimulate the appetite and aid digestion. The pungency of mustard is not fully developed until moistened with water; its flavour is best when freshly prepared. A pinch of salt added to mixed mustard will prevent it from becoming dry, and will, in some slight degree, preserve its aroma.

Nutmeg: Nutmegs are the seeds of the nutmeg tree. They are largely used as a flavouring. Nutmegs are sold whole or in ground form.

Pepper: This valuable condiment is produced from the seed of the berries of the plant *Piper nigrum.* The plant produces both white and black pepper. The berries, when ripe, are bright in colour, and each contains a single seed of globular form and brownish colour, which changes to nearly black when dried. This is the commercial black pepper, white peppercorns being produced by further treatment, and subjecting them to certain rubbing processes, by which their dark husks are removed. It is sold as whole peppercorns or ground pepper.

Owing to the high cost of peppercorns most of the so-called "pepper" now on the market is a mixture of other highly flavoured spices.

Salt: The importance of salt as a condiment, as an antiseptic, and as a food cannot be over-estimated.

Every other condiment, no matter how desirable, may be dispensed with, or one condiment may be substituted for another, but salt is indispensable, for it makes palatable food that would otherwise be uneatable. Salt, like all other seasonings, must be used with judgment.

It is sold as block or table salt. Block salt is the purer salt and is therefore better for cooking as table salt contains other ingredients to make it run freely.

Turmeric: Turmeric is the tuber of the *Curcuma longa,* a branch of the ginger family, extensively cultivated in the East Indies. The tubers are dried and then ground to a fine powder. It is a main component of curry powder.

Vanilla: Vanilla is the fruit of a tropical orchid plant. The dried, aromatic, sheath-like pod has a delicious fragrance. It is extensively used as a flavouring for cakes, custards, puddings, chocolate, liqueurs, etc.

A vanilla pod should be stored in the sugar jar. It may be used for custard, etc., in a pan of heating milk as an infusion (dried after use and returned to the sugar jar), but if the sugar is flavoured then anything the sugar is used for is also flavoured.

Vinegar: Vinegar serves many useful purposes in cookery: it is an ingredient in many sauces, and helps to soften the fibres of tough meat. Vinegar is also an antiseptic: and taken in small quantities it promotes digestion, by stimulating the digestive organs into greater activity; but, if taken to excess, it is highly injurious.

A LIST OF CULINARY HERBS AND THEIR USES

Herb	Part Used	Purpose
Angelica	Leaf stalks	These can be candied and used for flavouring and decorating cakes and fruit
	Midribs	As a vegetable
Anise	Leaves	Flavouring soups and sweets
	Seeds	Flavouring drinks
Balm	Leaves	Flavouring soups, stews, sauces and dressings
Basil	Leaves	In salads or for flavouring soups and sauces
Bay	Leaves	Flavouring stock, sauces, puddings and custard
Borage	Leaves	In salads
	Leaves and shoots	Flavouring fruit cups and other drinks
Caraway	Seeds	Flavouring cakes, soups and sauces
Chervil	Leaves	As a garnish, in salads or for flavouring soups, entrées and sauces
Chives	Leaves	In salads or for flavouring soups, omelettes and entrées
Coriander	Seeds	In pickles or for flavouring cakes, sauces and drinks
Dill	Leaves	Flavouring soups and sauces
	Seeds	In preserves or pickles
Fennel	Leaves	As a garnish or for flavouring sauces
Garlic	"Clove" (bulb)	In salads or for flavouring soups and stews
Horseradish	Root	Flavouring sauces
Hyssop	Leaves	Flavouring soups
Marjoram	Leaves	In stuffings or for flavouring soups, stews or sauces
Mint	Leaves	As a garnish or for flavouring sauces, soups or vegetables
Parsley	Leaves	As a garnish, in salads or for flavouring soups and sauces
Purslane	Leaves	In salads or for flavouring soups and sauces
Rosemary	Leaves and shoots	In salads or for flavouring stews, sauces and fruit cups
Rue	Leaves	Flavouring fruit cups—use sparingly
Sage	Leaves	In stuffings or for flavouring soups, sauces and stews
Savory	Leaves	As a garnish, in stuffings or for flavouring stews, sauces and vegetables
Sorrel	Leaves	In salads, as a vegetable or for flavouring soups
Southern-wood	Leaves	Flavouring cakes
Tansy	Leaves	As a garnish, in salads or for flavouring cakes, puddings and stews
Tarragon	Leaves	In salads, for making tarragon vinegar or flavouring omelettes, sauces and stews
Thyme	Leaves	In stuffings or for flavouring soups and stews

WEIGHTS AND MEASURES

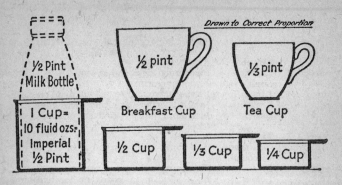

The British Standard measuring cup has a capacity of 10 fluid ounces, which is equal to the Imperial ½ pint.

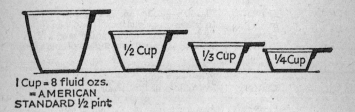

I Cup = 8 fluid ozs.
= AMERICAN
STANDARD ½ pint

The American and Canadian Standard measuring cup has a capacity of 8 fluid ounces, which is equal to the American ½ pint.

The British measuring tablespoon has a capacity of $\frac{1}{32}$ of the Imperial pint. Therefore 16 tablespoons equal the Imperial ½ pint. Three British Standard teaspoons equal the capacity of one British Standard tablespoon.

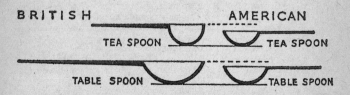

The American and Canadian Standard measuring spoons are slightly smaller in capacity than the British Standard measuring spoons. Three American Standard teaspoons equal one American Standard tablespoon.

Reproduced from Artistry in Cold Food Preparation published by The General Electric Co. Ltd. of England.

SOME HANDY MEASURES USED IN BAKING

Accurate weighing and measuring are absolutely essential to success. As many failures are due to "slapdash" weighing, it should be remembered that the food in the scale-pan must just "balance" the weight.

Ingredient	Standard Measuring Spoons			
	British Spoon		American Spoon	
		Weight		Weight
Sifted flour	3 tablesp.	1 oz.	4 tablesp.	1 oz.
Granulated, castor or superfine sugar . .	2 tablesp.	1¼ oz.	2 tablesp.	1 oz.
Sifted icing or confectioner's sugar .	3 tablesp.	1 oz.	4 tablesp.	1 oz.
Margarine or butter .	2 tablesp.	1¼ oz.	2 tablesp.	1 oz.
Rice, whole . . .	2 tablesp.	1¼ oz.	2 tablesp.	1 oz.
Cornflour or cornstarch	2 tablesp.	1 oz.	3 tablesp.	1 oz.
Syrup, treacle, molasses, warmed .	1 tablesp.	1 oz.	1 tablesp.	¾ oz.
Granulated or powdered gelatine .	4 teasp.	½ oz.	5 teasp.	½ oz.

All weights refer to level spoons. Approximate to the nearest ¼ oz.

The average modern tablespoon is equal in capacity to the British Standard measuring tablespoon and a large teaspoon is equal in capacity to the British Standard measuring teaspoon.

Spoons.—A rounded spoon means as much above the level of the spoon as below; for accuracy it is wise to measure in level teaspoons so that 1 rounded teaspoon will be 2 level ones. To talk of a "heaped" spoon is no guide at all, as one person's idea of a "heap" may be quite different from that of another person. Always divide a spoon by the length, e.g. ¼ oz. of cornflour will be half a level tablespoon—divided lengthwise.

Ingredient	Standard Measuring Cups		Homely Measures (British)	
	1 British Cup	1 American Cup	1 Breakfast-Cup	1 Teacup
	Weight	Weight	Weight	Weight
Sifted flour . . .	5 oz.	4 oz.	5 oz.	3 oz.
Granulated, castor or superfine sugar	9 oz.	8 oz.	9 oz.	6 oz.
Sifted icing or confectioner's sugar . . .	5 oz.	4½ oz.	5 oz.	3½ oz.
Margarine or lard .	9 oz.	8 oz.	9 oz.	6 oz.

All weights refer to level cups.

APOTHECARIES' MEASURES

MEASURES OF CAPACITY
60 minims = 1 fluid drachm
8 fluid drachms = 1 fluid ounce
20 fluid ounces = 1 pint
8 pints = 1 gallon

HOMELY WEIGHTS
3 halfpennies = ½ ounce (approx.)
3 farthings = ¼ ounce (approx.)

METRIC EQUIVALENTS
Weights (Approximate)
1 oz. = 30 grammes
½ lb. (8 oz.) = 225 grammes
1 lb. (16 oz.) = 453·5 grammes
2·205 lb. = 1 kilogramme
Fluid (Approximate)
½ Imperial pint = 2 2/25 decilitres
1¾ Imperial pints = 1 litre

LIQUID MEASURES
2 British Standard tablesp. = ¼ gill
4 British Standard tablesp. = ½ gill
6 British Standard tablesp. = ¾ gill
8 British Standard tablesp. = 1 gill = 5 fluid ounces = ¼ Imperial pint
4 gills = 20 fluid ounces = 1 Imperial pint
2 pints = 1 Imperial quart
4 quarts = 1 Imperial gallon

DRY MEASURES
2 pints = 1 quart
8 quarts = 1 peck
4 pecks = 1 bushel (bush.)
3 bushels = 1 sack

12 sacks = 1 chaldron
8 bushels = 1 quarter (qr.)
5 quarters = 1 load (ld.)

AVOIRDUPOIS WEIGHT
27 11/32 grains = 1 drachm
16 drachms = 1 ounce
16 ounces = 1 pound (lb.)
14 pounds = 1 stone

28 pounds = 1 quarter
4 quarters = 1 hundredweight (cwt.)
20 hundredweight = 1 ton

BRITISH CAN SIZES

No.	Approx. Net Weight	Used Principally for
Baby Food Can	4½ oz.	Strained Fruits and Vegetables
5 oz.	5 oz.	Baked Beans, Peas
8 oz.	8 oz.	Meat Puddings, Baked Beans, Spaghetti, Vegetables, Fruit
A 1	10 oz.	Baked Beans, Soups, Vegetables, Meats, Pilchards
E 1	14 oz.	Fruits, Vegetables
No. 1 Tall Can	1 lb.	Vegetables, Fruit, Meat, Soups, Pilchards, Milk, Cream, Fruit juices
1 lb. Flat Can	1 lb.	Sweet and Meat Puddings, Tongue, Galantine
A 2 Can	1½ lb.	Fruit and Vegetables, Fruit and Vegetable juices
A 2½ Can	1¾ lb.	Fruit and Vegetables
3 lb. HR.	3 lb.	Meat Rolls, etc.
A 10 Can	6¾ lb.	Fruit, Vegetables and Tongue

A 1, A 2 and A 2½ correspond with American sizes.

ABBREVIATIONS

The following abbreviations are used throughout the book, where spoonfuls are referred to, level spoons are meant unless otherwise stated.

sp.	spoonful	min.	minute
teasp.	teaspoonful	hr.	hour
dessertsp.	dessertspoonful	pt.	pint
tablesp.	tablespoonful	qt.	quart
oz.	ounce	wineglass	wineglassful
lb.	pound	liqueurglass	liqueurglassful
in.	inch		

OVEN CHART

The oven settings in the chart below have been used throughout the book. It must be noted however that the temperatures given are *indications* of oven heat conditions and, within limits, the cook can follow these safely; these limits however will vary from make to make and from one size of oven to another. Therefore the housewife must ascertain the individual variation of her oven, which, once found, can always be applied in future. For example, it may be found that a particular oven will need to be operated at a little higher or a little lower figure than that given in the recipe.

Thermostat Setting	Approximate Temperature Centre Oven	Heat of Oven
¼	240°	Very Cool
½	265°	Very Cool
1	290°	Very Cool
2	310°	Cool
3	335°	Warm
4	350°	Moderate
5	375°	Fairly Hot
6	400°	Fairly Hot
7	425°	Hot
8	450°	Very Hot
9	470°	Very Hot

Test for solid fuel or other oven without regulator:

Hot oven: (a) A piece of white paper put into the hottest part of the oven (usually the top) should become a good rich brown in 3 min.

(b) The hand held in the hottest part of the oven should begin to sting after an 8 or 9 seconds count. Suitable for bread, scones, pastry.

Fairly hot oven: The paper becomes light brown in 3 min. Suitable for small rich cakes, etc.

Moderate oven: The paper becomes yellow. Suitable for cakes of the sandwich type and for starting off large cakes.

Warm oven: The paper does not colour.

CARVING

GOOD carving is neither an art nor a science, but an acquired skill.

A knife is essentially a very finely toothed saw and it should be used in the same way, that is, drawn back and forth through the meat it is cutting. Never try to push even a sharp knife through meat without this sawing action. If the knife is sharp, the backward and forward motions can be long and light. In this way less-jagged slices are removed. Try to keep the knife at the same angle all the way through the joint and try to take a slice of equal thickness. This is not always possible, as with the first cut from a roast joint of beef.

Try always to cut across or away from yourself. Protect the left hand by using a fork, preferably a proper carving fork with a stout thumb-piece.

BEEF

When carving rolled joints of beef, leave the string and skewers in position until you have carved down to them and then if there are many, only remove those which impede the progress of further carving. Joints on the bone are carved from the outside fat towards the bone. When this is reached the knife is turned upwards and the slices gently detached. With sirloin and ribs try to carve the outside rib muscles first as these are better eaten hot. Save the central, least-cooked meat to be eaten cold for it will have a better flavour. As with most butcher's meat carve across the grain or run of the muscle. Generally this means cutting parallel to the rib bone. With boneless joints the obvious way to carve is usually the correct way.

Aitchbone of Beef: Set the joint on the wide, flat base. Take small slices towards the bone parallel to the base until a thick slice is being cut across the whole joint. At the end of each slice turn the knife blade upwards to separate the meat from the bone.

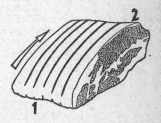

Fig. I.—Brisket of Beef

Beef Tongue: Unpressed, cut nearly through across the tongue at the thick part, and then serve a fairly thick slice. The carving may be continued in this way towards the point until the best portions of the upper side are served. The fat which lies about the root of the tongue can be served by turning it over. If *pressed,* carve thinly across the top, parallel to the round base.

Brisket of Beef (see Fig. I): The joint should be cut evenly and firmly across the bones (1–2), in slices the whole width of the joint.

Ribs of Beef (see Fig. II): Cut slices off the sides, starting at the thick end (3) and through to the other (4). The joint will be more easily cut if, before commencing to carve, the knife is slipped between the meat and the bone from (1) to (2).

Round of Beef (*see* Fig. III): A round of beef, or ribs rolled, are

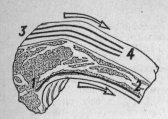

Fig. II.—Ribs of Beef

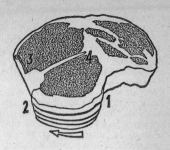

Fig. IV.—Sirloin of Beef

not so easily carved as some joints. A thin-bladed and very sharp knife should be used. Off the outside of the joint, at its top, cut a thick slice first, leaving the surface smooth: then thin and even slices should be carved to leave a level-topped joint.

Sirloin of Beef (*see* Fig. IV): Sirloin is seldom carved "on the bone" today. If it is, the carver should first slice the fillet or under-cut into a suitable number of pieces (1–2). It is best eaten hot (being rather flavourless cold).

meat from the backbone (3) and carve down towards the blade of the bone (4).

VEAL

Breast of Veal: The breast of veal consists of two parts—the rib-bones and the gristly brisket. These two parts should first be separated by sharply passing the knife through the centre of the joint; when they are entirely divided, the rib-bones should each be detached separately and served. The brisket can be helped by cutting pieces from the centre part of the joint. If boned and stuffed, carve by cutting downwards across the end of the rolled joint.

Fillet of Veal: The carving of this joint is similar to that of a round or roll of beef. The stuffing is inserted between the flap and the meat and a small portion of this should be served on each plate.

Knuckle of Veal: This is carved in the same way as a leg of lamb.

Loin of Veal: As is the case with a loin of mutton, the careful joint-ing of a loin of veal is more than half the battle in carving it. The butcher should be asked to do this. When properly jointed there is little difficulty in separating each chop. Each should carry a piece of the kidney and kidney fat.

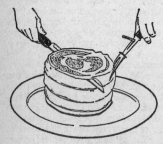

Fig. III.—Round of Beef

When the fillet has been used, turn the joint over, loosen the

MUTTON AND LAMB

Legs are cut perpendicularly to the bones inside the leg. Once one has been attempted the remainder will be easy. In the case of loins ask the butcher to "chine" them or saw across the blade parts of the bone or ask him to chop it through the joints for serving in cutlets. Should it be forgotten, use an old knife and knock the blade through between the joints where they are separated by white discs of gristle. Mutton, and to a lesser extent lamb, should always be served as quickly as possible and on very hot plates. The speed is necessary because the flavour of mutton is soon lost. The heat is required because mutton and lamb fat have a higher melting-point than other animal fats and on a cold plate solidify, leaving a semi-solid fat that coats the palate, producing a "furry" or diminished sense of taste.

Forequarter of Lamb: In carving a forequarter of lamb, separate the shoulder from the breast by raising the shoulder, into which the fork should be firmly fixed. It will come away easily by cutting round the outline of the shoulder and slipping the knife beneath it. The shoulder should be served cold. The remainder of the joint is then ready to be served as cutlets carved from the ribs.

Leg of Mutton (see Fig. V): This joint is almost invariably

Fig. V.—Leg of Mutton

carved by cutting a "V"-shaped piece down to the bone in the middle of the leg. Slices are then taken alternately from either side. Those from the thin or knuckle end will be the best-cooked. The fat will be found near the bottom corner of the thick end.

Loin of Mutton: Loin, and other similar joints, should be well jointed. Examine the loin before cooking it, and carefully joint any part that has been neglected. The knife should be inserted in the white gristle of the joint, and tapped between the bones with a steel or small hammer.

Saddle of Mutton (see Fig. VI): This consists of two loins con-

Fig. VI.—Saddle of Mutton

nected by the spinal bone. The method adopted in carving this joint, contrary to the general rule of cutting meat across the grain, is carved across the ribs, in slices running parallel with the backbone and the fibres or grain of the meat. Each long slice should be cut across into two or three pieces, according to its length; and with each portion is usually served a small piece of fat cut from the bottom of the ribs where the joint rests on the dish, and some good gravy. Red-currant jelly or mint sauce is served separately.

Shoulder of Mutton: The joint should be raised from the dish and

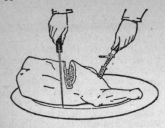

Fig. VII.—Shoulder of Mutton

slices cut parallel to the face of the meat (*see* Fig. VII). Lay the joint down and carve the meat lying on

Fig. VIII.—Shoulder of Mutton

either side of the bladebone from the knuckle end (Fig. VIII).

PORK

The remarks made about jointing loins of lamb are true of loins of pork. When carving a joint with crackling, remove a section of crackling first. Only remove as much as will expose that part of the joint to be carved hot.

Ham: In cutting a ham the carver must be guided by economy or the desire to have at once fine slices out of the prime part. To be economical commence at the knuckle end, and cut off thin slices towards the thick part of the ham, slanting the knife from the thick part to the knuckle. To reach the choicer parts, the knife, which must be very sharp and thin, should be carried quite down to the bone, at the centre of the ham.

Leg of Pork: This joint, which is such a favourite one with many people, is easy to carve. The knife should be carried sharply down to the bone, clean through the crackling, in exactly the same way as that described for leg of mutton. Carving is easier if a section of the crackling is removed.

Loin of Pork: As with a loin of mutton, it is essential that a loin of pork should be properly jointed before cooking, and the crackling must be scored. Divide into neat, even chops.

Sucking Pig: A sucking pig seems, at first sight, an elaborate dish, or rather animal, to carve; like small poultry it is mainly jointed rather than sliced. It is usually prepared by splitting in half, and the head is separated from the body. Separate the shoulder from the carcase, in the same way that the shoulder of a forequarter of lamb is raised. Then take off the hind leg; the ribs are then open to the knife and may be served as two or three helpings.

POULTRY

Larger birds are usually jointed at the wings and legs, which are served as portions or carved into slices. This is made easier if before the bird is placed on the table a small, pointed knife is worked between each joint. The joints occur at the natural bends of the limb and are quite easy to discover.

Roast Duck: A young duck or duckling is carved in the same way as a chicken. First remove the wings, then the breast should be cut off the bone in one slice, or several slices if very plump. The legs are next removed and divided at the joints. The foot, and the bone to which it is attached, is to-day rarely left on the dressed bird.

Boiled or *Roast Fowl* (see Fig. IX): Though the legs of a boiled fowl may be hidden beneath the skin, the method of carving is not affected, and the following directions may be applied to birds either roasted or boiled. The fork should be inserted firmly in the breast of the bird (1–2) and with a sharp knife a downward cut made between the thigh and the body, after which an outward turn

Fig. IX.—Roast Fowl

of the blade of the knife usually detaches the leg sufficiently to allow the joint connecting it to the body to be easily severed. Some carvers "open" the joint with a small knife before the bird is sent to table. With the fork still inserted in the breast, the next step should be to remove the wings (3–4). In doing this a good carver will contrive, by cutting widely, but not too deeply, over the adjacent part of the breast, to give to the wing the desired shape without depriving the breast of much of its flesh. When carving a large fowl the breast may be sliced (5–6), otherwise it should be separated from the back by cutting through the rib-bones near the neck. The breast should be cut across in half, thus providing two portions, to which may be added, when a larger helping is desired, a slice off the thigh. Cut length-wise into rather thin slices, the legs may be served as several portions or part-portions. To conclude the carving, the back should be turned over with the cut side to the dish, and if the knife is pressed firmly across the centre of it, and the neck raised at the same time with the fork, the back is easily dislocated about the middle. To remove the sockets of the thigh-joints (the side-bones to which are attached choice morsels of dark-coloured flesh), unless the joints have previously been opened, the tail part of the back must be stood on end, and held firmly with the fork, while the bones are cut off on either side. A fowl when boned and stuffed is usually cut across in slices.

Roast Goose: The breast of a goose is the part most liked. If the bird is large carve only the breast and save the legs and wings for cold or réchauffé dishes.

Pigeon: The knife is carried entirely through the centre of the bird, cutting it into two precisely equal and similar parts. If it is necessary to serve three, a small wing should be cut off with the leg on each side. There will be sufficient meat on the breast for a third portion.

Roast Turkey: A small turkey may be carved in the same way as a large fowl. No bird is more easily carved than a large turkey, for the breast alone may, when properly carved, supply several helpings. If more meat is required than the breast provides, the upper part of the wing should be served. When it is necessary for the legs to be carved, they should be severed from the body and then cut into slices. The forcemeat in the crop of the bird should be carved across in thin slices; and when the body is stuffed, serving is easiest with a spoon.

HORS D'ŒUVRES

THE hors d'œuvre of a meal today can either be an appetizer, grapefruit, melon, smoked salmon—or one of the dishes suggested in this chapter—or it can be a selection of these dishes, augmented by simple but colourful salads—diced beetroot, sliced tomato, Russian salad, etc. Hors d'œuvres present one of the best opportunities for the cook to show her skill and originality in combination and garnish.

When a large hors d'œuvre dish is used the ingredients should be arranged in their sections and each person left to help themselves. If, however, the proper dish is not available, then arrange the selection on individual plates.

Generally salads are "dressed" in oil and vinegar or mayonnaise, so there is no need to serve these separately.

A cold hors d'œuvre is not only an attractive, but also a very practical, first course to a meal when entertaining with little domestic help—for it can be prepared and set on the dining-table beforehand.

SIMPLE HORS D'ŒUVRES

ANCHOVIES

Lift the rolled or filleted anchovies out of the can—put on to crisp lettuce leaves. If wished coat with chopped parsley, chopped chives and a little cayenne pepper.

Allow about 3 anchovy fillets *or* rolled anchovies per person.

AVOCADO PEARS

These make an unusual ingredient for hors d'œuvres. Halve the pears and remove the stone, then cover the pear halves with oil, vinegar and seasoning. Allow to stand for a while. Alternatively try them filled with prawns as in the next recipe.

AVOCADO PEARS AND PRAWNS

2 large Avocado pears   2 tablesp. olive oil   2 tablesp. vinegar   good pinch of salt   good pinch of pepper a little mixed mustard   2 teacups (about ½ pt.) shelled prawns crisp lettuce leaves   lemon pinch of sugar (optional) ¼ crushed clove of garlic (optional)

Halve the pears. Blend the oil, vinegar and seasonings together. Toss the prawns in this, and then spoon into the pear halves. Put on to crisp lettuce leaves and garnish with wedges of lemon.

A pinch of sugar can be added to the dressing if wished, also a little garlic.
4 helpings

DEVILLED CRAB

1 medium-sized crab   1 teacup of breadcrumbs   1 teasp. mixed mustard   1 teasp. Worcester sauce 1 tablesp. oiled butter   cayenne pepper   salt to taste   cream or milk   2 tablesp. breadcrumbs extra butter

Remove the crab meat from the shell and claws, clean the shell and put it aside. Chop the meat of the crab, add the breadcrumbs, mustard, sauce, butter and a very liberal seasoning of cayenne and salt. Mix well, if necessary moisten with a little milk or cream, then turn the whole into the prepared shell. Cover lightly with breadcrumbs, add a few small pieces of butter, and brown in a fairly hot oven (375° F., Gas 5).

3 helpings
Cooking time—15 min.

CRAYFISH

Shell and serve on crisp lettuce, garnished with lemon or tossed in mayonnaise.

FOIE GRAS as Hors d'œuvre

Foie gras or goose liver, either in the form of pâté or sausage, is frequently served as hors d'œuvre. A pâté or terrine may be served plain after removing the fat on its surface, or scooped out with a dessertspoon previously dipped in hot water, and then dressed neatly on a dish and garnished with parsley. Foie gras sausage must be cut into thin slices, dished up and similarly garnished. In all cases, foie gras must be served very cold.

GRAPEFRUIT

Select sound, ripe fruit, wipe carefully, cut them in halves. Take out the pips and core; loosen the fruit from the skin. Cut the fruit into suitable small pieces but leave the pieces as if uncut in the halved skin. Sweeten to taste and, if liked, flavour with sherry poured over the fruit.

Serve in glass dishes and decorate with angelica. Keep in the refrigerator or on ice until required, if possible.

GRAPEFRUIT BASKETS

Remove grapefruit sections as described in previous recipe—mix with diced melon, diced pineapple, pieces of orange and Maraschino cherries but do not make too

sweet. Add sugar to taste. Replace in grapefruit halves. Serve in glasses topped with sprigs of mint.

SPICED GRAPEFRUIT

2 large grapefruit 1 oz. butter
1–2 oz. brown sugar ½–1 teasp.
mixed spice cherries—glacé or
Maraschino to decorate

Halve the grapefruit and loosen the pulp from the skins, discarding pips and pith. Spread with the softened butter and sprinkle sugar and spice over the top. Put for about 4 min. under a hot grill *or* for 10 min. in a fairly hot oven (400° F., Gas 6). Decorate with cherries and serve at once.

4 helpings

HERRING ROLLS

4 salt or rollmop herrings
8 anchovy fillets 2 hard-boiled eggs
1 oz. butter cayenne pepper
lemon 4–6 gherkins 1 small
beetroot parsley

If using salt herrings soak in cold water for several hours, fillet —removing all bones. If using rollmop herrings divide into 2 fillets. Mix chopped anchovy fillets with egg yolks, butter, pepper and little lemon juice. Put on to the herring fillets and roll firmly. Dip each end in finely chopped egg white. Sprinkle with lemon juice. Garnish with slices of lemon, sliced gherkin, diced beetroot and parsley.

8 savouries

LIVER PATE

1 lb. calf's or pig's liver or the livers
from poultry 4 oz. very lean ham
or bacon 1 small onion 3 oz.
butter seasoning pinch of mixed
herbs a few gherkins (optional)
1–2 hard-boiled eggs (optional)
a little cream (optional)
extra butter

Cut the liver, ham and onion into small pieces. Heat the butter in a pan and cook the liver, ham and onion for about 6 min.—no longer. Put through a very fine mincer twice to give a very smooth mixture. Add the seasoning, herbs and chopped gherkins or chopped hard-boiled eggs too if wished. For a very soft pâté also add a little cream. Put into a dish and cook for about ½ hr. in a moderate oven (350° F., Gas 4), covering with buttered paper and standing in a dish of cold water to prevent the mixture becoming dry. When the pâté is cooked, cover with a layer of melted butter.

Serve cut in slices on a bed of crisp lettuce and accompanied with hot toast and butter.

4–6 helpings

LOBSTER COCKTAIL

As for Prawn Cocktail, but use a small lobster instead of the prawns.

Garnish with the tiny lobster claws.

CREAMED LOBSTER

**1 small cooked lobster 1 oz. butter
2 egg yolks ½ gill cream or creamy
white sauce good pinch of salt
pinch of pepper pinch of grated
nutmeg 8–10 small rounds of fried
bread or toast ; or 2–3 slices of
toast parsley**

Remove the flesh of the lobster from the body and claws, and cut this into flakes. Cook in the butter for about 5 min. only—no longer as this toughens the lobster meat. Add the beaten egg yolks and cream or white sauce, the seasonings and nutmeg, and heat gently until the mixture thickens. Put on to the rounds of bread and garnish with parsley.

NOTE : Canned lobster could be used for this dish.

MELON

There are various kinds of melon served as hors d'œuvre, the cantaloup and rock melon being the most favoured. They must not be over-ripe, and should be served as fresh as possible and above all, very cold.

During the summer put crushed ice round the dish on which the slices of melon are served. Serve with powdered ginger and castor sugar.

MELON CANTALOUP AU MARASQUIN

**1 or more cantaloup or rock melons
Maraschino liqueur**

Cut the fruit in half, and put it into a glass bowl or deep dish, place it on another (flat) dish surrounded with crushed ice. Pour about 1 tablesp. of Maraschino liqueur in each half melon, then serve as hors d'œuvre with castor sugar.

If small melons are used allow ½ per person but otherwise slice in the usual way.

OYSTERS

English oysters are in season from September to the end of April and the best oysters to obtain to eat "au naturel" are the natives from Whitstable or Colchester—although during the close season in this country Continental oysters are imported.

All the oysters need, after being opened, is to be placed on the upper shell with a little of the liquor; they are then arranged on a dish, garnished with sprigs of fresh parsley, and, if possible, surrounded with ice. Thin slices of buttered brown bread, and quarters of lemon are handed round at the same time; also cayenne pepper and vinegar.

It is advisable to ask the fishmonger to open the shells for you.

PACIFIC PRAWNS

These make an unusual hors d'œuvre. If they are not already

boiled when bought, put into cold water, bring to the boil and simmer for not more than 8 min. They have a slightly sweet flavour but are not very interesting plain, they need to be served with a sauce or fried. *See* Scampi.

PRAWNS

These make an excellent hors d'œuvre—either by themselves or with a selection of some of the other small savouries in this section. Large Mediterranean prawns should be served in their shells, garnished with lettuce and lemon slices. Put finger bowls on the table in this case.

If preferred, shell the prawns, arrange on crisp lettuce, garnished with lemon. Serve with brown bread and butter and cayenne pepper.

Shrimps can be served in the same way.

PRAWN COCKTAIL

Heart of a small lettuce   ½ pt. picked prawns   ¼ gill mayonnaise 1 tablesp. tomato purée (see below) or tomato ketchup   1 teasp. chilli vinegar—if available   1 teasp. tarragon vinegar   good pinch of salt   good pinch of cayenne pepper lemon

Wash and dry the lettuce very well—pick out the tiny leaves and break into very small pieces. Arrange in cocktail glasses. Put the prawns on top. Mix the mayonnaise with the tomato ketchup or purée—to obtain this rub one large tomato through a fine sieve. Add the vinegars and seasoning. Put over the prawns and garnish with a piece of lemon and a dusting of cayenne pepper.

Serve very cold.

4 helpings

SCAMPI

These large prawns have become a very popular hors d'œuvre.

If you wish to buy fresh prawns then ask the fishmonger for Dublin Bay prawns, shell them and cook as individual recipes. If preferred, packets of quick frozen Scampi can be bought; these are uncooked, and need cooking as individual recipes. The ordinary boiled prawns are NOT suitable for these recipes.

FRIED SCAMPI

8 oz. frozen or fresh Dublin Bay prawns (weight when peeled) fat for frying   tartare sauce lemon wedges

BATTER
2 oz. flour   1 egg   ½ teacup milk salt and pepper

Separate the frozen prawns or dry the fresh prawns. To make the batter sift the flour, add the egg and milk gradually, giving a smooth thick batter. Season well. Dip each prawn in the batter and lower into really hot fat. Cook fairly quickly until golden brown. Drain on crumpled tissue or kitchen paper.

Serve on a hot dish with tartare sauce and garnish with wedges of lemon or serve with spinach (*see* p. 232).

SMOKED SALMON

1. Serve this with cayenne pepper, wedges of lemon and thin slices of brown bread and butter.

2. For an unusual hors d'œuvre, serve thin slices of smoked salmon with tiny crisp pastry cases filled with very hot and very creamy spinach.

3. Serve a mixture of smoked salmon and potted shrimp on a bed of crisp lettuce.

POTTED SHRIMPS

1 pt. shrimps—measure when picked 2–3 oz. butter   good pinch of cayenne pepper   pinch of salt grating of nutmeg   lettuce   lemon

Heat the butter and turn the shrimps in this until they are well coated, but do not cook them. Add the seasonings and nutmeg. Pour into small moulds or dishes and leave until the butter is set. Turn out on to a bed of crisp lettuce and garnish with lemon.

Serve with cayenne pepper and crisp toast.

SHRIMP MOULDS

½ pt. picked shrimps   3–4 Spanish olives   2 gherkins   1 tablesp. chutney   2 eggs   ½ pt. milk   pinch of cayenne pepper   pinch of salt 2 tablesp. cream   knob of butter

Chop the shrimps, olives and gherkins very finely. Mix with the chutney, the beaten eggs and milk and season well. Lastly stir in the cream. Coat 4 dariole moulds with butter and put in the mixture. Stand these moulds in a dish of cold water—to prevent the mixture curdling—and cook for about 25 min. in the centre of a moderate oven (350° F., Gas 4) until firm. Cool for a minute or two then turn out and serve.

These are a delicious start to a meal.
4 helpings

SOUSED FISH

1¼ lb. boiled fish or other fish left over   ½ gill fish stock   ½ gill vinegar   a few leaves of fennel (if obtainable)   2 bay leaves   2 cloves 1 dozen peppercorns   2 slices of lemon   salt   chopped parsley

Place the neatest pieces of fish in a deep dish. Boil up the fish stock with an equal quantity of vinegar, and the herbs, cloves, peppercorns, lemon and seasoning. Pour over the fish, turn fish over gently from time to time so that the seasoning gets thoroughly saturated. Serve in a little of the vinegar liquid—garnished with chopped parsley.

4 helpings

SMOKED TROUT

This makes a delicious hors d'œuvre. Buy the trout already smoked and remove the bones if possible. Serve with horseradish sauce, lemon, cayenne pepper and brown bread and butter.

SUGGESTIONS FOR SELECTION OF HORS D'ŒUVRES

ANCHOVY ROLLS

1 large thin or 2 small thin cucumbers   oil   vinegar   seasoning 1 teacup crab or lobster meat mayonnaise   small can anchovy fillets   stuffed olives   parsley

Peel the cucumbers and cut them into 1-in. thick slices. Cut out the centre portion, place rings on a dish, and pour over a little oil and vinegar; season well. Pound the crab or lobster meat, and mix with mayonnaise. Drain the cucumber shapes and fill the cavity with this mixture. Twist a whole anchovy fillet round each, and place a slice of stuffed olive on top. Garnish

with parsley.
About 10 savouries

BEETROOT CASSOLETTES

1 large cooked beetroot   vinegar oil   seasoning
FILLING
Small can anchovy fillets (well drained)   3–4 gherkins   1 hard-boiled egg   salt and pepper 1 teasp. chopped parsley   1 teasp. chopped chives if available pinch of mixed herbs

Cut 8 or so small cassolette shapes from the cooked beetroot, and cover them in vinegar, oil and seasoning. Prepare the filling by cutting the ingredients into thin strips, retaining the egg yolk for garnish. Season with a pinch of salt and pepper, oil and vinegar, and mix with the parsley and other herbs. Drain the cassolettes and fill them with the anchovy mixture. Dish, garnish with egg yolk.

8–9 savouries

CELERY A LA GRECQUE

The heart portion of 2 heads of white celery   vinaigrette sauce
1 dessertsp. finely-chopped chives or parsley

Clean the celery and shred finely. Put into a pie-dish and pour over the vinaigrette sauce. Sprinkle the chopped chives or parsley over and allow to stand for 2 hr. Arrange on a hors d'œuvre dish and serve.

About 6 helpings

CUCUMBER

1 large cucumber   salt   salad oil
vinegar or white wine vinegar
chopped parsley

Peel the cucumber thinly if wished and cut into thin slices. Place the slices on a dish and sprinkle with salt, cover, and let them remain for 1–2 hr. Drain well, dish up on small glass dishes, season with a little salad oil and vinegar. Sprinkle parsley over and serve.

10–12 helpings

EGG A LA DIJON

4 hard-boiled eggs   tomato garnish

FILLING
4 oz. cooked ham   2 oz. cooked mushrooms   seasoning

Cut the eggs in halves, remove the yolk and cut small thin slices off the bottom to make them stand properly. Make a purée of the minced or chopped ham, and mix with the egg yolks and chopped mushrooms and season. Fill the egg whites with the mixture. Garn-ish with tiny pieces of tomato and serve.

8 savouries

ROLLMOP HERRINGS

These make a most economical hors d'œuvre by themselves, and add flavour to a mixed hors d'œuvres.

6 large herrings   2 oz. kitchen salt
1 pt. water   1 pt. malt vinegar
2 large onions   2 bay leaves
4–6 small gherkins   chillies
1 tablesp. pickling spice

Clean, bone and fillet the herrings. Mix the salt and water together and put the herrings to soak in this for 2 hr. Lift out of the brine, drain and put into a shallow dish, covering with the vinegar and leaving for several hours. Shred the onions finely. Drain the herring fillets, reserving the vinegar, put 1 tablesp. of onion on to each fillet and roll firmly. Secure with small wooden cocktail sticks if possible. Put into jars with bay leaves, gherkins and chillies (use 1 per jar). Pour the vinegar from the dish into a saucepan and boil for a few minutes with the pickling spice. Cool and strain over the herrings. Cover the jars and store in a cool place. They will keep for 2–3 weeks prepared in this way. Note that the herrings are NOT cooked for this dish.

6–12 helpings—or fillets can be divided into halves for part of a mixed hors d'œuvres

OLIVES

Both Spanish and French olives are suitable for hors d'œuvres, the Spanish being considered better. Choose them large and firm and a nice green colour. Toss in a little oil and vinegar if wished but this is not essential. Those left over from a meal should be re-bottled at once otherwise they will turn black.

OLIVES A LA MADRAS

12 Spanish olives   1 oz. butter
1 tablesp. anchovy paste   2 hard-
boiled eggs   1 teasp. chutney
cayenne pepper   12 rounds fried
bread or crisp biscuits   12 anchovy
fillets   parsley

Stone the olives. Mix together the butter, anchovy paste, yolks of the eggs, chutney and seasoning. Spread a little of the purée on each croûte, and put a stoned olive filled with the rest of the mixture on each. Decorate with chopped egg white. Curl an anchovy fillet round the base of each olive, garnish with parsley.

12 savouries

RADISHES

Choose small, round and firm radishes of a light red and white colour. Trim and wash them in plenty of water. Dish up in little glass dishes. Keep in a refrigerator if possible until ready to serve.

SALADS TO SERVE IN AN HORS D'ŒUVRE

The following are suitable for serving in an hors d'œuvre: Potato Salad, Russian Salad, Tomato Salad, Cucumber Salad, Mixed Vegetable Salad, Cole Slaw, and Beetroot Salad. Recipes for these will be found in the Salad section, pp. 237–245.

SOUPS

Soup in the Menu: Soup may be served at the beginning of a dinner in which two or more other courses are to follow or it may be the main course of a simpler meal —a peasant-style lunch, a light supper or a snack meal. The soup that is the forerunner of the meal must stimulate the appetite and by the excellence of its flavour excite the gastric juices so that the following courses may be the better enjoyed and digested. The soup that forms the main course should contain a large proportion of solid foods, in fact it must be as much a stew as a soup.

The amount of soup to be served varies between $\frac{1}{4}$ pt. before a generous meal to over $\frac{1}{2}$ pt. as a main course.

Stock for Soup-making: Although it is not absolutely essential to the making of good soup, stock made from meat, bones and vegetables and, for certain recipes, from fish, provides a good basis of flavour for most soups and many sauces. An economical substitute for stock is the water in which any vegetables have been cooked.

For consommé, stock made from raw meat is essential, but for all other soups and sauces a household stock will suffice, and in this stock the inedible skin and gristle of raw meat, scraps and trimmings of cooked meat and raw or cooked bones may all be utilized.

In the making of stock (pp. 69–70) most of the flavour will be extracted from the meat in the first two or three hours of cooking. Subsequent simmering will not greatly improve the flavour of the stock although it may become more concentrated, but more gelatine and finally more calcium will be extracted, particularly if lemon juice or vinegar is added.

Classification of Soups: Although there are hundreds of different soups they can be divided into a few distinct classes. The two main groups of thin and thick soups may be sub-divided—thin soups into broths and clear soups; thick soups into purées and thickened soups.

There remains quite a large group of soups which fit into no one group; these may be termed "mixed" or "national" soups.

BROTHS are the uncleared liquids in which mutton, beef, veal, rabbit, sheep's head or chicken have been cooked. They are not thickened but may have such a large proportion of small pieces of meat, vegetables and pearl barley or rice that they may be confused with thick soups.

CLEAR SOUPS are made from good first stock and if cleared with egg white are known as consommés. Consommés must be sparkling clear; they may vary in colour from pale fawn to deep golden-brown according to the kind of meat used and they are always garnished. They take their distinguishing names from the different garnishes, of which there is an enormous variety.

PURÉES are soups in which the main ingredients are sieved to make them thick. They may often have an additional thickening, as have thickened soups. Purées are not garnished but are usually served with an accompaniment of croûtons of fried or toasted bread, or some form of rusked bread handed separately.

THICKENED SOUPS. These are thickened by various added ingredients, the chief of which are: cereal foods, such as flour, cornflour, arrowroot, barley or rice flour, semolina or fine tapioca; white or brown roux; kneaded butter and flour; egg yolk mixed with milk or cream; cream; blood, almost exclusively for hare soup. Thickened soups may or may not be garnished.

CREAM SOUP: Any thick soup, whether purée or thickened soup, may be termed a cream soup if cream has been added.

PROPORTIONS USED IN SOUP-MAKING

Meat: For first stock and meat purées and broths 1 lb. meat to 1 quart water.

Vegetables: 2 lb. vegetables to 1 quart stock *or* water.

Pulses: 4 oz. dry pulse to 1 quart stock *or* water.

Thickening: 1 oz. starchy ingredient to 1 quart of finished soup.

Approximately 2 egg yolks and ⅛ pint cream to each quart, but this may vary widely according to personal taste and economy.

2 oz. roux or kneaded butter and flour to each quart.

ACCOMPANIMENTS FOR SOUPS

Accompaniments are usually handed separately.

Forcemeat Balls are served with meat purées, notably with hare soup. *Croûtons of Bread:* Tiny cubes of bread, fried in deep or shallow fat, served hot, golden-brown. Or baked croûtons made by buttering a ¼-in. thick slice of bread, cutting it into cubes, arranging these, butter side up, on a tin and baking them in a moderate oven till golden and crisp. *Sippets or Croûtons of Toast:* The toast is to be fairly thin, crisp and golden, cut into fingers or tiny

cubes. *Fairy Toast:* Bread cut into very thin slices, baked in a slow oven till golden and very crisp. *Melba Toast:* Bread toasted golden on both sides, then carefully split into two thicknesses and slowly dried till crisp. *Pulled Bread:* The inside of a French roll pulled with a fork out of the crust, torn into rough pieces which are then dried in a slow oven until pale golden and very crisp. The crusts cut into fingers and dried make delicious rusks. *Grated Cheese:* Handed with Minestrone and other mixed vegetable soups. *Sour Cream:* Handed with Bortsch and with other Polish, Russian or Hungarian soups.

AUXILIARY RECIPES FOR SOUPS

BOUQUET GARNI or BUNCH OF FRESH HERBS or FAGGOT OF HERBS
1 sprig of thyme   1 sprig of marjoram   1 small sage leaf (optional)   1 strip of lemon rind (optional)   1 small bay leaf   a few stalks of parsley   a few chives (optional)   sprig of chervil (optional)

Tie all the herbs into a bunch with thick cotton or fine string, leaving a long piece free, which may be used to tie the bunch to the handle of the pan. Alternatively the herbs may be tied in a small square of muslin and fastened with string or cotton.

BROWNING

¼ lb. sugar   ¼ pt. water (approx.)

Dissolve the sugar very slowly in 1 tablesp. water, then boil it quickly till it is a dark brown. Add a little water and warm this gently till the caramel dissolves, then add enough water to make a thin syrup. Bring this to boiling-point, cool and bottle it. Use for colouring brown soups, sauces or gravies.

A better method of producing a brown colour and a good flavour is to fry the vegetables and meat, and often the flour, until all are of a pleasant nut-brown colour.

ESSENCES

This term means natural juices of meat and vegetables extracted by simmering in wine and then reducing them until the flavour is concentrated and the liquid slightly thick.

FUMETS

These are the same as essences but made from fish and vegetables instead of meat.

STOCKS FOR SOUP
BONE STOCK or HOUSEHOLD STOCK

(Also called Second Stock)

Cooked or raw bones of any kind of meat or poultry   cooked or raw skin, gristle and trimmings of lean meat   clean peelings of carrots, turnip, mushrooms   salt   1 outside stick of celery   1 onion   1 bay leaf   peppercorns

Break or chop the bones to 3-in. pieces and put them with the skin and trimmings into a strong pan. Cover with cold water and add ½ teasp. salt to each quart of water. Bring slowly to simmering point. Add the vegetables, including a piece of outer brown skin of onion, if a brown stock is required. Simmer for at least 3 hr., without a lid on top heat, or covered in a slow oven. Bones may be cooked until they are porous and so soft that they crumble when crushed, but they should be strained and cooled at the end of each day, the vegetables removed at once, and fresh water added next day. If the stock is not required at once it must be cooled quickly, kept cold —preferably in a refrigerator; and used within 24 hr. even in cool weather or within 3 days if kept in a refrigerator.

In warm weather it must be made as required and used at once. These precautions are necessary because stock provides an excellent medium for the growth of bacteria which can cause food-poisoning. Before use, skim the fat from the top of the stock. This fat may be clarified with other meat fat, or used as needed in meat cookery.

Quantity—1½ pt. from each 1 lb. bones, etc.

FIRST BROWN STOCK

(suitable for Consommé)

2 lb. veal and beef bones, mixed
1 lb. shin beef (lean only)   3 qt.
cold water   1½ teasp. salt   1 carrot
1 stick of celery   1 onion
½ teasp. peppercorns

Scrape the bones, remove fat and marrow and wash the bones in hot water. Wipe the meat with a damp cloth and cut it into small pieces, removing any fat. Put all into a pan and add the cold water and salt. Soak for ½ hr. Bring very slowly to simmering point and simmer 1 hr. Add the vegetables whole, including a piece of outer, brown skin of onion, and simmer for a further 3 hr. Strain the stock through a metal sieve and cool it. The remaining meat may be used in any dish requiring cooked meat. The bones should be used for household stock.

Quantity—5 pt.
Cooking time—at least 4 hr.

WHITE STOCK

2 lb. knuckle of veal   2 qt. cold water   1 teasp. salt   1 dessertsp. white vinegar or lemon juice 1 onion   1 stick of celery   ½ teasp. white peppercorns   small strip of lemon rind   1 bay leaf

Make as for Brown Stock

Quantity—about 3 pt.
Cooking time—at least 3 hr.

CHICKEN STOCK or GAME STOCK

Carcase of chicken or game bird
cleaned feet of bird   giblets   salt
cold water to cover   1 onion
white peppercorns

Make as for Brown Stock.

HARE or RABBIT STOCK

Bones of rabbit or hare   head,
heart and liver   "helmet" and flaps
salt   1 onion   1 bay leaf   1 blade
of mace   peppercorns

Make as for Brown Stock.

VEGETABLE STOCK

2 large carrots   ½ lb. onions
3 sticks of celery   2 tomatoes
outer leaves of 1 lettuce or ¼ small
cabbage   1 oz. butter or margarine
2 qt. boiling water   ½ teasp.
vegetable extract   bouquet garni
1 teasp. salt   ½ teasp. peppercorns
1 blade of mace   1 bay leaf

Clean the vegetables in the usual
way. Thinly slice the roots, cut
up the tomatoes and shred the lettuce or cabbage. Fry the roots
gently in the fat until golden
brown, add the tomatoes and fry
slightly. Add the boiling water, the
extract, bouquet garni, salt, peppercorns, mace and bay leaf and
simmer for 1 hr. Add the lettuce or
cabbage and simmer 20 min.
longer. Strain and use as soon as
possible.

NOTE: Water in which fresh
vegetables or pulses have been
boiled should always be utilized
for soups, sauces or gravy.

Quantity—4 pt.
Cooking time—1½ hr.

FISH STOCK

Bones, skin and heads from fish
which have been filleted or fish
trimmings or cod's or other fish
heads   salt   peppercorns   1 onion
1 stick of celery   1 blade of mace
1 bay leaf   bouquet garni

Wash the fish trimmings and
break up the bones. Cover them
with cold water, add salt and bring
slowly to simmering point. Add
the other ingredients and simmer
gently for no longer than 40 min.
Strain and use the same day, if
possible.

NOTE: If cooked for longer than
40 min. the fish stock will taste
bitter. Fish stock will not keep and
should be made as required.

Cooking time—50 min. altogether

BEEF BROTH

1 carrot   1 turnip (small)   1 onion
1 clove of garlic (optional)   1 oz.
butter or margarine   1 qt. brown
stock or bone stock   salt and
pepper   ½ small cabbage   a sprig of
parsley   a few chives   grated nutmeg
6 thin slices of French roll

Scrub and peel the carrot and
turnip, peel the onion and crush
the garlic (if used). Slice the vegetables in thin rounds. Melt the fat
and in it cook the vegetables gently for 10 min. with a lid on the
pan. Add the stock (boiling) and
½ teasp. salt. Simmer the whole
for 30 min.

Meanwhile wash the cabbage,
shred it finely and chop the parsley
and chives. Add the cabbage to the
broth and simmer for 20 min.
longer; then add seasoning, a little
grated nutmeg, and the chopped
parsley and chives. Toast or bake
the slices of roll till golden and
put one in each soup plate or cup;
pour the hot soup over them. If
liked, grated cheese may be handed
with this soup.

4–6 helpings
Cooking time—50 min.

BOUILLON EN TASSES

This is any good, well-flavoured
beef stock, or strong broth, served
in soup cups, without vegetables
of the broth. Usually served with

fingers of toast, Melba toast, or "pulled" bread (*see* p. 68).

CHICKEN BROTH

1 small old fowl   3–4 pt. water to cover   salt and pepper   1 onion 1 blade of mace   a bunch fresh herbs (thyme, marjoram, parsley stalks)   lemon rind   1 bay leaf 1 tablesp. rice (optional) 1 tablesp. finely-chopped parsley

Wash and joint the fowl, break the carcase bones, scald and skin the feet and wash the giblets. Put the pieces of fowl and the giblets into a pan and cover them with cold water. Add ½ teasp. salt to each quart of water and bring the whole very slowly to simmering point. Add the onion, peeled whole, the mace, herbs, lemon rind and bay leaf, and simmer very gently for 3–4 hr. Strain the broth through a colander, return it to the pan and sprinkle into it the washed rice, if used. Simmer for a further 20 min.

Meanwhile, the meat may be removed from the chicken bones and cut into small cubes, to be returned to the broth before serving, or the chicken may be finished and served as a separate dish. Just before serving the broth, season to taste and add the chopped parsley.

8 helpings
Cooking time—3–4 hr.

COCK-A-LEEKIE or COCKIE-LEEKIE

1 small boiling fowl   ½ lb. prunes salt and pepper   1 lb. leeks

Soak the prunes 12 hr. in ½ pt. water. Clean the fowl and truss it, wash the giblets, scald and skin the feet. Put the fowl, giblets and sufficient cold water to cover them in a pan, bring very slowly to simmering point, add 2 teasp. salt. Wash and trim the leeks thoroughly and cut them into thin rings. Add the leeks to the broth after

1 hr. cooking and simmer for 2–3 hr. more. Half an hour before serving add the soaked prunes; simmer till they are just tender but not broken. Lift out the fowl and the giblets and feet. Cut some of the flesh of the fowl into small cubes and return these to the broth. (The rest of the bird may be served with a suitable sauce as a separate course.) Season the broth carefully and serve it with the prunes.
Cooking time—3 hr.

HOTCH POTCH

2 lb. neck mutton (scrag and middle neck)   2 qt. water   salt and pepper bunch of fresh herbs   1 carrot 1 small turnip   1 very small cauliflower   1 small lettuce 6 spring onions   ½ pt. young shelled broad beans or ¼ lb. runner beans ¼ pt. shelled peas   chopped parsley

Wash the mutton, remove all fat and cut the lean meat into small pieces. Put bone and meat into a pan, add the cold water and bring very slowly to simmering point. Add 2 teasp. salt and the herbs, and simmer very gently for ½ hr.

Meanwhile, scrub and peel roots, wash cauliflower and lettuce. Cut the carrot and turnip into ¼-in. dice and the onions into thin rings; add them to the pan and simmer for 1½ hr. Break the cauliflower into small sprigs, shred the lettuce finely and shred the runner beans, if used. Add all these with the shelled beans and peas to the soup and simmer for ½ hr. longer. Season the broth, skim off the fat and remove the bunch of herbs and the bones. Add 1 tablesp. chopped parsley just before serving.

NOTE: The mixture of vegetables may be varied with the season. This soup may well be cooked in a cool oven (300°–310° *F., Gas* 1–2).

8 helpings as soup; or 4 as a thin

stew with extra stock for other soups

Cooking time—2½ hr.

MUTTON BROTH

1½ lb. neck of mutton or 1 lb. knuckle of mutton. 1 qt. water
1 teasp. salt and pepper 1 tablesp. pearl barley 1 carrot 1 onion or leek 1 small turnip 1 stick of celery chopped parsley

Wash the meat and remove all fat. Put the meat with the bones, water and salt into a stew pan and bring very slowly to simmering point. Blanch the barley by covering it with cold water in a small pan, bringing it just to boiling point, straining and rinsing it. Add barley to the pan and simmer all for 2 hr. Lift meat from broth, remove bones, cut meat into ¼-in. cubes and return to broth. If possible, let broth cool and remove the fat from the top: otherwise skim very thoroughly and draw pieces of absorbent paper over the top till it is free from fat. Scrub, peel and cut the vegetables into ¼-in. dice. Add them to the simmering broth and cook for 1 hr. longer.

Season the broth to taste and add 1 tablesp. chopped parsley before serving.

4–6 helpings
Cooking time—3 hr.

POT-AU-FEU

(2 dishes, a broth and a meat dish)

2 lb. brisket, topside or boned, top ribs of beef ½ lb. broken beef bones
2 teasp. salt 2 qt. water bunch of fresh herbs—parsley stalks, chervil, thyme, garlic, bay leaf 4 carrots
2 turnips 1 small parsnip 2 leeks
4 onions stuck with one clove each
6 peppercorns ½ cabbage
2 tomatoes potatoes (optional)
6 toasted slices of French roll

Wipe the meat with a damp cloth and remove some of the outside fat if this is excessive, tie the meat into shape. Wash the bones. Put the meat and bones in a large strong pan, add the salt and the cold water, and soak for ½ hr. Bring very slowly to simmering point, add the herbs and simmer very gently for 1 hr.

Meanwhile, scrub and peel the root vegetables; keep the onions whole but cut the others into large pieces and add these to the broth after the first hour's simmering. Put on the lid but leave it slightly tilted to allow steam to escape, and simmer very gently for another 2½ hr. Soak, wash and finely shred the cabbage, scald and skin the tomatoes and cut them into small pieces. Add these to the broth and, if liked, sufficient medium-sized peeled potatoes to serve with the meat. Continue gentle simmering for ½ hr.

To serve: strain the broth through a colander, return it to the pan and keep it hot. Dish the meat with the potatoes, some of the large pieces of vegetable round it and a little of the broth to moisten; keep this covered and hot. Remove the bones and herbs from the broth, cut 1 tablesp. of ¼-in. cubes from the carrot, leek, parsnip and turnip and add these to 1 qt. of the broth and reheat. Serve the broth with the toasted bread floating in it. There will be some broth left to use as stock, and the bones can be reboiled for stock.

Broth—6 helpings Stock—about 1½ pt. A meat dish—6 helpings
Cooking time—4 hr.

SCOTS or "SCOTCH" BROTH

1 lb. scrag neck of mutton 1 teasp. salt 1 qt. cold water 1½ oz. pearl barley 2 carrots 2 leeks 1 small turnip 1 stick of celery pepper
1 dessertsp. chopped parsley

Scrape and wipe the meat, remove outside fat and skin. Cut the lean meat into ½-in. cubes. Put the meat, bones and salt into a pan with the cold water; bring slowly to simmering point. Blanch the barley (see p. 35), and add it to the broth. Simmer very gently I hr.

Scrub and peel the vegetables and cut them into ¼-in. dice, except I carrot, which is grated and added later. Simmer for a further 2 hr., adding the grated carrot 20 min. before serving. Skim the fat from the surface and remove the bones. Season; add the chopped parsley and serve.

NOTE: To remove fat more completely, see Mutton Broth.

4–6 helpings
Cooking time—3 hr.

SCOTS KAIL BROSE or BROTH

2 lb. shin of beef or "hough" or half an ox head or 2 cow heels
2 qt. water   2 teasp. salt   2 leeks
2 lb. kail or 1 medium cabbage
2 oz. toasted oatmeal or 2 oz. pearl barley   pepper

Have the ox head thoroughly cleaned and blanched, or the cow heels scraped, cleaned and blanched. If shin of beef is used, keep it whole. Put the meat whole into a strong pan, add water, salt and the leeks, cut in 1-in. pieces, bringing slowly to simmering point and simmer gently till the meat is tender 3–4 hr. for shin or cow heel, 2–3 hr. for ox head. If barley is used, blanch it and simmer it in the broth for the last 2 hr. Strip the green from the ribs of the kail or cabbage, shred it finely and simmer it in the broth for 20 min. If oatmeal is added it should be toasted till golden-brown and cooked in the broth for 2–3 min. before serving. To serve, lift out the meat, dice some of the lean and return it to the broth. Season the broth and serve. The remainder of the meat may be used for another dish or served separ-

ately with a little of the broth.

6–8 helpings
Cooking time—3–4 hr.

SHEEP'S HEAD BROTH

1 sheep's head split in two   3 qt. water   3 teasp. salt   2 oz. pearl barley   2 leeks   1 turnip   2 carrots
1 tablesp. chopped parsley   pepper

Remove the brains and soak them in vinegar and water (these may be used for Brain Cakes to be served with Dressed Sheep's Head). Soak the head in salt water for I hr. Scrape the small bones and centre cartilage from the nostril and scour with salt. Scrape and scour the teeth. Blanch the head and rinse it (see p. 35). Tie the head with string, put it into a large pan with the water and 3 teasp. salt; bring very slowly to boiling point and simmer gently. Blanch the barley and add it to the broth. Cut the leeks, turnip and I carrot into ¼-in. dice and add them. Simmer the broth 3–4 hr. Half an hour before serving, grate and add the other carrot. When the head is tender lift it out and serve it as Dressed Sheep's Head (see p. 169). To serve the broth, skim off the fat, add the chopped parsley and season carefully. Some broth may be strained off for stock.

6–8 helpings, keeping 2–3 pt. of broth for stock
Cooking time—3–4 hr.

CONSOMMES OR CLEAR SOUP

For consommé it is essential to use stock made from raw meat, i.e. First Brown Stock: this is cleared by either of the two following methods except where otherwise stated in the recipes. The albumen in the egg whites coagulates at 160° F., and as the hardened particles rise to the surface they carry with them all the insoluble substances with which they come in contact, forming a thick "crust" of foam. The soup is then strained through a finely-woven linen cloth, the foam "crust" covers the bottom of the cloth and acts as a filter.

TO CLEAR FIRST BROWN
    STOCK
1 qt. stock (cold and free from fat)
1 small onion, scalded   1 small
carrot   1 small stick of celery   ½ lb.
lean shin of beef   ½ pt. water   1 egg
white   ⅛ teasp. salt   4 peppercorns
small piece of blade mace

Method 1. Scrub and peel vegetables and rinse them thoroughly. Scrape the lean beef into fine shreds with a sharp knife, discarding every scrap of fat, soak the beef in the water for ¼ hr. Put all the ingredients into a deep pan with the stock and whisk over moderate heat till almost boiling. Remove the whisk and let the stock boil till the froth rises to the top of the pan, then cover the pan and infuse the contents for ½ hr. Strain very slowly through a dry, finely-woven linen cloth.

6 helpings (with garnish)
Cooking time—about 35 min.

Method 2. Using the recipe above, prepare vegetables, shred and soak the beef as directed, beat the egg white. Put all the ingredients into a pan and bring them very slowly to simmering point. Simmer, without stirring or whisking, very gently for 1 hr. Strain as above.

NOTE: This method gives a better flavour and is almost as clear as the first.

Cooking time—1 hr.

CONSOMME A LA CELESTINE
    Clear soup with Cheese Pancakes.

1 qt. consommé

CHEESE PANCAKE BATTER
½ oz. flour   ½ teasp. melted butter
½ teasp. grated Parmesan cheese

1 teasp. chopped parsley   ½ beaten
egg   ⅛ pt. milk   salt and pepper

    Make a pancake batter with the ingredients. Fry very thin pancakes in the usual way and rinse them in hot water. Cut them in short strips ¼ in. wide, and serve them in the hot consommé.

6 helpings

CONSOMME FRAPPE
                        Iced clear soup

    Iced consommé may be made from either beef or chicken stock, in either case veal bones added to the stock will give a better jellied result. To serve it iced, the stock is cleared in the usual way and must be most carefully seasoned; it is then allowed to cool, sherry is added and finally it should be put in a refrigerator or packed into a colander with ice for 1–2 hr, before serving. It should be a soft jelly.

SUITABLE GARNISHES
Chopped parsley, chives and
tarragon or chervil to taste or tiny
dice of raw cucumber or chopped
hard-boiled egg white or small
squares of the fleshy part of scalded
tomato

    To serve consommé frappé the jelly should be lightly whipped so that it is not quite solid, and served with its garnish in soup cups.

CONSOMME A LA JULIENNE
1 qt. consommé

GARNISH
1 tablesp. shreds of carrot
1 tablesp. shreds of turnip
1 tablesp. shreds of green leek

    Cut the shreds 1/16 in. thick and 1–1¼ in. long. Boil them separately for a few minutes till just tender, drain them and put them into the soup tureen, pour on to them the hot consommé.
6 helpings

CONSOMME DE TORTUE FAUSSE

Clear Mock Turtle soup

2 qt. white stock (p. 69) made with ½ calf's head or 2 calf's feet instead of veal bones   1 egg white   1 glass sherry   2 teasp. lemon juice

Scrub, scrape, blanch the feet or have them prepared by the butcher. Cleanse the head as for sheep's head (p. 73). Remove the brains and the tongue to use for another dish. Wrap the head and tie it in clean muslin. Make the stock in the usual way; cool and skim it, clear it with the egg white as for consommé (p. 74). To 1 qt. of the cleared consommé, add 2 tablesp. neat cubes of meat from the head, the sherry and lemon juice.

8–10 helpings
Cooking time—3–4 hr.

CONSOMME A L'INDIENNE or A LA MULLIGATAWNY

Clear Mulligatawny soup

1 qt. first brown stock (p. 69)
2 level tablesp. curry powder   1 small onion   1 small apple   1 egg white juice of ½ lemon   salt

GARNISH
2 oz. cubes of cooked chicken

Mix the curry powder with a little of the stock. Add the peeled, chopped onion and apple with the curry paste and egg white to the stock. Clear the stock without whisking (p. 74). Flavour the consommé to taste with lemon juice and salt. It is well to make certain that the curry flavour is strong enough during the clearing process as no curry powder can be added later. Heat the dice of chicken for a few minutes in the consommé before serving.

6 helpings

CONSOMME DE QUEUE DE BŒUF

Clear Oxtail soup

1 ox tail   1 lb. shin of beef   3 qt. water   1 carrot   1 onion   1 stick of celery   1 blade of mace
6 peppercorns   3 teasp. salt   1 egg white   sherry (optional)

GARNISH
Small rounds from the thin end of the tail
1 tablesp. tiny dice of carrot

Joint the tail, remove solid fat, cover the tail with cold water, bring to the boil, drain and rinse it. Make the stock with the water and vegetables in the usual way (p. 69). Take the required amount of stock and a few pieces of the thin end of the tail for the soup; keep the rest of the tail and stock for other dishes. Clear the measured stock with the egg white (see p. 74). Add sherry to taste. Cook the diced carrot separately and add with the pieces of tail to the boiling consommé.

CONSOMME AUX PATES ITALIENNES or CONSOMME A L'ITALIENNE or CONSOMME AUX NOUILLES

Clear soup with Italian paste, Noodles, Spaghetti or Vermicelli.

1 qt. consommé   1 tablesp. Italienne paste: bought in tiny fancy shapes or as fancy shaped macaroni; or macaroni or spaghetti or vermicelli or home-made noodles (see p. 367)

Sprinkle the paste into the boiling consommé to allow it to cook before serving. Italian paste requires 3 min. boiling. Macaroni should be cut with scissors in ¼-in. rings after boiling for 20–30 min. in the consommé. Spaghetti should be cooked for 15–20 min. then cut into ¾-in. lengths. Break vermicelli into 1-in. pieces and sprinkle into the consommé 5 min. before serving.

CONSOMME ROYALE

Royal clear soup

1 qt. consommé
ROYAL CUSTARD
1 egg yolk   salt and pepper
1 tablesp. milk or stock

To make the custard: mix the
egg yolk with the seasoning and
milk or stock. Strain it into a
small greased basin. Stand the
basin in hot water and steam the
custard until it is firm. Turn out
the custard, cut it into thin slices
and from these cut tiny fancy
shapes with a "brilliant" cutter.
Rinse the custard shapes with hot
water, drain and add them to the
hot consommé.

6 helpings

THICK SOUPS
MEAT PUREES
CHICKEN PUREE

For the stock:
1 boiling fowl or carcase, giblets,
skin and legs of a fowl   ¼ lb. lean
bacon   2 onions   1 carrot   3 qt.
water   salt and pepper   a bunch of
herbs: parsley, thyme, marjoram
1 bay leaf   1 blade of mace
6 peppercorns   lemon juice
a strip of lemon rind

For each quart of chicken stock:
1 oz. butter or margarine   1 oz.
flour   lemon juice   nutmeg
½ gill cream or milk

Prepare the fowl, chop the
bacon, peel and slice the vegetables; put into a large pan with
the water, salt, herbs, spice, lemon
juice and rind. Cook until the flesh
of the chicken is absolutely white;
the addition of lemon juice makes
the flesh tender more quickly.
Cool the stock and skim off all fat.
Mince 4 oz. of the cooked chicken
and moisten it with a little stock.
Rub it through a coarse wire sieve.
Melt the fat, stir into it the flour
then the stock a little at a time;
boil well. Stir the hot soup gradu-

ally into the chicken purée. Season lightly with lemon juice, salt,
pepper and a trace of nutmeg. Add
the cream or milk and reheat without boiling.

4-6 helpings
Cooking time—stock 3-4 hr.;
soup 10 min.

GAME PUREE

1 qt. second stock and remains of 1
cold roast pheasant or 2-3 smaller
game birds; or 1 pheasant or 2-3
smaller game birds too old and tough
for roasting made into game stock
(see p. 70)   2 oz. lean bacon   1 oz.
butter or margarine   bunch of herbs
1 onion   1 carrot   1 bay leaf
1 blade of mace   1 chicken's liver
or 2 oz. calf's liver   salt and pepper
1 oz. flour   ½ glass port or sherry
(optional)

Lightly fry the pieces of game
and diced bacon in the fat. Drain
off the fat and keep it for thickening. Add the stock to the bones,
and bring to boiling-point, add the
vegetables, herbs and spices, and
simmer all for 2-2½ hr. Add the
liver and simmer for a further
15 min. Strain the soup. Lift out
the liver, lift out the meat, separate all meat from bones and mince
it. Melt the fat again, add to it the
flour and brown very slowly. Sieve
the meat through a wire sieve.
Stir the stock into the browned
flour, boil well, then stir this soup
gradually into the meat purée. Add
wine, season and reheat.

4-6 helpings
Cooking time—2½-3 hr.

GAME PUREE WITH
CHESTNUTS

1 lb. chestnuts   1 qt. stock   remains
of cold roast game   other ingredients as for Game Purée but omit
flour and liver

Score the chestnuts deeply on
the rounded side, boil them for 15
min., then drain, cool slightly and

remove shell and skin. Cook the chestnuts with the other ingredients in the stock and sieve them with the minced meat. Finish as for Game Purée.

4–6 helpings
Cooking time—2½–3 hr.

KIDNEY PUREE

½ lb. ox kidney   1 oz. dripping
1 onion   1 carrot   1 stick of celery
1 small turnip   1 oz. flour   1 qt.
second stock   a bunch of herbs
1 bay leaf   1 blade of mace
6 peppercorns   salt

Skin and wash the kidney; cut it in small pieces, removing the core. Melt the fat in a saucepan and when the fat hazes, lightly fry the kidney till just brown. Remove kidney and fry the vegetables, sliced. When the vegetables begin to brown, add the flour and carefully brown it without allowing it to become bitter. Add the stock and the pieces of kidney, herbs and spices, bring to simmering point and simmer for 3 hr. Remove herbs and spices, strain the soup, keep a few pieces of kidney for garnish, pass the rest through a wire sieve. Stir the soup into the purée and reheat it. Season carefully.

4–6 helpings
Cooking time—3½ hr.

LIVER PUREE

½ lb. calf's, ox, or lamb's liver
1 carrot   1 onion   1 oz. butter or
margarine   1 oz. flour   1 qt. stock
1 blade of mace   ¼ teasp. yeast or
meat extract   salt and pepper
2 tomatoes   lemon juice

Slice the carrot and onion, put the slices in a saucepan and fry them in the fat until beginning to brown; add the flour and brown it. Stir in the stock, bring to boil, stirring well. Add the mace, yeast or meat extract and salt and simmer the soup for 1 hr. Scald, skin and

cut up the tomatoes and add. Simmer for another ½ hr. Pass the soup through a nylon sieve, pressing through all the tomato. Mince the liver or chop it finely and whisk it into the soup with the lemon juice. Simmer the soup until the liver just loses its red colour. Season.

4–6 helpings
Cooking time—1½ hr.

THICKENED MEAT SOUPS
BARLEY SOUP

1½ oz. cream of barley or patent
barley   ½ pt. milk   1 qt. well-
flavoured stock   1 oz. butter or
margarine   ½ teasp. yeast or meat
extract (if needed)   salt and pepper
grated nutmeg

Blend the barley with the milk. Boil the stock with the fat and the yeast or meat extract, stir it into the barley and milk, return all to the pan and simmer until the barley thickens and becomes clear. Stir all the time as the barley easily forms lumps. Season very carefully, adding the merest trace of nutmeg.

Serve with croûtons of fried bread, handed separately.

6 helpings
Cooking time—20–30 mins.

EGG SOUP

1 pt. very full-flavoured stock
¼ teasp. yeast or malt extract   salt
and pepper   ⅛ pt. cream or milk
2 egg yolks   chopped parsley,
chives, chervil or tarragon (optional)

Heat the stock, add the yeast or meat extract, and season well. Mix the egg yolks with the cream or milk and stir this mixture into the stock, well below boiling-point. Stir the soup over gentle heat until the egg yolks thicken, but do not allow to boil or the eggs may curdle. Add chopped herbs if liked.

4 helpings
Cooking time—5–10 min.

GAME SOUP or HUNTER'S SOUP

Carcases and trimmings of
2 partridges or equivalent amount of
any game   1 oz. lean bacon   1 oz.
butter or margarine   1 onion
1 carrot   ½ parsnip   1 stick of celery
1 oz. flour   1 qt. stock   a bunch of
herbs   1 clove   some neat pieces
of breast of bird   salt and pepper

Put the pieces of carcase, the
trimmings, and the bacon, with the
fat in a saucepan and fry them till
brown. Remove the game and fry
the sliced vegetables till brown.
Add the flour and fry it till golden-
brown. Stir in the stock, bring to
the boil, add the herbs and clove,
return the game to the pan and
simmer for 1½–2 hr. Meanwhile
cut the pieces of breast meat into
¼-in. dice. Strain the soup, in it
reheat the diced game, season
carefully and serve.

4–6 helpings
Cooking time—about 2 hr.

GIBLET SOUP

2–3 sets chicken giblets or 1 set
turkey or goose giblets   1 qt. water
1 onion   1 carrot   1 stick of celery
a bunch of herbs   1 clove   small
blade of mace   6 peppercorns
1 teasp. salt   1 oz. flour
1 oz. butter or margarine

Prepare the giblets in the usual
way then cover them with cold
water, bring to simmering point
very slowly. Add the whole
vegetables, herbs, spice, peppercorns and salt, simmer for 2–3 hr.
Strain this stock. In a saucepan,
fry the flour in the fat till nut-
brown without being bitter, stir in
the stock, bring to the boil and
boil for 5 min. Cut tiny dice from
the best pieces of giblets, reheat
these in the soup. Season well and
serve.

4–6 helpings
Cooking time—2½–3½ hr.

GRAVY SOUP or SHIN OF BEEF SOUP

1 lb. lean shin of beef   1 oz. beef
dripping   1 onion   1 carrot
1 piece of turnip   1 stick of celery
1 qt. second stock or water
1 teasp. salt   a bunch of herbs
6 peppercorns   1 oz. flour

Cut the shin of beef in very thin
slices across the fibres. Make the
dripping smoking hot and in it fry
half the meat till brown, then remove it. Slice the vegetables and
fry them till golden-brown, then
remove them. Put the fried and
raw meat and the fried vegetables
into a deep pan, cover with the
liquid, bring very slowly to boiling-
point. Add the salt, herbs and peppercorns and simmer very gently for 3–4 hr. Meanwhile fry the
flour in the dripping until golden-
brown. Strain the soup, return to
the soup some of the pieces of meat
cut very small, and whisk in the
browned flour. Whisk till boiling,
season and serve. The remainder
of the meat may be minced and
served with another dish.

6 helpings
Cooking time—4½ hr.

HARE SOUP, THICKENED

Bones and trimmings of a hare
3 pt. second stock or water
1 onion   1 carrot   ½ turnip
small parsnip   1 stick of celery
1½ oz. dripping   a bunch of herbs
1 bay leaf   1½ teasp. salt
8 peppercorns   1½ oz. flour
¼ glass port

Collect the blood from the hare
by piercing the diaphragm. Carefully fillet the meat from the back
and legs to be used for Jugged
Hare (see p. 206). The head, flaps
and bones of the hare, with the
blood may be used for the soup.
Split the head, separate the bones,
cover them with the cold liquid,
add the blood and soak for 1 hr.
Fry the sliced vegetables in the

dripping then lift them out. Bring the panful of bones and liquid very slowly to simmering point; add the vegetables, herbs, salt and pepper-corns and simmer very gently for 3–4 hr. Meanwhile fry the flour till golden-brown in the dripping. Strain the soup. Remove from the bones any trimmings of meat, cut these neatly and return them to the soup. Whisk in the fried flour, whisk till boiling, add the port and season the soup.

8 helpings
Cooking time—4½ hr.

MULLIGATAWNY SOUP

1 lb. lean mutton or rabbit or stewing veal or shin of beef or ox tail
1 onion   1 small cooking apple
1 oz. butter or margarine
½ oz. curry powder   1 oz. flour
1 qt. bone stock or water   salt
1 carrot   ½ small parsnip
a bunch of herbs   lemon juice
¼ teasp. black treacle
2 oz. boiled rice

Cut the meat in small pieces. Chop finely the onion and the apple. Heat the butter in a deep pan and in it quickly fry the onion, then the curry powder. Add the apple and cook it gently for a few minutes, then stir in the flour. Add the liquid, meat and salt, and bring slowly to simmering point, stirring all the time. Add the other vegetables, the herbs tied in muslin and a few drops of lemon juice. Simmer until the meat is very tender. This will take be-tween 2 hr. for rabbit to 4 hr. for shin of beef. Taste the soup and add more lemon juice or add black treacle to obtain a flavour that is neither predominatingly sweet nor acid. Strain the soup, cut some of the meat in neat cubes and reheat them in the soup. Boil, drain and partly dry the rice as for curry (p. 38) and hand it with the soup.

NOTE: The amount of curry powder may be varied to taste; the quantity given is for a mild-flavoured soup.

4–6 helpings
Cooking time—from 2–4 hr. accord-ing to the meat used.

OXTAIL SOUP

1 ox tail   1 oz. beef dripping
1 onion   1 carrot   1 piece of turnip
1 stick of celery
1 qt. water or bone stock
1 teasp. salt   a bunch of herbs
6 peppercorns   1 oz. flour

Cleanse the ox tail, remove out-side fat and joint the tail. Make the dripping hot, in it fry half the meat till brown, then remove it. Slice the vegetables and fry them till golden-brown, then remove them. Put the fried and raw meat and the fried vegetables into a deep pan, cover with the liquid, bring very slowly to boiling-point. Add the salt, herbs and pepper-corns and simmer very gently for 3–4 hr. Meanwhile fry the flour in the dripping until golden-brown. Strain the soup, return to the soup some of the thinner pieces of meat and small rounds of carrot. Whisk in the browned flour. Whisk till boiling, season and serve. The thicker pieces of meat may be served as stewed ox tail.

6 helpings
Cooking time—4½ hr.

TURKEY SOUP

Carcase and trimmings of 1 turkey
1 oz. lean bacon
1 oz. butter or margarine
1 onion   1 carrot   ½ parsnip
1 stick of celery   1 oz. flour
1 qt. water to each 1 lb cooked turkey remains   a bunch of herbs
1 clove
some neat pieces of breast of bird
salt and pepper

Put the pieces of carcase, the trimmings, and the bacon, with

the fat in a saucepan and fry them
till brown. Remove the turkey and
fry the sliced vegetables till brown.
Add the flour and fry it till
golden-brown, stir in the stock,
bring to the boil, add the herbs and
clove, return the turkey to the pan
and simmer for 1½–2 hr. Meanwhile cut the pieces of breast meat
into ¼-in. dice. Strain the soup, in
it reheat the diced meat, season
carefully and serve.

NOTE: Scraps of forcemeat improve the flavour and help to
thicken.

4–6 helpings
Cooking time—about 2 hr.

BISQUES

Bisques are fish soups of a thick,
creamy consistency usually made
from molluscs or crustaceans, the
flesh of which is pounded and
sieved to form a purée.

BISQUE AUX HUITRES
                                   Oyster soup
1 doz. oysters, fresh or canned
1 qt. fish stock   ½ pt. cream
1 oz. butter   1 oz. flour
½ glass white wine   salt and pepper
lemon juice   grated nutmeg
1 egg yolk

Add the beards, buttons and
liquor of the oysters (fresh or
canned) to the simmering fish
stock. Cut the oysters into halves
and cover them with the cream.
Melt the butter in a deep pan, stir
in the flour, then the fish stock and
oyster liquor and the wine. Simmer the liquid for ½ hr. Season
carefully, adding a little lemon
juice and nutmeg to taste. Strain
the soup through a fine sieve.
Mix the egg yolk with the cream.
Boil the soup, remove it from the
heat and stir in the egg yolk, cream
and halved oysters. Cook the egg
without boiling.

6 helpings
Cooking time—40 min. for fish
    stock, 40 min. for bisque

BISQUE DE CREVETTES
                                   Shrimp soup
1½ pt. fish stock (p. 70) in which
the shells of the shrimps have been
cooked
3 tablesp. fresh breadcrumbs
2 oz. butter   1 pt. cooked shrimps
1 teasp. lemon juice   grated nutmeg
1 glass white wine or cider
1 egg yolk   ¼ pt. cream or milk
or ½ cream and ½ milk
salt and pepper

Heat ½ pt. of the fish stock and
in it soak the breadcrumbs. Melt
½ oz. butter in a deep pan and in
it toss the shrimps over gentle heat
for 5 min. Add lemon juice, nutmeg, breadcrumbs and ½ pt. stock,
heat gently for 5 min., beat in the
rest of the butter. Pound this
paste and rub it through a wire
sieve. Gradually add the wine and
the rest of the fish stock and bring
to boiling-point. Mix the egg yolk
with the milk or cream. Season
the soup carefully, remove it from
the heat, stir in the egg and cream
mixture and cook this without
allowing the soup to boil.

4–6 helpings
Cooking time—40 min. for fish
stock, 15–20 min. for the bisque

BISQUE D'HOMARD
                                   Lobster soup
The shell, trimmings and a little of
the flesh of a medium-sized lobster
1 onion   1 carrot   1 clove of garlic
1 bay leaf   1 blade of mace
lemon juice
1 teasp. anchovy essence
¼ pt. white wine   1¾ pt. fish stock
salt and pepper
1 tablesp. cooked lobster coral
2 oz. butter   1 oz. flour   ¼ pt. cream
a few drops carmine if needed

Crush the shell; flake the rough
pieces of flesh as finely as possible,
keeping neat pieces of the better
parts for garnish. Slice the vegetables finely, put them into a pan
with the spices, flavouring, shell,

flaked lobster and the wine. Heat all quickly and cook briskly for a few minutes. The alcohol in the wine should extract much of the flavour from the lobster and vegetables. Add the stock, and salt, bring to boiling-point; simmer 1 hr. Strain through a wire sieve, and rub through the sieve any of the scraps of lobster that are still firm. Pound the lobster coral with 1 oz. butter and rub through a nylon sieve. Melt the other 1 oz. butter, stir into it the flour, then the strained stock, bring to boiling-point. Whisk in, just at boiling-point, the lobster butter, then stir in the cream, off the heat. Season carefully, colour if necessary to obtain a deep orange-pink, reheat without boiling, adding any neat pieces of lobster.

NOTE: Live lobster may be used, see p. 139 for the methods of killing lobsters.

4–6 helpings
Cooking time—40 min. for fish stock, 1 hr. 20 min. for bisque

FISH SOUPS

BOUILLABAISSE

NOTE: This, the most famous of all fish soups, is made chiefly in the South of France, different districts having particular recipes. It is a kind of thick stew of fish which should include a very wide mixture of different kinds of fish. The original French recipes use many fish not available in Great Britain. The following recipe is adapted to use the available fish. In order to get a wide enough variety a large quantity must be made.

A mixture of 8 to 10 different kinds of fish, e.g.:

**Whiting   John Dory
Red mullet   Monk fish
Crawfish or lobster   Crab
Conger eel or eel   Bass
Gurnet   Sole**

To every 2 lb. fish allow:

**1 large onion   1 leek   1 clove of garlic   2 tomatoes   1 bay leaf
a sprig of parsley   a sprig of savory
a sprig of fennel or tarragon
¼ teasp. saffron   salt and pepper
¼ pt. olive oil   ¼ pt. white wine**

To each portion of bouillabaisse allow:

1 thick slice of French roll

Clean the fish, cut them into thick slices and sort them into 2 groups, the firm-fleshed kind and the soft kind. Chop the onion; slice the leek; crush the garlic; scald, skin and slice the tomatoes. In a deep pan make a bed of the sliced vegetables and the herbs, season this layer. Arrange on top the pieces of firm-fleshed fish; season them and pour over them the oil. Add to the pan the wine and enough cold water or fish stock barely to cover the top layer of fish. Heat as quickly as possible to boiling-point and boil briskly for 8 min. Now add the soft pieces of fish, forming a fresh layer. Boil for a further 5 min. Meanwhile toast the slices of bread and arrange them in the bottom of the soup tureen or individual bowls. Pour the liquid over the bread and serve it as a fish bouillon. Serve the fish separately.

NOTE: The vegetables and herbs are for flavour only, and need not be served, the olive oil should be distributed over the pieces of fish if cooking has been brisk enough.

The mixture suggested would probably weigh 4 lb.

**Sufficient for 8–10 helpings
Cooking time—15–20 min.**

FISH CHOWDER

This American dish is something between a soup and a fish stew.

**2 lb. filleted fresh cod or haddock, the head, bones and skin of the fish
¾ pt. water   salt and pepper**

lemon rind   a bunch of herbs
1 blade of mace   2 onions
1 lb. potatoes   ¼ lb. salt pork
1 oz. flour   1 pt. milk   1 oz. butter

Skin the filleted fish. Make a fish stock with the water, bones, head and skin of the fish, salt, lemon rind, herbs and mace, simmer gently for ½ hr. Cut the fillets into 2-in. strips, slice the onions thinly and dice the potatoes. Cut the pork in tiny cubes and heat it gently in a deep pan until the fat flows freely. In the pork fat cook the onion without browning for 10 min., then add the potatoes and shake them well in the fat for a few minutes. Sprinkle in the flour. Gradually add the hot, strained stock, then put in the pieces of fish and season the soup. Cook very gently for ½ hr. Heat the milk and butter and add them to the soup when the fish and potatoes are soft. Do not reboil. Serve at once.

4–6 helpings
Cooking time—1¼ hr.

FISH SOUP—HADDOCK, COD or SKATE

1½ lb. haddock, cod, skate or any available white fish   2 large onions
1 carrot   2 sticks of celery   ½ lb. potatoes   1 oz. butter   1 tablesp. olive oil   1 teasp. curry powder
1½ pt. boiling water   a bunch of herbs   salt and pepper   ½ glass white wine (optional)   1 oz. flour
¼ pt. milk   ⅛ pt. cream

Slice the onions, carrot and celery into thin rounds. Cut the potatoes into thick fingers. Heat the butter and olive oil together in a deep pan and in this toss all the vegetables over gentle heat for 10 min. Add the curry powder and stir the mixture over the heat for a few more minutes. Add the boiling water, the herbs, salt and pepper. Cut the fish into neat pieces and add to the soup. Sim-

mer until the fish is tender. Lift the best pieces of fish from the soup and keep them hot with a little of the liquid. Reduce the remaining liquid for 15 min.—pour it through a sieve and press through the potatoes and scraps of fish. Add the wine, if used, and reheat the soup. Blend the flour and milk, stir this into the soup and boil it. Return the pieces of fish and add the cream to the soup, just at boiling-point.

4–6 helpings
Cooking time—¾–1 hr.

SHELLFISH AND TOMATO SOUP

1 lb. cooked or 1 can of crawfish, crayfish or prawns   2 raw potatoes
1½ pt. fish stock (p. 70)   a bunch of herbs: fennel or tarragon, parsley, basil   1 bay leaf   lemon juice
lemon rind   1 lb. tomatoes or
1 medium-sized can   1 onion
2 oz. rice   ½ pt. white wine or cider   chopped parsley   paprika
pepper   ½ gill cream

Slice the potatoes thickly, and boil them till soft in ½ pt. fish stock with the herbs, lemon juice and a piece of lemon rind. Meanwhile cut up the tomatoes and chop the onion. Cook the tomatoes and onion without any other additions till they are quite soft. Sieve the potatoes and to them add all the stock. Bring the stock and potatoes to the boil, add the rice and cook till quite soft. Sieve the tomatoes and onion and add this purée to the thickened fish stock. Add the wine and the chopped fish and bring the soup to boiling-point. Grate in a little lemon rind, add the chopped parsley and season well. Off the heat, stir in the cream.

Serve at once.

4–6 helpings
Cooking time—30 min.

VEGETABLE PUREES AND CREAM SOUPS

VEGETABLE PUREE

Basic Recipe (1)

1 lb. vegetable flavouring vegetable
½–1 oz. butter, margarine or other
suitable fat 1 pt. stock—white for
white and pale green vegetables;
brown for dark-coloured vegetables;
or water; or vegetable boilings
flavouring herbs (optional) ¼ pt.
milk or ⅛ pt. milk and ⅛ pt. cream
for light-coloured soups ½ oz.
starchy thickening, e.g. flour,
cornflour, ground rice, tapioca or
potato to each pint of sieved soup
salt and pepper other flavouring or
colouring if required

For a Cream soup add:

⅛–¼ pt. cream (this may replace
some of the milk), sometimes
also 1 egg yolk

Slice or chop the main and
flavouring vegetables. Melt the
fat in a deep pan and in it cook the
vegetables over gentle heat for 10
min. Keep the lid on the pan and
shake it vigorously from time to
time. Boil the stock, add it to the
vegetables with the herbs and
other flavouring (if used) and
simmer the whole until the vegetables are quite soft. This cooking
time should be as short as possible
but will vary with the kind and age
of the vegetables used. Remove the
herbs, rub or press the vegetables
through a sieve (wire for soft,
pulpy or very firm vegetables;
nylon if a very smooth purée is
needed). Mix the liquid with the
purée and measure the soup.
Weigh or measure the thickening
in the proportion given above.
Blend the starch powder with cold
milk, stock or water and stir it into
the soup. Cook the soup until the
starch is thickened and no longer
tastes raw. Season carefully to
taste.

For a Cream soup:

After the starch thickening has
been cooked, remove the pan from
the heat. Mix the egg yolk and
cream together, stir them into the
soup, which should be well below
boiling-point. Stir over gentle heat
till the egg yolk thickens, but do
not boil. Serve the soup at once;
cream and eggs cannot be kept hot.
Cream when used alone may be
stirred into the soup just at boiling-
point, as it is removed from the
heat. It must not be allowed to
boil.

Serve separately with any vegetable purée, fried croûtons of
bread, pulled bread, Melba toast
or "fairy" toast (p. 68).

Basic Recipe (2)

1 lb. vegetable ½–1 oz. butter,
margarine or fat and/or ⅛ pt. boiling
stock or water 1 pt. thin sauce,
i.e. 1 oz. fat and flour to 1 pt.
Béchamel (p. 100) for light-coloured
purées, or Velouté (p. 103) for
dark-coloured purées

(Flavouring vegetables are included in the recipes for the foundation sauces.)

Cook the vegetable as in Basic
Recipe (1), adding only sufficient
boiling liquid to moisten it. Cook
very carefully without allowing it
to evaporate or burn. Rub this
concentrated purée through a sieve
and whisk it into the hot sauce.
Boil the soup and if required con-
vert it to a cream soup as in the
previous recipe.

BROAD BEAN PUREE

1 pt. shelled broad beans or if very
young, 1 pt. beans in the pod
1 oz. lean bacon scraps and rinds
½ oz. butter 1 onion 1 pt. stock
1 sprig of savory ½ pt. milk
cornflower to thicken salt and
pepper sugar lemon juice
1 teasp. chopped parsley

Unless the beans are young, boil

them for 10 min. in salted water and remove the skins. In a deep pan fry the bacon, butter and onion together for 10 min., add the stock and savory and when boiling add the beans. Simmer until the beans are soft, about 20 min. unless very old. Rub through a sieve, stir the milk into the purée and measure the soup. For each 1 pt. of soup blend ½ oz. cornflour with a little cold milk, stock or water, and stir into the soup. Cook until the soup is thickened. Season, add sugar and lemon juice to taste. Sprinkle the parsley over.

Decorate with piped double cream or a few cooked beans, if liked.

4 helpings
Cooking time—45–50 min.

CARROT SOUP

1 lb. carrots   1 onion   2 sticks of celery   ½ small turnip or swede
a few bacon rinds, bones or scraps
½ oz. butter or margarine   1 pt. brown stock   1 blade of mace
1 bay leaf   a bunch of herbs
peppercorns   a little yeast or meat extract   lemon juice   ¼ pt. milk
cornflour to thicken   salt

Proceed as for Basic Recipe (p. 83).

CELERY SOUP or CELERY CREAM SOUP

1 lb. outer sticks of celery   1 onion
¾ oz. butter or margarine   1 pt. white stock   lemon juice   ¼ pt. milk
cornflour to thicken   salt and pepper   ⅛ pt. cream (optional)

Proceed as in Basic Recipe (p. 83). Cook the celery without boiling or it will become stringy and difficult to sieve. If cut in ½-in. lengths it is easy to sieve.

4 helpings
Cooking time—1 hr.

CHESTNUT PUREE

1 lb. chestnuts after peeling (about

1½ lb. in shells)   1 onion   1 oz. butter   1 qt. stock   lemon juice
salt and pepper   a little yeast or meat extract   a pinch of sugar
a pinch of cinnamon   grated nutmeg
¼ pt. cream (optional)

Make an incision in the rounded sides of the chestnuts then drop them into fast boiling water and boil for 15 min. Drain them and while still warm remove shells and brown skins. Proceed as for Basic Recipe (p. 83). Add the spices so sparingly that they cannot be recognized but merely enhance the chestnut flavour. No added thickening is required except the cream which is optional.

CHICORY SOUP

2 large heads of chicory (Witloof) also called Belgian Endive   1 oz. butter   1 onion   1 pt. white stock
½ oz. flour   a bunch of herbs
1 blade of mace   salt and pepper
lemon juice   ¼ pt. milk or cream;
or ½ milk and ½ cream   1 egg yolk

Cut the chicory in ¼-in. slices and cook it with the onion gently in the butter for 10 min. Continue as for asparagus soup, reserving a few shreds of cooked chicory for garnish. Lemon juice added with the stock improves the flavour. The chicory must not be allowed to boil or it will become tough and stringy.

4 helpings

CREME VICHYSSOISE

½ lb. white leeks   ½ lb. potatoes
1 oz. butter   1 pt. stock   ¼ pt. milk
¼–⅛ pt. cream   salt and pepper.

Proceed as for Basic Recipe (p. 83).

NOTE: This soup may be served iced.

4 helpings

CUCUMBER CREAM SOUP

1 lb. cucumber   1 oz. butter
6 spring onions   1 oz. flour

1 pt. white stock   salt and pepper
lemon juice   green colouring
a sprig of mint   a sprig of parsley
⅛ pt. cream

Peel the cucumber, reserve a
2-in. length for garnish, slice the
rest. Melt the butter in a deep pan
and cook the onions gently, without browning, for 10 min. Stir in
the flour, then the stock and bring
to boiling-point. Add the sliced
cucumber and cook till tender.
Sieve through a nylon sieve. Season and add lemon juice to taste.
Cut the 2-in. piece of cucumber
into ¼-in. dice and boil these in a
little stock or water till just tender
and add them to the finished soup.
Five minutes before serving the
soup add the mint and parsley.
Tint the soup pale green. Stir the
cream into the hot soup immediately before serving.

4 helpings
Cooking time—20–30 min.

GREEN PEA SOUP

1½ lb. green peas in the pod
1 onion   ½ oz. butter   1 pt. white
stock   a few leaves of spinach
a sprig of mint   a few parsley
stalks   cornflour   salt and pepper
sugar to taste   green colouring, if
needed   ⅛ pt. cream or ⅛ pt. milk

Shell the peas, wash half the
shells, slice the onion. Melt the
butter in a deep pan and cook the
washed pods and onion very
gently for 10 min. Add the stock
and bring to boiling-point, add the
spinach leaves, the peas and the
herbs. Simmer only long enough
to cook the peas, from 10–20 min.
Sieve, add milk if used, and measure the soup. For every 1 pt. of
soup blend ½ oz. cornflour with a
little cold milk, stock or water and
stir into the soup. Cook until the
soup is thickened, season carefully,
add sugar to taste and colouring,
if required. If cream is used stir in
at boiling-point off the heat. A few

small cooked peas and a few blobs
of cream may be added to the
cooked soup.

4 helpings
Cooking time—30 min.

GUMBO SOUP (AMERICAN OKRA SOUP)

1 pt. or 1 medium can okra
2 large tomatoes   a few scraps of
bacon or bacon bone   parsley stalks
¼ pt. Lima or fresh haricot beans
1½ pt. brown stock   salt and pepper
chopped parsley

Slice the okra pods and cook
them with the sliced tomatoes,
bacon, parsley stalks and the beans
in boiling stock until tender. Rub
through a hair or nylon sieve; reheat and season. Sprinkle with
chopped parsley.

NOTE: See Okra in Vegetable
section (p. 223).

4 helpings
Cooking time—½ hr.

LEEK SOUP

1 lb. thick white leeks   ¾ lb.
potatoes   ½ oz butter or margarine
1 pt. stock or water   ½ pt. milk
salt and pepper   ⅛ pt. cream
(optional)   1 egg yolk (optional)

Proceed as for Basic Recipe (p.
83). The potatoes provide sufficient starch thickening. The leeks
should be cut into ½-in. lengths to
make sieving easier.

4–5 helpings
Cooking time—¾–1 hr.

MUSHROOM CREAM SOUP

½ lb. mushrooms   1 onion   1 clove
of garlic   2 oz. butter   ¾ pt. water
or white stock   a little yeast or
meat extract   ¾ pt. milk   1 oz. flour
salt and pepper   ¼ pt. cream
(optional)   1 egg yolk (optional)

Proceed as for Basic Recipe, p.
83, cooking the whole mushrooms
till tender, then chopping them
and returning them to the soup
before thickening it.

6 helpings
Cooking time—30–45 min.

NETTLE SOUP

1 lb. nettle tops   a few leaves of
sorrel or spinach   1 onion   1 oz.
butter   1½ pt. stock   salt and pepper
lemon juice   ¼ pt. milk or cream

Proceed as for Basic Recipe, p.
83.

4–6 helpings
Cooking time—½ hr.

ONION SOUP

3 large Spanish onions (about 2 lb.)
1 oz. butter or margarine or
dripping   1 qt. white stock or
1 pt. stock and 1 pt. milk   1 clove
1 bay leaf   1 blade of mace
flour to thicken   salt and pepper
¼ pt. milk or cream

Peel and slice the onions. Melt
the fat in a deep pan and lightly
fry the onions for 10 min., cook
slowly to prevent the onions
colouring. Boil the stock, add it to
the onions with the spices, and
simmer until the onions are tender.
Rub through a fine sieve, return
the purée to the pan and add milk
if used. To each 1 pt. of soup allow
½ oz. flour, blend the flour with a
little cold milk, water or stock and
stir into the soup. Cook until the
soup thickens, season to taste. If
cream is used, add it to the soup
before serving.

NOTE: For Brown Onion soup
use brown stock and brown the
onions very slowly in the fat (about
20 min.) before adding the stock.

6 helpings
Cooking time—1–1½ hr.

SAUERKRAUT SOUP

1 lb. sauerkraut (or medium-sized
can)   1 qt. stock or water   ½ lb.
potatoes   a few scraps of fat bacon
and bacon rinds   1 oz. mushrooms
or left-over mushroom stalks and
peelings from another dish   1 bay
leaf   1 blade of mace   salt and

pepper   a pinch of sugar
2 sausages—preferably Frankfurter
¼ pt. cream (optional)   grated cheese

Boil the stock, and add to it the
sauerkraut, sliced potatoes, bacon,
mushrooms, spices and salt. Simmer for ¾ hr. or until the sauerkraut is quite soft. Rub through a
sieve. Reheat, adding the sugar
and seasoning and the sausages
cut into ⅛-in. thick rounds. Simmer the soup 15–20 min. until the
sausage is cooked. Add the cream
if liked. Sprinkle cheese on top or
serve separately.

6 helpings
Cooking time—1 hr. 20 min.

SPINACH SOUP

2 lb. spinach   1 small onion   1 oz.
butter   1 qt. white or bone stock
¼ pt. milk   cornflour to thicken
salt and pepper   green colouring
¼ pt. cream (optional)
1 egg yolk (optional)

Shred the spinach, chop the
onion, and fry lightly in the
melted butter (see p. 83) for 10
min. Boil the stock and pour over
the spinach and onion; simmer for
10 min. Rub through a hair or
nylon sieve, add the milk to the
purée. Measure the soup and
thicken with ½ oz. cornflour to
each 1 pt. of soup, blended with a
little cold milk, stock or water.
Stir the cornflour paste into the
soup, reheat and season to taste,
colour if liked. If either cream or
egg yolk is used, stir in below
boiling point, reheat until egg is
cooked but do not allow to boil.

4–6 helpings
Cooking time—25 min.

TOMATO SOUP

1 lb. tomatoes (fresh or canned)
1 onion   1 carrot   ½ oz. margarine
1 oz. bacon scraps, rind or bone
1 pt. white stock or juice from
canned tomatoes   grated nutmeg
lemon juice   a bunch of herbs

minute tapioca or cornflour
salt and pepper sugar
red colouring, if needed

Slice the tomatoes, onion and carrot. If canned tomatoes are used, strain them and make the juice up to 1 pt. with stock. Melt the margarine in a deep pan and lightly fry the sliced vegetables and chopped bacon for 10 min. Boil the stock or tomato juice and add to the vegetables with the nutmeg, lemon juice and herbs and cook for ¾–1 hr. Sieve and thicken the soup with ½ oz. cornflour or minute tapioca to each 1 pt. soup, blended with a little cold milk, stock or water. Stir into the soup, cook till clear, season, add sugar to taste and colouring if needed.

4 helpings
Cooking time—¾–1 hr.

TOMATO SOUP—ITALIAN

1½ lb. ripe tomatoes 1 tablesp. olive oil 1 pt. stock 1 clove of garlic parsley basil marjoram 1 tablesp. ground rice salt and pepper ⅛ pt. cream (optional) 1 egg yolk (optional)

Proceed as for Basic Recipe (p. 83). Cook for 5 min. only, in stock before sieving. (The tomatoes should be chopped fine to hasten cooking.)

NOTE: If this soup is not thickened it may be served iced.

4 helpings
Cooking time—20 min.

PULSE PUREES
BUTTER BEAN PUREE

6 oz. butter beans 1 qt. water or bone stock a few scraps of bacon or a bacon bone or a few bacon rinds 1 onion 2 sticks of celery ½ small turnip 1 medium-sized potato ½ oz. bacon fat a bunch of herbs 1 blade of mace ½ pt. milk salt and pepper.

Wash the beans, boil the stock

or water. Soak the beans in the stock or water all night. Chop the bacon and slice the vegetables. Melt the fat in a deep pan and fry very gently the bacon, onion, celery, turnip and potato for 10 min. Add the water or stock, beans, herbs and mace; bring all to boiling-point and simmer for 2 hr. or until the beans are quite soft. Remove the herbs, sieve the vegetables and stir the milk into the purée. No starch thickening, other than the potato, should be needed. Reheat and season.

6 helpings
Cooking time—2½ hr.

HARICOT BEAN SOUP

See Butter Bean Purée.

HARICOT BEAN AND TOMATO SOUP

6 oz. haricot beans 1½ pt. water or ½ water and ½ stock ½ lb. tomatoes 1 onion 1 carrot 1 medium-sized potato ½ oz. butter or margarine or bacon fat salt and pepper a bunch of herbs 1 bay leaf 1 blade of mace

Wash the beans and soak them in water overnight. Drain, and put them in a pan with the 1½ pt. water, bring to boil and simmer for 1 hr. Meanwhile slice the tomatoes, onion, carrot and potato. Melt the fat and gently fry the sliced vegetables for 10 min. Add the fried vegetables to the beans with the herbs, bay leaf and mace, and simmer until the beans are quite soft. Remove the herbs, rub soup through a fine wire sieve; reheat and season.

6 helpings
Cooking time—2–2½ hr.

LENTIL SOUP

As for Butter Bean Purée opposite, substituting red Egyptian or brown lentils, and including carrot with the flavouring vegetables.

Cooking time—Egyptian lentils
1½ hr.; Brown lentils 2½ hr.

PEA SOUP

As for Butter Bean Purée, using
dried, whole or split peas and
adding a sprig of mint.

Cooking time—2 hr. (after 12 hr.
soaking)

THICKENED SOUPS
BONNE FEMME SOUP

½ lettuce, a few leaves of sorrel,
chervil, watercress or tarragon or
a mixture of these, 1½ in. length
cucumber; to make ½ pt. in all
½ oz. butter   1 qt. white stock
½ oz. flour   ¼ pt. milk   salt and
pepper   lemon juice   2 egg yolks
⅛ pt. cream

Shred the lettuce and other
leaves finely. Cut the cucumber
into match-like strips. Melt the
butter in a deep pan and fry the
vegetables very gently for 3 min.
Add the stock, boiling, to the
vegetables and simmer for 10 min.
Blend the flour with half the milk,
stir this into the soup and cook till
the flour thickens. Season very
carefully, add lemon juice to taste
and cook slightly. Mix the remaining milk with the egg yolks and
cream, add these to the cooked
soup and cook till the egg yolks
thicken, but do not allow to boil.

Serve at once.

6 helpings
Cooking time—20 min.

HOLLANDAISE SOUP

Carrot   cucumber   2 tablesp. small
green peas   ¾ oz. butter   ¾ oz. flour
1½ pt. white stock   2 egg yolks
⅛ pt. milk   ⅛ pt. cream   salt and
pepper   chopped tarragon

Cut out 2 tablesp. each of pea
shapes of carrot and cucumber.
Cook the vegetables in a little boiling stock till just tender. Melt the
fat in a deep pan and stir in the
flour, then the stock. Boil the

stock till the flour is completely
cooked, then cool it. Mix the egg
yolks, milk and cream and stir
them into the hot soup. Cook the
egg yolks without boiling. Season
and add the chopped tarragon and
the cooked vegetables.

6 helpings
Cooking time—about 20 min.

MILK SOUP WITH ONION

1 Spanish onion or 3 medium-sized
onions   ¾ oz. butter or other fat
¾ oz. flour or rice   1 pt. milk
1 bay leaf   1 clove   1 blade of mace
a little grated lemon rind   salt and
pepper   2 tablesp. sherry (optional)

Melt the fat in a deep pan and
cook the finely-chopped onion
gently for 10 min. Sprinkle and
stir in the flour, add the milk and
boil. Add the spices and lemon
rind; simmer till the onion is just
tender. Season and add sherry (if
used) before serving.

NOTE: If rice is used add it instead of flour and cook in the soup.

4 helpings
Cooking time—about ¾ hr.

VELVET SOUP

1 rounded teasp. curry powder
1 oz. flour   1 oz. butter   1 pt. milk
2 tablesp. boiled Patna rice   salt
and pepper   2 tablesp. cream

In a saucepan fry the curry
powder and flour in the butter for
a few minutes. Add the milk and
boil the soup; stir and simmer for
5 min. Cook the rice separately
and add it to the hot soup; season
to taste. Remove soup from heat
and stir in the cream.

4 helpings
Cooking time—10 min.

UNCLASSIFIED, NATIONAL OR REGIONAL SOUPS
BORTSCH, POLISH or RUSSIAN BEETROOT SOUP

4 raw beetroots   1 qt. brown stock
1 onion stuck with 1 clove   bunch

of herbs   a few caraway seeds
1 oz. goose fat or bacon fat
shredded white leek, cabbage,
beetroot, celery to make ½ pt. in all
salt and pepper   grated nutmeg
¼ pt. sour cream or
1 bottle yoghourt

Slice 3 of the beetroots and simmer them in the stock with the
onion, clove, herbs and caraway
seeds for about 1 hr. or until the
colour has run into the soup and
the flavour is no longer raw. Melt
the fat and in it cook the shreds of
vegetable and the finely-grated 4th
beetroot, very gently for 10–15
min. Strain the stock and press
the juice out of the beetroots into
it. Add the shreds of vegetable and
finish cooking them in the soup.
Season, add a trace of nutmeg to
the soup. Beat the sour cream or
yoghourt into the hot soup but do
not allow it to boil; or put a spoonful of yoghourt or sour cream into
each soup plate before pouring in
the soup.
6 helpings
Cooking time—1½ hr.

FRENCH ONION SOUP

2 oz. fat bacon   6 medium-sized
onions   ½ oz. flour   salt and pepper
½ teasp. French mustard   1½ pt.
stock   ¼ pt. white wine or cider
6 small slices of bread   2 oz. cheese :
Gruyère or Parmeson   a little butter

Chop the bacon and heat it
gently in a deep pan till the fat
runs freely. Slice the onions
thinly and fry them slowly in the
bacon fat till golden. Add the
flour, salt and pepper to taste and
continue frying for a few minutes.
Stir in the mustard, the stock and
the wine or cider. Simmer till the
onions are quite soft. Toast the
bread, grate the cheese. Butter
the toast and spread the slices
with grated cheese. Pour the soup
into individual fireproof soup-
bowls, float a round of toast on

each and brown it in a very hot
oven or under the grill.
6 helpings
Cooking time—about 1½ hr.

GOULASH SOUP—
HUNGARIAN

1 oz. dripping   1 onion   1 carrot
1 small parsnip   8 oz. meat (shin
of beef)   1 teasp. paprika
1 tomato   a few bacon rinds
¼ teasp. caraway seeds.   1½ pt.
water   salt and pepper   2 potatoes
¼ pt. sour milk or yoghourt

Melt the fat in a deep pan and
fry the sliced onion, carrot and
parsnip until they begin to brown.
Add the meat in ½ in. cubes, the
paprika, the tomato roughly cut
up, the bacon rinds and caraway
seeds. Heat gently, stirring for a
few minutes. Add the water and
a pinch of salt and bring very
slowly to simmering point. Simmer for 2 hr. Dice the potatoes
and add them to the soup; continue simmering for another hour.
Remove the bacon rinds. Season
soup to taste and stir in the sour
milk or yoghourt.
4–6 helpings
Cooking time—3 hr.

MINESTRONE—ITALIAN

¼ lb. haricot beans   3 pt. water
2 onions   1–2 cloves of garlic
1 oz. lean bacon scraps   2 tablesp.
olive oil   a bunch of herbs
2 large tomatoes   1 glass red wine
2 carrots   1 small turnip   2 sticks
of celery   2 small potatoes   ½ small
cabbage   2 oz. macaroni or fancy
shapes of Italian paste   salt and
pepper   grated cheese

Soak the beans overnight in ½
pt. of the water. Slice the onions,
crush the garlic, chop the bacon.
Heat the oil in a deep pan and fry
the onions very gently for 10 min.
Add the garlic, bacon, herbs, cut-
up tomatoes and the wine. Reduce this mixture by rapid boiling

for 5 min. Add the haricot beans and all the water and simmer for 2 hr. Dice the carrots, turnip and celery and add them to the soup; simmer for a further ½ hr. Add the potatoes, diced, and simmer for another ½ hr. Add the shredded cabbage and the macaroni and simmer for a final 10–15 min. Season the soup, stir into it a little grated cheese and serve the rest separately.

6 helpings
Cooking time—3½ hr.

SOUR CHERRY SOUP—
SCANDINAVIA

1 lb. morello or other acid variety of cherry   pinch of cinnamon
1 pt. water   to each pint of sieved soup : ½ oz. cornflour, arrowroot or minute tapioca   3–4 oz. sugar to taste   ½ pt. white or red wine (optional)   a little lemon rind   whipped cream (optional)

Halve the cherries and crack some of the stones. Put the cherries, stones, cinnamon and water into a pan and simmer till the cherries are soft. Rub the fruit through a hair or nylon sieve. Blend the cornflour with a little wine or water and stir it into the soup. Reboil and stir the soup till it thickens. Sweeten, add the wine (if used) and grated lemon rind. The soup may be served hot or iced. Whipped cream (served separately) makes a delicious accompaniment.

4 helpings
Cooking time—about 20 min.

SAUCES, GRAVIES AND FORCEMEATS

THE main tendency of modern British cookery is to conserve as much as possible of the natural quality and flavour of foods. It is today therefore held that a sauce should enhance and add to—but never overpower or disguise the flavour of the food with which it is served. Sauces should make the food they accompany, both look and taste more delicious and they should if possible add to its food value or make it more digestible.

GRAVIES

Gravy is really meat essence, usually diluted by washing and stirring round the cooking vessel with a little water, as in the making of gravy to serve with roast meat. Gravy may or may not be thickened according to custom in the accompaniments for different kinds of meat.

In the making of gravy for roast meat it is an excellent modern practice to use the water in which green vegetables have been cooked, the only other addition that is permissible is of a good meat or yeast extract.

FOUNDATION SAUCES— SAVOURY

From the following foundation sauces many variations in flavour, texture and colour can be evolved. In the later alphabetical list of recipes the foundation sauces will be referred to constantly.

1. ENGLISH FOUNDATION SAUCE
WHITE SAUCE

For a coating sauce:
2 oz. butter or margarine
2 oz. flour   1 pt. milk or fish stock or white stock or a mixture of stock and milk   salt and pepper to taste

For a pouring sauce:
1½ oz. butter or margarine   1½ oz. flour   1 pt. of liquid as for coating sauce   salt and pepper to taste

(1) *Roux Method*

Melt the fat in a deep saucepan, large enough to hold the amount of liquid with just enough room to spare for beating the sauce. Stir the flour into the fat and over gentle heat allow it to bubble for 2–3 min. On no account allow it to change colour; this is a White Roux. Remove from heat, stir in half the liquid. Return to moderate heat and stir the sauce briskly till it thickens, then beat it vigorously for a minute or two. Stir in the rest of the liquid, always adding the last portion with due regard to the required thickness of the sauce. Boil the sauce for 3 min., beating vigorously. Season and use the sauce at once. If a sauce must be kept hot cover it with wet greaseproof paper and a lid and before use beat it again in case skin or lumps should have formed.

A coating sauce should coat the back of the wooden spoon used for stirring, and should only just settle to its own level in the pan.

A pouring sauce should barely mask the spoon, flow freely, and easily settle to its own level in the pan.

Cooking time—15 min.

(2) *Kneaded Butter and Flour or Beurre Manié*

Knead the butter and flour, or work them together with a fork or spoon until they are quite smoothly mixed.

Heat the liquid, and when just below boiling-point, gradually whisk in the kneaded butter and flour. Whisk the sauce until it boils by which time all the thickening must be smoothly blended into the whole. Season and use.

NOTE: Both White Roux and Beurre Manié may be prepared in advance and stored for weeks, if necessary, in a refrigerator or cold larder. To use: allow 4 oz. to 1 pt. for a coating sauce, 3 oz. to 1 pt. for a pouring sauce.

SAUCES MADE FROM WHITE SAUCE FOUNDATION

ANCHOVY SAUCE

To ½ pt. white sauce made from fish stock *or* water *or* ½ milk and ½ water add 1 *or* 2 teasp. anchovy essence to taste and a few drops of lemon juice and a few drops of carmine to tint the sauce a dull pink.

Serve with fish.

BRAIN SAUCE

½ pt. white sauce (p. 91) made with the liquid in which sheep's head has been cooked   1–2 cooked onions
1 set of sheep's brains
a little vinegar *or* lemon juice
1 dessertsp. chopped parsley

To cook the brains, soak them in vinegar and water for 1 hr., then simmer them very gently in a little of the stock in which the head is being cooked, for 20–30 min. Chop the onion and brains and add them to the finished sauce with the vinegar and parsley.

CAPER SAUCE

To ½ pt. white sauce made with broth from boiled mutton *or* ½ broth and ½ milk, add 1 tablesp. capers and 1 teasp. vinegar in which the capers were pickled.

Serve with boiled mutton or fish.

CHEESE SAUCE

To ½ pt. white sauce (p. 91) made with vegetable boilings *or* milk *or* ½ milk and ½ vegetable liquid, add 2 heaped tablesp. grated cheese, seasoning, mixed English *or* French mustard and a grain or two of cayenne pepper.

Add the cheese to the cooked, seasoned sauce at boiling-point. Do not reboil the sauce, use at once.

EGG SAUCE

½ pt. white sauce made with milk
1 hard-boiled egg   1 teasp. chopped chives, if liked

Chop the hard-boiled egg, stir it, with the chives, into the hot, well-seasoned sauce. Reheat the whole.

FISH SAUCE

Make a white sauce (p. 91), using concentrated fish stock. A few drops of lemon juice improve the flavour.

HOT HORSERADISH SAUCE

To ½ pt. white sauce add 1 rounded tablesp. grated horseradish, 1 teasp. vinegar and ½ teasp. sugar.

LEMON SAUCE—SAVOURY

½ pt. white sauce made with chicken or fish stock, or milk and stock
1 lemon   1–2 tablesp. cream (optional)   1 tablesp. chopped parsley (optional)
½ teasp. sugar (optional)

Peel the rind from the lemon very thinly and simmer it in the milk or stock for 10 min. Strain the liquid and with it make the white sauce. Carefully stir the juice of the lemon and then the cream into the hot sauce but do not boil it again. Sweeten if liked.

Serve with fish, chicken or rabbit.

MAITRE D'HOTEL SAUCE

½ pt. white sauce made with milk or fish stock   1 rounded tablesp. very finely-chopped parsley   juice of ½ lemon   1 oz. butter

Add the lemon juice and chopped parsley to the hot sauce. Whisk the extra butter into the sauce just below boiling-point, adding it a small pat at a time.

Serve mainly with fish or with poultry.

MELTED BUTTER SAUCE

To ½ pt. white sauce (which may be savoury or sweet) made with milk or water, add flavouring as desired. Whisk an extra ounce of butter into the sauce just below boiling-point, a small pat at a time.

Serve with fish, poultry, rabbit and certain vegetables.

MUSHROOM SAUCE—WHITE

½ pt. white sauce
2–4 oz. mushrooms   ½–1 oz. butter

Cook the thinly sliced mushrooms very gently in the butter for 15–20 min. Stir the mushrooms with the butter and their juice into the hot sauce.

Serve with fish and meat entrées, poultry, etc.

MUSTARD SAUCE

½ pt. sauce made with meat or fish stock, milk or milk and stock
1 teasp. dry English mustard or 1 tablesp. French mustard   1 teasp. tarragon vinegar   1 teasp. sugar ½–1 oz. butter

Mix the dry mustard with the vinegar. Whisk the mixed mustard and sugar into the hot sauce. Whisk the butter into the sauce just below boiling-point, adding it a small pat at a time.

Serve with boiled beef, herring or mackerel.

ONION SAUCE—WHITE

To ½ pt. white sauce made from ½ milk and ½ liquor in which onions were boiled, add 2 chopped, cooked onions and a few drops of lemon juice.

Serve with mutton, rabbit or tripe.

OYSTER SAUCE

½ pt. white sauce made with fish stock   6 oysters, fresh or canned liquor from the oysters   salt and pepper   lemon juice

For fresh oysters: strain the liquor from the deep shell, beard the oysters, drop them into the boiling fish stock and simmer them with the lid on the pan very gently 20–30 min., do not allow to boil. Strain the stock and with it make the white sauce. Cut the oysters into 3–4 pieces each and return them to the sauce. Season and add lemon juice. For canned oysters: cut the oysters in 3–4 pieces and add them, together with the liquid from the can, to very thick white sauce. Season and add lemon juice.

PARSLEY SAUCE

½ pt. white sauce made with stock, fish stock or water   1 heaped tablesp. finely-chopped parsley 1 oz. butter

Add the chopped parsley to the boiling sauce, then whisk in the butter, a small pat at a time, at just below boiling-point.

Serve with fish, white meat or vegetables.

SHRIMP SAUCE

To ½ pt. white sauce made with ½ fish stock and ½ milk, add ¼ pt. picked or canned shrimps and a few drops of anchovy essence and lemon juice to taste. Season with cayenne pepper. Serve with fish.

SOYER SAUCE

½ pt. white sauce made with fish stock   2 shallots   ½ oz. butter

1 tablesp. finely-chopped herbs:
thyme, marjoram, tarragon, fennel,
sorrel, parsley   lemon juice
1–2 egg yolks   2 tablesp. cream

Finely chop the shallots and
cook them gently in the butter till
soft; add these to the sauce. Add
herbs and lemon juice to the sauce
and reheat for 2–3 min. Cool the
sauce; mix a little cool sauce with
the egg yolks and cream; stir into
the sauce.

WHITE WINE SAUCE

½ pt. white stock or fish stock
2 oz. butter   1 oz. flour
⅛ pt. white wine   1–2 egg yolks
juice of ½ lemon   salt and pepper

Make a white sauce with the
stock, half the butter and the flour.
To this add the wine and simmer it
for 10 min. Whisk in the remaining butter just below boiling-point,
then stir in the egg yolks mixed
with lemon juice; season. Thicken
the egg yolks without boiling.

Serve with fish or white meat.

2. ENGLISH FOUNDATION SAUCE

BROWN SAUCE

1 small carrot   1 onion
1 oz. dripping   1 oz. flour
1 pt. household stock
salt and pepper.

Thinly slice the carrot and
onion. Melt the dripping and in it
slowly fry the onion and carrot
until they are golden brown. Stir
in the flour and fry it even more
slowly till it is also golden brown.
Stir in the stock, bring to simmering point, season then simmer for
½ hr. Strain the sauce before use.
As the frying of the flour is a long
process, extra colour may be given
to the sauce by adding a piece of
brown onion skin, or a little gravy
browning or a little meat or vegetable extract which will also add
to the flavour.

Cooking time—40 min.–1 hr.

SAUCES MADE FROM BROWN SAUCE FOUNDATION

CIDER SAUCE

½ pt. brown sauce   ¼ pt. cider
½ bay leaf   ¼ clove   salt and pepper

Mix all the ingredients and simmer the sauce to reduce it to the
required thickness. Strain the
sauce.

Serve with braised ham, pork or
duck.

MUSHROOM SAUCE—BROWN

½ pt. brown sauce
2–4 oz. mushrooms

Fry the mushroom stalks with
the other vegetables when making
the brown sauce. Add the mushroom skins and the sliced mushrooms with the stock when making
the sauce, and simmer them for
½ hr. Strain the sauce, lift out and
chop the mushrooms and return
them to the sauce.

NOTE: This sauce may also be
made with Espagnole sauce foundation (p. 101).

ONION SAUCE—BROWN

½ pt. brown sauce using 2 medium-
sized onions (chopped) and omitting
the carrot   nutmeg   salt and pepper
1 teasp. wine vinegar
½ teasp. French or mixed mustard

Make the sauce in the usual way.
Do not strain it. Add nutmeg,
vinegar and mustard at the end of
cooking. Season to taste.

PIQUANT SAUCE

½ pt. brown sauce   1 onion or
2 shallots   1 oz. mushrooms   1 bay
leaf   1 blade of mace   2 tablesp.
vinegar   1 tablesp. halved capers
1 tablesp. chopped gherkins.
1 dessertsp. mushroom ketchup
½ teasp. sugar (optional)

Finely chop the onion or shallots, chop the mushrooms coarsely.
Simmer the onion or shallots, the
bay leaf and mace in the vinegar

for 10 min. Add this mixture and the chopped mushrooms to the brown sauce and simmer till the mushrooms are soft. Add all the other ingredients. Do not strain the sauce but lift out bay leaf and mace.

Serve with pork, mutton or vegetables.

NOTE: This sauce may also be made with Espagnole foundation (p. 101).

SAGE AND ONION SAUCE

½ pt. brown sauce 2 onions 1 oz. butter or pork or goose dripping ½ teasp. chopped fresh sage 1 tablesp. fresh crumbs

The onions may either be boiled till tender and then chopped, or chopped fine and cooked very gently till quite tender, but not brown, in the fat. Add onion, sage and crumbs to the brown sauce and cook it gently for a further 10 min.

Serve with pork, goose or duck.

WALNUT SAUCE

To ½ pt. brown sauce add 4 pickled walnuts, 1 tablesp. walnut vinegar and sugar to taste (optional).

MISCELLANEOUS, UNCLASSIFIED SAUCES
AGRO-DOLCE

Bitter-sweet Sauce

1 onion 1 carrot 1 clove of garlic (optional) 1 bay leaf 6 peppercorns 1 tablesp. olive oil ¼ pt. red wine ⅛ pt. wine vinegar 2 oz. sugar 2 tablesp. water ¼ pt. good meat gravy

SWEETENING

Any one or any mixture of the following to taste: 1 teasp. chopped mint; 1 teasp. finely-shredded candied orange peel; 1 dessertsp. chopped nuts; 1 dessertsp. sultanas; 1 tablesp. grated bitter chocolate

Chop the onion and carrot, crush the garlic. Cook them with the bay leaf and peppercorns very gently in the oil for 15–20 min. Drain off the oil and add the wine and vinegar. Simmer gently ½ hr. In a separate pan boil the sugar, dissolved in the water until it turns golden brown. Add to this the wine mixture. Add the gravy and any one or any mixture of the sweetening ingredients to taste.

Serve with braised meat.

AIOLI

4–6 cloves of garlic or 4 shallots 1 egg yolk salt ⅛ pt. olive oil lemon juice or wine vinegar 1 medium-sized cooked potato cayenne pepper

Crush and pound the garlic to a smooth pulp. Mix with it the egg yolk and salt. Proceed as for mayonnaise (p. 104). Finally work the sauce gradually into the sieved cold potato. Season to taste.

Serve with salads, vegetables, fish or meat.

BOAR'S HEAD SAUCE

Rind of 2 large oranges 1 shallot ½ lb. redcurrant jelly ½ glass port 1 oz. sugar ¼ teasp. mixed mustard cayenne pepper juice of 1 orange

Grate the rind of the oranges, carefully avoiding any pith. Chop the shallot. Put the jelly, port, rind and shallot in a small pan; heat slowly to simmering point, cover, and infuse for ½ hr. over a very gentle heat. Add sugar, mustard, cayenne and orange juice, strain the sauce and cool it. This sauce may be bottled and stored for future use.

Serve with game, venison or mutton.

BREAD SAUCE

1 large onion 2 cloves 1 blade of mace 1 bay leaf 4 peppercorns 1 allspice berry ½ pt. milk 2 oz. dry white breadcrumbs ½ oz. butter

salt and pepper
2 tablesp. cream (optional)

Put the onion and spices into the milk, bring them very slowly to boiling-point. Cover the pan and infuse over a gentle heat for $\frac{1}{2}$–1 hr. Strain the liquid. To it add the crumbs and butter, and season to taste. Keep the mixture just below simmering point for 20 min. Stir in the cream if used, serve the sauce at once.

Serve with roast chicken or turkey.

CHESTNUT SAUCE

$\frac{1}{2}$ lb. chestnuts $\frac{3}{4}$ pt. stock
1 oz. butter   a trace of ground cinnamon   a small strip of lemon rind   salt and pepper
$\frac{1}{8}$ pt. cream (optional)

Score the rounded side of the shells of the chestnuts and bake or boil them for 15–20 min. Remove shells and skins. Simmer the chestnuts until soft in the stock, about $\frac{1}{2}$ hr. Rub them through a fine wire sieve. Reheat the sauce with the butter and flavourings, season to taste. Add the cream just below boiling-point. Serve at once.

Serve with roast chicken or turkey.

CURRY SAUCE

1 medium-sized onion   1 oz. butter or margarine   1 small cooking apple
$\frac{1}{2}$ oz. curry powder $\frac{1}{2}$ oz. rice flour or flour $\frac{1}{2}$ pt. white stock, coconut infusion (see below) or water $\frac{1}{2}$ teasp. black treacle
1–2 teasp. lemon juice
1 dessertsp. chutney   salt

Chop the onion, put it into a saucepan and fry it very gently in the butter for 10 min. Chop the apple and cook it in the butter with the onion for a further 10 min. Stir in the curry powder and heat it for a few minutes. Add the flour and then stir in the liquid. When boiling, add all the other

ingredients and simmer the sauce for at least $\frac{1}{2}$ hr., or better $1\frac{1}{2}$ hr.

To make the coconut infusion: Soak 1 oz. desiccated *or* fresh grated coconut in $\frac{1}{2}$ pt. water for a few minutes, bring slowly to boiling-point and infuse it for 10 min. Wring the coconut in a piece of muslin to extract all the liquid.

DEVIL SAUCE

1 oz. butter, margarine or beef dripping   1 oz. flour $\frac{1}{2}$ pt. good meat gravy   1–2 tablesp. Worcester or other commercial sauce   2 teasp. lemon juice $\frac{1}{4}$ teasp. anchovy essence   1 teasp. mixed mustard
$\frac{1}{4}$ teasp. pepper $\frac{1}{2}$ teasp. grated lemon rind $\frac{1}{2}$ teasp. chopped shallot   1 teasp. chopped capers
$\frac{1}{2}$ teasp. chilli vinegar
a very little cayenne pepper

Make a brown sauce with the fat, flour and gravy (*see* p. 94). Add all the other ingredients to taste and simmer them together for 5–10 min.

Serve with fried or grilled beef, or mutton.

CHAUDFROID SAUCES

WHITE CHAUDFROID SAUCE

$\frac{1}{2}$ pt. Béchamel sauce $\frac{1}{4}$ pt. aspic jelly $\frac{1}{4}$ oz. powdered gelatine salt and pepper   1 teasp. wine vinegar *or* lemon juice
1 tablesp. thick cream

Have the sauce just warm. Heat the jelly over hot water and in it dissolve the gelatine. Cool the jelly until it also is just warm. Fold the jelly into the sauce and season the mixture, add the vinegar or juice. Wring the sauce through muslin, fold in the cream.

Use the sauce for masking fish, poultry or veal served en chaudfroid, using it when cold but liquid.

Brown Chaudfroid Sauce: As above substituting Espagnole sauce for Béchamel sauce.

Use for masking beef, mutton or game.

Fawn Chaudfroid Sauce: Use Velouté sauce in place of Béchamel sauce.

Use for lamb, veal, poultry instead of white chaudfroid.

Green Chaudfroid Sauce: As for White Chaudfroid Sauce, using 1 tablesp. of spinach purée or green colouring with the Béchamel sauce.

Tomato Chaudfroid Sauce: Substitute Tomato sauce for Béchamel sauce.

FRUIT SAUCES TO SERVE WITH MEAT

APPLE SAUCE

1 lb. apples 2 tablesp. water
½ oz. butter or margarine rind and juice of ½ lemon sugar to taste

Stew the apples very gently with the water, butter and lemon rind until they are pulpy. Beat them quite smooth or rub them through a hair or nylon sieve. Reheat the sauce with the lemon juice and sweeten to taste.

Serve with roast pork, roast goose or pork sausages. Excellent also as a sweet sauce with ginger pudding.

APPLE SAUCE WITH HORSE-RADISH

As for apple sauce with the addition of 1–2 tablesp. grated horseradish.

Serve with pork or beef.

CHERRY SAUCE

½ lb. freshly-stewed or bottled cherries, morellos for preference
¼ pt. juice in which cherries were cooked or bottled sugar to taste
2 tablesp. redcurrant jelly pepper
1–2 teasp. vinegar 2 tablesp. red wine ½ teasp. arrowroot (optional)

Stone the cherries. Heat all the ingredients together and simmer the sauce till the juice is slightly syrupy, or blend the arrowroot with 1 teasp. cold water and add it to thicken the liquid.

Serve with braised game or rabbit.

CRANBERRY SAUCE

½ lb. cranberries ¼–½ pt. water
sugar to taste

Stew the cranberries till soft, using ¼ pt. water and adding more if needed. Rub the fruit through a hair or nylon sieve. Sweeten to taste. For economy, half cranberries and half sour cooking apples make an excellent sauce.

Serve with roast turkey, chicken or game.

GOOSEBERRY SAUCE

½ lb. green gooseberries ¼ pt. water
½ oz. butter 1 oz. sugar lemon juice nutmeg salt and pepper
½ teasp. chopped chives (optional)
a few chopped leaves of sorrel (optional)

Stew the gooseberries very gently with the water and butter until they are pulpy. Beat them quite smooth or rub them through a hair or nylon sieve. Reheat the sauce, stir in the sugar, add lemon juice and grated nutmeg to taste, season. Stir in the chives and sorrel if used.

Serve with mackerel.

REDCURRANT SAUCE

¼ lb. redcurrant jelly ⅛ pt. port or other red wine

Heat the two ingredients together gently until the jelly is melted.

Serve with game, venison *or* as a sweet sauce with puddings.

GRAVIES

GRAVY—

for any Roast Joint except Pork
Meat dripping from the roasting tin
flour essences from the joint
water in which vegetables have been boiled *or* stock salt and pepper

Drain the fat from the roasting tin, carefully saving any sediment and meat juices. Dredge into the thin film of dripping sufficient flour to absorb it all. Brown this flour slowly till of a nut brown colour. Stir in water in which green vegetables or potatoes have been cooked, or stock, allowing ½ pt. for 6 persons. Boil the gravy and season it to taste.

To obtain a brown colour without browning the flour add a few drips of gravy browning from the end of a skewer. To improve the flavour add a meat or yeast extract.

GRAVY (thickened)

(for a Stuffed Joint or for Roast Pork)

Bones and trimmings from the joint
cold water salt

To each pint of gravy:
1 oz. dripping 1 oz. flour

Make a stock from the bones, allowing at least 2 hr. simmering —much longer if possible (*see* p. 69). Melt the dripping and sprinkle in the flour. Brown the flour slowly until a nut brown colour. Stir in the stock, boil up and season to taste.

GIBLET GRAVY for poultry

1 set of giblets 1 onion (optional)
cold water to cover flour
salt and pepper

Simmer the giblets very gently in the water with the onion (if liked) for at least 2 hr.—much longer if possible. Drain the fat from the tin in which the bird has been roasted, carefully saving the sediment. Dredge into the thin film of dripping only sufficient flour to absorb it all. Brown this flour until a nut brown colour. Stir in the liquid from the giblets, boil up and season to taste.

GRAVY for Game

Bones, giblets or trimmings of game

cold water to cover 1 bay leaf
thyme 1 clove 6 peppercorns and
1 piece of onion to each pt. of water
salt

Make stock from the above ingredients. Drain all the fat from the roasting-tin and rinse the tin with the game stock, using no flour. Boil the gravy and skim it.

GRAVY for Hare—JUGGED GRAVY

½ lb. shin of beef 1 pt. water
small piece of lean ham or bacon
bone and rinds ½ carrot 2 in. of
celery 1 blade of mace 4 peppercorns a bunch of herbs 1 clove
dripping flour salt 2 tablesp. redcurrant jelly 1–2 tablesp. port wine

Make stock with the beef, water, ham or bone, vegetables, spices and herbs (*see* p. 70). Make a thickened brown gravy (opposite) and add to it the jelly and port.

Use also for venison.

HOLLANDAISE SAUCE

See also Mock Hollandaise (p. 101)

2 tablesp. wine vinegar 2 egg yolks
2–4 oz. butter salt and pepper
lemon juice

Boil the vinegar till it is reduced by half; allow to cool. Mix the cool vinegar with the egg yolks in a basin and place this over hot water. Whisk the egg yolks till they begin to thicken, then whisk in the butter gradually until all is absorbed. Season, add lemon juice to taste and serve immediately.

Serve with fish or vegetables.

HORSERADISH CREAM (COLD)

2 tablesp. grated horseradish
1 tablesp. wine vinegar or lemon
juice 2 teasp. castor sugar salt
and pepper to taste mixed mustard
to taste ¼ pt. cream

Mix all ingredients except the cream. Half-whip the cream, i.e. until the trail of the whisk just shows on the surface. Lightly fold the horseradish mixture into the cream. Serve the sauce very cold. It may be chilled in a refrigerator and served semi-solid.

Serve with beef.

MINT SAUCE

3 heaped tablesp. finely-chopped mint   a pinch of salt   2 teasp. sugar 2 tablesp. boiling water ¼ pt. vinegar

The mint should be young and freshly gathered if possible. Wash well, pick the leaves from the stalks and chop the leaves finely.

Mix the mint, salt and sugar in the sauce-boat. Pour on to them the boiling water and leave the mixture to cool. Add the vinegar and if possible leave the sauce for 1 hr. to infuse the flavour of mint into the vinegar.

Serve with roast lamb.

MOUSSELINE SAUCE— SAVOURY, HOT

2 egg yolks   ¼ pt. cream   1 tablesp. stock   grated nutmeg   cayenne pepper   salt   ½ oz. butter   lemon juice   1 whipped egg white

Put all the ingredients except butter, lemon juice and egg white into a china basin. Place the basin over boiling water and whisk the mixture briskly till it thickens. Remove from heat and whisk in the butter and lemon juice. Fold in the egg white. Serve at once.

Serve with fish, poultry or vegetables.

PORT WINE SAUCE

1 tablesp. redcurrant jelly ¼ pt. good mutton or venison gravy ⅛ pt. port wine

Heat all the ingredients together until the jelly is melted.

Serve with roast mutton or venison.

SHARP SAUCE—HOT or COLD

1 shallot   2 hard-boiled egg yolks 4 anchovies   ½ teasp. mixed mustard

2 teasp. vinegar   1 teasp. chopped capers   salt and pepper sugar to taste For a cold sauce. ¼ pt. thin cream For a hot sauce : ¼ pt. good meat gravy

Chop the shallot finely. Crush and pound the hard-boiled egg yolks, anchovies and shallot together. Add the other ingredients to this paste. For a cold sauce, half-whip the cream and fold it carefully into the other ingredients. For a hot sauce, add the gravy (boiling) and reheat the sauce. Serve with meat, fish or vegetables.

SOUR–SWEET SAUCE

2 onions   1½ oz. butter or margarine 1½ oz. flour   ¾ pt. water or stock 4 tablesp. vinegar   1–2 teasp. any good commercial bottled sauce 2 tablesp. sugar   1 level teasp. French mustard   1 level teasp. yeast or meat extract   salt and pepper

Chop the onions, put into a saucepan and fry them till tender and golden-brown in the butter. Add the flour and brown it a very little. Stir in the liquid, bring to the boil, stirring all the time. Add the other ingredients and simmer the sauce for 15–20 min.

Serve with boiled beef or other meat, fish or vegetables.

TOMATO SAUCE

1 onion   1 small carrot   1 oz. bacon scraps or bacon bone or rinds ½ oz. butter or margarine 4 medium-sized tomatoes, fresh, bottled or canned   ½ oz. rice flour ½ pt. white second stock or liquid from canned or bottled tomatoes salt and pepper   lemon juice   sugar grated nutmeg

Slice the onion and carrot. Put them into a saucepan with the bacon and fry them in the fat without browning them for 10 min. Slice and add the tomatoes and cook them for 5 min. Sprinkle in the rice flour, add the stock or juice, stir till the sauce boils. Simmer the sauce for 45 min. Rub the sauce through a hair or nylon sieve. Reheat, season and add lemon juice, sugar and nutmeg to taste.

TOMATO SAUCE—CLEAR
(*quick method*)

½ pt. canned tomato juice 1 heaped teasp. arrowroot 1 onion or shallot salt and pepper grated nutmeg lemon juice sugar

Blend the arrowroot with a little cold juice. Slice the onion and simmer it for 10 min. in the juice. Stir in the blended arrowroot and boil it for a minute. Season the sauce, add nutmeg, a few drops of lemon juice and sugar to taste. Strain the sauce.

THE FRENCH FOUNDATION SAUCES (GRANDES SAUCES)

These important sauces are internationally famous. The white Béchamel, the brown Espagnole and the fawn Velouté form the bases of hundreds of more complex sauces; while Mayonnaise, though not lending itself to so many additions still has a number of variations. A representative selection of the sauces derived from each is given here under the foundation or "parent" sauce.

1. BECHAMEL SAUCE

1 pt. milk 1 small onion 1 small carrot 2 in. celery stick 1 bay leaf 1 clove 1 blade of mace salt 6 peppercorns a small bunch of herbs 2 oz. butter 2 oz. flour ⅛ pt. cream (optional)

Warm the milk with the vegetables, herbs, salt and spices, and bring it slowly to simmering point. Put a lid on the pan and stand it in a warm place on the cooker to infuse for ½ hr. Strain the milk, melt the butter, add the

flour, cook this roux for a few minutes without browning it. Stir the flavoured milk gradually into the roux. Bring the sauce to boiling-point, stirring vigorously. For an extra smooth result, wring the sauce through damp muslin. If cream is used, add it to the sauce just at boiling-point and do not reboil it.

Serve with chicken, veal, fish or white vegetables.

NOTE: Béchamel sauce may be made with ½ white stock and ½ milk, the result will have a good flavour but will not be so creamy in texture.

Cooking time—40 min.

SAUCES MADE FROM BECHAMEL FOUNDATION

BEARNAISE SAUCE

¼ pt. Béchamel sauce 2 shallots sprig of tarragon sprig of chervil 6 peppercorns ⅛ pt. white wine or wine vinegar 2–3 egg yolks 4 oz. butter 2 teasp. lemon juice salt and pepper

Chop shallots and herbs. Put wine in a pan with shallots, herbs and peppercorns and simmer gently till reduced by half, then strain. Mix egg yolks and sauce and heat in a double boiler. Add wine and whisk in the butter, a pat at a time. The water must not be allowed to boil or sauce will curdle. Season sauce and add lemon juice, add a little chopped tarragon and chervil and use sauce at once.

CARDINAL SAUCE

¼ pt. Béchamel sauce ¼ pt. well-reduced fish stock cayenne pepper salt ⅛ pt. cream 1 dessertsp. lemon juice 1–2 oz. lobster butter

Heat sauce and stock together and season. Just below boiling-point stir in cream and lemon juice and whisk in the lobster butter, a small pat at a time. Do not allow sauce to boil. Cardinal sauce may be made with Velouté sauce made from fish stock.

HOLLANDAISE SAUCE— ECONOMICAL or "MOCK" HOLLANDAISE

See also p. 98.

½ pt. Béchamel sauce   1–2 egg yolks
2 tablesp. cream   1 dessertsp. lemon juice or wine vinegar   cayenne pepper   salt

Mix the egg yolks and cream, stir them into the hot sauce—well below boiling-point and cook the egg yolk without boiling it. Add the lemon juice and seasoning to taste. Use the sauce at once.

Serve with salmon or other fish, or with delicately flavoured vegetables such as asparagus and seakale.

MORNAY SAUCE

½ pt. Béchamel sauce   1 egg yolk
¾ oz. Parmesan cheese   ¾ oz. Gruyère or Cheddar cheese   ⅛ pt. cream (optional)   cayenne pepper

For a fish dish:

¼ pt. fish stock reduced to 2 tablesp. or 2 tablesp. fish fumet (p. 69)

Add the egg yolk mixed with a little cooled sauce to the Béchamel sauce well below boiling-point. Cook the egg yolk without boiling it. Stir in the grated cheese and the cream, season and serve the sauce at once. If fish fumet is used add it hot, before the cream.

Serve with fish or vegetables.

SOUBISE SAUCE

½ pt. Béchamel sauce   ½ lb. onions
1½ oz. butter   1–2 tablesp. stock
salt and pepper   sugar   nutmeg

Peel and slice the onions and cook them gently in ½ oz. of the butter and just enough stock to moisten them. When they are tender, sieve them. Have the sauce very thick, add to it the onion purée, reheat, season and add sugar and nutmeg to taste. Whisk the remaining 1 oz. butter into the sauce at boiling-point, adding a small pat at a time. Do not allow the sauce to boil.

Serve at once.

TARTARE SAUCE—ECONOMICAL (HOT)

½ pt. Béchamel sauce   1–2 egg yolks
1 tablesp. cream   1 heaped teasp.
chopped gherkin   1 heaped teasp.
chopped capers   1 dessertsp.
chopped parsley
lemon juice or wine vinegar

Mix the egg yolks and cream, stir them into the hot sauce well below boiling-point. Cook the egg yolk without boiling it. Add the gherkin, capers and parsley and flavour with lemon juice or vinegar. Serve at once.

Serve with salmon and other fish.

2. ESPAGNOLE SAUCE

Spanish Brown sauce

1 onion   1 carrot   2 oz. mushrooms or mushroom trimmings   2 oz. lean raw ham or bacon   2 oz. butter or dripping   2 oz. flour   1 pt. brown stock   bouquet garni   6 peppercorns   1 bay leaf   ¼ pt. tomato pulp salt   ⅛ pt. sherry (optional)

Slice the vegetables, chop the ham. Melt the fat and fry the ham for a few minutes and then, very slowly, the vegetables until they are golden brown. Add the flour and continue frying very slowly till all is a rich brown. Add the stock, herbs and spices and stir till the sauce simmers; simmer for ½ hr. Add the tomato pulp and simmer the sauce for a further ½ hr. Wring the sauce through a tammy cloth or rub it through a fine hair or nylon sieve. Season, add the sherry, if used, and reheat the sauce.

SAUCES MADE FROM ESPAGNOLE FOUNDATION

BROWN CAPER SAUCE

½ pt. Espagnole sauce or Brown
sauce (p. 94)   1 onion or shallot
1 tablesp. halved capers   1 teasp.
caper vinegar   1 teasp. anchovy
essence   cayenne pepper
lemon juice to taste

Chop the onion or shallot and
simmer it in the sauce for 10 min.
then strain. Add the other ingredients, reheat the sauce.

Serve with steak, kidneys or fish.

DEMI-GLACE SAUCE

Half glaze

½ pt. Espagnole sauce   ¼ pt. juices
from roast meat or ¼ pt. stock and
1 teasp. good beef extract or
meat glaze

Boil the sauce and meat juices
together until well reduced. Skim
off any fat before serving the sauce.

Serve with meat, poultry, game,
etc.

GAME SAUCE

½ pt. Espagnole sauce   trimmings
and carcase of strong-flavoured roast
game   1 onion   2 shallots   1 blade
of mace   4 peppercorns   ¼ clove
parsley stalks   sprig of thyme
1 bay leaf   ¼ pt. sherry or stock

Break the game carcase into
small pieces, chop the onion and
shallots. Put the vegetables, game
scraps, spices and herbs into a pan
with the sherry or stock and simmer very slowly for ½ hr. Strain
the liquid into the hot Espagnole
sauce and reduce it slightly.

ITALIAN SAUCE—BROWN

½ pt. Espagnole sauce   4 shallots
6 mushrooms   1 tablesp. olive oil
⅛ pt. stock   ⅛ pt. white wine
(optional)   parsley stalks   sprig of
thyme   1 bay leaf   salt and pepper

Chop the shallots and mushrooms and very gently cook them

for 10 min. in the olive oil. Add
the stock, wine (if used), herbs and
spices and simmer gently until reduced by half. Add the Espagnole
sauce and cook gently for 20 min.
Season and lift out the herbs.

Serve with fish and meat.

MADEIRA SAUCE

½ pt. demi-glace sauce (opposite)
⅛ pt. Madeira wine   1 teasp. meat
glaze or good beef extract
salt and pepper

Simmer the sauce, wine and
extract (if used) together until well
reduced. Season to taste, put in
the meat glaze (if used), stir until
dissolved; strain and use as required.

Serve with meat, poultry and
game.

MUSHROOM SAUCE—BROWN

See p. 94.

OLIVE SAUCE

½ pt. Espagnole sauce   12 French
olives   lemon juice to taste

Rinse the whole olives to remove the preserving vinegar,
stone them. Heat the olives carefully in the Espagnole sauce for
10 min. Add lemon juice to taste.

ORANGE SAUCE—SAVOURY

½ pt. Espagnole sauce   ½ orange
½ lemon   ⅛ pt. red wine (optional)
2 tablesp. redcurrant jelly   salt
cayenne pepper   pinch of sugar

Remove the outer orange rind
without the pith, and cut it in neat
thin strips. Cover the orange rind
with a little cold water; stew till
just tender; then strain. Squeeze
the orange and lemon juice into
the sauce, add the orange rind.
Reheat, add the wine (if used), the
redcurrant jelly, season with salt,
pepper and sugar to taste.

Serve with roast duck, goose or
wild duck.

POIVRADE SAUCE (PEPPER SAUCE)

½ pt. Espagnole sauce   2 shallots
1 sprig of thyme   1 bay leaf
12 peppercorns   ½ glass red wine
2 tablesp. wine vinegar
ground pepper to taste

Finely chop the shallots and simmer them with the herbs and spices in the wine and vinegar until reduced by half. Strain the liquid into the hot Espagnole sauce and add extra ground pepper to taste.

REFORM SAUCE

½ pt. Poivrade sauce   ½ small glass
port   1 tablesp. redcurrant jelly
1 dessertsp. shredded gherkin
1 dessertsp. shredded cooked
mushroom   1 dessertsp. shredded
cooked tongue   1 dessertsp.
shredded hard-boiled egg white

Gently heat all the ingredients in the hot Poivrade sauce.
Serve with cutlets.

SALMI SAUCE

½ pt. Espagnole sauce (p. 101)
2 shallots   a few mushroom
trimmings   1 tablesp. olive oil
¼ pt. game stock   ⅛ pt. red wine
(optional)   sprig of thyme   1 bay
leaf   1 dessertsp. redcurrant jelly

Chop the shallots, put them in a saucepan and fry them with the mushrooms in the olive oil until they are golden brown. Add the stock and wine (if used) with the herbs. Simmer till reduced by half. Add the Espagnole sauce and simmer very gently for 10 min. Strain, add the redcurrant jelly.

Serve with game or duck "en casserole".

3. VELOUTE SAUCE
French Fawn sauce

2 oz. butter   6 button mushrooms
or mushroom trimmings
12 peppercorns   a few parsley stalks
2 oz. flour   1 pt. good white stock

(p. 69)   salt and pepper   lemon
juice   ⅛–¼ pt. cream

Melt the butter in a saucepan and gently cook the mushrooms, peppercorns and parsley for 10 min. Add the flour and cook for a few minutes without browning it. Stir in the stock, bring the sauce to simmering point and simmer for 1 hr. Wring the sauce through a tammy cloth or damp muslin. Season, add lemon juice, and reheat. Just at boiling-point stir in the cream. The mushrooms may be rinsed and used as garnish for the dish.

Serve with chicken, veal, sweetbreads, fish or vegetables.

SAUCES MADE FROM VELOUTE FOUNDATION

PAPRIKA SAUCE

½ pt. Velouté sauce   1 small
red pimento or sweet pepper, fresh
or canned   paprika pepper to taste
2 tablesp.–⅛ pt. cream

Shred the pimento into neat, equal-length strips. If raw pimento is used it may be necessary to simmer it for 10 min. and to remove the skin before shredding it. Add paprika pepper to the sauce to give it a pink colour and desired flavour. Carefully reheat the pimento strips in the sauce. Stir in the cream when the sauce is below boiling-point.

Serve with veal or beef:

RAVIGOTE SAUCE—HOT

½ pt. Velouté sauce
1 tablesp. Ravigote butter
1 tablesp. wine vinegar   nutmeg
sugar   salt and pepper

RAVIGOTE BUTTER

1 heaped tablesp. of a mixture of
picked parsley, chervil leaves,
chopped shallot, tarragon leaves,
chopped chives, crushed garlic
½ oz. butter

To make the Ravigote butter,

scald the herbs, shallot and garlic in a little boiling water; drain them and wring dry in muslin. Pound the herbs and butter together, then rub through a fine sieve. Heat the Velouté sauce, add to it the vinegar, nutmeg, sugar and seasoning. Whisk the Ravigote butter into the sauce, adding a small pat at a time, keeping the sauce almost at boiling point but not allowing it to boil. Serve the sauce at once.

SUPREME SAUCE

½ pt. Velouté sauce   2 tablesp.–⅛ pt. cream   1 egg yolk   ½–1 oz. butter nutmeg to taste   lemon juice salt and pepper

Heat the Velouté sauce, preferably in a double boiler. Mix the egg yolk and cream, and stir into the sauce, cook without boiling, till the egg yolk thickens. Whisk in the butter, a small pat at a time. Add a pinch of nutmeg, a few drops of lemon juice, season and use the sauce at once.

Serve with any meat, poultry, fish or vegetables.

4. MAYONNAISE

1–2 egg yolks (new laid)   salt and pepper   mustard   ½–¾ pt. best olive oil   mixed vinegars to taste— 4 parts wine vinegar or lemon juice, 2 parts tarragon and 1 part chilli vinegar

The eggs and oil should be at the same temperature and that not too cold. In summer it is easier to make a good mayonnaise beginning with 2 egg yolks.

Remove every trace of egg white from the yolks. Put the yolks in a thick basin which will stand steady in spite of vigorous beating. Add to the egg yolks the pepper, salt and mustard to taste. Drop by drop add the olive oil, beating or whisking vigorously all the time. As the mayonnaise thickens the olive oil can be poured in a thin, steady stream but whisking must never slacken. When the mixture is really thick a few drops of vinegar or lemon juice stirred in will thin it again. Continue whisking in the oil, alternately with a little vinegar until the whole amount is added.

To store the mayonnaise cover it with damp muslin and store in a cool larder or refrigerator.

To use after storing, whisk it again and add a drop or two more vinegar.

If the mayonnaise should curdle, break fresh egg yolk and beat into this the curdled mixture just as the oil was added originally.

COLD SAUCES MADE FROM MAYONNAISE

ANDALUSIAN SAUCE

½ pt. mayonnaise   2 tablesp. concentrated tomato purée 1 small, sweet, red pepper (pimento)

Cut the pimento in thin strips and stir into the mayonnaise with the tomato purée.

ASPIC MAYONNAISE

½ pt. mayonnaise   ¼–½ pt. aspic jelly

Have the mayonnaise really stiff and the jelly liquid but cold. Fold the jelly carefully into the mayonnaise. Use the aspic mayonnaise when it is beginning to thicken.

NOTE: The smaller proportion of jelly gives a mixture which may be piped through a forcing tube and bag; the higher proportion of jelly gives a mixture for coating cold foods served with salad.

COLD GREEN MOUSSELINE SAUCE

½ pt. mayonnaise 1 tablesp. cooked spinach purée 2 tablesp. whipped cream

Fold the cold purée and then the whipped cream into the mayonnaise. Serve with fish.

ESCOFFIER SAUCE (MAYON-NAISE)

¼ pt. mayonnaise ½ teasp. horse-radish cream 1 teasp. chopped parsley 1 teasp. chopped chervil

Fold the horseradish cream into the mayonnaise, then the parsley and chervil.

REMOULADE SAUCE

¼ pt. mayonnaise 1 teasp. French mustard a few drops of anchovy essence 1 dessertsp. mixed chopped: gherkins, capers, parsley, tarragon, chervil

Stir the mustard, essence and herbs into the mayonnaise.

TARTARE SAUCE—COLD

¼ pt. mayonnaise 1 teasp. each of chopped gherkin, chopped olives, chopped capers, chopped parsley, chopped chives a little French mustard 1 dessertsp. wine vinegar a little dry white wine (optional)

Mix the chopped ingredients into the mayonnaise, add the mustard. Thin to the required consistency with vinegar and wine.

Serve with fried and grilled fish and meat.

TOMATO MAYONNAISE

¼ pt. thick mayonnaise ½ pt. tomato purée, canned or fresh, or ⅛ pt. cold tomato sauce or bottled tomato sauce

Fold the tomato purée carefully into the mayonnaise.

NOTE: If fresh tomatoes are used some of the juice must be pressed out and kept apart from the firm flesh before sieving.

SWEET SAUCES TO SERVE WITH PUDDINGS

APPLE SAUCE

See p. 97.
Serve with hot gingerbread or steamed ginger pudding.

APRICOT SAUCE

½ lb. apricots, fresh or canned
¼ pt. water or syrup from can
1–2 oz. brown sugar lemon juice
1 teasp. Maraschino (optional)
1 level teasp. arrowroot

Stone the apricots and stew them till soft in the water. When soft rub them through a hair or nylon sieve. Meanwhile crack the stones, scald and skin the kernels: Add sugar, lemon juice, liqueur (if used) and kernels to the sauce. Reheat the sauce, stirring in the arrowroot blended with a little cold water. Bring to the boil and serve the sauce.

See also Jam Sauce, p. 108.

ARROWROOT SAUCE—CLEAR

1 rounded teasp. arrowroot ½ pt. fruit juice or white wine and fruit juice or cider lemon rind sugar lemon juice

Blend the arrowroot with a little cold liquid. Boil the rest of the liquid with lemon juice and rind to taste. Remove rind and stir the boiling liquid into the blended arrowroot, return the mixture to the pan and bring it just to boiling-point. Sweeten to taste.

BRANDY BUTTER (Hard Sauce)

See p. 401.

BRANDY SAUCE (1)

1 level teasp. arrowroot or cornflour
½ pt. milk 1 egg yolk ⅛ pt. good brandy 1 teasp. sugar, Barbados if possible

Blend the arrowroot with a little cold milk. Heat the rest of the milk and when boiling stir it into the blended arrowroot. Return mixture to pan and bring to boil-ing-point. Mix together the egg yolk, brandy and sugar. Cool the arrowroot sauce a little, then stir into it the egg mixture. Cook without boiling until the egg yolk thickens.

BRANDY SAUCE (2)—RICH

¼ pt. thin cream   2 egg yolks
1 dessertsp. light Barbados sugar
⅛ pt. good brandy

Mix all the ingredients in a basin. Set the basin over a saucepan of boiling water and whisk steadily until the mixture thickens.

BUTTERSCOTCH SAUCE

4 oz. moist, dark brown sugar
¼ pt. water   1 oz. butter   1 strip of lemon rind   1 teasp. arrowroot
a few drops of vanilla essence
a few drops of lemon juice

Dissolve the sugar in the ¼ pt. water, add the butter and lemon rind and boil for 5 min. Remove lemon rind. Blend the arrowroot with 2 teasp. water; thicken the sauce with the blended arrowroot. Add vanilla and lemon juice to taste.

CARAMEL SAUCE

2 oz. sugar or golden syrup
½ pt. water   ½ pt. custard sauce
lemon juice or vanilla essence

Put the sugar and 2 tablesp. water in a small pan; dissolve the sugar over gentle heat, then boil the syrup so made until it is a deep golden brown. Add to the caramel the rest of the water and leave it in a warm place to dissolve. If golden syrup is used heat it without water until of a golden-brown colour, then dissolve it in the water. Add the dissolved caramel to the custard sauce and flavour to taste.

CHANTILLY SAUCE—COLD

1 lb. cooking apples   1½ oz. sugar
1 oz. butter   ¼ pt. cream

Peel, core and slice the apples, put them in a saucepan with 2–3 tablesp. cold water. Add the butter and sugar, cook gently until tender, then rub through a nylon sieve. Whip the cream stiffly, stir it into the apple purée, use as required.

CHOCOLATE SAUCE (1)

3 oz. bitter chocolate or cooking chocolate or 1 heaped tablesp. cocoa
½ pt. water   ¼ oz. cornflour or custard powder   sugar if required
vanilla essence   1 teasp. rum (optional)   a few drops of coffee essence (optional)

Break the chocolate in rough pieces and warm them gently with a very little water. When melted, beat the chocolate mixture till smooth, adding the rest of the water gradually. Thicken the sauce with the cornflour or custard powder blended with a little cold water. Flavour and sweeten to taste.

If cocoa is used, mix it with the dry cornflour before blending with water.

CHOCOLATE SAUCE (2)—RICH

¼ lb. chocolate   ½ pt. milk
2–3 egg yolks   vanilla essence
1 teasp. rum   sugar, if required
1 egg white (optional)

Dissolve the chocolate in the milk. Make a custard with the egg yolks and the chocolate-flavoured milk—see Custard Sauce. Flavour and sweeten to taste. If liked one egg white may be whipped to a stiff froth and folded into the finished sauce.

CHRISTMAS PUDDING SAUCE

2 eggs   ⅛ pt. rum or brandy
1½ oz. castor sugar   ⅛ pt. water

Whisk all the ingredients in a basin placed over a pan of boiling water. Whisk vigorously all the time until the sauce is thick and frothy. Serve at once.

COFFEE SAUCE

¼ pt. very strong coffee   ¼ pt. milk
1 heaped teasp. cornflour or custard powder   1 egg yolk   sugar to taste

vanilla essence (optional)
1 teasp. rum (optional)

Thicken the coffee and milk
with the cornflour or custard
powder (see Cornflour Sauce).
Cool the sauce, add the egg yolk
and cook it without boiling.
Sweeten and flavour to taste.

CORNFLOUR CUSTARD

½ oz. lightweight cornflour or
custard powder   ½ pt. milk
1 dessertsp. sugar   flavouring
1 egg yolk

Blend the cornflour with a little
of the cold milk. Boil the rest of
the milk with thinly cut lemon
rind if used for flavouring. Remove rind and stir the boiling
liquid into the blended cornflour.
Rinse the pan and return the
sauce to it. Just bring it to boiling-
point for custard powder; boil for
3 min. for cornflour. Sweeten and
flavour the sauce unless lemon
rind has been used. Cool the sauce,
add the egg yolk and sugar and
cook gently until the egg thickens
without boiling. At once pour out
of pan into a basin or the sauce-
boat. Flavour and add extra
sweetening if required.

CORNFLOUR SAUCE

½ pt. milk   ½ oz. cornflour
1 dessertsp. sugar   lemon rind or
any flavour to blend with the flavour
of pudding which it accompanies

Blend the cornflour with a little
of the cold milk. Boil the rest of
the milk with the thinly cut lemon
rind if used. Remove rind and stir
the boiling liquid into the blended
cornflour. Rinse the pan and return the sauce to it. Bring to boiling-point and boil for 3 min.
Sweeten and flavour the sauce,
unless lemon rind has been used
for flavouring.

CUSTARD SAUCE

1 dessertsp. sugar   2 egg yolks or
1 whole egg   ½ pt. milk   flavouring

Mix together the sugar and egg
yolks or whole egg. Warm the
milk until about at blood heat.
Stir the milk into the egg, return
the whole to the rinsed pan and
cook gently until the egg thickens,
without boiling or the egg will
curdle. At once pour out of the
pan into a basin or the sauceboat.
Flavour and add extra sweetening
if required. If the custard should
curdle, whisk it vigorously just
before serving.

FROTHY SAUCE

½ pt. milk   1 tablesp. sugar   2 eggs
¼ pt. sherry or white wine
flavouring of lemon rind or any
spice, if liked

Heat the milk. Dissolve the
sugar in the milk; then allow to
cool a little. Whisk the eggs and
sherry together, add the warm
milk. In a basin, placed over boiling water, whisk all the ingredients until the sauce is thick and
frothy. Serve at once.

FRUIT SAUCE

Fruits suitable are: Damsons,
Plums, Raspberries, Redcurrants,
Blackberries.

1 lb. bottled or fresh fruit   a very
little water to stew   sugar to sweeten
lemon juice, if liked   1 teasp.
(rounded) arrowroot to each ½ pt.
purée

Stew the fruit in the water till
soft, sieve it. Sweeten, flavour and
thicken the sauce with arrowroot
blended with a little cold water or
fruit juice.

FRUIT AND YOGHOURT
SAUCE—COLD

½ pt. fruit purée   1 bottle plain
yoghourt   sugar to sweeten

Carefully mix the cold fruit
purée and yoghourt together.
Sweeten well as the mixture will
be very sour.

See also Fruit Sauces to Serve

with Meat; *also* Apple and Apricot Sauces in this section.

GINGER SAUCE

½ pt. cornflour or custard sauce
1 level teasp. ground ginger   golden syrup to sweeten   lemon juice
½ teasp. grated lemon rind (optional)

Stir the ginger into the sauce, sweeten and flavour with lemon juice and rind if liked.

NOTE: Caramel sauce with the addition of ginger is also good.

JAM SAUCE

4 good tablesp. jam   ½ pt. water
sugar   lemon juice   1 heaped teasp. arrowroot   colouring, if needed

Boil the jam and water together, add sugar and lemon juice to taste, and thicken with the arrowroot blended with a little cold water. Strain the sauce if the jam has pips. Colour if necessary.

MARMALADE SAUCE (1)

As for Jam Sauce above substituting marmalade for jam. Do not strain the sauce.

MARMALADE SAUCE (2)

4 tablesp. stiff marmalade
⅛ pt. white wine

Heat the marmalade and wine together.

LEMON SAUCE

½ pt. milk   ½ oz. cornflour or custard powder   rind of 1 lemon
sugar or golden syrup
juice of ½ lemon

Blend the cornflour with a little cold milk. Boil the rest of the milk with the thinly cut lemon rind. Strain the boiling milk on to the blended cornflour and stir well. Rinse the pan and return the sauce to it. Just bring to boil for custard powder, boil 3 min. for cornflour, then add the lemon rind, sugar or golden syrup to taste, stir in the lemon juice.

ORANGE SAUCE

As for Lemon sauce but use much less sugar.

RUM BUTTER

See p. 402.

SABAYON SAUCE—HOT or COLD

2 egg yolks   1 oz. castor sugar
¼ pt. Marsala wine or Madeira

In a saucepan whisk the egg yolks and sugar till very light and frothy. Stir in the wine and over very gentle heat continue whisking briskly until the sauce rises; it must not boil. Serve at once.

SWEET MELTED BUTTER SAUCE

To ½ pt. white sauce (p. 91) add 1 oz. butter extra, sweeten to taste and add any sweet flavouring desired.

SWEET WINE SAUCE

¼ pt. water   ¼ pt. sherry   2 tablesp. any jam or jelly   sugar to taste
lemon juice to taste

Boil all the ingredients together for 5 min. Rub through a hair or nylon sieve or strain the sauce. Adjust the flavour, reheat if necessary. If liked this sauce may be thickened as Jam sauce opposite.

SAVOURY VINEGARS AND STORE SAUCES

CELERY VINEGAR

¼ lb. celery or ½ oz. celery seed
1 pt. vinegar, wine or white
½ teasp. salt

Chop the celery if used. Boil the vinegar with the salt. Pour the hot vinegar on to the chopped celery or seed, cover and leave till cold. Bottle and leave the vinegar for 3 weeks, then strain and rebottle. Cork securely.

Use in salad dressings.

CHILLI VINEGAR

6 fresh chillies (small red peppers)
1 pt. vinegar

Chop the chillies roughly. Boil the vinegar, pour it hot on to the chillies, cover and allow to cool. Bottle the vinegar for 3 weeks, strain and rebottle.

Use in salad dressing.

CRESS VINEGAR

½ oz. crushed cress seed
1 pt. vinegar

Proceed as for chilli vinegar.

CUCUMBER VINEGAR

6 cucumbers   1 qt. vinegar   2 teasp. salt   2 teasp. white peppercorns
4 shallots   2 cloves of garlic

Boil the vinegar, salt and peppercorns together for 20 min., then allow the mixture to become quite cold. Slice the cucumbers without peeling them into a wide-necked bottle or jar, add the shallots and garlic, and the vinegar when cold. Cover closely and leave for 14 days, then carefully strain off into smaller bottles. Cork tightly, and store in a cool, dry place.

ESCAVEEKE SAUCE

1 pt. wine vinegar   rind of 1 lemon, grated   6 shallots   1 clove of garlic
1 tablesp. coriander seed
½ teasp. ground ginger   ½ teasp. salt
⅛ teasp. cayenne pepper

Pound all the dry ingredients well together. Boil the vinegar and pour it boiling on to the pounded mixture. Bottle when cold. Store for 1 month before use.

HERB VINEGAR

1 pt. malt vinegar   2 oz. grated horseradish   1 teasp. chopped
shallot   rind and juice of ½ lemon
2 cloves   a sprig each of thyme, basil, savory, marjoram, tarragon
1 bay leaf

Simmer all the ingredients for 20 min. Cool and then strain the vinegar. Bottle when cold.

Use a very little with other vinegar in salad dressings.

HORSERADISH VINEGAR

1 pt. vinegar   2 oz. grated horseradish   ½ oz. chopped shallot
½ teasp. salt $\frac{1}{16}$ teasp. cayenne
1 oz. sugar

Boil the vinegar; mix together the other ingredients. Pour the boiling vinegar on to the mixture, cover. When cool bottle the mixture and store for 10 days. It may now be used unstrained as horseradish sauce. To store the vinegar, strain, boil it and bottle it in hot, dry sauce bottles. Screw them down at once.

MINT VINEGAR or BOTTLED MINT SAUCE

1 pt. wine vinegar   ½ pt. chopped mint   1 oz. sugar

Make this exactly like mint sauce, omitting any water and drying the mint leaves completely before chopping them. The mint should be young and fresh. The vinegar may be strained and used for salad dressings, the mint in vinegar will keep through the winter months.

RASPBERRY VINEGAR

Raspberries   malt, wine or cider vinegar   sugar

To each pound of ripe fruit allow 1 pt. wine or malt vinegar. Pick over the raspberries, cover them with vinegar, and allow to stand for 4 days. Strain through a fine hair or nylon sieve (do not press the fruit). To each pint of strained vinegar add 4–5 oz. sugar. Simmer gently for 10 min.; bottle.

TARRAGON VINEGAR

1 pt. vinegar   2 oz. tarragon leaves

Bruise the tarragon leaves slightly. Put them into a bottling jar, pour in the vinegar and screw down the cap. Store the vinegar for 6 weeks, then strain and re-bottle it. Store in a cool dry place.

NOTE: If using home-grown tarragon, the leaves should be gathered on a dry day about the end of July, just before the plant begins to bloom.

WORCESTER SAUCE

4 shallots   1 qt. best brown vinegar
6 tablesp. walnut ketchup
5 tablesp. anchovy essence
4 tablesp. soy   ½ teasp. cayenne
pepper   salt to taste

Chop the shallots very finely. Put with all the other ingredients into a large bottle, and cork it closely. Shake well 3 or 4 times daily for about 14 days, then strain the sauce into small bottles, cork tightly, store in a cool, dry place.

FORCEMEATS OR STUFFINGS

Forcemeat, or *Farcemeat* as it was originally called, derives its name from the French verb *farcie*, to stuff.

The excellence of forcemeat depends on flavouring and seasoning. The flavouring should enhance the flavour of the dish with which the stuffing is to be used, e.g. lemon flavouring with sweet dishes, anchovy flavouring with white fish, etc.

Many forcemeats may be made into balls the size of a walnut and baked, fried or poached to serve with roast, braised or stewed meats. For this purpose the mixture must be bound with egg and should be stiff enough to shape into balls. The balls may be coated with egg and crumbs before frying or baking.

APPLE AND CELERY STUFFING

2 oz. chopped salt pork or bacon diced or pork sausage meat
2 onions   4 tablesp. chopped celery

4 medium cooking apples   3 oz. stale breadcrumbs   2 tablesp. chopped parsley   sugar to taste salt and pepper

Brown the pork, bacon or sausage in its own fat, lift it out of the pan. Chop the onion. In the pork fat cook the onion and celery for 5 min., then remove them. Dice the apples and in the same fat fry them till tender and brown. Mix all the ingredients together.

Use with duck, goose or pork.

APPLE AND WALNUT STUFFING

1 onion   ½ oz. butter   1 large, sour apple   12 walnuts   2 oz. pork sausage meat   2 oz. breadcrumbs
½ teasp. powdered, mixed herbs salt and pepper   1 egg
milk if needed to mix

Finely chop the onion. Fry it very gently till soft and light golden in the butter. Peel, core, chop the apple, peel and chop the walnuts. Mix all the ingredients together and bind them with beaten egg and as much milk as necessary.

Use for stuffing roast goose or duck.

CHESTNUT STUFFING

2 lb. chestnuts   1–1½ pt. stock   2 oz. butter   salt and pepper   a trace of powdered cinnamon   ½ teasp. sugar

Slit the chestnuts and bake or boil them for 20 min. Remove shells and skins. Stew the chestnuts till tender in sufficient stock barely to cover them. Rub them through a fine wire sieve. Add the butter, seasoning, flavouring, sugar, and sufficient stock to make a soft dough.

Use for roast turkey, also good with chicken.

FISH FORCEMEAT

½ lb. raw white fish without bone or skin   1 oz. butter   1 oz. flour
¼ pt. fish stock or milk   1–2 eggs

salt and pepper   grated lemon rind
lemon juice

Melt the butter in a saucepan,
stir in the flour, then the stock, and
beat the mixture over heat till it
forms a stiff ball. Cool this panada,
then beat into it the beaten eggs
and seasoning. Flake the fish, removing all small bones. Beat the
fish into the egg mixture. Add
grated lemon rind and lemon juice
to taste.

GIBLET STUFFING

Cooked giblets   1 onion, cooked
2–4 oz. breadcrumbs $\frac{1}{8}$–$\frac{1}{2}$ pt. boiling
stock   1–2 oz. butter   1 egg
1 teasp. mixed fresh herbs or
$\frac{1}{2}$ teasp. dried herbs   1 tablesp.
chopped parsley   a little grated
lemon rind (if liked)
salt and pepper

The giblets are stewed for 1$\frac{1}{2}$ hr.
or until tender, with the onion.
The liquid in which they are
cooked makes the gravy for the
roast bird. Remove all bones from
the neck and the lining of the
gizzard and chop or mince the
flesh of the giblets. Soak the
crumbs in sufficient boiling stock
to moisten them. Melt the fat.
Beat the egg. Mix all the ingredients together and season the mixture to taste.

Use for chicken or turkey.

HAM STUFFING or FORCE-MEAT

4 oz. lean ham or bacon   2 oz. suet
or margarine   4 oz. breadcrumbs
1 tablesp. chopped parsley   1 teasp.
mixed fresh herbs or $\frac{1}{2}$ teasp. dried
herbs   grated rind of 1 lemon
a little grated nutmeg $\frac{1}{16}$ teasp.
powdered allspice   1 egg   a little
milk or stock   salt and pepper

Chop or mince the ham and
chop or grate the suet. Mix all the
dry ingredients and bind with the
egg and stock or milk. Season
well.

When the mixture is intended
for balls, the consistency should be
tested by poaching a small quantity in boiling water.

Use for veal, poultry or hare.

LIVER FARCE or STUFFING

$\frac{1}{2}$ lb. calf's or chicken's liver $\frac{1}{4}$ lb.
bacon or pork sausage meat   1 very
small onion   1 oz. butter $\frac{1}{2}$ beaten
egg $\frac{1}{2}$ teasp. chopped fresh herbs
1 teasp. chopped parsley
salt and pepper

Cut the liver and bacon into
$\frac{1}{4}$-in. dice. Chop the onion. Melt
the butter and in it cook the
bacon, liver and onion gently for
10 min. Chop them still more
finely and add the other ingredients. Use for poultry or game.

RICE STUFFING for chicken

2 oz. rice   the liver of the chicken
1 small onion   2 oz. raisins
2 oz. ground or chopped almonds
2 tablesp. chopped parsley
1 oz. butter   1 sprig of thyme
salt and pepper   1 egg (optional)

Boil the rice till just tender.
Chop the liver and the onion.
Mix all the ingredients, mashing
the butter into the mixture with a
fork. Season and bind well. Use
also for meat, fish or vegetables.

SAGE AND ONION STUFFING

$\frac{1}{2}$ lb. onions   4 young sage leaves or
$\frac{1}{4}$ teasp. powdered sage
2 oz. breadcrumbs   1 oz. butter
salt and pepper $\frac{1}{2}$ egg (optional)

Slice the onions thickly, parboil them 10 min. in very little
water. Scald the sage leaves. Chop
the onions and sage. Mash and
work all the ingredients together
and season to taste.

Use for pork, goose or duck.

SAUSAGE STUFFING

$\frac{1}{2}$ lb. lean pork   2 oz. breadcrumbs
$\frac{1}{2}$ teasp. mixed fresh herbs or
$\frac{1}{4}$ teasp. dried herbs   2 small sage

leaves   salt and pepper   grated
nutmeg to taste   liver of bird   stock

Mince the pork. Chop the liver.
Mix all the ingredients, using
enough stock to bind the mixture.
Season to taste. Use for turkey or
chicken. NOTE: A good bought
pork sausage meat mixed with the
liver of the bird makes a quick
stuffing for poultry.

TOMATO STUFFING

1 large ripe tomato   ½ sweet, red
pepper or pimento   ½ clove of
garlic   2 tablesp. breadcrumbs
salt and pepper

Scald, skin and chop the tomato.
Remove the seeds from the
pimento and chop it. Crush and
chop the garlic. Mix the ingredients, using enough crumbs to
absorb the juice of the tomato.
Season to taste. Use with pigeon
or other small birds.

VEAL STUFFING or FORCE-
   MEAT

4 oz. breadcrumbs   2 oz. chopped
suet or margarine   1 tablesp.
chopped parsley   1 teasp. chopped
mixed herbs   nutmeg   grated rind
of ½ lemon   salt and pepper
1 beaten egg

Mix together all the ingredients
and season to taste. Use for veal
and poultry, fish or vegetables.

FISH

PERHAPS it is because fish must be handled and cooked with care that it does not figure on the menu as often as it might. Yet fish is as rich in protein—one of the best body-building foods—as meat. Oily fish, such as salmon, grilse (young salmon), herring, mackerel and sprats, where the fat is distributed throughout the flesh, provide valuable quantities of vitamins A and D. The flesh of white fish, such as cod, haddock and whiting, contains very little fat, most of the oil being stored in the liver. Canned fish are often packed in oil, thus adding extra fat, and as the bones are usually sufficiently soft to be eaten, they also provide calcium and phosphorus—both bone- and teeth-building materials.

Most varieties of white fish (particularly whiting), because of their lack of fat, have less flavour than oily fish but are easily digested, and it is for this reason that white fish figures in the diet of invalids and convalescents.

SEA AND FRESH WATER FISH

CHOOSING FISH—POINTS TO LOOK FOR

1. Fish should first of all be fresh. The flesh should be firm, not flabby.
2. There should be no stale smell.
3. The gills of most varieties should be bright red.
4. The eyes should be bright and not sunken in the head.
5. A "slimy" skin is a sure sign of freshness, providing it is not a decomposed yellowish slime.

Buying Fish: The housewife should not set out with the fixed intention of buying a certain kind of fish, but be guided in her selection by the state of the market. Many circumstances combine to make the variations in the price of fish greater than in the case of any other food commodity. The fact that fish is a most perishable article of food and is usually caught while travelling in shoals results in alternate scarcity and over-supply of a particular kind. More often than not the housewife will find that some particular fish is scarce, and that in consequence it is priced far beyond its worth, and quite out of comparison with the price of other kinds of fish which are plentiful in the market.

Smaller, younger fish are to be preferred. A flat fish should be thick in proportion to its size. In buying a slice of fish it is better to choose a thick slice from a small fish than a thin slice from a large one. Avoid cuts of fish with too much bone or waste tissue.

All fresh fish should be cooked the day it is bought as it quickly loses its freshness and flavour. If fish is put into a refrigerator it must be covered to prevent the fish smell tainting other foods. Quick frozen fish should be stored in the "freezer" compartment; it can be kept 48 hr. and once it has thawed out it must not be re-frozen.

PREPARING FISH

Fishmongers are only too glad to prepare fish ready for the housewife to cook, but if for some reason that is impracticable here are the simple ways of doing it.

To Clean Whole Fish: Scrape off any scales on both sides of the fish with the back of a knife. Hold the fish by the tail and scrape from the tail towards the head. Rinse often whilst working to remove loose scales.

Round Fish: With a pair of kitchen scissors or sharp knife slit the belly from just below the head to half-way to the tail, remove and discard the entrails, reserve the roe. Wash well. Rub with a little salt to remove any black tissues. If the head is to be left on take out the eyes, if the head is to be removed cut across behind the gills.

Flat Fish: Cut off the fins, remove the gills. Cut open the belly which is just under the head, on the dark side, and remove and discard the entrails. Wash with cold water. To remove the head make a semi-circular cut below the head.

To Skin Whole Flat Fish: The dark skin of sole is always removed but not necessarily the white. The skin of turbot is usually cut off after filleting.

To skin any fish it must be kept wet. With whole flat fish begin at the tail. Cut the skin across, but do not cut into the flesh, and loosen the skin along the fins on either side with the fingers. Then tear off the skin with the left hand, keeping the thumb of the right hand well pressed over the backbone to prevent the removal of the flesh with the skin.

To Skin Whole Round Fish: Cut off a narrow strip of skin over and along the backbone near the tail. Make another cut just below the head and loosen the skin below the head with the point of a sharp knife. Dip the fingers in salt to give a better grip and gently pull off the skin, working towards the tail. Keep the thumb of the right hand well pressed over the backbone to prevent the removal of the flesh with the skin. Remove the skin from the other side in the same way.

Filleting: Flat Fish: Place the fish flat on a board or table, and with the point of a sharp, flexible knife cut the flesh from head to tail down the backbone. Next insert the knife in the slit made, and carefully separate the flesh from the bone, keeping the knife pressed lightly against the bone meanwhile. Remove the fillet, turn the fish round, remove the second fillet from tail to head, then turn the fish over and remove the other two fillets in the same way.

Round Fish: With a sharp knife slit the fish down the centre back to the bone. Working from head end to tail, cut along the belly, cutting the flesh cleanly from the bones by keeping the knife pressed against the bones. Remove the fillet from the other side in the same way.

To Skin Fillets: Place the fillets on a board skin side down. Rub a little salt on the fingers of the left hand, take a firm hold of the tail in the left hand, and with a knife in the right hand, and using a "sawing" movement, peel the flesh away from the skin, working from tail to head.

Always use the skin and bones for making fish stock.

It is a common error to wash fish too much. Usually whole fish are washed and dried, but portions of cut fish are wiped with a clean damp cloth.

COOKING FISH

As fish can so easily be spoiled by over or under cooking, it is essential to know when it is sufficiently cooked. Test for readiness by pressing gently in the thickest part. The flesh will readily separate from the bones when fully cooked. When cooking fillets or cutlets the presence of a white "curd" like substance between the flakes is an indication that the fish is cooked.

Of the various ways in which fish may be cooked, boiling or poaching is the least recommended as more flavour is lost by these methods.

Boiling or Poaching—suitable for whole fish or cuts of large fish, e.g. cod and haddock. The term "boiled" fish is really a misnomer, strictly speaking fish should *never be boiled*, the water should just simmer gently *below boiling*-point.

The ideal way to poach fish is to use a fish-kettle, i.e. a large pan fitted with a strainer so that the fish can be gently lifted out without breaking. If no fish-kettle is available, use a large saucepan, tie the fish loosely in clean muslin (for easy removal) and place on a plate on the bottom of the pan.

Salmon and salmon trout should be put into boiling salted water, to preserve their colour; but other kinds of fish should be placed in warm water, because boiling water has a tendency to break the skin, and cold water extracts much of the flavour.

Cook the fish in just sufficient water to cover the fish (this should afterwards be used as a basis for fish soup or fish sauce) as soluble nutrients diffuse out into the cooking water. For each quart of water add 1 tablesp. vinegar and 2 level teasp. salt. Lemon juice added to the water when cooking white fish tends to increase its whiteness.

When boiling-heat is reached, reduce heat immediately and allow fish to simmer gently in water just off the boil. The time required for cooking depends more on the thickness than on the weight of the fish, allow 10–15 min. per lb.

Frying—suitable for fillets, steaks and small whole fish. Fish to be fried should be well dried after washing or wiping, and should first be coated to prevent the fat from soaking into the fish. It may coated with egg and breadcrumbs, milk or beaten egg and seasoned flour; or if to be fried in deep fat, coated with batter. *See also* notes on frying (p. 34).

Shallow frying is better for thick slices or steaks, which require longer cooking to ensure that they are cooked through.

There should be enough fat in the pan to come half-way up the fish. Heat the fat, put in the coated fish and fry until golden brown on one side, then turn and brown the other side. Allow 6–8 min. for fillets and 8–12 min. for larger pieces.

Deep frying requires a deep frying-pan with a frying basket or a perforated spoon to remove the fish from the hot fat. Heat the fish basket, if used, in the fat, but gently drop the coated fish into the fat—do not place directly on the fish basket or the coating will stick to the wires of the basket.

Grilling—suitable for steaks, cutlets or fillets and small whole fish, e.g. herring, plaice and sole. The fish should be thoroughly dried, then liberally brushed over with a little oil or melted fat and seasoned with salt and pepper. Score deep gashes across whole fish to allow the heat to penetrate, or the outside may dry up before the fish is cooked.

Heat the grill and grease the grill rack to prevent the fish sticking. Cook the fish rather slowly, turning carefully until done. Allow 7–8 min. for thin fillets and 10–15 min. for steaks and thicker fish.

Steaming—suitable for fillets or thin slices. This is a very favourite and excellent way of cooking fish, as although it is a rather slower process than boiling, the flavour is better preserved, and the danger of the fish being broken is eliminated. If using a steamer a piece of greased greaseproof paper placed in the bottom will facilitate removal of the fish after cooking. Season the prepared fish and sprinkle with lemon juice.

Stewing—suitable for steaks, fillets and small pieces of cod. In stewing, a gentle simmering in a small quantity of fish stock made from bone and fish trimmings, or in milk and water, until the flesh comes easily away from the bones, is all that is required. This is one of the most economical and tasty ways of cooking fish. Cook slowly. Fish should invariably be stewed in a fireproof glass or an earthenware dish. The liquid in which the fish has been simmered may be flavoured and thickened and used as a sauce.

Baking—This is a very satisfactory method of cooking almost any whole round white fish or a middle cut from a large fish, or steaks or fillets. Place the prepared fish in a well-greased baking-tin or fireproof dish with a very little fat, cover with greased greaseproof paper. Bake in a fairly hot oven (375° F., Gas 5). Cooking time will vary according to thickness and weight, but average times are 10–20 min. for fillets, depending on thickness; allow about 10 min. per lb. and 10 min. over for whole fish weighing up to 4 lb.

BARBEL

BARBEL

1–2 barbel, according to size
1 tablesp. salt   2 small onions, sliced
2 anchovies   2 tablesp. vinegar   juice of 1 lemon   bouquet garni   grated nutmeg to taste   pinch of mace

Soak the fish in slightly salted water for 2–3 hr. Put into a fish-kettle or saucepan with warm water and the salt, and poach gently until done. Take 1 pt. of the water in which the fish was cooked and add to it the other ingredients. Simmer gently for about 15 min., then strain, and return to the saucepan. Put in the fish and let it heat gradually in the flavoured liquor.

4 helpings

BLOATERS

GRILLED BLOATERS

Break off the head, split the back, remove the roe and take out the backbone. Rub over with a little fat, place the fish, inside down, on a grill pan grid. Cook until nicely browned, turn over and cook the back. If preferred place 2 bloaters with the insides together, and cook as above. The roes should be cooked and served with the bloaters.

Cooking time—7 min.

BREAM

Sea Bream is available all the year but best from June to December. Fresh-water Bream is in season July–February. Bream can be baked or grilled. It is often sold ready filleted.

BAKED SEA BREAM

1 bream about 2 lb. weight
salt and pepper   cayenne pepper
2 oz. butter or cooking fat (approx.)

Thoroughly wash the bream, but do not remove the scales, dry thoroughly with a clean cloth. Season inside and out with salt and pepper and place in a well-greased baking-dish. Place the butter in small pieces on the fish and bake in a fairly hot oven (375° F., Gas 5) for a little more than 30 min.

4 helpings

BAKED STUFFED SEA BREAM

One 3–4 lb. sea bream (cleaned)
3 rashers streaky bacon

STUFFING

2 oz. margarine   1 medium-sized onion   2 sticks celery   4 oz. cooked rice   ¼ level teasp. sage   ½ level

teasp. thyme 1½ oz. chopped stuffed
olives (optional) seasoning to taste

GARNISH
Parsley or watercress

Scale the fish and trim the fins
and tail. Leave the head on, but
remove the eyes. To make the
stuffing, melt the margarine in a
pan, add the chopped onion and
celery and fry gently for about 3
min. Add the rice and remaining
ingredients and mix thoroughly
over the heat for 2–3 min. Stuff
fish with some of the mixture and
spread the remainder over the
bottom of a shallow fire-proof dish.
Place the fish on top and cover
with the bacon, cut in long thin
strips, arranged in a criss-cross
pattern. Bake in a fairly hot oven
(375° F., Gas 5) for 30–40 min.
(allowing 10 min. per lb.). Serve in
the same dish, garnished with
parsley or watercress.
4 helpings
Cooking time—30–40 min.

BRILL

In season practically all the year,
but only small quantities landed.

BRILL
1 small brill lemon juice salt
vinegar

Clean the brill, cut off the fins,
and rub a little lemon juice over it
to preserve its whiteness. Barely
cover the fish with warm water,
add salt and vinegar to taste and
simmer gently until done (allow
about 10 min. per lb.). Garnish
with cut lemon and parsley, and
serve with either fish, Hollandaise
or melted butter sauce.
NOTE: This fish is also nice
baked or grilled.
Allow 4–6 oz. per helping

BRILL A LA CONTI
1 brill weighing about 2½ lb.
1 glass white wine (optional)

salt and pepper 1½ pt. stock
1 teasp. finely-chopped parsley

Clean and skin the fish and cut
some slits down the back. Add the
wine (if used) and salt and pepper
to the stock; when warm, put in
the fish and simmer gently until
done. Remove the fish and keep it
hot; boil the stock rapidly until
reduced to half its original quantity; then add the parsley and pour
over the fish.
6 helpings
Cooking time—20 min.

CARP
BAKED CARP
1 carp egg and breadcrumbs
butter for basting

FORCEMEAT
8 sauce oysters 3 anchovies, boned
2 tablesp. breadcrumbs 1 teasp.
finely-chopped parsley 1 shallot
salt cayenne pepper 1 egg yolk

SAUCE
1 oz. butter 1 tablesp. flour ⅜ pt.
good stock 1 teasp. mixed mustard
1 tablesp. lemon juice
½ tablesp. Worcester sauce

Clean and scale the fish. Remove the beards of the oysters and
simmer for 15 min. in a little fish
stock or water. Cut the oysters
into small pieces, but do not cook
them; also cut the anchovies into
small pieces. Mix together the
breadcrumbs, oysters, anchovies,
parsley, finely-chopped shallot and
seasoning; add the egg yolk, the
liquor of the oysters and the stock
in which the oyster beards were
simmered. Put the forcemeat inside the fish and sew up the opening; brush over with egg and coat
with breadcrumbs. Place in a
baking-dish and cook gently for
about 1 hr., basting frequently
with hot butter. To make the
sauce: melt the butter in a saucepan, stir in the flour, add the stock
and stir until the sauce boils.

Simmer for 2–3 min., then add the mustard, lemon juice, Worcester sauce and the liquor (strained) in which the fish was cooked. Garnish the fish with cut lemon and parsley, and serve the sauce in a sauceboat.

NOTE: The fish may be stuffed with veal forcemeat instead of oyster forcemeat if liked.

4–5 helpings
Cooking time—1¼–1½ hr.

STEWED CARP

1 large carp   vinegar   2–3 small onions   2 oz. butter   1 pt. stock
12 small button mushrooms
bouquet garni   a good pinch of grated nutmeg   salt and pepper
1 tablesp. flour   toasted bread

Wash the fish in vinegar and water and cut it into thick slices. Slice the onions. Melt 1½ oz. of the butter in a saucepan, fry the onion until brown, then add the stock, mushrooms, herbs, nutmeg and seasoning. When warm, add the fish and simmer gently for 30–40 min. Meanwhile knead together the flour and remaining butter. Take out the fish and keep it hot. Add the butter and flour to the contents of the saucepan, simmer and stir until the sauce is cooked smoothly. Place the fish on a hot dish, strain the sauce over and garnish with the mushrooms and sippets of toasted bread.

5–6 helpings

CATFISH

See Rockfish

COALFISH

See Saithe

COD

Cod is available all the year; best from October to February. It is suitable for all methods of cooking, and is good cold with salad. Also smoked and sold as Smoked Cod Fillet.

COD A LA PROVENCALE

2 lb. middle cut cod (approx.)   salt and pepper   ½ pt. Velouté or other rich white sauce   1 gill white stock
2 small shallots   a small bunch of parsley   bouquet garni   1 egg yolk
2 oz. butter   1 teasp. anchovy paste
1 teasp. chopped parsley
2 teasp. capers

Wash and wipe the fish well and place in a saucepan. Season with pepper and salt, and add the sauce, stock, finely-chopped shallots, bunch of parsley and the bouquet garni. Simmer slowly until the fish is done, basting occasionally. Remove the fish to a hot dish, and keep it warm. Reduce the sauce until the desired consistency is obtained. Remove the herbs, add the egg yolk, work in the butter, and pass through a strainer. Return to a smaller saucepan, add the anchovy paste, chopped parsley and capers, stir over heat for a few minutes but do not allow to boil, then pour over the fish.

5–6 helpings
Cooking time—35–40 min.

COD STEAKS

Four 4–6 oz. cod steaks   flour
salt and pepper   fat for frying parsley

Make a rather thin batter of flour and water, season well with salt and pepper. Melt sufficient clarified fat or dripping in a frying-pan to form a layer about ½ in. deep. Wipe the fish, dip each piece separately in the batter, place these at once into the hot fat, and fry until light-brown, turning once during the process. Drain well, and serve garnished with crisply-fried parsley. If preferred, the fish may be coated with egg and breadcrumbs and fried in deep fat.

Serve with anchovy or tomato sauce.

4 helpings

CURRIED COD

2 lb. cod   2 oz. butter   1 medium-sized onion   1 tablesp. flour
1 dessertsp. curry powder   1 pt. white stock (fish or bone)   1 tablesp. lemon juice   salt and pepper
cayenne pepper

Wash and dry the cod, and cut into pieces about 1½ in. square. Melt the butter in a saucepan, fry the cod slightly, then take out and put aside. Add the sliced onion, flour and curry powder to the butter in the saucepan and fry 15 min., stirring constantly to prevent the onion becoming too brown, then pour in the stock. Stir until boiling, then simmer gently for 20 min. Strain and return to the saucepan, add lemon juice and seasoning to taste, bring nearly to boiling-point, then put in the fish. Cover closely, and heat gently until the fish becomes thoroughly impregnated with the flavour of the sauce. An occasional stir must be given to prevent the fish sticking to the bottom of the saucepan.

NOTE: Remains of cold fish may be used for this dish in which case the preliminary frying may be omitted.

5–6 helpings

GOLDEN GRILLED COD

4 cutlets or steaks of cod about 1 in. thick   1 oz. butter or margarine
1–2 oz. grated cheese   2 tablesp. milk (optional)   salt and pepper

Place the prepared fish in a greased fireproof dish and grill quickly for 2–3 min. on one side. Meanwhile soften the fat and cream the cheese and the fat together, then work in the milk if used and season to taste. Turn the fish over and spread the cheese mixture over the uncooked side and return to the grill. Reduce the heat slightly and cook gently for a further 10–12 min. until the coating is brown and the fish cooked

through. Serve at once.

NOTE: Cod fillet can be used instead of cutlets. Allow 1–1½ lb., cut into 4 portions before cooking.

4 helpings

The topping can be varied:

Devilled Grill

1 oz. butter or margarine   1 level teasp. chutney   1 level teasp. curry powder   1 level teasp. dry mustard
1 teasp. anchovy essence (optional)
salt and pepper to taste

Surprise Grill

1 oz. butter or margarine   2 teasp. lemon juice   3 level tablesp. grated onion   salt and pepper

HASHED COD

2 lb. cooked cod   1½ oz. butter
1½ oz. flour   1 pt. milk   ¼ pt. picked shrimps   salt and pepper
mashed potatoes   chopped parsley

Remove skin and bone and flake the fish into small pieces. Blend the butter and flour in a saucepan, and fry for a few minutes without browning. Add the milk and stir until boiling. Then put in the cod and the shrimps. Cook until thoroughly hot and season carefully. Make a deep border of mashed potatoes on a hot dish, pour the hash in the centre and sprinkle a little chopped parsley over the top.

4–5 helpings
Cooking time—½ hr.

COD'S ROE

1 lb. cod's roe   salt   vinegar
melted butter sauce or other white sauce   a little milk or cream
brown breadcrumbs

Wash and wipe the cod's roe and poach for 10 min. in water with a little salt and vinegar. Dice the roe and put into melted butter sauce or other white sauce diluted with a little cream or milk. Butter 3–4 scallop shells, put in the roe, cover with brown breadcrumbs and brown in the oven, or serve on hot buttered toast.

3–4 helpings

SALT COD AND PARSNIPS

2 lb. salt cod　12 young parsnips
egg sauce (p. 92)

Wash the fish and soak it in cold water for 12 hr. or longer if very salty, changing the water every 3 or 4 hr. Cover the fish with cold water and bring slowly to simmering point, then reduce heat and cook very gently for 20 min., or until the fish leaves the bones. Meanwhile boil the parsnips, if small cut them lengthwise into 2, or if large into 4 pieces. Drain the fish well, place it on a hot dish, pour the egg sauce over and garnish with parsnips.

4–5 helpings

CONGER EEL

This forms the basis of the well-known soup of the Channel Islands and is made into pies in the West of England. Like a tough steak, it always needs long stewing or cooking, as the flesh is remarkably firm and hard. It can be cooked like a fresh-water eel. Available all the year; best from March to October.

BAKED CONGER EEL

2 lb. conger eel　suet forcemeat see
Baked Stuffed Plaice　butter or fat
flour

Wash and dry the fish thoroughly, skin and stuff with forcemeat and bind it with tape. Melt the butter or fat in a baking-dish or tin, put in the fish and baste well. Bake gently for 1 hr., basting occasionally with fat and dredging the surface with flour.

Serve with the gravy poured round, or if preferred with tomato, brown caper, or a suitable fish sauce.

4–5 helpings

CONGER EEL PIE

1 small conger eel　salt and pepper
1 teasp. finely-chopped onion
1 teasp. finely-chopped herbs
1 teasp. finely-chopped parsley
1 tablesp. vinegar　rough puff or
puff pastry, using 4 oz. flour, etc.

Wash and dry the fish thoroughly, remove all skin and bones and cut into neat pieces. Place in layers in a pie-dish, sprinkling each layer with salt, pepper, onion, herbs and parsley. Add water to $\frac{3}{4}$ fill the dish and mix with it the vinegar. Cover the pie-dish with pastry and bake in a very hot oven (450° F., Gas 8) until pastry is set, then reduce heat to moderate (350° F., Gas 4).

Serve either hot or cold.

6–8 helpings
Cooking time—about $\frac{3}{4}$–1 hr.

DABS

Dabs are available all the year; best from June to February. They are suitable for frying, steaming or poaching.

DOGFISH

See Flake

EELS

Eels are available practically all the year; least seasonable in winter. Suitable for baking, frying, poaching or serving cold jellied.

FRIED EELS

1–2 medium-sized eels　1 tablesp.
flour　$\frac{1}{2}$ teasp. salt　$\frac{1}{8}$ teasp. pepper
egg and breadcrumbs　fat for frying
fried parsley for garnish

Wash, skin and thoroughly dry the eels. Divide them into pieces $2\frac{1}{2}$–3 in. long. Mix the flour, salt and pepper together, and roll the pieces of eel separately in the mixture. Coat carefully with egg and breadcrumbs, fry in hot fat until crisp and lightly-browned, drain well.

Allow 2 lb. for 5–6 helpings
Cooking time—about 20 min.

JELLIED EELS

Live eels are usually purchased. The fishmonger will prepare them for you, but if you prefer to do it at home, this is the method: Prepare by half-severing the head and slitting down the stomach. Scrape away the gut, etc., and cut off with the head. Cut into 2-in. lengths. Put in a pan with sufficient water to just cover, boil for about ½ hr., turn into a bowl and leave to set. If the liquor does not look thick enough, add a little gelatine, but normally it will "jell" on its own.

STEWED EELS

2 lb. eels 1 pt. good stock small glass port wine or claret 1 onion 2 cloves strip of lemon rind salt cayenne pepper 1 oz. butter 1 oz. flour 2 tablesp. cream 1 teasp. lemon juice

Wash and skin the eels. Cut into pieces about 3 in. long. Put into a saucepan, add the stock, wine, finely-chopped onion, cloves, lemon rind and seasoning. Simmer gently for ½ hr., or until tender, then lift carefully on to a hot dish. Meanwhile knead together the butter and flour, add it to the stock in small portions, stir until smoothly mixed with the stock. Boil for 10 min., then add the cream and lemon juice and a little more hot stock if the sauce is too thick. Season and strain over the fish.

5–6 helpings
Cooking time—¾ hr.

FLAKE
(sometimes called DOGFISH)

Available all the year; best from October to June. Suitable for frying, poaching, steaming and for made-up dishes.

FLOUNDERS

Flounders are available in small quantities most of the year, but are not at their best in March and April. Suitable for frying, steaming and poaching.

FLOUNDERS

3–4 flounders ½ carrot ½ turnip 1 slice parsnip water or fish stock 1 small onion 1 small bunch herbs 6 peppercorns salt parsley

Cut the carrot, turnip and parsnip into very fine strips and cook till tender in slightly-salted water or fish stock. Trim the fish and place in a deep sauté-pan, with the onion cut up in slices, the bunch of herbs and peppercorns. Add a little salt and pour on sufficient water to cover the fish well. Bring to the boil and cook gently for about 10 min. Lift out the fish and place in a deep entreé dish, sprinkle over the shredded cooked vegetables and some finely-chopped parsley, add a little of the fish liquor and serve.

3–4 helpings

FRIED FLOUNDERS

Flounders salt egg and bread-crumbs fat for frying fried parsley

Clean the fish and 2 hr. before required rub them inside and out with salt, to make them firm. Wash and dry them thoroughly, dip into beaten egg and coat with breadcrumbs. Fry in hot fat. Serve garnished with parsley.

6 oz.–7 oz. per helping for breakfast; rather less when served in the fish course of a dinner
Cooking time—10–15 min. according to size

GARFISH

STEWED GARFISH

2 medium-sized garfish 1 pt. stock or water 1 onion bouquet garni

1 blade of mace 2 cloves salt and
pepper 1½ oz. butter 1½ oz. flour

Remove the skin, which would
impart a disagreeable oily taste to
the dish, and cut the fish into
pieces 1½ in. long. Bring the stock
or water to simmering point, put
in the fish, onion (sliced), herbs,
mace, cloves, a little salt and
pepper and simmer gently for 20
min. Meanwhile melt the butter
in a saucepan, add the flour, stir
and cook slowly for 3 min., without browning. Strain on the
liquor from the fish, stir until
boiling, boil for 5 min., then season to taste. Strain over the fish
and serve.

4 helpings

GRAYLING

BAKED GRAYLING

2 medium-sized grayling butter for
basting salt and pepper
½ pt. melted butter sauce

Empty, wash and scale the fish.
Dry well, place in a baking-dish in
which a little butter has been previously melted and baste well.
Season with salt and pepper, cover
with a greased paper and bake
gently for 25–35 min., basting
occasionally. Make the melted
butter sauce very thick and a few
minutes before serving strain and
add the liquor from the fish. Place
the fish on a hot dish, strain the
sauce over and serve.

4 helpings

FRIED GRAYLING

4 small grayling flour salt and
pepper egg and breadcrumbs
fat for frying parsley sauce

Empty, scale, wash and dry the
fish, remove the gills and fins, but
leave the heads. Roll in flour
seasoned with salt and pepper, coat
carefully with egg and breadcrumbs and fry in hot fat until
nicely browned. Serve with pars-

ley sauce, or any other sauce
preferred.

4 helpings
Cooking time—8–9 min.

GUDGEON

GUDGEON

Gudgeon egg and breadcrumbs
frying-fat

Clean the fish, remove the inside
and gills, but do not scrape off the
scales. Dry well, dip in egg and
breadcrumbs and fry in hot fat
until nicely browned.

Cooking time—4–6 min.

GURNET or GURNARD

Gurnet are available all the year.
Out of condition April to June.
Suitable for baking, frying and
poaching. Excellent cold with
salad.

BAKED GURNET

1 medium-sized gurnet veal forcemeat butter or fat for basting
2–3 rashers bacon

Empty and wash the fish, cut off
the fins and remove the gills.
Leave the head on. Put the forcemeat inside the fish and sew up
the opening. Fasten the tail in the
mouth of the fish, place in a pie-
dish or baking-dish, baste well
with hot fat or butter. Cover with
bacon and bake in a moderate
oven (350° F., Gas 4) for 30–45
min. Serve with either parsley or
anchovy sauce.

2–3 helpings

HADDOCK

Haddock are available all the
year; best from May to February.
Extensively used for smoking to
produce Smoked Haddock, Smoked
Haddock Fillets and Golden Cutlets. Suitable for cooking by all
methods; often sold ready filleted.

BAKED HADDOCK AND ORANGE

1 orange   1½ lb. fillet of haddock
salt   juice of 1 lemon   2 level
teasp. cornflour   ½ level teasp. sugar

Grate the rind from the orange, remove pith and cut pulp across into slices. Cut the fish into convenient portions for serving and arrange in a greased dish. Sprinkle with a little salt, add the lemon juice and arrange the slices of orange over the top. Cover with greased paper and cook in a fairly hot oven (400° F., Gas 6) for 15–20 min. Strain off the liquor and make up to ¼ pt. with water. Blend the cornflour with this, add the grated orange rind and sugar and bring to the boil, stirring constantly. Boil gently for 3 min., correct the seasoning and serve with the fish.

4 helpings

SMOKED HADDOCKS
(Finnan Haddocks)

Smoked haddocks are best cooked either in the oven or on the top of the cooker in a dish with a little water to create steam, to prevent the surface of the fish becoming hardened. Medium-sized haddocks should be cooked whole, and before serving an incision should be made from head to tail and the backbone removed. The fish should be liberally spread with butter, sprinkled with pepper and served as hot as possible.

HAKE

Available all the year; best from June to January. Suitable for baking, frying and steaming. It is often sold ready filleted, or cut into steaks or cutlets.

BAKED HAKE STEAKS

4 medium-sized hake steaks   flour
salt and pepper   1 teasp. finely-chopped parsley   1 teasp. finely-chopped onion   1 oz. butter

Wipe the steaks and place them side by side in a greased baking-dish. Dredge well with flour, season with salt and pepper, sprinkle over the parsley and onion and add the butter in small pieces. Bake gently for ½ hr., basting occasionally, then place the fish on a hot dish, strain the liquor over it and serve.

4 helpings

HALIBUT

Available all the year; best from July to March. Suitable for cooking by all methods. Excellent cold with salad.

BAKED HALIBUT

2 lb. halibut, cut in one thick slice
salt and pepper   flour
1 oz. butter or dripping

Wipe the fish well, sprinkle liberally with salt and pepper and dredge with flour. Place in a baking-dish or pie-dish, add the butter in small pieces and bake gently for about 1 hr. Serve on a hot dish with the liquid from the fish strained and poured round.

4–5 helpings
Cooking time—30–40 min.

BOILED HALIBUT

3–4 lb. halibut   salt   1 lemon
parsley   ½ pt. anchovy or
shrimp sauce

Add salt to hot water in the proportion of 1 oz. to 1 qt., and put in the fish. Bring slowly to boiling-point and simmer very gently for 30–40 min., or until the fish comes away easily from the bone. Drain well, arrange on a hot dish garnished with slices of lemon and parsley, and serve the sauce separately.

8–12 helpings (or 3 helpings per lb.)
Cooking time—30–40 min.

HALIBUT BRISTOL

1 lb. halibut (centre cut)   salt and
pepper   ¼ pt. milk and water

½ oz. butter or margarine
½ oz. flour   1½ oz. grated cheese
12 mussels (fresh-cooked)

Place the halibut in a greased
fireproof dish, sprinkle with a little
seasoning and add the liquid.
Cover with greased paper and cook
for 20 min. in a fairly hot oven
(375° F., Gas 5). Remove from the
oven, strain off the liquid and remove the centre bone from the
fish. Use the liquid to make a
creamy sauce with the fat and
flour, add 1 oz. cheese and seasoning if necessary. Arrange the
mussels round the halibut, cover
all with the sauce and sprinkle
over the remaining cheese. Return the dish to a very hot oven
(450° F., Gas 8) for a further 10
min. to brown.

NOTE: Turbot may be used if
halibut is not available.

4 helpings

HERRINGS

Supplies of herring are difficult
in early January, late March and
April, September and late December. Herrings are extensively used
for smoking into Kippers, Bloaters,
Buckling, etc. Suitable for cooking
by all methods, including sousing
and serving cold with salad.

BAKED STUFFED FRESH
HERRINGS

6 herrings   2 tablesp. breadcrumbs
1 tablesp. finely-chopped suet
1 teasp. chopped parsley   ¼ teasp.
grated lemon rind   salt and pepper
milk

Wash and split the herrings and
remove the backbone. Mix together the breadcrumbs, suet, parsley and lemon rind, season to taste
and add enough milk to moisten.
Season each herring with salt and
pepper, spread on a thin layer of
the forcemeat and roll up tightly,
beginning with the neck. Pack
closely in a greased pie-dish, cover
with greased paper and bake 30–40

min. in a moderate oven (350° F.,
Gas 4). Serve hot.

5 helpings

SOUSED HERRINGS

8 fresh herrings   1 spanish onion
salt and pepper   1 bay leaf   1 level
dessertsp. mixed pickling spice
vinegar

Wash and scale the herrings,
cut off the heads, split the herrings
open and remove the gut and
backbone. Put a slice of onion in
the centre of each fish, roll up
tightly, beginning with the neck.
Pack the herrings closely in a pie-
dish, sprinkle with salt, pepper,
bay leaf and spice, half-fill the dish
with equal quantities of vinegar
and water, and bake in a moderate
oven (350° F., Gas 4) for 40 min.

Serve cold with salad, or cut up
for hors d'œuvre; or eat plain, hot
or cold, with bread and butter.

6 helpings

RED HERRINGS

Red herrings   milk or water   oil
vinegar   egg yolk and gherkins or
diced boiled potatoes

Cover the herrings with boiled
water and after several minutes,
drain. Soak in milk or water for
1 hr. Skin and fillet, then cut into
pieces and dress with oil and vinegar. The herrings can be garnished with sieved egg yolk and
chopped gherkins. Alternatively
mix the herring pieces with diced
boiled potatoes and dress the
whole with oil and vinegar.

JOHN DORY

John Dory is best from January
to April, but landings are light and
erratic.

JOHN DORY

This fish is dressed in the same
way as turbot, which it resembles
in firmness but not in richness.
Wash it thoroughly, cut off the

fins but not the head, place in a pan and cover with warm water, adding salt to taste. Bring gradually to near boiling-point and simmer gently for 20–30 min. for a 2–3-lb. fish.

Serve garnished with cut lemon and parsley. Anchovy or shrimp paste sauce, and plain melted butter, should be served with it.

NOTE: Small John Dorys are excellent baked.

6–7 helpings

LING

BAKED LING

2 lb. ling   3 oz. butter   ground mace   salt and pepper   1 oz. flour
¾ pt. milk

Wash and dry the fish, cut it into slices ¾ in. thick. Put into a fireproof dish with 2 oz. butter, a good pinch of mace and a liberal seasoning of salt and pepper. Cover and cook gently for 1 hr., basting occasionally. When the fish is rather more than half cooked, melt the remaining butter in a saucepan and add the flour. Cook for 2–3 min., put in the milk and stir until boiling. Pour the sauce over the fish and continue to cook gently until done.

4–6 helpings

FRIED LING

2 lb. ling   salt and pepper   flour
egg and breadcrumbs   fat for frying

Wash and dry the fish and cut it into slices. Sprinkle with salt and pepper, dredge well with flour, brush over with beaten egg and coat with breadcrumbs (when well coated with flour the fish browns nicely without the addition of egg and breadcrumbs). Fry in hot fat, drain well and serve with a suitable fish sauce.

4–6 helpings
Cooking time—about 20 min.

MACKEREL

Mackerel is most seasonable in winter and spring. Suitable for all methods of cooking.

BAKED MACKEREL

2 large-sized mackerel   veal forcemeat   1 oz. butter or sweet dripping
flour   salt and pepper

Clean the fish and take out the roes. Stuff with the forcemeat and sew up the opening. Put them with the roes into a fireproof dish. Add the butter or dripping, dredge with flour, sprinkle well with salt and pepper and bake for 30–40 min., basting occasionally.

Serve with parsley sauce, or melted butter to which a little lemon juice has been added, and finely-chopped parsley.

3–4 helpings

BOILED MACKEREL WITH PARSLEY SAUCE

2 large mackerel   salt
parsley sauce

Remove the roes, wash the fish, put them into the pan with just sufficient hot water to cover and add salt to taste. Bring the water gently to near boiling-point, then reduce heat and cook very gently for about 10 min. If cooked too quickly, or too long, the skin is liable to crack and spoil the appearance of the fish. The fish is sufficiently cooked when the skin becomes loose from the flesh. Drain well, place the mackerel on a hot dish, pour a little parsley sauce over and serve the remainder of the sauce separately.

Fennel and anchovy sauces may also be served with boiled mackerel.

4 helpings
Cooking time—10–15 min.

GRILLED MACKEREL WITH GOOSEBERRY SAUCE

2 large mackerel   1 tablesp.
seasoned flour   1 oz. margarine
tomatoes   gooseberry sauce (p. 97)

Trim, clean and fillet the mackerel. Dip each fillet in seasoned flour. Melt the margarine in the bottom of the grill pan, add the fillets, brush them with the melted fat and grill for 8–10 min., turning once. Cut the tomatoes in half and grill at the same time, for garnish. Meanwhile prepare the gooseberry sauce. Serve the fillets on a hot dish, garnished with the tomatoes and serve the sauce separately.

NOTE: Grilled mackerel may be served with Maître d'Hôtel butter or Maître d'Hôtel sauce if preferred to gooseberry sauce.

4 helpings
Cooking time—8–10 min.

MEGRIM

This is a flat fish which can be cooked by any of the methods given for sole. *See* pp. 131–2.

MULLET

GREY MULLET

4 grey mullet

Clean and scale the fish. If very large, place them in warm salted water; if small, they may be put into hot water and cooked gently for 15–20 min. Serve with anchovy or melted butter sauce.

NOTE: Grey mullet may also be grilled or baked.

4 helpings
Cooking time—15–20 min.

MULLET—FRIED A LA MEUNIERE

4 mullet   seasoned flour   butter
lemon juice   parsley

Prepare the fish, then coat with seasoned flour. Fry them gently in the melted butter, turning until cooked on either side, about 12–15 min. Arrange on a hot flat dish, sprinkle with lemon juice and chopped parsley. Add a large nut of fresh butter to the pan, heat until nut brown in colour, then pour over the fish and serve.

4 helpings

GRILLED RED MULLET

4 small red mullet   salt and pepper
olive oil   parsley

Scrape the scales from the fish, cut off the fins and remove the eyes, but leave the head and tail on. Gut the fish if necessary and keep the liver. Wash well. Season the inside of each fish and replace the liver. Brush the fish with olive oil and put a little oil in the grill-pan before putting in the fish. Grill quickly for 3 min., then turn the fish over and baste well. Reduce the heat and continue grilling until the mullet are cooked, about a further 15 min. Serve on a hot dish with the remaining oil poured over. Garnish with parsley.

4 helpings

PERCH

BOILED PERCH

4 perch   salt

The scales of perch are rather difficult to remove; the fish can either be boiled and the scales removed afterwards, or a better method is to plunge the fish into boiling water for 2–3 min., then scale.

Before cooking, the fish must be washed in warm water, cleaned, and the gills and fins removed. Have ready boiling water to cover the fish, add salt to taste, put in the fish, reduce heat and simmer gently for 10–20 min., according to size. Serve with Hollandaise or melted butter sauce.

4–5 helpings

PIKE

BAKED PIKE

1 medium-sized pike (about 4 lb.)
4 oz. veal forcemeat   1 egg
brown breadcrumbs
butter or fat for basting

Wash, clean and scale the fish and remove the fins and gills. Fill the inside with forcemeat, sew up the opening, brush over with beaten egg and coat with breadcrumbs. Sometimes the fish is trussed in a round shape, the tail being fastened in the mouth with a skewer. Before putting the fish in the oven it should be well basted with hot fat or butter, and as this fish is naturally dry it must be frequently basted and kept covered with greased paper while cooking. Bake gently for 40–45 min.

8–10 helpings

STEWED PIKE

1 small pike (2–3 lb.)   ½ oz. butter
rashers of bacon   ½ pt. stock or
water   1 teasp. lemon juice or
1 tablesp. vinegar   salt and pepper

Wash, clean and dry the pike. Melt the butter in a saucepan, put in the pike and cover with rashers of bacon. Put on a close-fitting lid, let the fish cook gently in the steam for 15 min., then add the stock, lemon juice or vinegar and season to taste. Simmer very gently for about ¼ hr., then serve on a hot dish with the liquor strained round.

6 helpings

PILCHARDS

The taste of pilchards is very similar to that of herrings, but more oily. They may be dressed according to the directions given for cooking herrings. Pilchards are very often canned in either oil or tomato sauce and may be served cold with salad, or as hors d'œuvre, or on toast as a savoury.

PLAICE

Plaice is available all the year; best from May to January. Most plentiful of the flat fish varieties. Suitable for all methods of cooking, including serving cold.

BAKED STUFFED PLAICE

1 medium-sized plaice   2 tablesp.
white breadcrumbs   1 tablesp.
finely-chopped suet   1 dessertsp.
finely-chopped parsley   ¼ teasp.
mixed herbs   a pinch of nutmeg
salt and pepper   1 egg   milk
pale brown breadcrumbs
a little butter or fat

Mix the white breadcrumbs, suet, parsley, herbs and nutmeg together, season well with salt and pepper, add half the egg and enough milk to moisten thoroughly. Make an incision down the centre of the fish as for filleting, raise the flesh each side as far as possible and fill with forcemeat. Instead of drawing the sides of the fish close together, fill up the gap with forcemeat and flatten the surface to the level of the fish with a knife. Brush over with the remaining egg, coat lightly with pale brown breadcrumbs, put into a fireproof dish and dot a few small pieces of butter on top. Bake for 20–30 min. in a moderate oven (350° F., Gas 4).

NOTE: The forcemeat may be varied by using shrimps or oysters.

3–4 helpings

FILLETS OF PLAICE WITH LEMON DRESSING

4 fillets of plaice (4 oz. each
approx.)   seasoning   1 oz. butter or
margarine   juice of ½ lemon
chopped parsley

Season the fish. Melt the fat in the grill pan and place the fish skin side uppermost in the pan. Cook for 1 min., then turn with flesh side up and grill steadily until golden brown and cooked, about 5–8 min., depending on thickness of fillets. Remove to a hot serving dish, keep hot. Add the lemon juice to the remaining fat in the pan, reheat and pour over the fish. Sprinkle liberally with chopped parsley.

4 helpings

FRIED PLAICE

Four 4 oz. fillets of plaice 1 tablesp. flour salt and pepper a little milk or water egg and breadcrumbs frying-fat parsley

Wipe the fillets with a clean damp cloth. Season the flour with salt and pepper to taste and dip each fillet in it. Beat the egg, mix with a little milk or water and brush over each fillet. Coat the fillets with breadcrumbs, press on firmly and fry in hot fat until nicely browned. Garnish with fresh or fried parsley, and serve plain with cut lemon or with anchovy, shrimp or melted butter sauce.

4 helpings

PLAICE MORNAY

Four 4 oz. fillets of plaice mornay sauce (p. 101)

Fold the fillets in half and steam between two plates. Meanwhile make the sauce. Arrange the cooked fish in a shallow fireproof dish, coat with sauce and sprinkle with the remaining cheese. Place under a hot grill until golden brown.

Serve with grilled half tomatoes and mashed potatoes.

4 helpings

ROCK SALMON

See Saithe

ROCKFISH

(sometimes called CATFISH)

Rockfish are available all the year; best from February to July. Suitable for frying, steaming, poaching and for made-up dishes. Usually sold skinned.

SAITHE

(sometimes called ROCK SALMON or COALFISH)

Saithe is available all the year; best September to February. Suitable for all methods of cooking.

SALMON

Seasons: English and Scottish, February to August; Irish, January to September. Suitable for poaching, grilling, baking; excellent served cold.

BAKED SALMON

2 lb. salmon (middle) (approx.) salt and pepper grated nutmeg 2 small shallots 1 teasp. chopped parsley a little butter 1 small glass claret or cider (optional) tomato sauce

Cut the fish into 2–3 even-sized slices and place in a well-buttered fireproof dish. Season with salt, pepper and a little grated nutmeg. Chop the shallots and sprinkle over with the parsley. Dot a little butter on top of the fish. Moisten with the wine or cider (if used), and bake for about 15 min. in a fairly hot oven (375° F., Gas 5), basting the fish frequently. When done, dish up and pour some tomato sauce over the slices of salmon. Use the essence left in the dish in which the fish was baked to flavour the sauce.

6–8 helpings

BOILED SALMON

Salmon salt boiling water

Scale and clean the fish, and put into a saucepan or fish-kettle with sufficient *boiling* water just to cover, adding salt to taste. The boiling water is necessary to preserve the colour of the fish. Simmer gently until the fish can be easily separated from the bone.

Drain well. Dish, garnished with cut lemon and parsley. Serve with fish sauce, and a dish of thinly-sliced cucumber.

Allow 4–6 oz. per helping
Cooking time—allow 10 min. per lb.

BOILED SALMON—in Court Bouillon

Salmon

COURT BOUILLON

To each quart of water allow:
1 dessertsp. salt   1 small turnip
1 small onion   ½ leek   1 strip of
celery   6 peppercorns   bouquet garni

Put into the pan just enough water to cover the fish, and when boiling add the prepared vegetables and cook gently for 30 min. In the meantime, wash, clean, and scale the fish and tie it loosely in a piece of muslin. Remove any scum there may be on the court bouillon, then put in the fish and boil gently until sufficiently cooked (the time required depends more on the thickness of the fish than the weight; allow 10 min. for each lb. when cooking a thick piece, and 7 min. for the tail end). Drain well, dish, garnished with parsley.

Serve with sliced cucumber, and Hollandaise, caper, shrimp or anchovy sauce.

Allow 4–6 oz. per helping

POTTED SALMON

Cold salmon   salt and pepper
cayenne pepper   ground mace
anchovy essence   clarified butter

Free the fish from skin and bone, and pound it thoroughly. Add the seasoning by degrees, add anchovy essence to taste and clarified butter a few drops at a time, until the right consistency and flavour is obtained. Rub the ingredients through a fine sieve, press into small pots and cover with a good layer of clarified butter. Fresh salmon may also be potted.

SALMON CUTLETS EN PAPILLOTES

Slices of salmon, about ¾–1 in. thick
salt and pepper   butter
anchovy or caper sauce

Season the slices with salt and pepper. Butter some pieces of greaseproof paper or aluminium foil. Enclose a slice of fish in each, secure the ends of the paper case by twisting tightly, and bake for 15–20 min. in a moderate oven (350° F., Gas 4). Serve with anchovy or caper sauce.

Allow 4–5 oz. per helping

SALMON MOUSSE

1 lb. cooked salmon (approx.) or
one 16-oz. can   1 oz. gelatine   1 pt.
clear fish stock   salt and pepper
2 egg whites

Dissolve the gelatine in the stock and season to taste. Cook the egg whites in a dariole mould or small cup until firm; when cold cut into thin slices and cut out into fancy shapes. Drain the oil from the salmon and remove all skin and bones. Cover the bottom of a mould with the jellied stock, let it set, and then decorate with egg-white shapes. Set the garnish with a little jelly, allow to set. Add a layer of salmon, cover with jelly and put aside until set. Repeat until the mould is full. Keep in the refrigerator or in a cool place until wanted, then turn out and serve.

NOTE: 1 tablesp. sherry or Marsala can be added to the jelly to give it additional flavour.

6–8 helpings

DEVILLED SMOKED SALMON

½ lb. smoked salmon (approx.)
3–4 slices toasted bread
1 oz. fresh butter   salt and pepper
curry butter

Trim the slices of toast, cut each into 3 even-sized pieces and butter one side of each. Sprinkle with salt and pepper, cover with thin slices of smoked salmon, then spread with curry butter. Place in a hot oven for a few minutes. Dish up neatly, garnish with sprigs of parsley and serve hot.

5–6 helpings

SALMON TROUT

Salmon trout is of the same species as river trout and is related to the salmon; it is very similar in appearance to grilse. It is in season March to August, its average weight being 2–4 lb., and its average length 1 ft. 6 in.–2 ft. 6 in.

POACHED SALMON TROUT

Clean the fish, removing the gills, intestines and eyes, but leaving on the head and tail. If a fish kettle with drainer is not available, cradle the fish in muslin and cook in a large saucepan or preserving pan. Lower the fish into simmering, lightly salted water (1 teasp. per qt.) and poach, allowing 10 min. per lb. and 10 min. over. As soon as cooked, lift carefully from the water and drain. To serve cold, cool a little and then neatly remove the skin from one side. When serving hot, skinning is optional.

To serve hot: Arrange on a flat dish, garnish with sliced cucumber, parsley, lemon and new potatoes. Serve with melted butter or Hollandaise sauce.

To serve cold: 1. Serve quite plain, garnished with salad and accompanied by mayonnaise.

2. Glaze the cold fish with aspic jelly made with the liquor in which the fish was cooked, garnish with chopped aspic, stuffed tomatoes and sliced cucumber.

SHAD
BAKED SHAD

One 2–3-lb. shad   3–4 oz. veal
forcemeat   2–3 rashers bacon

Wash, clean, scale and dry the fish. Stuff the fish with forcemeat and sew up the opening. Place in a fireproof dish or baking-tin, lay the slices of bacon on top and bake gently in a moderate oven (350° F., Gas 4) for 25–30 min.

4 helpings

SKATE

Skate is available all the year; spawns in March and April. Excellen for poaching or frying, or cold with salad. Only the "wings" are eaten.

BOILED SKATE

One 5–8 oz. piece of skate wing
salt

Wash the skate, put into a saucepan containing sufficient salted warm water just to cover, and simmer gently for about 15 min. or until the fish separates easily from the bone. Drain well, dish and serve with shrimp, or caper sauce.

1 helping

SKATE AU BEURRE NOIR

1¼ lb. skate wing (approx.)
1½ oz. butter   1 tablesp. vinegar
chopped parsley
COURT BOUILLON
1 small carrot   1 small onion
1 pt. water   1 dessertsp. vinegar
1 level teasp. salt   ½ bay leaf
sprig of parsley   2 peppercorns

Peel and slice the carrot and onion. Place all the ingredients for the court bouillon in a pan, bring to the boil and boil for 5 min., strain and return to the pan.

Cut the skate into convenient portions for serving and poach in the court bouillon for 10–15 min. Remove the pieces of fish carefully, drain and place on a hot dish. Heat the butter in a small, strong pan until it begins to turn brown, remove from the heat and add the vinegar very gradually to prevent spluttering. Pour over the fish, sprinkle with a little chopped parsley and serve.

4 helpings

SMELTS

BAKED SMELTS

12 smelts   breadcrumbs
2 oz. fresh butter
salt and cayenne to taste

Wash and dry the fish thoroughly with a cloth; arrange them in a flat baking-dish. Cover with fine breadcrumbs and place dabs of butter over them. Season and bake for 15 min. Just before serving, add a squeeze of lemon juice and garnish with fried parsley and cut lemon.

4 helpings

FRIED SMELTS

12 smelts   a little flour   egg and breadcrumbs   fat or oil for frying

Smelts should be very fresh and not washed more than is necessary to clean them. Dry in a cloth, flour lightly, dip them in egg and coat with very fine breadcrumbs. Put them into hot fat or oil and fry until pale brown. Drain well and serve with plain melted butter. This fish is often used as a garnish.

4 helpings
Cooking time—5 min.

SOLE

The true sole is the Dover Sole, the so-called Lemon Sole is a different species but can be cooked by the same methods.

Sole is seasonable all the year: it spawns February to May, sole without roe are superior. Sole is suitable for all methods of cooking.

Allow one 3–4-oz. fillet per helping when served as the fish course of a 4-course menu and 2 fillets when a main dish.

BAKED FILLETS OF SOLE WITH FORCEMEAT

4 fillets of sole   2 tablesp. bread-crumbs   1 tablesp. finely-chopped suet   1 dessertsp. finely-chopped parsley   ¼ teasp. mixed herbs   1 egg salt and pepper   pale-brown breadcrumbs   butter

Wipe fillets with a clean, damp cloth. Mix the other ingredients together with sufficient beaten egg to moisten. Spread a thin layer of forcemeat on each fillet and fold in two. Place the fillets in a fireproof baking-dish and fill up the spaces between with the rest of the forcemeat. Sprinkle lightly with pale-brown breadcrumbs, add a few small pieces of butter and bake for about 30 min. in a moderate oven (350° F., Gas 4). Serve in the cooking dish.

4 helpings

FILLETS OF SOLE AUX FINES HERBES

Eight 2 oz. fillets of sole   salt and pepper   4 tablesp. fish stock
½ pt. white wine sauce (p. 94)
1 tablesp. finely-chopped fresh herbs

Wipe the fillets with a clean, damp cloth, season with salt and pepper and fold in three. Place in a greased fireproof dish, add the fish stock, cover, and cook in a fairly hot oven (375° F., Gas 5) for 15–20 min. Drain the fillets well and place on a dish, coat with white wine sauce and sprinkle with the finely chopped fresh herbs.

4 helpings

FILLETS OF SOLE BONNE FEMME

4 fillets of sole   4 oz. mushrooms
1 shallot   1 teasp. chopped parsley
salt and pepper   ¼ pt. white wine
¼ pt. fish Velouté sauce
a little butter

Wipe the fillets with a clean, damp cloth. Put them flat in a shallow pan with the sliced mush-rooms, sliced shallot, parsley and seasoning. Add the wine, cover and poach for 10–15 min. Drain the fish from the wine, place on a fireproof dish and keep warm. Boil the wine rapidly until it is reduced by half, then stir it into the hot Velouté sauce and thicken with a little butter. When thoroughly blended pour the sauce over the fillets and place under a hot grill until lightly browned. Serve at once in a border of sliced, steamed potatoes.

4 helpings

FILLETS OF SOLE MEUNIERE

4 large or 8 small fillets of sole
a little seasoned flour   3 oz. butter
1 tablesp. lemon juice
1 level tablesp. chopped parsley
lemon "butterflies" (see p. 40)

Dredge the fillets lightly, but thoroughly, with seasoned flour. Heat the butter in a frying-pan and when hot fry the fillets until golden brown and cooked through —about 7 min. Arrange the fillets on a hot dish. Reheat the fat until it is nut brown in colour and then pour it over the fish. Sprinkle the lemon juice and parsley over the fillets, garnish with lemon "butter-flies" and serve at once.

4 helpings

FRIED SOLE

1–2 medium-sized soles   salt and
pepper   1 tablesp. flour   egg and
breadcrumbs   deep fat for frying

Wash and skin the soles, cut off the fins, and dry well. Add a liberal seasoning of salt and pepper to the flour. Coat the fish with seasoned flour, then brush over with egg, and coat with fine bread-crumbs. Lower the fish carefully into the hot fat and fry until golden brown.

Soles may also be fried, though less easily, and sometimes less satisfactorily, in a large frying-pan. The oval form is preferable for the purpose; and in frying, care should be taken to cook first the side of the sole intended to be served uppermost, otherwise breadcrumbs that have become detached from the side first fried may adhere to the side next cooked, and spoil its appearance. Drain well on kitchen paper and serve garnished with fried parsley.

1–2 helpings

Cooking time—about 10 min.

SOLE AU GRATIN

3 fillets or 1 large sole   salt and
pepper   ¼ glass white wine   lemon
juice   mushroom liquor   1 teasp.
chopped parsley   preserved mushrooms, sliced   Italian sauce (p. 102)
brown breadcrumbs   butter

If using a whole sole, skin both sides, cut off the head and fins and make several incisions with a knife across one side of the fish. Place fish on a well-buttered, fireproof dish (if using whole fish place cut side uppermost), season with pepper and salt, add the white wine, a few drops of lemon juice, a little mushroom liquor and some chopped parsley. Slice the mush-rooms and place in a row down the centre of the fish; cover with a rich Italian sauce. Sprinkle with brown breadcrumbs, dot a few tiny bits of butter on top of the fish and bake in a moderate oven (350° F., Gas 4) for 20–30 min., according to size of sole.

2–3 helpings

SPRATS

Choose sprats with a silvery appearance, brightness being a sign of freshness. They are best from November to March. Sup-plies are rather erratic, as they are affected by weather.

Sprats should be cooked very fresh. Wipe dry; fasten in rows by a skewer run through the eyes;

dredge with flour and grill under a red-hot grill. The grill rack should first be rubbed with suet. Serve very hot, with cut lemon and brown bread and butter.

Allow 1 lb. for 3 helpings
Cooking time—3-4 min.

FRIED SPRATS

3 doz. sprats (approx.)   2 tablesp.
flour   salt and pepper   ½ oz.
cooking fat   lemon wedges

Wash and dry the sprats thoroughly, mix the flour with the salt and pepper to season. Dip the sprats in the seasoned flour and fry them in the hot fat. Serve as quickly as possible on a hot dish with a wedge of lemon per helping.

5 helpings
Cooking time—20 min.

STURGEON
BAKED STURGEON

2 lb. sturgeon   salt and pepper
1 small bunch of herbs
juice of ½ lemon   ½ pt. white wine
½ lb. butter

Clean the fish thoroughly and skin it. Lay the fish in a large fire-proof dish, sprinkle over the seasoning and herbs very finely minced, and moisten with the lemon juice and wine. Place the butter in small pieces over the whole of the fish, put into a moderate oven (350° F., Gas 4) for about 30–40 min., and baste frequently. Bake until brown, then serve with its own gravy.

5–6 helpings

STURGEON CUTLETS

1½ lb. sturgeon   ½ teasp. finely-
chopped parsley   ½ teasp. finely-
grated lemon rind   egg and
breadcrumbs   salt and pepper
fat for frying

Cut the fish into thin slices, flatten them with a heavy knife, and trim them into shape. Add

the parsley and lemon rind to the breadcrumbs, and season with salt and pepper. Brush over with beaten egg, coat carefully with the seasoned breadcrumbs, and fry in hot fat until cooked and lightly browned on both sides. Drain free from fat, and serve with piquant or tomato sauce.

6–8 helpings
Cooking time—about 10 min.

TENCH
BAKED TENCH

1 tench   juice of 2 lemons
2 oz. butter or fat   salt and pepper
2 shallots   1 tablesp. coarsely-
chopped gherkin   ½ pt. white sauce

Scale and clean the fish thoroughly, remove the gills, which are always muddy, sprinkle the fish liberally with lemon juice, reserving 1 tablesp. of juice, put the fish aside for 1 hr. Then melt the butter in a baking-dish, put in the fish and baste it well, sprinkle with salt and pepper and add the finely-chopped shallots. Cover with greased paper and bake gently for 25–35 min., according to taste. Add the gherkin and 1 tablesp. lemon juice to the sauce and season to taste. Serve the fish with the sauce poured over.

2–3 helpings

TROUT

River trout are available all the year. Serve grilled, baked, fried or cold with salad.

BAKED STUFFED TROUT

2 large trout   veal forcemeat
3 oz. butter   1 oz. flour
1 dessertsp. capers   1 teasp. lemon
juice   ½ teasp. anchovy essence
salt and pepper

Clean, scale, empty and dry the fish. Make the forcemeat stiff. Stuff the trout with forcemeat, and sew up or skewer the openings.

Place in a baking-tin or dish with 2 oz. of butter and bake in a moderate oven (350° F., Gas 4) for about ½ hr., basting frequently. Fry the flour and the rest of the butter together. When the fish is ready, remove it to a hot dish and strain the liquor in the baking-dish on to the flour and butter. Stir until boiling and smooth, then add the capers, lemon juice, anchovy essence and season to taste. Simmer for 2–3 min., then pour over the fish and serve.

5–6 helpings

TRUITES AU BLEU

One 6–8 oz. trout   vinegar   salt   parsley

The essential factor of this famous dish is that the trout should be alive until just before cooking. In continental restaurants they are often kept in a tank from which the customer selects his fish, which is then stunned, cleaned and cooked immediately.

The fish should be stunned, cleaned (gutted) and immediately plunged into a pan of boiling salted water to which a little vinegar has been added. (The fish are not scaled or washed as this would spoil the blue colour.) Draw the pan aside or reduce the heat and poach the fish for about 10–12 min. Drain and serve garnished with parsley and accompanied by melted butter, Hollandaise sauce and small boiled potatoes.

TRUITES A LA MEUNIERE

As for Mullet à la Meuniere (p. 126) substituting trout for mullet.

TURBOT

Turbot is considered by many to be the finest of the flat fish. It is notable for the small bony tubercles on the dark skin surface and for the complete absence of scales. Turbot often grow to considerable size—25 lb. is not unusual—and are usually sold cut in thick slices or cutlets.

Young turbot are referred to as Chicken Turbots and they are cut entirely into fillets.

Turbot is seasonable most of the year; normally cheapest when salmon is in season. It can be cooked by any method, and is excellent cold with salad. It must be noted that if cooking a whole turbot, a turbot-kettle (shaped) will be required.

POACHED TURBOT

1 chicken turbot or a cut, 1½–2 lb. in weight   lemon   salt

Wipe the fish thoroughly and trim the fins. Make an incision down the middle of the back, to lessen the possibility of the skin cracking; and rub the white side of the fish with a cut lemon to retain its whiteness. Have ready a pan containing sufficient warm water to cover the fish, add salt to taste, put in the fish, bring gradually to near boiling-point, then simmer very gently for 15–20 min. Drain the fish and dish up neatly.

Garnish with lobster coral, parsley and cut lemon, and serve with Hollandaise, anchovy or shrimp sauce.

5–6 helpings

TURBOT A LA DUGLERE

Four 5–6 oz. pieces of turbot (skinned)   ½ lb. tomatoes   1 small onion   1 level tablesp. chopped parsley (optional)   ¼ pt. dry white wine   salt and pepper   1 oz. butter or margarine   1 oz. flour

Place the fish in a greased casserole. Skin and chop the tomatoes, peel and finely chop the onion. Mix the tomatoes, onion, parsley (if used) and wine together, season and pour over the fish. Cover the casserole and cook in a fairly hot oven (400° F., Gas 6) for 30–35 min. Remove from the oven, lift the fish on to a hot dish and keep hot while making the sauce. Measure the tomato mixture and make up to $\frac{1}{2}$ pt. with water if necessary. Melt the fat, add the flour and cook for 1–2 min. Add the tomato mixture, bring to the boil, stirring all the time and boil gently for 5 min. Season to taste, then pour over the fish and serve at once.

4 helpings

WHITEBAIT

Whitebait is most seasonable from February to July. Best deep fried.

WHITEBAIT

Whitebait ice flour deep fat for frying cayenne or black pepper salt lemon

Frying whitebait is a difficult task for inexperienced cooks. The following is a well-tried method which, if carefully followed, never fails to produce satisfactory results. Put the whitebait with a piece of ice in a basin, which must be kept cool. When required for cooking, spread the fish on a cloth to dry, dredge well with flour, place in a wire basket and shake off the superfluous flour. Plunge the basket into a pan of clean, very hot lard and fry rapidly for 3–4 min. Keep moving the basket all the time whilst frying. Lift the basket, shake it to strain off the fat, and turn the fish on to grease-proof paper. Place on a warm dish and repeat until all the whitebait are fried. Season with cayenne or black pepper and fine salt. Serve garnished with quarters of lemon.

Cooking time—3–4 min.

WHITING

Whiting is available all the year; best in winter months. It is the traditional fish for invalids. It can be served poached, steamed, baked or fried.

BAKED WHITING

As for Sole au Gratin (p. 132), substituting skinned whiting for sole.

BAKED WHITING AUX FINES HERBES

As for Sole aux Fines Herbes (p. 131).

FRIED WHITING

3–4 whiting 1 tablesp. flour salt and pepper egg and breadcrumbs deep fat or oil for frying parsley

Wash, clean and dry the fish. Remove their skins and fasten the tail in the mouth with a small skewer. (The fishmonger will usually do this for you.) Season the flour with salt and pepper and coat the fish with it. Brush them over with egg, coat with breadcrumbs and fry in hot fat until nicely browned. Serve on a fish paper, garnished with sprigs of fresh or crisp-fried parsley.

3–4 helpings

Cooking time—6–7 min.

WITCH

Available all the year: best from August to April. Suitable for all methods of cooking.

See also recipes for cooking sole.

MISCELLANEOUS FISH DISHES

FISH PUDDING

1 lb. any kind of white fish
4 oz. finely-chopped suet
2 oz. breadcrumbs 1 teasp. finely-chopped parsley salt and pepper
a few drops of anchovy essence
2 eggs $\frac{1}{4}$ pt. milk or
stock made from fish bones

Grease well a plain mould or basin. Free the fish from skin and bones, chop the fish finely and rub through a fine sieve. Add to the suet with the breadcrumbs, parsley, salt, pepper and anchovy essence, and mix well. Beat the eggs slightly, add the milk or fish stock and stir into the mixture. Put into the mould or basin, cover with greased paper, and steam gently for nearly 1½ hr.

4–5 helpings

FRICASSEE OF FISH

1 lb. white fish   ½ pt. milk   ¼ pt. water   salt and pepper   ½ bay leaf   a small piece of mace   a pinch of nutmeg   1 oz. butter   1 oz. flour   lemon juice

Divide the fish into pieces about 1½ in. square. Put the milk, water, salt and pepper, bay leaf, mace and nutmeg into a saucepan, and when warm add the fish. Bring to the boil and simmer for 10 min., then remove the bay leaf and mace. Meanwhile knead together the butter and flour, add in small portions to the contents of the saucepan and stir gently until the flour is mixed smoothly with the liquor. Simmer for 10 min., then add lemon juice, season to taste and serve.

2–3 helpings

SEA-FOOD CHOWDER

1 smoked haddock (1–1¼ lb.) 1–2 sliced onions   1 breakfast-cup diced raw potatoes   2–3 skinned tomatoes   1–1½ oz. butter or margarine   1 tablesp. flour   3–4 tablesp. cream   salt and pepper   ½ pt. shelled prawns or shrimps   ½ A1 can peas 1 dessertsp. freshly-chopped parsley

Cover the well-washed haddock with cold water, bring slowly to boil, then remove and wash again. Skim off scum from the stock. Cook onions in a little of the stock until almost soft. Add potatoes and cook until soft. Cut tomatoes into eighths, discard seeds; simmer in remaining stock. Add tomatoes to other vegetables and cook a little. Meanwhile, free the haddock flesh of skin and bones. Melt the fat, add flour and cook for a

few min. without browning. Remove from heat. Slowly stir the strained remaining stock into this roux. Cook gently for a few min., while stirring. Stir in the cream and season to taste. Add the vegetable mixture, then the haddock and prawns or shrimps, reserving a few. Add the drained peas. Heat through but do not boil. Sprinkle in the parsley, turn into a serving dish and garnish with the reserved shellfish.

4–5 helpings

WATER SOUCHET

Flounders, plaice, soles, perch or tench   parsley   salt   carrot

Any of the above-named fish will be suitable. Wash and clean the fish, put into a saucepan with just sufficient cold water to cover, add a small bunch of parsley and salt to taste. Cook gently until done, then transfer the fish carefully to a serving dish. Sprinkle over some finely-chopped parsley and finely-shredded cooked carrot. Strain and add the liquor, then serve. Serve with thinly-cut brown bread and butter.

SHELLFISH

The shellfish commonly eaten are the lobster, crab, crayfish, oyster, cockle, mussel, escallop, shrimp and prawn. Prawns are much sought after for garnishing.

COCKLES

Cockles are available all the year and are normally sold cooked. Serve cold with vinegar or hot in sauces, pies, etc.

CRABS

Crabs are on sale all the year round, but are at their best from May to October. It is usual to buy crabs which have been boiled by the fishmonger. Choose crabs which are heavy for their size.

Avoid crabs which are attracting flies, especially around the mouth, as this is a sign of deterioration; choose a crab which looks and smells fresh. The hen crab may be distinguished from the cock crab by its broader tail flap. Normally the flesh of the cock crab is more reliable for quality than the hen, the cock crab usually yields more meat for its size and is therefore a more economical buy. An average crab about 6 inches across should weigh 2½–3 lb., this will be found sufficient for 4 people. It is illegal to sell "berried" or "rush" crab.

TO PREPARE A CRAB

After wiping well with a damp cloth, place the crab on its back with tail facing, and remove claws and legs by twisting them in the opposite way to which they lie. Place the thumbs under flap at tail and push upwards, pull flap away upwards so that the stomach contents are not drawn over the meat, and lift off. (The fishmonger will always do this on request.) Reverse the crab so that the head is facing, then press on the mouth with the thumbs pushing down, and forward, so that the mouth and stomach will then come away in one piece. Remove the meat from the shell by easing round the inside edge of the shell to loosen the tissues with the handle of a plastic teaspoon, and the meat will then come away easily. Keep the dark and the white meat separate. With the handle of a knife, tap sharply over the false line around the shell cavity, press down and it will come away neatly. Scrub and dry the shell, then rub over with a little oil. Remove the "deadmen's fingers" (the lungs) and discard, then scoop out the meat from the claw sockets. Scoop out as much as possible but keep it free of bone. Twist off first joint of large claws and scoop out meat.

Tap sharply round the broad shell with back of knife until halves fall apart. Cut the cartilage between the pincers, open pincers and meat will come away in one piece.

DRESSED CRAB

One 2½–3-lb. crab   salt and pepper
fresh breadcrumbs (optional)
a little lemon juice (optional)
French dressing (p. 245)
1 hard-boiled egg   parsley

Pick the crab meat from the shells. Mix the dark crab meat with salt and pepper, fresh breadcrumbs and a little lemon juice if liked. The breadcrumbs are optional but they lessen the richness and give a firmer texture. Press the mixture lightly against the sides of the previously cleaned shell. Flake out the white meat, mix with French dressing and pile in the centre of the shell. Garnish with sieved egg yolk, chopped egg white, chopped parsley, sieved coral if any, and decorate with small claws. Make a necklace with the small claws, place on a dish and rest the crab on this. Surround with salad.

4 helpings

POTTED CRAB

2 crabs   salt   cayenne pepper
powdered mace
about 4 oz. clarified butter

Pick the crab meat from the shells, mix with salt, cayenne and mace to taste, rub through a fine sieve. Press into small pots, cover with melted butter and bake in a moderate oven (350° F., Gas 4) for ½ hr. When cold, cover each pot with clarified butter.

CRAYFISH

Crayfish are freshwater shellfish closely resembling lobsters but much smaller in size. They are in season June–March.

TO BOIL CRAYFISH

Wash thoroughly, remove the intestinal cord, then throw the fish into fast-boiling salted water. Keep boiling for about 10 min.

POTTED CRAYFISH

4 doz. live crayfish salt and pepper
a little vinegar ½ lb. butter (approx.)
ground mace clarified butter

Put the crayfish into boiling water to which has been added a good seasoning of salt and a little vinegar. Cook for about 15 min., then drain and dry. Pick the meat from the shells, pound to a fine paste, adding gradually the butter and mace, salt and pepper to taste. Press into small pots, cover with clarified butter and use when cold.

ESCALLOPS OR SCALLOPS

Escallops are usually opened by the fishmonger and displayed in their flat shells. If the escallops are to be served in their shells ask the fishmonger for the *deep* shells. If however it is necessary to open escallops they should be put over a gentle heat to allow the shells to open. When they have opened, remove from the shells, trim away the beard and remove the black parts. Wash the escallops well, drain and dry. Wash and dry the shells; keep the deep shells for serving-dishes.

Escallops are in season from November to March. They can be served baked, fried, poached or grilled.

BAKED ESCALLOPS

4 large escallops cider (optional)
2½ oz. bacon fat or margarine
2 oz. breadcrumbs (approx.)
1 teasp. finely-grated onion a little
lemon juice salt and pepper
grating of nutmeg
sprigs of watercress or parsley

Prepare the escallops. Separate the roes (orange tongue) and place in a casserole with just enough cider or water to prevent sticking and a shaving of fat on top; cover. Melt the rest of the fat, add sufficient breadcrumbs to give a moist texture, then add onion, lemon juice and seasoning. Cut the escallops in half horizontally; season. Cover the bottom of each shell with a thin coating of the breadcrumb mixture and place the fish on top. Coat with the remaining breadcrumb mixture. Bake shells and roes in a fairly hot oven (375° F., Gas 5) for 25–30 min. Serve each fish garnished with a roe and a spring of watercress or parsley.

4 helpings

ESCALLOPS IN SHELLS

1½ doz. small escallops 1 oz. butter
1 cup fresh breadcrumbs cayenne
pepper a little chopped parsley
a little lemon juice salt and pepper
1 gill white sauce

Prepare the escallops and 6 shells. Butter the shells and sprinkle in a few breadcrumbs. Put 3 escallops in each and season with cayenne, chopped parsley and a drop or two of lemon juice. Mix a little pepper and salt with the remaining breadcrumbs. Cover the escallops with white sauce, sprinkle with breadcrumbs, place bits of butter on top and bake for about 20 min. in a fairly hot oven (375° F., Gas 5).

6 helpings

LOBSTERS

Lobsters can be obtained all the year round, but are scarce from December to March. They are cheapest during the summer months. Lobsters are usually bought already boiled, but live lobsters can be obtained to order if a few days' notice is given to the fishmonger. Choose one of medium size and heavy in weight, it is illegal to sell lobsters less than 9 inches in length, or to offer "berried" or "spawny" fish, i.e. when the coral is visible outside the shell. If fresh, the tail of a cooked lobster will be stiff, and if gently raised, will return with a spring. The narrowness of the back part of the tail and the stiffness of the two uppermost fins (swimmerettes) in the tail distinguish the cock lobster from the hen.

TO BOIL LOBSTERS

Method 1: Wash the lobster well before boiling, tie the claws securely. Have ready a saucepan of boiling water, salted in the proportion of ¼ lb. salt to 1 gallon water. Throw the lobster head first into the water (this instantly destroys life), keep it boiling for 20–45 min., acording to size, and skim well. Allow 20 min.–½ hr. for small lobsters and ½–¾ hr. for large lobsters. If boiled too long the meat becomes thready, and if not done enough, the coral is not red. Rub the shells over with a little salad oil to brighten the colour.

Method 2: Put the lobsters into warm water, bring the water gradually to the boil and boil as above. This is believed by many to be a more humane method of killing, as the lobster is lulled to sleep and does not realize it is being killed.

TO PREPARE LOBSTER

Wipe the lobster well with a clean, damp cloth and twist off claws and legs. Place lobster on a board parallel to the edge with back uppermost and head to left. Cut along the centre of back, from junction of head with body to tail, using a sharp, stainless knife. Reverse so that tail is to left and cut along head; the stomach, which lies just behind the mouth, is not cut until last. Remove intestinal cord, remove stomach and coral (if any) and keep for garnish. Meat may be left in shell or removed and used as required. Knock off the tips of the claws with the back of a knife and drain away any water. Tap sharply round broadest part of each claw and shell should fall apart. Cut cartilage between pincers, open pincers and meat can be removed in one piece. Remove meat from smaller joints of claws.

BAKED LOBSTER

1 boiled lobster   1½ oz. butter
½ teasp. finely-chopped shallot
2–3 tablesp. white sauce
1 dessertsp. finely-chopped parsley
juice of ½ lemon   pinch of nutmeg
salt and pepper   1 egg
browned breadcrumbs

Remove the lobster meat from the shells (*see* above) and mince or chop it coarsely. Clean the two halves of the large shell. Melt the butter in a saucepan, fry the shallot for 2–3 min. without browning, then add the lobster meat, white sauce, parsley, lemon juice, nutmeg and salt and pepper to taste. Stir and heat until thoroughly hot. Beat the egg slightly, add it to the mixture and cook until it begins to bind. Put the mixture into the shells, cover lightly with brown breadcrumbs, put 3–4 very small pieces of butter on top and bake for 10–15 min. in a moderate oven (350° *F.*, *Gas* 4).

4–5 helpings
Cooking time—½ hr.

COQUILLES OF LOBSTER

1 boiled or canned lobster
mushrooms   butter   white sauce
salt and pepper   nutmeg   cayenne
pepper   8 baked shell-shaped pastry
cases   fried breadcrumbs   parsley

Dice the meat of the lobster and put it in a saucepan with some chopped mushrooms and butter, allowing 8 mushrooms and $\frac{1}{2}$ oz. butter to every $\frac{1}{2}$ lb. of lobster. Heat, stirring all the time, until thoroughly hot, then moisten with white sauce. Season with salt, pepper, a little grated nutmeg and a pinch of cayenne. Keep the mixture hot so that it is ready for use when required. Warm the baked shells in the oven, fill them with the mixture and sprinkle over some fried breadcrumbs. Dish up on small plates and garnish with parsley.

NOTE: A little anchovy essence added to the mixture will improve the flavour considerably.

8 helpings

DEVILLED LOBSTER

1 boiled lobster   butter   3 tablesp. white breadcrumbs   2 tablesp. white sauce or cream   cayenne a few browned breadcrumbs

Cut the lobster in two lengthwise, remove the meat carefully, as the half-shells must be kept whole, and chop the meat finely. Melt $1\frac{1}{2}$ oz. butter and pour it on the lobster. Add the white breadcrumbs and the sauce, season rather highly with cayenne and mix well. Press the mixture lightly into the shells, cover with brown breadcrumbs, put 3 or 4 pieces of butter on top and bake for about 20 min. in a moderate oven (350° F., Gas 4). Serve hot or cold.

LOBSTER MAYONNAISE

1 boiled lobster   mayonnaise   salad

Lobster Mayonnaise may be served in either of the following ways:

(a) Cut the lobster in half lengthways, scoop out the meat from the body, mix with a little mayonnaise and return. Carefully remove the meat from the tail, slice and return to the shell, arranging it in overlapping slices with the red part uppermost. Serve on a bed of salad, garnished with the claws. Serve mayonnaise separately.

(b) Remove all the meat from the shell and claws. Arrange on a bed of salad, either cut into slices or roughly flaked and coat with mayonnaise.

The coral can be used, sieved, as a garnish or for making butter.

LOBSTER MORNAY

2 small boiled lobsters $\frac{1}{2}$ pt. cheese sauce   2–3 tablesp. grated cheese

Cut the lobsters in half lengthwise. Remove the meat from the tail and cut into slices, keeping the knife on the slant. Place a little of the sauce at the bottom of each shell and arrange the meat on top, overlapping the slices slightly. Pour a little sauce over the top and sprinkle with grated cheese. Brown in a hot oven (450° F., Gas 8) for about 10 min.

4 helpings

LOBSTER THERMIDOR

2 small boiled lobsters   1 shallot
1 wineglass white wine
$1\frac{1}{2}$ oz. butter $\frac{1}{4}$ pt. Béchamel sauce
1 level teasp. mixed mustard
pinch of cayenne pepper
a little grated cheese

Cut the lobsters in half lengthwise and remove the stomach and the intestinal cord. Remove the meat from the shell and cut into slices, keeping the knife on the slant. Chop the shallot very finely. Put the white wine in a small saucepan and cook the shallot until it is tender and the wine reduced to half. Meanwhile, melt the butter and heat the meat very carefully in this. Add the shallot and wine mixture to the lobster meat with the sauce, mustard and pepper, mix and return to the shells. Sprinkle with grated cheese and brown under a hot grill.

4 helpings

MUSSELS

Mussels are bought while still alive and their shells should be tightly shut. Discard any that do not shut immediately when given a sharp tap, as they are probably dead. Mussels are in season from September to March. They can be served cold with vinegar or hot in soups, sauces or pies.

TO PREPARE MUSSELS

Allow 1–1½ pt. mussels per person. Scrape and clean the shells thoroughly in several lots of cold water. Mussels are not opened with a knife like oysters, but open themselves during cooking. The only part of a mussel which needs to be removed is the breathing apparatus, which is found in the form of a black strip known as the "beard". This is removed after the shells have been opened.

TO OPEN

There are two simple methods of opening mussels:

English method—For a small quantity of 1–2 pt., place the mussels (after cleaning) in a rinsed wide pan and cover them closely with a folded damp tea-cloth. Heat quickly, shaking the pan at intervals, and at the end of 5–7 min. the shells will open. Remove from the heat promptly as overcooking toughens them.

French method—To 3½ pt. of cleaned mussels in a wide pan, add 1 shallot, finely chopped, 5–6 stalks of parsley, a sprig of thyme, ⅓ of a bay leaf, a pinch of pepper and ¼ pt. dry white wine (½ water and ½ dry cider could be used). Cover the pan tightly and cook over a sharp heat for 5–6 min., shaking the pan from time to time. Remove from the heat as soon as the shells open.

MOULES MARINIERES

3½ pt. mussels   1 shallot, chopped finely   5–6 stalks of parsley
⅓ of a bay leaf   sprig of thyme
pinch of pepper   ¼ pt. dry white wine (½ water and ½ dry cider can be used)   1 oz. butter   chopped parsley

Open the mussels by the French method. Strain the liquid through muslin, to remove any traces of sand, then return the liquid to the pan with the butter and boil rapidly until reduced by half. Meanwhile, remove the beards from the mussels, and return the mussels to their half-shell, discard empty shells. Arrange in soup plates, pour the reduced liquor over the mussels and sprinkle with chopped parsley.

MUSSELS

1 qt. mussels   1 oz. butter   ½ oz. flour   2 egg yolks   1 tablesp. vinegar   1 teasp. chopped parsley
salt and pepper

Open the mussels by the English method. Take them out of the shells and strain the liquor into a basin. Carefully remove the beards. Melt the butter, add the flour and cook for 3–4 min., then pour in the mussel liquor and stir until boiling. Cool slightly, then add the egg yolks, vinegar, and parsley, season to taste and stir over a low heat until the egg yolks thicken. Put in the mussels to reheat and serve in the sauce.

2–3 helpings
Cooking time—about ½ hr.

OYSTERS

Oysters have the best reputation of the bi-valve shellfish, for flavour and digestibility, and are for that reason given to invalids. They are in season from September to April, and can be served raw or baked, stewed, or in sauces, pies, etc. Oysters should be opened as near as possible to the time of eating.

Do not try to open them yourself unless you are an expert: ask your fishmonger either to loosen the shell for you or to open them completely and put the oyster with its liquor in the deep shell.

DEVILLED OYSTERS

1 dozen oysters   salt   cayenne pepper   1 oz. butter

Open the oysters carefully so as to preserve as much of the liquor as possible, or ask your fishmonger to open them for you and leave them in their shells. Sprinkle lightly with salt, and more liberally with cayenne, and put a small piece of butter on top of each one. Place the oysters on a baking-sheet and put in a hot oven until thoroughly heated.

3-4 helpings
Cooking time—4 min.

OYSTER FRITTERS

12 large oysters   ¼ pt. tepid water
1 tablesp. salad oil or oiled butter
3 oz. flour   salt   2 egg whites
frying fat

Make a batter by stirring the water and salad oil gradually into the flour; when perfectly smooth add a pinch of salt and lastly the stiffly-whisked egg whites. Beard the oysters, dip them in the batter and fry in hot fat until golden brown. Serve immediately.

6 helpings

OYSTERS A LA MARINIERE

18 sauce oysters   ½ glass Chablis or cider   1 tablesp. chopped parsley
1 tablesp. chopped shallots   1 oz. fresh breadcrumbs   salt and pepper
1 oz. butter   lemon juice

Beard the oysters and put the oysters with their liquor in a basin, pour the wine over and allow to stand for about 1 hr. Mix the parsley, shallots and bread-crumbs, and season to taste with salt and pepper. Arrange the oysters in a buttered fireproof dish, pour over a little of the liquor and wine and cover with the bread-crumb mixture. Place the remaining butter in small pieces on top. Bake in a fairly hot oven (375° F., Gas 5) for about 15 min. Squeeze a little lemon juice on top and serve in the dish.

5-6 helpings

PRAWNS

Prawns are available all the year. They are usually sold cooked, and can be served cold, fried, or in soups, sauces and in made-up dishes.

To boil freshly-caught prawns: Cooked prawns should be very red and have no spawn when cooked; much depends on their freshness and the way in which they are cooked. Wash well, then put into boiling salted water and keep them boiling for about 7-8 min. They are ready when they begin to change colour; do not overboil or they will become tasteless and indigestible.

To shell prawns: To shell prawns, take the head between the right-hand thumb and second finger, take the tip of the tail between the left thumb and fore-finger; with the nail on the right forefinger raise the shell at the knee or angle, pinch the tail and the shell will come apart, leaving the prawn attached to the head.

CURRIED PRAWNS

2 doz. prawns   1½ oz. butter
1 small onion   1-1½ level dessertsp. curry powder (depending on strength)   1 level dessertsp. flour
½ pt. stock   1 sour apple
1 tablesp. grated coconut   salt
1 teasp. lemon juice

Shell the prawns and put them aside. Melt the butter in a saucepan, fry the chopped onion without browning, then add the curry powder and flour and fry slowly for at least 20 min. Add the stock, coarsely-chopped apple, coconut and a little salt. Simmer gently for $\frac{1}{2}$ hr., then strain and return to the saucepan. Season to taste, add the lemon juice, put in the prawns and when thoroughly hot serve with well-boiled rice.

4 helpings
Cooking time—about 1 hr.

POTTED PRAWNS or SHRIMPS

1 qt. fresh prawns or shrimps
$\frac{1}{2}$ lb. fresh butter   cayenne pepper
ground mace or nutmeg   a little salt
clarified butter

The fish should be perfectly fresh and as large as possible. Boil, then shell and divide them slightly. Pound to a paste with the butter and seasoning. Rub through a fine sieve, press into small pots, cover with clarified butter, and when cold tie down closely.

Cooking time—8 min.

SCALLOPS

See Escallops

SHRIMPS

Shrimps are available all the year. They are usually sold cooked and served cold in soups, sauces, etc.

To boil freshly-caught shrimps: Throw the shrimps into boiling salted water, and keep them boiling for about 5 min. Care should be taken that they are not over-boiled, as they then become tasteless and indigestible; they are done when they begin to change colour.

To shell shrimps: Take the head between the right thumb and forefinger and with the left forefinger and thumbnail raise on each side the shell of the tail, pinch the tail, and the shell will at once separate.

MEAT

Meat, in terms of money alone, is one of the most expensive purchases made by the housewife. Yet a closer appreciation of it shows that, valued as calories per penny, or body-building value per ounce consumed, or even as satisfaction per meal eaten, it is still among the cheapest of our foods.

The cost of weekly meat purchases can be much reduced if experience accompanies the shopping basket. Experience can only be gained by trial and error: best of all it is to be found vested in a friendly butcher, one who will anxiously advise and teach his customer all she may wish to know or indeed may be able to absorb.

Cooking Meat: Two factors influence the final cooked product: the first is the temperature; the second is the time. The meat may be brought to any given temperature by a number of means: by radiant heat (grilling or broiling), by hot air (roasting or baking), by hot water (casseroling, boiling, stewing and braising) or by contact with hot metal and fat (frying). For full details of these methods *see* p. 31.

Joints for roasting should always enter the oven so that the cut faces of the meat are exposed to direct heat. A rib, cooked on the bone, should be prepared by the butcher so that it will stand upright. A rolled piece of beef should be slightly flattened on one side so that it will stand erect. If the outside covering of fat varies in thickness, then the thickest part should go to the top of the oven. The initial heat is essential to seal the outside face of the meat. Properly done this prevents undue escape of the meat juices and results in a roast that is moist inside. Never prod roasting (or baking) meat with a knife or skewer to see if it is done. Through the hole will ooze the juice vital to its palatability.

IMPORTED MEAT

Frozen: Up to and sometimes beyond the point of retail sale frozen meat is solid and needs thawing before it can be successfully cooked. The freezing naturally produces ice crystals within the muscle tissue and damages it. On thawing the meat "drips" and so loses some of its goodness. The amount of damage done by the ice formation depends to a large extent on the rate of freezing. Smaller carcases fare better than large and for this reason frozen lamb suffers much less damage than frozen beef. In cooking either lamb or beef in the oven, basting is essential to replace as far as possible the flavour lost by the tendency to "drip". A hot oven is needed as with other meat to seal the outside, but in this case it is especially necessary to prevent loss of nutritive value.

Chilled: Meat that is chilled is kept as nearly as possible to the freezing-point without freezing (and hence ice formation) taking place. Occasionally there is a slightly objectionable flavour to the fat. This can be masked by seeing that the fat is well salted prior to roasting. It also helps to ensure that the outside of the joint is well crisped.

OFFALS

Liver: That of the lamb, calf,

pig and ox is usually the order of preference. Liver from any animal is the only offal which tastes better in cooking than in eating. The word taste is used rather than smell, for both senses are closely associated.

Ox tail: Properly cooked this is a delicacy and, in terms of edible meat obtained on cooking, is proportionately expensive. Ox tails should be cooked until the meat just leaves the bone. Overcooking ruins the flavour. Tails should be brightly coloured and should carry a reasonable quantity of creamy white fat.

Hearts: Those of the pig, calf and lamb may be roasted. They are best served (and cooked) with a herb-flavoured stuffing. If ready prepared stuffings are used it is an advantage to "lard" the mixture with a little fat before placing in the heart.

Sweetbreads: Butchers will often speak of two sweetbreads. In fact "they" are one gland, the thymus, which in young animals consists of two portions, one known as the throat bread and the other the heart bread. Sweetbreads should be used very fresh. The heart sweetbread of the calf is firm, white, broad and rather thick. It is most suitable for serving whole. The throat sweetbread is longer, less compact and dark in colour and is more suitable for cutting into pieces. The pancreas or stomach bread is often referred to as a sweetbread but is a very different organ with a very different though not unpleasant flavour.

Kidneys: These have a marked flavour and are useful for flavouring steak pies and puddings. Their proper place in the cuisine may be considered to be as part of a mixed grill.

Tongues: Although tongues can be consumed either fresh or salted they are usually eaten after brining.

Most commonly sold is salt boiled ox tongue. It is an excellent dish if not overcooked. Tongues from sheep, pigs and calves can be similarly treated and as they are small can be used as a kitchen "experiment" at very little cost.

Feet: Today it is uncommon for the feet of cattle to be stewed into "cow-heel". Ox, cows' or calves' feet can provide an excellent base for aspic jellies. Pigs' feet or pettitoes are a delicacy but it is perhaps now considered indelicate to eat them; the only method is with the teeth and fingers.

Tripe: This again is a connoisseur's dish little eaten, it would seem, today. Most generally cooked are three of the four stomachs of the ox. That from the sheep is also popular in Scotland.

Head: The use of head meats varies with the animal. From the ox the best-known meat is ox cheek. This needs prolonged cooking but has an excellent flavour. (Tongues have been separately dealt with.) The equivalent from the pig is the Bath chap, which is the cheek meat salted and boiled. Sheep's heads are generally cooked by boiling either fresh or salted after they have been split in half. The meat is stripped from the bones and a brawn of fine flavour produced from the meat and the rendered stock. From all heads, brains are obtainable.

Suet: This is the hard internal fat of the sheep and ox. Calves have little internal fat and that of the pig is oily and of little use in cooking. Lamb or sheep suet is hard, white and usually carries too much flavour to be useful to the cook. Beef suet however is excellent. Its slow melting makes it invaluable in pudding crusts and in Christmas puddings.

Lights: These are the lungs of the animal and although perfectly edible they are usually set aside

BEEF

BEEF is obtained from adult bovine animals, usually designated "cows" by the uninitiated. The cow proper is the mother animal. Female bovines which have not borne young are characterized in the trade as heifers.

The father of cattle is the bull. Bull beef is rarely met on sale in retail shops. The flesh is dark, strong in taste and usually extremely lean. In the Jewish section of the meat trade there is however a leaning towards young bull meat. This is usually well fatted but still possesses a strong flavour and is unsuitable for normal Gentile methods of cooking.

The prime supplier of quality beef is the oxen or steer or bullock. These alternative terms, of which the last is the most common, apply to a male animal castrated at an early age. The flesh should ideally be bright red when freshly cut, but, after exposure to the air for a short while, the lustre of colour is lost and it assumes a colour hard to describe. The term "creamy red" may perhaps convey the colour. Certainly it is not a pink or beige red, and there should be no trace of mauve in it.

The carcase of the animal, that is the animal after the removal of head, feet, skin and internal organs, is split down the backbone into two halves called sides. Each side is then divided into two halves by cutting between the tenth and eleventh rib bone. (The cuts and cutting described are London style. Wherever it is necessary reference will be made to the terms used in other areas.) The piece that contains the forelimb and first ten rib bones is called the forequarter, and the other half of the side is called the hindquarter.

THE HINDQUARTER

The cuts into which the hindquarter is divided will be better understood from the accompanying diagram than from a description.

(1) The *undercut* or *fillet* is the most suitable meat for frying. Having a very delicate flavour it is unsuitable for any other treatment. There are, however, only 5–7 pounds of fillet in a carcase of 600–700 lb. Certainly not enough to satisfy the potential demand.

(2) The *sirloin* may be considered to be the next most suitable frying cut and, on the grounds of its superior flavour, is preferred to fillet by many people. It is not often cut in England, where the most usual practice is to roast the sirloin.

(3) *Rump steak* is the most common frying cut, and the prime end of the rump is to be found in the small slices which are removed from the hip-bone.

(4) The *topside*, which is the muscle of the inside leg, (5) the *top rump*, which is the muscle of the front of the thigh, are suitable for slow frying from the highest quality of fat animal. In nearly all cases, however, they are, together with the rump, better cooked in the oven with a small quantity of water.

The muscle of the outside of the thigh and the buttock is sold as *silverside* (6). It is today common for this joint to be roasted, but it is at best suitable only for casseroling if tenderness is desired, and is eminently suitable for salting and boiling.

For those who have acquired the taste for beef fat, (7) the *hindquarter flank* (the belly of the animal) yields a cheap and delicious joint for boiling or casserole.

(8) The *leg of beef* is only suitable for boiling. There is little to

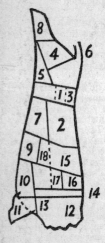

choose between the leg and the foreleg or shin except that the leg is larger and will yield bigger pieces of meat for stewing where this is required.

Several terms are now in growing use for various types of beefsteaks. They are not new terms and some have already been mentioned. *Fillet:* This term is used in two ways. Correctly it refers to the meat found beneath the blade part of the loin bones. It is also used for the continuation of this same muscle which is part of a whole unboned rump steak or steakpiece. This part is properly called the undercut. Fillet or undercut may be served in several ways and under several names. *Châteaubriand:* A very thick piece

of fillet sufficient for two people and cut at the time of serving into two portions. *Tournedos:* Thick slices of fillet for one person. Usually ¾ in. thick and a nice round shape, they are perhaps the most usual way in which the steak is cooked. They are sometimes tied to preserve their shape. *Noisettes:* Neatly trimmed, round or oval shapes of fillet between half and three-quarters of an inch in thickness. *Mignons:* Very fine fillet steaks which should be cooked quickly. These are often referred to as minute steaks. *Porterhouse:* A steak from the wing end (wing rib) of the sirloin or forerib. In fact a slice from the part of the loin which contains no undercut or fillet. *T-bone steak:* A steak cut through the sirloin so that it contains on one side at least the "T"-shaped loin bone. It has two "eyes", that of the loin meat and that of the fillet. *Entrecôte:* This is a sirloin steak without the undercut and without the bone. In other words the eye meat of the loin cut into steaks.

THE FOREQUARTER

As in the case of the hindquarter the diagram fully explains the position of the various cuts. Commencing with:

(9) the *flank* and (10) *brisket*, two joints suitable for salting and boiling, and for casseroling. When tender they may be finished for a short while in a very hot oven to simulate the flavour and appearance of roast beef. Whether purchased with the bone or boneless they are extremely economical joints. Properly cooked they yield a slice of meat little fatter than that obtained from the sirloin of the same animal, and have the advantage of providing at the same time an extremely fine and nutritious beef dripping.

The remarks made above about

leg of beef apply equally well to (11) the *shin* or *foreleg*.

(12) The *sticking* or *neck* of the animal and (13) the *clod* or front chest muscles provide meat suitable for casseroling rather than boiling.

(14) The *chuck* and *blade bone* lie on the dividing line between casserole steak and roasting meat. Though sold for stewing, they need a shorter cooking time than any other cut of oven stewing meat with the possible exception of the top rump and topside.

The *foreribs* (15) are merely an extension of the sirloin and the *backribs* (16) an extension of the forerib. Since they are nearer to the harder working part of the animal than the sirloin (the forequarter is more exercised in feeding by the constant lifting and dropping of the head), they require rather more care in roasting, that is to say a lower heat, a longer time, and the addition of a little water to the pan.

The last cuts of the forequarter, the *top ribs* (17) and *flat ribs* (18), come halfway between the two types of cut and may be very slowly roasted.

BEEF A LA MODE

2 lb. rump of beef 1 glass claret
juice of ½ lemon 1 small onion
2 cloves salt and pepper
bouquet garni 1 oz. butter or fat
10 button onions 1 oz. flour
1½ pt. stock 2 bacon rashers
2 carrots

Trim and bone the meat. Place it in a bowl with a marinade made from the claret, lemon juice, finely-chopped onion, cloves, salt, pepper and bouquet garni. Leave for 2 hr., basting frequently. Melt the fat in a stewpan, drain the beef well and fry until brown. Fry the button onions at the same time. Remove both from the pan, add the flour and fry until nut

brown. Then add the stock and the marinade in which the meat was soaked and stir until boiling. Replace the meat and the onions and season to taste. Cover the meat with the bacon rashers. Add the carrots, thinly sliced, and cook gently for 2½ hr., stirring occasionally. When tender, place on a hot dish, strain the liquid in the saucepan and pour over the meat.

8 helpings

BEEF OLIVES

1½ lb. good stewing steak cut in
6 slices 4 oz. veal forcemeat
¾ pt. Espagnole or brown sauce

Wipe and trim the slices of meat, flatten them with a wet cutlet bat or rolling-pin. Spread a little forcemeat on each slice, roll up tightly and tie securely with fine string or cotton. Place the sauce in a saucepan, bring to the boil, and add the "olives". Simmer gently for about 1 hr. When cooked, untie the olives; serve on a bed of mashed potatoes.

6 helpings

Basic Recipe
BEEFSTEAK PIE

1½ lb. lean beefsteak seasoned flour
2 onions stock or water flaky,
rough puff or short pastry, using
8 oz. flour, etc. egg or milk

Wipe the meat, remove the skin and superfluous fat and cut meat into small cubes. Dip the cubes in the seasoned flour and place in a pie-dish, piling them higher in the centre. Peel and finely chop the onions; sprinkle them between the pieces of meat. Sprinkle any remaining seasoned flour between the meat. Add enough stock or water to quarter fill the dish. Roll out the pastry ¼–½ in. thick to the shape of the pie-dish, but allow an extra 2 in. all round. Cut a strip about ¾ in. wide from around the edge of the pastry to cover the rim of the pie-dish. Damp the rim, place the strip of pastry around with the cut side out and allow it to overlap the rim a little. Damp the join and the rest of the pastry and cover with the pastry lid. Press the edges lightly together. Trim, make a small round hole in the centre of the pie, and decorate with pastry leaves. Brush with beaten egg or milk. Place in a hot oven (450° F., Gas 8) until pastry is set and then reduce heat; if necessary place the pie on a lower shelf and cover with greased paper to prevent pastry becoming too brown. Heat the stock. Make a hole in the pie and pour in the hot stock before serving.

6 helpings
Cooking time—about 2 hr.

Beefsteak and Kidney Pie: As for Beefsteak Pie, but add 2 sheep's or 6 oz. ox kidneys. Soak the kidneys, remove the skins and cores and cut into slices. Then proceed as directed in the preceding recipe, adding the sliced kidneys with the steak and onions.

Beefsteak and Potato Pie: As for Beefsteak Pie, adding potatoes to taste. Cut the meat in slices and dip in the seasoned flour. Cut the potatoes into slices. Place a layer of sliced potato on the bottom of the pie-dish, season, and cover with a layer of meat. Add a little onion, finely chopped. Repeat with layers of potato, meat, onion and seasoning until the dish is full. Add stock or water to one-third the depth of the dish. Then cover with pastry and cook as directed for Beefsteak Pie.

BEEFSTEAK PUDDING

1½ lb. good stewing steak
seasoned flour   suet pastry (p. 342), using 8 oz. flour, etc.
3 tablesp. stock or water (approx.)

Wipe the meat; remove any superfluous skin and fat. Cut the meat into narrow strips or cubes and dip in the seasoned flour. Cut off one-third of the pastry for the lid. Roll the remainder out into a round about ¼ in. thick and line a greased pudding-basin with it. Press well in to remove any creases. Half-fill the basin with the prepared meat and add the stock or water. Then add the remainder of the meat. Roll out the pastry reserved for the lid. Damp the edges, place the lid on top and press the edges well together. Cover with greased greaseproof paper if pudding is to be steamed, or with a pudding cloth if it is to be boiled. Place in boiling water and steam for about 3½ hr.—keep the water boiling, if necessary add more *boiling* water; *or* boil for 3 hr. Serve in the pudding-basin, or turn out on to a hot dish.

6 helpings

Beefsteak and Kidney Pudding: As for Beefsteak Pudding but add 2 sheep's or 6 oz. ox kidneys. Soak the kidneys, remove the skins and cores and cut into thin slices 3 in. by 2 in. Dip in seasoned flour, place a slice of kidney on each slice of meat, roll up tightly and place the rolls on end in the basin. Proceed as directed for Beefsteak Pudding.

BOILED BEEF

2½–3 lb. brisket, aitchbone or round of beef   salt   3 cloves   10 peppercorns   a bunch of herbs   carrots   turnips   onions
suet dumplings (optional)

Wipe the meat with a damp cloth and tie into a neat shape with string. Put into a pan and cover with boiling salted water. Bring to the boil again and boil for 5 min. to seal the surface. Reduce to simmering point, add the cloves, peppercorns and herbs and simmer for the remainder of the time, allowing 20 min. per lb. and 20 min. over. Skim when necessary. Add the sliced vegetables, allowing enough time for them to be cooked when the meat is ready. Place the meat on a hot dish. Remove string and re-skewer meat if necessary. Arrange vegetables neatly round and serve some of the liquid separately in a sauce boat.

If suet dumplings are to be served, put them into the liquor 20 min.–½ hr. before serving.

Salt beef silverside or topside: if very salt cover with unsalted cold water, otherwise use warm water. Bring slowly to boiling-point and skim well. Continue as for fresh meat, allowing a little extra boiling time.

Suet dumplings: 3–4 oz. suet; ½ lb. flour; ¼ teasp. salt; 1 teasp. baking-powder; cold water. Make as for suet pastry (p. 342); form into small balls and drop into boiling stock; after 3 min. reduce heat and simmer for remainder of time.

BRAISED BEEF

3 lb. brisket of beef   1 large carrot
1 large turnip   18 button onions
2 leeks   a few sticks of celery
¼ lb. fat bacon rashers
1 oz. dripping   bouquet garni
6–12 peppercorns   salt   stock

Wipe and trim the meat and tie into a good shape. Dice a little of the carrot and turnip and put aside with the onions for garnish. Thickly slice the remainder of the carrot, turnip, leeks and celery and fry slightly in a stewpan with the bacon trimmings in the hot dripping. Place the meat on top and cover with slices of bacon. Add the bouquet garni and peppercorns tied in muslin, salt to taste and enough stock nearly to cover the vegetables. Cover with a well-fitting lid and cook as slowly as possible for about 3 hr., basting occasionally and adding more stock if necessary. When nearly ready,

cook the diced vegetables and onions separately in well-flavoured stock. Make a brown gravy, adding any strained stock left in the stewpan. Place the meat on a hot dish, remove string and garnish with the diced vegetables and onions. Serve the gravy separately.

BRISKET OF BEEF

3 lb. brisket of beef   bacon rashers
2 onions   bouquet garni   2 cloves
1 blade of mace   allspice
peppercorns   stock or water
¾ pt. brown sauce   2 carrots

Wipe and trim the meat. Cover the bottom of a stewpan with rashers of bacon, place the meat on them and lay more bacon on top. Add the onions, bouquet garni, cloves, mace, allspice, peppercorns and trimmings from the vegetables. Nearly cover with stock or water. Cover closely and cook very gently for 2½–3 hr., adding more boiling liquid if necessary. In the meantime make the brown sauce, using stock from the stewpan if liked. Peel and dice the carrots and cook them separately. Place the meat on a hot dish, remove any string and re-skewer if necessary. Glaze and garnish with the diced carrots. Serve with the sauce.

CURRIED BEEF

1½ lb. lean beef   2½ oz. butter or fat
1 large onion   1 sour apple
2 teasp. curry powder   1¼ oz. flour
1½ pt. strained stock or coconut
infusion   1–2 teasp. curry paste
2 teasp. chutney   salt and pepper
4–6 oz. patna rice   juice of ½ lemon
2 teasp. jam or jelly   paprika
gherkins

Cut the meat into 1-in. cubes. Melt the fat in a stewpan; fry the meat lightly on both sides, then remove and keep hot. Peel and chop the onion; peel, core and slice the apple. Fry them in the fat until golden brown. Add the curry powder and flour and fry gently for 5 min. Add the strained stock or coconut infusion, curry paste, chutney and seasoning; stir until boiling. Replace the meat, cover closely, and simmer gently for 1½–2 hr. Meanwhile, boil the rice in boiling salted water for about 15–20 min. Drain on a sieve, separate the grains by pouring boiling water over; dry thoroughly. Arrange in a border on a hot dish. Add lemon juice, jelly and extra seasoning, if required, to the curry. Pour the curry into the middle of the rice border. Garnish with paprika and gherkins.

6 helpings

FILLETS OF BEEF— PORTUGUESE STYLE

1½–2 lb. fillet of beef   oil or melted butter   salt and pepper
Maître d'hôtel butter (p. 401)
stuffed tomatoes (p. 233)

Wipe and trim the meat and cut into neat fillets. Beat to flatten slightly and brush with oil or melted butter. Season to taste. Grill, then place on a hot dish. Put a pat of Maître d'hôtel butter on each fillet and serve with baked stuffed tomatoes.

6 helpings
Cooking time—according to taste

FILLETS OF BEEF WITH FRIED BANANAS

1½ lb. fillet beef   salt and pepper
3 bananas   egg and breadcrumbs
deep fat butter or fat   meat glaze
½ pt. brown sauce

Wipe, trim and cut the meat into neat fillets; season. Peel and cut the bananas in quarters, coat with egg and breadcrumbs and fry in deep fat. Drain and keep hot until required. Fry the fillets in hot butter or fat for about 7 min., turning frequently. Drain, glaze and arrange in a circle on a hot dish. Place the bananas in the centre and pour some of the sauce

round. Serve the remainder of the sauce separately.

6 helpings

FRIED BEEFSTEAK

1½ lb. frying beefsteak, 1 in. thick
salt and pepper   fat

Wipe the meat, remove and discard any skin, beat lightly and season to taste. Put in sufficient fat barely to cover the bottom of a frying-pan. When hot, fry the steak quickly on both sides to seal the surface. Then cook more slowly until cooked to taste.

For a good gravy to serve with the steak, drain any fat from the frying-pan, keeping back the sediment. Add salt and pepper and about 1½ gills of boiling water. Boil up, skim and strain.

6 helpings
Cooking time—about 7–10 min.

GRILLED BEEFSTEAK

1½ lb. rump or fillet steak or sirloin
oil or butter   salt and pepper
Maître d'hôtel butter

Wipe and cut the meat across the grain into suitable slices. Beat on both sides with a cutlet bat or rolling-pin. Brush with oil or melted butter and sprinkle with salt and pepper. Place under a red-hot grill and grill quickly on both sides to seal the surfaces, thus preventing the juices from escaping. Then grill more slowly until cooked as required; a "rare" steak requires 3–4 min. for each side. Turn frequently, using tongs or 2 spoons, never pierce with a fork as this would make holes through which the meat juices would escape. Serve at once with a pat of Maître d'hôtel butter.

6 helpings

HOT POT

1½ lb. lean beef   3 onions   3 carrots
2 lb. potatoes   salt and pepper
stock or water

Remove any fat and cut the meat into pieces. Cut the onions and carrots into thin slices and the potatoes into thicker slices. Arrange the meat, onion, carrots and potatoes in layers in a casserole and season well. The top layer should be of potatoes neatly arranged. Three-quarters fill the casserole with cold water or stock, adding more later if the dish appears to be dry. Cover and bake in a warm oven (335° F., Gas 3) for 2 hr. Uncover ½ hr. before serving to allow the top layer of potatoes to brown. Serve in the casserole.

MIGNONS OF BEEF— BOURGEOISE STYLE

1½ lb. fillet of beef 3 large carrots
24 button onions 2 medium-sized
turnips stock ½ pt. brown sauce
2 tablesp. tomato purée salt and
pepper butter or fat

Wipe the meat and cut into neat 2-in. pieces or small round fillets. Prepare the carrots, onions and turnips and cook them in strong stock until about half cooked. Place the brown sauce in a saucepan, add the tomato purée, boil up and season to taste. Fry the mignons of meat in hot fat for about 6 min., drain and place in one large casserole or individual casseroles. Cover the mignons with vegetables, add the sauce and cook gently on the cooker or in the oven for 20 min. If preferred the fat may be drained from the mignons when cooked and the sauce and vegetables added to the pan and cooked on the stove. In this case, serve the mignons on a hot dish, pour the sauce over and arrange the vegetables in heaps around the meat.

6 helpings

MINCED COLLOPS

1½ lb. rump steak 1 onion or
3 shallots 1½ oz. butter or fat

1¼ oz. flour ½ pt. stock or water
salt and pepper 1 tablesp. mushroom ketchup or lemon juice or vinegar

GARNISH
Sippets of toast parsley

Mince the meat very finely. Finely chop the onion, heat the fat and fry the onion until lightly browned, then add the flour and fry lightly. Put in the minced meat and cook lightly. Add the stock or water, seasoning and the mushroom ketchup, lemon juice or vinegar. Cook very gently for 20 min., stirring occasionally. Then serve on a hot dish and garnish with sippets of toasted bread and parsley.

6 helpings

MINIATURE ROUND OF BEEF

1 large rib of beef 1 gallon water
2 lb. coarse salt ½ oz. saltpetre
6 oz. brown sugar 12 peppercorns
a bunch of mixed herbs 2–3 onions
vegetable trimmings
diced carrot and turnip

Boil the water, salt, saltpetre and sugar together for ½ hr., skimming when necessary, then allow to become cold. Bone the meat, rub well with salt, roll up lightly and tie securely with string. Place in the cold brine and leave for 6 days, turning each day. Then drain well and wash in cold water. Place in a pan, cover with cold water, add the herbs and peppercorns and bring slowly to the boil. Boil for 5 min. Skim, add the onions and vegetable trimmings and simmer for the required time, allowing 25 min. per lb. and 25 min. over. When ready, place on a hot dish, remove the string and skewer if necessary. Serve, garnished with diced vegetables.

NOISETTES OF BEEF WITH MUSHROOMS

1½–2 lb. fillet of beef 2 mushrooms

1 shallot   ½ teasp. finely-chopped
parsley   salt and pepper   2 oz.
butter or fat   spinach or mashed
potatoes   ½ pt. brown sauce

Wipe the meat and cut into
round even fillets not less than ½
in. thick. Finely chop the mushrooms and shallot and mix well
together with the parsley, salt and
pepper. Place a round pat of this
mixture in the centre of each fillet.
Heat the fat in a sauté pan, put in
the fillets with the stuffing side
down, fry quickly, then turn and
fry the other side a little more
slowly. When cooked, arrange in a
row on a foundation of spinach or
mashed potatoes. Pour some sauce
round the noisettes and serve the
rest of the sauce separately.

6 helpings
Cooking time—about 7 min.

PORTERHOUSE STEAK

1 steak about 1½ in. thick cut from
the thick end of sirloin; allow
4–6 oz. steak per person   salt and
pepper   melted butter or oil

Season and brush the steak over
on both sides with melted butter or
oil. If possible leave oiled for 1 hr.
before cooking. Grill and serve
plain or with Maître d'hôtel butter,
button onions fried in butter and
small stuffed tomatoes or horseradish sauce.

Cooking time—about 10 min.

ROAST BEEF

Joint of beef suitable for roasting
(p. 147)   salt and pepper   beef
dripping (allow 1 oz. per lb. of meat)

Weigh meat to be able to calculate cooking time. Wipe with a
damp cloth. Place joint in a roasting-tin, season and add dripping.
Roast according to one of the
methods outlined below.

Method 1. Put into a very hot
oven (450° F., Gas 8) for 10–15
min. to brown or "sear" the meat.
Then reduce heat to fairly hot

(375° F., Gas 5) and baste every
20 min. for the first half of the
cooking time and afterwards every
30 min. Allow 20 min. per lb. and
another 10 min. over for solid
joints, i.e. joints without bone: and
15 min. per lb. and 15 min. over for
thick joints, i.e. joints with bone.

Method 2. Calculate the cooking
time as in Method 1, but cook the
whole time in a fairly hot oven
(375° F., Gas 5). This method is
more suitable for large joints, as
small joints will not be in the oven
long enough to brown properly.

Method 3. Cook the meat slowly
in a covered tin in a warm to moderate oven (335°–350° F., Gas
3–4), allowing 30 min. per lb. plus
30 min. over for joints without
bone; and 20 min. per lb. and 20
min. over for joints with bone.

Remove on to a hot dish when
cooked, remove string and skewer
with a metal skewer if necessary.
Keep hot. Drain off fat from tin
and make gravy from sediment.

ROAST FILLET OF BEEF

1½–2 lb. fillet of beef   meat glaze
½ pt. demi-glace sauce

MARINADE
2 tablesp. olive oil   1 tablesp. lemon
juice or vinegar   1 teasp. chopped
onion   1 teasp. chopped parsley
a good pinch of powdered herbs
a pinch of ground cloves
salt and pepper

Wipe, trim and tie the meat into
a good shape, place on a dish and
pour over the marinade. Allow to
soak in the marinade for 2–3 hr.,
turning and basting frequently.
Drain off half the liquid and fold
the remainder with the meat in a
thick sheet of well-greased greaseproof paper or aluminium foil,
fastening all ends securely. Roast
for 1 hr. and remove the paper to
allow the meat to brown. Place on
a hot dish and brush with meat
glaze. If liked a little sauce may be

poured round the dish, the rest being served separately. Serve with horseradish sauce.

6 helpings

ROLLED STEAK

1½–2 lb. stewing steak about ¾ in. thick, cut in 1 piece   salt and pepper   6–8 oz. veal forcemeat
1½ oz. fat   1 pt. stock or water
1 oz. flour

Wipe and trim the meat and flatten it with a rolling-pin. Season the forcemeat well, spread it on the meat, and roll up tightly and tie securely. Heat the fat in a saucepan until very hot and fry meat quickly until the whole surface is browned. Add the hot stock or water, cover closely and cook very slowly for about 2 hr. When ready, place the meat on a hot dish. Thicken the gravy with the flour which has been blended to a smooth paste with a little cold stock or water and boil for 4 min. Season to taste, strain and pour some over the meat. Serve the remainder separately. If preferred, the roll may be baked in a moderate oven (350° F., Gas 4) in which case it must be well basted with stock or fat.

6 helpings

SCOTCH COLLOPS

1½ lb. good stewing steak
2 oz. butter or fat   2 teasp. finely-chopped onion or shallot   2 teasp. flour   ½ pt. stock   salt and pepper gravy browning   mushroom ketchup   sippets of fried or toasted bread   parsley

Cut the meat into small, neat dice. Heat the fat in a stewpan and fry the onion or shallot lightly. Add the flour and cook for about 5 min., stirring all the time. Add the stock, seasoning, a little brown colouring, and the meat. Bring slowly up to the boil, add the mushroom ketchup and simmer

very slowly for 1 hr., or until tender. Season if necessary and place on a hot dish. Arrange sippets of bread around the dish and garnish with chopped parsley.

6 helpings

SMOTHERED BEEFSTEAK

1½ lb. rump steak   salt and pepper
4 Spanish onions   seasoned flour
2 oz. dripping   ½ pt. stock or water

Wipe the meat, beat well, then season. Cut the onions into rings and dip in seasoned flour. Melt the dripping, and, when hot, fry the onion rings until crisp and lightly browned. Remove the onions, and keep hot. Fry the meat quickly on both sides to seal the surfaces, and then more slowly for about 15 min. or until tender (adding more fat if necessary). Drain and keep hot. Drain off most of the fat, add some flour and fry until brown. Add boiling stock or vegetable water, a little gravy browning, if necessary, and stir and boil for 2–3 min. Season to taste and strain. Place the meat on a hot dish, cover with the onion rings and pour the gravy over. Serve very hot.

6 helpings

STEAK PUDDING

½ lb. good stewing steak   ½ lb. ox kidney   salt and pepper   dripping
6 oz. flour   2 eggs
¾ pt. milk or water

Cut the steak into finger-shaped pieces. Cut the kidney into thin slices and season well. Fry the steak for a few minutes in the dripping to seal the surface. Mix the flour, eggs and milk or water into a smooth batter and season. Melt about ½ oz. dripping in a casserole or pie-dish and put in half the batter and bake until set. Place the steak and the kidney on top of the batter, fill up the dish with the remainder of the batter and bake in a hot oven (425° F., Gas 7) for

10 min.; then reduce to moderate
(350° F., Gas 4) for about 1 hr.
until set and well browned. Serve
with a good gravy.

6 helpings

STEWED STEAK

**1½ lb. stewing steak   2 large carrots
2 large turnips   1½ oz. fat
1 large onion   1½ oz. flour   1½ pt.
water or stock   salt and pepper**

Wipe the meat, cut off any
superfluous fat, and cut the meat
into neat pieces. Cut the vegetables into dice or Julienne strips
and keep in water until required.
Put the trimmings aside for adding
to the stew. Heat the fat in a
saucepan and, when smoking hot,
fry the meat until lightly browned
on both sides, then remove from
the pan. Slice the onion and fry
until lightly coloured. Add the
flour, mix well, and cook slowly
until a good brown colour. Add
the water or stock, the vegetable
trimmings and stir until boiling.
Season, replace the meat, cover
with a tightly fitting lid and simmer gently for about 2–2½ hr. or
until tender. Have ready the dice
or strips of vegetable which have
been cooked in boiling salted
water. Arrange the meat in the
centre of a hot dish, pour the stock
over and garnish with the vegetables.

6 helpings

TENDERLOIN OF BEEF

**A thick piece of well-hung sirloin
olive oil, melted mutter or fat
salt and pepper**

Wipe the meat and beat it well.
Brush both sides with oil or fat
and season with salt and pepper.
Grill as for grilled beefsteak (*see*
p. 152). Serve immediately with
Maître d'hôtel butter and fried
potatoes or other accompaniments
if preferred.

TOURNEDOS OF BEEF A LA BECHAMEL

**1½–2 lb. fillet of beef   salt and
pepper   butter or fat   ½ pt.
Béchamel sauce (p. 100)   mashed
potatoes   ¼ pt. demi-glace sauce**

Trim the fillet of beef into
rounds (tournedos) about 2 in. in
diameter and 1 in. thick and
season with salt and pepper. Grill
or fry in hot fat. Cover one side of
the tournedos with thick Béchamel
sauce, arrange on a bed of mashed
potatoes and pour a little demi-
glace sauce around.

If liked, the tournedos can be
served on croûtes of fried bread.
Brush over with meat glaze, arrange in a circle on a hot dish.
Place a heap of cooked small
potatoes in the centre and sprinkle
the potatoes with parsley. Pour a
little Béchamel sauce round and
serve the rest separately.

6 helpings

STEWS AND OFFAL DISHES

BROWN STEW

**1½ lb. neck of beef   vinegar
2 carrots   1 turnip   2 onions
1½ oz. dripping   1½ oz. flour   1½ pt.
stock or water   salt and pepper**

Wipe the meat and trim off any
skin and superfluous fat. Cut the
meat into pieces suitable for serving and place in a dish with the
vinegar. Leave for about 1 hr.,
turning 2 or 3 times; then drain
well and dry. Cut the carrots and
turnip into dice or Julienne strips
for garnishing and keep the trimmings. Slice the onions. Heat the
fat in a saucepan and fry the meat
quickly until lightly browned, then
remove from the pan. Fry the
sliced onion until lightly browned;
add the flour and cook slowly, mixing well, until a good brown
colour. Add the water or stock and
bring to the boil, stirring all the
time. Replace the meat, add the

vegetable trimmings and seasoning, cover with a lid and simmer gently for about 2½ hr. or until the meat is tender. Before serving, cook the diced carrots and turnip separately. Arrange the meat in the centre of a hot dish and pour the gravy over. Garnish with the drained, diced vegetables.

6 helpings

EXETER STEW

1½ lb. lean beef   1½ oz. dripping
3 medium-sized onions   1½ oz. flour
1 teasp. vinegar   salt and pepper

SAVOURY BALLS

4 oz. flour   ¼ teasp. baking-powder
1½ oz. finely-chopped suet
1 tablesp. finely-chopped parsley
½ teasp. mixed herbs   1 teasp. salt
¼ teasp. pepper   egg or milk

Wipe the meat and remove all the fat. Cut the meat into pieces about 2 in. by 2½ in. Heat the fat in a stewpan until smoking hot and fry the meat until brown. Remove the meat and fry the sliced onions. Then add the flour and cook, stirring until brown. Add 1¼ pt. water and bring to the boil, stirring constantly. Simmer for a few minutes. Add the vinegar and seasoning, return the meat and simmer gently for about 2 hr. Mix the ingredients for the savoury balls together, bind with the egg or milk into a stiff mixture and make into 12 balls. Bring the stew to boiling-point about 30 min. before time for serving and drop in the balls. Simmer for the remainder of the time. Pile the meat in the centre of a hot dish, pour the gravy over and arrange the balls neatly round the base.

6 helpings

GOULASH OF BEEF

1½ lb. lean beef   2 oz. dripping
2 onions   1½ oz. flour   1 pt. stock
¼ pt. red wine (optional)   2 tomatoes
salt   paprika   bouquet garni
6 diced potatoes
2 tablesp. sour cream (optional)

Wipe and trim the meat, removing any skin and fat. Cut into neat pieces. Heat the fat and sauté the sliced onions with the meat, until the meat is evenly browned. Add the flour and stir until brown. Then add the stock, wine, skinned and diced tomatoes, salt, paprika, and bouquet garni. Stir, bring to the boil. If liked, transfer to a casserole and cook slowly for 1½–2 hr. in the oven, stirring occasionally, or continue cooking in saucepan for the same time. Add the diced potatoes about ½ hr. before the goulash is ready. They should be cooked but not broken. If liked, 2 tablesp. sour cream may be stirred in before serving.

6 helpings

SEA PIE

1½ lb. stewing steak   seasoned flour
1 large onion   1 carrot   1 small
turnip   hot stock or water
suet pastry (p. 342), using 8–12 oz.
flour, etc.

Cut the steak into thin slices about 2 in. square. Dip the meat in the seasoned flour. Cut the prepared vegetables into thin slices or dice and place in a stewpan with the meat and cover with the hot stock or water. Simmer very gently for about 1½ hr. Roll out the suet pastry to a round a little less than the top of the stewpan and place on top of the stew. Continue cooking for 1 hr. Garnish with chopped parsley.

6 helpings

BEEF SAUSAGES

2 lb. lean beef   1 lb. beef suet
¼ teasp. powdered allspice   salt and
pepper   sausage skins   fat for frying

Mince the beef and grate the suet finely or use shredded suet. Add the allspice, salt and pepper to taste and mix well. Press the mixture lightly into the prepared skins and prick well with a fork. Fry in hot fat until well browned and cooked. If preferred the mixture may be shaped into small cakes and floured before being fried.

BULLOCK'S HEART— STUFFED AND BAKED

**1 bullock's heart   veal forcemeat or sage and onion stuffing
2–3 oz. dripping   1 oz. flour
1 pt. stock or vegetable water
redcurrant jelly or apple sauce**

Wash the heart thoroughly under running water or in several changes of cold water. Cut off the flaps and lobes and remove all pieces of gristle. Cut away the membrane which separates the cavities inside the heart and see that it is quite free from blood. Soak for at least ½ hr. Drain and dry the heart thoroughly and stuff with the forcemeat or stuffing. Sew up the ends with fine string and place in a baking-tin with smoking-hot dripping. Baste well and cook in a warm to moderate oven (335°–350° F., Gas 3–4) for 3 hr. Baste frequently and turn occasionally. When tender remove the string, place the heart on a hot dish and keep hot. Pour away most of the fat, retaining about 1 tablesp. of the sediment. Add 1 oz. flour and stir and cook until brown. Add 1 pt. of stock or vegetable water, gradually at first, blend well and stir until boiling. Boil for 4 min. Pour a little round the heart and serve the rest separately. Serve redcurrant jelly with the heart if it is stuffed with veal forcemeat and apple sauce if sage and onion stuffing is used.

6 helpings

Cow Heel
BOILED COW HEEL

**2 cow heels   stock or water
1 oz. butter or fat   1 oz. flour**

**1 dessertsp. finely-chopped parsley
salt and pepper**

Wash and blanch the heels. Put in a saucepan and cover with cold water or stock and simmer very gently for about 3 hr. Melt the fat in a saucepan, add the flour and cook without colouring. Add 1 pt. of the stock in which the cow heels were cooked, stir well until boiling, simmer for 5 min., add parsley and seasoning to taste. Remove the bones from the meat and arrange the pieces of meat on a hot dish. Pour the sauce over and serve hot.

6 helpings

FRIED COW HEEL

**2 cow heels   1½ tablesp. seasoned flour   1 egg   1 teasp. finely-chopped parsley   finely-grated rind of ½ lemon   milk if necessary
breadcrumbs   deep fat
fried or fresh parsley**

Wash and blanch the heels, and simmer gently in stock or water until the bones can be easily separated from the meat—about 3 hr. Remove the bones and press the meat between 2 plates until cold. Then cut into pieces about 1½ in. square. Dip the pieces into the seasoned flour. Beat the egg and add to it the finely-chopped parsley and lemon rind. Add a little milk if mixture is too dry. Coat the pieces of meat thickly with the egg mixture and toss in breadcrumbs. Fry in hot, deep fat until golden brown. Serve hot, garnished with parsley.

6 helpings

Ox kidney
KIDNEY HOT POT

**1 lb. ox kidney   ¼ lb. lean bacon rashers   2 large onions   3 tomatoes
3 oz. mushrooms   salt and pepper
stock   1½ lb. potatoes   bacon fat
parsley**

Soak the kidney in tepid salt water for 15 min. Wash well, skin if necessary, remove the core and any fat and cut the kidney into slices about ¼ in. thick. Cut the bacon into pieces and the onions, tomatoes and mushrooms into slices. Put alternate slices of kidney, bacon, onion, tomatoes and mushrooms in a casserole, seasoning each layer. Three-quarters fill the casserole with stock and cover the top with a thick layer of sliced potatoes. Place some bacon rinds on top. Cover and cook in a moderate oven (350° F., Gas 4) for 2½ hr. Remove the lid and bacon rinds ½ hr. before serving. Dot the top with small pieces of bacon fat and allow the potatoes to brown. Sprinkle with finely-chopped parsley.

6 helpings

STEWED KIDNEY

1½ lb. ox kidney   2 oz. seasoned flour   2 oz. dripping   1 onion   1½ pt. water or stock   3 teasp. tomato or mushroom ketchup border of rice or mashed potatoes green peas

Prepare the kidney as directed for Kidney Hot Pot. Coat the slices of kidney with seasoned flour. Heat the dripping in a stewpan and fry the kidney until browned on both sides. Chop the onion finely and fry at the same time until lightly browned. Stir in any remaining flour and brown. Add the stock and ketchup and stir until boiling. Cover with a lid and simmer very gently for about 1½–2 hr. If cooked too quickly the kidney will become tough. When ready re-season if necessary and serve on a hot dish with a border of rice or mashed potato. Garnish with green peas.

6 helpings

Ox Liver
LIVER HOT POT

1¼ lb. ox liver   1 oz. seasoned flour   4 oz. bacon rashers   3 large onions   2 lb. potatoes   1½ teasp. powdered sage   salt and pepper   stock or water   chopped parsley

Prepare the liver by washing thoroughly in tepid water and removing any tubes. Dry well, cut into slices ¼ in. thick and toss in the seasoned flour. Cut the bacon in pieces, slice the onions thinly, slice the potatoes. Place alternate layers of liver, bacon, onions and potatoes in a pie-dish or casserole and sprinkle with sage and seasoning. Add enough stock barely to cover the contents and place a thick layer of sliced potato on top. Cover with a lid and cook in a moderate oven (350° F., Gas 4) for about 2 hr. Remove the lid ½ hr. before serving, place small pieces of dripping on top and allow the potatoes to brown. Sprinkle with chopped parsley.

6 helpings

LIVER SAVOURY

1½ lb. ox liver   flour   veal forcemeat   ¼ lb. thin bacon rashers stock   1 oz. flour   salt and pepper

Wash the liver thoroughly in tepid water, cut out any tubes and dry thoroughly. Cut into slices about ¼ in. thick and coat lightly with flour. Spread each slice with a thin layer of forcemeat and cover with bacon. Put into a large baking-tin, cover with a slice of bacon and pour in stock to half cover the liver. Cover with a greased paper and cook in a moderate oven (350° F., Gas 4) for about 1½–2 hr. Add more stock as necessary. Arrange the liver on a hot dish and keep hot. Mix the 1 oz. flour to a smooth paste with a little cold stock, add ¼ pt. boiling stock or water, pour into the tin and boil up. If too thick, add more stock or water, season if necessary and strain round the liver.

6 helpings

ROAST LIVER

1–1½ lb. ox liver   ½ lb. fat bacon
stock or water   seasoned flour
parsley

Wash the liver in tepid salt water, remove any skin and tubes and cut the liver in slices. Place in a deep baking-tin or dish. Lay the rashers of bacon on top and add enough stock or water to half cover the liver. Bake gently for 1½–2 hr., basting well and dredging frequently with seasoned flour. Dish neatly and strain the gravy round. Garnish with parsley.

NOTE: The bacon may be cut into dice and served as a garnish, in which case it must be kept covered with 2–3 thicknesses of greaseproof paper while cooking, or it will become too crisp.

Marrow
MARROW TOAST

Beef marrow bones   salt and
pepper   lemon juice   hot buttered
toast   parsley

Season the marrow with salt, pepper and lemon juice, breaking down the marrow with a fork. Spread on fingers of hot buttered toast. Place in a hot oven to heat and serve very hot. Sprinkle with finely-chopped parsley.

Cooking time—20–25 min.

GRILLED OX TAIL

2 ox tails   1½ pt. well-flavoured
stock   egg and breadcrumbs
oil or butter   parsley
½ pt. piquant sauce or good gravy

Wash and dry the tails and divide them at the joints. Put into a saucepan with the stock which must be well flavoured, otherwise vegetables and herbs must be added. Simmer gently for 2½ hr.,

and when tender drain well and put aside until cold. Coat carefully with egg and breadcrumbs, brush with melted butter or oil and grill until brown. Place on a hot dish and garnish with the parsley. Serve with piquant sauce or a good gravy.

6 helpings

STEWED OX TAIL

2 small ox tails   2 oz. fat   2 onions
1½ oz. flour   1½ pt. stock or water
salt and pepper   bouquet garni
cloves to taste   mace to taste
juice of ½ lemon

GARNISH
Croûtons of fried bread   dice or
Julienne strips of carrot and turnip

Wash the tails, dry well and remove any superfluous fat. Cut into joints and divide the thick parts in half. Melt the fat in a saucepan, fry the pieces of tail until brown, then remove from the pan. Slice the onions and fry them until light brown, add the flour, mix well and fry slowly until a good brown colour. Add the stock or water, salt, pepper, bouquet garni, cloves and mace and bring to boiling-point, stirring all the time. Return the pieces of tail and simmer gently for about 2½–3 hr. Remove the meat and arrange on a hot dish. Add the lemon juice to the sauce, correct the seasoning, strain and pour over the meat. Garnish with croûtons of fried bread and diced or thin strips of cooked carrot and turnip.

6 helpings

Ox Tongue
BOILED TONGUE

1 ox tongue   1 onion   1 carrot
1 turnip   a bunch of mixed herbs

Wash the tongue thoroughly and soak for about 2 hr. If the tongue is dry and rather hard soak for 12 hr. If pickled, soak for about 3–4 hr. Put the tongue into a large pan of cold water, bring slowly to the boil, skim and add the onion, carrot, turnip and bunch of herbs. Cook gently, allowing 30 min. per lb. and 30 min. over. When ready, lift out tongue, remove the skin very carefully.

The tongue can then be garnished with tufts of cauliflower or Brussels sprouts and served hot with boiled poultry or ham.

To serve cold (1). After skin has been removed, shape tongue on a board by sticking a fork through the root and another through the top to straighten it. Leave until cold, trim and then glaze. Put a paper frill around the root and garnish with parsley. Decorate with a savoury butter if liked.

To serve cold (2). When skin has been removed put the tongue in a bowl or flat tin, curling it round tightly, cover with stock, put a saucer on top and press with a weight on top. Leave until cold, then turn out.

Tripe

TRIPE AND ONIONS

**1½ lb. tripe   ½ pt. milk   1 teasp. salt
2 large onions   1 oz. flour
salt and pepper**

Blanch the tripe and cut into 3-in. squares. Put in a saucepan with the milk, ½ pt. water and the salt; bring to the boil. Peel and slice the onions finely. Add them to the tripe and simmer very slowly for 2 hr. Mix the flour to a smooth paste with a little cold milk and add to the pan. Stir with a wooden spoon until boiling. Simmer for another 10 min., season to taste and serve.

6 helpings

LAMB

THE colour of good-quality lamb meat should be cherry red. There is a considerable difference in the colour of English and imported lamb due to the effect of freezing. Lamb fat should be creamy white. A brittle white fat is indicative of age, and an unduly yellow tinge is usually accompanied by an unpleasant "muttony" flavour.

The skeletal structure of the lamb is similar to that of the bullock and the cutting into sides and

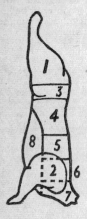

quarters follows the same pattern.

The *leg* (1) or hind limb is leaner, tougher and drier than the *shoulder* (2). It is also dearer. Both contain about the same amount of bone and both are eminently suitable for roasting.

(3) The *chump*, which is equivalent to the rump of beef, (4) the *loin* and the *best end neck* (5) are all used for chops and all equally suitable for frying. There is little to choose in tenderness, but it is

generally considered that the best end provides the sweetest eating, and the loin the most tender chops.

(6) The *middle neck* and *scrag* (7) are both used for stewing, but in the case of the middle neck it is possible to cut two or three chops from the end remote from the scrap which are suitable for frying or grilling.

(8) The *breast* may be either roasted or boiled. If roasted with stuffing to which no fat has been added much of the lamb fat is absorbed, giving rise to a more palatable dish.

Three distinct types of lamb *chop* are available, chump, cut from the leg end of the loin, loin chops proper and best end neck chops. Best end chops are often served as cutlets or *noisettes*. They are prepared by removing the chine bone (back bone) and trimming away some of the meat at the rib end. Cutlets should be carefully beaten so that the meat is uniform in thickness. Best end neck may also be served as a *crown roast*. This is a double neck, i.e. the adjoining pieces from each side of the lamb cut so that it can be formed into a ring. The ends of the bones are trimmed as in the case of cutlets.

BLANQUETTE OF LAMB

2 lb. fleshy lamb-loin, neck or breast
salt and pepper   1 large onion
bouquet garni   6 peppercorns
pinch of grated nutmeg   stock or
water   1½ oz. butter   1 oz. flour
1 egg yolk   2 tablesp. cream or milk

GARNISH
Croûtes of fried bread or fleurons
of pastry   button mushrooms

Cut the meat into pieces about 2 in. square and put into a stewpan with salt, sliced onion, herbs, peppercorns and nutmeg. Just cover with cold stock or water and simmer until tender—about 2 hr. When the meat is cooked, melt the butter in a saucepan and stir in the flour. Cook for a few minutes without browning. Strain ½ pt. liquor from the meat and add to the blended flour and butter. Stir until boiling, then simmer for 3 min. Beat together the egg yolk and cream and add to the sauce. Stir and cook gently for a few minutes, do not allow to boil or it may curdle. Correct the seasoning. Arrange the meat on a hot dish, piling it high in the centre and strain the sauce over.

Garnish with neatly shaped croûtes of fried bread or fleurons of pastry and grilled mushrooms. Serve hot.

5–6 helpings

DUTCH STEW

1½ lb. middle neck mutton   1 oz. dripping   2 onions   ½ pt. water or white stock   salt and pepper
1 small cabbage   6 potatoes

Cut the meat into slices. Melt the dripping in a saucepan and fry the meat with chopped onions, stirring occasionally. Add the stock or water and seasoning, and simmer for 1 hr. Lift out the meat and add the shredded cabbage and the potatoes. Add more stock if needed. Place the meat on top of the vegetables and braise until the contents are tender. Serve the meat on the cabbage, with the potatoes and gravy.

6 helpings
Cooking time—about 2 hr.

FRICASSEE OF LAMB

A breast of lamb   1 onion   2 oz. butter or fat   2 bay leaves   2 cloves
1 blade of mace   6 peppercorns salt and pepper   1 pt. boiling stock

or water   1 oz. flour
1 dessertsp. roughly-chopped capers

Prepare the meat and cut into 2-in. squares. Slice the onion, melt the fat, add the onion, bay leaves, cloves, mace, peppercorns, salt, pepper and meat. Cover and cook very gently for about ½ hr., stirring frequently. Add boiling stock or water and simmer for about 1½ hr. or until tender. Mix the flour smoothly with a small quantity of cold water. Gradually add to it, stirring all the time, about ½ pt. of the liquor from the saucepan. To this sauce add the meat, bring to the boil and simmer until tender. Serve on a hot dish within a border of mashed potatoes, sprinkle the capers over the meat.

4–6 helpings, depending on the quantity of meat

KEBABS

6 neat pieces mutton from the leg
3 sheep's kidneys   6 small bacon rashers   6 small sausages   6 small mushrooms   6 small tomatoes
oil or melted butter   12 bay leaves

Trim the meat into neat even-shaped pieces. Skin the kidneys, remove the cores and cut the kidneys in halves. Soak in cold water for 5 min. Curl the bacon into rolls, prick the sausages and peel the mushrooms. Brush them all (including tomatoes) with oil or butter and thread on to 6 skewers with a bay leaf at each end. Grill for 10–15 min., turning as required. Serve on their skewers and, if liked, on a bed of risotto (rice cooked in stock in a casserole until stock is absorbed).

6 helpings

LAMB CHOPS AND SPAGHETTI

6 lamb chops   ½ oz. butter
3 oz. spaghetti   6 tomatoes
salt and pepper   parsley

Trim, wipe and bone the chops. Secure in a neat shape with string or skewers. Place the chops on a buttered plate in a steamer, cover with greased greaseproof paper and steam for 1–1¼ hr., according to thickness. If a steamer is not available the plate may be placed on top of a saucepan of boiling water and the chops covered with greased greaseproof paper and a lid. If cooked this way, turn the chops when half cooked. Cook the spaghetti for about 15 min. by simmering in salt water. Drain well. Grill the tomatoes. Season the liquid from the plate on which chops were cooked, mix with the spaghetti and reheat. Place in the bottom of a gratin dish. Arrange the chops neatly on the spaghetti with half a grilled tomato on each and the rest of the tomatoes round, sprinkle with parsley.

6 helpings

LAMB CUTLETS—MALMAISON STYLE

6 lamb cutlets from the best end of neck   salt and pepper   1 egg
breadcrumbs   cooked lentils
cooked green peas   6 small stuffed
tomatoes   potatoes   2 oz. butter or
fat   ½ pt. demi-glace sauce (p. 102)

Trim the cutlets to a neat uniform shape. Season with salt and pepper and coat with egg and breadcrumbs. Rub the cooked vegetables through a fine sieve, season to taste, and bind with a little egg yolk. Press into small dariole moulds and keep hot until needed. Prepare and bake the stuffed tomatoes. Cook and mash the potatoes, make into a border, brush over with egg yolk and brown in the oven. Then heat the fat in a frying-pan and fry the cutlets until lightly browned. Drain well. Arrange on the potato border. Garnish with the tomatoes and small timbales of

vegetables. Serve the hot sauce separately.

6 helpings

LAMB SHASHLIK

1½ lb. lamb from leg or shoulder
1 thinly-sliced onion   ¾ teasp. salt
pinch of pepper   juice of 1 lemon
2 tablesp. wine or cider   6 small
tomatoes   6–9 small mushrooms
butter or good dripping

Cut the meat in 1½-in. cubes, trimming off most of the fat. Place in a bowl with the sliced onion, seasoning, lemon juice and wine or cider. Mix well together and leave to stand overnight. When ready to cook, arrange the meat on skewers, alternating pieces of meat with a whole tomato or a mushroom. Brush with butter or dripping and grill for 15 min., turning frequently. Serve on the skewers with vegetables and potatoes or savoury rice.

6 helpings

LEG OF LAMB—FRENCH STYLE

A small leg of lamb (boned)
1 carrot   1 onion   1 shallot
1 teasp. chopped parsley   1 clove
of bruised garlic   salt and pepper
2 oz. good dripping

Slice the carrot and onion and finely chop the shallot. Mix together the parsley, shallot, garlic, salt and pepper, and then sprinkle the mixture on the inner surface of the meat. Bind into a good shape. Place in a covered baking-tin with the dripping, onion and carrot. Season well with salt and pepper. Bake for 20 min. in a fairly hot oven (400° F., Gas 6), then reduce heat to moderate (350° F., Gas 4) for the remainder of the time, allowing 20 min. per lb. and 20 min. over. For the last 10 min. remove the covering and allow the meat to brown and become crisp.

Serve on a hot dish with gravy made from the bones and the sediment in the baking-tin.

6–8 helpings

NAVARIN OF LAMB

1 large breast or boned neck of lamb
a good pinch of sugar   1 large
tablesp. flour   ½ lb. skinned
tomatoes   1 crushed clove of garlic
salt and pepper   bouquet garni
8–10 small onions   8–10 small
potatoes   one A1* can peas
one A1 can small whole carrots
chopped parsley

Cut the lamb into about 2½-oz. pieces and gently fry them in some of the fat trimmed off them. Transfer to a casserole. Pour off the fat. Sprinkle the sugar into the pan and heat until it becomes a deep gold. Work in the flour and then the chopped tomatoes (seeds discarded), then stir in enough hot water to make a sauce to cover the meat. Pour over the meat. Add the crushed garlic, a little pepper and salt and the bouquet garni. Cover, cook for a further ½–¾ hr. Add the drained peas and carrots and heat through. Sprinkle with parsley and serve.

* *See* Chart of Can Sizes, p. 53.

NOISETTES OF LAMB

These are the neatly trimmed round or oval-shaped pieces cut from the fleshy part of the loin of lamb. They may be cooked in the same way as cutlets but are not usually coated with egg and crumbs.

NOISETTES A LA JARDINIERE

Prepare the noisettes as above and place on a bed of mashed potatoes. Garnish attractively with vegetables to choice and pour a good brown gravy around the noisettes.

6 helpings

STEWED LAMB

1½–2 lb. loin, neck or breast   1 oz.
dripping   a few young carrots
1 onion   bouquet garni (parsley,
thyme, bay leaf, 6 peppercorns)
2 sprigs of mint   stock or water
peas   1 oz. flour   salt and pepper

Trim the meat and cut into portions suitable for serving. Heat the dripping in a stewpan and put in the meat, diced vegetables, and the bouquet garni and mint tied in muslin. Cover closely and cook very gently for 10 min., stirring occasionally. Add stock or water just to cover the meat, cover closely and simmer gently until tender (about 2 hr.). About ½ hr. before cooked, add the peas a few at a time so that the temperature is not much reduced. Blend the flour to a smooth paste with a little cold water, add some of the hot liquid from the pan and stir well. Return to the stewpan and stir until boiling. When cooked, remove the herbs, season to taste and serve hot.

6 helpings

Lamb's Liver
STUFFED LIVER

¾ lb. lamb's liver   seasoned flour
4–6 oz. bacon   ½ pt. stock
browned breadcrumbs   parsley
1 teasp. Worcester sauce

STUFFING

3 oz. breadcrumbs   3 teasp.
chopped parsley   2 teasp. finely-
chopped onion   salt and pepper

Wash the slices of liver, dry, and dip in the seasoned flour. Place in a greased meat-tin or fireproof dish. Mix all the ingredients for the stuffing and spread some on each slice of liver. Arrange pieces of bacon to cover the stuffing. Pour in the stock carefully, cover and cook in a moderate oven (350° *F.*, *Gas* 4) for ½–¾ hr., depending on the thickness of the liver. Serve the slices sprinkled with some browned breadcrumbs and a little chopped parsley. Boil up the stock with a little thickening and add the Worcester sauce. Pour a little round the liver and serve the rest separately.

6 helpings

Lamb's Sweetbreads
FRIED SWEETBREADS

1½ lb. lamb's sweetbreads   seasoned
flour   egg and breadcrumbs
butter or fat   ½ pt. good brown
gravy or tomato sauce

Prepare the sweetbreads as follows: wash and soak in cold water for 1–2 hr. until free from blood. Put into a pan, cover with cold water, bring to boil and simmer for 3–5 min., then plunge into cold water. Discard fat and skin and any gristle. Press between 2 dishes until cold. Roll in seasoned flour and coat with egg and breadcrumbs. Fry in hot fat until golden brown. Serve the sauce or gravy separately.

6 helpings
Cooking time—to fry about 8 min.

MUTTON
BOILED BREAST OF MUTTON

A breast of mutton   2 tablesp.
breadcrumbs   1 tablesp. finely-
chopped suet   1 dessertsp. chopped
parsley   ¼ teasp. mixed herbs
salt and pepper   a little milk
stock or water with vegetables,
10 peppercorns, and salt

Remove all the bones and surplus fat; flatten the meat and season well. Make the stuffing by mixing the breadcrumbs, suet, parsley, herbs, salt and pepper together. Moisten with milk. Spread the mixture on the meat, roll up lightly and bind securely with string. Put into the boiling stock or water and vegetables, and simmer for 2–3 hr., according to size.

Pour caper sauce over the meat, if liked.

NOTE: Leg and neck of mutton can be cooked in the same way.

6–8 helpings

BOILED KNUCKLE OF MUTTON

A knuckle of mutton   1 onion
1 carrot   ½ turnip   good stock or
water   salt   bouquet garni
8 peppercorns

Prepare the vegetables and meat. Place the meat in the stock or water with the salt, sliced vegetables, and the flavourings tied in muslin. Simmer very gently until tender—about 1¾ hr. Remove the flavourings, serve the vegetables with the meat. If liked, the stock in which the mutton is cooked may be used for making onion sauce to be served with the dish.

2–3 helpings

BRAISED LEG OF MUTTON

A small leg of mutton   2 onions
1 turnip   2 carrots   1 oz. dripping
stock   bouquet garni   10 peppercorns   2 shallots   1½ oz. butter
1½ oz. flour   salt and pepper

Thickly slice the onions, turnip and carrots. Melt the dripping in a saucepan and sweat the sliced vegetables in it with the lid on, over a gentle heat for 5–10 min. Almost cover with stock or water, add the bouquet garni and peppercorns. Place the prepared meat on top, put a piece of greased greaseproof paper on top of the pan and cover with a well-fitting lid. Cook gently for 3–3½ hr., basting occasionally with the stock and adding more stock if necessary. About ½ hr. before serving, chop the shallots very finely, melt the butter and fry the shallots lightly. Then add the flour and cook until a good brown colour. Keep the meat hot, strain the stock and make up to

1 pt. Add the stock to the browned flour and butter and stir until boiling. Season to taste and pour a little over the meat. Serve the remainder in a sauceboat.

Cooked tomatoes, mushrooms, diced turnips and carrots, peas, timbales of spinach or green pea purée are all suitable garnishes for this dish.

If preferred, the leg may be boned and the cavity filled with a forcemeat made as follows: equal quantities of ham and trimmings from the leg finely chopped, finely-chopped onion and a little garlic, if liked. Allow an extra ½ hr. for cooking.

8–12 helpings

BRAISED MUTTON CUTLETS

6 cutlets from the best end of neck
larding bacon   1 onion   1 carrot
½ turnip   2 sticks of celery
bouquet garni   1½ oz. dripping
½ pt. stock   salt and pepper
meat glaze

Trim and flatten the cutlets. Insert about 5 strips of larding bacon into the lean part of each cutlet. Thickly slice vegetables and lightly fry them with the bouquet garni in the dripping. Then add stock to three-quarters cover them; season to taste. Lay the cutlets on top, cover with greased paper and a well-fitting lid. Cook gently for about 50 min., adding more stock as necessary. When cooked, brush one side of the cutlets with meat glaze and put into a hot oven to crisp the bacon.

Serve on a bed of mashed potato garnished with diced vegetables. Tomato or caper sauce are suitable for serving with this dish.

6 helpings

CASSEROLE OF MUTTON

1½ lb. middle neck of mutton
1 onion   good gravy or stock
salt and pepper   suet pastry

(p. 342), **using 4 oz. flour, etc.**

Cut the meat into neat chops and remove the bones and surplus fat. Place the meat in a casserole so that it is about half full. Thinly slice the onion and place on top and barely cover with gravy or stock. Season carefully. Cover and cook gently in a moderate oven (350° F., Gas 4), for about 1½ hr. Roll the suet pastry to the shape of the casserole—but slightly smaller. Lay the pastry on top of the meat, replace the lid and cook gently for 1 hr. longer. Before serving, divide the pastry crust into suitable portions.

NOTE: If a casserole is not available this may be cooked in a saucepan on top of the cooker.

6 helpings

GRILLED MUTTON

6 slices about ¾ in. thick cut from
the middle of the leg
3 tablesp. salad oil or oiled butter

MARINADE
2 dessertsp. vinegar   1 teasp. very
finely-chopped onion   ½ teasp. salt
1 teasp. finely-chopped parsley
a pinch of powdered mixed herbs
⅛ teasp. pepper

Put the slices of meat into a dish and cover with the marinade. Leave for at least 2 hr., turning and basting occasionally. When ready, drain, dry and brush with the salad oil or melted butter. Grill, turning several times, for about 10–15 min.

Suitable accompaniments are tomato sauce and chipped potatoes; or mushroom sauce, baked tomatoes and chipped potatoes; or stewed mushrooms and brown sauce.

6 helpings

HARICOT MUTTON

6 small chops from the middle neck
or 2 lb. scrag end   1 oz. butter or

good dripping   1 large onion
1 oz. flour   1½ pt. stock   salt and
pepper   bouquet garni

Trim off the skin and surplus fat and cut the meat into small pieces or cutlets. Put the butter or dripping into a saucepan and, when smoking, fry the meat quickly and lightly. Remove the meat, chop the onion finely and fry slowly in the same fat without browning. Add the flour and fry slowly until a rich brown. Cool slightly and add the stock, seasoning and bouquet garni. Bring to the boil, put in the meat and simmer gently until tender—about 2 hr. Cut the carrots and turnip into neat dice for garnish. Add the rough trimmings to the meat. Cook the diced carrot and turnip separately in boiling salted water until just tender. Arrange the meat on a hot dish. If necessary rapidly boil the liquid in the saucepan to reduce and then strain over the meat. Garnish with diced carrot and turnip.

6 helpings

IRISH STEW

2 lb. best end of neck   1 lb. onions
salt and pepper   3 lb. potatoes
1½ pt. stock or water   parsley

Cut the meat into neat cutlets and trim off the surplus fat. Arrange in a saucepan layers of the meat, thinly-sliced onions, seasoning and half the potatoes cut in slices. Add stock or water just to cover and simmer gently for about 1½ hr. Add the rest of the potatoes —cut to a uniform size to improve the appearance on top. Cook gently in the steam for about ¾ hr. longer. Serve the meat in the centre of a hot dish and arrange the potatoes round the edge.

Pour the liquid over the meat and sprinkle with finely-chopped parsley.

Alternative method of serving:

Place the meat in the centre of a hot dish. Arrange half the potatoes round the edge. Then sieve the liquid—onions and remaining potatoes—and pour over the meat. Sprinkle with chopped parsley.

6 helpings

LANCASHIRE HOT POT

2 lb. best end of neck   2 lb. potatoes
3 sheep's kidneys   1 large onion
salt and pepper   stock   1 oz. butter
or margarine   ½ pt. good gravy

Divide the meat into neat cutlets. Trim off the skin and most of the fat. Grease a fireproof baking-dish and put in a layer of sliced potatoes. Arrange the cutlets on top, slightly overlapping each other, and cover with slices of kidney and slices of onion. Season well. Add the remainder of the potatoes. The top layer should be of small potatoes cut in halves, uniformly arranged to give a neat appearance to the dish. Pour down the side of the dish about ½ pt. hot stock seasoned with salt and pepper. Brush the top layer of potatoes with warmed fat and cover with greased greaseproof paper. Bake for about 2 hr. in a moderate oven (350° F., Gas 4). Then remove the paper to allow the potatoes to become crisp and brown, cooking for a further 20 min. When ready to serve, pour some gravy down the sides of the dish and serve the rest in a gravy-boat. Serve the hot pot in the dish in which it is cooked.

6 helpings

MUTTON PIES—
CUMBERLAND STYLE

12 oz. minced mutton   shortcrust
pastry using 12 oz. flour, etc.
1 onion   4 oz. mushrooms
1 dessertsp. chopped parsley
a pinch of thyme   salt and pepper
a little good stock   egg or milk

Chop and lightly fry the onion. Line 12 small round tins or small saucers with half the pastry. Mix together the minced mutton, chopped onion, chopped mushrooms, parsley, thyme and seasoning. Divide the mixture between the tins. Add to each a little stock to moisten. Cover with lids made from the rest of the pastry. Brush with egg or milk and bake in a moderate oven (350° F., Gas 4) for about 30–45 min.

6 helpings

MUTTON PUDDING

1 lb. lean mutton   salt and pepper
suet pastry using 9 oz. flour, etc.
1 or 2 kidneys

Follow the directions for preparation and cooking given for Beefsteak Pudding (p. 150).

5–6 helpings

SCRAG OF MUTTON

Scrag end of neck of mutton
2 onions   2 carrots   ½ turnip
bacon rashers   bouquet garni
10 peppercorns   stock or water
egg and breadcrumbs
2 oz. dripping

Wash the meat in warm salt water. Slice the onions, carrots and turnip and put in a saucepan. Lay the meat on top, cover with slices of bacon. Add the bouquet garni, peppercorns and enough stock or water nearly to cover the vegetables. Cover with a close-fitting lid and cook gently for 2½ hr. Remove the meat, brush with beaten egg and coat with breadcrumbs. Put in a tin with the hot dripping and cook in a fairly hot oven (400° F., Gas 6) for about ½ hr. until nicely browned. Baste occasionally. Serve with brown gravy made from the stock in which the meat was cooked.

6–8 helpings

STUFFED AND ROAST LOIN OR SHOULDER OF MUTTON

A loin or shoulder of mutton
veal forcemeat or sage and onion
stuffing   salt and pepper
2–3 oz. dripping

Remove all the bones from the meat. Trim off any skin and surplus fat and flatten the meat with a rolling-pin. Season the meat well with salt and pepper and spread on the forcemeat or stuffing. Roll up and tie securely with string. Melt the dripping in a covered meat-tin, put in the meat and roast in a moderate oven (350° F., Gas 4) until tender. Allow 25 min. per lb. and 25 min. over. Baste occasionally. A good gravy or brown sauce may be served with the meat.

Sheep's Brains

BRAIN AND TONGUE PUDDING

3 sheep's brains   3 sheep's tongues
suet pastry using 6 oz. flour, etc.
1 teasp. finely-chopped parsley
1 shallot   1 teasp. flour   salt and
pepper   1 hard-boiled egg
¼ pt. milk.

Prepare the brains as in the following recipe. Wash the tongues and simmer until the skin can be removed. Line a greased basin with suet pastry. Fill with layers of sliced tongue, cleaned and roughly-chopped brains, seasoning of parsley, finely-chopped shallot, flour, and salt and pepper, and slices of hard-boiled egg. Add the milk and cover with suet pastry. Cover with greased greaseproof paper and steam for 3–3½ hr.

6 helpings

Sheep's Head

SHEEP'S HEAD

A sheep's head   bouquet garni
10 peppercorns   salt and pepper
2 tablesp. pearl barley or rice
2 onions   1 small turnip   2 small

carrots   1 oz. butter or fat
1 oz. flour   parsley

If necessary, split the head and remove the brains. Wash the head several times, taking care to remove all splintered bones. Scrape the small bones from the nostrils and brush the teeth. Soak in salt water for 30 min. Cover with cold water and bring to the boil. Pour away the water and replace with fresh cold water and add the bouquet garni, peppercorns and salt. Boil up and skim well. Add the barley (blanched) or rice. Cook slowly for about 3 hr. Meanwhile prepare the vegetables and cut into dice; these should be added about 1 hr. before serving. Remove the skin and fibres from the brains with salt and wash in cold water. Tie the brains in muslin and cook with the head for about 15–20 min. Then chop coarsely. Heat the fat in a saucepan and add the flour. Stir over the heat and cook without browning for about 3 min., then add ¾ pt. of liquid in which the head is cooking. Stir until boiling, correct the seasoning and add the brains. Remove the head and take all the flesh from the bones. Skin and slice the tongue. Place the meat neatly on a hot dish. Pour the brain sauce over. If liked, garnish with some of the sliced tongue, vegetables and chopped parsley. Serve the broth separately.

3 helpings

Sheep's Heart
SHEEP'S HEART
1 sheep's heart   veal forcemeat
2 oz. dripping   ½ pt. good stock
¾ oz. flour   salt and pepper

Soak the heart for about ½ hr. Wash well in clean water. Cut the pipes from the top, leave the flaps to fasten down and cut the dividing walls of the chambers. Dry thoroughly and fill the heart with forcemeat, fold over the flaps and tie or skewer to keep it in. Heat the dripping in a small meat-tin. Put in the heart, baste well and bake in a cool to moderate oven (310°–350° F., Gas 2–4) for 1½ hr. Gentle cooking and frequent basting are necessary to prevent the heart from becoming dry and hard. When cooked, place the heart on a hot dish and keep hot. Drain off most of the fat but keep back any sediment. Blend the flour and stock and add to the sediment to make thickened gravy. Season carefully. Pour a little round the heart and serve the rest in a gravy-boat.

NOTE: Sheep's heart may be stuffed with sage and onion stuffing and cooked in a saucepan on top of the cooker. This must be done very carefully over a very gentle heat.

Sheep's Kidneys
DEVILLED KIDNEYS
6 sheep's kidneys   1½ oz. butter or fat   1 tablesp. chopped onion
salt   cayenne pepper   3 teasp. chutney   2 teasp. lemon juice
½ teasp. mixed mustard   ¼ pt. stock
2 egg yolks   breadcrumbs   buttered toast or potato border

Skin and well wash the kidneys. Split open and remove the cores. Cut the kidneys into neat pieces. Melt the fat in a small pan, put in the onion and cook without browning. Then add the kidney, salt, cayenne, chutney, lemon juice, mustard and stock. Cover and stew for a short time over moderate heat until the kidney is cooked. Cool slightly and stir in the egg yolks. Sprinkle in enough breadcrumbs to make a soft consistency and correct the seasoning. Serve on buttered toast or in a mashed potato border.

6 helpings
Cooking time—about 20 min.

KIDNEY AND BACON CROUTES

3 sheep's kidneys   3 bacon rashers
4 oz. mushrooms   3 skinned
tomatoes   salt and pepper   6 eggs
6 large croûtes of bread
2 oz. butter or fat   paprika

Skin the kidneys, remove the cores and soak in cold water for 5 min. Chop the kidneys and bacon. Fry the bacon until crisp and keep hot. Fry the chopped mushrooms and kidney for 5 min. in the bacon fat. Halve and grill the tomatoes and season carefully with salt and pepper. Poach the eggs. Fry croûtes of bread in the fat until golden on both sides, and keep hot in the oven. Reheat the bacon in the fat and add the kidneys and mushrooms. Correct the seasoning and spread equally on the croûtes. Place an egg on each one and dredge with paprika pepper. Garnish each with ½ tomato. Serve at once.

6 helpings

SAUTED KIDNEYS

6 sheep's kidneys   2 shallots
1 oz. butter or fat   ¼ pt. brown
sauce   1 tablesp. sherry (optional)
salt and pepper   watercress
croûtes of fried or toasted bread

Skin the kidneys and remove the cores. Soak for 5 min. in cold water. Dry and cut into ¼-in. slices. Finely chop the shallots, heat the fat in a sauté pan and fry them slightly. Then put in the sliced kidney and shake and toss over the heat for about 5 min. Drain off the surplus fat and add the brown sauce, sherry (if used) and salt and pepper. Stir over a gentle heat until thoroughly hot, but take care not to let the mixture boil. Serve hot on toast or fried bread, garnished with watercress.

6 helpings
Cooking time—about 10 min.

Sheep's Liver

LIVER A LA PROVENCALE

1½ lb. sheep's liver   4 oz. bacon
1½ lb. onions   salt and pepper
1 oz. flour   ½ pt. stock   parsley

Wash the liver well. Dice the bacon and fry in a saucepan until crisp. Remove and keep hot. Chop the onions and fry in the bacon fat (covered) until tender but not brown. Season with salt and pepper. Dust in the flour, add the stock and stir until boiling. Place the slices of liver on top, cover and simmer for ¾ hr. Serve the slices of liver on a hot dish with the bacon on top and the onions heaped neatly at each end, sprinkled liberally with parsley.

6 helpings

LIVER AND BACON

1 lb. sheep's liver   ½ lb. bacon
rashers   seasoned flour   ¾ pt. stock

Remove the rind and rust from the bacon. Wash the liver in cold water and remove any tubes or blood vessels. Dry the liver and, if necessary, cut in slices ½ in.—¾ in. thick. Dip each slice of liver in seasoned flour. Fry the slices of bacon and remove to a hot dish and keep hot until required. Fry the liver in the fat from the bacon lightly and quickly so that it is browned on both sides without hardening or overcooking. Remove to the hot dish, placing the bacon neatly on top. Drain off all but about 1 dessertsp. of fat, add about ¾ oz. flour and stir until browned. Add about ¾ pt. stock. Boil and season to taste. Strain round the liver.

Calves' liver may be used equally well.

6 helpings
Cooking time—about 10 min.

HAGGIS

1 sheep's paunch and pluck
1 lb. oatmeal   1 lb. beef suet

2 Spanish onions   1 teasp. pepper
2 tablesp. salt   ½ nutmeg, finely
grated   juice of 1 lemon
1½ pt. good stock or gravy

Soak the paunch for several
hours in salt and water. Then turn
it inside out and wash thoroughly
several times. Wash the pluck well,
just cover the liver with cold water
and boil for about 1½ hr. After ¾
hr. add the well-cleaned heart and
lights. Chop half the liver coarsely
and chop the other half with the
heart and lights, very finely. Mix
all together and add the oatmeal, finely-chopped suet, finely-
chopped onions, salt, pepper, nutmeg, lemon juice and stock. Press
this mixture lightly into the
paunch and sew up the opening,
allowing space for the oatmeal to
swell. (If overfilled, the paunch is
likely to burst.) Put the haggis into
boiling water and cook gently for
about 3 hr. During the first hour
prick occasionally and carefully
with a needle to allow the steam to
escape. Usually no sauce or gravy
is served with haggis. If a smaller
dish is required use a lamb's
paunch and pluck instead of a
sheep's.

Sheep's Tongues

BRAISED SHEEP'S TONGUES

4 sheep's tongues   1 oz. butter
or margarine   1 onion   1 turnip
1 carrot   2 sticks of celery
bouquet garni   6 peppercorns
½ pt. stock   2 bacon rashers
meat glaze

Soak the tongues well in salt
water for 1 hr., then blanch and
dry them. Melt the fat in a stewpan and add the roughly sliced
vegetables. Put on a tightly fitting
lid and toss for 10 min. over a very
low heat. Lay the tongues on top,
add the bouquet garni, peppercorns and enough stock almost to
cover the vegetables. Place the
bacon on top of the tongues. Cover
with greased greaseproof paper,
and the lid, and cook gently for
about 2 hr. or until the tongues are
tender. When ready, skin the
tongues, cut in halves lengthwise
and brush with warm glaze. Place
on a greased paper in a baking-tin
and put in a warm oven for a few
minutes to reheat.

Serve on a bed of mashed potatoes or spinach purée. Serve with
brown sauce.

6 helpings

PORK

MORE and more people today realize that with the development of cold storage it is now perfectly safe to eat pork at any time of the year.

The appearance of the *leg* (1) and *loin* (2) are well known. They may be either baked, the leg boiled or in the case of cutlets and chops, fried.

(7) The *belly*, comparable to the streak in bacon, is usually salted and boiled. It is perfectly suitable

for roasting and if bought in the form of thin strips or rashers, may be grilled.

(3) The *spare rib* of the pig is almost a parallel cut to the middle neck of lamb. It is a moist-eating tender joint, equally pleasant whether roasted or grilled.

From immediately above the spare rib is lifted the *blade-bone* (4). A parallel joint to this, the blade half shoulder, may also be found in lamb. The blade-bone is

a roasting joint and is especially tasty if the bone is removed and the resulting space filled with stuffing.

A joint which is much neglected today is (5) the *hand* and *spring* of pork. This constitutes the fore leg of the animal and in bone structure is akin to the knuckle half shoulder of lamb. Although a large joint for the smaller family to buy it is extremely cheap and may be most economically used. The knuckle portion is best removed and set aside in strong salt water for two or three days ready for boiling. The remainder may be roasted and if suitably boned and rolled it is an easy joint to carve, even for beginners.

In London and the South of England the pig carcase is the only one delivered to shops with (6) the *head* attached. The effect of this is that, on the whole, the specialized offal butcher is usually the only one to stock sheep's heads and ox cheek, together with tongues and brains. In the case of pigs' heads, however, every butcher who sells pork will have the head. The large piece of cheek meat provides the Bath chap when salted and boiled. The remainder of the head may be boiled, when it is easily removed from the bones, and used for brawn.

The flesh of pork should be a pale pink colour. Whenever it has a dark red tinge the pork should be avoided. The fat should be white and firm to the touch. It should never be greyish in colour. Occasionally pork may be found with small black spots in the fat, particularly in the belly. This is due to a carry-over of black pigment from the skin of black or brown pigs. Although unsightly, it is in no way harmful.

BACON AND HAM

Bacon is obtained from a side of pork from which the head and feet have been removed. The side is then salted for a suitable time to provide green bacon. In the South of England much bacon is further treated by smoking, exposure for 24 to 48 hours to the smoke from slow-burning hardwood dust such as oak. The chine or back bone is removed prior to processing, and before slicing the other bones (rib, shoulder and thigh bones).

Bacon is usually cut into the following joints, pork equivalents are given in brackets: *gammon* (leg), boiled for ham or baked; best *back* and *long* (loin of pork), used for back rashers; *streaky* (belly of pork), cut as streaky rashers or cut with the loin as long back; *collar* (spare rib of pork), used as a boiling joint or for very lean rashers; *hock* (hand and spring of pork), used as a boiling joint.

Strictly speaking, ham should be so called only when it is obtained from the gammon. It may be cooked before or after smoking and can be specially prepared by dry salting process (York hams) or by special smoking (Bradmun hams).

BOILED PICKLED PORK

A joint of pickled or salt pork
broad beans   10 peppercorns
1 carrot   1 onion   ½ turnip   salt
parsley sauce (p. 93)

Soak the beans overnight. Soak the meat in cold water. Cover the pork with cold water and simmer gently, allowing 25–30 min. per lb. and 25–30 min. over. When the liquid is boiling, add the peppercorns, and the carrot, onion and turnip cut in thick slices. About ½

hr. before the pork is cooked, cook the beans in boiling salted water, simmer gently until tender but whole. Drain the beans well and coat with parsley sauce. Pease pudding (p. 226) may be served in place of the beans if liked. Serve the pork in a hot dish, garnished with the vegetables.

The liquor in which the pork is cooked can be made into good pea soup.

BRAISED PORK, COUNTRY STYLE

4 pork chops   4 tablesp. cider
bouquet garni   3 onions   2 cooking
apples   good pinch of ground
cinnamon   salt and pepper
2–3 large dark mushrooms
1 breakfastcup or A1 can garden
peas   1 breakfastcup or A1 can
beetroots   6–8 oz. noodles

Trim off rind and excessive fat and quickly fry chops in them until golden brown. Place in a casserole, add cider and bouquet garni, cover and cook gently on the cooker or in a cool oven (310°–335° F., Gas 2–3). Meanwhile, pour off excess fat from frying-pan; peel, chop, then fry the onions and apples for a few minutes. Add the cinnamon and water to cover them, put on a lid and simmer until soft. Sieve, season to taste and turn on to the chops. Cover and cook for 1¾–2 hr. in all, adding the thickly-sliced mushrooms ½ hr. before the end. Heat the peas and beetroots separately. Trickle the noodles in salted boiling water and boil until, on testing a piece, the centre is slightly firm. Drain the noodles, peas and beetroots. Dish the noodles with the chops on top and garnish with the mushrooms, peas and beetroots.

FRIED or GRILLED PORK CUTLETS or CHOPS

6 bones neck or loin of pork
1 egg   1 teasp. powdered sage

salt and pepper   breadcrumbs
1½ oz. butter or fat

Trim the cutlets, removing most
of the fat. Beat the egg and add
to it the sage, salt and pepper.
Brush each cutlet with this and
then coat carefully with breadcrumbs. Heat the fat and gently
fry, or grill, the cutlets for about
20 min., turning frequently until
golden brown.

PORK PIE

1 lb. lean pork   powdered herbs
salt and pepper   1 small onion
½ gill water or stock   hot water
crust pastry using 8 oz. flour, etc.

Cut the meat into neat small
dice and season to taste with herbs,
salt and pepper. Place the bones,
finely-chopped onion, salt and
pepper in a saucepan with the
water or stock and simmer for 2
hr., so that the gravy when cold
will form a firm jelly. Mould the
pastry with the hands or line a
pie mould. Put in the filling, add
some stock and cover with pastry
lid. (The remainder of the stock
should be reheated and added after
the pie is baked and still hot.) 3 or
4 folds of greased greaseproof
paper should be fastened round
the pie to preserve its shape and
prevent it becoming too brown.
Brush the top of the pie with egg
or milk, and make a hole in the
centre. Bake in a hot oven (425°
F., Gas 7) at first and reduce heat
as soon as pastry is set to moderate
(350° F., Gas 4) for about 1½ hr.
Remove the greaseproof paper or
mould for the last ½ hr. and brush
the sides with egg or milk.

NOTE: If preferred, small individual pies may be made. Cook
for about 1 hr.

6 helpings

SAVOURY LOIN OF PORK

3 lb. loin of pork   ½ teasp.
powdered sage   1 saltsp. dry

mustard   1 tablesp. finely-chopped
onion   ½ teasp. salt   ¼ saltsp.
pepper   apple sauce
brown gravy (p. 98)

Score the pork with narrow
lines. Mix the onion with the
sage, salt, mustard and pepper and
rub the mixture well into the meat.
Wrap the joint in greased greaseproof paper and roast in a covered
tin in a hot oven (425° F., Gas 7)
for 10 min. and then reduce heat
to moderate (350° F., Gas 4) for
the remainder of the time. Allow
25 min. per lb. and 25 min. over.
About ½ hr. before serving, remove
the paper and lid and continue
cooking to crisp the crackling.
Serve the apple sauce and gravy
separately.

6 helpings

SAVOURY TENDERLOIN OF
   PORK

6 pork chops from the spare rib,
tenderloin or neck   2 lb. Spanish
onions   salt and pepper   ⅛ teasp.
sage   1 oz. dripping   mixed herbs
½ oz. flour

Dice the onions and mix with a
small teasp. salt, ⅛ teasp. pepper,
sage and ⅛ teasp. mixed herbs. Put
in a casserole with ¼ pt. cold water,
cover and cook gently for 1½ hr.,
stirring occasionally. When the
onions are about half cooked, place
the chops with a little hot dripping
in a meat-tin. Season with salt,
pepper and a pinch of herbs. Roast
in a moderate oven (350° F., Gas
4) for 15 min., then turn them,
season the other side and cook for
a further 15 min. Remove the
chops when cooked and pour off
all the fat, leaving any sediment.
Sprinkle in the flour and return to
the oven to brown. Add the onions
to the browned flour, mix well together and reheat. Dish the chops
neatly on a hot dish, serving the
onion gravy in the centre.

6 helpings

BACON AND HAM

BOILED BACON

Soak the bacon for at least 1 hr. in warm water—if very dry or highly salted longer is needed, and the water should be changed. Scrape the underside and the rind as clean as possible. Put into a pan with cold water, just to cover. Bring slowly to the boil and re-move any scum. Simmer gently until tender, allowing about 25 min. per lb. and 25 min. over, e.g. 2 lb. will take 75 min. or 1 hr. 15 min. if a thick piece, and rather less if a thinner piece. Take joint out and remove the skin—this comes off easily when the bacon is done. If to be eaten cold, allow to cool in the water in which it was cooked. To finish—drain well, then sprinkle the fat thickly with a mix-ture of browned breadcrumbs and brown sugar.

NOTE: Bacon can be cooked very successfully in a pressure cooker. Remove the trivet, cover joint with water, bring to boil, then throw the water away. Cover again with water and pressure cook at 15 lb. pressure, allowing 12 min. per lb.

BAKED HAM

A ham   flour   brown sugar   cloves

Soak the ham in water for at least 12 hr. Wipe well and trim off any rusty bits. Coat with a flour and water paste crust which must be sufficiently thick all over to keep in the gravy. Place the ham in a fairly hot oven (400° F., Gas 6) for about 15 min., then reduce heat to cool (310° F., Gas 2) and cook for the remainder of the time, allow-ing 30 min. per lb. Remove the crust and skin, score squares in the fat and place a clove in each square, sprinkle brown sugar over the fat. Garnish the knuckle with a paper frill. Pieces of ham will need less time to cook.

BAKED HAM LOAF

8 oz. ham   4 oz. browned breadcrumbs   2 oz. sultanas 1 large cooking apple   4 oz. corned beef   1 tablesp. finely-chopped parsley   1 teasp. grated lemon rind pinch of allspice   pinch of grated nutmeg   salt and pepper   2 eggs milk

Well grease a bread-tin and coat with browned breadcrumbs. Wash the sultanas well; peel, core and grate the apple. Mince the ham and corned beef and mix with the parsley, lemon rind, bread-crumbs, apple, sultanas, allspice, nutmeg and seasoning. Bind with the beaten eggs and a little milk if needed. Carefully put into the prepared bread-tin and bake in a cool oven (310° F., Gas 2) for about 40 min. Serve hot with gravy, or cold with salad.

6 helpings

BOILED HAM

Ham   glaze or raspings   brown sugar

If the ham has been hung for a long time and is very dry and salt, soak for 24 hr., changing the water as necessary. For most hams about 12 hr. soaking is suffi-cient. Clean and trim off the rusty parts. Put into a saucepan with sufficient cold water to cover and simmer gently until tender, allow-ing 30 min. per lb. When cooked, remove the ham and strip off the skin. Sprinkle the ham with a mix-ture of equal quantities of raspings and brown sugar. If to be eaten cold, after removing skin, put the ham back into the water until cold to keep it juicy. Before serving sprinkle on the raspings and sugar, or glaze, if preferred.

NOTE: To ensure that the ham is sweet insert a sharp knife close to the bone—when withdrawn there should be no unpleasant smell.

PINEAPPLE HAM SLICES

12 oz. cooked ham   1 teasp. mixed
mustard   1 tablesp. mayonnaise
3 tablesp. sherry, cider or pineapple
juice   6 slices of pineapple
4 gherkins (optional)

Mince the ham and mix with the
mustard, mayonnaise and sherry,
cider or juice. Drain the pineapple
slices and cover neatly with ham
mixture. Place in a greased fireproof dish or meat-tin and bake in
a moderate oven (350° F., Gas 4)
for 10–15 min. Serve garnished
with slices of gherkin if liked.

6 helpings

Pig's Cheek

PIG'S CHEEK

A pig's cheek   browned
breadcrumbs

If the cheek has been cured and
dried, soak it for 5–6 hr., if not,
wash well in several waters. Cover
the meat with warm water and
simmer gently for 2½ hr. Then remove the cheek, strip off the skin
and cover the cheek thickly with
lightly browned crumbs. Bake for
about ½ hr. in a moderate oven
(350° F., Gas 4). Serve hot or cold.
Baking the meat is not essential
and can be omitted if liked.

3–4 helpings

Pig's Feet

STUFFED PIG'S FEET

4 pig's feet   salt   1 tablesp. flour
1 egg   breadcrumbs   frying fat

STUFFING

2 tablesp. cooked and finely-chopped
onion   1 tablesp. breadcrumbs
1 tablesp. oiled butter   ½ teasp. salt
½ teasp. powdered sage   ½ teasp.
mixed mustard   ¼ teasp. pepper

Put the feet into a saucepan with
1 teasp. salt. Cover with cold
water and simmer for about 3 hr.
Mix the ingredients for the stuf-

fing. When the feet are done, split
them, remove the bones and press
the stuffing into the cavities. Replace the halves together and press
between 2 dishes with a weight on
top until cold. When ready for use,
cut the feet into slices about 1 in.
thick. Roll each piece in flour and
brush with beaten egg and coat
with breadcrumbs. Fry in hot fat
until golden brown. Serve hot
garnished with parsley.

6 helpings

Pig's Fry

PIG'S FRY

1½–2 lb. pig's fry, which consists of
the heart, lights, liver and
sweetbread   salt and pepper   flour
sage   frying fat

Wash the fry, well. Cover with
cold water, add a little salt and
boil gently for ½–¾ hr. Drain, dry
well, and cut into thin slices. Coat
lightly with flour seasoned with
salt and pepper and a little sage.
Fry in hot fat until nicely browned,
then remove and keep hot.
Sprinkle a little flour on the bottom of the frying-pan, let it brown,
then pour in some of the stock in
which the fry was boiled; season
to taste. Serve the fry with a little
of the gravy poured round and
serve the rest separately.

6 helpings

Pig's Head

BOILED PIG'S HEAD

A pig's head   salt

Clean the head thoroughly.
Remove the hair, eyes, snout and
brains if this has not been done
by the butcher. Soak well in salt
water for 2 hr., changing the water
3 or 4 times. Drain the head well,
place in a large saucepan and just
cover with cold water. Simmer for
3–3½ hr. or until tender.

Pig's Liver
FAGGOTS or "SAVOURY DUCKS"

1 lb. pig's liver or fry   2 medium-sized onions   4 oz. fat pork
a pinch of thyme   ½ teasp.
powdered sage   a pinch of basil
salt and pepper   a pinch of grated
nutmeg   1 egg   breadcrumbs
a pig's caul

Slice the liver, onions and pork thinly. Put in a saucepan with the thyme, sage, basil, salt, pepper and nutmeg and barely cover with water. Simmer for ½ hr., then strain off the liquid and save for the gravy. Mince the contents of the stewpan finely. Add the beaten egg and sufficient breadcrumbs to make into a fairly firm mixture and mix thoroughly. Form into balls and enclose each one in a piece of caul. Place in a baking-tin, and add a little gravy. Bake in a fairly hot oven (400° *F.*, *Gas* 6) until nicely browned. Serve with a good thickened gravy. If preferred, the mixture can be pressed into a well-greased baking-tin and marked into squares. Cover with caul and cut into squares after cooking.

6 helpings

SAUSAGES—to make
1 lb. pork   1 lb. lean veal

1 lb. beef suet   ½ lb. breadcrumbs
grated rind of ½ lemon   ⅛ teasp.
grated nutmeg   salt and pepper
6 sage leaves (optional)   ⅛ teasp.
marjoram (optional)   ¼ teasp.
savoury herbs (optional)   sausage skins

Remove all the skin and gristle from the pork. Chop or mince the pork, veal and suet together very finely. Add the breadcrumbs, lemon rind, nutmeg, seasoning and the herbs if desired, which must all be very finely chopped. Mix together very thoroughly and then put into skins. Alternatively, the mixture may be formed into meat cakes, floured and fried.

SAUSAGES—to boil

Prick the sausages with a fork, throw them into boiling water, and cook gently for 15 min. Serve on hot buttered toast or mashed potato.

SAUSAGES—to fry

Prick the sausages well with a fork, as this prevents the skins breaking. Put into a frying-pan containing a little hot fat and fry gently, turning 2 or 3 times, to brown them equally.

Serve on hot buttered toast or with mashed potatoes.

VEAL

ONCE the preceding facts about beef, pork and lamb have been acquired there is little that needs to be added on veal. The carcase is only sparsely fatted in all except the largest calves and even in these there is not the same percentage of fat as would be found on other meat. The flesh is usually described as pink but the colour is darker than that of pork. The cuts follow the same pattern as lamb cutting and are described by the same names. Occasionally the shoulder is called an *oyster of veal* after the fore knuckle has been removed.

The meat from the hind and fore knuckles, equivalent to the shin and leg of beef together with the scrag and middle neck are used for stewing. All the other cuts are suitable for roasting or frying. Due to the absence of fat, veal is rather dry and tasteless unless cooked with a moist, fat-containing stuffing, or served with a sauce. The breast, stuffed and roasted, is probably the most tasty and the most economical cut.

BRAISED NECK OF VEAL

2½ lb. best end of neck of veal
1½ oz. fat   2 oz. bacon   2 onions
2 carrots   1 small turnip   bouquet
garni   2 cloves   1 blade of mace
12 peppercorns   salt and pepper
stock   ¾ oz. flour   meat glaze
1 tablesp. capers
1 teasp. lemon juice

Detach the short pieces of rib bones which have been sawn across and fold the flap under. Melt ¾ of the fat in the stewpan and fry the bacon and vegetables slightly. Add the bouquet garni, cloves, mace, peppercorns, and seasoning, nearly cover with stock and bring slowly to the boil. Place the meat on the bed of vegetables, cover with greased paper and a well-fitting lid and cook gently for about 2 hr., adding more stock as necessary and basting occasionally. Then place in a moderate oven (350° F., Gas 4) for ½ hr., removing the lid for the last 15 min. Meanwhile melt the remaining ¾ oz. fat in a small pan, add the flour and fry gently until nut brown. When the meat is tender, remove to a hot dish, brush over with glaze and keep hot. Strain the liquid, add to the brown roux and stir until smooth. Add more stock if necessary and simmer for 5 min. Add the capers and lemon juice, season to taste and serve separately. Garnish the meat with the vegetables and serve very hot.

6 helpings

CURRIED VEAL

1½ lb. lean veal   2½ oz. butter or
margarine   2 onions   2 apples
1 clove of garlic (optional)   1 oz.
flour   1-2 heaped teasp. curry
powder   1½ pt. light stock or
coconut infusion   2 heaped teasp.
curry paste   2 heaped teasp. chutney
salt   6 oz. rice   2 heaped teasp.
redcurrant jelly   lemon juice
cayenne pepper

GARNISH
Chilli skins or paprika pepper
sliced gherkin   crimped slices of
lemon   parsley

Trim, wipe and cut the meat into 1-in. cubes. Heat the fat and fry the meat lightly until sealed and lightly browned. Then remove. Fry the finely chopped onions and apples and the minced garlic for about 7 min. without browning too much. Add the flour and curry powder to the apple and cook for at least 5 min. to get rid of the raw flavour. Add the stock or coconut infusion, curry paste, chutney and salt and whilst stirring bring slowly to the boil. Return the meat to the pan and simmer very slowly for about 2 hr., stirring occasionally. Cook the rice and arrange as a border on a hot dish and keep hot. Add to the curry the redcurrant jelly, lemon juice, cayenne pepper to taste and place in the centre of the dish. Garnish with chilli skins or paprika pepper, gherkin, lemon and parsley.

NOTE: Curry can be served with any of the following accompaniments: poppadums; slices of hard-boiled egg; cubes of cucumber in coconut milk; green olives; Bombay duck; shredded coconut; cubes of salted almonds; sliced banana; variety of chutneys; fresh melon; chillies; silver onions; guava jelly; preserved ginger; diced pineapple.

6 helpings

To make coconut infusion

Add 1½ pt. boiling water to 2 heaped tablesp. coconut. Infuse for 15–20 min., strain and use as stock.

ESCALLOPS OF VEAL— VIENNESE STYLE

1¼–1½ lb. fillet of veal cut in 6 slices   salt and pepper   flour
egg and breadcrumbs   oil or butter for frying   lemon juice

BEURRE NOISETTE
2 oz. butter   salt and pepper
cayenne pepper

GARNISH
6 stoned olives   6 boned anchovy fillets   1 hard-boiled egg
1 tablesp. chopped parsley
crimped slices of lemon

Wipe the meat, season, dip in flour and coat with egg and breadcrumbs. Heat the oil or butter and fry the escallops for about 5 min. until golden brown. Make the beurre noisette by heating the butter in a saucepan until golden brown, then seasoning with salt, pepper and cayenne. Place the escallops slightly overlapping on a hot dish. Sprinkle with lemon juice and pour over the beurre noisette. Garnish with olives wrapped in anchovy fillets. Place the chopped egg white, sieved egg yolk and chopped parsley at either end of the dish. Serve with crimped lemon slices.

6 helpings

FILLETS OF VEAL

1¼–1½ lb. fillet of veal   1 egg
½ teasp. finely-chopped parsley
¼ teasp. thyme   2 teasp. grated lemon rind   1 teasp. lemon juice
breadcrumbs   2 oz. butter or fat
bacon rolls   mashed potatoes

SAUCE
½ oz. flour   ½ pt. white stock
½ teasp. lemon juice   a little gravy browning   salt and pepper
1–2 tablesp. cream (optional)

Cut the veal into slices about ½ in. thick, then cut each slice into rounds of about 2¼–2½ in. diameter. Beat with a wooden spoon or rolling-pin. Beat the egg and add to it the parsley, thyme, lemon rind and lemon juice. Soak the fillets in this mixture for about ½ hr., then coat with crumbs. Fry in the hot fat until golden brown on both sides, then reduce heat and cook more slowly for 7–10 min. in all. Drain thoroughly and keep hot together with the fried or grilled bacon rolls. To make the sauce, add the flour and the fat remaining in the pan and fry lightly. Add the stock, stir until it boils; then add the lemon juice, gravy browning and seasoning and simmer for 3 min. Add the cream, if liked. Serve the fillets in a circle on a border of mashed potatoes, pile the bacon rolls in the centre and pour the strained sauce round.

6 helpings

FLADGEON OF VEAL

¾ lb. lean veal   ¼ lb. suet   3 oz. breadcrumbs   1 teasp. finely-grated lemon rind   pinch of nutmeg salt and pepper   2 eggs   gravy or milk   ¼ pt. stock   parsley

Finely mince the veal and suet and mix with the breadcrumbs, lemon rind, nutmeg and seasoning to taste. Stir in 1 egg and as much gravy or milk as is required to thoroughly moisten the mixture. Half-fill a greased pie-dish with the mixture and bake for 1 hr. in a fairly hot oven (375° F., *Gas* 5). Beat up the other egg, add stock, seasoning to taste, and pour over the contents of the pie-dish. Bake until set. Garnish with parsley and serve in the dish.

4 helpings

LARDED AND ROAST VEAL

2½–3 lb. neck of veal   larding bacon 2 carrots   1 onion   1 small turnip 2 sticks of celery   salt and pepper bouquet garni   10 peppercorns stock   fat for basting   1 oz. butter or margarine   1 oz. flour

Fold the flap of the joint under if not already done. Lard the upper surface in close rows with thin 1½-in. strips of bacon. Slice the carrots, onion, turnip and celery and place in a saucepan with the salt, bouquet garni, peppercorns and enough stock barely to cover the vegetables. Lay the meat on top, cover with greased paper, put on the lid and cook gently for 2 hr., adding more stock when necessary. Heat some dripping in a baking-tin, put the meat in, baste well and bake in a moderate oven (350° F., *Gas* 4) for

½ hr., basting after 15 min. Have ready a brown roux made from the 1 oz. fat and flour, add ¾ pt. of stock from the saucepan and stir until boiling. Then simmer for 5 min. and season to taste. Serve the meat on a hot dish and serve the sauce separately.

6 helpings

POT PIE OF VEAL

1½ lb. lean veal   ½ lb. pickled pork salt and pepper   stock   1 lb. potatoes   puff or rough puff pastry using 6 oz. flour, etc.

Cut the meat into pieces convenient for serving and cut the pork into thin, small slices. Place the meat and pork in layers in a large pie-dish, seasoning each layer well with salt and pepper, and fill the dish ¾ full with stock. Cover with a lid and cook in a moderate oven (350° F., *Gas* 4) for 1½ hr. Meanwhile parboil the potatoes and cut in thick slices. After cooking for 1½ hr., allow the meat to cool slightly. Add more stock if necessary, place the potatoes on top, cover with pastry and make a hole in the top. Bake in a very hot oven (450° F., *Gas* 8) until the pastry is set, reduce heat and cook more slowly for the remainder of the time, making 40–50 min. altogether. Add more hot stock through the hole in the top. Garnish with parsley and serve.

6 helpings

RAGOUT OF VEAL

2½ lb. neck, breast or knuckle of veal   1½ oz. dripping   1 onion hot water   salt and pepper   1½ oz. butter or fat   1½ oz. flour

GARNISH
2 carrots   2 turnips   chopped parsley   bacon rolls

Cut the meat into pieces convenient for serving. Heat the dripping in a saucepan, fry the meat until lightly browned, then re-move it. Fry the sliced onion for a few minutes, then drain off the surplus fat. Return the meat to the saucepan, cover with hot water and add seasoning. Cover with a lid and cook slowly until a pale brown colour. Meanwhile dice the vegetables for the garnish and add the trimmings to the meat. Cook the diced vegetables separately, strain, then toss in a little butter. Add the chopped parsley and keep hot. When pale brown, remove the meat and keep hot. Strain the liquid in the saucepan and make up to $\frac{3}{4}$ pt. with water, if necessary. Add to it the blended fat and flour and cook and stir for 4 min. Season to taste, return the meat and sim-mer gently for $\frac{1}{2}$ hr. Garnish with grilled bacon rolls and the diced vegetables.

6 helpings

STEWED BREAST OF VEAL

2½ lb. breast of veal   2 onions
2 small carrots   1 small turnip
12 peppercorns   salt   1 pt. parsley
sauce or piquant sauce

Wipe the meat and place in a pan with as much cold water as will cover it. Bring to the boil and skim. Add the vegetables, cut into dice, peppercorns and salt to taste. Cover with a well fitting lid and simmer gently for 2½–3 hr. Pre-pare the sauce, using some of the veal stock. Place the veal on a hot dish, pour over sufficient sauce to cover the meat and serve the re-mainder in a sauce-boat.

6 helpings

STEWED KNUCKLE OF VEAL

A large knuckle of veal   1 onion
1 carrot   ½ turnip   2 sticks of celery
bouquet garni   salt and pepper
1½–2 oz. rice   1 pt. parsley sauce

GARNISH
Boiled bacon, ham or bacon rolls
grilled or fried   slices of lemon

Wipe the meat, separate the shank bone and put it with the meat into a saucepan with enough water to cover. Bring to the boil, skim well, add the vegetables cut into dice, the bouquet garni and salt. The ham or bacon for the garnish should be boiled separate-ly and served on a separate dish. Simmer the veal gently until tender—about 3 hr.—add the washed rice ½ hr. before serving. Remove the meat from the broth and keep it hot. Take out the bones and bouquet garni, season the broth to taste, and serve it separately. Pour a little parsley sauce over the meat and serve the rest in a sauce-boat. If boiled bacon is not being served, garnish with bacon rolls and slices of lemon.

6 helpings

VEAL CUTLETS

1½ lb. fillet or neck of veal   2 eggs
or 1 egg and milk   1 teasp. finely-chopped parsley   ¼ teasp. powdered thyme   ½ teasp. finely-grated lemon rind   salt and pepper   ½ oz. butter
breadcrumbs
butter or fat for frying

GARNISH
Parsley   slices of lemon

Cut the meat in slices about ½ in. thick and trim into neat fillets. Beat the eggs, or egg and milk, and mix with the parsley, thyme, lemon rind, seasoning and ½ oz. melted butter. Brush the cutlets with this mixture and coat care-fully with breadcrumbs. Fry in hot butter or fat for about 10–15 min. Fry both sides quickly first, then cook more slowly, turning as re-quired until golden brown. Drain well and place on a hot dish. Garnish with parsley and slices of lemon. Serve with tomato, demi-glace or piquant sauce, or gravy.

6 helpings

VEAL OLIVES

1½ lb. fillet of veal   8 thin bacon
rashers   4–6 oz. veal forcemeat
1½ oz. butter or fat
1 pt. brown sauce

GARNISH
Mashed potatoes   green peas
slices of lemon   spinach purée

Prepare the veal and cut it into
8 thin slices about 4 in. by 3 in.
and season. Place a slice of bacon
on each piece of meat and spread
with a thin layer of forcemeat.
Then roll up tightly and fasten
securely with fine string. Heat the
fat in a saucepan and fry the rolls
(olives) until lightly browned.
Pour off the surplus fat and add
the hot brown sauce to the olives.
Cover and simmer gently for
about 1½ hr. When tender, remove the string and place the
olives on a bed of mashed potato
and pour the sauce over. Garnish
with green peas and slices of lemon
and serve with spinach purée.

6 helpings

VEAL PARISIAN

1½ lb. fillet of veal   salt and pepper
2 tablesp. olive oil   1 tablesp.
finely-chopped onion   ¾ pt. Madeira
sauce.   1 dessertsp. chopped parsley
croûtons of fried bread
Parisian potatoes

Wipe, trim and cut the meat
into neat fillets. Season well. Heat
the oil and fry the fillets lightly.
Fry the chopped onion lightly.
Then add the sauce and cook
gently for ½–¾ hr. until the meat
is tender. Add the chopped parsley
and arrange on a hot dish. Serve
with croûtons of fried bread and
Parisian potatoes.

6 helpings

Calves' Brains
CALVES' BRAIN CAKES

2 calves' brains   2 small onions
pinch of sage   salt and pepper

1–2 teasp. lemon juice or vinegar
8 peppercorns   1 bay leaf   fat
2–3 eggs   breadcrumbs   parsley

Wash the brains under running
cold water or in several changes of
water, and remove any clots of
blood, loose skin and fibres. Then
soak in cold water for at least 1 hr.,
changing the water 2 or 3 times.
Put the brains in a saucepan, cover
with cold water, and add the
sliced onions, sage, salt, lemon
juice or vinegar. Add the peppercorns and bay leaf tied in muslin.
Bring to the boil and simmer for
about 10 min. or until firm. Remove the muslin bag and allow the
mixture to cool. Chop the brains,
add seasoning to taste and sufficient beaten egg to bind the ingredients. Stir well over a low
heat until the mixture thickens.
Then spread on a plate in the form
of a large round cake and allow to
cool. When cold divide into equal
small portions and form each into
a cake. Coat with egg and breadcrumbs and fry in hot fat until
light golden brown. Drain well and
serve on a hot dish garnished with
parsley.

6 helpings

Calves' Kidneys
CALVES' KIDNEYS—STEWED

3 calves' kidneys   seasoned flour
1 onion   2 oz. butter or dripping
6 mushrooms   ½ pt. stock or gravy
1 tablesp. sherry (optional)   salt
and pepper   1 dessertsp. finely-
chopped parsley
croûtons of fried bread or pastry

Wash the kidneys well, remove
any skin and cut out the cores with
scissors. Soak in tepid salt water
for 10–15 min. Wash well in clear
tepid water. Cut the kidneys in
halves lengthwise. Cut each half
into slices about ⅛ in. thick and
toss in seasoned flour. Chop the
onion finely, heat the fat and cook
it until lightly coloured. Then add

the sliced mushrooms and prepared kidney and cook quickly
until browned. Pour off any surplus fat and add the stock or
gravy, the sherry (if used) and seasoning. Stir until boiling and
simmer very gently for ½ hr. Add
the chopped parsley, stir well and
serve on a hot dish. Garnish with
croûtons of fried bread or pastry.

6 helpings

Calf's Liver

CALF'S LIVER AND SAVOURY RICE

1½ lb. calf's liver   1½ oz. butter or
margarine   1 onion   2 cloves of
garlic (optional)   6 oz. Patna rice
¾ pt. well-flavoured white stock
salt and pepper   ¼–½ teasp.
powdered saffron   seasoned flour
butter or oil for frying
½ pt. brown sauce
juice of ½ lemon or 2 tablesp. wine

GARNISH
Fried or grilled bacon rolls
paprika   green peas

Wash the liver well in tepid salt
water, remove any skin and tubes
and dry well. Heat 1 oz. of the fat
in a saucepan and sauté the finely
chopped onion and garlic without
colouring it. Add the well-washed
rice, mix well and cook for a few
minutes. Add the stock, seasoning
and saffron and cook very slowly
for about ¼–¾ hr. on top of the
cooker, or in the oven until the rice
is tender and has absorbed all the
stock. Add the remaining fat, mix
well and press well into a border
mould or 6 individual moulds. Put
aside until set. Slice the liver
finely, dip in seasoned flour and fry
in a little butter or oil. Drain well.
Bring the brown sauce to the boil,
add the lemon juice or wine and
the liver and heat. Turn the rice
on to a hot dish and heat in the
oven. Place the liver and sauce in
the centre (if a border mould) or

round the rice, and garnish with
grilled or fried bacon rolls, paprika
and peas.

6 helpings

Calves' Sweetbreads

BRAISED SWEETBREADS

2 calves' heart sweetbreads   1 oz.
fat   1 small onion   1 small carrot
½ small turnip   bouquet garni
6 peppercorns   salt and pepper
¾ pt. stock   croûte of fried bread

Prepare the sweetbreads as follows: wash and soak in cold water
for 1–2 hr. until free from blood.
Put into a pan, cover with cold
water, bring to boil and simmer
for 3–5 min., then plunge into
cold water. Discard fat and skin
and any gristle. Press between
two plates to retain shape.
Melt the fat in a stewpan or
meat-tin, add the sliced vegetables
and fry for about 10 min., then add
the bouquet garni, peppercorns,
salt and pepper and almost cover
with stock. Place the sweetbreads
on top of the vegetables and cover
with greased greaseproof paper.
Bring to the boil, baste the sweetbreads well and cook in a moderate
oven (350° F., Gas 4) for about 1
hr. with the lid on. Add more stock
as necessary and baste occasionally. Meanwhile cut a croûte of
bread 2 in. thick and fry until
golden brown. Drain well. Place
the croûte on a hot dish with the
sweetbreads on top.

6 helpings

VARIATIONS
1. Brush the sweetbreads with
glaze or tomato sauce and serve
with peas or a macédoine of vegetables.
2. Serve with Italian sauce and
mushrooms.
3. Serve with mushrooms
cooked in sauce Suprême, peas,
haricot beans or a macédoine of
vegetables.

FRIED SWEETBREADS

2 calves' sweetbreads 1 pt. white stock ; or water with vegetables to flavour salt and pepper egg and breadcrumbs butter or deep fat parsley

Method 1. Prepare and blanch the sweetbreads as directed for Braised Sweetbreads. Place the sweetbreads in a saucepan, with the stock, seasoning if required, and simmer gently for 40 min. Press between 2 plates until cold, then cut into slices. Brush with beaten egg and coat with breadcrumbs. Fry in butter in a shallow pan or in a pan of hot deep fat until golden brown. Drain well and garnish with sprigs of fresh or fried parsley.

Method 2. After blanching, boil the sweetbreads in slightly salted water for 10 min. and allow to cool. Cut into $\frac{1}{4}$-in.-thick slices and season. Coat both sides with thick Béchamel sauce ($\frac{1}{2}$ pt.). Place in a refrigerator or cool place until the sauce is set. Then fry as before.

Method 3. After coating the sweetbreads with thick Béchamel sauce (*see above*) they may be covered with batter, then fried. Drain well, sprinkle with salt and pepper and pile on a hot dish. Garnish with parsley.

6 helpings

COLD DISHES AND POTTED MEATS

Beef
GALANTINE OF BEEF

1 lb. good stewing steak $\frac{1}{2}$ lb.
bacon 6 oz. breadcrumbs salt
and pepper 1 egg $\frac{1}{4}$ pt. stock
raspings or meat glaze and a little
butter or aspic jelly

Cut the steak and bacon into
very small pieces. Add the breadcrumbs, season liberally and mix
well together. Beat the egg, add to
it the stock and stir into the dry
ingredients. Shape the mixture into
a short thick roll and tie tightly
in a greased cloth in a good shape.
Boil gently in stock, or in water
with vegetables added for flavour,
for about 2 hr., or, if preferred,
steam for 2½–3 hr. When cooked,
tightly retie in a dry cloth and
press until cold. Before serving,
roll in raspings or brush over with
dissolved meat glaze and decorate
with creamed butter or chopped
aspic jelly.
6 helpings

POTTED BEEF

2 lb. lean beef a pinch of
powdered cloves a pinch of
powdered mace a good pinch of
powdered allspice salt and pepper
$\frac{1}{2}$–1 teasp. anchovy essence
clarified butter

Wipe, trim and cut the meat
into small pieces. Put into a stone
jar or casserole with 1 tablesp.
water, the cloves, mace, allspice,
salt and pepper. Cover with several
thicknesses of greased paper and a
lid and place in a pan of boiling
water, or in the oven in a tin of

boiling water. Cook gently for
about 3 hr., replenishing the water
as it reduces. Then pound the
meat well, adding juice from the
meat and a few drops of anchovy
essence by degrees. Season to taste,
rub through a fine wire sieve, press
into pots and cover with melted
clarified butter.

PRESSED BEEF

Salt brisket of beef 1 onion
1 carrot $\frac{1}{2}$ turnip bouquet garni
10 peppercorns meat glaze

Weigh the meat. Wash it well,
or if very salt soak for about 1 hr.
in cold water. Put into cold water
and bring slowly to boiling-point.
Skim well. Cut the prepared vegetables into large pieces, add to the
meat with the bouquet garni and
peppercorns, and simmer gently,
allowing 25 min. per lb. and 25
min. over. Take the meat out, remove the bones and press between
2 boards or dishes until cold.
Then brush over with meat glaze.

POTTED OX TONGUE

1 cooked ox tongue 3 oz. clarified
butter to each 1 lb. of tongue
powdered mace cloves nutmeg
cayenne pepper salt and pepper
extra clarified butter

Chop the tongue finely, then
pound it well. Add gradually the
clarified butter in the proportion
stated above and the flavourings
and seasoning to taste. When the
mixture is reduced to a moist
smooth paste, rub through a fine
sieve, press into pots and cover
with melted clarified butter.

SAVOURY ROLLED OX TONGUE

1 pickled ox tongue   bouquet garni
2 onions stuck with 2 cloves
2 sliced carrots   1 sliced turnip
aspic jelly

Wash the tongue, put into tepid water and bring slowly to the boil. Skim well and add the herbs, onions, carrots and turnip. Simmer gently until tender, allowing 3–4 hr., according to size. Skim when necessary. When cooked, the tip of the tongue should be easily pierced with a metal skewer. Plunge the tongue into cold water and remove the skin. Trim the root, reserving the edible parts. Roll up the tongue and put into a greased cake-tin. Place the trimmings in the centre and leave with a weighted dish on top. When cold, pour on enough cold, liquid aspic to fill the tin. Turn out carefully when set and garnish with salad.

6 helpings

Lamb

COLD LAMB CUTLETS

Lamb cutlets   salt and pepper
aspic jelly   cooked peas and beans
mayonnaise or French salad
dressing   lettuce

Prepare the cutlets by trimming to a neat uniform shape. Beat them with a cutlet bat or rolling-pin. Then season with salt and pepper and cook either by grilling, or by frying in smoking hot oil or fat, or by braising. Grilling or frying are more simple methods, but braising is recommended because of the fine flavour imparted by this method of cooking. Press between 2 dishes with a weight on top until quite cold. Dissolve the aspic and pour a ⅓ into a sauté pan or large dish rinsed out with cold water. Allow to set. Brush the cutlets with cold, liquid aspic and lay them about ½ in. apart on the jelly with the bones all curving the same way.

Pour the remaining jelly gently over and leave to set. Then turn out on to a sheet of greaseproof paper rubbed with ice. With a sharp knife, dipped in hot water, cut out the cutlets and arrange them in a circle on a round dish, with the bones pointing to the inside of the circle. Fill up the centre with the cooked vegetables mixed with mayonnaise or French dressing. Shredded lettuce may be arranged outside the circle of cutlets. Garnish with neatly cut cubes of aspic or small piles of chopped aspic.

Mutton

CHAUFROID OF MUTTON CUTLETS

6 cutlets from the best end of neck
mirepoix   salt and pepper   6 oz.
liver farce   ½ oz. gelatine   ⅓ pt.
Béchamel sauce   ⅓ pt. tomato sauce

Braise the neck as directed for Braised Mutton Cutlets. When cold, cut into neat cutlets and remove all the surplus fat. Season on both sides with salt and pepper. Cover one side of the cutlets with a thin layer of liver farce. Carefully dissolve the gelatine in 2 tablesp. cold water and divide equally between the Béchamel and tomato sauces, which should be warm when the gelatine is added. Cool the sauces slightly, then coat the covered sides of the cutlets, making ½ red and the other ½ white. Leave in a cool place until set, then arrange in a circle in alternate colours and place a frill on each cutlet. Serve with dressed salad in the centre.

NOTE: Other sauces may be used in place of those mentioned above—brown sauce instead of Béchamel and Green Chaudfroid Sauce as a substitute for tomato.

Noisettes of mutton may also be served in this way.

6 helpings
Time—2 hr.

Pork

BRAWN

A pig's head weighing about 6 lb.
2 tablesp. salt   ¼ teasp. powdered
cloves   ⅛ teasp. powdered mace
1½ lb. lean beef   1 teasp. pepper
1 onion

Clean the head well and soak in
water for 2 hr. Place in a saucepan with the rest of the ingredients
and almost cover with cold water.
Boil for about 3 hr. or until quite
tender. Take out the head and
remove all the flesh. Put the bones
back into the liquid and boil
quickly until well reduced so that
it will form a jelly when cold.
Roughly chop the meat with a
sharp knife, work quickly to prevent the fat settling in and put
into a wet mould, basin or cake-
tin. Pour some of the hot liquid
over the meat through a strainer.
Leave until quite cold and turn
out when set.

The liquor in which the meat
was cooked will make excellent
soup, and the fat, if skimmed off
and clarified well, will answer the
purposes of lard.

GALANTINE OF PORK

1½ lb. belly pork (preferably salted)
salt and pepper   gherkins   stock or
water with 2 onions, 1 carrot and
½ turnip   meat glaze (optional)
parsley (optional)

Season the inside of the meat
well with salt and pepper and arrange thin slices of gherkin all
over it. Roll up tightly and secure
with string, then secure tightly in
a cloth. Just cover with stock or
water and vegetables and simmer
gently for about 3 hr. When
cooked, press between 2 dishes
until cold, then remove the cloth.

The meat may be brushed with
glaze and served garnished with
parsley.

6 helpings

POTTED HAM

2 lb. lean ham   ½ lb. fat ham
¼ teasp. ground mace   ¼ teasp.
pepper   ¼ teasp. grated nutmeg
⅛ teasp. cayenne pepper
clarified butter

Pass the ham through a mincing
machine 2 or 3 times or chop
very finely. Then pound well and
rub through a fine sieve. Add
gradually the mace, pepper, nutmeg and cayenne and mix well
together. Put into a well greased
pie-dish, and cover with greased
greaseproof paper. Bake in a
moderate oven (350° F., Gas 4)
for about ¾ hr. When cooked,
press into small pots and cover
with clarified butter.

Cooking time—about ¾ hr.

Veal

PRESSED VEAL

A breast of veal   salt and pepper
1 large onion   a few sticks of
celery or ¼ teasp. celery seeds
1 carrot   ½ turnip   bouquet garni
10 peppercorns

Wipe the meat and remove the
skin, bones and gristle. Trim the
meat neatly, season well, roll up
tightly and tie with string. Slice
the onion, celery, carrot and turnip
and put into a saucepan with the
bones and trimmings, bouquet
garni, peppercorns and salt and
put the meat on top. Add water
to the depth of the vegetables.
Cover the meat with greased
paper, put on the lid and cook
gently for 3 hr., basting occasionally. When the meat is tender,
place it between 2 dishes or boards
with weights on top, until quite
cold. Strain the stock and on the
following day boil rapidly until
reduced to a glaze. Add colouring
if liked. Trim the meat and brush
it over with the glaze.

RAISED VEAL, PORK AND EGG PIE (Plate 5)

Hot water crust pastry (p. 341) using 12 oz. flour, etc.   1 lb. stewing veal   1 lb. lean stewing pork   1 oz. flour   1½ level teasp. salt   ¼ level teasp. pepper   3 hard-boiled eggs   ½ pt. (approx.) seasoned stock from veal and pork bones.

Grease a 7-in. tin with lard. Make the pastry and, when cool enough to handle, knead well. Cut off a quarter of the dough and keep this covered in a warm place until required. Roll out remaining dough to a round 2 in. wider than the base of the tin. Line the tin with the dough, working up the sides with the fingers.

Cut the meat into small pieces, removing any gristle and fat. Mix together the flour, salt and pepper and toss the pieces of meat in this. Put half the meat into the pastry case and put in the peeled eggs. Add the remainder of the meat and 2 tablesp. water. Roll out the remaining piece of pastry to a round slightly larger than the top of the tin. Damp the edges and cover the pie. Pinch the edges. Brush with beaten egg. Bake for 15 min. in a very hot oven (450° F., Gas 8), then reduce heat to very cool (290° F., Gas 1), and continue cooking for 2½ hr. The bones from the veal and pork should meanwhile be cooked with a little water in a covered saucepan or casserole in the oven while the pie is cooking. When the pie is cooked it should be filled with the seasoned stock from the bones. Allow to cool completely before serving.

Individual pies. If preferred, the above amounts may be made into 6 individual pies. The egg should be cut into small pieces for the smaller pies.

VEAL AND HAM PIE

¾ lb. sliced York ham   ¾ lb. fillet of veal   2 hard-boiled eggs   ½ teasp. mixed herbs   ½ teasp. pepper   ¼ teasp. ginger and nutmeg (mixed together)   jelly stock   ½ lb. puff pastry

Line a pie-dish with slices of ham. Fill with small slices of ham and ¼-in.-thick slices of the veal fillet. With each layer place thick slices of the eggs and sprinkle with the mixed herbs and seasoning. When the dish is filled moisten with the stock, cover with puff pastry and cook in a medium oven until the pastry is just browned. Remove and cook slowly on a low heat for a further 15 min. When cold pierce the crust in 2 places and fill with stock to replace that which has evaporated. Allow to set, serve cold.

VEAL CAKE or VEAL MOULD

1 lb. lean fillet of veal   ½ lb. lean bacon   2 hard-boiled eggs   1 teasp. finely-chopped parsley   2 teasp. finely-grated lemon rind   salt and pepper   ¾ pt. jellied veal stock   ¼ oz. gelatine (if required)   parsley or salad

Dice the veal and bacon. Cut the eggs into slices and arrange some of them in a pattern on the bottom of a greased mould. Mix the parsley, lemon rind and seasoning together. Place a thick layer of veal in the mould, cover with a thin layer of bacon, a layer of sliced egg and a layer of the parsley and lemon mixture. Repeat the layers until the mould is full. Pour in the jellied stock, cover with greased greaseproof paper and bake in a moderate oven (350° F., Gas 4) for 2–2½ hr. Fill up the mould with extra stock, adding ¼ oz. gelatine to ½ pt. stock if the stock is not stiff enough. When cold, turn out the mould and garnish with parsley or salad.

6 helpings

POULTRY

THERE is no bird, nor any bird's egg, that is known to be poisonous, though they may, and often do, become unwholesome because of the food that the birds eat, which at all times greatly changes the quality of the flesh, even in birds of the same breed.

Wild ducks and other aquatic birds are often rank and fishy-flavoured. Pigeons fatten and waste in the course of a few hours. The pronounced flavour of grouse is said to be due to the heather shoots on which they feed.

Age and Flavour of Chickens: The flesh of young chickens is the most delicate and easily assimilated of bird meats, which makes it especially suitable for invalids and people with weak digestion.

Few birds undergo so great a change with regard to the quality of their flesh as the domestic fowl. When quite young, cocks and hens are equally tender, but as chickens grow older the flesh of the cock is the first to toughen, and a cock over a year old is fit only for conversion into soup. A hen of the same age affords a substantial and palatable dish.

Birds of all sizes may now be obtained all the year round, so that a variety of recipes may be used, according to the bird chosen. The youngest birds may be called Baby Chicks, Spring Chickens or Squabs (French—*poussins, petits poulets*); these are usually grilled or fried and have a delicate flavour.

The birds likely to be the most popular in the average household are cockerels, roasting chickens and fowls and capons (French—*poulets de grain, poulets reine, poulardes, chapons*). These may be cooked in a number of ways, two of the most popular being roasting and braising.

Older birds used for boiling may also be an economical purchase for the housewife (French—*poules*).

To Choose Poultry: As a rule small-boned birds are an economical purchase; they should be plump and not devoid of fat.

When fresh, they should be free from any tainted smell, the eyes clear and not sunken, the feet limp and pliable. The legs should be soft and smooth, and the breastbone and wing-tips pliable. The signs of an old fowl are its stiff, horny-looking feet, long spurs, dark-coloured and hairy thighs, stiff beak and hard bones.

CHAPONS AND POULARDES: The male fowl, the capon (chapon), and the female bird, the poularde, are both, by treatment while young, made incapable of generating, with the result that their size is increased, and they become fatter than ordinary fowls. The flesh of these birds does not toughen with age, and even when three years old they are as tender as chicken—with a delicate flavour. The flavour of the poularde is considered more delicate than that of the capon (chapon), but the latter is the larger bird. They may be boiled, braised, roasted or otherwise prepared, according to the directions given for cooking chickens and fowls.

TURKEYS: These when young have smooth black legs and short spurs. The eyes of a fresh bird are bright and not sunken. Choose one which has a broad, plump breast and white flesh, the best being from seven to nine months old. The flesh of the hen is usually found to be more tender than the cock.

An old bird will have pale or reddish, rough legs, and the spurs will be long.

DUCKS: When young these usually have yellow feet and bills. The underbill should be so soft that it will bend back easily, and the webbing of the feet should be soft; the breast should be meaty. (French: duck—canard: duckling —caneton.)

GEESE: The signs of freshness in a goose are the same as those in a duck, and the former should still have some down on its legs. A gosling or green goose is one up to four months old.

DRESSING POULTRY (see plates 8 and 9)

Plucking: If a strong hook firmly fixed to a wall is available, plucking can be facilitated by tying the two feet of the bird together with strong string, and hanging the bird over the hook. Draw out one wing and pull out the under feathers, taking a few at a time. Work towards the breast and then down to the tail. Repeat on the other side. Small hairs may be singed away with a taper; burnt feathers, however, will impart an unpleasant flavour to the bird.

Drawing: Half-way along the neck, cut a ring round the outer skin and pull or cut off the head. Slip the knife under the skin and cut back towards the body. Holding the neck in a dry cloth, pull the skin loose. At the base of the neck cut through the meat and then, still holding the neck in a dry cloth, twist firmly round until it is detached from the body. (Keep the neck for stock.) Push the index finger into the crop cavity to loosen the crop and gizzard.

Turn the bird around and with a sharp knife cut the skin on the leg, place over a board or table edge and snap the bone. Grasp the foot in one hand and the thigh of the bird in the other and pull off the foot with the tendons. There should be 7 tendons.

To remove the viscera make a slit of about 2–3 in. above the vent, taking care not to cut into the rectal end of the gut. Insert the first two fingers of the right hand, knuckles upwards, and gently draw out the intestines. Several attempts will have to be made in the first instance to remove all the organs, including the crop, which has to be pulled with the gizzard from the neck end, out to the back of the bird. When they are free, trim the end of the intestines and the vent away. The liver can now be separated from the gall bladder, taking care not to break the latter. The meaty underside of the crop can be skinned or cut away from the gritty contents.

The lungs, which are bright red, lie close to the ribs. They are best removed by wrapping the index finger in a dry cloth and pushing in turn down from the back bone and out along each rib.

Burn the inedible waste, i.e. head, intestines, lungs, crop, feet, container of grit from the gizzard, etc., immediately. The giblets, i.e. the neck, gizzard, liver and heart should be kept away from the bird so that its flesh will not be discoloured.

Wipe the inside of the bird with a dry cloth. Do not wet it by washing unless the bird is to be cooked immediately.

Trussing: The object of trussing a bird is to ensure that when cooked it looks attractive. The easiest way to truss is with a needle, similar in size to a packing needle. When the bird is clean lay it down with the breast uppermost and away from you. Thread the needle and pass it through the left leg just above the thigh bone and near to the joint between the thigh and leg bone. (When the leg is folded down against the bird these two bones form a "V" shape with the apex of the "V" pointing towards the front of the bird.) Pass the needle on through the body, out the other side, and through the other leg joint. The legs should be pushed tight against the body during this operation.

The string should now be passing through the body and the leg joints. Leaving sufficient on either side, turn the bird breast downwards and carry the string through the elbow joint of the wing on each side, then twist the end of the wing under the neck of the bird to hold the neck flap of skin. The two ends may now be drawn together not too tightly and tied off. It now only remains to tie down the legs. This may simply be done by looping the string over the ends of the drumsticks and drawing them together, tying off round the tail end of the "parson's nose". To make this operation easier a slit may be cut in the flesh above the original vent cut and the "parson's nose" pushed through. The legs may also be tied down, using the needle on each leg end in turn. The packing needle and string can also usefully be used to repair any tears that have occurred during plucking or drawing. When trussed the skin should be as complete as possible in order to prevent the loss of fat from the bird during cooking, so resulting in over-dryness and an unpalatable meat.

Boning poultry and game: Birds are invariably plucked and singed before boning, but not drawn. The crop, however, should be removed, the wings and legs cut off at the first joint, and the tendons of the legs carefully drawn at the same time. To bone the bird, use a small sharp knife, and first remove the merry-thought at the neck. Cut the skin down the centre of the back and raise the flesh carefully on either side, sever the wing joints, and continue to detach the flesh, keeping the blade of the knife close to the bone. When the legs are reached, dislocate the joints, cut the connecting tendons, but leave both wings and legs intact until the breast and backbones have been removed, together with the viscera. Turn the body completely inside out; take the thigh bones of one of the legs in the left hand and strip the flesh downwards. Repeat this until all the small bones are removed. The bird may then be turned right side out again, when it will be found completely boned and should be quite whole.

Both large and small birds may be boned in this way. They are then stuffed, re-shaped and trussed, or rolled into gallantines.

Jointing poultry: See plate 7.

ACCOMPANIMENTS

ROAST CHICKEN: Thin brown gravy, bread sauce, bacon rolls, green salad, game chips, watercress to garnish, veal forcemeat stuffing.

ROAST DUCK: Thickened gravy, sage and onion stuffing, apple-cranberry- *or* orange-sauce, watercress to garnish.

ROAST WILD DUCK: Port wine- *or* orange-sauce *or* orange salad.

ROAST TURKEY: Thickened gravy, veal *or* chestnut stuffing, sausage-meat stuffing, bacon rolls, grilled sausages, bread- *or* cranberry sauce.

ROAST GOOSE: Thickened gravy, sage and onion stuffing, apple sauce.

GENERAL HINTS

(*a*) Chicken is stuffed at the neck-end, duck and goose are stuffed from the vent-end, turkey is stuffed with veal *or* chestnut stuffing in the crop and with sausage-meat stuffing in the body.

(*b*) Chickens and game birds may be roasted for a little while at the beginning of the cooking time, on the breast. This will make the breast-meat more moist. It should not be done with duck or goose. All birds should be roasted on a trivet, not resting in the tin in basting fat.

(*c*) Sufficient garnish should be served with each dish to provide some with each portion served. When dishes are to be served hot, the garnish must be ready in advance and arranged quickly. If the process takes time, the serving dish may be placed in a shallow tin of hot water to ensure that the food is served very hot.

(*d*) Frozen chickens or chicken portions can be utilized in many of the following recipes.

(*e*) The use of metal foils for cooking can be recommended (1) to ensure a tight-fitting lid when stewing or braising, (2) to wrap birds during roasting when a covered roaster is not available or proves too small. Before cooking is completed the foil should be turned back from the breast and legs of the bird to allow the skin to become crisp and brown.

(*f*) If a good stock is not available it may be produced quickly by using one of the reliable makes of consommé soup-mix now on the market.

(*g*) When the method of cooking is in a casserole or by stewing, some dry cider or dry wine may be substituted for some of the stock.

CHICKEN

BOILED CHICKEN

See recipe for Boiled Fowl.

CANNELONS OF CHICKEN

Chicken rissole mixture (p. 373)

rough puff pastry (p. 341) using 4 oz. flour, etc egg and breadcrumbs frying fat

Roll out pastry as thinly as possible. Cut into $1\frac{1}{2}$ in. squares. Place a little chicken mixture in centre of each square, roll up rather tightly. Coat with egg and fresh breadcrumbs, fry in hot, deep fat until golden brown, drain well. Serve very hot, garnished with parsley.

6–8 helpings
Cooking time—15 min.

CHICKEN A LA MARENGO

1 chicken $\frac{1}{4}$ pt. olive oil 1 pt. Espagnole sauce (p. 101) salt and pepper 2 ripe tomatoes $\frac{1}{2}$ glass sherry (optional) 1 doz. button mushrooms 6 stoned olives 1 truffle

GARNISH

Fleurons of pastry *or* croûtes of fried bread olives truffle mushrooms

Joint chicken (plate 7). Remove skin and excess fat. Fry joints in oil until golden brown, drain well, pour away oil. Heat Espagnole sauce with tomato pulp, add chicken, sherry (if used), whole olives and mushrooms, truffle in large pieces, and season. Simmer gently until chicken is tender—about $\frac{3}{4}$ hr.

Pile in centre of hot dish, strain sauce over and garnish. Place fleurons *or* croûtes round the dish.

6 helpings

CHICKEN CREAM

$\frac{1}{2}$ lb. raw chicken 1 egg $\frac{1}{8}$ pt. coating Béchamel sauce (p. 100) $\frac{1}{8}$ pt. double cream salt and pepper 1 pt. pouring Béchamel sauce

GARNISH

Truffles *or* mushrooms

Brush 1 large mould (approx. 5 in. diameter, 3–4 in. deep) with clarified butter. (Individual moulds may be used if preferred.)

Chop and pound chicken until smooth, add egg and coating sauce gradually, sieve, if desired, very smooth. Whip cream stiffly, fold into mixture, season. Put mixture into prepared mould, cover with buttered paper, steam gently until firm—25 to 30 min. Meanwhile, make 1 pt. Béchamel sauce. Dish the cream, pour some sauce over. Garnish with truffles or mushrooms. Serve remainder of sauce in a sauce-boat.

4 helpings

CHICKEN EN CASSEROLE

1 chicken   1 oz. flour   salt and
pepper   2 oz. butter or dripping
4–6 oz. streaky bacon   1 shallot
2 oz. chopped mushrooms
1 pt. stock

Joint the chicken, dip joints in flour and seasoning. Melt the fat in a casserole; fry the bacon, cut in strips; add chicken, mushrooms and chopped shallot. Fry until golden brown, turning when necessary. Add hot stock, sufficient just to cover the chicken, simmer until tender—about 1½ hr. Correct the seasoning. Serve in the casserole.

6 helpings

CHICKEN ESCALOPES

2 large raw chicken legs   ¼ lb. lean
veal and ¼ lb. bacon or ¾ lb.
sausage meat   6 mushrooms
1 truffle (optional)   salt and pepper
1 egg   3 oz. butter   1 onion
1 carrot   ½ small turnip   1 stick
celery   bouquet garni   1 pt. stock
1½ oz. flour   lemon juice
1 tablesp. sherry (optional)
spinach purée

Chop and pound veal and bacon until smooth. Add the diced mushrooms and truffle, season well, bind with egg. Bone chicken legs, stuff with farce, shape into rolls. Put 1½ oz. butter and the vegetables, sliced, into saucepan,

lay chicken legs on top; cover, fry gently for 20 min., add bouquet garni. Add stock to ¾ the depth of the vegetables; place a buttered paper over; put on lid, simmer gently for 1 hr. Meanwhile, melt remaining butter, stir in flour, cook very gently (about ½ hr.) until a brown roux is formed. Remove chicken legs when cooked, keep them hot. Gradually strain stock on to roux, stirring (or pour on rapidly, whisking at the same time). Bring to boiling-point, simmer 20 min.; add lemon juice and sherry; season to taste. Cut chicken legs into ½-in. slices, arrange slightly overlapping on bed of spinach; strain sauce over.

4–6 helpings
Cooking time—2 hr.

CHICKEN FORCEMEAT

½ lb. raw boneless chicken   1 oz.
butter   1 oz. flour   ½ gill stock
1 egg   salt and pepper   nutmeg

Melt the butter, stir in the flour, add stock (chicken stock if possible), boil 3–5 min., allow panada to cool. Chop and pound chicken, add egg and panada gradually, season well. Sieve, if required, very smooth.

NOTE: Before moulding or shaping the farce, test the consistency (it should not crack when handled and should retain an impression of the spoon). If necessary, soften with cream or milk.

Use for quenelles, cutlets, boudins, bombes, timbales.

CHICKEN MAYONNAISE

1 cold boiled chicken or fowl
½ pt. aspic jelly   ¾ pt. mayonnaise
sauce (p. 104)   truffle or pickled
walnut   chervil

Joint chicken (plate 7), remove skin and excess fat, and as much bone as possible. Trim joints to a neat shape. Melt aspic jelly; when almost cool, blend ¼ pt. carefully into mayonnaise. A smooth glossy sauce will be obtained by passing it through a tammy cloth (i.e. a piece of well-washed flannel). This is most easily done by twisting the ends of the cloth containing the sauce in opposite directions. Place the pieces of chicken on a wire cooling-tray, and mask them with the sauce when it is of a good coating consistency. Use a small ladle or tablespoon. Decorate when almost set with cut shapes of truffle (pickled walnut is cheaper, but must previously be drained on clean blotting-paper) and chervil *or* other colourful garnish. Mask with a thin layer of the remaining aspic jelly.

Arrange on a bed of dressed salad, *or* on a dish flooded with coloured aspic. Decorate the edge of the dish with endive, cucumber and blocks of aspic jelly, if liked.

6 helpings

CHICKEN PILAFF

1 chicken or fowl   3 pt. stock or 3 pt. water and 2 lb. scrag-end neck of mutton   2 large Spanish onions 1 carrot   1 blade mace   6 black peppercorns   4 oz. butter   6 oz. Patna rice   salt and pepper 1 tablesp. curry paste 2 small onions (shallots)

Joint the chicken (plate 7), put the backbone, giblets, bones and trimmings and stock (*or* water and the mutton cut into small pieces) into a saucepan; add outside layers of Spanish onions, carrot, mace and peppercorns. Simmer gently 2–3 hr., strain. Dice remainder of Spanish onions, fry in a saucepan until lightly browned in 2 oz. of the butter, add the washed and drained rice, 1½ pt. stock and seasoning. Cook gently until rice has absorbed stock. Fry chicken slowly in remaining butter until lightly brown, put into rice with curry paste and mix well, retaining the butter. Cook gently until chicken and rice are tender, adding

more stock if necessary. Cut small onions into rings, fry until golden brown in the butter in which the chicken was fried.

Pile the pilaff on a hot dish, pile rings of fried onion on top. Serve very hot.

6 helpings
Cooking time—about 1½ hr., excluding stock

CHICKEN RAMAKINS

6 oz. raw chicken   2 eggs   salt and pepper   2 mushrooms   1 truffle or extra mushrooms   2 tablesp. cream ½ oz. butter

Chop or mince chicken very finely, add egg yolks gradually, making mixture as smooth as possible. (Sieve if desired.) Season well. Add chopped mushrooms and truffle to the chicken mixture, lightly stir in half-whipped cream. Fold stiffly-beaten egg whites into mixture, add more liquid (milk) if stiff. Three-quarters fill 8 well-buttered china or paper ramakin cases with the mixture. Cook in a fairly hot oven (375° *F.*, *Gas* 5) 15–20 min. until well risen, firm and well browned. Serve at once.

8 helpings

CHICKEN SAUTE

See Chicken à la Marengo, p. 193, and Fried Fowl with Peas, p. 374.

CHICKEN SOUFFLE

½ lb. raw chicken meat   1½ oz. butter   1 egg yolk   salt and pepper 2 tablesp. cream   2 egg whites ½ pt. Béchamel sauce

Mince chicken finely, gradually add butter and egg yolk, season well, sieve if desired. Stir in half-whipped cream, fold in stiffly-beaten egg whites. Place in a well-buttered soufflé mould or straight-sided tin; cover with greased paper and steam gently and evenly 50–60 min. (Individual moulds 25 min.)

Turn out on to a hot dish, coat quickly with sauce. Garnish with mushrooms and serve at once.

6 helpings

CHICKEN SPATCHCOCK

**1 spring chicken   1 oz. butter
salt and pepper   bacon rolls**

Split the prepared bird in half, cutting through the back only, cut off the legs and wings at the first joints, flatten as much as possible and keep in shape with skewers. Brush with melted butter, season lightly and grill until flesh is cooked—about 20 min. Brush with more butter if necessary and turn frequently to ensure even browning.

Remove skewers, dish up, garnish with bacon rolls; serve with Tartare *or* Piquant sauce.

1–2 helpings

CHICKEN WITH MACARONI

**1 chicken   1½ pt. stock (approx.)
4 oz. macaroni   ¼ pt. tomato sauce
(p. 99)   ¼ pt. Espagnole sauce
(p. 101)   lemon juice *or* tarragon
vinegar   salt and pepper**

Truss the chicken (p. 191), boil until half-cooked, in stock (*or* water flavoured with vegetables). Put macaroni in boiling salted water and cook rapidly for 15–20 min., drain well, cut into short lengths. Heat sauces together, cut the chicken into convenient pieces for serving and put them in the sauce; add macaroni, lemon juice (*or* tarragon vinegar), season to taste, and simmer ½–¾ hr.

Place the macaroni in an entrée dish, pile chicken on top, strain sauce over and serve while hot.

6 helpings

CHICKEN WITH RICE AND TOMATOES

1 chicken   larding bacon   2 onions
**2 carrots   1 turnip   bouquet garni
(p. 68)   10 peppercorns   1½ pt.
stock (approx.)   ½ lb. rice   ¼ pt.
tomato purée
3 oz. grated Parmesan cheese**

Truss the chicken (p. 191), lard the breast closely (p. 36) or lay fat bacon over; wrap in greased paper. Cut vegetables into thick slices, place in pan with bouquet garni, peppercorns and sufficient stock to cover vegetables, not more. Put chicken on bed of vegetables, cover with a tightly-fitting lid, cook gently for about 1½ hr., until bird is tender, adding more stock if necessary. Wash and blanch rice; cook in good stock until tender and dry; then stir in tomato purée and cheese; season to taste. Remove paper and trussing strings from chicken; place in a hot oven (425°– 450° F., Gas 7–8) until bacon is crisp.

Serve in a border of the rice mixture.

6 helpings

CURRIED CHICKEN

**1 chicken   2 oz. butter   1 chopped
onion   1 dessertsp. flour   1 tablesp.
curry powder   1 dessertsp. curry
paste   ¾ pt. white stock   1 chopped
apple   1 dessertsp. chutney
1 tablesp. lemon juice   salt and
pepper   1 oz. sultanas   1 oz.
blanched almonds   1 dessertsp.
desiccated coconut
2 tablesp. cream *or* milk (optional)**

GARNISH

**Fans of lemon   gherkin fans
red pepper**

Divide chicken into neat joints, remove skin, fry joints lightly in hot butter, remove from saucepan and drain. Fry onion lightly, add flour, curry powder and paste, and fry very well, stirring occasionally. Stir in stock, bring to boil. Put in all other ingredients except the cream, put in chicken joints. Have the coconut tied in muslin, and remove after 15 min. Simmer gently about 1¼ hr., adding a little more stock if necessary. Dish the chicken, add the cream to the sauce and pour the sauce over the chicken, straining if liked. Garnish.

ACCOMPANIMENTS: Dry boiled Patna rice sprinkled with paprika pepper, mango chutney, Bombay Duck, poppadums, fresh grated coconut, gherkins and pickled pimentoes. These are served separately, not in the dish with the curry. Bombay Duck and poppadums are grilled before serving.

6 helpings

Cooking time—1¾ hr.

FONDUE OF CHICKEN

See Chicken Ramakins, p. 195.

FRICASSEE OF CHICKEN

1 boiled or 1 lb. can of chicken
1 pt. Velouté sauce   ½ gill cream or milk   1 egg   salt and pepper
juice of 1 lemon

GARNISH
Chopped parsley   sippets of fried bread, or potato border

Before chicken is quite cold, cut into joints, remove skin and excess fat. Make sauce, thoroughly heat chicken in it, add cream and egg, stir over a low heat until the sauce thickens (do not boil). Season, add lemon juice. Arrange chicken in entrée dish, strain sauce over and garnish.

NOTE: If a potato border is used, pipe or fork this into the dish, before arranging the chicken for serving.

6 helpings

Cooking time—20 min. (excluding sauce)

GRILLED CHICKEN—WITH MUSHROOM SAUCE

1 chicken   ½ pt. Espagnole sauce (p. 101)   1 can button mushrooms

salt and pepper   croûte of fried bread   ½ lb. lean raw ham   salad oil or butter for frying and grilling

GARNISH
Ham   mushrooms

Make Espagnole sauce, add mushrooms to it, correct seasoning and keep the sauce hot. Divide chicken into pieces convenient for serving, brush them with salad oil or oiled butter. Cut a slice of bread to fit the serving dish; fry this until lightly browned. Cut the ham into short strips and fry this. Grill prepared chicken until tender—about 15–20 min.

Pile chicken on the croûte, strain sauce round, and garnish.

4 helpings

Cooking time—about 30 min.

POTTED CHICKEN

Trimmings of cold roast chicken
3 oz. cooked ham   salt and pepper
nutmeg   2 oz. butter
clarified butter (p. 37)

Mince chicken and ham very finely, season well, add pinch of nutmeg, and work in butter gradually, making the mixture as smooth as possible. Press paste into small pots, cover contents with clarified butter.

RECHAUFFE OF CHICKEN

See Hashed Fowl, p. 374.

ROAST CHICKEN

1 roasting chicken   salt and pepper
2–3 rashers of bacon   ½ pt. stock
fat for basting

GARNISH
Bunches of clean watercress

Truss chicken for roasting, season lightly and cover with bacon. Roast on a trivet in the roasting tin in a fairly hot oven (375°–400° F., Gas 5–6) until tender, 1–1½ hr. Baste frequently. The chicken may be roasted on the breast for a little while at the beginning, this will make the breast-meat more moist. (Prick the thigh to test for tenderness—if there is any trace of blood the chicken is not cooked.) The bacon may be removed 10–15 min. before serving, to allow the breast to brown. When the chicken is cooked, place on a hot meat-dish, remove trussing string, and keep hot. Make the gravy: pour excess fat from roasting tin but retain sediment; pour in stock, boil 2–3 min. Season to taste, strain into a hot sauce-boat.

Have ready the watercress, washed, drained and lightly seasoned, garnish the chicken; serve with the gravy and bread sauce (p. 95). See also Accompaniments (p. 192).

ROAST CHICKEN—STUFFED WITH HERBS

1 chicken   1½ oz. butter   1 tablesp. chopped onion   2 tablesp. chopped carrot   1 oz. flour   ¾ pt. stock salt and pepper   1 glass white wine or cider (optional)   1 teasp. parsley 1 teasp. chervil   1 teasp. tarragon

FORCEMEAT

2 tablesp. breadcrumbs   1 teasp. each of chopped shallot, chopped tarragon, chopped parsley, and chopped chervil   salt and pepper liver from chicken 1 oz. oiled butter (approx.)

Remove gall bladder, wash and chop the liver finely. Mix the chopped liver with breadcrumbs, forcemeat, herbs, seasoning and sufficient oiled butter to moisten. Stuff the bird with forcemeat, truss for roasting. Roast in moderately hot oven (350°–375° F., Gas 4–5) until tender, 1–1½ hr., basting frequently. Melt 1½ oz. butter in a saucepan; fry onion and carrot lightly, stir in flour, cook gently until lightly browned. Stir in stock, boil until cooked, add seasoning and wine (if used) together with

1 teasp. each of parsley, chervil, tarragon or other herbs, as liked. Simmer sauce gently ¼ hr. Remove trussing strings from bird.

Serve with a little sauce poured round; and serve remainder of sauce in a sauce-boat.

4–6 helpings

TIMBALES OF CHICKEN

½ lb. raw chicken   3 oz. macaroni 1½ oz. butter   1 egg yolk   salt and pepper   2 tablesp. cream   2 egg whites   ½ pt. Béchamel sauce

Put macaroni into rapidly-boiling salted water and cook until tender—about 15 min. Drain well. Cut macaroni into thin rings and line six well-buttered timbale moulds as evenly as possible with the rings (use the point of a needle to fix them in position). Prepare chicken mixture as for Chicken Soufflé (p. 195) and fill the moulds. Cover moulds with buttered paper, steam 25–35 min.

Serve hot with sauce poured round.

6 helpings

DUCK

BRAISED DUCK—WITH CHESTNUTS

1 duck   1 pt. stock   larding bacon (optional)   2 oz. butter ¾ pt. Espagnole sauce (p. 101) 1 glass port wine (optional) 1 dessertsp. redcurrant jelly

MIREPOIX

2 onions   1 small turnip   2 carrots 1 stick celery   bouquet garni 6 black peppercorns   2 cloves

STUFFING

1 lb. chestnuts   1 Spanish onion salt and pepper   1 egg

Boil chestnuts, remove skins and chop or mince nuts finely for stuffing. Cook Spanish onion in water until tender, chop finely, add to chestnuts, season well and bind with egg. Stuff duck with chestnut mixture, truss, lard with bacon, if liked. Slice vegetables for mirepoix (foundation), place in a large saucepan with butter, lay duck on vegetables, cover pan, fry gently for 20 min.; then add bouquet garni, spices, and enough stock to come three-quarters of the depth of mirepoix. Cover with a buttered paper, put on lid, simmer gently until duck is tender—about 2 hr. Add more stock if necessary to prevent burning. Heat Espagnole sauce, add wine (if used) and jelly, reheat and season to taste. Remove paper and trussing string from duck, and place it in a hot oven (425°–450° F., *Gas* 7–8) to crisp the bacon. Serve on a hot dish, with a watercress garnish, if liked: serve sauce separately.

4–5 helpings
Cooking time—about 3 hr. in all

DUCK EN CASSEROLE

1 duck ¾ oz. flour salt and pepper
4 oz. mushrooms 4 shallots ¾ pt.
stock (approx.) ½ pt. green peas
1 teasp. chopped mint

Cut duck into joints, remove all skin, dip the joints in seasoned flour. Place duck, chopped mushrooms and chopped shallots in a casserole. Just cover with stock, put on a tightly-fitting lid and cook in a fairly hot oven (375°–400° F., *Gas* 5–6) about ¾ hr. Add shelled peas and mint and continue cooking until duck is tender—about another ½ hr. Correct seasoning. Serve from the casserole.

4–5 helpings

HASHED DUCK

1 cold roast duck 1 onion
1 oz. butter 1 oz. flour 1 pt. stock
1 orange 1 glass claret
salt and pepper

Carve duck ready for serving. Chop onion finely, put into a saucepan, fry in butter, stir in flour

and cook gently until brown. Add stock, stir until boiling, allow to simmer 10 min. Cut orange rind into very thin strips, add to the sauce with the orange juice, claret and pieces of duck. Season. Simmer very gently for ½ hr. Dish the meat and pour sauce over.

4 helpings
Cooking time—about 1 hr.

ROAST DUCK

1 duck fat for basting sage and
onion stuffing (p. 111) ½ oz. flour
½ pt. stock salt and pepper
apple sauce (p. 97)

Fill duck with sage and onion stuffing, truss for roasting. Baste well with hot fat, roast in a fairly hot oven (375°–400° F., *Gas* 5–6) 1–1½ hr., basting frequently. Keep duck hot, pour fat from roasting-tin, sprinkle in flour and brown it. Stir in stock, simmer 3–4 min., season and strain. Remove trussing strings from duck.

Serve gravy and apple sauce separately. *See also* Accompaniments (p. 192).

4–5 helpings
Cooking time—1½ hr.

ROAST DUCK—WITH ORANGE

1 duck fat for basting
1 large orange
1 tablesp. brandy *or* red wine

Truss and roast duck in a fairly hot oven (375°–400° F., *Gas* 5–6) for 1–1½ hr., until tender, basting if necessary. Meanwhile, stand the orange in a pan of boiling water for about 3 min., remove skin, cut orange into sections, soak these in brandy *or* wine. Remove all white pith from the skin, cut the latter into thin strips, boil in a little water for about 5 min., drain. Heat the orange sections gently in the brandy. Remove trussing strings from duck. Serve with strips of rind and hot orange sections as a garnish.

4–5 helpings

SALMI OF DUCK

1 duck (or trimmings from 2 cold roast ducks)   1 Spanish onion
fat for basting   1½ oz. butter
1 oz. flour   ¾ pt. stock
12 stoned French olives

Slice onion into roasting-tin, put prepared duck on top, baste with hot fat and roast in a fairly hot oven (375°–400° F., Gas 5–6) until tender. Melt butter, add flour and cook slowly until the roux browns, stir in stock and simmer until required. If a whole duck has been used, remove trussing string, cut duck into small joints and add with the olives to sauce, season and re-heat thoroughly. Sieve (or finely chop) the onion, add to the duck. Drain off the fat and add the sediment from the roasting tin to the sauce.

The salmi may be dished on a croûte of fried bread placed in the centre of a hot dish with sauce and olives poured over, if liked.

4 helpings
Cooking time—about 1 hr.

STEWED DUCK (Whole)

1 duck   fat for basting   2 onions
2 oz. butter   1½ oz. flour   1 pt. stock
4 sage leaves   2–3 strips lemon-thyme
salt and pepper

Truss duck, baste with hot fat, cook in a hot oven (425°–450° F., Gas 7–8) until well browned, basting frequently. Slice onions, fry until golden brown in butter, remove them, and brown the flour in the butter. Place duck in a large saucepan, barely cover it with hot stock, add fried onions, sage and lemon-thyme. Cover with a closely fitting lid, and simmer gently until tender—about ¾ hr. When duck is cooked, strain sauce from pan, and stir ¾ pt. of it into the brown roux;

stir until boiling, cook 5 min. and season. Serve the duck with gravy and 1 pt. green peas, handed separately.

4–5 helpings
Cooking time—1½–1½ hr.

STUFFED DUCKLING

1 large "Rouen" duckling   fat for basting   ¾ pt. brown sauce (p. 94)
sections of 1 large orange

STUFFING

1 chicken liver   1 duckling liver
½ teasp. parsley   ¼ teasp. thyme
3 oz. breadcrumbs   salt and pepper
nutmeg   1 oz. butter   1 egg

Blanch chicken and duckling livers, chop them finely, add herbs, breadcrumbs, melted butter, pinch of nutmeg, salt and pepper, then bind with egg. Stuff duckling with liver mixture; truss, baste well with hot fat, roast in hot oven (425°–450° F., Gas 7–8) for ½ hr., basting frequently. Drain off all fat, pour hot brown sauce into baking-tin and continue cooking until duckling is tender—about 20 min. Baste frequently with sauce.

Serve on a hot dish. Strain a little sauce round, garnish with orange (heated in a little wine or stock, over a pan of hot water), and serve remainder of sauce separately.

4 helpings
Cooking time—1 hr.

FOWL
BOILED FOWL

1 fowl   1 onion   1 carrot   ½ lemon
salt   bouquet garni   1½ oz. butter
1½ oz. flour   ¾ pt. stock

GARNISH

Truffle or mushroom   sprigs of parsley or sieved yolk of hard-boiled egg

Truss the fowl, inserting some pieces of vegetable in the body. Rub breast of bird with lemon, wrap in buttered paper and put in pan with sufficient stock or water to cover. Add remainder of vegetables (sliced), salt and bouquet garni and cook gently until fowl is tender (about 2 hr.). Meanwhile melt butter in a saucepan, add flour and cook without browning; gradually stir in the stock and boil for 10 min., stirring all the time; season. Use some of the liquor from stewpan if no stock is available. Remove trussing string from fowl.

Place on a hot dish, coat with sauce; garnish.

5–6 helpings

CURRIED FOWL

Remains of 2 cold roast fowls
1 sliced onion   2 oz. butter
1 tablesp. flour   1 tablesp. curry powder   ¾ pt. stock   1 sliced apple
1 teasp. chutney or redcurrant jelly
1 dessertsp. lemon juice
salt and pepper

Cut fowl into neat pieces (use bones and trimmings for stock). Fry sliced onion lightly in butter in a saucepan, stir in flour and curry powder, cook 3 min. Stir in stock, bring to boil. Add sliced apple, chutney, lemon juice and seasoning; simmer gently for ½ hr. Put in fowl, keep hot, but not simmering, for ½ hr. Dish fowl, pour sauce over (strain if liked). Garnish and serve accompaniments as for Curried Chicken (p. 196).

GALANTINE OF FOWL

1 boned fowl   salt and pepper
1 lb. sausage meat   ¼ lb. boiled ham or tongue   2 hard-boiled eggs
2 truffles or 6 mushrooms
½ oz. pistachio nuts or almonds
1½ pt. stock (approx.)   1 pt. chaudfroid sauce   ½ pt. aspic jelly

GARNISH—selection of:
Pimento   truffle   mushroom
lemon rind   hard-boiled egg

Bone the fowl (p. 192), cut down the centre of the back (this may be done before boning, as it makes the process easier), spread it out, and distribute the flesh as evenly as possible, season well. Spread with half of sausage meat, arrange narrow strips of ham or tongue, slices of egg, chopped truffles or mushrooms and chopped, blanched nuts on the sausage, season well, then cover with remainder of sausage. Fold over the back skin and stitch firmly. Wrap bird in clean cloth and fasten securely. Simmer gently in stock 2½ hr.; allow to cool a little in the stock, then press between 2 large boards or plates until quite cold. Unwrap, skin, and wipe free from excess grease.

Coat with chaudfroid sauce, garnish, and mask with aspic jelly.

If preferred the galantine may be brushed with glaze, instead of using chaudfroid sauce, and garnished with aspic jelly.

8–10 helpings

RAGOUT OF FOWL

1 fowl   2½ oz. butter   1 onion
salt and pepper   1½ oz. flour
1¼ pt. stock   ¼ lb. ham or bacon

Joint fowl (plate 7), heat the butter in a saucepan, fry the joints in this until lightly browned; remove and keep them hot. Fry the sliced onion lightly, sprinkle in the flour, and brown this slowly; add the stock, stir until boiling, season carefully. Replace the joints in the sauce, add diced ham or bacon, cover with a tightly-fitting lid and cook gently until fowl is tender—2–2½ hr. Correct the seasoning, serve with the sauce strained over.

5–6 helpings

ROAST FOWL—STUFFED

1 roasting fowl   veal forcemeat
(p. 112)   salt and pepper
fat for basting

GARNISH

Bacon rolls   watercress

Make the forcemeat rather moist, and press lightly into the bird, rounding it under the skin. Any extra may be formed into small balls, coated with egg and breadcrumbs and baked or fried. A good flavour is imparted if the bird is stuffed some hours before cooking. Truss the bird, roast it in a fairly hot oven (375°–400° F., Gas 5–6) until tender (test the thigh of the bird with a thin skewer for tenderness), about 1½–2 hr. Remove trussing string.

Garnish bird and serve with gravy and bread sauce (p. 95) handed separately.

5–6 helpings

STEWED FOWL—WITH RICE

1 fowl   2 onions   3–4 sticks of celery   2 pt. stock   bouquet garni 4 oz. rice   salt and pepper

Slice the vegetables and place a few pieces inside the body of the fowl. Truss the bird for boiling, place in a large saucepan or casserole, add the stock and bring to boiling-point. Add remainder of vegetables, and bouquet garni, tied in muslin. Cover closely, and cook very gently for 1 hr., then add well-washed rice and seasoning. Continue cooking gently until fowl and rice are tender—about 2 hr. The rice should absorb nearly all the stock. Dish the fowl, removing strings. Remove vegetables and bouquet garni from the rice, correct the seasoning of this, and serve with the bird.

5–6 helpings

Cooking time—about 2–2½ hr.

GIBLETS

GIBLET PIE

1 set of goose giblets   1 onion, sliced   bouquet garni   salt and pepper   1 lb. rump steak   puff

pastry (p. 340) using 6 oz. flour, etc. egg or milk for glazing

Wash the giblets, put in a saucepan with sliced onion, bouquet garni and seasoning, cover with cold water, simmer gently 1½–2 hr. Slice the steak thinly, and season it. Place alternate layers of steak and giblets in a pie-dish (approx. 1½ pt. size) which should be filled, and strain over enough stock to come three-quarters of the way up the dish. Cover the pie with puff pastry (allowing the meat to cool first, if possible) and bake in a hot oven (425°–450° F., Gas 7–8) until pastry is set—about 20 min.—then lower heat to moderate (350°–375° F., Gas 4–5) and continue cooking until meat is tender—about 60 min. more. Fill up the pie with the remainder of the hot stock.

The pie may be glazed with egg or milk, about 20 min. before it is ready.

6 helpings

Cooking time—1¼–1½ hr.

STEWED GIBLETS

1 set of goose giblets   stock   1 oz. butter   1 oz. flour   salt and pepper

Wash the goose giblets. Cover with stock and water and stew until tender. Remove the liver, neck and tendons as soon as tender, leaving the gizzard until it can be pierced with a fork. Heat butter in a saucepan, stir in flour and brown slowly. Strain ¾ pt. of stock from giblets, and stir into roux. Bring to boiling-point, season, add giblets and reheat thoroughly. Serve very hot.

3–4 helpings

Cooking time—about 1½ hr.

GOOSE

ROAST GOOSE

1 goose   sage and onion stuffing (p. 111)   fat for basting   flour

Prepare the goose, make the stuffing and insert this in the body of the bird. Truss the goose (p. 191), and prick the skin of the breast. Roast bird in a fairly hot oven (375°–400° F., Gas 5–6) 2½ hr.—until tender. When almost cooked, dredge breast with flour, baste with some of the hot fat and finish cooking. Remove trussing string; dish the bird. Serve with apple sauce (p. 97) and beef gravy handed separately.

Gravy made from goose giblets is very rich, but may be served instead of beef gravy, if desired.

8–10 helpings

ROAST GREEN GOOSE OR GOSLING

Geese are called green until about 4 months old—they are not stuffed usually.

1 green goose   2 oz. butter
salt and pepper

GARNISH
Watercress

Prepare the goose, mix together the butter, salt and pepper, and place this in the body. Truss the bird, and cook in a moderate oven (350°–375° F., Gas 4–5) for about 1 hr., basting with fat if necessary. Dish the bird. Garnish with the watercress.

Brown gravy and gooseberry jelly, or gooseberry sauce (p. 97) may be served, if desired.

5–6 helpings

GUINEA FOWL
ROAST GUINEA FOWL

1 guinea fowl   2 oz. butter
salt and pepper   2 slices fat bacon

GARNISH
Watercress   French dressing

Prepare the bird (p. 191), mix the butter and seasoning, place in body of bird. Truss the bird, lay slices of bacon over the breast, and roast in a moderately hot oven (350°–375° F., Gas 4–5) 1–1½ hr., basting frequently. When the bird is almost cooked, "froth" the breast, i.e. dredge with flour, baste and finish cooking. Wash and dry watercress, toss lightly in French dressing (p. 245). Remove trussing strings from bird and garnish. Serve with browned crumbs, bread sauce, and Espagnole sauce (p. 101) handed separately.

4–5 helpings

TURKEY
BOILED TURKEY

1 turkey   1 lb. sausage meat
stock or water   2 onions   2 carrots
1 small turnip   bouquet garni   salt

GARNISH
Veal forcemeat   boiled celery
egg and breadcrumbs

Stuff the turkey with seasoned sausage meat, truss for boiling (p. 191). Place in a large pan, cover with boiling stock or water; add large pieces of onion, carrot, turnip, the bouquet garni and a little salt. Cover, boil gently until tender—about 2½ hr. for 9-lb. bird (this may vary considerably—test the thigh of the bird with a thin skewer). Make forcemeat into small balls, egg and crumb, fry in deep fat, also cook celery and make sauce. Remove trussing strings from bird. Garnish with forcemeat balls; and serve celery separately.

Boiled ham or tongue is usually served with this dish.

DEVILLED TURKEY LEGS

2 turkey legs   salt and pepper
cayenne pepper   mixed mustard or
French mustard   butter

Remove skin from turkey, crisscross with deep cuts. Sprinkle well with seasoning and a little cayenne, if required, very hot. Spread with mixed mustard (or French mustard) pressing well into the cuts and leave for several hours. Grill 8–12 min. until crisp and brown, spread with small pieces of butter mixed with cayenne, and serve immediately.

4 helpings

FRICASSEE OF TURKEY

See Fricassée of Chicken (p. 197).

ROAST TURKEY

1 turkey   1–2 lb. sausage meat
1 lb. veal forcemeat (p. 112)
2–3 rashers streaky bacon
fat for basting

Stuff crop of bird with veal forcemeat and put seasoned sausage meat inside body of bird. Truss for roasting (p. 191). Lay bacon rashers over the breast, roast in a pre-heated hot oven (425° F., *Gas* 7) for 15–20 min., then reduce heat to moderate (350° F., *Gas* 4), basting frequently. The cooking time will vary according to the size and quality of the bird—as a general guide, allow 15 min. per lb. for a turkey under 14 lb. weight, and 12 min. per lb. if over 14 lb. About 20 min. before serving remove the bacon to allow the breast to brown. Remove trussing string; serve on a hot dish.

Serve with gravy, sausages and bread sauce (p. 95) if liked, or cranberry sauce (p. 97). *See also* Accompaniments (p. 192).

ROAST TURKEY—WITH CHESTNUTS

1 turkey   2 lb. chestnuts   ½ pt. stock
2 oz. butter   1 egg   salt and pepper
cream or milk   1–1½ lb. sausage
meat or 1 lb. veal forcemeat
2–3 slices bacon   fat for basting

Slit the skins of the chestnuts, cook in boiling water for 15 min., then remove skins. Now stew chestnuts in stock for 1 hr.—drain and chop or sieve them. Add melted butter, egg, seasoning and sufficient cream or milk to moisten the stuffing. Fill the crop of the bird with the chestnut stuffing, and the body of the bird with seasoned sausage meat. Truss the bird for roasting. Cover the bird with bacon, roast in a moderate oven (350° F., *Gas* 4) until tender (allow 15 min. per lb. for a turkey weighing under 14 lb., and 12 min. per lb. for a turkey over 14 lb.). Baste well. Remove bacon towards end of cooking to allow the breast to brown. Remove trussing string, dish. Serve gravy separately.

NOTE: If the turkey is large the breast meat may dry up in a small oven before the legs and thighs are cooked. Either remove legs before roasting and cook separately, or take turkey from oven when breast is ready and cook the legs according to any suitable recipe, for use at another meal.

See also General Hints, p. 192.

HARE AND RABBIT

HARES may be roasted or jugged when young, and made into soup when old. The young ones have smooth sharp claws, a narrow cleft in the lip and soft ears which will tear readily; they have short, stumpy necks and long joints. A leveret is a hare up to 1 year old; it will have a small bony knot near the foot, which is absent in a full-grown hare. Hares should be well hung, for 7 or 8 days, in a cool dry place. They should hang, unskinned, by the hind legs, with the head in a tin cup, to catch the blood. Hares are not paunched until required for cooking.

Skinning hares: In many respects the dressing of a hare resembles that of poultry. The main difference is that a furry skin has to be removed instead of feathers. This is achieved by first cutting off the feet above the foot joint. The feet can be jointed off with a small thin-bladed knife. Next carefully cut through the skin straight down the belly, taking care not to cut into the meat. Then gently ease back the skin away from the flesh and work round each side until the centre of the hare is completely freed from its skin. Now push forward one hind leg and work the skin free. Repeat with the other and then pull the skin away from the tail. Holding the skinned hindquarters in the left hand, gently pull the skin up the back and over the shoulder, working each foreleg through in turn. The skin must now be eased with a knife from the neck and head. Cut carefully round the base of each ear to free the fur, but take care not to cut off the ears, which are left on for cooking.

When free of skin, carefully cut through the skin of the belly from the chest to the legs and draw out the viscera (this is known as paunching). Wipe dry with a clean cloth. The kidneys, found in the back embedded in a little fat, are left in position. The liver and heart are cooked and care should be taken in detaching the greenish gall-bladder from the liver. See plate 10.

Trussing hares: A hare may be trussed with a needle and string. The desired effect is of the animal crouching prone on the dish. Sew a back leg into each side and also a foreleg (shoulder). Pass a string from front to rear, passing round the neck, and draw tight to cause a small arch in the back.

Jointing hares: See plate 11.

Rabbits have the same characteristics, when young, as hares. They are paunched before being hung and they should not be hung for longer than a day. Young ones the suitable for roasting, older ones for stewing, or boiling.

They are dressed as for hares except that the ears and eyes are removed. They may be trussed like a hare. In this case the forelegs are jointed off and sewn back in position. Either rabbit or hare may easily be jointed with a stout-bladed knife which can be tapped through the bones.

Many of the rabbits now on sale are frozen imported animals.

GRILLED HARE

Remains of roast hare   butter   salt   cayenne pepper

Separate meat into neat pieces, brush with oiled butter and season highly. Grill under a hot grill until

well browned, turning frequently
and brushing with more butter if
necessary.

Serve very hot. Serve with
sauce or gravy.

Cooking time—about 10 min.

HARE EN CASSEROLE

**1 hare   3 oz. butter   1 onion
3 cloves   bouquet garni   salt and
pepper   1½ pt. stock** or **equal
quantities stock and stout** or **cider
1 oz. flour   veal forcemeat (p. 112)
fat for frying**

Prepare the hare and cut into
pieces convenient for serving. Fry
pieces in 2 oz. of the butter until
brown, then pack closely in a casserole. Slice and fry onion, add to
casserole with cloves, bouquet
garni, seasoning, stock (*or* equal
quantities stock and stout, *or*
cider). Cover closely, simmer
about 2½ hr., until hare is tender.
Knead remaining 1 oz. butter and
flour together, divide into small
pieces, drop into casserole, about ½
hr. before serving. Shape forcemeat into small balls, fry in hot fat,
drain well, add to casserole 5 min.
before serving. Remove bouquet
garni, correct seasoning. Serve
with redcurrant jelly handed
separately.

**6 helpings
Cooking time—about 3 hr.**

JUGGED HARE

**1 hare   3 oz. butter   salt and pepper
1 onion   4 cloves   1 glass port** or
**claret (optional)   1 tablesp. lemon
juice   12 peppercorns   bouquet
garni   1½ pt. stock   1 oz. flour
veal forcemeat (p. 112)
fat for frying**

Prepare hare as in Notes on
Trussing (p. 205), and cut into
neat small pieces. Heat 2 oz. of
the butter, fry the pieces of hare
in it until brown. Put hare in a
casserole with salt, onion stuck
with cloves, half the wine (if used),

lemon juice, peppercorns, bouquet
garni and hot stock. Place a tight
lid on the casserole, cook in a
moderate oven (350° *F.*, *Gas* 4)
about 3 hr. Knead flour and remaining butter together, stir into
the stock about ½ hr. before serving. Add remaining wine and
season to taste. Make forcemeat,
form into small balls and fry.
Gently heat blood from hare, stir
into gravy, allow to thicken.

Serve hare piled on a hot dish,
strain sauce over, arrange forcemeat balls round dish. Serve with
redcurrant jelly handed separately.

5–6 helpings

ROAST HARE

**1 hare   veal forcemeat (p. 112)
fat bacon   milk   2 oz. butter
1 teasp. chopped shallot   ½ teasp.
chopped parsley   pinch of thyme
1½ oz. flour   ¾ pt. stock   1 glass
port (optional)   salt and pepper
redcurrant jelly**

Skin, draw and truss the hare
(p. 205), reserving the liver. After
inserting the forcemeat, sew up the
hare, cover with bacon, bake in a
fairly hot oven (375°–400° *F.*, *Gas*
5–6) 1½–2 hr. until tender, basting
frequently with milk, and a little
butter, if liked. Meanwhile, remove
gall-bladder from liver, wash the
liver, put into cold water, bring to
the boil and boil for 5 min.; chop
very finely. Melt the butter, add
the liver, shallot, parsley and
thyme. Fry for 10 min. Lift the
liver mixture from the butter, put
in the flour, brown the roux. Stir
in the stock (*or* milk used for basting), bring to boiling-point; add
the liver mixture, season, simmer
for 10 min.; add wine if used. Remove bacon from hare, dredge
with flour, baste and allow to
brown. Remove trussing strings
and cotton. Serve on a hot dish.
Serve the liver sauce and redcurrant jelly separately.

5–6 helpings

LEVERET
ROAST LEVERET

2 leverets   butter or dripping for basting   flour   redcurrant jelly

Prepare and truss as for a hare (p. 205), but do not stuff the leverets. Roast them in a fairly hot oven (375°–400° F., Gas 5–6) 40–50 min., basting them well with butter or dripping. A few minutes before serving, dredge with flour, rebaste and leave to brown. Remove trussing strings.

Serve with plain gravy in the dish; serve the redcurrant jelly separately.

5–6 helpings

RABBIT
CURRIED RABBIT

1 rabbit   2 oz. butter   1 chopped onion   1 dessertsp. flour   1 tablesp. curry powder   1 dessertsp. curry paste   ¾ pt. white stock   1 chopped apple   1 dessertsp. chutney   1 tablesp. lemon juice   salt and pepper   1 oz. sultanas   1 oz. blanched almonds   1 dessertsp. desiccated coconut   2 tablesp. cream or milk (optional)

GARNISH

Fans of lemon   red pepper   gherkin fans

Wash, dry and joint the rabbit. Heat the butter in a saucepan, fry joints lightly, remove and drain. Fry onion lightly, add flour, curry powder and paste, and fry very well, stirring occasionally. Stir in stock, bring to boil. Put in all other ingredients except the cream; put in rabbit joints. Have the coconut tied in muslin, and remove after 15 min. Simmer gently about 1½ hr., adding a little more stock if necessary. Add cream or milk (if used).

Dish the rabbit, pour the sauce over, straining if liked. Garnish.

3–4 helpings

RABBIT EN CASSEROLE

1 large rabbit   strips of fat bacon (optional)   2 oz. butter   2 onions   2 slices lean bacon   salt and pepper   1 oz. flour   1 pt. stock   bouquet garni

Wash and joint the rabbit. If desired, lard the joints with strips of fat bacon (see p. 36). Heat the butter in a casserole and brown in it the rabbit, sliced onions and lean bacon (diced). When well browned, add salt and pepper; sprinkle in flour, and when this has browned, stir in stock. Bring to boiling-point, add bouquet garni. Cover tightly and cook slowly in a moderate oven (350° F., Gas 4) for 2–2½ hr. Remove bouquet garni and correct seasoning. Serve from the casserole.

4–5 helpings

RABBIT PIE

1 rabbit   ½ lb. beef steak   ½ lb. bacon or pickled pork   salt and pepper   ½ pt. stock   puff pastry (p. 340) using 8 oz. flour, etc.   egg for glazing

Wash, dry and joint the rabbit, dice the beef and bacon or pork. Place these ingredients in layers in a pie-dish, season well, ¾ fill dish with stock. Cover with pastry. Bake 1¾–2 hr. in a hot oven (425°–450° F., Gas 7–8) for 15 min., and in a moderate oven (350° F., Gas 4) for the remainder of the time. Glaze with egg 20 min. before pie is cooked. Add remainder of seasoned stock and serve hot or cold. If the pie is required cold, forcemeat balls and sliced, hard-boiled egg will be an improvement.

6–8 helpings
Cooking time—1¾–2 hr.

RAGOUT OF RABBIT

1 rabbit   4 oz. streaky bacon   2 oz. butter   1 onion   1½ oz. flour

1 pt. stock   salt and pepper
1 carrot   ½ small turnip
6 peppercorns

GARNISH
Macédoine of vegetables

Wash, dry and joint the rabbit; dice the bacon. Heat the butter in a saucepan, fry rabbit in it until well browned; remove rabbit and keep hot. Fry diced onion, put in flour, stir and fry until well browned. Add boiling stock; boil for 10 min. Return rabbit to pan, add seasoning, diced carrot and turnip, bacon and peppercorns Cover tightly. Stew gently until rabbit is tender—about 2 hr. Correct seasoning.

Serve rabbit on a hot dish with sauce strained over. Garnish at either end with macédoine of vegetables.

3–4 helpings

VEGETABLES

COOKING VEGETABLES

Vegetables can form one of the most interesting parts of the meal, yet they are all too often considered by the cook to be the least important part.

The general level of vegetable culture is high, but there is a tendency for most growers to keep back vegetables until they are of large size and have really passed the stage at which they should be eaten. Small young peas, carrots, new potatoes and Brussels sprouts have a flavour entirely different from that of the large, fully grown vegetable. This excellent flavour is also partly the result of being able to reduce cooking time to a minimum.

Vegetables may be insipid in flavour through lack of seasoning. Sufficient salt should be used during the cooking and the vegetable tasted and re-seasoned, if necessary, before serving. Potatoes, particularly when served as mashed potatoes, often lack flavour and are much improved by the addition of grated nutmeg. Vegetables which have little flavour in themselves are improved by being served with a well-flavoured sauce, which should be made with part, at any rate, of the cooking liquid from the vegetable.

The flavour of vegetables can be fully appreciated only if they are served *immediately* cooking is completed.

Value of Vegetables: Vegetables are essential to the diet because they are a most valuable source of Vitamin C. They also contain Vitamins A and B1 (thiamine); certain mineral elements, chiefly calcium, phosphorus and iron; carbohydrate in the form of starch, sugar and roughage and a small quantity of useful second-class protein.

Green Vegetables: Green vegetables are of nutritional importance chiefly because of the Vitamins C and A which they contain. Unfortunately, however, Vitamin C is rapidly lost after the vegetable is cut or pulled from the ground. Where possible, therefore, it is desirable to grow vegetables in the garden and to cook them within an hour of cutting.

Green vegetables should be soaked for the minimum of time and cooked in only a small quantity of water until just tender. The cooking liquid should be used for gravies or soups.

Vitamin A is present in the form of carotene in green vegetables. The amount present is proportional to the greenness of the vegetable.

Green vegetables are quite good sources of Vitamin B1 (thiamine). Like Vitamin C it is very easily soluble and is rapidly destroyed in the presence of bicarbonate of soda. Green vegetables also contain mineral elements.

Lastly, green vegetables have their value in the diet as suppliers of indigestible cellulose or roughage which stimulates the muscles of the digestive tract and has a laxative effect.

Roots and Tubers: Potatoes are the most important of these vegetables. The high proportion of starch which they contain makes them a valuable source of calories in the diet. The starch cells must be ruptured by cooking before the starch can be eaten and digested.

The potato contains Vitamin C, not in a large quantity, but, owing to the amount of potato eaten in the diet, it forms a useful contribution. Where possible potatoes should be cooked in their skins to retain maximum food value and flavour.

Beetroots, carrots, swedes, parsnips and onions all provide sugar in the diet. The sugar is very soluble, hence the undesirability of boiling these vegetables in a large quantity of water for a long time. Beetroots retain their sweet flavour if baked or cooked in a pressure cooker rather than boiled in the usual way. Carrots are exceptional among root vegetables in containing a large amount of Vitamin A in the form of carotene.

Like green vegetables, root vegetables also supply roughage in the diet which has a useful laxative effect.

Peas and Beans: Fresh peas and beans contain the vitamins and mineral salts to be found in green leafy vegetables. Their Vitamin B1 content is higher, however, and peas contain the same percentage of iron as watercress.

Peas and broad beans contain sugar and rather a higher percentage of second-class protein than most other vegetables.

Dried peas and beans (usually called pulses) must not be confused with the fresh vegetables, particularly from a dietetic point of view. They contain no Vitamin C and very little Vitamin A. Pulses are palatable only when really well cooked and, though sometimes served as a separate vegetable, they are probably enjoyed and digested best if sieved and served in the form of soup.

Dehydrated Vegetables: Dehydrated carrot and other root vegetables, including potato, dehydrated cabbage and mixtures of these vegetables, cut in strips, are now available in the shops. They are dried in such a way that the Vitamin C is unharmed and carotene and other nutritive factors are not affected. Their flavour and appearance when cooked is excellent. Clear instructions as to amount of liquid and time for cooking are supplied with the vegetables.

Frozen Vegetables: The popularity of frozen vegetables is no doubt due to the fact that no preparation is needed before cooking them, and to the excellent quality of the vegetables. Their value in the diet is equal to that of fresh vegetables, provided that they are cooked before they have thawed out.

Canned and Bottled Vegetables: Present-day canned and bottled vegetables contain the same amount of Vitamin C as well-cooked vegetables. During processing, both Vitamin B1 and C diffuse out of the vegetable into the surrounding liquid, so this should be utilized. After the can is opened the vegetable should be used as soon as possible. If kept hot in the presence of air the vegetables will lose Vitamin C just as freshly cooked vegetables do.

ARTICHOKES

Globe artichokes are in season from July to October.

BOILED GLOBE ARTICHOKES

6 globe artichokes   salt   1 tablesp. lemon juice   ¼ pt. Hollandaise sauce (p. 98) or ½ pt. mushroom sauce (p. 4) or 2 oz. melted butter

Soak the artichokes in cold, salt water for at least 1 hr. to ensure the removal of all dust and insects. Wash them well. Cut off the tails and trim the bottoms with a sharp knife. Cut off the outer leaves and trim the tops of the remaining ones with scissors. Put into a pan with just sufficient boiling water to cover them, adding salt and the

lemon juice. Cook until tender,
15–45 min., according to size and
freshness (when cooked the leaves
pull out easily). Test frequently
after 15 min. as they are apt to
break and become discoloured if
over-cooked. Remove from water
and drain them well by turning
them upside down.

Serve with Hollandaise sauce or
melted butter or mushroom sauce.

6 helpings
Cooking time—15–45 min.

ARTICHOKE BOTTOMS

Where economy does not have
to be considered, globe artichokes
may be cooked as in the preceding
recipe and only the bottoms or
"fonds" used. After cooking, the
leaves are carefully pulled out of
the artichokes so that the bottoms
are retained, unbroken.

The bottoms may be served
quite simply, tossed in hot butter
or coated with a good sauce; they
may be fried; or they may be
stuffed with vegetable, meat or
cheese fillings piled into the
natural cavity in the centre of each.

JERUSALEM ARTICHOKES

Jerusalem artichokes are seasonable from October to April.

BOILED JERUSALEM ARTICHOKES

1½–2 lb. Jerusalem artichokes
white vinegar or lemon juice   salt
¾ pt. white sauce (p. 91)

Scrub, scrape and rinse the artichokes, using 1 teasp. of white
vinegar or lemon juice in each
water to keep the vegetable white.
Put into sufficient boiling, salted
water to cover the vegetable, adding 1 teasp. white vinegar or
lemon juice to each quart of water.
Simmer gently till just tender,
about 20 min. Drain well and
serve in a hot vegetable dish with
the white sauce poured over.

5–6 helpings
Cooking time—about 20 min.

FRIED JERUSALEM ARTICHOKES

1½ lb. Jerusalem artichokes
coating batter (double quantity
(p. 258)   fried parsley (p. 225)

Prepare and parboil the artichokes (about 15 min.). Cut them
into slices ½ in. thick and season
them well. Make the batter, dip
in the slices of artichokes and fry
in hot fat, at 340° F. until golden
brown (5–7 min.), turning them
during cooking. Drain well and
serve very hot with fried parsley.

6 helpings
Cooking time—15 min. to parboil
   artichokes
5–7 min. to fry them

MASHED JERUSALEM ARTICHOKES

2 lb. Jerusalem artichokes   lemon
juice or white vinegar   1 oz. butter
or margarine   2 tablesp. milk
salt and pepper   chopped parsley

Prepare and cook as in Boiled
Jerusalem Artichokes (opposite).
Drain well and shake the pan over
a low heat to dry the artichokes
slightly. Mash with a fork or
potato-masher or rub through a
nylon sieve. Heat the butter or
margarine in the pan and beat in
the purée. Stir over heat until
thoroughly hot. Season well. Serve
in a hot vegetable dish and sprinkle
with chopped parsley.

5–6 helpings
Cooking time—30–35 min.

ASPARAGUS

Asparagus is in season from
March to July.

ASPARAGUS—BOILED

1 bundle of asparagus   salt
2 oz. butter   lemon juice

Trim the hard white ends of the
asparagus to suitable lengths for

serving Scrape the stalks with a sharp knife, working downwards from the head. Wash them well in cold water. Tie them into small bundles with the heads in one direction. Re-trim the stalks evenly. Keep them in cold water until ready to cook. Cook very gently, with the heads off the source of heat, in just enough salted, boiling water to cover. When tender (in about 15–20 min.), drain and serve on a folded table napkin. Serve with melted butter, seasoned and lightly flavoured with lemon.

NOTE: To ensure that the tender point of the asparagus is not overcooked by the time that the stem is ready, the asparagus should be cooked "standing". This can be achieved in an "asparagus boiler", a narrow, very deep pan. A bottling jar half-filled with boiling water, stood in a deep saucepan of boiling water, serves as a very good substitute. The asparagus is placed stems down in the jar and the points cook more slowly in steam only. Allow 30 min. for this method of cooking.

Allow 6 or 8 medium-sized heads per person

ASPARAGUS POINTS

Asparagus   melted butter   salt and pepper   chopped shallot and chopped parsley (optional)

Cut the points and tender green parts of the asparagus into short pieces, place them in slightly salted, boiling water, and cook gently 5 to 10 min., according to size and age. Drain well, put the asparagus into a saucepan containing a little melted butter, sprinkle with pepper and toss over heat for a few minutes. Serve as a garnish or a vegetable or as a filling in omelets.

NOTE: It is a mistake to add anything which will impair the delicate flavour of the asparagus, but a little chopped shallot and parsley may be fried in the butter before adding the asparagus.

Allow 12 points per helping
Cooking time—15 min.

AUBERGINE (EGG PLANT)

Aubergines are used extensively in the East, where they are considered a great delicacy. It is essential that they should be fresh and they are at their best in July and August before the seeds form in them. Fresh aubergines have a smooth, very glossy skin and are firm to the touch.

BAKED AUBERGINE WITH CHEESE

4 aubergines   1 heaped tablesp. grated Parmesan cheese   ½ pt. Béchamel sauce (p. 100)   salt and pepper   1 tablesp. breadcrumbs ½ oz. butter

Parboil the aubergines for 10 min., then slice rather thickly, remove the seeds, if any, and arrange slices neatly in a fireproof dish. Mix the cheese into the Béchamel sauce, season to taste, and coat the aubergines with it. Cover lightly with the breadcrumbs, sprinkle the surface with the melted butter. Bake in a fairly hot oven (375° F., Gas 5) for ½ hr.

6 helpings

FRIED AUBERGINE

4 aubergines   flour   cayenne pepper salt   1 finely-chopped onion salad oil or butter

Slice the aubergines about ½ in. thick, lay them out on a flat dish, sprinkle with salt and put on a weight (this hastens the process of removing the moisture). After ½ hr. wipe them with a cloth, then coat them lightly with flour seasoned with cayenne and salt. Fry the onion in the oil or butter until lightly browned, drain and keep the onion hot. Replace the butter in the pan and fry the aubergine until both sides are lightly browned. Drain and dish. Sprinkle the onion on the aubergine; serve with tomato sauce, if liked.

6 helpings
Cooking time—to fry the aubergine, about 15 min.

BEANS

French beans are in season from May to November. Runner beans are in season from August to October. Broad beans are in season from June to August.

BOILED FRENCH or RUNNER BEANS

1½ lb. French or runner beans
1 oz. butter or margarine salt

Wash, top and tail and string the beans. Do not cut up French beans *or* young runner beans as they lose their flavour in cooking. For older scarlet runners, slice thinly, or, for better flavour, cut into diamonds, i.e. slice them in a slanting direction. Have ready just enough boiling, salted water to cover them and cook them with the lid on the pan. When tender (15–20 min.), drain and reheat in butter or margarine. Serve immediately.

4–6 helpings

BROAD BEANS WITH PARSLEY SAUCE

2–3 lb. broad beans salt
2–3 savory leaves (if available)
parsley sauce (p. 93)

Wash the beans and shell them. If not to be cooked immediately, cover down with some of the washed pods as this prevents the skins of the beans from drying out and becoming slightly toughened. Cook gently in just enough boiling, salted water to cover, with the savory leaves in the water. When tender, 15–35 min. according to size and age, drain well. Make a good parsley sauce with ½ milk and ½ bean water and well flavoured with lemon juice. Reheat the beans in the sauce and serve immediately.

NOTE: When really young, broad beans should have heads, tails and strings removed as for runner beans, and be cooked whole in the pods. The pods are eaten after tossing them in melted butter. The pod is quite tender, with an excellent flavour, and a very economical dish can be produced by this method.

When really mature, it is often necessary to skin the beans after cooking and before tossing them in the parsley sauce.

4–6 helpings (according to yield)

HARICOT BEANS

The two following recipes given for Haricot Beans may be used for similar beans such as Butter Beans, American Lima Beans, Flageolets (green haricots), etc.

BOILED HARICOT BEANS

½ lb. haricot beans 1 oz. butter or margarine salt and pepper
chopped parsley

Soak the beans overnight in boiling water. Drain them and well cover with cold, salted water. Bring slowly to boiling-point and simmer very slowly until tender, 2–2½ hr. Drain off the water and shake them gently over the low heat to dry them. Toss them in butter and season with pepper and salt. Serve hot, sprinkled with freshly chopped parsley.

6 helpings

HARICOT BEANS AND MINCED ONIONS

½ lb. haricot beans 2 medium-sized onions (minced or chopped very finely) 1 oz. butter or margarine
seasoning chopped parsley

Cook the beans. Fry the onions slowly in the butter until tender and golden brown. Mix together the onions and beans, season and serve hot sprinkled with parsley.

6 helpings
Cooking time—2–2¼ hr.

BEETROOT

When small, young and juicy, this vegetable makes a very excellent addition to winter salads, and may easily be converted into an economical and quickly-made pickle (*see* p. 393). Beetroot is more often served cold than hot; when served hot it should be served with sour-sweet sauce (p. 99) or melted butter.

Beetroot is obtainable throughout the year.

BAKED BEETROOT
Small young beetroots

Wash the beetroots carefully. If the skin has been damaged in any way, cover the damaged part with a little flour-and-water paste. Put them into a baking-dish and bake in a moderate oven (350° *F.*, *Gas* 4), until tender, about 1 hr. This method is excellent for young beetroots, all the flavour and sweetness of the beetroot being retained.

NOTE: The beetroots may be wrapped in greased papers or covered with aluminium foil before baking.

BOILED BEETROOT
Beetroots

Wash the beetroots very carefully, but do not break the skins, or they will lose colour and flavour during cooking. Put them into sufficient boiling water to cover them and boil them gently until tender, 1½–2½ hr., according to size and age. Unless to be served as a hot vegetable, leave them to cool in the cooking water before rubbing off the peel. If to be served hot, serve them with melted butter.

Beetroots are cooked most successfully and quickly in a pressure cooker, taking 15–40 min., according to size and age, with the cooker set at 15 lb. pressure.

Cooking time (in a pressure cooker)
Small beetroots 15 min., *medium* beetroots 20 min., *large* beetroots 35–40 min.

BROCCOLI

This vegetable is known to the cook in three different forms:

(1) Most of the cauliflowers which are sold between October and June come from the broccoli plant, which is very hardy. (The cauliflower plant proper is less hardy and supplies the typical white heads during the summer and early autumn, before the frosts appear.) This form of broccoli is cooked by the methods suggested for CAULIFLOWER (p. 217).

(2) The Calabrese, green or Italian sprouting broccoli, produces a medium-sized green central head which is usually available in March. It is cooked like cauliflower and served with melted butter.

After the central head is cut, shoots appear from every leaf joint, each shoot having a tiny head. The shoots are cut with about 6 in. of stem and provide an excellent vegetable for two or three months. The stems should be cut into short lengths and cooked, with the tiny heads, in boiling, salted water as for any green vegetable; or they can be tied in bundles and cooked and served like asparagus.

(3) Early purple sprouting and white sprouting broccoli come into season at the beginning of April. The tiny heads should be cut off with about 2 in. of stem and adjoining leaves and cooked whole in boiling salt water like any other green vegetable.

As purchased from the greengrocer, there is often a great deal of stem and leaf with the heads. The really coarse stems should be discarded and the rest shredded with the leaves and added to the pan before the small heads.

BRUSSELS SPROUTS

Sprouts are in season from September to March.

BOILED BRUSSELS SPROUTS

1½ lb. Brussels sprouts   salt
1 oz. butter or margarine (optional)

Choose small, close, sprouts. Remove shabby outer leaves by cutting the end, then make a cross cut on the bottom of each stalk. Soak in cold water, containing 1 teasp. of salt per quart, for 10 min. only. Wash thoroughly under running water if possible. Choose a suitably sized pan and put in enough water to quarter fill it only, with ½ teasp. salt to 1 pt. of water. When boiling, put in half the sprouts, the largest ones if variable in size, put on lid and bring quickly to boil again. Add rest of sprouts and cook until all are just tender, with the lid on the pan all the time. Drain in a colander and serve immediately in a hot vegetable dish or toss in melted butter before serving. Sprouts should be served quickly as they soon cool.

NOTE: By this method the sprouts retain their maximum colour, flavour and nutritive value.

6 helpings
Cooking time—15 min.

FRIED BRUSSELS SPROUTS

1 lb. small, tight Brussels sprouts, cooked   coating batter or
yeast batter

YEAST BATTER

½ oz. margarine   ½ pt. milk   ½ lb.
flour   ¼ oz. yeast   ¼ teasp. salt

Prepare the batter, if using yeast batter: warm the milk to blood heat with the margarine, and cream the yeast with a little of it. Add the rest of the milk to the yeast, then add all to the warmed flour and salt. Beat till smooth. Put to rise in a warm place till doubled in size. Cook the sprouts so that they are just tender. Drain well. Dip them in the batter on a skewer and lower each piece carefully into hot, deep fat at 340° F. Turn them during frying as they will float, and when golden brown, 5–7 min., remove from the fat. Drain well and serve garnished with fried parsley.

NOTE: The yeast batter gives a pleasant, very crisp result. Tomato sauce is an excellent accompaniment if the sprout fritters are to be served as a separate course.

4 helpings

CABBAGE

Cabbage is obtainable throughout the year.

BOILED CABBAGE

1 large, fresh cabbage (about 2 lb.)
salt

Cut across the end and remove only the very thick, coarse piece of stalk and shrivelled or discoloured outer leaves. Pull off the green leaves and put to soak, with the heart cut into 4 pieces, in cold water with 1 teasp. of salt per quart of water. Soak for 10 min. only. Wash thoroughly under running water if possible. Choose a suitably-sized pan and put in enough water to ¼ fill it only, with ½ teasp. of salt to 1 pt. of water. Cut out the stalk from the green leaves and heart of the cabbage, shred it and put on to cook with the lid on the pan. Shred the green outer leaves and add these to the pan. Replace lid and bring to boil again quickly, while shredding the cabbage heart. Add the heart to the pan a handful at a time so that the water barely goes off the boil. Cook with lid on pan until the cabbage is just tender. Drain well in a colander but do not press out liquid. Serve in a hot dish and send to table immediately.

NOTE: *See* Boiled Brussels Sprouts.

6 helpings
Cooking time—10–15 min.

STUFFED CABBAGE

6 large leaves of cabbage 4 oz. cooked rice 2 teasp. very finely-chopped onion 4 oz. fresh minced meat powdered mace pepper and salt Worcester sauce stock arrowroot

Wash and boil the cabbage leaves for 5 min. in salt water. Drain. Mix the filling, moistening it with stock and flavouring it carefully. Form into rolls. Remove a little of the coarse vein of the cabbage leaves. Wrap each roll of filling in a cabbage leaf and tie with cotton or secure with a cock-tail stick. Place in a saucepan, barely cover with stock, put on lid and simmer very gently 45 min. Lift on to a hot dish and thicken stock by boiling it with blended arrowroot (1 teasp. to $\frac{1}{4}$ pt. of stock). Season carefully. Pour sauce over cabbage rolls and serve immediately.

6 helpings
Cooking time—about 1 hr. (approx.)

RED CABBAGE

STEWED RED CABBAGE

1 small red cabbage 1 slice of ham $\frac{1}{4}$ oz. butter or margarine 1 pt. stock $\frac{1}{4}$ pt. vinegar salt and pepper 1 tablesp. granulated sugar

Soak, wash and slice the cabbage thinly. Put into a stewpan with the ham (diced), the butter, $\frac{1}{2}$ pt. of stock, and the vinegar. Put on the lid and stew gently 1 hr. When very tender, add the rest of the stock, sugar and seasoning. Mix and stir over heat until nearly all the liquor has dried away. Serve at once.

This is an excellent dish to serve with sausages.

6 helpings
Cooking time—1$\frac{1}{2}$ hr.

CARDOONS

This is a very good vegetable, not used sufficiently by most cooks. In the South of France, where the very prickly variety, *Cardon de Tours*, is grown, it is a very highly favoured vegetable, and both roots and stalks are used.

Cardoons are in season from October throughout the winter.

BOILED CARDOONS

2 lb. cardoons $\frac{3}{4}$ pt. white sauce (p. 91) salt 1 tablesp. lemon juice

Discard the outer stems, which are very tough. Cut the inner stalks into 3-in. lengths, remove the prickles, cover with boiling salted water and lemon juice and cook very gently for 15 min. Drain and rub off the skins with a cloth. Put into fresh, boiling, salted water and continue to cook very gently for another 1–1$\frac{1}{2}$ hr. Drain well and coat with white sauce. Serve immediately.

6 helpings
Cooking time—1$\frac{1}{4}$–1$\frac{1}{2}$ hr.

CARROTS

Carrots are obtainable through-out the year.

CARROTS—CONSERVATIVELY COOKED

1$\frac{1}{2}$ lb. carrots 1 oz. butter or margarine $\frac{1}{2}$ teasp. salt $\frac{1}{2}$–1 gill boiling water chopped parsley

Cut off the green tops, scrub and scrape the carrots. Slice them thinly if old carrots (or leave whole if really young). Fat steam the carrots for 10 min., i.e. shake them in the melted fat, well below frying temperature, with the lid on the pan until the fat is absorbed. Add the liquid (less for young carrots) and the salt, and simmer

PLATE 1
Gas, Electric, and Solid Fuel Cookers

1 has a built-in high-level barbecue grill which can be used
for normal grilling or spit
roasting. The burners are easily
removed for cleaning.

2 A rotating spit can be fitted,
when required, into the oven
of this electric cooker. It is
linked with the oven timer so
that oven heat and spit start
operating together.

3 This open-fire cooker is
equipped with two ovens and
a trivet which can be used
either as an extra boiling plate
or as a fire-guard.

PLATE 2

Kitchen Utensils
1 Funnel
2 Strainer
3 Vegetable masher
4 Ladle
5 Carving fork
6 Carving knife
7 Cook's vegetable knife
8 Set of measuring spoons
9 Icing syringe
10 Icing pipes or tubes
11 Icing nails
12 Grater
13 Palette knife
14 Cylindrical grater
15 Nylon sieve

PLATE 3
Cake Tins, Moulds, etc.

1 patty tins; 2 éclair tins; 3 raised pie mould; 4 caramel mould;
5 dariole or castle pudding mould; 6 and 8 vol au vent
cutters; 7 madeleine or shell mould; 9 border or ring mould;
10 set of fluted pastry cutters; 11 gugelhupf or fluted timbale
mould; 12 soufflé dish; 13 cutlet bat; 14 set of cake decoration
markers; 15 cake decoration markers; 16 jelly mould.

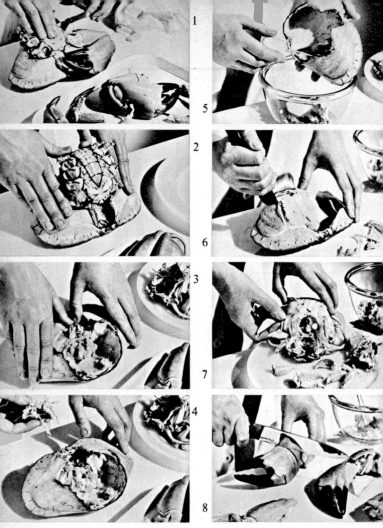

PLATE 4 Dressing a Crab

1 Wipe crab with damp cloth and remove claws and legs by twisting inwards.
2 Place thumbs under tail flap and push up until body breaks from shell.
3 and 4 Remove mouth and stomach bag.
5 Loosen meat round inside of shell, put into a basin.
6 Trim shell by tapping 'false' line round shell cavity with knife handle, press till edges of shell wall break away.
7 Discard 'dead men's fingers'. Remove meat. Scoop white meat from leg sockets, keeping free of bone.
8 Twist off joint from claws and empty meat into basin. With back of knife tap sharply round centre of broadest part of claws till shell cracks apart.

PLATE 5
Making a Raised Pie

1 Pour the boiling lard and water or milk on to the sifted flour and salt, mixing well with a wooden spoon or a palette knife.

2 When the mixture is cool enough, knead it thoroughly with the hands. Cut off a quarter of the dough and keep covered in warm place till needed.

3 Roll out the remaining dough to a round and line greased tin, working the dough up the sides of tin.

4 Roll the chopped meat in seasoned flour, put half into lined tin with the shelled eggs, fill with the remaining meat. Damp edge of the pastry lining the tin and cover with the remaining rolled-out pastry.

5 When the pie is baked fill up with stock poured through a funnel made of clean greaseproof paper.

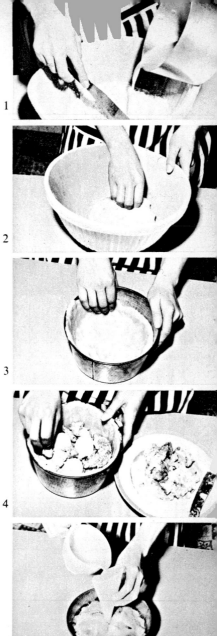

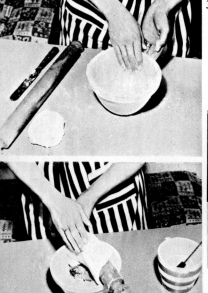

1

2

3

4

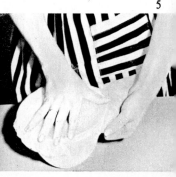

5

PLATE 6
Making Beefsteak Pudding

1 Cut the beefsteak into strips or cubes and toss in seasoned flour.

2 Cut off a third of the pastry for the lid, roll out the remainder into a round of about ¼ inch thickness.

3 Line the greased pudding basin with pastry, pressing out creases.

4 Fill with meat, adding the stock. Damp the edge of the pastry, roll out the lid and place on the top.

5 Press the edges together, cover with greased greaseproof paper, folding surplus under basin rim.

PLATE 7
Jointing a Chicken

1. Pull the leg away from body, cut through skin. Break leg from body at joint and cut through joint.

2. Cut thigh from the drum-stick at the joint. Repeat with the other leg. Turn the carcase so that neck end is towards you. Cut off extreme wing tips and cook with the giblets.

3. Cut the breast meat straight down to the wing joint. Break joint and cut so that the wing and the piece of breast meat are all in one piece.

4. With a heavy knife, cut down back of carcase, cut from vent to neck end. Cut breast into 2 or 4 pieces, according to size. For dishes where joints are to be coated they should be skinned. Remove all small bones.

5. Eight separate joints of chicken.

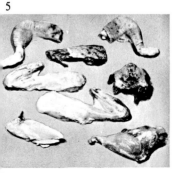

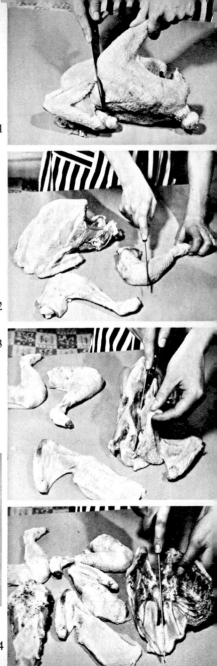

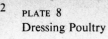

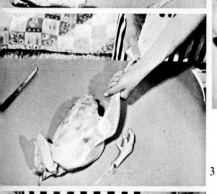

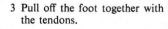

PLATE 8
Dressing Poultry

1 Halfway along the neck of the plucked chicken, cut a ring round outer skin and pull or cut off the head. Holding the neck with a dry cloth, pull the skin loose. Twist the neck round until it is detached from the body. Push index finger into crop cavity to loosen crop and gizzard.

2 With a knife cut the skin on the leg, place the leg over the table edge and snap the bone.

3 Pull off the foot together with the tendons.

4 Make a slit of from 2 to 3 inches above the vent to enable the viscera to be removed.

5 Insert the first two fingers of the right hand. Draw out intestines —with knuckles upwards.

PLATE 9
Dressing Poultry

6 Trim the end of the intestines and vent away with a sharp knife. Separate the liver from the gall-bladder, do not break the latter.

6

7 Skin the meaty outside of the crop from the gritty contents. Remove and discard the lungs.

8 Wipe the inside with a dry cloth.

7

9 Pass a threaded needle through the left leg just above thigh bone; pass through body, and through other leg joint. Turn breast downwards, carry string through the elbow joint of the wing on each side, twist end of wing under the neck of the bird to hold the neck flap of the skin. Draw the two ends together and tie up.

8

10 Cut a slit in the flesh above the original vent-cut and push parson's nose through. Loop the string over the ends of the drum-sticks, draw together and tie off round tail end of parson's nose.

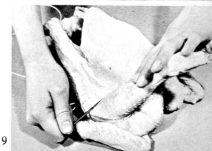

9

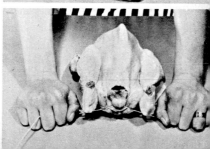

10

PLATE 10
Dressing a Hare

1 With a sharp knife cut off the feet just below the foot joint.

2 Cut carefully through the skin straight down the belly; ease back the skin from the flesh. Work round the body until the flesh is freed from the skin.

3 Push forward each hind leg in turn and work the skin free of flesh. Pull the skin from tail. Holding the skinned hindquarters in the left hand, gently pull the skin over the back and shoulders.

4 Work each foreleg free in turn.

5 If head is to be left on remove skin; otherwise cut off the head.

6 Cut through the skin of the belly. Slit the belly from the chest to the legs and draw out the viscera.

PLATE 11
Jointing a Hare or Rabbit

This sequence of photographs takes up where the sequence on Plate 10 ends. Before starting the following set of operations the hare or rabbit should be thoroughly washed in salt water.

1 With a sharp knife cut off the side flaps, then the hind legs.

2 Cut off front legs at the joint.

3 Chop the back sharply once or twice (depending on size of the animal), and separate the body into fairly even parts as shown.

4 This photograph shows nine separate joints which can be cut from a hare or rabbit. In foreground are the liver and kidneys.

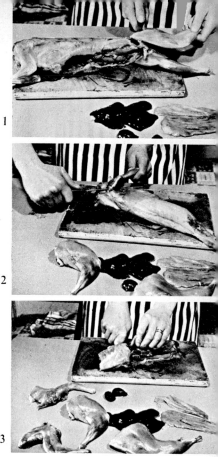

PLATE 12
Making Short Crust Pastry

1 Ensure all utensils are cold. Sift flour and salt into a bowl.

2 With a sharp knife cut, or use a grater to shred in the fat.

1

2

3 Rub in the fat with the finger tips until the mixture looks like fine breadcrumbs. Lift the hands up from the bowl so that the air is entrapped as the flour falls back into the bowl.

4 Using a knife, mix to a stiff dough with only the necessary amount of freshly-drawn cold water. Gather the mixture together, leaving the bowl clean. Dough should feel damp but not sticky.

4

3 5

5 On a floured surface, press the dough lightly with the fingers into rough shape required.

PLATE 13
Making Flaky Pastry

1 Sift the flour and salt into a bowl. Divide fat into four equal portions. Lightly rub quarter of the fat into the flour. Next mix to a soft dough with cold water and lemon juice.

2 Roll dough out into an oblong shape.

3 Place quarter of the fat in small pieces on the top two-thirds of the pastry.

4 Fold the bottom third of the pastry up and the top third downwards.

5 With the rolling pin, press edges lightly together, make a half turn, and press ridges in the pastry to distribute the air evenly. Allow dough to relax. Roll out and repeat with the other two portions of fat.

PLATE 14
Icing a Cake

1 Using a pastry-brush, brush top and side of cake with apricot glaze. Roll out the almond paste to a round shape about 4 in. wider than the diameter of the cake. Place the cake in the centre of the almond paste, top-side down.

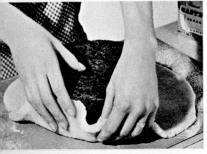

2 With the hands work the paste up side of the cake until it is within ½ inch of the top edge.

3 Using a straight-sided jar, roll round the side, holding the cake firm with the other hand.

4 Take a spoonful of icing and smooth with a palette knife; do the top first, then side.

5 Decorate, using a forcing bag and pipe. Draw design first on greaseproof paper cut to fit top and side of cake. Prick the lines of the design through with a pin. Decorate top, then side, then base.

PLATE 15
Making a Flan Case
("Blind" Baking)

1 Roll out the pastry and line a greased flan ring with it. Press to fit bottom and side so that no air bubbles form underneath.

2 Trim off surplus pastry by rolling across with the rolling-pin or cut it off with a sharp knife.

3 Cover bottom of flan with a piece of greaseproof paper and weight it to keep shape during baking.

4 Remove paper, rice, beans, etc., and flan ring when pastry is cooked.

1

2

3

4

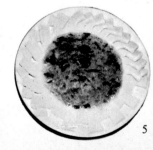

PLATE 16

Decorating Tarts

A few simple finishing touches like the ones outlined below will soon transform even the plainest tarts and pies into fancy party dishes.

1. With a sharp knife make even cuts about 1 inch apart and 1 inch in depth round the edge of the tart. Damp with a pastry-brush and fold alternate pieces down, pressing them only very lightly.

2. Roll out pastry trimmings to a thickness of $\frac{1}{8}$ inch and cut out small circles. Damp the edge of the tart and press cutouts on edge so that they overlap.

3. Make cuts as in 1. Moisten and fold pieces so that they overlap to give sunray effect.

4. Decorate the edge with a fork, then arrange fleurons (cut with a fluted pastry cutter from pastry scraps) on the filling.

5. Three ways of folding an edge after cutting (see 1 above).

gently until the carrots are tender —15–30 min., according to age of carrots. Serve hot, with the small amount of liquid remaining, and garnished with parsley.

NOTE: This method should be employed for cooking most root vegetables, e.g. parsnips, turnips, swedes, onions, etc., and should replace "boiling". Both flavour and food value are conserved.

6 helpings

GLAZED CARROTS

1½ lb. young carrots   2 oz. butter
3 lumps sugar   ¼ teasp. salt
good stock   chopped parsley

Melt the butter in a saucepan. Add the scraped, whole carrots, sugar, salt and enough stock to come half-way up the carrots. Cook gently, without a lid, shaking the pan occasionally until tender. Remove the carrots and keep them hot. Boil the stock rapidly until reduced to rich glaze. Replace the carrots 2 or 3 at a time, turn them until both sides are well coated with glaze. Dish, sprinkle with chopped parsley and serve.

6 helpings
Cooking time—about ¾ hr.

CAULIFLOWER

Cauliflowers are in season from June to October. *See* Broccoli (p. 214).

BOILED CAULIFLOWER WITH WHITE SAUCE

1 large cauliflower   ½ pt. white sauce made with half milk and half cauliflower water   salt

Trim off the stem and all the leaves, except the very young ones. Soak in cold water, head down, with 1 teasp. salt per qt. of water, for not more than 10 min. Wash well. Choose a suitably sized pan and put in enough water to ¼ fill it, with ½ teasp. salt to 1 pt. water. Put in cauliflower, stalk

down, and cook with lid on pan until stalk and flower are tender. Lift out carefully and drain. Keep hot. Coat the cauliflower with the sauce and serve immediately.

NOTE: To reduce cooking time, the cauliflower may be quartered before cooking or broken into large sprigs.

6 helpings
Cooking time—20–25 min.

CAULIFLOWER WITH CHEESE

1 large cauliflower   ¾ pt. cheese sauce (p. 92)   salt   1 heaped tablesp. grated cheese (dry Cheddar) or 1 dessertsp. grated Cheddar cheese and 1 dessertsp. grated Parmesan cheese

Cook the cauliflower as in preceding recipe, drain well and dish up in a fireproof dish. Coat with thick cheese sauce. Sprinkle with grated cheese and immediately brown under a hot grill or in the top of a hot oven (425° F., Gas 7). Serve immediately.

4 helpings
Cooking time—25–30 min.

CELERIAC or TURNIP ROOTED CELERY

This vegetable with its flavour of celery has many uses. It can be grated raw in salads, used for flavouring soups and is excellent cooked in various ways. The thick root only is used. It stores well.

Celeriac is in season from October to April.

CELERIAC WITH WHITE SAUCE

3 roots of celeriac   ¾ pt. good white sauce (p. 91)   salt
lemon juice

Scrub the roots well, then peel thickly. (If the roots are spongy discard them as useless.) Cut into ½-in. slices and stew them slowly in boiling, salted vegetable stock or water till tender—about 45 min.

Drain. Make a good white sauce with ½ pt. milk and cooking liquid. Season and add a little lemon juice. Coat the celeriac and serve immediately.

NOTE: The vegetable stock can be water in which onions, Jerusalem artichokes, etc., have been cooked.

6 helpings
Cooking time—45 min. (approx.)

CELERY

This vegetable is most commonly eaten raw. It may be cooked in a variety of ways and the outer stems, unsuitable for eating raw, should always be used in soups, stews and for flavouring in some sauces and fish dishes.

Celery is in season from September to February.

BRAISED CELERY

4 heads of celery   stock
glaze (if available)

MIREPOIX
½ oz. dripping   ½ oz. bacon   2 large carrots   1 small turnip   2 onions
bouquet garni (thyme, marjoram, sage, parsley)   1 blade of mace
6 white peppercorns   1 bay leaf   salt

Trim the celery but leave the heads whole. Wash them well and tie each securely. Prepare the mirepoix. Fry the bacon in the dripping in a large saucepan, then fry all the vegetables cut in pieces ¾ in. thick, until lightly browned. Add herbs, spices and ½ teasp. of salt and enough stock to come ¾ of the way up the vegetables. Bring to boiling-point. Lay the celery on top. Baste well with the stock in the pan and cover closely with greased paper or metal foil. Put on lid and cook until the celery is soft (about 1½ hr.). Baste several times during cooking. Dish the celery and keep hot. Strain the liquor, put it back in the pan and add 1 teasp. of glaze if available. Reduce by boiling quickly until of glazing consistency. Pour over the celery.

NOTE: Use the coarse outer stems of the celery for soups. A few pieces may be cut up and fried for the mirepoix. The cooked mirepoix can be served sprinkled with parsley, as a separate vegetable dish or, if sieved and thinned down with stock, it makes an excellent soup.

CELERY WITH WHITE SAUCE

2 large heads of celery
½ pt. good white sauce (p. 91)   salt
lemon juice

Trim off the green tops of the celery, reserving a few pale green ones. Remove the very tough outer stalks. Separate the other stalks and wash or, if necessary, scrub in cold water. Rinse and reserve the tender hearts for eating raw. Scrape the stalks to be cooked, cut into suitable lengths for cooking and tie in bundles. Stew in barely sufficient boiling water, slightly salted, to cover the celery. If possible, cook in vegetable water from cooked artichokes, onions, etc. When tender (in about 1 hr.), drain. Make a good white sauce with half milk and half cooking liquid. Season and add a little lemon juice. Coat the celery with the sauce, garnish with some of the pale green leaves and serve immediately.

NOTE: The celery may be cooked in milk, with the addition of 1 finely chopped onion. When cooked, the celery may be served as above, with the addition of 2 tablesp. of cream to the sauce just as the pan is removed from the heat.

4–6 helpings
Cooking time—1 hr.

CHESTNUTS
CHESTNUTS AU JUS

2 lb. chestnuts   2 cloves   1 small onion   1 outside stick of celery

1 bay leaf   1 blade of mace   1 pt.
good brown stock   cayenne pepper
salt   1 dessertsp. glaze (if available)
fleurons of pastry

Take a sharp knife and make an
incision in each chestnut, in the
shell only. Put into a saucepan and
cover with cold water. Bring to the
boil and cook for 2 min. Drain and
peel and skin them while very hot.
Stick the cloves into the onion and
put chestnuts, onion, celery, bay
leaf and mace into the boiling
stock. Season. Simmer about 1 hr.
until the chestnuts are tender.
Strain and keep the chestnuts hot.
Return stock to pan, add the glaze
if available and reduce to a glazing
consistency. Pile the chestnuts in a
hot vegetable dish, pour the glaze
over and decorate with fleurons.

6 helpings
Cooking time—1¼ hr.

CHESTNUT PUREE

2 lb. chestnuts   veal or chicken
stock   ½ oz. butter   1 tablesp. cream
seasoning

Peel and skin chestnuts as in
preceding recipe. Put them into
the boiling stock with a little salt
and stew gently until tender (use
barely enough stock to cover).
Strain. Put the chestnuts through
a wire sieve. Put them back into
the pan, add the butter and
enough of the cooking liquor to
give a thick purée. Add the cream
and season carefully. Serve in a
hot vegetable dish. Put tiny pieces
of butter on the surface to prevent
a crust forming, if the purée must
be kept waiting.

CHICORY

This vegetable is used extensively in France, particularly in its
raw state, with a French dressing.
It is an excellent vegetable either
raw or cooked. The bitter flavour,
disliked by some, is disguised by
the French dressing and can be
removed from cooked chicory by
blanching for five minutes prior to
the cooking process itself. Chicory
is in season from September to
April.

CHICORY AND WHITE SAUCE

6 large heads of chicory
¾ pt. good white sauce (p. 91)   salt
lemon juice

Cut off the end of the chicory
and the outer leaves. Split each
head to within ½ in. of the end and
wash well between the leaves.
Blanch, by bringing to the boil in
just enough water to cover and
boiling 5 min. Drain, then tie the
heads together in bundles of 2 and
cook in boiling, salted water until
just tender. Finish and serve as
for Celery with White Sauce (p.
218).

6 helpings
Cooking time—30–40 min.

CORN, INDIAN CORN, SWEET CORN, or MAIZE

In cookery corn always means
Maize or Indian Corn. It is grown
extensively in America, where it is
considered a great delicacy. Early
ripening varieties from America
have made it a fairly well known
vegetable with British cooks. It is
not, however, eaten at its best in
Britain, as it is often allowed to
ripen too long, and it should be
freshly cut when cooked. When
ripe enough to cut, the milk of the
grain should exude when the grain
is pierced with the finger-nail.
After this stage it is useful only as
food for poultry.

Corn is seasonable from May to
August.

BAKED CORN ON THE COB

6 ears or cobs of corn, freshly picked
2 oz. butter   seasoning

Method 1. Remove outer and
inner husks and the silk. Melt the
butter in a roasting-dish. Roll the
cobs in it, so that they are lightly

coated with butter. Season. Roast
in a fairly hot oven (375° F., Gas
5), turning them frequently.

6 helpings
Cooking time—35 min. (approx.)

Method 2. Prepare as above but
place the cobs in the roasting-dish
(without butter) and just cover
them with milk. Bake for about
45 min. Drain; season with salt
and pepper. Toss in melted butter
and place under a hot grill for a
few minutes before serving.

6 helpings
Cooking time—1 hr. (approx.)

BOILED CORN ON THE COB

6 ears or cobs of corn, freshly picked
seasoning   butter

Remove the outer husks of the
corn. Open the tender, pale green
inner husks and take away all the
silk surrounding the corn. Replace
the inner husk and tie securely;
place the ears in a saucepan with
sufficient boiling water to cover
them. Simmer gently 15–20 min.
Drain and remove strings and
husks. Serve with melted, seasoned
butter. The flavour is always best
if the corn is torn from the cob
with the teeth, each guest being
supplied with melted butter in
which to dip the corn.

6 helpings
Cooking time—about 20 min.

CUCUMBER

Cucumbers are usually eaten uncooked or pickled. Cucumber is
most digestible if the skin is left on
and the cucumber sliced thickly to
ensure that it is well chewed. The
rind is rich in salts and flavour,
and contains minute amounts of
substances which help in digestion
of the pulp of the cucumber.

There are a number of pleasant
ways of using cucumber as a
cooked vegetable. As with marrow,
which, like the cucumber, contains
a high percentage of water, it

should be steamed rather than
stewed or boiled.

Cucumbers are obtainable all the
year round but are cheapest in July
and August.

CUCUMBER WITH SAUCE

2 large cucumbers   1 oz. butter or
margarine   1 teasp. finely-chopped
shallot   ¾ pt. white sauce (p. 91)
1 egg   1 teasp. finely-chopped
parsley   salt and pepper

Peel the cucumbers and steam
until tender (about 20 min.).
Drain well and cut into 1-in. slices.
Melt the butter in a saucepan, put
in the shallot and cook it without
browning. Add the sliced cucumber, toss over heat for a few
minutes, then stir in the white
sauce. Just before boiling-point is
reached, add the well-beaten egg
and parsley, stir and cook gently
until the egg thickens. Season and
serve hot.

6 helpings
Cooking time—30 min. (approx.)

STUFFED CUCUMBERS

2 large cucumbers   1 oz. margarine
¼ lb. minced cold meat, e.g. ham,
veal, beef, chicken   2 heaped
tablesp. fresh breadcrumbs
1 tablesp. finely-chopped parsley
¼ teasp. mixed herbs   1 egg   a little
stock   seasoning   Worcester sauce
croûtes of fried bread

Wash and peel the cucumbers
and cut into 2-in. lengths. Scoop
out the centres with a teaspoon.
Steam until soft—about 15 min.
While the cucumber is cooking,
heat the margarine in a saucepan.
Stir in the meat, breadcrumbs,
parsley and herbs, heat thoroughly,
add the beaten egg and enough
stock to give a soft stuffing. Season
well, adding Worcester sauce for
extra flavour, if necessary. Drain
the cucumber and put each piece
on a croûte of bread. Fill with the
hot stuffing, which should be piled

up high. Garnish with chopped parsley.

Serve tomato sauce (p. 99) or brown sauce (p. 94) with the stuffed cucumber.

6 helpings
Cooking time—35 min. (approx.)

NOTE: Other fillings for stuffed cucumber are as follows:

(1) Hard-boiled eggs, finely chopped and mixed with thick cheese sauce.

(2) Macédoine of vegetables in a thick cheese sauce.

(3) Finely chopped cooked mushrooms mixed with chopped onion and bacon and thickened with breadcrumbs or white sauce.

DANDELION LEAVES

STEWED DANDELION LEAVES

2 lb. young, tender dandelion leaves
1 oz. butter or margarine   salt and
pepper   1 tablesp. cream

Wash the leaves thoroughly and soak in cold water for 1 hr. Cook in boiling, salted water, the water should come ¼ of the way up the pan before the leaves are put into it. When tender (in 20–30 min.) drain them well, like spinach. Chop them and reheat with butter and cream. Season and serve hot.

NOTE: Dandelion leaves are suitable for cooking in the Spring.

6 helpings

EGG PLANT (see Aubergine)

ENDIVE

This vegetable is generally served as a salad but may also be served as a hot vegetable.

Endive is in season from November to March.

BRAISED ENDIVE

6 heads of endive   stock
glaze, if available
mirepoix (see Braised Celery, p. 218)

Cut off the stumps of the endive and discard any outer leaves that

are discoloured or tough. Wash in several waters, then parboil in salted water 10 min. to remove bitter flavour. Drain well, pressing out water with the fingers. Braise and serve as for Braised Celery (p. 218).

6 helpings
Cooking time—approx. 1½ hr.
altogether

KOHL-RABI

This is a vegetable which resembles turnip in flavour, but is grown much more easily and should be eaten soon after it is taken from the ground, as its flavour is spoilt by storing.

It may be served in any way suitable for turnips, but as its characteristic flavour is in and near the skin, it should, where possible, be cooked in the skin.

LEEKS

Leeks are in season from August to May.

BOILED LEEKS

12 leeks   salt
¾ pt. white sauce (p. 91)

Trim off the roots and outer leaves and as much of the tops as necessary. Split from the top to within 1 in. of the bottom. Wash very thoroughly under running water, separating each leaf with the fingers to ensure that no grit is left between the leaves. Drain and tie in bundles. Boil in as little water as possible (barely enough to cover), with 1 teasp. salt to 1 pt. water. Cook until tender—30–40 min. Drain well and coat with white sauce made with half milk and half leek water.

6 helpings

LENTILS

BOILED LENTILS

¾ lb. lentils   bouquet garni   1 ham
bone (if available) or bacon rinds

1 onion 1 clove salt and pepper
½ oz. butter or margarine

Put the lentils into cold water
with the herbs, ham bone, onion
stuck with the clove, and a little
salt. Bring to boiling-point and
cook until the lentils are soft—
about 1 hr. Strain the lentils, toss
in a little melted butter or margarine; season and serve. If preferred,
sieve the lentils before tossing in
butter.

6 helpings

LETTUCES

Though generally served as the
principal ingredient in a salad,
lettuces may also be served as a
cooked vegetable.

STEWED LETTUCE

6 small lettuce 1 oz. butter or
margarine 1 oz. flour ½ pt. stock
1 dessertsp. chopped chives 1 bay
leaf 1 dessertsp. chopped parsley
salt and pepper

Wash the lettuces well. Plunge
into boiling salt water and simmer
2 min. Plunge into cold water,
drain. Melt the butter in a saucepan, add the flour, mix well, then
add stock and stir until smooth and
thick. Add chives, bay leaf, parsley,
and a little salt and put in the lettuces. Cook gently for ½ hr., stirring from time to time. Re-season
and serve.

6 helpings
Cooking time—½ hr. (approx.)

LIMA BEANS (see Haricot
Beans, p. 213)

MUSHROOMS

Mushrooms are obtainable all
the year.

BAKED MUSHROOMS

18–24 flap mushrooms salt and
pepper powdered mace
butter or margarine

Wash the mushrooms under
running water, peel the caps and
trim the ragged ends of the stalks.
Put into a baking-dish, gills of the
mushrooms uppermost, sprinkle
with salt and pepper and a very
little mace and put a tiny piece of
butter on each. Cover and cook
25–30 min. in a fairly hot oven
(375° F., Gas 5).

If possible, cook in a fireproof
glass dish with a lid and serve in
the same dish, thus retaining all
the flavour of the mushrooms.

6 helpings

GRILLED MUSHROOMS

12 flap mushrooms salt and pepper
butter or bacon fat buttered toast
chopped parsley lemon juice

Wash, peel and trim the stalks.
Season and brush with melted
butter or bacon fat. Cook under a
hot grill, turning them once.
Serve in a hot dish or on rounds of
buttered toast, with a sprinkling
of chopped parsley and a squeeze
of lemon juice.

6 helpings
Cooking time—10 min. (approx.)

MUSHROOMS STEWED WITH WINE

1 lb. button mushrooms 6 rashers
of streaky bacon 1 teasp. finely-
chopped chives 1 teasp. finely-
chopped parsley salt and pepper
white wine or cider flour

Wash and peel the mushrooms,
trim the stalks. Cut up the bacon
into small pieces and cook in a
saucepan 15 min. Add the mushrooms, chives and parsley and a
little salt. Moisten with white wine
or cider, dredge lightly with flour
and stew very gently until the
sauce is quite thick. Re-season.

6 helpings
Cooking time—40 min. (approx.)

PRESERVED MUSHROOMS WITH BROWN SAUCE

1 small can or bottle of mushrooms
stock 1 oz. butter or margarine

1 oz. flour   1 tablesp. sherry
(optional)   salt and pepper

Strain the liquor from the can
or bottle and add to it sufficient
stock to make up to ½ pt. Fry the
butter and flour together until well
browned, add the liquor and stir
till the mixture boils. Add sherry
and mushrooms and heat thoroughly. Season and serve.

4–5 helpings
Cooking time—about 30 min.

STEWED MUSHROOMS

1 lb. flap or button mushrooms
2 oz. butter or margarine
1 dessertsp. arrowroot   ¼ pt. stock
lemon juice   2 tablesp. cream
salt and pepper   chopped parsley
fleurons of pastry

Wash and peel the mushrooms,
trim the stalks. Melt the butter in
a saucepan and fry the mushrooms
in it slowly, about 10 min. Blend
the arrowroot with the stock. Add
to the pan and stir till boiling.
Simmer 20–30 min. Add lemon
juice and cream and season carefully. Dish and garnish with
parsley and fleurons of pastry.

NOTE: This mixture may be
used to fill small French rolls.

6 helpings
Cooking time—30–40 min.

NETTLES

Young nettles are very pleasant
to eat, resembling spinach. The
young tops should be gathered,
washed and cooked like spinach,
cooking them over a low heat at
first until the water has run off the
leaves and there is no fear that they
will burn on the bottom of the pan.

Gloves must be worn when gath-
ering and preparing the nettles.

OKRA (*Gumbo*)

This is an aromatic bean native
to the West Indies, where it is
known as Gumbo. It is now grown
extensively in India, West Africa
and the Southern States of
America, and to a lesser extent in
the South of France. The young
green pods are sometimes pickled
and the older pods preserved in
cans for export. Okra has a peculiar flavour, often thought disagreeable to an unaccustomed
palate. It is exceedingly mucila-
ginous, the pods in the tin being
surrounded by a substance of
greater viscidity than gum.

BOILED OKRA

24 fresh okras   2 oz. butter
2 tablesp. cream or milk
salt and pepper

Wash the okras in cold water,
drain them well and trim both
ends. Place in barely enough salted
water to cover, cook gently for 15
min., or until tender, and drain
well. Heat the butter and cream
in the saucepan, put in the okras,
sprinkle with salt and pepper,
shake over heat for a few minutes,
then serve.

6 helpings
Cooking time—20–30 min.

CANNED OKRAS
(*to serve as a vegetable*)

1 can okras   ½ oz. butter or
margarine   salt and pepper

Turn the contents of the can
into a saucepan and heat. Drain.
Toss in melted butter or margarine. Season and serve.

ONIONS

The name Spanish onion is
often given to any large onion of
mild flavour.

If strong onion flavour is disliked, onions should be blanched
prior to the actual cooking.

BAKED ONIONS

6 large onions   salt and pepper
a little margarine or butter
a little milk

Method 1. Peel the onions and
cook in boiling, salted water 20

min. Drain and place in a fireproof dish. Sprinkle with salt and pepper. Put a small pat of margarine *or* butter on the top of each and pour enough milk in the dish to come a third of the way up the onions. Cover with a greased paper. Bake in a moderate oven (350° F., Gas 4) until tender, basting frequently with the milk. Serve with any milk and onion liquor in the dish.

6 helpings

Cooking time—to bake the onions about 1½ hr.

Method 2. Boil the onions till tender, in their skins. Drain and dry in a cloth and wrap each onion in well-greased paper or in "cropar" paper. Bake in a moderate oven (350° F., Gas 4) for an hour. Unwrap and serve in their skins with butter or margarine.

6 helpings

Cooking time—to boil 1½ hr.; to to bake 1 hr.

Method 3. Trim off the roots of the onions, wipe, but do not skin. Put a little margarine, butter *or* dripping in a fireproof dish, or roasting-tin. Place the onions in it and bake until tender in a fairly hot oven (375° F., Gas 5). Take out the onions and peel them. Put them back in the dish, season with salt and pepper, and baste well, using a little extra fat if necessary. Reheat for 10 min.

6 helpings

Cooking time—to bake 1½–2 hr.

BOILED ONIONS

**6 large onions   salt and pepper
¾ pt. white sauce (p. 91)
lemon juice**

Cut off the root and top of the onions, the brown skin and inner layer of skin. Put into cold water, bring to the boil and strain if a mild flavour is required. Put into boiling water (just enough to cover) with 1 teasp. salt to 1 pt. of

water. Boil gently 1½–2 hr., according to size. Make a white sauce with half milk and half onion water. Season and flavour with a little lemon juice. Coat the onions and serve very hot.

6 helpings

Cooking time—1½–2 hr.

FRIED ONIONS

**6 large onions   frying fat
salt and pepper**

Peel and slice the onions. Heat enough frying fat in a frying-pan to cover the bottom of the pan. Fry the onions slowly until golden brown and quite soft, stirring them occasionally during frying. Drain well, season and serve hot.

6 helpings

Cooking time—20 min.

STEWED ONIONS

**6 large onions   1 pt. brown stock
salt and pepper
small bunch of herbs**

Peel the onions and blanch them. Put them into a pan which will just hold them standing side by side. Add the stock, bunch of herbs, and a little salt and put on the lid of the pan. Simmer gently 1½ hr. Season and serve in a hot dish with the cooking liquid poured round.

6 helpings

Cooking time—about 1½ hr.

STUFFED ONIONS

**6 large onions   4 tablesp. finely-chopped liver or cooked ham or any cooked meat   1 tablesp. finely-chopped cooked onion   1 tablesp. breadcrumbs   ½ teasp. finely-chopped fresh sage or ½ teasp. dried sage   salt and pepper   1 egg butter or margarine
¾ pt. brown sauce (p. 94)**

Peel and steam the onions gently until almost soft, about 1 hr. Lift out the centre of each onion with a teaspoon handle.

Chop the onion centres and add to the stuffing. Mix the stuffing ingredients with the beaten egg. Season well. Press it firmly into each onion and pile neatly on top. Sprinkle the top of each onion with a little melted butter or margarine. Pin a band of stiff, greased paper round each onion to prevent splitting. Put into a greased, fireproof dish and bake 30–40 min. in a moderate oven (350° F., *Gas* 4). Serve with the sauce poured round.

6 helpings
Cooking time—about 1¾ hr.

PARSLEY

Parsley is used extensively by the cook as a garnish for all types of savoury dishes and adds considerably to their Vitamin C value. If chopped by the method on p. 40 it is bright green in colour, retains most of its Vitamin C and is chopped quickly, without leaving a stain on the chopping board.

FRIED PARSLEY

Remove stalks from the parsley, leaving it in sprigs. Wash it, shake well and dry in a cloth for at least 1 hr. before frying. Put into the basket of a deep-fat pan. Dip the basket just into the hot fat at 340° F., remove quickly, dip again and remove, then plunge into the fat and leave it in until most of the bubbling has ceased and the parsley is bright green and crisp. Drain very well on absorbent paper. Serve hot with many savoury dishes, particularly with fish.

NOTE: The high water-content of parsley causes hot fat to bubble fiercely and, if the parsley is plunged straight into the fat and left there, the fat may come over the top of the pan and cause a fire.

PARSNIPS

Parsnips are in season from October to March.

PARSNIPS—CONSERVATIVELY COOKED

2 lb. parsnips   1 oz. butter or margarine   ½ teasp. salt   1 gill boiling water   chopped parsley

Scrub and scrape the parsnips and slice them thinly. Fat steam the parsnips for 10 min., i.e. shake them in the melted fat, well below frying temperature, with the lid on the pan until the fat is absorbed. Add the boiling water and the salt, and simmer gently until the parsnips are tender.

Serve hot with the small amount of liquid remaining, and garnish with chopped parsley.

6 helpings
Cooking time—30–45 min.

MASHED PARSNIPS

2 lb. parsnips (conservatively cooked)   1 oz. butter or margarine 2 tablesp. milk   salt and pepper chopped parsley

Prepare the parsnips and cook them as in Parsnips—Conservatively Cooked. Drain off any liquid left in the pan and reserve it for a soup or gravy. Mash with a fork or rub through a nylon sieve. Heat the butter or margarine in a pan and beat in the purée, add the milk, stir over heat until thoroughly hot. Season well. Serve in a hot vegetable dish and sprinkle with chopped parsley.

6 helpings
Cooking time—35–50 min.

PEAS

Peas are in season from May to September.

GREEN PEAS

2 lb. peas   salt   sprig of mint a little sugar   ½ oz. butter or margarine

Shell the peas. Have sufficient boiling, salted water to cover the peas. Add the peas, mint and sugar. Simmer gently until soft, from 10–20 min. Drain well. Re-heat with butter *or* margarine and serve in a hot vegetable dish.

NOTE: If the peas must be shelled some time before cooking, put them in a basin and cover them closely with washed peapods.

4–6 helpings (according to yield)
Cooking time—10–20 min.

CANNED or BOTTLED PEAS
(*to dress*)

1 can or **bottle of peas   butter** or **margarine   sprig of mint   sugar   salt and pepper**

Strain the peas and rinse them well. Melt ½–1 oz. butter *or* margarine in a saucepan (the amount depends upon the size of the can of peas). Add a sprig of mint, the peas, salt and little sugar. Cover down closely with a butter or margarine paper, then the tightly-fitting lid of the pan. Leave over a very low heat, shaking the pan occasionally until the peas are hot, about 15–20 min. Re-season and serve.

NOTE: If available 1 or 2 outside lettuce leaves may be put into the pan (whole) and removed before serving the peas.

DRIED PEAS

Dried peas   2 qt. boiling water to each 1 lb. peas   ½ level teasp. bicarbonate of soda or **a piece of washing soda the size of a cherry**

Pour the boiling water on to the required weight of peas, add the soda, and leave to soak overnight.

Rinse the peas thoroughly after soaking, cook in plenty of boiling, salted water until the peas are soft —1 to 1½ hr. approximately.

To improve the flavour, add a sprig of mint, bunch of herbs (a small sprig of marjoram, sage, thyme and a few parsley stalks) or an onion stuck with 2 or 3 cloves.

PEASE PUDDING

1½ pt. split peas   1 small onion small bunch of herbs   2 oz. butter or **margarine   2 eggs   salt and pepper**

Soak the peas overnight; remove any discoloured ones. Rinse and cover with cold, salted water. Bring slowly to boiling-point in the water, to which has been added the onion (whole) and the bunch of herbs. Simmer very slowly until tender—2–2½ hr. Drain well and rub through a sieve. Add the but-ter, cut in small pieces, the beaten eggs, pepper and salt. Beat well until the ingredients are well in-corporated. Tie tightly in a floured cloth and simmer in water for an hour. Turn out and serve very hot.

NOTE: Pease pudding is served with hot pickled pork.

6 helpings
Cooking time—about 3½ hr.

PEPPERS or CAPSICUMS

The large peppers used as a vegetable are variously known as Spanish peppers, Long peppers, Green or sweet peppers, Bell peppers or Red peppers according to their shape and colour. They are a very popular vegetable in America and Spain and are being used more extensively than for-merly in Britain.

Peppers are in season from August to November.

FRIED PEPPERS

4 green peppers   butter or **margarine** or **deep fat   egg and breadcrumbs (if to be fried in deep fat)**

Wash the peppers. Parboil in salted water for 5 min. Drain and cut into strips or rings. Remove seeds and inner partitions. Toss in hot butter *or* margarine in a fry-ing-pan for 5–10 min. *or* dip in egg and breadcrumbs and fry in deep fat (360° F.) 5–7 min. Drain well and serve hot.

4–6 helpings

POTATOES

ANNA POTATOES

**2 lb. even-sized waxy potatoes   salt
and pepper   melted clarified butter
or margarine**

Grease a thick cake-tin and line
the bottom with greased paper.
Peel and trim the potatoes so that
they will give equal-sized slices.
Slice them very finely and arrange
a layer of slightly overlapping
slices. Sprinkle with clarified fat
and seasoning. Make a second
layer of potato and repeat. Continue until the tin is full, pressing
each layer well into the tin. Cover
with greased paper and a lid and
bake in a fairly hot oven (375° F.,
Gas 5) for about 1 hr. Look at the
potatoes from time to time and add
more clarified butter if they become dry. Turn out onto a hot dish
and serve at once.

**6 helpings
Cooking time—about 1 hr.**

BAKED POTATOES—IN THEIR JACKETS

**6 large potatoes   butter or margarine
or bacon fat**

Scrub the potatoes, rinse and
dry them. Brush with melted butter, *or* margarine, *or* bacon fat or
rub with a greasy butter paper.
Prick with a fork. Bake on the
shelves of a fairly hot oven (375°
F., Gas 5) until soft—about 1½ hr.,
turning them whilst they are cooking. Cut a cross in the top of each,
insert a pat of butter *or* margarine.
Serve in a hot vegetable dish.

**6 helpings
Cooking time—about 1½ hr.**

BAKED AND STUFFED POTATOES

6 large potatoes

STUFFING, choice of:

(1) **3 oz. grated cheese ; 1 oz. butter
or margarine ; a little milk ;
seasoning ; nutmeg**

(2) **3 oz. chopped, fried bacon ; a
little milk ; seasoning**

(3) **3 oz. mashed, cooked smoked
haddock ; chopped parsley ;
lemon juice ; a little milk ;
nutmeg**

(4) **2 boned kippers, cooked and
mashed ; a little milk**

(5) **2 oz. grated cheese ; 1 oz.
butter ; chopped parsley ; a little
milk ; seasoning ; 2 egg yolks
stirred into the filling ; 2 egg
whites folded in at the end**

Scrub, rinse and dry the potatoes and grease as in preceding
recipe. With a small sharp knife,
cut through the skin of the
potatoes to give the appearance of
a lid. Bake as for Potatoes in
Jackets. Lift off lids carefully,
scoop out cooked potato from
skins, including lids, taking care
not to split the skins. Mash the
potato in a basin and add the ingredients of any one of the stuffings listed above. Mix well and
season thoroughly. Fill the potato
skins with the mixture, piling it
high. Fork the tops and brush with
a little egg, or sprinkle with a little
grated cheese (if an ingredient of
the stuffing). Put back in the oven
and bake till thoroughly hot and
golden brown. Serve in a hot dish
garnished with parsley and with
the skin "lids" replaced, if liked.

NOTE : A stuffing consisting of
cooked minced meat in a sauce or
gravy, *or* of cooked mixed vegetables *or* flaked fish in a sauce may
replace the floury meal of the
potato entirely. The latter should
then be mashed and served separately *or* mashed and piped round
the opening of the potato after it
has been stuffed and before returning it to the oven.

**6 helpings
Cooking time—about 2 hr.**

BOILED POTATOES

**2 lb. even-sized potatoes   salt
chopped parsley**

Scrub the potatoes. Peel thinly. Rinse and put into a saucepan with sufficient *boiling* water just to cover them and 1 teasp. salt to each quart of water. Boil gently 25–40 min., according to age and size. Test with a fine skewer and, if tender, drain off the water and put the saucepan back on a very low heat, with the lid tilted to allow steam to escape. Serve hot, sprinkled with chopped parsley.

NOTE: The potatoes have a better flavour if boiled in their skins. In this case peel off a thin strip of skin, round the middle of each potato. This facilitates skinning after cooking.

6 helpings
Cooking time—25–40 min.

DUCHESS POTATOES

1 lb. old potatoes   1 oz. butter or
margarine   cream or top of milk
2 yolks or 1 whole egg   salt and
pepper   grated nutmeg

Prepare and cook the potatoes as for Boiled Potatoes. Put through a sieve. Mash with the fat, beaten egg and sufficient cream to give a smooth mixture, which stands up in soft peaks when drawn up with the wooden spoon. Season well and add grated nutmeg. Pipe through a star vegetable pipe, on to a greased baking-sheet. Sprinkle with a little beaten egg and bake in a hot oven (400° F., Gas 6), until crisp and brown. Serve in a hot uncovered dish.

NOTE: If a "pipe" is not available, keep the mixture a little stiffer and shape on a floured board into small cork shapes, diamonds, rounds or triangles. Decorate the tops with criss-crosses made with the back of a knife.

If more convenient, the mixture may be shaped or piped on to the tin and left in a cool place for baking at a later time.

6 helpings
Cooking time—to bake, 15 min.

MASHED POTATOES

2 lb. potatoes   1 oz. butter or
margarine   chopped parsley
a little milk   salt and pepper
grated nutmeg

Prepare and cook potatoes as for Boiled Potatoes. Pass them through a wire sieve or through a potato masher, or mash with a fork or the end of a rolling-pin. Melt the fat (in one corner of the pan if the potatoes have been mashed in the pan itself) and beat in the potatoes. Add milk gradually and beat well until the mixture is thoroughly hot, and smooth. Season well and add a little grated nutmeg. Serve in a hot dish. Sprinkle with chopped parsley.

NOTE: If mashed potatoes are to be served with sausages, use a little of the sausage fat instead of butter or margarine.

Successful mashed potato depends upon the use of a floury type of potato, thorough drying of potatoes after the water has been strained off them, and the thorough mashing of the potatoes before fat and milk are added.

6 helpings
Cooking time—30–45 min.

NEW POTATOES—BOILED

2 lb. new potatoes, even-sized   salt
and pepper   mint   1 oz. butter or
margarine   parsley

Where possible dig the potatoes just before cooking. Scrub with a stiff brush. (This should be sufficient to remove the skin. If the potatoes are not freshly dug, scrape them to remove skins.) Rinse. Cook as for old potatoes but with mint in the water. When dried, add fat, chopped parsley and chopped mint to the saucepan. Toss the potatoes gently in the fat. Serve hot.

New potatoes are in season from May to July.

4–6 helpings

Cooking time—15-30 min., according to size and freshness

POTATO BALLS or CROQUETTES

1 lb. cooked potatoes 1 oz. butter or margarine 2 egg yolks or 1 whole egg salt and pepper (optional : 1 teasp. chopped parsley or 2 tablesp. dry grated Cheddar cheese or 2 tablesp. grated Parmesan cheese) egg and breadcrumbs deep fat

Put the potatoes through a sieve and mash in a saucepan with the fat, beaten egg, and parsley or cheese if used. Season well. Form into small balls or into rolls. Coat twice with egg and crumbs. Fry in hot deep fat at 380° F. for 4-5 min. Drain well and serve immediately.

6 helpings

POTATOES—BAKED IN FAT

2 lb. even-sized potatoes salt and pepper dripping

Peel the potatoes and cut in halves or even in quarters if very large. Parboil and strain off the water and dry the potatoes over a low heat. Put into hot dripping in a roasting-tin, or in the tin containing the roast joint. Roll the potatoes in the fat and cook till tender and brown.

Cooking time—to parboil, 10 min.; to bake, 1 hr. (approx.)

FRIED POTATOES
LYONNAISE POTATOES

2 lb. potatoes ½ lb. onions 3 oz. butter or margarine chopped parsley salt and pepper

Cook the potatoes in their skins until nearly soft. Peel and slice thinly. Slice the onions thinly across and cook them slowly in the butter in a frying-pan until just golden coloured. Remove the onions and keep them hot. Toss the potatoes in the fat as for Sauté Potatoes. Add the onions to them and mix. Season well with salt and pepper. Serve in a hot dish and sprinkle with chopped parsley.

6 helpings
Cooking time—to fry, 15 min.

PARISIAN POTATOES

2 lb. potatoes 2-3 oz. butter or margarine salt

Scrub, rinse and peel the potatoes. Using a round vegetable scoop, scoop small balls from the potatoes. Boil them until nearly tender and drain them well. Heat the butter in a frying-pan or sauté pan and fry the potatoes in it, tossing them all the time until they are brown. Season and serve.

6 helpings
Cooking time—to fry, about 10 min.

POTATO CHIPS and POTATO STRAWS

6 medium-sized potatoes deep fat salt

Scrub and rinse the potatoes. Peel them thinly. For chips—cut into sticks about 2 in. long and ½ in. wide and thick. For straws—cut into strips the size of a wooden match. Drop them into cold water as they are cut. Rinse and drain and dry in a clean cloth. Put them into the frying-basket and lower them gently into hot deep fat at 360° F. (Keep the heat fairly high, as the potatoes will have cooled the fat.) When the potatoes are soft but *not* brown—about 3 min. for chips and 1 min. for straws—lift out the basket and heat the fat to 375° F. Put back the basket and leave in the fat until the potatoes are crisp and golden brown—about 3 min. for chips and 2 min. for straws.

Drain on absorbent paper, sprinkle with salt and serve immediately.

NOTE : If potato chips or straws are to be served with fried fish or any other fried dish, the second frying of the potatoes to brown and crisp them should be done after the fish, etc., is fried. In this way the potatoes will be sent to table in their best condition.

6 helpings
Cooking time—for chips, about 6 min.; for straws, about 3 min.

POTATO CRISPS

6 egg-sized, waxy potatoes   deep fat
salt

Scrub and rinse the potatoes but do not peel unless the skins are very tough and blemished. Slice very thinly with a sharp knife or on a potato slicer bought for the purpose. Drop them into cold water as they are cut. Drain and rinse and dry well between the folds of a clean cloth. Sprinkle gradually into hot deep fat, at 320° F., and fry till golden and crisp. Remove from the fat as they brown and drain on absorbent paper. Keep them hot while frying the rest. Sprinkle with salt.

They can be kept in an air-tight tin for some time and be reheated when necessary.

NOTE: To the professional cook or chef these are known as "chips". They are served with grills and with poultry and game but may also be served with many meat and fish dishes.

6 helpings
Cooking time—3–4 min.

POTATO PUFFS

9 medium-sized potatoes   deep fat
salt

Scrub, peel and rinse the potatoes. Cut them lengthwise into slices about $\frac{3}{16}$ in. thick. Trim into ovals or oblongs; drop into cold water. Rinse and drain. Dry in a clean cloth. Put the potato slices into the frying-basket and lower them gently into hot, deep fat at 320° F. Cook until just soft but

not coloured. Lift out the basket. Reheat the fat to 350° F., put in the basket and fry until the potatoes begin to brown. Lift out again and heat the fat to 380° F. Fry the potatoes a third time till golden brown. Drain carefully, sprinkle with salt and dish.

6 helpings
Cooking time—about 25 min.

SAUTE or TOSSED POTATOES

6 medium-sized potatoes (waxy ones)
1–2 oz. butter or margarine
seasoning

Cook the potatoes, preferably in their skins, until only just soft. Let them dry thoroughly, then peel and slice them $\frac{1}{4}$ in. thick. Heat the fat in a frying-pan and put in the potatoes. Season them with salt and pepper. Toss in the fat until they are light brown and have absorbed all the fat. Serve at once.

4–6 helpings

PUMPKIN

Pumpkin may be served as a vegetable or as the main ingredient of the filling for Pumpkin Pie or with equal quantities of apple as a Pumpkin and Apple Pie.

Pumpkin is in season from July to October.

FRIED PUMPKIN

2 very small pumpkins   coating
batter or yeast batter, see Fried
Brussels Sprouts (p. 215), or
egg and breadcrumbs

Peel and boil the pumpkins in salt and water until tender. Drain well. Cut in $1\frac{1}{2}$-in. squares or into strips; remove the seeds. Coat with egg and crumbs or dip in batter and fry in deep hot fat at 340° F. Turn them during frying as they will float, and when golden brown remove from the fat. Drain well, serve hot.

6 helpings
Cooking time—to fry, 7 min.

PUMPKIN PIE

½ pt. pumpkin (cooked and sieved)
¼ teasp. ground ginger   ½ teasp.
nutmeg   good pinch of cinnamon
3 eggs   2 tablesp. brandy   ¼ pt. milk
(approx.)   4 oz. castor sugar
(approx.)   short crust pastry (p. 341),
using 8 oz. flour, etc.

Put the pumpkin in a mixing-
bowl. Stir in the spices, the well
beaten eggs, the brandy and sufficient milk to give a consistency of
thick batter. Sweeten to taste.
Turn into a deep 9-in. pie-plate
lined with pastry. Cover with
pastry. Bake in a fairly hot oven
(375° F., Gas 5) about 45 min.
Serve hot.
NOTE: Pumpkins should be
peeled, sliced and the seeds removed before boiling in slightly
salted water until tender.
5–6 helpings

RADISHES (Radis)

Although generally eaten raw,
radishes can be used very successfully as a flavouring and as a
garnish in place of turnip, particularly when turnips are poor in
quality or when new turnips are
very expensive.

Radish tops are a valuable
source of Vitamin C and may be
cooked as a green vegetable.

SALSIFY, SALSAFY or VEGETABLE OYSTER

This vegetable is very popular
on the European continent. It is
an excellent root vegetable. The
name Vegetable Oyster or Oyster
Plant was given to it many years
ago when it must have had a
flavour somewhat resembling
oysters. It does not possess that
flavour today.

The young leaves of salsify may
be used in salads.

Salsify is seasonable from December to March.

BOILED SALSIFY

2 lb. salsify   white vinegar or lemon
juice   salt   ¾ pt. white or
Béchamel sauce (p. 100)

Wash and scrape the roots, using
vinegar or lemon juice in the
water (see Boiled Jerusalem Artichokes). Scrape gently so that only
the outside peel is removed. Cut
into 4-in. lengths, cook and serve
as for Jerusalem Artichokes (p.
211).
6 helpings
Cooking time—30–40 min.

SAVOY

See recipes for cooking Cabbage,
p. 215.

SEAKALE

This is an excellent vegetable
and can be used raw in salads, or
cooked and served with a good
sauce. It grows in the wild state
on the beaches of certain parts of
Hampshire and on the sea-coasts
of Western Europe. Its high price
when bought probably prevents
cultivated seakale from being a
more popular vegetable.

Seakale is in season from December to May.

BOILED SEAKALE

2 lb. seakale   salt   ¾ pt. white sauce
(p. 91) or ¾ pt. Béchamel sauce
(p. 100) or ½ pt. Hollandaise sauce
(p. 98) or melted, seasoned butter

Cut off the stump and any
broken or discoloured leaves.
Wash. Tie into bundles. Cook very
gently in just enough boiling,
salted water to cover, until tender,
25–30 min. Seakale hardens if
cooked longer. Drain and serve
with melted butter, or coat with
one of the sauces suggested.
6 helpings
Cooking time—25–30 min.

SORREL

Sorrel is in season from May to
October.

SORREL PUREE

3 lb. sorrel   1 oz. butter or
margarine   1–2 tablesp. cream
a little flour   salt and pepper

Pick over the sorrel, remove the
stalks and wash it in several
waters. Put into a large saucepan
enough water to cover the bottom.
Bring to the boil. Add the sorrel
and cook it gently about 20 min.,
turning it over and pressing it
down repeatedly with a spoon, to
equalize the cooking. Drain well
and rub through a fine sieve.
Return it to the pan with the
butter, cream and salt and pepper.
Stir over heat for about 8 min.,
dredging in gradually enough
flour to give a thick consistency.

NOTE: A little sugar may be
added during cooking to counter-
act the acidity of the vegetable.
Sorrel is excellent served with
eggs, veal or white fish.

6 helpings
Cooking time—about 30 min.

SPINACH

Spinach is in season all the year
as there are winter and summer
varieties.

BOILED SPINACH (1)

3 lb. spinach   1 oz. butter or
margarine   2 tablesp. cream
(optional)   salt and pepper

Pick over the spinach carefully
and wash it in at least 3 waters.
Break off the stalks and at the same
time pull off the central ribs if
coarse. (Young, summer spinach
need not be stripped of the central
ribs.) Put the wet leaves into a
saucepan, without additional water.
Cook slowly until tender, about 15
min., stirring the spinach in the
pan occasionally. The pan should
have a tightly-fitting lid. Drain
well, pressing out the water. Reheat in the butter. Add the cream,
if used, and mix it well with the
spinach. Season and serve hot.

5–6 helpings
Cooking time—about 25 min.

BOILED SPINACH (2)

3 lb. spinach
(a) 1 oz. butter or margarine and a
    little cream or
(b) a roux : 1 oz. butter or
    margarine and 1 oz. flour or
(c) a panada : 2 rounded teasp.
    cornflour and 1 gill spinach
    liquor
salt and pepper

GARNISH
Fleurons of pastry, or sieved egg
yolk, or crescents of fried bread

Cook as for Boiled Spinach (1)
and drain well. Chop finely with
a stainless knife or rub through a
hair, nylon or stainless metal sieve.
Reheat with either (a) the butter
and a little cream if liked, or (b)
with the roux, or (c) with the
panada. Season well. Serve hot.
Garnish if liked, with fleurons of
pastry, sieved egg yolk or crescents
of fried bread.

NOTE: If the spinach is to be
sieved, the central rib need not be
stripped from the spinach. A little
grated nutmeg may be added for
additional flavour.

5–6 helpings
Cooking time—25 min.

SPRING GREENS

(See Cabbage, p. 215.)

SWEET POTATOES

Sweet potatoes may be served as
a vegetable or in the sweet course
and are in season from September
through the winter.

BAKED SWEET POTATOES

6 even-sized sweet potatoes   butter
or margarine   salt and pepper

Scrub the potatoes well and rub
them all over with a greasy butter
or margarine paper. Bake in a

fairly hot oven (375° F., Gas 5),
until soft. Serve with butter, salt
and pepper or scrape out the soft
inside, mash with butter, season
and serve hot.

6 helpings
Cooking time—about 1 hr.

TOMATOES
BAKED TOMATOES

6 large tomatoes   a little butter or
margarine   salt and pepper   castor
sugar   finely-chopped tarragon
(optional)

Wash the tomatoes and cut
them in halves. Put them in a
greased, deep fireproof dish. Season and sprinkle each with a pinch
of sugar and a pinch of chopped
tarragon, if used. Put a tiny piece
of butter on each or cover with a
well-greased paper. Bake in a
moderate oven (350° F., Gas 4)
until soft—about 20 min.

6 helpings

DEVILLED TOMATOES

6 tomatoes   2 oz. butter or
margarine   yolks of 2 hard-boiled
eggs   salt   cayenne pepper
½ teasp. mixed mustard   a little
sugar   2 tablesp. vinegar   2 eggs

Peel and slice the tomatoes and
cook them slowly in a saucepan
with ½ oz. of the butter. Mix the
rest of the butter with the hard-
boiled egg yolks, stir in the salt,
pepper, mustard, about 1 saltsp. of
sugar and the vinegar. Lastly add
the beaten eggs. Put the mixture
into another small pan and stir
over a gentle heat until it thickens.
Re-season. Place the tomatoes in a
hot dish and pour the sauce over
them.

5–6 helpings
Cooking time—about 30 min.

STUFFED TOMATOES

6 large, firm tomatoes   1 teasp.
finely-chopped onion   1 teasp.

finely-chopped mushroom   ½ oz.
butter or margarine   1 heaped
tablesp. finely-chopped cooked ham
1 tablesp. fresh breadcrumbs
½ teasp. chopped parsley   salt and
pepper   1 teasp. dry grated cheese
6 rounds of fried or toasted bread

Wash and dry the tomatoes. Cut
a small round from each tomato at
the end opposite the stalk. Scoop
out the centre with the handle of a
teaspoon. Fry the onion and the
mushroom in the butter or margarine until cooked. Add the ham,
crumbs, parsley and sufficient
tomato pulp to bind the mixture
Season well. Fill the tomatoes with
the mixture, piling some on top.
Bake in a moderate oven (350° F.,
Gas 4) until the tomatoes are soft
—about 20 min. Sprinkle the tops
with cheese, replace the lids and
serve on the fried or toasted bread.
Garnish with parsley.

NOTE: For alternative fillings
see Stuffed Cabbage, p. 216,
Stuffed Vegetable Marrow, p. 234.

For a vegetarian filling replace
the ham and cheese in the above
recipe with chopped mushrooms
or chopped nut meat.

6 helpings
Cooking time—to bake, about
   20 min.

TURNIPS AND
SWEDE-TURNIPS

Swedes differ from turnips in
that the flesh is orange in colour,
and not the pure white of that of
the turnip. Swedes have a sweeter,
milder flavour than the turnip.
There are two varieties of turnip
—the summer ones, which do not
store well and are pulled when
about the size of a tennis ball, and
main-crop turnips, which are much
larger in size and are left in the
ground or pulled about November
for storage. Swedes are left in the
ground to mature fully and are
always large in size.

In certain parts of England, e.g.

Cornwall, the term "turnip" is applied to the orange-fleshed swede, the white turnip finding no favour there.

Swedes may be cooked and served in the way described for turnips.

They are in season in late autumn and winter.

TURNIPS—CONSERVATIVELY COOKED

2 lb. turnips   1 oz. butter or margarine   ½ teasp. salt   ½–1 gill boiling water   chopped parsley

Scrub and peel the turnips thickly. If large, cut into quarters, then slice thinly (if young turnips, slice the whole turnip). Fat steam the turnips for 10 min., i.e. shake them in the melted fat, well below frying temperature, with the lid on the pan until the fat is absorbed. Add the liquid and the salt, and simmer gently until the turnips are tender, 15–30 min., according to age of turnips. Serve hot with the small amount of liquid remaining, and garnished with chopped parsley.

6 helpings

TURNIP GREENS

These, when young, provide a most pleasant green vegetable, very rich in Vitamin C.

The stalks should be removed and the leaves shredded and cooked like cabbage (p. 215).

VEGETABLE MARROW

Vegetable marrows should be cut and used as a vegetable when small and young. The tiny French marrows known as "Courgettes" and the Italian "Zucchini" are better flavoured, and much more interesting as a vegetable than the large English marrow. Vegetable marrow is in season from July to October.

FRIED VEGETABLE MARROW

2 very small marrows   coating batter or yeast batter, see Fried Brussels Sprouts (p. 215), or egg and breadcrumbs

Peel and boil the marrows in salt and water until tender. Drain well. Cut into 1½-in. squares or into strips, remove the seeds. Coat with egg and breadcrumbs or dip in batter and fry in hot deep fat at 340° F. Turn them during frying as they will float, and when golden brown remove from the fat. Drain well, serve hot.

6 helpings
Cooking time—to fry, 7 min.

STUFFED VEGETABLE MARROW

2 small vegetable marrows
¾ pt. brown sauce or tomato sauce

STUFFING
1 small finely-chopped onion
¼ lb. cooked ham or nut meat for vegetarians   6 mushrooms, chopped
2 oz. butter or margarine   1 tablesp. chopped parsley   2 oz. breadcrumbs
1 egg   seasoning   1 gill stock (approx.)

COATING
Browned crumbs   melted butter or margarine

Peel the marrows and cut into halves lengthwise or cut into rings, about 2 in. thick. Remove the seeds with a tablespoon and steam the marrow until almost soft. Drain carefully. Fry the chopped mushrooms and onion in the butter until cooked—about 10 min. Add all the other ingredients and bind with the egg and enough stock to make a soft stuffing. Season well. Stuff the marrow halves or rings of marrow with filling. Sprinkle browned crumbs on top, then a little melted butter. Bake in a fairly hot oven (375° F., Gas 5) Serve with brown or tomato sauce.

6 helpings
Cooking time—about 1 hr.

VEGETABLE MARROW— CONSERVATIVELY COOKED

2 small marrows   1 oz. butter or
margarine $\frac{1}{2}$–1 gill boiling water
$\frac{1}{2}$ teasp. salt $\frac{3}{4}$ pt. white sauce
(p. 91)

Peel the marrows. Cut into
halves lengthwise and scrape out
the seeds and pith with a tablespoon. Cut into pieces, about 2 in.
square. Fat steam the pieces for
10 min., i.e. shake them in the
melted fat, well below frying
temperature, with the lid on the
pan until the fat is absorbed. Add
the liquid and the salt, and simmer
gently until the marrow is tender,
about 15 min. Drain well, retaining the cooking liquor for use in
making the white sauce. Dish the
marrow in a hot dish and coat with
the sauce. Serve immediately.

6 helpings
Cooking time—about 25 min.

YAMS

The yam resembles the potato
but has a thicker skin and often
weighs as much as 2 lb. The flesh
is very white and floury when
cooked and is sweeter in flavour
than potato.

BAKED YAMS

Yams   butter or margarine
salt and pepper

Scrub and rinse the yams. Bake
in a fairly hot oven (375° F.,
Gas 5) until soft. Serve with
butter, salt and pepper.

1 yam for 2 to 3 helpings
Cooking time—about 2 hr.

BOILED YAMS

Yams   salt

Scrub, peel and rinse the yams.
Boil as for potatoes (p. 227). Drain
dry and serve or mash as potatoes.

NOTE: Yams may also be cooked
in most of the ways suitable for
potatoes.

1 yam for 2 to 3 helpings
Cooking time—about 35 min.

MIXED VEGETABLES

MIXED VEGETABLES CONSERVATIVELY COOKED

1$\frac{1}{2}$ lb. mixed vegetables.
In winter: parsnip, turnip, carrot,
leek, cauliflower
In summer: new carrots, new
turnips, broad beans, peas, spring
onions, tomatoes
1 oz. butter or margarine $\frac{1}{2}$–1 gill
boiling water   salt and pepper
chopped parsley

Prepare all the vegetables. Cut
the winter vegeables into thin
slices, cutting the slices in halves
or quarters when large. Break the
cauliflower into sprigs. Leave most
of the summer vegetables whole,
cutting the carrots in thick slices,
if not really small, trimming the
spring onions rather short and
cutting the tomatoes into wedges.
Melt the fat in a saucepan. Add
the vegetables to it at intervals,
starting with the ones which take
the longest time to cook. Put the
lid on the pan after each addition
and toss the vegetables in the fat.
(Do not add the tomatoes to the
summer vegetables until 5 min.
before serving.) Add the liquid
and the salt (use very little water
with the summer vegetables), and
simmer gently until the vegetables
are tender. Serve hot, sprinkled
with chopped parsley.

6 helpings
Cooking time—winter vegetables,
about $\frac{3}{4}$ hr.
summer vegetables, about $\frac{1}{2}$ hr.

MIXED VEGETABLES FOR GARNISH

Carrots   turnips   peas   cauliflower
French or runner beans   salt

Wash and scrape or peel the carrots and turnips. Dice them very neatly or cut out small balls with a vegetable scoop. Wash and divide cauliflower into neat sprigs. Cut beans into diamond shapes.

Cook each vegetable separately in the minimum of boiling, salted water until just tender. Drain well. Use one vegetable only as a garnish *or* mixtures of any *or* all of the above.

SALADS

ALTHOUGH lettuce frequently forms the foundation of salads, there are few vegetables and edible plants that may not be used in salad-making. Originally a salad consisted of uncooked, edible leaves of various plants, but today the name is applied to mixtures which may include cooked and uncooked vegetables, herbs, fruits, meat and fish.

To ensure success in salad making it is essential that all vegetables and fruits used are in perfect condition. Leafy salad plants should be young, crisp and freshly gathered. They must be properly washed in several waters or under running water. As much water should be removed as possible, after washing, by shaking the plants in a salad-shaker or colander, allowing them to drain well and then drying in a clean cloth held by the corners. If possible they should be put into a covered container in the refrigerator to crisp them before use. Lettuce leaves which need to be mixed into a salad should always be cut with a stainless knife or torn with the fingers.

Vegetables which are usually eaten cooked should be very finely divided when to be eaten raw in a salad, or they will be indigestible. Carrots and young turnips should be grated; cabbage should be finely chopped; and cauliflower grated or broken into tiny sprigs.

All salads should be mixed with a dressing just before serving. The dressing adds considerably to their flavour, digestibility and food value.

AMERICAN CABBAGE SALAD

½ small white cabbage 1 tablesp.
vinegar 6 peppercorns good pinch
of salt 1 teasp. melted butter
2 tablesp. cream 1 egg

Chop the cabbage very finely and put into a china bowl. Boil 1 tablesp. of vinegar for 2 min. with the peppercorns and salt, then strain it and put into a basin. Melt the butter, add the cream and the egg yolk and well-beaten egg white; stir into the cooled vinegar. Put the basin over hot water and stir the sauce continually until it thickens, but do not let it boil. When cold, pour over the cabbage. Serve very cold.

4–6 helpings

APPLE AND CUCUMBER SALAD

1 cucumber 3 dessert apples
salt and pepper lemon juice
cream or evaporated milk
finely-chopped mint (optional)

Slice the cucumber thinly; quarter, core and slice the apples. Season lightly and sprinkle with lemon juice. Stir in a little cream or evaporated milk. Pile in a salad bowl. Sprinkle with a little mint, if liked.

6 helpings

BANANA SALAD

6 bananas lemon juice
mayonnaise sauce (p. 104) or salad
dressing (p. 245) chopped parsley
watercress French dressing (p. 245)

Cut the bananas into rounds ⅛ in. thick and put them into a salad bowl containing about 1 tablesp. lemon juice. Mix lightly, and pile in the dish. Coat with salad dressing or mayonnaise, sprinkle with parsley. Arrange watercress around the dish and sprinkle it with French dressing.

NOTE: Coarsely chopped walnuts may be added to this salad.

6 helpings

BEETROOT AND CELERY SALAD

2 cooked beetroots   2 dessert apples
2 oz. shelled walnuts   1 large celery
heart or 2 heads chicory   chopped
parsley   French dressing (p. 245)
1 bunch watercress

Cut neat rounds of beetroot for garnish, then dice the rest. Mix the diced apples, chopped walnuts, diced celery or chicory, beetroot and chopped parsley. Toss lightly in the French dressing. Pile in a salad bowl. Make a border of the rounds of beetroot and tiny bunches of watercress. Decorate the top with curled celery.

NOTE: This is an excellent salad for winter.

6 helpings

BEETROOT SALAD

2 cooked beetroots   French dressing
(p. 245)   grated horseradish

Slice or dice the beetroot and arrange neatly. Baste with French dressing, after sprinkling with freshly grated horseradish.

NOTE: If preferred, dry mustard may be added to the French dressing and the horseradish omitted.

6 helpings

CABBAGE, BEETROOT AND CARROT SALAD

¼ of the heart of a white cabbage
1 celery heart   1 tablesp. raisins or
sultanas   1 small cooked beetroot
2 carrots   fine cress   salad dressing
1 teasp. lemon juice
chopped parsley

Chop the cabbage very finely. Shred the celery; chop the raisins. Cut the beetroot into tiny dice. Grate the carrots finely. Mix the cabbage lightly with most of the beetroot and carrot and with all the celery and raisins and some salad dressing. Pile on a flat salad dish. Garnish with small heaps of beetroot and carrot, separated by little bunches of cress. Sprinkle the carrot and beetroot with a little lemon juice and finely-chopped parsley before serving.

6 helpings

CARROT SALAD

3 large carrots   1 lettuce
French dressing (p. 245)
finely-chopped parsley

Grate the carrots finely and serve on a bed of lettuce leaves. Sprinkle with the French dressing. Garnish with chopped parsley.

NOTE: Grated, raw carrot can be used with success in many salads. It should be grated very finely to be digestible and sprinkled with lemon juice or French dressing as soon as grated to retain its bright colour.

6 helpings

CELERY AND CHESTNUT SALAD

½ lb. stewed chestnuts   1 dessert
apple   2 celery hearts   salad dressing
(pp. 244-5)   crisp lettuce leaves

Cut the chestnuts into fairly large pieces. Dice the apple, shred the celery. Mix lightly with the dressing. Pile on a dish decorated with small, crisp lettuce leaves. Garnish with curled celery, see p. 39.

4-6 helpings

CHERRY SALAD

1 lb. Morello cherries   1 tablesp.
olive oil   1 teasp. lemon juice
3 or 4 drops of tarragon vinegar
1 dessertsp. brandy or Kirsch
finely-chopped tarragon   finely-
chopped chervil   1 teasp. castor sugar

Stone the cherries. Crack some of the stones and mix the kernels with the cherries. Mix the oil, lemon juice, vinegar, brandy or Kirsch, a very small quantity of tarragon and chervil and the sugar. Pour over the cherries.

Serve with roast game or duck.

4–6 helpings

CHICKEN SALAD

1 small cooked boiling fowl or remains of a cooked chicken or turkey   1 celery heart (if in season)   1 large lettuce   1 dessertsp. caper vinegar   salt and pepper   ½ pt. mayonnaise sauce (p. 104)   2 hard-boiled eggs   olives or gherkins   1 tablesp. capers

Cut the chicken into neat, small pieces. Shred the celery and the outer leaves of lettuce. Mix lightly with the vinegar and a little salt and pepper. Pile in a salad bowl and coat with the mayonnaise sauce. Garnish with lettuce leaves, slices of hard-boiled egg, stoned olives or strips of gherkins and capers.

6 helpings

CHICORY SALAD

6 heads of chicory   French dressing (p. 245) or Vinaigrette sauce (p. 245)

Prepare, wash and drain the chicory well, having split each head in half lengthwise. Toss in the French dressing.

NOTE: Chicory cut in shreds may be added to many salads, its crisp texture making it a very pleasant addition. It is most useful as a substitute for celery when the latter is of poor quality.

6 helpings

CRAB SALAD

1 large cooked crab or 2 small cooked crabs   2 celery hearts or the heart of 1 endive   2 tablesp. olive oil   2 tablesp. tarragon vinegar   1 tablesp. chilli or caper vinegar

1 dessertsp. chopped parsley   salt and pepper   crisp lettuce leaves   2 hard-boiled eggs   1 tablesp. capers   12 stuffed olives

Cut the meat of the crabs into convenient-sized pieces. Shred the celery or endive, add to the crab meat and mix lightly with the oil, vinegar, parsley and seasoning. Serve on a bed of lettuce leaves; garnish with slices of hard-boiled egg, capers and stuffed olives.

6 helpings

CUCUMBER SALAD

1 large cucumber   salt   French dressing   chopped parsley   chopped tarragon

Slice the cucumber ("Ridge" cucumbers must be peeled prior to slicing. For other cucumbers see note in Vegetable Section under Cucumber, p. 220). Put on a china plate and sprinkle with salt. Tilt the plate slightly so that the water may drain off easily and leave for ½ hr. Rinse quickly in a colander and drain. Dish and pour over the French dressing. Sprinkle with parsley and tarragon.

6 helpings

DANISH SALAD

4 tomatoes   1 lb. cooked French beans   ½ pt. cooked green peas   ¼ pt. pickled button onions   mayonnaise sauce (p. 104)   sprigs of dill

Skin and slice the tomatoes; cut the beans into thick slices. Mix the beans, peas and onions with mayonnaise sauce. Pile on a dish and garnish with sliced tomato and sprigs of dill.

4–6 helpings

DUTCH SALAD or FLEMISH SALAD

1 cooked beetroot   2 cooked potatoes   1 heart of celery   French dressing with mustard (p. 245)   6 anchovy fillets   watercress

Cut the beetroot, potatoes and celery into strips. Mix lightly with the dressing and pile in a salad bowl. Decorate with strips of anchovy fillets and small bunches of watercress.

4–6 helpings

EGG SALAD

6 hard-boiled eggs   2 tablesp. cream
(optional)   mayonnaise sauce (p. 104)
1 tablesp. chopped parsley   1 crisp
lettuce   salt and pepper   1 tablesp.
capers   beetroot

Slice the eggs thickly. Whip the cream (if used) till stiff and add to the mayonnaise sauce with 1 teasp. of the parsley. Arrange a layer of lettuce leaves in the salad bowl, add a layer of mayonnaise, then a layer of slices of egg and so on until all the egg and lettuce is used, piling the centre high. Season each layer. Garnish with capers and neat slices of beetroot, sprinkle with rest of the parsley.

6 helpings

ENGLISH SALAD or SUMMER SALAD

1 large lettuce   ½ small cucumber
3 tomatoes   ½ bunch radishes
a few spring onions   salad dressing
(pp. 244–5)   bunch of watercress or
box of mustard and cress
2 hard-boiled eggs (if liked)

Reserve the best lettuce leaves and shred the rest. Slice the cucumber thinly, skin and slice the tomatoes, slice the radishes. Leave the onions whole. Mix the shredded lettuce leaves lightly with some of the cucumber, radishes and salad dressing. Line a salad bowl with the lettuce leaves. Pile the mixture in the middle and garnish with small bunches of watercress, sliced tomatoes, radishes, cucumber and hard-boiled egg. Hand the onions separately or arrange on the salad so that they may be avoided if not liked.

6 helpings

FISH SALAD

Cold cooked fish   salt and pepper
⅛ pt. tartare sauce (p. 105) or ⅛ pt.
mayonnaise sauce (p. 104)   1 lettuce
1 lemon

Use any cold cooked fish divided into large flakes. Season it and mix with the tartare sauce and a little shredded lettuce. Decorate a dish with the crisp, inner lettuce leaves and slices of lemon and arrange the fish on the dish.

4 helpings

FRENCH SALADS

A typical French salad consists of one vegetable only, dressed with a simple French dressing comprising oil, vinegar, seasonings and a little mustard if liked, or with a Vinaigrette sauce.

FRENCH CARROT SALAD

1½ lb. young carrots
1 dessertsp. French mustard

MARINADE
¼ pt. water   ¼ pt. wine vinegar
¼ pt. white wine   1 level teasp. salt
1 level teasp. sugar   sprig of parsley
sprig of thyme   1 bay leaf
1 crushed clove of garlic   good
pinch cayenne pepper   ¼ pt. olive oil

Mix all the ingredients of the marinade and bring to the boil. Slice thickly or quarter the carrots and cook them in the marinade until just soft. Drain them and strain the liquor. Mix the mustard into the liquor and pour over the carrots. Leave till quite cold. Serve.

NOTE: This salad is improved if prepared the day before it is to be served.

6 helpings

GAME SALAD

**1 lb. of remains of cold game
2 lettuces   1 hard-boiled egg
mayonnaise sauce (p. 104)
cayenne pepper and salt   beetroot**

Dice the meat. Shred the lettuce finely. Stamp out star-shaped pieces of egg white and beetroot. Mix the meat and chopped egg yolks and remains of whites. Arrange meat, lettuce and mayonnaise in alternate layers in a salad bowl, seasoning each layer, and pile in pyramid shape. Cover the surface with a thin layer of mayonnaise sauce. Garnish with the stars of beetroot and egg white.

6 helpings

GRAPE SALAD

**1 lb. green grapes
French dressing (p. 245)**

Skin, halve and remove pips from the grapes. Place the grapes in a salad bowl and mix lightly with the dressing.

4–6 helpings

HAM SALAD WITH PINEAPPLE

**½ lb. cooked ham   1 small fresh
pineapple or 1 small can of pineapple
mayonnaise sauce (p. 104) or salad
dressing (pp. 244–5)   sliced gherkins**

Cut the ham into short strips. Cut the pineapple into small dice. Toss lightly with mayonnaise sauce or salad dressing. Garnish with slices of gherkin.

4–6 helpings

ITALIAN SALAD

**½ lb. cold roast veal   ½ lb. cooked
potatoes   ¼ lb. beetroot   ¼ lb.
gherkins   1 tablesp. capers   salt and
pepper   mayonnaise sauce or salad
dressing   12 stoned olives   crisp
lettuce leaves   12 slices salami
sausage   1 lemon**

Dice the veal, potatoes and beetroot. Slice the gherkins. Mix them with the capers and seasoning and pile in a salad bowl. Pour over the mayonnaise and garnish with the olives, lettuce leaves, salami sausage and slices of lemon.

6 helpings

LETTUCE SALAD

Lettuce, of the cabbage or cos variety, prepared correctly and dressed with a French dressing *or* Vinaigrette sauce, provides the finest of all salads.

To prepare lettuce: 1. Cut off the stump of the lettuce and discard the coarse outer leaves only. 2. Separate all the leaves and wash them leaf by leaf under running water if possible, otherwise in several waters in a basin. 3. Put into a salad shaker or a clean teatowel and swing them to shake out the water. 4. Leave to drain. 5. If possible put into a covered box *or* into a casserole with a lid in the refrigerator for at least ½ hr. before dressing them for table.

The salads in which lettuce is used as a foundation are so numerous that it is unnecessary to name them all here.

LOBSTER SALAD

**1 large cooked lobster   1 endive
1 lettuce   ½ pt. mayonnaise sauce
(p. 104)   salt and pepper   2 hard-
boiled eggs   12 stoned olives
3–4 gherkins   1 teasp. capers
12 anchovy fillets
½ bunch watercress**

Remove all the meat from the lobster and cut into neat pieces. Break the endive into tufts, shred the lettuce coarsely. Arrange the lobster and salad in layers with a little mayonnaise and seasoning. Coat with mayonnaise. Decorate with slices of hard-boiled egg, olives, gherkins, capers, anchovy fillets, the small inner lettuce leaves and watercress.

6 helpings

MIXED VEGETABLE SALAD
(*using cooked summer vegetables*)

3 large new potatoes   3 new turnips
½ pt. shelled peas   ½ bunch new
carrots   1 tablesp. chopped parsley
1 teasp. chopped mint   salad
dressing (p. 245)

Cook the vegetables and slice the
carrots, potatoes and young turnips. Save some of each vegetable
for garnish and toss the rest in the
salad dressing with the herbs. Put
the mixture in a suitable dish and
garnish with the remainder.

4–6 helpings

MIXED VEGETABLE SALAD
(*using cooked winter vegetables*)

1 cauliflower   2 large carrots
1 parsnip or 2 turnips   1 cooked
beetroot   1 small can of peas
salad dressing (pp. 244–5)
watercress or fine cress
a little French dressing

Steam the cauliflower, carrots,
parsnip or turnips. Divide the
cauliflower into sprigs. Dice the
carrots, parsnip or turnip, and
beetroot, or cut into neat rounds
with a cutter. Rinse and drain the
peas. Mix all trimmings and uneven pieces of vegetable lightly
with salad dressing—include some
of the peas. Put this mixture into
a dish, preferably oblong in shape.
Cover with lines of each vegetable,
very neatly arranged and with suitable colours adjoining. Garnish the
edges with watercress or fine cress.
Baste the surface with French
dressing.

6 helpings

ORANGE SALAD

4 sweet oranges   ½ teasp. castor
sugar   1 tablesp. French dressing
(p. 245)   chopped tarragon and
chervil or chopped mint

Peel the oranges thickly with a
saw-edged knife, so that all pith is
removed. Cut out the natural
orange sections. Place in a salad
bowl, sprinkle with sugar. Pour
the dressing over and sprinkle with
tarragon and chervil, if obtainable,
or with chopped meat.

4–6 helpings

PEARS FILLED WITH NUT
AND DATE SALAD

3 ripe dessert or canned pears
1 small crisp lettuce   4 oz. chopped
dates   2 oz. chopped walnuts
chopped parsley   French dressing
(p. 245) or salad dressing (pp. 244–5)

Peel and halve the pears. Remove the cores with a sharp teaspoon, then scoop out a little of the
pulp of the pears to leave a hollow
for the filling. Shred a few lettuce
leaves very finely and mix with
dates, walnuts, chopped parsley
and finely diced pear pulp and
French dressing *or* salad dressing.
Place the halved pears on small
crisp lettuce leaves on individual
plates. Pile the mixture on each
piece of pear.

NOTE: If fresh pears are used,
squeeze lemon juice over them to
prevent discoloration.

6 helpings

POTATO SALAD

6 large new potatoes or waxy old
potatoes   French dressing or
Vinaigrette sauce (p. 245)   2 heaped
tablesp. chopped parsley   1 teasp.
chopped mint   1 teasp. chopped
chives or spring onion
salt and pepper

Cook the potatoes until just soft,
in their skins. Peel and cut into
dice whilst still hot. Mix while hot
with the dressing and the herbs
and a little seasoning. Serve cold.

6 helpings

POTATO SALAD—HOT

6 large new potatoes or waxy old
potatoes   salt and pepper
1 heaped tablesp. chopped parsley
1 tablesp. chopped chives or

spring onion   4 tablesp. French
dressing (p. 245)
1 tablesp. lemon juice

Cook the potatoes as in preceding recipe. Peel and slice and put
a layer of slices in a hot fireproof
dish. Sprinkle with mixed parsley
and chives and lemon juice. Continue until all the potato is used.
Bring the French dressing to the
boil and baste over the potatoes.
Cover and put into a moderate
oven (350° F., Gas 4) until the
contents are very hot.

6 helpings

RUSSIAN SALAD

1 small cauliflower $\frac{1}{4}$ pt. peas
$\frac{1}{4}$ pt. vegetables (carrot, turnip,
French beans)   3 potatoes   1 small
cooked beetroot   2 tomatoes
aspic jelly   2 oz. diced ham or
tongue   2 oz. cooked fish (shrimps,
prawns, lobster)   2 oz. smoked
salmon (optional)   3 gherkins
1 dessertsp. capers   a few lettuce
leaves   mayonnaise sauce or salad
dressing   1 hard-boiled egg (white
only)   6 stoned olives
6 anchovy fillets

Method 1. Prepare and cook all
the vegetables (or use canned or
bottled vegetables). Drain them
well. Divide the cauliflower into
small sprigs, dice all the other
vegetables except the peas. Skin
and slice the tomatoes. Line a
border mould with aspic jelly and
decorate it with a little of the
diced vegetables. Set layers of
vegetables, meat, fish and pickles
alternately with jelly in the
mould; do not use all the vegetables. When set, turn out. Toss
shredded lettuce and remaining
vegetables in mayonnaise or salad
dressing and pile in the centre of
the mould. Decorate with egg
white, olives and anchovy fillets.

Method 2 (without aspic jelly).
Put layers of vegetables, meat and
fish in a salad bowl, season with

salt and pepper and a pinch of
castor sugar and cover each layer
with mayonnaise sauce. Arrange
in pyramid form. Cover lightly
with mayonnaise. Decorate with
beetroot, diced egg white, olives,
capers, anchovies and shredded
salmon. Serve mayonnaise separately.

Method 3. Mix the vegetables
lightly and stir into them aspic
mayonnaise (p. 104). Pour into a
cylindrical mould. Turn out when
set and decorate as in preceding
method.

6 helpings

STUFFED CUCUMBER SALADS

1 large cucumber   tomatoes
macédoine of vegetables, cooked
and cold   salad dressing (pp. 244–5)
or mayonnaise sauce (p. 104)
parsley   fine cress

Cut the cucumber into 1-in.
rings and scoop out the centres
with a teaspoon. Peel the tomatoes and cut into slices, one for
each ring of cucumber. (Any
tomato left over should have pips
and pulp removed and be neatly
diced and added to the macédoine.)
Mix the macédoine of vegetables
with mayonnaise or salad dressing
and chopped parsley. Place the
tomato slices on a flat dish; put a
cucumber ring on each; fill with
the vegetable mixture. Decorate
with tiny bunches of cress.

6 helpings

STUFFED TOMATO SALADS

6 large firm tomatoes
crisp lettuce leaves

STUFFING, choice of:
1. Finely-shredded lettuce leaves;
   cold cooked asparagus tips;
   salad dressing or
2. Chopped celery, finely-diced
   cooked carrot; canned peas;
   salad dressing or
3. Chopped hard-boiled egg;
   chopped gherkins; salad dressing
   or

4. Chopped shrimps or prawns;
finely-shredded lettuce leaves;
salad dressing

Cut off the tops of the tomatoes,
take out the centres and the pulp.
Use a little of the pulp with the
stuffing. Mix the chosen stuffing
and fill the tomatoes. Put back the
tops. Garnish with tiny sprigs of
parsley or with a suitable ingredient of the filling. Dish on crisp
lettuce leaves on individual dishes
or plates.

6 helpings

SWEDISH SALAD

4 oz. cold roast beef   1 pickled
herring   4 oz. cooked potatoes
4 oz. cooking apples   4 oz. cooked
or pickled beetroot   1 tablesp.
chopped gherkin   1 tablesp.
chopped capers   chopped chervil
chopped tarragon   oil   vinegar
1 hard-boiled egg   3 anchovy fillets
6 bearded oysters (optional)

Dice the beef, herring, potatoes,
apples and beetroot. Mix with the
gherkin, capers, herbs and moisten
with a little oil and vinegar. Pile
in a dish and garnish with hard-
boiled egg, anchovy fillets and, if
liked, 6 bearded oysters.

NOTE: This salad is often served
with stiffly-beaten sour cream coloured with pickled beetroot juice.

4–6 helpings

TOMATO IN SALADS

For all salads containing sliced
tomatoes, the tomatoes should be
skinned first. The removal of the
pips from the tomatoes is a matter
for personal choice.

To skin tomatoes

There are three methods of skinning tomatoes. The 1st and 2nd
methods listed below are excellent
where only a few tomatoes have to
be skinned. The 3rd method is
preferable where a large number
of tomatoes have to be skinned.

1. Rub the surface of the tomatoes
   firmly with the back of a knife.
   Slit and remove the skin.
2. Impale the tomato on a fork
   and hold over a low gas flame,
   turning it in the flame until
   the skin wrinkles and splits. (A
   gas taper may be used instead
   of the gas burner.) Remove the
   skin and cool the tomato.
3. Cover the tomatoes with boiling water and leave for 1 min.
   Drain and plunge the tomatoes
   immediately into cold water.
   Slit and remove the skins.
   Care must be taken to avoid
   leaving the tomatoes too long
   in the boiling water and thus
   partially cooking them.

TOMATO SALAD

6 large firm tomatoes   salt and
pepper   French dressing   finely-
chopped parsley

Skin and slice the tomatoes.
Season lightly. Pour the dressing
over the tomatoes. Sprinkle with
chopped parsley.

6 helpings

SALAD DRESSINGS (see also p. 104)

Lemon juice may be used in all
the following recipes, in place of
vinegar, if preferred.

CREAM SALAD DRESSING

½ level teasp. mixed mustard or
French mustard   1 level saltsp. salt
1 saltsp. castor sugar   4 tablesp.
double cream   1 tablesp. vinegar
(wine or malt with a little tarragon)

Mix the mustard, salt and sugar
smoothly together. Stir in the
cream. Add the vinegar drop by
drop, beating mixture all the time.

EVAPORATED MILK
DRESSING

4 tablesp. evaporated milk
1 tablesp. vinegar (wine or malt)
1 level saltsp. mixed mustard

good pinch castor sugar
1 level saltsp. salt

Whisk the milk until thick. Add the vinegar drop by drop, stirring vigorously. Add the flavourings.

FRENCH DRESSING

2–3 tablesp. olive oil   pepper and salt   1 tablesp. wine vinegar

Mix the oil and seasoning. Add the vinegar gradually, stirring constantly with a wooden spoon so that an emulsion is formed.

NOTE: A pinch of sugar, a little mustard and one or two drops of Worcester sauce may be added.

Where suitable, orange or grapefruit juice may also be used.

A graduated medicine bottle is most useful for making French dressing. The oil and vinegar can be measured accurately without waste, and the dressing vigorously shaken to mix it. It can be stored in the larder or refrigerator, the bottle being well shaken before the dressing is used.

MAYONNAISE—COOKED

1 teasp. castor sugar   1 teasp. salt
1 level teasp. dry mustard   good pinch pepper   1 tablesp. salad oil
3 egg yolks   ⅛ pt. vinegar (1 teasp. to be tarragon)
½ pt. milk or single cream

Mix the sugar, salt, mustard and pepper. Stir in the oil, then the well-beaten egg yolks. Add the vinegar gradually and lastly the milk or cream. Cook in the top of a double saucepan, or in a basin placed in a saucepan containing sufficient boiling water to come half-way up the basin, stirring it all the time until the mixture thickens like custard. Re-season when cold.

NOTE: This salad dressing will keep well if put in a cool larder or in the refrigerator.

MAYONNAISE

3 rounded teasp. flour   1 teasp. castor sugar   1 teasp. salt   1 level teasp. dry mustard   good pinch pepper   1 tablesp. melted butter or margarine   1 egg yolk
⅛ pt. vinegar   ½ pt. milk

Proceed as in preceding recipe, mixing the flour with the sugar, salt, mustard and pepper, and adding the melted butter or margarine before the egg yolk, etc. Bring just to the boil to cook flour.

SALAD DRESSING (with foundation of Béchamel sauce)

This is the best dressing to use for a potato salad.

1 egg or 2 yolks   ½ pt. Béchamel sauce (made with all milk) (p. 100)
2 tablesp. wine or malt vinegar
1 tablesp. tarragon vinegar   salt and pepper   a little castor sugar

Beat the egg or egg yolks. Cool the Béchamel sauce until the hand can be placed in comfort on the bottom of the pan. Stir in the egg and cook without boiling. Wring through muslin and, when cooled a little, stir in the vinegars gradually and the seasoning and sugar. Leave until quite cold, then taste and re-season if necessary.

VINAIGRETTE SAUCE

This consists of a simple French dressing to which add:

1 teasp. finely-chopped gherkin
½ teasp. finely-chopped shallot or chives   ½ teasp. finely-chopped parsley   1 teasp. finely-choped capers   ½ teasp. finely-chopped tarragon and chervil (if available)

HOT SWEETS

MILK PUDDINGS

MILK puddings are basically made with a farinaceous ingredient, sugar and milk. Eggs may be added, if liked, or any other suitable flavouring.

Skimmed and dried milk can be used for making milk puddings, and $\frac{1}{2}$–1 oz. butter or suet added to each pint of milk will make up the deficiency of fat. If *sweetened condensed milk* is used the amount of sugar in the recipe should be decreased accordingly. *Evaporated and condensed milks* should be made up to the equivalent of fresh milk by following the directions on the tin.

The addition of egg to a milk pudding increases the nutritive value and the pudding is made much lighter if the whites are whisked before being added. The egg must not be added until the grain is fully cooked otherwise the prolonged cooking necessary to cook the grain would overcook the eggs and cause them to curdle. Baking for about 30 min. in a warm oven (335° F., *Gas* 3) is usually long enough to cook the eggs and brown the top of a one-pint pudding.

Steamed Milk Puddings: Milk puddings can also be steamed and unmoulded provided that they contain at least 2 eggs to each pint of liquid in addition to the farinaceous ingredient. The basin or mould must be well greased, the pudding covered with greased paper and allowed to steam very gently until set.

GENERAL HINTS

1. Avoid using thin saucepans; rinse out the saucepan with cold water before using, *or* lightly grease with butter to lessen the risk of burning.
2. Puddings cooked in a saucepan must be stirred well from the bottom of the pan and allowed only just to simmer.
3. If a double saucepan is used, little attention is required, but the pudding will take longer to cook.
4. A pinch of salt added to all puddings improves the flavour.
5. Finely-shredded suet, *or* flakes of butter *or* margarine, put on to the top of all baked puddings, improves the flavour and also increases the fat content. Grease the pie-dish to facilitate cleaning afterwards.
6. In puddings where eggs are included, the mixture must be cooled slightly before the egg yolks are added.

FLAVOURINGS

Ground cinnamon: Sprinkle on top of large grain puddings *or* mix with any type of milk pudding. *Nutmeg:* Grate on top of large grain milk puddings and baked puddings. *Lemon* or *orange rind:* Cut thin strips of lemon *or* orange rind, avoiding white pith. Add at commencement of cooking and remove before serving. *Lemon* or *orange rind (grated):* Add to milk pudding just before serving. *Dried fruit:* Sultanas, seedless and stoned raisins, chopped dates and finely-chopped candied peel can be added to all puddings at start of cooking. *Essences:* Add to small- and powdered-grain puddings at the end of boiling. *Cocoa:* Blend first with a little of the milk: then add to the rest of the milk. Extra sugar may be required. *Chocolate:* Grate plain chocolate and dissolve in a little warm milk, add to rest of milk.

LARGE GRAIN PUDDINGS

(Large sago, whole rice (Carolina or short grain), flaked tapioca, flaked rice)

Basic Recipe

4 oz. grain   2 pt. milk   2–3 oz. sugar   ½ oz. finely-shredded suet or butter (optional)   grated nutmeg or other flavouring (see above)

Grease a pie-dish with butter. Wash the grain in cold water if necessary, and put it into the pie-dish with the milk. Leave to stand for about ½ hr. Add the sugar, flake the fat on to the top and add any flavouring required. Bake slowly (310° F., Gas 2) until the pudding is brown on top and of a thick creamy consistency.

6 helpings
Cooking time—about 2½ hr.

LARGE GRAIN PUDDINGS —WITH EGGS

(Large sago, whole rice, flaked tapioca, flaked rice)

Basic Recipe

4 oz. grain   2 pt. milk   2–4 eggs 2–3 oz. sugar
flavouring (see above)

Wash the grain in cold water, if necessary. Put the grain and milk into a strong *or* double saucepan and cook slowly until the grain is tender. Remove from the heat and allow to cool slightly. Separate the eggs and whisk the whites stiffly. Stir into the pudding the egg yolks, sugar and flavouring, and lastly stir in lightly the stiffly-whisked whites. Pour into a well buttered pie-dish and bake in a warm oven

(335° F., Gas 3) about 30–40 min. until the top is brown.

6 helpings

Variations
APPLES AND RICE

3 oz. rice   pinch of salt   1½ pt. milk   rind of 1 lemon   1 oz. butter 3 oz. granulated sugar   6 cooking apples   2 tablesp. raspberry jam or butter and sugar

Wash the rice and simmer it in the milk (with the salt and strips of lemon rind) until tender and most of the milk has been absorbed. Stir in the butter and granulated sugar and remove the lemon rind. Peel and core the apples and place them in a large pie-dish. Fill the cavities with raspberry jam *or* butter and sugar. Carefully fill the spaces between the apples with rice. Bake in a cool oven (310° F., Gas 2) for about ¾–1 hr. until the apples are tender but not broken.

6 helpings

APPLE SNOWBALLS

To each apple allow:
1½ oz. rice   ½ pt. milk or milk and water   pinch of salt   1½ oz. sugar 1 clove (optional)

Simmer the rice in the milk with the salt until the rice is tender and all the milk is absorbed. (1 tablesp. of sugar to every pt. of milk may be added, if liked.)

Peel and core the apples, keeping them whole. Put a clove (if used) into the centre and stand each apple on a base of cooled rice on a pudding-cloth. Fill the centre of the apple with sugar and then cover the apple with rice. Tie the apples in the pudding-cloth and drop into boiling water. Boil very gently for about 45 min. Serve with castor sugar.

1 apple per helping

GENEVA PUDDING

3 oz. rice   1½ pt. milk   pinch of

salt   3 oz. sugar   2 lb. cooking
apples   1 oz. butter   ¼ teasp.
ground cinnamon   3 tablesp. water

Wash the rice and let it simmer
in the milk with the salt until
cooked. Add ½ oz. sugar. While the
rice is cooking wipe the apples and
chop them roughly; put them in a
saucepan with the butter, cinnamon and 3 tablesp. of water. Simmer very gently until tender; then
put the mixture through a fine
sieve. Add the rest of the sugar (2½
oz.). Well grease a pie-dish with
butter and arrange the rice and
apple purée in alternate layers,
with rice forming the bottom and
top layers. Bake in a moderate oven
(350° F., Gas 4) until brown.

6 helpings
Time—1¼ hr.

MACARONI or SPAGHETTI
   PUDDING

4 oz. macaroni or spaghetti   salt
1½ pt. milk   2 oz. sugar   grated
rind of 1 lemon   1½ oz. butter or
margarine   1–3 eggs

Break the macaroni into ½-in.
lengths and throw into boiling,
salted water. Cook for 10 min.
until just tender. Strain the
macaroni and put it into the saucepan with the milk and simmer
until soft. Cool slightly. Add
the sugar, lemon rind and butter.
Separate the eggs and stir in the
beaten yolks, stir for a few minutes
but do not let it boil. Whip the egg
whites stiffly and fold lightly into
the mixture. Remove the lemon
rind. Pour into a buttered pie-dish
and cook until brown in a moderate oven (350° F., Gas 4)—about
20–30 min.

6 helpings

TAPIOCA CREAM PUDDING

2½ oz. tapioca   1½ pt. milk   pinch
of salt   ½ oz. butter or margarine
1½ oz. sugar   ¼ teasp. almond

essence   3 eggs
3 oz. crushed ratafias

Wash and soak the tapioca in the
milk with the salt for 1–2 hr.
Simmer the tapioca in the milk
until cooked. Add the butter, sugar
and almond essence. Separate the
eggs and add the egg yolks. Pour
into a well-buttered pie-dish and
bake in a moderate oven (350° F.,
Gas 4) until just set. Stiffly whisk
the egg whites and fold in lightly
the crushed ratafias. Pile on top of
the tapioca. Reduce the heat of the
oven to cool (290°–310° F., Gas
1–2) and bake until a pale golden
brown on top; about 30 min.

6 helpings

VERMICELLI PUDDING

1½ pt. milk   1 bay leaf or pinch of
ground cinnamon or orange or
lemon rind   3 oz. vermicelli
pinch of salt   1½ oz. sugar   2–3 eggs

Bring the milk slowly to the
boil, with the flavouring ingredient (not ground cinnamon);
then remove the flavouring. Add
the vermicelli, broken into short
pieces, and the salt. Simmer until
tender, then cool slightly. Separate the eggs. Add the sugar,
ground cinnamon (if used) and egg
yolks and stir well. Lightly stir in
the stiffly-whipped egg whites.
Pour into a well-buttered pie-dish
and bake in a moderate oven
(350° F., Gas 4) until golden
brown—about 20–30 min.

6 helpings
Cooking time—about 1 hr. altogether

MEDIUM OR SMALL
   GRAIN PUDDINGS
(Semolina, ground rice, small sago,
crushed tapioca)
Basic Recipe

2 pt. milk   flavouring (see p. 246)
3 oz. grain   2–3 oz. sugar

Heat the milk and infuse the

flavouring for about 10 min., then remove the flavouring. Sprinkle the grain into the milk, stirring quickly to prevent lumps forming. Continue stirring until the mixture has simmered long enough for the grains to become transparent and cooked through—usually about 15 min. Add the sugar and essence (if used for flavouring). The pudding can then be (a) served as it is, or (b) poured into a well-buttered pie-dish, and put into a moderate oven (350° F., Gas 4) for 20-30 min. until the top is browned.

6 helpings

SMALL GRAIN PUDDINGS —WITH EGGS

(Semolina, ground rice, small sago, crushed tapioca)

Basic Recipe

2 pt. milk   flavouring (see p. 246)
3 oz. grain   2-4 eggs   2-3 oz. sugar

Heat the milk, and infuse the flavouring for about 10 min., then remove it. Sprinkle the grain into the flavoured milk, stirring quickly to prevent lumps forming. Continue stirring until the mixture has simmered long enough for the grain to become transparent and cooked through—about 15 min. Leave to cool slightly. Separate the eggs and stir in the egg yolks. Add the sugar and flavouring essence (if used), and lastly stir the stiffly-beaten egg whites into the pudding. Pour into a well-buttered pie-dish and bake in a warm oven (335° F., Gas 3) until the top is nicely brown—about 30-40 min.

6 helpings

HASTY PUDDING

1½ pt. milk   2½ oz. sago or semolina or ground rice
1 oz. sugar

Heat the milk to almost boiling, then sprinkle in the sago, semolina or ground rice, stirring briskly. Simmer until the grain is cooked and the mixture begins to thicken —about 10-15 min. Add the sugar.

Serve with cream, sugar, jam or treacle.

6 helpings

HONEY PUDDING

1 gill milk   1 oz. semolina   1 oz. butter   4 oz. honey   grated rind of ½ lemon   ½ teasp. ground ginger
2 eggs   6 oz. breadcrumbs

Grease a 1-1½ pt. mould or basin.

Heat the milk in a saucepan; sprinkle in the semolina, and, stirring well, cook for 10 min. Add the butter, honey, lemon rind, ginger, the egg yolks and the breadcrumbs. Beat well. Whisk the egg whites stiffly and stir them lightly into the rest of the ingredients. Turn the mixture into the mould or basin; cover. Steam gently for 1¾-2 hr.

5-6 helpings

POWDERED GRAIN PUDDINGS

(Arrowroot, cornflour, custard powder, finely ground rice, powdered barley, fine oatmeal)

Basic Recipe

2½ oz. powdered grain   2 pt. milk
2-3 oz. sugar
flavouring (see p. 246)

Mix the grain to a smooth paste with a little of the milk and put the rest of the milk on to boil. Pour the boiling milk quickly on to the blended paste, stirring vigorously to prevent lumps forming. Return the mixture to the saucepan, heat until it thickens, then simmer for 2-3 min. to completely cook the grain, stirring continuously. Add the sugar. The pudding can then be served as it is, or poured into a well-buttered pie-dish and baked in a moderate oven

(350° F., Gas 4) until the top is browned, about 20–30 min.

6 helpings

POWDERED GRAIN PUDDINGS—WITH EGGS

(Arrowroot, cornflour, custard powder, finely ground rice, powdered barley, fine oatmeal)

Basic Recipe

2½ oz. powdered grain   2 pt. milk
2–4 eggs   2–3 oz. sugar
flavouring (see p. 246)

Mix the grain to a smooth paste with a little of the milk and put the rest of the milk on to boil. Pour the boiling milk quickly on to the blended paste, stirring vigorously to prevent lumps forming. Return the mixture to the saucepan, heat until it thickens, then simmer for 2–3 min. to completely cook the grain, stirring continuously. Allow the mixture to cool. Separate the eggs and whisk the whites stiffly. Stir into the pudding the egg yolks, sugar, any flavouring essence and lastly stir in lightly the stiffly-whisked egg whites. Pour into a well-buttered pie-dish and bake in a warm oven (335° F., Gas 3) until the top of the pudding is nicely browned, about 30–40 min.

6 helpings

Variation

ARROWROOT PUDDING— STEAMED

1½ oz. arrowroot   1½ pt. milk
2 oz. castor sugar   ¼ teasp. vanilla
essence or grated lemon rind
3 eggs

Mix the arrowroot to a smooth paste with a little of the milk. Boil the remainder of the milk and pour over the arrowroot paste, stirring well. Return to the saucepan, stir, and simmer gently until the mixture thickens. Leave to cool slightly and stir in the flavouring, sugar and well-beaten eggs. Pour into a 2-pt. greased basin, cover with greased paper and steam for 1½ hr.

Turn out and serve with custard or wine sauce (p. 108).

6 helpings

CUSTARDS AND CUSTARD MIXTURES

Custards can be cooked by "boiling", baking or steaming, but they must be cooked very carefully and slowly since over-cooking will cause the mixture to curdle. A custard which is to be turned out requires at least the equivalent of 4 eggs to 1 pt. of liquid, otherwise it is liable to break .

Pouring Custards: These are made by heating and maintaining the mixture at a temperature below boiling-point until the eggs cook evenly through the mixture. The use of a double saucepan for this purpose lessens the risk of curdling.

Baked Custards: The pie-dish should be well greased and then placed in a tray of warm water and baked slowly at about 335°–350° F., Gas 3–4, until the custard is set. Take out of the water immediately to prevent further cooking.

Steamed Custards: The basin must be well greased and the custard covered with greased paper to prevent the condensing steam from dripping into it. Only a very gentle flow of steam should be maintained to prevent overcooking.

Flavourings: Custards can be flavoured with grated nutmeg; cinnamon; vanilla, lemon *or* almond essence; or by infusing a bay leaf *or* thinly-cut strips of lemon rind (avoid the white pith) in the milk for a few minutes, then removing them.

BAKED CUSTARD

1½ pt. milk   flavouring (see p. 250)
3 eggs   1½ oz. castor sugar

Beat the eggs with the sugar. Add the warmed milk and flavouring. Strain into a greased pie-dish. Stand the pie-dish in a tray of warm water and bake slowly in a warm-moderate oven (335°–350° F., Gas 3–4) until the custard is set in the centre—about 50 min.

6 helpings

CUP CUSTARD

To make ¾ pt.

½ pt. milk   flavouring: lemon rind or vanilla essence   1 egg and
1 yolk or 3 egg yolks
1 oz. castor sugar
2 tablesp. double cream (optional)

Warm the milk, infusing the lemon rind if used. Mix eggs and sugar to a liquid. Pour the warmed milk over the eggs and strain the custard into a pan previously rinsed with cold water. Cook the custard gently until the eggs have coagulated and thickened the milk. To ensure that this occurs evenly and forms a smooth creamy texture, stirring should be brisk and thorough. If the custard is cooked in a saucepan, a wooden spoon will be found most suitable for this, as the thick edge of the spoon works smoothly over the base of the pan, keeping it clear. If the custard is cooked in a double saucepan over hot water, a whisk is better, as thickening takes place from the sides as well as from the base. Do not let the custard boil. When the custard coats the spoon, pour into a cool bowl, and add the vanilla, if used. Add the cream (if used) and stir in lightly. Stir frequently during cooling so that a skin does not form on the surface.

NOTE: A thinner pouring custard can be made by using 1 pt. milk and 2 eggs.

Time—15 min.

STEAMED CUSTARD

1 pt. milk   flavouring (see p. 250)
4 eggs   1 oz. castor sugar

Warm the milk and flavouring. Beat the eggs and sugar together. If bay leaf or lemon rind has been used to flavour, remove from the milk before pouring it on to the eggs and sugar; stir well. Pour the mixture into a buttered mould, cover with greased paper and steam very gently for about 40 min. Turn out and serve with wine sauce (p. 108).

5–6 helpings
Time—50 min.

Variations

BORDER OF PEARS

½ lb. loaf sugar   1 pt. water
a few drops of cochineal
2 lb. small stewing pears   2 eggs
1 egg yolk   1 gill milk   2 oz. castor sugar   grated rind of ½ lemon
1 oz. butter
3 individual sponge cakes

Make a syrup by slowly heating together the loaf sugar and water and then boiling rapidly for a few minutes; add a few drops of cochineal just to colour the syrup pink. Peel, halve and core the pears and put immediately into the syrup and stew until tender: about ½ hr. Take out the pears and reduce the syrup by rapid boiling to just over ½ pt., reheat the pears in the syrup before serving. Meanwhile, beat together the eggs, warmed milk, castor sugar, lemon rind and melted butter. Slice the sponge cakes and arrange them in a buttered border mould. Pour the custard on to the sponge cakes. Stand the mould in a tray containing sufficient cold water to come about half-way up the sides of the mould. Bake 40 min. in a warm oven

($335°$ F., *Gas* 3) until set.

Turn out on to a hot dish, arrange the pears on the border or in the centre and pour the syrup round.

Serve either hot or cold.

6 helpings

Cooking time—altogether $1\frac{1}{4}$ hr.

BREAD AND BUTTER PUDDING

6 thin slices of bread and butter
2 oz. sultanas or currants or stoned raisins or chopped candied peel
3 eggs $1\frac{1}{2}$ oz. sugar $1\frac{1}{2}$ pt. milk

Grease a 2-pt. pie-dish. Cut the bread into squares or triangles and put them neatly in the dish. Remove the crust, if preferred. Sprinkle the fruit over. Beat the eggs with the sugar, add the milk and pour over the bread; it should only half-fill the dish. Leave to soak at least 30 min. Bake in a moderate oven ($350°$ F., *Gas* 4) until the custard is set; about 1 hr.

5–6 helpings

CABINET PUDDING—PLAIN

4 oz. stoned raisins $\frac{1}{2}$ lb. bread
4 eggs   1 oz. sugar   1 pt. milk
vanilla essence

Grease a 2-pt. pudding-basin and decorate the base and sides by pressing on some halved raisins.

Cut the bread into $\frac{1}{4}$-in. dice. Beat the eggs. Heat the sugar and milk slightly and stir into the beaten egg. Add vanilla essence to taste. Add the bread and rest of the raisins and leave to soak for $\frac{1}{2}$ hr. Pour into the basin, cover with greased paper and steam gently $1\frac{1}{4}$–$1\frac{1}{2}$ hr. until the pudding is firm in the centre.

Serve with jam sauce.

6 helpings

Cooking time—$1\frac{1}{4}$–$1\frac{1}{2}$ hr.

CANADIAN PUDDING

1 oz. stoned raisins   6 oz. corn meal   2 pt. milk   rind of 1 small lemon   2 oz. sugar   3 eggs

Grease, then decorate a basin with the raisins. Mix the meal with a little of the cold milk; infuse the lemon rind in the remainder of the milk for 15 min. Remove the lemon rind; pour the boiling milk over the blended corn meal, stirring well. Return to the pan, add the sugar, and simmer gently for 10 min. When cool, add the well-beaten eggs. Pour the mixture carefully into the decorated mould. Cover. Steam slowly for $1\frac{1}{2}$–2 hr. until firm to the touch.

6–7 helpings

CARAMEL CUSTARD

4 eggs   1 oz. castor sugar
$\frac{3}{4}$ pt. milk
a few drops of vanilla essence

CARAMEL

3 oz. loaf sugar $\frac{1}{2}$ gill cold water

Have ready a warm charlotte *or* plain mould and a thickly-folded band of newspaper to encircle it so that the mould can be firmly held in one hand. Prepare the caramel by heating the loaf sugar and water together, stir until it boils, then remove the spoon and allow to boil without stirring until it is golden brown. Pour the caramel into the warm mould and twist round until the sides and base are well coated with caramel.

Work together the eggs and sugar without beating them and pour on to them the warmed milk. Add the vanilla essence. Strain the custard into the mould and cover with greased paper. Steam very slowly for about $\frac{3}{4}$ hr. until the custard is firm in the middle; *or* the caramel custard may be baked by leaving it uncovered, standing it in a tray of warm water, and baking in a warm oven ($335°$ F., *Gas* 3) until the custard is set in the centre: about 40 min. Turn out carefully, so that the caramel runs off and serves as a sauce.

NOTE: Small caramel custards can be made in dariole moulds; cook for about 20 min.

6 helpings

CREME BRULEE

½ pt. milk   ½ oz. cornflour   ½ pt. cream   a few drops of vanilla essence   3 eggs   2 oz. castor sugar ground cinnamon

Mix the cornflour with a little of the milk and put the rest of the milk and cream on to boil. When boiling, pour on to the cornflour paste, stirring well. Return to the pan and simmer for 2–3 min. Add the vanilla essence and stir in the well-beaten eggs. Whisk over a low heat until the mixture thickens, but do not allow to boil. Add 1 oz. sugar to sweeten. Pour into a well-greased soufflé dish, sprinkle well with cinnamon and the rest of the sugar and bake in a fairly hot oven (400° F., Gas 6) until the mixture is set and well browned, about ¼ hr., or brown under the grill.

6 helpings

CUSTARD PIE

3 level tablesp. cornflour   1½ pt. milk   3 eggs   1½ oz. castor sugar a little grated nutmeg short crust pastry using 6 oz. flour

Blend the cornflour with a little of the cold milk and put the rest of the milk to boil. Pour the boiling milk on to the blended cornflour, stirring well. Return to pan, re-boil 2–3 min.; remove from heat. Work together the eggs and sugar, and when the cornflour mixture is cooler add this to the worked eggs.

Line a 9-in. flan ring or a shallow heat-proof glass dish with short crust pastry and prick the base finely. Pour in the custard mixture, dust with a little grated nutmeg, if liked, and bake in a fairly hot oven (375° F., Gas 5) until the pastry is browned, then reduce the heat to 335° F., Gas 3,

until the custard is set—45 min.

NOTE: To ensure that the base of the pastry case is cooked through place the flan ring or dish on a solid baking sheet in the oven.

6 helpings

FOREST PUDDING

4 stale individual sponge cakes jam   grated rind of ½ lemon 1 oz. sugar   3 eggs   1½ pt. milk

Slice the sponge cakes thinly, spread half of them with jam, cover with the remaining halves and put into a well-buttered pie-dish, which they should half-fill. Sprinkle with lemon rind. Beat together the sugar and eggs and pour on the milk. Pour the custard over the sponge cakes and leave to stand for 1 hr. Bake very slowly for 40–50 min. in a warm–moderate oven (335°–350° F., Gas 3–4) until the custard is set and the pudding browned on top.

6 helpings

ITALIAN PUDDING

2 eggs   ½ oz. castor sugar   ¾ pt. milk   2 oz. cakecrumbs   ½ lb. stoned dates   ½ lb. stoned raisins 2 oz. finely-chopped mixed peel ¼ teasp. ground nutmeg 1 lb. cooking apples

Make a custard by beating together the eggs and sugar and pouring on the warmed milk. Stir in the cakecrumbs. Mix together the dates, raisins, peel and nutmeg. Peel, core and slice the apples thinly. Put the apple slices at the bottom of a well-buttered pie-dish, add the mixed fruit and then cover with the custard mixture. Bake in a warm oven (335° F., Gas 3) for ¾–1 hr., until firm and set. Serve hot or cold.

5–6 helpings

JENNY LIND PUDDING

4 stale individual sponge cakes

4 coconut cakes   12 ratafias
1 oz. desiccated coconut   1 pt. milk
2 eggs   ¾-1 oz. castor sugar

Slice the sponge cakes and put them in a buttered pie-dish interspersed with the coconut cakes and ratafias Simmer the coconut in the milk until tender—about 15 min., cool slightly. Beat the eggs and sugar together and add to the milk and coconut. Pour the custard over the other ingredients and bake gently (about 335° F., *Gas* 3) until the mixture is set.

5–6 helpings .
Time—50–60 min.

MADEIRA PUDDING

6 oz. bread, cut into ½-in. dice
3 oz. castor sugar   1 teasp. grated
lemon rind   ¾ pt. milk   3 eggs
1 wineglass sherry or Madeira
(optional)

Mix together in a basin the bread, sugar and lemon rind. Heat the milk to about blood heat and pour it on to the well-beaten eggs. Add the sherry *or* Madeira, if used, and pour this over the bread, sugar and lemon rind mixture. Leave to soak for 15–20 min. Pour into a well-buttered mould or basin, cover and steam very gently for 2 hr.

Serve with custard, wine or jam sauce (pp. 107, 108).

5–6 helpings

MARMALADE PUDDING (1)

4 tablesp. marmalade   1 oz. butter
or margarine   1 pt. milk   1 oz.
sugar   ½ pt. breadcrumbs   3 eggs
2–4 oz. castor sugar

Butter a 2-pt. pie-dish and cover the bottom of the dish with a layer of marmalade. Heat together the butter, milk and 1 oz. sugar. Add the breadcrumbs and leave to stand for about 10 min. Beat together 1 whole egg and 2 egg yolks and stir well into the breadcrumb mixture. Pour half the

breadcrumb mixture into the dish; add another layer of marmalade, and put the remainder of the breadcrumb mixture on top. Bake in a moderate oven (350° F., *Gas* 4) until the mixture is set. Whip the egg whites stiffly, fold in the 2–4 oz. castor sugar and pile on top of the pudding. Dredge well with castor sugar. Bake in a very cool oven (290° F., *Gas* 1) for about 20–30 min. until the meringue is fawn and crisp.

Cooking time—1 hr.

5–6 helpings

NOTE: *See* p. 269 for Marmalade Pudding (2).

QUEEN OF PUDDINGS

1 pt. milk   ½ pt. breadcrumbs
2 oz. butter or margarine   grated
rind of 2 lemons   2 oz. granulated
sugar   2 eggs   3 tablesp. jam
2–4 castor sugar

Heat the milk and add to it the breadcrumbs, fat, lemon rind and granulated sugar. Leave to soak for 30 min. Separate the eggs and stir in the yolks. Pour the mixture into a buttered pie-dish and bake in a moderate oven (350° F., *Gas* 4) until set—about ¾ hr. When the pudding is set, spread the jam on top. Whip the egg whites very stiffly, add 1 oz. of castor sugar and whip again until stiff; then stir in lightly the rest of the sugar. Spread over the pudding, put into a very cool oven (265° F., *Gas* ½) until the meringue is set and golden brown.

5–6 helpings

QUEEN'S PUDDING

¼ lb. biscuit- or cakecrumbs
1 pt. milk   2 oz. sugar   2 eggs
vanilla essence   6–9 apricot halves
(preserved, i.e. canned or bottled)
glacé cherries for decoration
apricot sauce (p. 105)

Rub the biscuit- or cakecrumbs

through a fine sieve. Heat the milk, add the crumbs, leave to stand for 10–15 min. until soft; then beat until smooth. Beat in the sugar and eggs. Flavour with vanilla essence. Grease a plain mould or basin with butter, line the base with a round of greased paper and sprinkle with castor sugar. Pour in the mixture and cover with paper. Stand the mould in a tin of hot water, and bake in a warm oven (335° F., Gas 3) until the mixture is firm to the touch; about $\frac{3}{4}$ hr.

Meanwhile make the apricot sauce. When the pudding is set in the middle, leave it to stand a few minutes and then carefully un-mould on to a dish. Tear off the paper, arrange apricot halves round the dish, decorate pudding with cherries, and pour round it the apricot sauce.

6 helpings

SAVOY PUDDINGS

8 oz. stale savoy or sponge cake
2 oz. finely chopped mixed peel
1½ gill milk   2 oz. warmed butter
1 wineglass sherry or Marsala
(optional)   4½ oz. castor sugar
3 eggs

Pass the cake through a fine wire sieve. Add the peel, milk, warmed butter, wine and 1½ oz. of the sugar. Separate the eggs and add the yolks to the mixture. Beat well and pour the mixture into a buttered pie-dish. Bake in a moderate oven (350° F., Gas 4) until the pudding is set—about $\frac{3}{4}$ hr. Stiffly whisk the egg whites, stir in the remaining 3 oz. of sugar lightly, and pile on top of the pudding.

Bake in a very cool oven (265°–290° F., Gas $\frac{1}{2}$–1) to set and colour the meringue, about $\frac{1}{2}$ hr.

5–6 helpings

BATTERS

Batters are made from a basic mixture of flour, milk and egg. The flour (with salt added for flavouring) is worked to a slack consistency with the eggs and some of the liquid, so that it can be beaten more easily until smooth and viscous. The rest of the liquid is then stirred in. The mixture is left to stand for $\frac{1}{2}$ hr. before use.

The lightness of a batter depends on the quick formation of steam within the mixture and the quick cooking of the flour. A baked batter therefore requires a hot oven (425° F., Gas 7); the temperature can be reduced when the flour is almost cooked. It is best to put the batter at the top of the oven to begin with; then to move it to a lower shelf at reduced heat (375° F., Gas 5) to finish cooking.

Batter mixtures may also be steamed. See notes on steaming (p. 264).

Coating batters are dealt with in the section on fritters (p. 257).

Basic Recipe

BATTER PUDDING

¼ lb. plain flour   ¼ teasp. salt
2 eggs   1 pt. milk
1 tablesp. cooking fat or lard

Sift the flour and salt into a basin. Make a well in the centre of the flour and break the eggs into this. Add about a gill of the milk. Stir gradually, working the flour down from the sides and adding more milk, as required, to make a stiff batter consistency. Beat well for about 5 min. Add the rest of the milk. Cover and leave to stand for 30 min. Put the fat into a Yorkshire pudding tin and heat in the oven until hot. The fat should just be beginning to smoke. Quickly pour in the batter and leave to cook in a hot oven (425° F., Gas 7) at the top of the oven until nicely browned. Reduce the heat to 375° F., Gas 5, and finish cooking through for 10-15 min. Serve with wine- or jam-sauce.

6 helpings

Time (Large pudding)—35-40 min.
(Individual puddings)—20-25 min.

STEAMED BATTER PUDDING

1 pt. milk   ¼ teasp. salt   2 eggs
½ lb. plain flour

Prepare the mixture as in previous recipe. Pour it into a well-greased pudding basin. Cover with a greased paper and steam for 2 hr. Serve with a fruit- or sweet-sauce.

6 helpings

Cooking time—2 hr.

CREPES SUZETTE

½ pt. batter   icing sugar
brandy or rum

FILLING

2 oz. butter   3 oz. castor sugar
rind of ½ orange, grated   2 teasp.
orange juice   1 teasp. lemon juice
1 tablesp. kirsch or Curaçao

Make the batter and leave it to stand. Cream together the butter and sugar for the filling until very soft, then work in the orange juice, orange rind, lemon juice and liqueur. Make a very thin pancake, spread with some of the filling, roll up and dredge with icing sugar. Put into a warm place while the rest of the pancakes are being made. Just before serving pour over the rum or brandy and light up. Serve immediately.

FRENCH PANCAKES

½ pt. milk   2 oz. butter or
margarine   2 oz. castor sugar
2 eggs   2 oz. plain flour
a little grated lemon rind
4 tablesp. jam (approx.)

Warm the milk. Cream the fat and sugar until soft. Well whisk the eggs and beat them gradually into the creamed fat and sugar. Stir in the flour. Add the warmed milk and lemon rind. Beat well. Leave to stand for ½ hr.

Grease 6 small deep plates *or* large saucers and pour an equal quantity of batter into each. Bake in a fairly hot oven (400° F., Gas 6) for about 5-10 min., until the batter rises; then more slowly (350° F., Gas 4) for about another 10 min., until firm and brown on top.

Turn a pancake out on to a hot dish, spread quickly with melted jam; lay another pancake on top, and so on until the last pancake is put on top.

Dredge well with castor sugar and serve quickly.

NOTE: This is sometimes known as ANGEL PUDDING.

5-6 helpings

PANCAKES

Batter as for Batter Pudding (p. 255)
a little cooking fat   lemon
castor sugar

Prepare the batter. Leave to stand for ½ hr., then pour into a jug. Use a small clean frying-pan or omelet pan.

If the pan is new or has been washed frequently, melt in it about ½ oz. cooking fat; heat until it is smoking hot, twisting the pan so that the sides are coated with fat. Pour away all the fat and wipe the pan clean with a soft cloth or pieces of kitchen paper, otherwise the pancakes may stick.

Put about ¼ oz. of cooking fat into the cleaned frying-pan and heat until it is just beginning to smoke. Quickly pour in enough batter to coat thinly the bottom of the pan, tilting the pan to make sure that the batter runs over evenly. Move the frying-pan over a quick heat until the pancake is set and browned underneath. Make sure that the pancake is loose at the sides and either toss or turn with a broad-bladed knife or fish slice. Brown on the other side and turn on to a sugared paper. Sprinkle with sugar and lemon juice, roll up and keep hot while cooking the rest.

Serve dredged with castor sugar and pieces of cut lemon.

6 helpings

Jam pancakes: Spread with jam before rolling up.

Orange pancakes: Make the pancakes but sprinkle with orange juice and serve with pieces of cut orange.

Tangerine pancakes: Add grated tangerine rind to the batter. Sprinkle with tangerine juice before rolling up.

With *brandy filling:* Cream together 2 oz. butter and 1 oz. castor sugar until soft. Work in 1 tablesp. brandy and 1 teasp. lemon juice. Spread the pancakes with this mixture. Roll up and put immediately into the serving dish.

YORKSHIRE PUDDING

1 pt. batter as for Batter Pudding (p. 255)   2 tablesp. dripping

Prepare and cook as for Batter Pudding but cook the pudding in meat dripping. Start cooking on the top shelf above the meat and finish off below the meat on a lower shelf.

Serve with roast beef.

NOTE: In Yorkshire this pudding is served with gravy, as a separate course, before the meat.

6 helpings
Cooking time—about 35 min.

FRITTERS

Fritters are usually made from a batter mixture, used as a coating or as a means of cohering a mixture. They are fried in fat.

Fritters can be varied by using: dessert *gooseberries*; *prunes* soaked, the stones removed and the cavity filled with an almond *or* marzipan; ripe *pears* cut into quarters soaked in a little liqueur *or* lemon juice before coating; *strawberries*; *figs*; *stale cake* or *pudding*, cut into suitable pieces, soaked lightly in fruit syrup *or* liqueur; *small fresh fruit*, coated and dropped into the fat in spoonfuls.

GENERAL HINTS

1. The batter should be thick enough to coat the food to be fried.
2. The frying fat should be at least one inch in depth. Coated food can be fried in deeper fat.
3. The fat must be hot enough to seal the batter immediately so that the food inside does not become greasy, but not so hot as to burn the coating before the filling is cooked or heated through.
4. When hot enough the fat should just show signs of hazing. It can be tested by dropping a small spot of batter into the fat. If the fat is at the correct temperature the batter will sink, rise to the surface immediately and then begin to colour.
5. Cook only small amounts at a time and finish cooking on one side before turning the food over.
6. Allow the fat time to reheat before putting in another batch.
7. Drain the fried food well on kitchen paper, which will ab-

sorb the surplus fat before serving.

8. Strain the fat after use.

COATING BATTER (1)

2 oz. plain flour   pinch of salt
1 dessertsp. salad oil or oiled butter
¼ gill warm water   1 egg white

Sift together the flour and salt. Mix to a smooth consistency with the oil and water. Beat well and leave to stand for at least 30 min. Just before using, stiffly whisk the egg white and then stir it lightly into the batter.

COATING BATTER (2)

4 oz. plain flour   pinch of salt
1 tablesp. salad oil or melted butter
1 gill warm water (approx.)
1 teasp. baking powder

Sift together the flour and salt. Mix to a smooth consistency with the oil and water until the mixture is thick enough to beat. Beat well; then add water until the mixture is of a consistency to coat the back of a wooden spoon. Leave to stand for at least 30 min. Just before using, stir in the baking powder.

COATING BATTER (3)

4 oz. plain flour   pinch of salt
1 egg   1 gill milk

Sift together the flour and salt. Make a well in the centre of the flour and add the egg and some of the milk. Mix gradually to a stiff consistency, using more milk as required. Beat well. Add the rest of the milk. Leave to stand for about 30 min. before using.

ALMOND FRITTERS

2 eggs   1 oz. castor sugar   ½ oz.
cornflour   2 oz. ground almonds
a few drops of vanilla   frying-fat

Beat the egg yolks and the sugar together until thick and creamy. Stiffly whisk the egg whites. Stir the cornflour, almonds and vanilla essence into the creamed yolks and sugar. Lightly stir in the egg whites. Drop the mixture in teaspoonfuls into frying fat (which is just beginning to haze and which is at least 1 in. in depth). Fry until golden brown underneath. Turn, and when cooked on the other side drain well.

Dredge with castor sugar and serve at once.

5–6 helpings
Time—30 min.

APPLE FRITTERS

1 lb. cooking apples   castor sugar
deep fat   coating batter
lemon juice

Peel the apples, core them with an apple corer and cut into rings about ¼ in. thick. Put the apple rings on to a plate and sprinkle with lemon juice and sugar. Let them stand for a few minutes. Using a skewer, dip them into the batter, then drop them into deep fat which should just be beginning to haze. Cook until golden brown —about 4 min., and then lift out with a skewer.

Dredge well with castor sugar before serving.

4 helpings
Time—20 min.

APRICOT FRITTERS

12 apricot halves (fresh or
preserved)   fat for frying
castor sugar   ground cinnamon

YEAST BATTER

½ oz. yeast   ¼ teasp. castor sugar
1½ gill warm milk (approx.)
6 oz. plain flour   pinch of salt
1 oz. melted butter

Make the batter by creaming the yeast and sugar and adding a little milk. Sift together 2 oz. of the flour and the salt into a warm bowl. Mix to a batter consistency with the yeast mixture, adding more milk if required. Leave to rise until double its size. Meanwhile, drain the apricots from the syrup. When the dough is risen, add the rest of the flour and warm milk to make a batter consistency, and work in the melted butter. Leave to rise again in a warm place. Coat the apricots thinly with the batter and place them on a well-buttered paper. Leave in a warm place for 30 min. Fry in hot fat until nicely brown.

Drain well and dredge with plenty of castor sugar and cinnamon, before serving.

12 fritters

BANANA FRITTERS

4 firm bananas   coating batter (p. 258)   frying-fat   castor sugar

Prepare the batter. Cut each banana lengthwise and across the middle, making four portions. Coat with batter. Fry in hot fat, which is just beginning to haze.

Sprinkle well with castor sugar and serve immediately.

6 helpings

Orange Fritters: Remove peel and pith from 4 oranges; divide these into pieces of 3-4 segments. Carefully cut into centre to remove pips. Dip into batter and fry as above.

Pineapple Fritters: Use canned pineapple rings; drain well, dip into batter and fry as above. Serve with pineapple sauce made from the syrup.

BREAD AND BUTTER FRITTERS

Coating batter (p. 258)   6 thin slices of bread and butter   jam fat for frying   castor sugar ground cinnamon

Make the batter. Spread the slices of bread and butter well with jam. Make into sandwiches and cut into four. Dip into the batter and fry in fat which is at least 1 in. deep and which is just showing

signs of smoking or hazing. Turn and fry to a golden brown. Drain well. Dredge with plenty of castor sugar and cinnamon. Serve immediately.

4-5 helpings
Cooking time—5 min.

BREAD FRITTERS

6 slices of bread, about ½ in. thick, cut into halves or 3 French dinner rolls cut into slices   1 egg   1 egg yolk   ¾ pt. milk   ½ teasp. ground cinnamon   ½ oz. castor sugar ½ small glass of maraschino (optional)
clarified butter or frying-fat

Cut the crusts off the bread and place the bread in a deep dish. Beat the egg and egg yolk, add the milk, cinnamon, sugar and maraschino, if used. Stir well, and pour over the bread. Leave to soak for 10 min. Carefully lift out the slices of bread and let them drain. Fry in hot fat or clarified butter until golden brown on both sides. Drain, sprinkle with castor sugar and cinnamon. Serve immediately.

6 helpings
Cooking time—10 min.

GOOSEBERRY FRITTERS

1 lb. large gooseberries
fat for frying

BATTER

2 oz. plain flour   pinch of salt
2 tablesp. cream or milk
2 tablesp. water   2 eggs

Sift together the flour and salt. Mix to a stiff batter with the milk, water and egg yolks (*see* p. 258). Beat well and leave to stand for at least ½ hr.

Top, tail, wash and dry the gooseberries. Stiffly whisk the egg whites and stir into the batter, then add the gooseberries. Take up 2-3 gooseberries at a time, using a greased tablespoon, and lower them into the deep fat, which should just be beginning to haze, without separating them. Fry a golden brown, drain well.

Sprinkle with plenty of sugar and serve.

6–7 helpings
Cooking time—6–8 min.

SOUFFLE FRITTERS

4 oz. flour   pinch of salt   ½ pt.
water   4 oz. butter or margarine
3 large eggs   vanilla essence
fat for frying   castor sugar

Make choux pastry: sift the flour and salt. Put the water and fat in a saucepan and when the fat has melted bring to boiling-point. Add the sifted flour all at once and beat well over the heat until the mixture leaves the sides of the pan —about 1 min. Allow to cool slightly and add the beaten eggs

gradually and then vanilla essence to taste, beating well.

Heat the deep fat until it is just beginning to haze. Grease a dessertspoon and, with it, drop small spoonfuls of the pastry into the fat. Cook gently until crisp and lightly browned. Drain well.

Dredge with castor sugar and serve hot.

NOTE: It is advisable to test a fritter from each batch to ensure that the centre is cooked, since the time of cooking depends on the temperature of the fat.

5–6 helpings
Cooking time—7–10 min.

STRAWBERRY FRITTERS

Proceed as for Gooseberry Fritters (p. 259), substituting strawberries for gooseberries.

Cooking time—6–8 min.

HOT SOUFFLES

Soufflés can be either steamed or baked. The mixture depends for its lightness on the introduction of air incorporated into the egg whites by whisking.

Preparation of Soufflé Tin or Mould: Grease with clarified butter or a tasteless cooking fat. If to be steamed, tie a band of greased paper to come 3 in. above the top and half-way down the side of the tin, to support the mixture as it rises. The cut edges of the paper should be at the top. Cut a circle of greased paper for the top of the tin to prevent condensing water dripping on to the soufflé during steaming.

Steamed Soufflés: These are cooked in a steamer *or* a saucepan containing sufficient boiling water to come half-way up the sides of the pan. To prevent the soufflé tin from being in direct contact with the bottom of the saucepan, stand it on an upturned saucer or plate.

Steam gently but steadily and avoid moving or jolting the steamer in any way. When cooked, the soufflé should be well risen and just firm to touch. Turn out immediately on to a hot dish and serve at once with a suitable sauce.

Baked Soufflés: These are served in the dish in which they are baked —either in a large dish, in individual fireproof china dishes or in paper cases. The mixture should only three-quarters fill the dish before cooking. Soufflés tend to sink very easily, so during cooking avoid unnecessary opening of the oven door; close it gently, as a sudden cold draught or jolting of the oven could cause the mixture to fall. When cooked, the soufflé should be well risen and firm. Serve at once with a suitable sauce.

GENERAL HINTS
1. Before beginning to make the

souffle, prepare the tin or mould, and see that the steamer or oven is on.

2. Whisk the egg whites as stiffly as possible, until they stand up in points. Fold them very carefully into the mixture, taking care not to push out the entrapped air. Cook straight away.

3. Time the preparation and cooking so that the soufflé can be served as soon as it is cooked. The mixture falls very quickly after removal from the heat.

APRICOT SOUFFLE

¾ pt. apricot purée   1½ oz. butter
1½ oz. plain flour   4 egg yolks
2 oz. castor sugar   cochineal
6 egg whites

Prepare the soufflé tin (see p. 260). Make the apricot purée by rubbing either stewed or tinned apricots through a fine sieve and thinning down the purée with some of the syrup.

Melt the butter in the saucepan, add the flour and cook slowly for a few minutes. Stir in gradually the apricot purée; continue cooking until the mixture thickens. Leave to cool. Beat in the egg yolks singly and the sugar. Add a few drops of cochineal to bring up the apricot colouring. Stiffly whisk the egg whites; fold them into the mixture. Pour into the soufflé mould, cover and steam gently, about 50–60 min.

Turn out and serve at once with apricot- (p. 105) or custard- (p. 107) sauce.
6 helpings

CHOCOLATE SOUFFLE

2 oz. finely-grated plain chocolate
⅔ pt. milk   1½ oz. butter
1½ oz. plain flour   4 egg yolks
3 oz. castor sugar   ½ teasp. vanilla
essence   5 egg whites

Prepare the soufflé tin (p. 260). Dissolve the chocolate in the milk.

Melt the butter, add the flour and let it cook for a few minutes without colouring. Add the milk and beat well until smooth. Reheat until the mixture thickens and comes away from the sides of the pan. Allow to cool slightly. Beat in the egg yolks well, one at a time, add the sugar and vanilla essence. Stiffly whisk the egg whites and fold them lightly into the mixture. Turn into the mould; cover, and steam very gently for about 1 hr.
6 helpings

CUSTARD SOUFFLE

Butter   3 oz. plain flour   ⅔ pt. milk
4 eggs   2 oz. castor sugar

Well butter a pie-dish. Melt 3 oz. butter in a saucepan, add the flour and stir over the heat until well cooked but not coloured. Add the milk; beat well until smooth. Reheat, stirring continuously until the mixture thickens and comes away from the sides of the pan. Let it cool slightly. Beat in the egg yolks singly and add the sugar. Stiffly whisk the egg whites and fold them lightly into the mixture. Turn into the pie-dish and bake in a fairly hot oven (375° F., Gas 5) for 25–30 min.

Serve with a wine- or fruit-sauce.
6 helpings

ORANGE SOUFFLE

Butter   1½ oz. plain flour
⅔ pt. milk   5 egg yolks
finely-grated rind of 1½ oranges
juice of ½ orange   1½ oz. castor
sugar   6 egg whites

Butter and prepare a soufflé tin (see p. 260). Melt 1½ oz. butter, stir in the flour and cook for a few minutes. Add the milk gradually, beating well. Continue cooking until the mixture thickens. Leave it to cool, then beat in the yolks one at a time. Stir in the orange rind, juice and sugar. Stiffly whisk the egg whites and fold these into the mixture. Pour the mixture into the mould; cover with a buttered paper. Steam for 50–60 min. until firm on top.

Serve immediately.

5–6 helpings

PINEAPPLE SOUFFLE

1½ oz. butter 1½ oz. plain flour
⅜ pt. milk 4½ egg yolks 1½ oz. castor sugar a few drops of vanilla essence 3 oz. preserved pineapple
6 egg whites angelica (optional)

Well butter and prepare a soufflé tin (see p. 260). If liked, the bottom can be decorated with angelica and pineapple. Melt 1½ oz. butter, stir in the flour and cook very slowly for a few minutes. Add the milk gradually, beating all the time, continue cooking for a minute longer. Let the mixture cool slightly. Beat in the egg yolks one at a time, then add the sugar, vanilla essence and diced pineapple. Stiffly whisk the egg whites and fold them lightly into the mixture. Pour the mixture into the prepared soufflé tin; cover with a buttered paper. Steam gently for 45–60 min. until firm on the top. Unmould and serve immediately, with pineapple sauce.

NOTE: If canned pineapple is used, drain the fruit well and substitute half the milk with pineapple juice.

5–6 helpings

STRAWBERRY SOUFFLE

Strawberries to make ¼ pt. pulp
1½ oz. butter 2 oz. plain flour
¼ pt. cream or top of milk 3 eggs
2 oz. castor sugar

a few drops of cochineal
½ lb. strawberries, cut into dice

Butter a soufflé dish. Reduce strawberries to a ¼ pt. pulp by crushing them with a fork, sweeten to taste. Melt the butter, add the flour and cook for a few minutes. Stir in the milk or cream and continue cooking until the mixture thickens. Leave to cool. Beat in the egg yolks. Work in the strawberry pulp and sugar. Add a few drops of colouring, if necessary, and the ½ lb. diced strawberries. Stiffly whisk the egg whites and fold these into the mixture. Turn into the mould and bake in a fairly hot oven (400° F., Gas 6) 35–40 min.

6–7 helpings

VANILLA SOUFFLE

1½ oz. butter 1½ oz. plain flour
⅜ pt. milk 4 egg yolks 1½ oz. castor sugar ½ teasp. vanilla essence 5 egg whites

Prepare the soufflé tin according to the method of cooking. If the soufflé is to be baked, butter the mould well, if steamed, see p. 260.

Melt the butter, stir in the flour and cook gently for a few minutes without colouring. Add the milk, stir well until smooth. Reheat, stirring continuously until the mixture thickens and leaves the sides of the pan. Leave to cool. Beat in the egg yolks, sugar and vanilla essence. Whisk the egg whites stiffly and fold them in lightly. Pour the mixture into the mould or tin and cover.

Steam for ¾–1 hr. or bake in a fairly hot oven (375° F., Gas 5) for 30–35 min.

6 helpings

SWEET OMELETS

GENERAL HINTS

1. The pan should be the correct size for the number of eggs

used. A two-egg omelet requires a pan of about 6 in. diameter.

2. The pan should be absolutely clean and should be kept only for omelet making. Do not wash it after use but wipe it out with a clean dry cloth, rubbing off any burnt egg with a little salt.

3. An old pan is better for omelets; a new pan needs to be proved. Heat a little fat (about $\frac{1}{2}$–1 oz.) in a new pan until a haze appears; pour off the fat and wipe the pan with a clean dry cloth.

4. A palette knife or fish slice is useful for folding the omelets.

5. Overcooking will make the omelet tough. It is cooked when the egg on top is just set. When making an omelet in which the yolks and whites of egg have been separated to finish cooking it under the grill for a minute.

6. Serve an omelet as soon as it is cooked.

JAM OMELET

2 eggs   1 oz. castor sugar
a few drops of flavouring, if liked
$\frac{1}{2}$ oz. unsalted butter
1 tablesp. warmed jam

Cream together the egg yolks, sugar and flavouring. Whisk the whites stiffly and mix them lightly with the yolks and sugar. Heat the butter in the omelet pan and take off any scum. Pour in the omelet mixture and cook without stirring over a moderate heat until it just sets. Brown off the top by putting it into a hot oven ($425°$ $F.$, Gas 7) or by putting it under a hot grill for a minute. Spread the jam in the centre and fold the omelet over, away from the handle of the pan, and then tip it out on to a hot dish. Dredge with sugar and serve at once.

2 helpings
Time—15 min.

RUM OMELET

3 eggs $\frac{1}{2}$ oz. castor sugar
1 tablesp. cream   2 tablesp. rum
$\frac{1}{2}$ oz. unsalted butter

Beat the eggs well and stir in thoroughly the sugar, cream and one tablesp. of rum. Heat the butter and take off any scum. Pour in the egg mixture and cook over a fairly quick heat. Stir until the mixture begins to set; then fold it over, away from the handle of the pan. Cook for another minute and then tip it out on to a hot dish.

Pour round a tablesp. of rum and light, if liked. Serve at once.

NOTE: This omelet can be varied by using a liqueur instead of rum for flavouring.

2 helpings

SWEET OMELET

2 eggs   pinch of salt   1 tablesp.
cream or top of the milk $\frac{1}{2}$ oz.
castor sugar $\frac{1}{2}$ oz. unsalted butter

Beat the eggs thoroughly with the salt, cream and castor sugar. Heat the butter in an omelet pan and remove any scum. When the butter is really hot pour in the omelet mixture and stir until it begins to set. Fold away from the handle of the pan. Cook for another minute and then tip out on to a hot dish.

Dredge with castor sugar and serve at once.

NOTE: Any sweet filling can be added, such as warmed jam, fruit purée or diced soft fruit. It should be spread evenly in the centre just before the omelet is folded over.

2 helpings

PUDDINGS

Puddings are made basically from flour, breadcrumbs or cakecrumbs, fat, sugar, eggs and a raising agent. When the proportion of baking-powder to flour is 1 teasp. to $\frac{1}{2}$ lb., self-raising flour is a satisfactory alternative.

The fat is worked into the mixture in various ways.

(a) *Chopped-in Method (Suet):* Either beef or mutton suet can be used, although beef suet is generally preferred. Shredded packet suet is, of course, ready for use and requires no further chopping.

To prepare suet remove the skin and fibrous tissue from the suet. Sprinkle the suet liberally with some of the measured flour or breadcrumbs. Shred or cut it down in flakes; then chop it finely. Add more measured flour if the suet becomes sticky. Mix all the other dry ingredients with the suet. Stir in the eggs and sufficient milk to obtain the consistency required by the recipe.

(b) *Rubbed-in Method:* Sift the flour, salt and raising agent into a mixing bowl. Cut the fat into small pieces. With the tips of the fingers, rub the fat into the flour. Continue this until all the lumps of fat have been worked down and the mixture resembles breadcrumbs. Add the rest of the dry ingredients. Stir in the beaten eggs and liquid, according to the recipe.

(c) *Creaming Method:* This method is used for richer puddings, where the amount of fat is often too great to be rubbed in, or where flour is not used in the recipe. Castor sugar should be used, as the small crystals are more easily dissolved.

Work the fat and sugar well together—using either a wooden spoon or the hand—until the mixture is lighter in colour and of the consistency of thick cream. Add any essences at this stage. (In cold weather, a warm bowl or hot dish-cloth round the bowl will facilitate the creaming, but on no account should the mixture be allowed to oil as a result of too much heat.)

Beat the eggs. Add the beaten egg a little at a time, beating well between each addition so that the mixture remains smooth. Curdling of the mixture may occur if the egg is added too quickly or if the egg used has come direct from the refrigerator. Sift in the flour, salt and baking-powder. Stir in lightly, adding the rest of the ingredients.

(d) *Creaming of Yolks and Sugar Method:* Put the yolks into a basin with the sugar. Whisk until lighter in colour and frothy. Stir in lightly the other ingredients, proceeding according to the recipe.

Consistencies of Mixtures: A *dropping consistency* is reached when the mixture will just drop off a spoon when it is shaken lightly. For a *soft dropping consistency* the mixture should drop easily from the spoon. For a *slack consistency* the mixture should fall easily from the spoon.

STEAMED AND BOILED PUDDINGS

The mould or basin in which a pudding is cooked should be well greased with fresh butter, clarified butter *or* margarine, *or* cooking fat. Always prepare the mould or basin and the covering before the pudding is mixed.

STEAMED PUDDINGS

1. Have the steamer ready before the pudding is mixed. There should be plenty of boiling water in the steamer. If a steamer is not available, the pudding can be *partly steamed* by standing it on an old plate, saucer or pastry cutter (to prevent direct contact with the source of heat) in a saucepan, with just enough water to reach half-way up the mould or basin. Put a tightly fitting lid on the saucepan and simmer gently. If the water boils away, add

more *boiling* water to replace it.

2. Where gentle steaming is indicated in the recipe, the water below the steamer should only simmer.

3. The basin or mould should not be more than three-quarters full.

4. Always cover the pudding with greased paper before steaming; this acts as a waterproof cover against condensing steam. Use a piece of strong paper, such as greaseproof, grease it well and place it greased side down on the basin. Turn the edges under and twist them securely below the rim of the basin.

5. After taking the pudding out of the steamer, leave it for a minute or two, to allow it time to shrink slightly from the sides of the mould or basin, before turning it out.

BOILED PUDDINGS

1. The pudding can be boiled in a basin covered with a cloth *or* in a cloth only. The cloth should be clean and well floured before use. Roly-poly types of puddings are rolled in the floured cloth, forming a sausage-shape, and tied loosely at either end, to allow room for the pudding to swell.

2. If a basin is used, fill it completely.

3. The water must be boiling rapidly when the pudding is put in and then should simmer gently. The water must completely cover the pudding, and be deep enough to float those boiled in cloths; otherwise a plate or saucer must be placed at the bottom of the pan. As the water boils away, *boiling water* must be added.

4. The pudding should be allowed to stand a minute or two before being turned out in order that some of the steam may escape,

causing the pudding to shrink and thus be less liable to break.

Christmas Puddings: After the first boiling, the cloth should be taken off and a clean, dry, well-floured cloth tied on to the pudding. Cover or wrap in greaseproof paper and store in a cool larder. Give at least another 1½ hours' boiling before serving.

APPLE DUMPLINGS—BOILED

6 apples   suet crust pastry (p. 342) using 12 oz. flour, etc.   3 oz. moist or brown sugar   6 cloves

Core and peel the apples. Divide the pastry into 6 portions and roll each into a round. Put an apple into the centre of the round of pastry and work the pastry round the apple until it nearly meets. Fill the centre of the apple with sugar and a clove. Damp the edges of pastry and join them firmly together. Tie each apple dumpling in the corner of a well-floured pudding cloth. Put the dumplings into boiling water and boil gently, from 40–50 min.

6 helpings

APPLE PUDDING—STEAMED

4 oz. apples (after peeling and coring)   4 oz. breadcrumbs 4 oz. finely-chopped suet   4 oz. moist sugar   pinch of nutmeg pinch of salt   2 eggs   ¼ pt. milk

Chop the apples coarsely. Mix together the breadcrumbs, suet, sugar, nutmeg and salt. Add the apples. Beat the eggs. Stir in the eggs and milk, and mix well. Leave to stand for 1 hr. to allow the bread to soak. The mixture should then drop easily from the spoon. If it is too stiff, add a little more milk. Pour into a well-greased basin, cover, and steam for 2 hr. Serve with custard sauce (p. 107).

NOTE: *See also* Fruit Pudding with Suet Crust (p. 268).

5–6 helpings

BACHELOR'S PUDDING (1)

3 oz. dried fruit   6 oz. plain flour
pinch of salt   1 teasp. baking-
powder   3 oz. sugar
2 oz. breadcrumbs
3 oz. finely-chopped suet   1 egg
milk to mix (about 1 gill)

Grease a pudding basin. Clean
the fruit. Mix together the sifted
flour, salt, baking-powder, sugar,
breadcrumbs and suet. Stir in the
dried fruit. Add the well-beaten
egg and some of the milk. Stir,
adding more milk as required,
until the mixture drops easily
from the spoon. Turn the mixture
into the basin; cover with greased
paper, and steam for 2–2½ hr.
When ready, turn out of the basin
and dredge well with sugar.

4–5 helpings

BARONESS PUDDING

4 oz. finely-chopped suet   6 oz.
stoned raisins   8 oz. plain flour
2 oz. castor sugar   1 rounded
teasp. baking-powder   pinch of salt
1 gill milk (approx.)

Grease a 1½-pt. pudding basin.
Prepare the suet and raisins. Mix
together the sifted flour, baking-
powder and salt with the raisins,
suet and sugar. Add enough milk
to mix to a soft dropping consistency. Put the mixture into the
basin; cover with a greased paper.
Steam 1½–2 hr. Serve with custard,
brandy- or lemon-sauce or well
dredged with sugar.

6 helpings
Cooking time—1½–2 hr.

CANARY PUDDING

6 oz. butter or margarine   6 oz.
castor sugar   3 eggs   grated rind
of ½ lemon   6 oz. plain flour
1 level teasp. baking-powder

Grease a 1½-pt pudding basin or
mould. Cream together the fat and
sugar until soft and lighter in
colour. Beat in the eggs gradually.

Add the lemon rind. Stir in lightly
the sifted flour and baking-powder.
Pour into the basin or mould.
Cover with a greased paper. Steam
1½ hr. Turn out and serve with
jam sauce (p. 108).

6 helpings

CHOCOLATE PUDDING (1)

8 oz. plain flour   1 teasp. baking-
powder   pinch of salt   4 oz. butter
or margarine   4 oz. castor sugar
1 oz. cocoa   2 eggs   milk to mix
a few drops of vanilla essence

Grease a 2-pt. basin. Sift together the flour, salt and baking-
powder. Rub in the fat. Add the
sugar and cocoa. Mix to a soft
dropping consistency with the
beaten eggs and milk. Add vanilla
essence to taste. Put the mixture
in the basin; cover. Steam for 2 hr.
Serve with chocolate sauce (p.
106).

6 helpings

CHRISTMAS PUDDING

(1) Fruitarian Plum Pudding
(without suet)

½ lb. figs   8 oz. peeled sweet
almonds   4 oz. shelled Brazil nuts
4 oz. pine kernels   4 oz. currants
8 oz. raisins, stoned and halved
4 oz. sultanas   2 small cooking
apples   1 teasp. mixed spice
4 oz. moist brown sugar
½ lb. breadcrumbs   4 oz. chopped
candied peel   pinch of salt
rind and juice of 1 large lemon
4 oz. butter or margarine
4 oz. honey   3 eggs

Grease two 1½-pt. basins. Wash,
chop (or mince) the figs; chop the
nuts; prepare the dried fruit; core,
peel and chop the apples.
Mix together the fruit, nuts,
spice, sugar, breadcrumbs, candied
peel, salt and grated lemon rind.
Warm the butter and honey together. Beat the eggs and add them
to the butter and honey. Stir into
the dry ingredients. Add the lemon

juice and stir well to mix the ingredients thoroughly. Put the mixture into the basins; cover. Boil for 3 hr.

12 helpings

CHRISTMAS PUDDING
(2) Rich

10 oz. sultanas   10 oz. currants
½ lb. raisins   2 oz. sweet almonds
(skinned and chopped)   1 level
teasp. ground ginger   ½ lb. plain
flour   pinch of salt   1 lb. soft
brown sugar   ½ lb. mixed, finely-
chopped candied peel.   1 level
teasp. mixed spice   1 level teasp.
grated nutmeg   ½ lb. breadcrumbs
10 oz. finely-chopped or shredded
suet   6 eggs   ½ gill stout   juice of
1 orange   1 wineglass brandy
½ pt. milk (approx.)

Grease three 1-pt. pudding
basins. Prepare the dried fruit;
stone and chop the raisins; chop
the nuts.

Sift the flour, salt, spice, ginger
and nutmeg into a mixing bowl.
Add the sugar, breadcrumbs, suet,
fruit, nuts and candied peel. Beat
the eggs well and add to them the
stout, orange juice and brandy, and
stir this into the dry ingredients,
adding enough milk to make the
mixture of a soft dropping consistency. Put into the basins. Cover
and boil steadily for 6–7 hr. Take
the puddings out of the water and
cover them with a clean dry cloth
and, when cold, store in a cool
place until required.

When required, boil the puddings for 1½ hr. before serving.

3 puddings (each to give 6 medium helpings)

CHRISTMAS PUDDING
(3) Inexpensive

1 apple   1 lb. mixed dried fruit
(sultanas, currants, raisins)   4 oz.
plain flour   1 oz. self-raising flour
pinch of salt   4 oz. breadcrumbs
4 oz. moist brown sugar   ½ lb.

shredded suet or finely-chopped suet
6 oz. mixed chopped candied peel
juice and rind of 1 lemon   2 eggs
milk to mix   a little caramel or
gravy browning
a few drops of almond essence

Grease two small basins or one
large basin; peel, core and chop the
apple; prepare the dried fruit.

Sift together the plain flour,
self-raising flour and salt into a
mixing bowl. Add the breadcrumbs, dried fruit, sugar, suet,
candied peel and grated lemon
rind. Beat the eggs and milk
together and stir them into the dry
ingredients with the lemon juice,
adding more milk to make the
mixture of a soft dropping consistency. Add a little caramel or
gravy browning to slightly darken
the mixture (about a level teasp.),
and the almond essence. Mix well
in. Turn into the basin, cover and
boil for 4 hr.

12 helpings

COCONUT PUDDING

6 oz. flour   pinch of salt
1 rounded teasp. baking-powder
2 oz. butter or margarine   2 oz.
sugar   2 oz. desiccated coconut
1 egg   milk to mix

Grease a 1½-pt. pudding basin.
Sift together the flour, salt and
baking-powder. Rub in the fat
and add the sugar and coconut.
Mix to a soft dropping consistency
with the beaten egg and milk. Put
the pudding mixture into the basin
and cover with a piece of greased
paper. Steam for 1½–2 hr.

4–6 helpings

CURRANT PUDDING

12 oz. plain flour   2 rounded teasp.
baking-powder   pinch of salt
6 oz. currants   6 oz. finely-chopped
suet.   1½ gill water (approx.)
lemon   castor sugar

Sift together the flour, salt and
baking-powder. Add the suet and

currents and mix with the water to make a soft pliable dough. Form into a roll and put into a floured pudding cloth. Roll up loosely and tie at each end to form a sausage-shape. Put the pudding into boiling water and let it boil gently for 2–2½ hr. Turn out and serve with cut lemon and castor sugar.

6 helpings

DATE ROLY POLY

6 oz. dates   12 oz. plain flour
2 rounded teasp. baking powder
¼ teasp. salt   4–6 oz. finely-chopped suet   water to mix

Chop the dates. Sift together the flour, baking-powder and salt. Add the suet and dates. Add sufficient water to mix to a soft, but firm, dough. Form into a roll and place at the end of a well-floured pudding cloth. Roll up loosely and tie firmly at either end, into a sausage-shape. Drop into boiling water and simmer 2–2½ hr. Serve with custard.

NOTE: For dates the same weight of the following may be substituted—*currants, sultanas, stoned raisins or figs,* and the pudding named accordingly.

FIG PUDDING

8 oz. dried figs   4 oz. plain flour
4 oz. finely-chopped suet   4 oz. breadcrumbs   1 level teasp. baking-powder   4 oz. castor sugar   pinch of salt   pinch of ground nutmeg
1–2 eggs   1½ gill milk (approx.)

Grease a 2-pt. basin. Wash, dry and chop the figs. Mix the flour, suet, breadcrumbs, baking-powder, sugar, salt, nutmeg and figs. Beat the egg with some of the milk and stir into the mixture. Add milk as necessary to make the mixture of a dropping consistency. Put it in the basin; cover. Steam for 2½ hr. Serve with a custard or sweet sauce.

6 helpings

FINGER PUDDING

3 eggs   4½ oz. castor sugar   4½ oz. ground almonds   ½ teasp. grated lemon rind   ¼ teasp. ground cinnamon   pinch of ground cloves
2 oz. melted butter or margarine
1½ oz. crushed savoy or finger biscuits

Grease a mould. Separate the eggs. Beat the yolks and sugar together until light and creamy. Add the ground almonds, lemon rind, cinnamon, cloves, the melted fat and the crushed biscuits. Mix well. Stiffly whisk the egg whites and fold them in lightly. Pour the mixture into a well-greased mould. Steam gently for 1–1¼ hr.

5–6 helpings

FRUIT PUDDING WITH SUET CRUST

1–1½ lb. fresh fruit (see p. 269)
2–3 oz. granulated sugar

SUET CRUST PASTRY
½ lb. plain flour   1 teasp. baking-powder   pinch of salt
3 oz. finely-chopped suet

Prepare the fruit and mix it with the sugar.

Sift the flour and baking-powder, add the suet and salt. Mix with sufficient water to make a soft, but firm, dough. Grease and line a basin (*see* below). Fill to the top with the fruit and sugar and add ¼ gill of cold water. Put on the top crust.

To boil: Cover with a well-floured cloth and boil for 2½–3 hr.

To steam: Cover with greased paper and steam for 2½–3 hr.

6 helpings

NOTE: *To line a basin*—cut off one quarter of the pastry for the top. Roll the remaining pastry ½ in. larger than the top of the basin, drop the pastry into the greased basin, and with the fingers work the pastry evenly up the

sides to the top. Roll out the lid
to the size of the top of the basin,
wet the edges and secure it firmly
round the inside of the pastry lining the basin.

SUGGESTED FILLINGS:
Apples blackberries and apples
blackcurrants cranberries
damsons gooseberries plums

GINGER PUDDING

½ lb. plain flour 1 level teasp.
ground ginger pinch of salt
1 level teasp. bicarbonate of soda
4 oz. finely-chopped suet 3 oz.
sugar 1 tablesp. treacle 1 egg
milk to mix

Grease a 2-pt. basin. Prepare the
suet. Sift the flour, ginger, salt and
bicarbonate of soda into a bowl.
Add the finely-chopped suet and
sugar. Stir in the treacle, beaten
egg and sufficient milk to make a
soft dropping consistency. Put the
mixture into the basin; cover.
Steam for 2 hr. Turn out and serve
with a sweet sauce.

6 helpings

GOLDEN PUDDING

4 oz. marmalade 4 oz. plain flour
4 oz. breadcrumbs 3 oz. finely-
chopped suet 2 oz. castor sugar
1 rounded teasp. baking-powder
pinch of salt 2 eggs
1 gill milk (approx.)

Grease a 2-pt. pudding basin.
Put 2 oz. marmalade at the base.
Mix together the flour, breadcrumbs, suet, sugar, baking-powder and salt. Beat together the
eggs, remaining 2 oz. marmalade
and a little of the milk. Stir this
into the dry ingredients and, using
milk as required, mix to a very
soft dropping consistency. Put the
mixture into the basin, cover with
greased paper. Steam for 1½-2 hr.
Serve with marmalade sauce (p.
108).

6 helpings

LEMON PUDDING (1)

6 oz. flour pinch of salt
1 rounded teasp. baking-powder
2 oz. butter or margarine
2 oz. sugar juice and rind of
1 lemon 1 egg milk to mix

Grease a 1½-pt. pudding basin.
Sift together the flour, salt and
baking-powder. Rub in the fat
and add the sugar and grated
lemon rind. Mix to a soft dropping consistency with the beaten
egg, lemon juice and milk. Put the
pudding into the greased basin and
cover with a piece of greased
paper. Steam for 1½-2 hr.

4-6 helpings

MARMALADE PUDDING (2)

Rind of 1 lemon 4 oz. plain flour
pinch of salt 1 level teasp. baking-
powder 4 oz. breadcrumbs
4 oz. finely-chopped suet
4 oz. sultanas 2 oz. castor sugar
4 tablesp. marmalade 2 eggs
1 gill milk (approx.)

Grease a basin. Grate the lemon
rind. Sift together the flour, salt
and baking-powder. Mix with the
breadcrumbs, suet, lemon rind,
sultanas and sugar. Stir in the
marmalade, beaten eggs and milk.
Use enough milk to make the mixture of a dropping consistency.
Put into the basin; cover; steam
for 1½-2 hr. Serve with marmalade
sauce.

6 helpings

NOTE: See p. 254 for Marmalade Pudding (1).

PLUM PUDDING

4 oz. finely-chopped suet 4 oz.
raisins 4 oz. currants 4 oz. plain
flour pinch of salt 1 rounded
teasp. baking-powder 4 oz.
breadcrumbs 4 oz. moist sugar
¼ teasp. ground mace ¼ teasp.
grated nutmeg 1 egg
1 gill milk (approx.)

Grease a 2-pt. basin. Prepare the suet, raisins and currants. Sift the flour, salt and baking-powder and mix with the breadcrumbs, suet, sugar, raisins, currants, ground mace and grated nutmeg. Stir in the beaten egg and milk and mix to a dropping consistency. Turn into a well-greased basin; cover. Boil for 4–5 hr. *or* steam for at least 5 hr. Serve with melted butter sauce (p. 93).

6 helpings

POUND PUDDING

½ lb. finely-shredded suet ½ lb. raisins, stoned and halved ½ lb. currants 1 oz. finely-chopped candied peel pinch of salt ½ lb. plain flour 1 level teasp. ground ginger ½ lb. sugar ½ lb. breadcrumbs ¼ of a nutmeg, grated 1 egg ½ pt. milk

Grease a 2-pt. mould or basin. Prepare the suet, raisins, currants and peel. Sift together the salt, flour and ginger and mix with the sugar, breadcrumbs, raisins, currants, candied peel and nutmeg. Stir in the beaten egg and milk; mix to a dropping consistency, adding more milk as necessary. Turn into a well-buttered mould *or* basin; cover. Boil for 3–3½ hr.

5–6 helpings

ROLY POLY

12 oz. plain flour 2 rounded teasp. baking-powder 6 oz. finely-chopped suet pinch of salt water to mix jam

Sift the flour and baking-powder, add the suet and salt. Mix with sufficient water to make a soft, but firm, dough. Roll it into a rectangle about ¼ in. thick. Spread with jam almost to the edge. Damp the edges and roll up lightly. Seal the edges. Wrap the pudding in a scalded, well-floured cloth; tie up the ends. Put into

fast boiling water. Simmer for 2–2½ hr.

6 helpings

SNOWDON PUDDING

4 oz. raisins 1 oz. glacé cherries 4 oz. finely-chopped beef suet 4 oz. breadcrumbs 1 oz. ground rice 4 oz. castor sugar rind of 1 lemon pinch of salt 2 eggs 2 tablesp. marmalade ½ gill milk (approx.)

Grease a 2-pt. mould (or basin) with butter. Prepare the raisins and halve the cherries. Decorate the bottom and sides of the mould with some of the raisins and cherry halves.

Put the remainder of the fruit into a mixing bowl. Add the suet, breadcrumbs, ground rice, sugar, grated lemon rind and salt. Beat together the eggs, marmalade and a little of the milk. Add to the other ingredients; use sufficient milk to moisten, and mix well. Pour the mixture into the prepared mould. Cover with a greased paper. Steam for 2–2½ hr.

Serve with marmalade sauce.

6 helpings

SUET PUDDING

12 oz. plain flour ¼ teasp. salt 2 rounded teasp. baking-powder 4–6 oz. finely-chopped suet water to mix

Sift the flour, salt and baking-powder. Mix in the suet. Add cold water, stirring gradually until a stiff dough is formed. Shape the dough into a roll. Put the dough into a scalded, well-floured pudding cloth and roll up loosely. Tie the ends securely with string. Put into a saucepan of boiling water and boil gently for 1½–2 hr., adding more boiling water, if necessary, to keep the pudding covered.

Serve with jam-, treacle-, fruit- or marmalade-sauce.

6–7 helpings

SYRUP SPONGE PUDDING

6 oz. plain flour 6 oz. breadcrumbs
4 oz. finely-chopped suet. 2 oz.
castor sugar 1 teasp. ground
ginger 1 level teasp. bicarbonate of
soda pinch of salt 1 egg
2 tablesp. golden syrup 1 tablesp.
treacle milk to mix

Grease a basin and, if liked, put an extra tablesp. of golden syrup in the bottom. Mix together the flour, breadcrumbs, suet, sugar, ginger, bicarbonate of soda and salt. Beat the egg with the golden syrup, treacle and a little of the milk. Stir this into the other ingredients, using more milk if required, to mix to a very soft dropping consistency. Put the mixture into the basin; cover with greased paper. Steam for 1½–2 hr.

6–7 helpings

TRANSPARENT PUDDING

3 oz. butter or margarine
3 oz. sugar 3 eggs
2 tablesp. apricot jam

Well butter 6 dariole moulds. Cream together the fat and sugar until lighter in colour and quite soft. Add each egg separately and beat well. One-third fill each mould with this mixture and put a dessertsp. of apricot jam on top; then cover with the remaining mixture, so that the moulds are about ¾ full. Cover with greased paper. Steam slowly for about 25 min. Let the puddings cool slightly before turning them out, to lessen the risk of their breaking. Serve at once with custard.

6 helpings

TREACLE LAYER PUDDING

2 oz. breadcrumbs rind of 1 lemon
½ lb. treacle or golden syrup
(approx.) suet crust pastry using
12 oz. flour, etc.

Divide the suet pastry into two equal portions, using one portion to line a 2-pt. basin. From the other portion cut off enough to make the lid; roll out the remainder thinly.

Mix the breadcrumbs and grated lemon rind. Put a layer of treacle in the basin; sprinkle well with the breadcrumbs. Cover with a round of the thinly-rolled pastry. Moisten the edge of it with water and join securely to the pastry at the side of the basin. Add another layer of treacle, crumbs and pastry; then more treacle and crumbs. Finally cover with the rolled-out top as the last layer of pastry Cover with greased paper. Steam for 2½ hr.

6–7 helpings

WASHINGTON PUDDING

As for Canary Pudding (p. 266) but add 2 tablesp. of raspberry jam.

BAKED PUDDINGS

GENERAL HINTS

1. Well butter the dish, tin or mould, so that the pudding is easily turned out or served.
2. Wipe round the edges of the pie-dish before baking.
3. The pudding is easier to handle if it is placed on a baking sheet while cooking.
4. Oven settings may vary with different cookers, so that the average settings in the recipes are given for general guidance.

ALMOND CASTLES

3 oz. butter 3 oz. castor sugar
3 eggs 3 tablesp. cream or milk
1 tablesp. brandy (optional)
6 oz. ground almonds

Grease 8 dariole moulds. Cream together the butter and sugar. Stir in the egg yolks, cream or milk, brandy (if used) and almonds. Whisk the egg whites to a stiff froth and add lightly to the rest of the ingredients. Three-quarters fill the moulds. Bake in a warm oven (335° F., Gas 3) 20–25 min., the puddings are firm in the centre and golden brown. Turn out and serve with custard.

If liked, the puddings may be steamed—cover with greased paper and steam 40–50 min., until firm.

8 helpings

APPLE CHARLOTTE

2 lb. cooking apples   4 oz. brown sugar   1 lemon   8 thinly-cut slices of bread and butter   castor sugar

Grease a 2-pt. pie-dish with butter. Peel, core and slice the apples. Place a layer in the bottom of the pie-dish and sprinkle with sugar, grated lemon rind and lemon juice. Cover with thin slices of bread and butter. Repeat until the dish is full, finishing with a layer of bread and butter. Cover with greased paper. Bake in a moderate oven (350° F., Gas 4) for ¾–1 hr. Turn out of the dish and dredge well with castor sugar before serving.

5–6 helpings

APPLE CRUMBLE

1½ lb. apples   4 oz. brown sugar a little grated lemon rind   ½ gill water (approx.)   3 oz. butter or margarine   6 oz. plain flour   3 oz. castor sugar   ¼ teasp. ground ginger

Peel, core and slice the apples into a pan. Add ½ gill water, 4 oz. brown sugar and lemon rind. Cook gently with lid on the pan until soft. Place in a greased 2-pt. pie-dish. Rub the fat into the flour until of the consistency of fine breadcrumbs. Add the castor sugar, ground ginger and mix well. Sprinkle the crumble over the apple; press down lightly. Bake in a moderate oven (350° F., Gas 4) until golden brown, and the apples are cooked—about 30–40 min., de-

pending on the cooking quality of the apples.

Dredge with castor sugar and serve with custard or cream.

NOTE : For apples the same weight of the following may be substituted: *damsons, gooseberries, plums, raspberries* or *rhubarb*, and the crumble named accordingly.

6 helpings

APPLE DUMPLINGS

Short crust pastry (p. 341), 12 oz. for large apples or 8 oz. for small apples   2 oz. brown sugar   a little grated lemon rind or ground cinnamon   6 cooking apples 12 cloves (optional)

Make the short crust pastry; divide into six portions, shaping each into a round.

Mix the sugar and grated lemon rind or cinnamon. Peel and core each apple and put it on a round of pastry. Work the pastry round the apple until it is almost covered. Press the cloves, if used, into the centre of the apple; then fill the cavity with the sugar mixture. Seal the pastry edges by moistening slightly with water. Place the dumplings, join downwards, on a greased baking sheet. Brush them with milk and dredge with castor sugar. Bake for about 30 min. in a fairly hot oven (400° F., Gas 6).

6 helpings

APPLE PUDDING

2 lb. cooking apples   ½ gill water 6 oz. castor sugar   2 oz. butter or margarine   1–2 eggs 4 oz. breadcrumbs

Peel, core and cut the apples into slices, stew with ½ gill water until tender. Stir in the sugar, fat, and well-beaten egg. Butter a 2-pt. pie-dish. Coat the bottom and sides thickly with the crumbs. Add the apple pulp and finish with a layer of crumbs. Put a few flakes of butter on the top and bake in a moderate oven (350° F., Gas 4) for ¾ hr.

4–5 helpings

BACHELOR'S PUDDING (2)

8 oz. plain flour pinch of salt 4 oz. castor sugar 1 teasp. baking-powder 3–4 oz. chopped suet 2 oz. sultanas 2 oz. raisins, stoned and halved 1 egg 1 gill milk (approx.)

Butter a pie-dish. Mix sifted flour, salt and baking-powder with the sugar, suet, sultanas and raisins. Beat the egg with some of the milk and add to the mixture. Mix to a soft dropping consistency, adding more milk if necessary. Put into the pie-dish. Bake in a moderate oven (350° F., Gas 4) for 1–1½hr.

When ready, turn out of the dish, dredge with castor sugar, serve with a fruit sauce.

5–6 helpings

NOTE: See p. 266 for Bachelor's Pudding (1).

BAKED APPLES

6 cooking apples 2 oz. demerara sugar ½ gill water

FILLING, choice of:—

1. 2 oz. moist sugar and 2 oz. butter
2. Blackcurrant or raspberry or strawberry or apricot jam
3. 3 oz. stoned dates or sultanas or currants or raisins, 2 oz. moist sugar and 1 teasp. ground cinnamon

Prepare the filling. Wash and core the apples. Cut round the skin of the apple with the tip of a sharp knife, ⅔ of the way up from the base. Put the apples into a fireproof dish and fill the centres with the chosen filling. Sprinkle with the demerara sugar. Add the water. Bake in a moderate oven (350° F., Gas 4) until the apples are soft in the centre—about ¾–1

hr., depending on the cooking quality of the apples.

BAKED JAM ROLL

12 oz. plain flour 1 teasp. baking-powder pinch of salt 6 oz. finely-chopped suet jam

Mix the flour, baking-powder, salt and suet with sufficient water to make a soft, but firm, dough. Roll the dough into a rectangle about ¼ in. thick. Spread with jam almost to the edges, damp the edges and roll up lightly. Seal the edges. Put on to a well-greased baking sheet. Cook in a fairly hot oven (400° F., Gas 6) until cooked through; about 1 hr.

6 helpings

BREAD PUDDING

8 oz. stale bread 4 oz. currants or raisins or sultanas 2 oz. brown sugar 2 oz. finely-chopped suet 1 oz. chopped peel ½ teasp. mixed spice 1 egg a little milk

Break the bread into small pieces and soak in cold water for at least ½ hr.; then strain and squeeze as dry as possible. Put into a basin and beat out the lumps with a fork. Add the dried fruit, sugar, suet, peel and mixed spice and mix well. Add the egg and enough milk to enable the mixture to drop easily from the spoon. Put into a greased tin. Bake in a warm oven (335° F., Gas 3) for about 1 hr. When done, turn out on to a hot dish. Dredge with sugar and serve with custard.

5–6 helpings

CASTLE PUDDINGS

4 oz. butter or margarine 4 oz. castor sugar 2 eggs 4 oz. plain flour 1 level teasp. baking-powder grated rind of ½ lemon or a few drops of vanilla essence

Grease 6–7 dariole moulds. Cream together the fat and sugar until soft and lighter in colour. Beat in the eggs gradually. Stir in the sifted flour, baking-powder, lemon rind *or* vanilla essence. Three-quarters fill the moulds. Bake in a moderate oven (350° *F.*, *Gas* 4) until set and golden brown —about 25 min. Turn out and serve with jam sauce.

NOTE: These may be steamed: cover with greased paper; steam for about 50 min.

CHERRY PUDDING

1 lb. cooking cherries   ½ gill water
3 oz. moist sugar   3 oz. plain flour
2–3 tablesp. milk (approx.)   1 gill cream *or* milk   2 oz. castor sugar
pinch of salt   3 eggs   grated rind of ¼ lemon   pinch of ground cinnamon

Stone the cherries and stew them very gently (to keep them whole) in a small saucepan with the water and moist sugar. Allow to cool. Blend the flour with the 2–3 tablesp. of milk, so that it is smooth and "runny". Boil the cream *or* milk and add to it the blended flour, beating well to keep the mixture smooth. Bring to the boil again and add the castor sugar and salt. Cool the mixture. Separate the eggs. Beat the egg yolks into the mixture. Add the lemon rind and cinnamon, and lastly the stiffly-whisked egg whites. Put into a well-greased mould or pie-dish a layer of cherries and a layer of mixture alternately until the mould is full. Cover with greased paper. Bake in a fairly hot oven (400° *F.*, *Gas* 6) for about 40 min.

Serve with a sweet sauce or fruit syrup.

5–6 helpings

CHESTNUT PUDDING

6 oz. chestnuts, weighed after the skins have been removed   pinch of salt   1 oz. plain chocolate   ½ pt. milk   2 oz. butter *or* margarine
2 oz. flour   2 oz. cakecrumbs
3 eggs   ½ teasp. vanilla essence
1 oz. castor sugar

Wash the chestnuts, make a slit in each and boil in water for about 10 min. Remove both skins and put the chestnuts into a saucepan with a very little water and the salt. Cook until tender, strain, dry and rub through a fine sieve.

Grate the chocolate and put it in the milk and simmer until dissolved. Allow to cool slightly.

In another pan melt the fat, stir in the flour, cook for 2–3 min. Work in the milk and chocolate gradually, keeping the mixture smooth; stir until it boils. Add the cakecrumbs and continue cooking until the mixture leaves the sides of the pan. Allow to cool. Separate the eggs. Beat into the mixture the egg yolks, chestnut purée, vanilla essence and sugar. Whisk the egg whites to a stiff froth and fold them lightly into the mixture. Pour into a well-buttered mould. Cover with buttered paper. Bake in a fairly hot oven (375° *F.*, *Gas* 5) for 1 hr. or steam for 1½ hr.

Serve with custard sauce.

6–7 helpings

CHOCOLATE PUDDING (2)

6 oz. plain flour   pinch of salt
1 rounded teasp. baking-powder
3 oz. butter *or* margarine   4 oz. castor sugar   1 oz. cocoa   1 egg
milk to mix
a few drops of vanilla essence

Sift together the flour, salt and baking-powder. Rub in the fat. Add the sugar and cocoa; mix well. Add the beaten egg and milk and mix to a dropping consistency. Add the vanilla essence. Put into a greased tin or pie-dish. Bake in a fairly hot oven (375° *F.*, *Gas* 5) for 30–40 min.

Dredge well with castor sugar and serve with chocolate *or* custard sauce.

6 helpings

NOTE: *See* p. 266 for Chocolate Pudding (1).

COLLEGE PUDDING

4 oz. flour   ½ teasp. baking-powder
pinch of salt   ½ teasp. mixed spice
4 oz. breadcrumbs   3 oz. finely-
chopped suet   3 oz. castor sugar
2 oz. currants   2 oz. sultanas
1–2 eggs   1 gill milk (approx.)

Grease 6–7 dariole moulds. Sift
together the flour, baking-powder,
salt and spice. Add the breadcrumbs, suet, sugar, currants and
sultanas, and mix well together.
Well beat the eggs. Add to the dry
ingredients and mix to a soft
dropping consistency, adding milk
as required. Half-fill the moulds
with the mixture. Bake in fairly
hot oven (375° F., Gas 5) for about
25 min.; or cover with greased
paper and steam for 35–40 min.
Serve with wine-, orange-, brandy-
or custard-sauce.

COTTAGE PUDDING

½ lb. plain flour   pinch of salt
1 rounded teasp. baking-powder
4 oz. butter or margarine   3 oz.
sugar   4 oz. raisins   1 egg
¼ gill milk (approx.)

Grease a Yorkshire pudding tin
(10 in. by 8 in.). Sift together the
flour, salt and baking-powder.
Rub the fat into the flour. Add
the rest of the dry ingredients.
Mix to a stiff consistency with the
egg and milk, so that the mixture
will just drop from the spoon.
Spread in the tin. Bake in a fairly
hot oven (375° F., Gas 5) until
firm in the centre and golden
brown; about 35–40 min.

5–6 helpings

EVE'S PUDDING

1 lb. apples   1 tablesp. water
2–4 oz. granulated or demerara
sugar   4 cloves (optional)   4 oz.
butter or margarine   4 oz. castor
sugar   2 eggs   grated rind of
½ lemon   4 oz. plain flour
1 level teasp. baking-powder

Peel, core and thinly slice the
apples. Put them into a small
saucepan with the water, granulated or demerara sugar, and
cloves if used. Cook very slowly
(with the lid on the pan) until the
apples are soft, stirring occasionally to prevent them from burning.
Remove the cloves. Put the apples
into the bottom of a well-greased
pie-dish.

Cream together the fat and
castor sugar. Beat in the eggs
gradually. Add the grated lemon
rind. Sift in the flour and baking-
powder. Mix to a soft dropping
consistency. Spread this mixture
over the apples. Bake in a moderate oven (350° F., Gas 4) for 40–45
min.

4 helpings

EXETER PUDDING

5 oz. breadcrumbs   1 oz. ratafias
3½ oz. finely-shredded suet   2 oz.
sago   3 oz. castor sugar   ½ teasp.
grated lemon rind   3 eggs
2–3 tablesp. milk or cream
1 wineglass rum (optional)
2 individual sponge cakes   jam

SAUCE
3 tablesp. blackcurrant jelly
3 tablesp. water
1 wineglass sherry (optional)

Coat a well-buttered mould or
pie-dish with some of the breadcrumbs. Cover the bottom with
some of the ratafias.

Mix together the rest of the
breadcrumbs, suet, sago, sugar and
grated lemon rind. Stir in the
well-beaten eggs, milk and rum
(if used). Put some of the mixture
into the lined dish. Cover with
slices of sponge cake. Spread
thickly with jam and place a few
ratafias on top. Repeat this until
all the ingredients are used up,
finishing with the breadcrumb
mixture. Bake gently in a moderate oven (350° F., Gas 4) for about
1 hr.

Make the sauce by boiling together the blackcurrant jelly, water and sherry (if used).

5–6 helpings

FRUIT SPONGE

1 lb. fresh fruit (e.g. apricots, peaches, gooseberries) sugar to taste 3 oz. butter or margarine
3 oz. castor sugar 2 eggs
4 oz. self-raising flour

Prepare the fruit according to kind. Grease a 1½-pt. pie-dish and arrange the fruit in the bottom. Sprinkle with sugar to taste and add a little water if required. Cream together the fat and 3 oz. sugar. Add the well-whisked eggs gradually, beating well between each addition—if sign of curdling, add some flour. Sift flour and stir lightly into the creamed fat and egg. Spread the sponge mixture over the fruit, and bake in the middle of a moderate oven (350° F., Gas 4) for 35–40 min. Serve hot or cold.

NOTE: This can be made with canned fruit if liked, drain the fruit from the juice before arranging in the pie-dish.

LEMON PUDDING (2)

2 oz. butter or margarine 4 oz. castor sugar 3 eggs rind and juice of 1½ lemons 6 oz. plain flour
½ pt. milk

Grease a 2 pt. pie-dish.
Cream together the butter and sugar until soft. Beat in the egg yolks. Add the grated lemon rind and the sifted flour. Stir in the milk and lemon juice. Fold in the stiffly-whisked egg whites. Pour the mixture into the buttered pie-dish. Bake in a moderate oven (350° F., Gas 4) for 45 min., until firm and brown.

4 helpings

NOTE: See p. 269 for Lemon Pudding (1).

RAISIN PUDDING

See Cottage Pudding (p. 275).

SWISS PUDDING

8 oz. breadcrumbs 2 lb. cooking apples 6 cloves 6 oz. brown sugar
2 oz. butter or margarine

Butter a 2-pt. pie-dish. Cover the bottom with a layer of crumbs. Peel, core and thinly slice the apples. Put in the pie-dish a layer of apple, with 1–2 cloves, sugar and a little water to moisten. Add a layer of breadcrumbs, and repeat the layers of apple mixture and crumbs alternately, finishing with a layer of crumbs. Melt the fat and pour over the mixture. Bake gently in a moderate oven (350° F., Gas 4) for ¾ hr., until the apple is cooked.

5 helpings

YEAST MIXTURES

BABAS WITH RUM SYRUP

½ lb. plain flour pinch of salt
½ oz. yeast 1 oz. castor sugar
1 gill milk 4 eggs 4 oz. butter
2 oz. currants

RUM SYRUP

3 oz. granulated sugar 1 gill water
rind of ½ lemon 1 wineglass rum
1 wineglass sherry

Grease 9 dariole or baba moulds. Sift the flour and salt into a warm basin. Cream the yeast with a pinch of castor sugar, and add to it the gill of warm milk. Mix this into the flour to form a soft dough. Beat well until the dough leaves the sides of the basin clean. Cover the basin with a damp cloth and leave the dough to rise in a warm (but not hot) place until about twice its size. When the dough has risen sufficiently add 2 eggs, the melted butter and castor sugar, beat well in. Then add the rest of the eggs and the currants and beat again for 5–10 min., until the dough is smooth and glossy. Half-fill the moulds with the mixture. Put them in a warm place until the mixture has risen to the top of the moulds. Bake in a fairly hot oven (425° F., Gas 7) for about 20–25 min. until brown and firm.

Put the granulated sugar and water into a pan with the thinly peeled lemon rind. Boil for 10 min., add the rum and sherry; strain.

Reheat the syrup. Soak the babas in it for a minute; lift them out and serve immediately, with the syrup poured round.

9 babas

NORFOLK DUMPLINGS
Boiling water   salt

BREAD DOUGH
8 oz. plain flour   ½ teasp. salt
½ oz. yeast   small pinch of sugar
½ oz. lard   ¼ pt. warm water
(approx.)

Make the dough: sift the flour and salt into a basin. Cream the yeast with the sugar and add the warm water and the melted fat. Mix to an elastic dough. Knead well until smooth, cover with a cloth, and set in a warm place to rise to double its size. Knead again until there are no large holes in the dough when cut.

Roll into small balls. Leave in a warm place to rise slightly. Drop into gently boiling, salted water. Simmer for 6–7 min. Strain.

Serve with one of the following: jam, treacle, golden syrup, *or* butter and sugar.

8 helpings

SAVARIN
4 oz. plain flour   pinch of salt

¾ oz. yeast   ¼ gill warm water
1 egg   ¼ oz. sugar   1½ oz. butter

RUM SAUCE
3 oz. loaf sugar   ¼ pt. water
1–2 tablesp. rum   juice of ½ lemon

DECORATION
Apricot jam
blanched almonds, browned

Sift the flour and salt into a basin and put it to warm. Cream the yeast with the tepid water. Make a well in the centre of the flour and pour in the yeast mixture. Sprinkle over the top with a little of the flour from the side of the bowl. Leave to prove for 10–15 min. in a warm place. Add the egg gradually, beating well to a smooth elastic dough, using a little more tepid water if necessary. Knead well. Put the dough back into the basin and press down, sprinkle the sugar on the top and put on the butter in small pieces. Cover with a damp cloth and leave in a warm place to double its size. Beat well again until all the sugar and butter is absorbed. Grease a border mould and fill it one-third of the way up with the mixture. Leave to prove in a warm place until the mixture just reaches the top of the mould. Then bake in a fairly hot oven (400° F., Gas 6) for about 20 min.

Make the sauce: boil the water and sugar steadily for about 10 min. Add the rum and the lemon juice.

Turn the savarin out on to a hot dish, prick with a needle or hat-pin and soak well in the sauce. Coat with hot sieved apricot jam and decorate with spikes of almonds, etc. Serve with the rest of the sauce poured round.

4 helpings

COLD SWEETS

CEREAL MOULDS

CEREAL moulds are composed of whole or ground cereals, milk and sugar, flavouring and sometimes a little gelatine to ensure a firm set.

Whole grain, such as rice (Carolina), large sago, large tapioca, and barley, should be simmered gently in the milk until every grain is soft and the milk is almost absorbed. To accomplish this without burning, and without excessive evaporation, use (a) a double saucepan, or (b) a thick-bottomed pan, standing over low heat or in a cool oven. Keep covered and stir occasionally to ensure even cooking of the grain. Cooking time $1\frac{1}{2}$–2 hr.

Small grain, such as semolina, ground rice, small sago and tapioca should be sprinkled dry into near-boiling milk and cooked gently until the grain is soft and clear. Continuous stirring is necessary to ensure smoothness, and excessive evaporation must be avoided by keeping the heat low. Cooking time 10–15 min.

Powdered grain, such as cornflour, arrowroot, custard powder and flour, should be blended with sufficient cold milk to make a thin cream. The rest of the milk is heated almost to boiling-point and poured on to the blended grain, stirring continuously. Pour back into the pan and boil gently, still stirring, until all the starch grains are quite cooked. Cooking time 4–5 min.

Choose china or glass moulds, as the cold wetted surface causes instant gelatinization of the surface starch and imparts a clean, glossy surface to the mould when turned out. Pour in quickly and from a slight height. If cereal mixtures are to be set in border moulds, which are metal, a little margarine or butter or, best of all, pure olive oil, should be used to grease the inside. A sharp tap on the side of this type of mould should be all that is necessary to dislodge the mixture.

A china or glass mould may be turned out quite cleanly if the cereal mixture is first gently loosened from the lip of the mould with the tips of the fingers, then inverted on to the hand or dish and dislodged by a sharp jerk of the wrist. If the surface of the dish is moistened the mould can be moved to an exact position.

WHOLE GRAIN MOULDS
(Rice, large sago, large tapioca)

Basic Recipe
WHOLE RICE MOULD
6 oz. rice   1 qt. milk   3 oz. castor sugar   flavouring (see p. 279)
$\frac{1}{4}$–1 oz. fresh butter (optional)

Wash the rice and put it with the milk into a double saucepan, or a thick pan standing over a very low heat. Simmer very gently, with the lid on the pan to prevent undue evaporation. Stir occasionally to prevent the rice from settling on the bottom of the pan, and cook until the rice is quite tender and the milk almost absorbed. Sweeten to taste, add flavouring if required, stir in the butter if used. Pour quickly into a cold, wet basin or mould. Turn out when set and serve with stewed, canned, or fresh fruit, jam, jelly, etc.

6 helpings
Cooking time—2–3 hr.
Setting time—2 hr.

FLAVOURINGS

Lemon or *Orange:* Wash fruit, dry well and grate rind finely; stir into the cooked mixture just before moulding. Alternatively, peel rind in thin strips, avoiding white pith, and infuse in mixture during cooking; remove before adding sugar and butter.

Coffee: Add coffee essence to taste, with the sugar.

Variations

CREAMED RICE

To 1 pint of cold rice mould, add whipped cream *or* cream and custard, to produce a soft, creamy consistency. Pour into serving dishes and flavour and decorate in any of the following ways:

1. *Chocolate:* Grate chocolate coarsely over the top.
2. *Coffee:* Stir in coffee essence to taste.
3. *Orange:* Stir in finely-grated orange rind just before serving.
4. *Fruit* (fresh, canned, preserved *or* stewed, e.g. peaches, pineapple, dessert apples, dates).
   (a) Drain the fruit from the juice, chop or shred, and stir into the rice.
   (b) Arrange fruit attractively on top of the rice, either in slices, quarters, halves *or* even a purée. The dish may be finished by piling up on top a meringue (p. 39) and drying it to a golden brown in a cool oven (310 ° F., Gas 2) *or* finished as for Peach Condé (*see below*).

4 helpings

PEACH CONDE

1 pt. cold rice mould   ⅛ pt. double

cream or cream and custard
1 small can peaches
1 level teasp. arrowroot

Stir the cream into the cold rice mould to produce a soft, creamy consistency. Pour into serving dishes. Drain the fruit from the juice and arrange attractively on top of the rice. Make up the fruit juice to ¼ pt. with water. Blend the arrowroot with the fruit juice and boil until clear. Pour carefully over the fruit. Finish by decorating with whipped cream.

NOTE: Apricots or pineapple may be substituted for peaches.

4 helpings

SMALL GRAIN MOULDS
(Semolina, ground rice, tapioca, small sago)

Basic Recipe
SEMOLINA MOULD

1 qt. milk   4 oz. semolina
3 oz. castor sugar   flavouring

Rinse a thick saucepan, put in the milk and heat to boiling-point. Sprinkle in the semolina, stirring continually. Boil gently, stirring all the time, until the grain is quite cooked, and appears transparent when lifted on the back of a spoon (7–8 min.). Add sugar and stir well. Pour quickly into a cold, wet mould.

6 helpings
Cooking time—10 min.
Setting time—2 hr.

FLAVOURINGS

Lemon or *Orange:* Infuse thin strips of rind with the milk during heating. Remove before adding the grain.

Coffee: Add 1 tablesp. coffee essence, with the sugar.

Chocolate: Melt 3 oz. chocolate in the milk, *or* blend 1½ oz. cocoa with some of the milk. Add rum, brandy, sherry *or* vanilla essence.

Variations
BANANA AND TAPIOCA SPONGE

6 bananas (not over-ripe) 2 oz.
granulated sugar ¼ pt. water
juice of ½ lemon 1 pt. milk
2 oz. tapioca sugar to taste
2–3 egg whites

Slice bananas and cook to a
purée with the granulated sugar
and water (5–10 min.). Add
strained lemon juice and beat to a
smooth cream. Boil the milk,
sprinkle in the tapioca and cook
gently for about 15 min., stirring
all the time. Add banana purée,
taste and re-sweeten if necessary.
Whisk egg whites stiffly and fold
lightly into the banana tapioca
mixture. Stir lightly until cool and
serve piled up in a glass dish. Chill
if liked.

6 helpings
Cooking time—35 min.

CARAMEL MOULD
1 lemon 1½ pt. milk 3 oz. ground
rice 1 oz. castor sugar

CARAMEL
2 oz. loaf or granulated sugar
1 tablesp. cold water

Heat a tin charlotte or soufflé
mould and have ready a thickly
folded band of newspaper so that
the hot tin may be encircled with
it and held firmly in one hand.
Melt loaf sugar in the water in a
thick, very small pan, and, when
dissolved, boil quickly until it becomes dark golden brown. Do not
stir. Pour at once into the hot tin
mould and rotate quickly to coat
the sides and base of the mould.
Finally, place mould on a firm flat
board so that excess caramel may
flow to the base and set level. Keep
in a warm place, as draughts may
cause the caramel coating to crack.

Cut thin strips of lemon rind
and infuse in the milk, slowly.
Remove the rind when the milk

boils, sprinkle in the rice, stirring
all the time, and cook until grain is
soft and smooth, about 8–10 min.
Sweeten to taste. Pour into the
coated mould and leave in a cool
place to set. Turn out and serve
with cream.

6 helpings

CREME DE RIZ
1 pt. milk 2 oz. ground rice ½ oz.
powdered gelatine 2 tablesp. cold
water 2 oz. castor sugar flavouring
(see p. 279) ¼–½ pt. double cream

Heat the milk and, when boiling, sprinkle in the rice. Cook
gently, stirring continuously, until
quite soft and smooth—15–20
min. Avoid too much evaporation.
Soak gelatine in the 2 tablesp. cold
water, for 5–10 min., then warm
until dissolved. Sweeten and flavour the rice, stir in the gelatine
and allow to cool, stirring lightly
from time to time. When quite
cool, but not set, fold in the
whipped cream. Pour into a cold
wet mould and leave to set.

NOTE: This recipe may be used
for whole rice, or for semolina.

4 helpings
Cooking time—½ hr.
Setting time—2 hr.

TAPIOCA CREAM
½ pt. packet red jelly 1 tablesp.
sherry (optional) 1 tablesp.
redcurrant or crab-apple or bramble
jelly rind of ½ lemon 1 bay leaf
2 pt. milk 1½ oz. tapioca
2 oz. castor sugar 2 egg yolks
2 tablesp. double cream

Make the jelly to just less than
½ pt., inclusive of sherry (if used)
and preserves, and add these when
jelly is cool. Pour into a wet
border mould and leave to set. Cut
thin strips of lemon rind without
white pith; infuse in the milk with
the bay leaf. When milk boils, remove flavourings and sprinkle in
tapioca, stirring continuously.

Cook gently 15-20 min., until smooth and soft. Add sugar, cool slightly, and add beaten egg yolks. Reheat to cook the yolks, but do not boil. Allow to cool, then lightly stir in whipped cream. Pour into the border mould and leave to set.

6 helpings
Cooking time—1 hr.
Setting time—2 hr.

POWDERED GRAIN MOULDS
(Cornflour, arrowroot)
Basic Recipe

CORNFLOUR MOULD

3 oz. cornflour   2 pt. milk   2 oz. castor sugar   flavouring (see below)

Blend cornflour with a little cold milk to a thin cream. Boil remainder of milk and pour on to the blended cornflour, stirring continuously. Return mixture to the pan and heat until boiling. Cook gently for 4 min., stirring all the time. Add sugar to taste, and flavouring essences, if used. Pour quickly into a wetted mould. Turn out when set.

6 helpings
Cooking time—15 min.
Setting time—2 hr.

FLAVOURINGS

Lemon or *orange:* Infuse thinly-cut strips of lemon *or* orange rind with the milk. Remove rind before pouring milk on to cornflour.

Chocolate: Blend 1½ oz. cocoa with the cornflour. Extra sugar may be desired, and also a flavouring of vanilla, rum *or* coffee essence.

Coffee: Add 1 tablesp. coffee essence with the sugar, and taste before adding more, as essences vary in strength.

Custard: Add beaten egg yolk to cooled mixture and reheat until cooked; *or* replace 1 oz. cornflour with 1 oz. custard powder.

Variations

AMBROSIA MOULD

3 oz. cornflour   2 pt. milk   2 oz. butter   4 oz. sugar   ¼ pt. sherry

Blend cornflour with a little of the milk to a thin cream. Boil remainder of the milk with the butter. Pour over blended cornflour, return to pan and cook thoroughly. Add sugar and sherry; pour into a wetted mould. Turn out when cold and serve with wine sauce (p. 108).

6 helpings
Cooking time—10 min.
Setting time—2 hr.

COCONUT MOULD

2½ oz. cornflour   2 pt. milk   2 oz. butter   2 oz. desiccated coconut   2-3 oz. castor sugar   carmine colouring   pink desiccated coconut

Blend cornflour with sufficient of the milk to mix to a smooth cream. Heat remaining milk with butter and proceed as for cornflour mould. Add coconut and sugar and colour a very pale pink. Pour quickly into a wet mould. Turn out when set and sprinkle pale pink coconut lightly all over.

6 helpings
Cooking time—15 min.
Setting time—2 hr.

To colour coconut: Tint 1 teasp. cold water with 2-3 drops only of colouring. Stir into white desiccated coconut until evenly coloured. Spread thinly over a sheet of greaseproof paper to dry well. Store in a stoppered jar.

FRUIT MOULD

1 pt. mixture as for cornflour mould (opposite)   ½ lb. stewed fruit

Put a thick layer of cornflour mixture at the bottom of a mould. When set, place a tumbler in the centre, and fill the space between the two with cornflour mixture. When the mixture is firm, remove the tumbler, fill the cavity with stewed fruit, and cover with a layer of cornflour mixture. When set, turn out, and serve with custard or whipped cream.

NOTE: If liked, Ground Rice Mould can be substituted for cornflour mould.

5–6 helpings
Time—about 2 hr.

GOLDEN MOUSSE PRALINE

4 oz. almond brittle or almond rock 1 egg 1½ oz. loaf sugar
1 orange 1 dessertsp. powdered gelatine ½ pt. water 1 dessertsp. cornflour pinch of salt
½ pt. evaporated milk
one No 1 tall can strawberries

Pass the almond brittle through a mincing machine or crush it with a rolling-pin between 2 sheets of greaseproof paper. Beat the egg into it. Rub the lumps of sugar hard on the orange rind to absorb its zest. Wet the gelatine with half the water and heat only enough to dissolve it. Add the orange-flavoured sugar and break it down. Add to the almond brittle-egg mixture. Blend the remaining water with the cornflour and stir over a low heat until cooked. Add the salt and stir into the other mixture. Leave until lukewarm, then stir in the evaporated milk. When cold and beginning to thicken, whip until very frothy. Turn into a greased mould and leave to set.

Turn out and garnish with the strawberries in their syrup.

5–6 helpings

SWISS CREAM

¼ lb. ratafia biscuits or sponge cake
3–4 tablesp. sherry 1½ oz. cornflour
1 pt. milk 1 lemon 2 oz. castor sugar ¼–½ pt. double cream
2 teasp. chopped or grated nuts or glacé fruits

Put the ratafia biscuits or cake in the bottom of a glass dish, or individual dishes, and soak with sherry. Blend the cornflour with sufficient of the milk to make a smooth cream. Heat the remainder of the milk slowly with thin strips of lemon rind. Strain on to the blended cornflour, return to the pan and cook thoroughly but gently for 3–4 min. Stir in the sugar. Allow to cool. Whip the cream slightly and add it and the juice of the lemon gently and gradually to the cool cornflour cream. Re-sweeten if necessary. Pour over the soaked biscuits or cake and leave to go cold.

Decorate with chopped nuts, or glacé cherries and angelica.

4–6 helpings
Cooking time—25 min.

JELLIES

Jellies may be made from fruit juices, fruit purées, milk flavoured with essences, or water and wine set into a jellied form by the addition of gelatine. To be palatable, a jelly should be only just sufficiently set to stand upright when turned out, and to achieve this consistency the measuring of ingredients must be exact.

Jelly Moulds: All moulds must be scrupulously clean. They must be quite cold when used and should be rinsed out with cold water immediately before use.

Unmoulding Jellies: This can only be successfully achieved by one single, quick, and total immersion in very hot water. As the whole is immersed, the top of the jelly must be dried afterwards with a clean cloth.

AMBER JELLY

¾ pt. water   1 wineglass sherry
(optional)   ¼ pt. lemon juice
(2 lemons)   6 oz. loaf sugar
1 oz. gelatine   3 egg yolks
thin rind of 1 lemon

Put all ingredients into a pan
and allow to soak 5 min. Whisk
over gentle heat until near boiling-
point. Do not boil or the eggs will
curdle. Strain through muslin and
pour into a prepared mould.

This is a delicious and nutritious
sweet for an invalid.

4–6 helpings
Cooking time—½ hr.

BANANA JELLY WITH CREAM

1 pt. lemon or orange jelly   ½ oz.
peeled pistachio nuts   6 bananas
¼ pt. double cream

Make the jelly and allow to
cool. Chop green pistachio nuts
finely and stir into 2 tablesp. jelly.
Set the nut jelly in the bottom of
a mould. Beat the bananas to a
purée and half-whip the cream.
Stir the banana purée into the remaining jelly; add cream and fold
together lightly. Fill up the mould
and turn out when set.

6 helpings
Cooking time—5 min.
Setting time—2 hr.

DUTCH FLUMMERY

1 lemon   1 pt. water   1 oz. gelatine
2 eggs   1 small wineglass of
sherry or Madeira wine
castor sugar to taste

Wash lemon and cut thin strips
of rind; infuse the rind in water.
Add gelatine and simmer gently
until dissolved. Beat the eggs, add
wine, juice of the lemon and water
with the gelatine. Strain all into
a pan and stir over gentle heat
until thick. Sweeten to taste and
pour into a 2-pt. wetted mould.
Turn out when set.

6 helpings

Cooking time—about 40 min.
Setting time—2–3 hr.

HONEYCOMB MOULD

1 pt. milk   flavouring: vanilla
essence or lemon or orange rind
2 large eggs   1 oz. castor sugar
½ oz. gelatine   4 tablesp. water

If orange or lemon rind is being
used for flavouring, slowly infuse
thinly-cut strips of rind in the
milk. Remove the rind and make
a custard with the egg yolks,
sugar and flavoured milk. If
using essence add to the custard
after the sugar. Dissolve gelatine
in measured water and while still
warm stir into the custard. Allow
to cool. When just beginning to
set, fold in the stiffly-whisked egg
whites. Pour into a quart border
mould and leave to set.

Turn out and serve with fruit
salad piled up in the hollow.
Decorate with whipped cream.

4–6 helpings

LEMON CURD JELLY

3 large lemons   1½ pt. milk
7–8 oz. sugar   1 oz. gelatine
(light-weight)   4 tablesp. water

Wash lemons and remove rind
in thin strips from two of them.
Infuse rind in the milk with the
sugar until the latter is dissolved.
Soak the gelatine in the water and,
when soft, stir into the warm milk.
Do not allow the milk with gelatine to boil or curdling may occur.
Strain into a bowl and allow to
cool to blood-heat. Stir in the
strained juice of three lemons and
mould. Turn out when set.

NOTE: If curdling should occur,
whisk vigorously before moulding
and a fine, spongy texture will be
formed.

6 helpings
Cooking time—½ hr.
Setting time—2 hr.

MILK JELLY (INVALID)

½ oz. gelatine   4 tablesp. water

lemon rind   ½ pt. milk
1 teasp. castor sugar

Heat the gelatine gently in the water until dissolved. Add the milk, sugar and thinly-cut strips of lemon rind. Stir over a gentle heat until sugar is dissolved—do not let it boil or it will curdle. Strain into a basin and stir from time to time until it attains the consistency of thick cream. Pour into a wet mould.

NOTE: The jelly may be flavoured with vanilla *or* coffee essences, if liked.

2 helpings
Cooking time—5 min.
Setting time—1 hr.

ORANGE JELLY

1 pt. water   3–4 oz. sugar   1½ oz.
gelatine   6 oranges (1 pt. juice)
2 lemons   angelica (optional)

Put water, sugar and gelatine into a pan. Wash fruit and cut thin strips of outer rind from 3 oranges, avoiding white pith. Add strips to the pan and bring slowly to the boil. Leave to infuse, with the lid on, for 10 min. Squeeze juice from oranges and lemons and strain on to juice. Then either: (*a*) pour into a wet metal mould; *or* (*b*) prepare orange-skin "cups" made from half-sections of peel freed from pulp. Fill with liquid jelly, stand in patty-tins to hold upright until set, and decorate with piped cream and angelica-strip "handles" to form baskets; *or* form baskets as shown on p. 40; *or* (*c*) allow to set in orange-skin cups, then cut the halves into quarters and arrange as boats.

6 helpings
Cooking time—10 min.
Setting time—2 hr.

PORT WINE JELLY

1 pt. water   2 oz. sugar   2 tablesp.
redcurrant jelly   1 oz. gelatine
½ pt. port wine   cochineal

Put water, sugar, redcurrant jelly and gelatine into a pan and leave to soak for 5 min. Heat slowly until dissolved. Add half the port wine and colour dark red with a few drops of cochineal. Strain through double muslin; add the rest of the wine. Pour into a wet mould.

6 helpings
Cooking time—10 min.
Setting time—2 hr.

"CLEARED" JELLIES

"Cleared" jelly is filtered through a foam of coagulated egg whites and crushed egg-shells. The pan, whisk and metal jelly-mould to be used must first be scalded. The egg whites are lightly whisked until liquid, then added with the washed and crushed egg-shells to the cooled jelly. The mixture is heated steadily and whisked constantly until a good head of foam is produced, and the contents of the pan are hot, but not quite boiling. The albumen in the egg-whites and egg-shells coagulates, forming a thick crust of foam. The correct temperature is reached when the foam begins to set, and care must be taken not to break up, by whisking too long, a completely coagulated foam. The whisk is removed, and heating continued to allow the foam crust to rise to the top of the pan. The heat is then lowered and the contents of the pan left to settle in a warm place, covered with a lid, for 5–10 min. The jelly is then poured through a scalded jelly cloth while the cloth is still hot, into a scalded bowl below. The bowl of strained jelly is replaced with another scalded bowl, and the jelly re-strained very carefully by pouring through the foam crust which covers the bottom of the cloth and acts as a filter.

The filtering is most easily caried out using a jelly bag and stand made for the purpose, but if these are not available the four corners of a clean cloth can be tied to the legs of an upturned stool, and a bowl placed below the cloth.

Moulds: All moulds must be scrupulously clean, and should be scalded, as the merest trace of grease may cause cloudiness.

To Line a Mould thinly and evenly with jelly, it is essential that it should be rotated quickly; therefore it is better to choose a round mould and to prepare a bed of crushed ice, into which the mould is set on its side in such a position that it can be spun by the thumbs. Care must be taken to prevent ice from entering the mould during spinning. The jelly should be cold but liquid.

Decorating a Mould: Decorations may be placed in the base or on the lined sides of a mould, and must be covered by another thin coating of jelly before the filling is put in, otherwise, when the mould is turned out, they will appear to have sunk into the filling. When the sides of the mould are set, use a teaspoon to place jelly in the base. On no account should jelly be poured into the mould.

Decorations should be chosen for their colour-contrast, or if decorating a cream they could indicate the flavour of the cream filling; but in all cases they must be very neatly cut. Each piece of decoration is dipped into cold liquid jelly before being set in place. Two hat-pins will be found most suitable for this meticulous work.

Filling the Mould: Moulds should always be filled to the brim, and if when moulding a cream there is insufficient cream, the space should be filled with jelly.

Unmoulding Jellies and Creams: The unmoulding of jellies and creams can only be successfully achieved by one single, quick, and total immersion in very hot water. Charlottes lined with sponge fingers are dipped only to the rim, as any dampening of the sponge would cause the charlotte to collapse. After total immersion, quickly absorb any surface moisture with a clean cloth, and with one sharp jerk, turn out the mould on to the serving dish by gently sliding the fingers of the supporting hand from underneath the loosened jelly.

Mask the dish surrounding the jelly with piped cream or chopped jelly and, if a silver dish, rub lightly to remove any spot or mark before serving.

LEMON JELLY

4 lemons   sherry (optional)   1½ pt. water   6 oz. sugar   4 cloves   1 in. cinnamon stick   1¾–2 oz. gelatine shells and whites of 2 eggs

Scald a large pan, whisk and metal jelly-mould. Wash lemons and cut thin strips of rind, avoiding white pith. Extract juice and measure. Make up to ½ pt. with water *or* sherry, but if the latter is to be used, do not add until just before clearing the jelly. Put the 1½ pt. water, ½ pt. juice, rinds, sugar, flavourings and gelatine into the scalded pan and infuse, with a lid on, over gentle heat until sugar and gelatine are dissolved. Do not let the infusion become hot. Wash egg-shells and crush. Lightly whisk the whites until liquid and add, with shells, to the infusion. Heat steadily, whisking constantly, until a good head of foam is produced, and the contents of the pan become hot, but not quite boiling. Strain through the crust (*see* p. 284), and add sherry if used, to the jelly as it goes through the filter.

6 helpings
Time—1–1½ hr.

WINE JELLY

4 lemons (¼ pt. juice)   ½ lb. sugar
1½–2 oz. gelatine   1 pt. water
whites and shells of 2 eggs
¼ pt. brandy   ½ pt. sherry

Infuse the thinly cut lemon rinds, sugar and gelatine in the measured water until dissolved. Add lemon juice, whites and crushed shells of the eggs and whisk steadily until boiling-point is almost reached. Remove whisk and boil to the top of the pan. Pour in the brandy and sherry without disturbing the foam crust. Boil again to the top of the pan. Remove from the heat, cover, and leave to settle for 1 min. Strain carefully (see p. 284). Cool, remove froth, and mould in scalded individual moulds.

4–6 helpings
Time—1–1½ hr.

FRUIT IN JELLY

1½ pt. very clear lemon jelly or wine jelly, using white wine instead of sherry and brandy   selected pieces of fruit, e.g. bananas, black and green grapes, tangerines, cherries, apricot, pineapple, etc.

Scald a metal mould, then rinse it with cold water. Cover the bottom with a thin layer of cool jelly (about ⅛ in. thick). Avoid the formation of bubbles in the jelly by tilting the mould and placing the jelly in spoonfuls in the bottom. Leave to set. Cut pieces of fruit to suit the hollows and spaces of the mould, dip each piece into cold liquid jelly and set in place around and on the jelly layer. Leave to set and cover carefully with a layer of clear jelly. Allow to set. Repeat, taking care that each layer of fruit is quite firm before adding a layer of jelly—otherwise the fruit may be "floated" from its position. Fill the mould to the top.

When quite set, turn out and decorate with piped cream.

6 helpings
Time (without ice)—3–4 hr. (with ice packed around the mould)— 1 hr.

WHIPPED JELLIES

If jelly is whipped or whisked just prior to setting, tiny bubbles of air are enclosed. These impart a lightness of texture both stimulating and refreshing to the palate. The addition of egg white, slightly whisked and then whipped with the cold liquid jelly, increases the volume of the jellied foam and also adds to its nutritive value without unduly diluting the flavour, although a strongly-flavoured jelly is necessary if more than 1 egg white is used. This is a sweet very suitable for, and popular with, children and invalids.

BLACKCURRANT WHIP

½ pt. blackcurrant purée and ½ pt. water or ¾ pt. blackcurrant juice
½ oz. gelatine   sugar to taste

Heat the gelatine slowly in the juice or purée and water until dissolved. Add sugar if necessary. Cool, then whisk briskly until a thick foam is produced. When the whisk leaves a trail in the foam, pile quickly into a glass dish.

6 helpings
Time—½ hr.

COFFEE WHIP

1 pt. milk   1 tablesp. coffee essence
sugar to taste   ¾ oz. gelatine soaked and dissolved in 4 tablesp. water
1–2 egg whites (optional)

DECORATION

Chopped nuts

Heat together the milk, coffee essence and sugar. Heat the gelatine in the water until dissolved, then cool slightly. Add to the cooled, coffee-flavoured milk. Whisk strongly. If egg whites are used, whisk them until liquid and slightly frothy, and stir into the cool jelly just before whisking. When thick, pile into a dish and scatter chopped nuts over the top.

6 helpings
Cooking time—10 min.
Setting time—½ hr.

LEMON WHIP

One 1-pt. lemon jelly tablet
sugar if necessary   ¾ pt. water
1 tablesp. lemon juice

Melt the jelly tablet in ¼ pt. water. Stir in ½ pt. cold water and strained lemon juice. Sweeten if necessary. When cool, whisk briskly until a thick foam is produced. When the whisk leaves a trail in the foam, pile quickly into a glass dish.

6 helpings
Time—½ hr.

ORANGE WHIP (1)

One 1-pt. orange jelly tablet
water and orange juice to make ¾ pt.

Proceed as for Lemon Whip.

ORANGE WHIP (2)

¾ pt. strained orange juice
½ oz. gelatine   castor sugar to taste

Proceed as for Blackcurrant Whip.

PINEAPPLE WHIP (1)

One 1-pt. pineapple jelly tablet
½ pt. canned pineapple juice
¼ pt. water   sugar if necessary

Proceed as for Lemon Whip.

PINEAPPLE WHIP (2)

¾ pt. pineapple juice   ½ oz. gelatine

Proceed as for Blackcurrant Whip.

CREAMS

Creams can be divided into two types: full creams and half-creams.

Full Creams: These consist wholly of cream flavoured with essence or liqueurs, set with gelatine.

Half-Creams (also known as *Bavaroise* or *Bavarian Creams*) are compounds of custard, cream and flavouring, the last being in the form of fruit purées, juices, essences, etc.

Fresh cream cannot be equalled in texture and flavour by any synthetic cream, but substitutes can be used without any modification of the recipe provided certain precautions are taken in using them:

1. *Evaporated Unsweetened Milk:* Boil the can of milk, unopened, for 20 min., then cool quickly. If possible chill for 24 hr., in a refrigerator.

2. *Synthetic Cream:* Whip the cream as it is. Any sugar required for sweetening should be stirred in after whipping.

The inclusion of milk, custard, cream or ice cream in a jellied liquid increases its density and therefore less gelatine is required to set 1 pt. of this thicker consistency, as little as a ¼ oz. being sufficient to set 1 pt. of a really thick liquid such as a mixture of cream and rich custard. The gelatine, dissolved in a little water, must be added at a certain temperature; if it is too hot it causes the cream to lose some of its lightness, and if too cold, it sets in small hard lumps before it is evenly distributed (should this happen whip the mixture over a bowl of hot water). Egg also has a thickening capacity as it coagulates when heated and in this state is able to hold liquid. One egg will "set" ¼ pt. of liquid and if eggs are being added to jellies for nutritional purposes the proportion of gelatine should be adjusted accordingly.

Full creams

PISTACHIO CREAM

4 oz. pistachio nuts   ½ oz. gelatine
4 tablesp. water   2 oz. castor sugar
1 pt. double cream
sap-green colouring

Blanch, skin and finely chop the pistachio nuts. Soak gelatine in the water, heat to dissolve. Add sugar and stir until dissolved. Whip the cream, fold in the liquid gelatine and chopped nuts, and colour pale green, adding the colouring a drop at a time. Pour into a prepared mould and leave to set.

6 helpings
Setting time—1-2 hr.

VELVET CREAM

½ oz. gelatine   4 tablesp. water
1½-2 oz. castor sugar   sherry, or
vanilla essence   1 pt. double cream

Soak the gelatine in the cold water for 5 min. Heat gently until quite dissolved and clear. Stir in the sugar until dissolved. Add the sherry or vanilla. Whip the cream until thick and fold into it the flavoured liquid gelatine. Pour into a prepared mould and leave to set.

6 helpings
Setting time—1 hr.

Half creams

CHOCOLATE CREAM

4 oz. plain chocolate   ½ pt. milk
3 egg yolks or 1 whole egg and
1 yolk   2–3 oz. castor sugar
½ oz. gelatine   4 tablesp. water
1 teasp. vanilla or coffee essence
½ pt. double cream

Grate the chocolate and dissolve in the milk. Beat eggs and sugar until liquid and make a thick pouring custard with the flavoured

milk, straining back into the pan to cook and thicken. Do not allow to boil or the eggs may curdle. Allow to cool. Soak gelatine in the water for 5 min., then heat to dissolve. Stir the vanilla or coffee essence gently into the cooled custard, and add the dissolved gelatine, stirring again as it cools. Whip the cream and fold lightly into the custard mixture just before setting. Pour into a prepared mould or into glass dishes.

6 helpings
Setting time—1-2 hr.

COFFEE CREAM

3 egg yolks or 1 whole egg and
1 yolk   2–3 oz. castor sugar   ½ pt.
milk   ½ oz. gelatine   4 tablesp.
water   2–3 teasp. coffee essence
½ pt. double cream

Beat the eggs and sugar until liquid. Heat the milk almost to boiling-point and pour over the egg mixture. Strain the egg and milk back into the pan, and cook gently until thick, stirring all the time. Allow to cool. Soak the gelatine in the water for 5 min., then heat to dissolve. Stir the coffee essence into the cooled custard, and add the dissolved gelatine, stirring again as it cools. Whip the cream and fold lightly into the custard mixture just before setting. Pour into a prepared mould or into glass dishes.

6 helpings
Setting time—1-2 hr.

GINGER CREAM

2-3 oz. chopped preserved ginger
½ pt. milk   3 egg yolks or 1 whole
egg and 1 yolk   castor sugar to
taste   ½ oz. gelatine   4 tablesp.
water   2–3 tablesp. ginger syrup
½ pt. double cream

Infuse the preserved ginger in the milk. Beat the eggs and sugar until liquid and make a thick pouring custard with the flavoured

milk, straining back into the pan
to cook and thicken. Allow to cool.
Soak gelatine in the water for 5
min., then heat to dissolve. Stir
the ginger syrup gently into the
cooled custard, and add the dissolved gelatine, stirring again as it
cools. Whip the cream and fold
lightly into the custard mixture
just before setting. Pour into a
prepared mould or into glass
dishes.

6 helpings
Setting time—1-2 hr.

RUM CREAM

1 bay leaf   ½ pt. milk   3 egg yolks
or 1 whole egg and 1 yolk   2–3 oz.
castor sugar   ½ oz. gelatine
4 tablesp. water   1 wineglass of rum
½ pt. double cream

Infuse the bay leaf in the milk
for 20 min. Beat eggs and sugar
until liquid and make a thick
pouring custard with the flavoured
milk, straining back into the pan
to cook and thicken. Allow to
cool. Soak gelatine in the water for 5
min., then heat to dissolve. Stir
the dissolved gelatine into the
cooled custard. Stir in the rum.
Whip the cream and fold lightly
into the custard mixture just before setting. Pour into a prepared
mould, or into glass dishes.

6 helpings
Setting time—1-2 hr.

VANILLA CREAM

3 egg yolks or 1 whole egg and
1 yolk   2–3 oz. castor sugar   ½ pt.
milk   ½ oz. gelatine   4 tablesp.
water   2 teasp. vanilla essence
½ pt. double cream

Beat the eggs and sugar until
liquid. Heat the milk to almost
boiling-point and pour over the
egg mixture. Strain the egg and
milk back into the saucepan, and
cook very gently until thick, stirring all the time. Allow to cool.
Soak the gelatine in the water for

5 min., then heat to dissolve. Stir
the vanilla essence into the cooled
custard, and add the dissolved
gelatine, stirring again as it cools.
Whip the cream and fold lightly
into the custard mixture just
before setting. Pour into a prepared mould or into glass dishes.

6 helpings
Setting time—1-2 hr.

FRUIT CREAMS

½ pt. fruit purée (see below)   ½ pt.
thick, rich custard   castor sugar to
sweeten   lemon juice (optional)
½ oz. gelatine   4 tablesp. water or
thin fruit juice   colouring (optional)
½ pt. double cream

Purée the fruit through a very
fine sieve—nylon mesh if possible,
as fresh fruit is acid. Blend with
the cool custard, sweeten, and
flavour with lemon juice if required. Soak the gelatine in the
water or juice for a few minutes
and heat to dissolve. Pour, while
steaming hot, into the custard and
fruit mixture, and stir to keep well
blended until the mixture begins
to feel heavy and drags on the
spoon. Colour if necessary. Stir
in, lightly, the whipped cream and
pour into a prepared mould.

NOTE: *Apricots, blackcurrants,
damsons, gooseberries, greengages,
peaches, raspberries* or *strawberries* may be used for the purée,
and the cream named accordingly.

6 helpings
Setting time—1-2 hr.

ORANGE CREAM (1)

3 large oranges   ½ pt. milk   3 egg
yolks or 1 egg and 1 yolk
2 oz. castor sugar   ¾ oz. gelatine
¼ pt. double cream

Infuse thin strips of rind from 2
oranges in the milk. Remove the
rind, and make into a thick pouring custard with the egg yolks and
sugar. Soak the gelatine in the
orange juice and add sufficient

water to make ½ pt. Heat to dissolve, and strain into the orange-flavoured custard. Whip the cream and fold in when the gelatine-custard mixture is thick but not set. Pour into a prepared mould and turn out when quite cold.

6 helpings
Setting time—1–2 hr.

ORANGE CREAM (2)

Two 1-pt. orange jelly tablets   ¼ pt. water   ½ pt. orange juice or squash
1 pt. thick pouring custard
½ pt. double cream

Melt the jellies in the water and juice. Make the custard and stir into the jelly when both are slightly cooled. Whip the cream and fold in.

8 helpings
Setting time—1–2 hr.

Pineapple Cream: Substitute pineapple jelly and juice for orange, stir in 4 oz. chopped pineapple before the cream.

ORANGE CREAM (3)

Two 1-pt. orange jelly tablets   ¼ pt. water   ¼ pt. orange juice or squash
12-oz. family block of ice cream
juice of ½–1 lemon to taste
½ pt. milk

Melt the jellies in the water and juice. Stir in the ice cream quickly and, if the mixture sets at this stage, place the bowl over a pan of hot water and stir until liquid again. Add lemon juice as required as this mixture will be very sweet. Stir in the milk, and pour into a prepared mould. Turn out when set.

8 helpings

Pineapple Cream: Substitute pineapple jelly and juice for orange.

CHARLOTTES

Charlottes are moulds lined with sponge fingers, savoy fingers, *or* wafers, and filled with various creams. Choose a mould with straight sides.

GOOSEBERRY CHARLOTTE

20 savoy fingers
1½ pt. gooseberry cream (p. 289)

DECORATION
½ pt. clear lemon jelly   3 glacé cherries   angelica

Thinly coat the bottom of a mould with jelly, and, when set, decorate with neatly-cut slices of cherry and leaves of angelica. Both these fruits should be cut thickly as they are translucent and will not show clearly if too thin. Re-coat with a second layer of cold liquid jelly, sufficient only to cover the decoration. When the jelly has set, line the sides of the mould with savoy fingers, having trimmed the ends so that they fit closely on to the jelly. Remove any crumbs from the surface of the jelly with the tip of a dry pastry brush. Pour the gooseberry cream into the lined mould and leave to set. Trim the fingers level with the rim. Turn out and decorate with piped cream. If preferred, the base of the mould may be lined with sponge fingers.

NOTE: A quicker but less satisfactory method is to pour the gooseberry cream into the mould unlined, and after turning out press trimmed savoy fingers, sugar side outwards, around the sides. Tie a ribbon round to ensure a neat finish.

6 helpings

Charlotte Russe: As for Gooseberry Charlotte, but fill the prepared mould with vanilla cream.

CHARTREUSE
CHARTREUSE OF BANANAS

2 pt. clear lemon or wine jelly (pp. 285–6)   1 oz. pistachio nuts

4 bananas   ½ pt. double cream
vanilla essence   castor sugar to taste

Line a 1-qt. border mould with
jelly. Blanch, skin, chop and dry
the pistachio nuts, mix with 2
tablesp. jelly and run smoothly
over the base of the mould. When
set, cover with a ½-in. layer of
clear jelly. Slice a banana evenly,
dip each slice in jelly and arrange
them, slightly overlapping, in an
even layer on the jelly when set.

Cover with another ½-in. layer of
clear jelly and allow to set. Repeat
with fruit and jelly until the
mould is full, the last layer being
jelly. When set, turn out and pipe
the whipped cream, sweetened,
and flavoured with vanilla, into
the centre. Surround with chopped
jelly.

6 helpings
Setting time (without ice)—2–3 hr.
   (with ice)—¾ hr.

COLD SOUFFLES

Soufflés are extremely light in texture because of the air which is
entrapped by whisking the ingredients and retained either by
the use of gelatine, or by freezing.
The eggs are separated, the yolks
being whisked with the sugar and
flavouring over hot water until
very thick and "ropey". On no
account should the bowl containing the egg and sugar be allowed
to become hot, as this would cook
the egg and make the inclusion
of air impossible. The container
holding the hot water should be
deep enough for the bowl holding
the mixture to rest firmly in the
rim without touching the water.
Whisking should continue until
the mixture is cool, so that the dissolved gelatine, which must be
added steaming hot in order to
ensure even distribution throughout the mixture, does not raise the
temperature of the whole too
much. This is very important, as a
too-warm mixture necessitates prolonged stirring in order to keep
the various ingredients blended,
and during this operation most of
the air so carefully whipped in will
be lost.

The cream is half-whipped—to
blend easily with the thickly-
whisked mixture, and the egg
whites stiffly whipped. These are
folded in just before setting, as they

hold most of the air. Pour immediately into a prepared soufflé
dish.

Tie a double band of greaseproof
paper around a 1-pt. china soufflé
dish, so that 3 in. of the paper
extends above the rim. This is so
that the soufflé mixture will set
when it is at least 1 in. above the
rim, and, on removal of the paper,
will appear to have risen above
the dish.

Basic Recipe
MILANAISE SOUFFLE

2 lemons   3–4 eggs, according to
size   5 oz. castor sugar   ½ oz.
gelatine   ¼ pt. water
½ pt. double cream

Wash lemons, dry, and grate
rind finely. Whisk the egg yolks,
sugar, rind and lemon juice over
hot water until thick and creamy,
then remove bowl from the hot
water and continue whisking until
cool. Soften the gelatine in the
¼ pt. water, and heat to dissolve.
Half-whip the cream. Whisk the
egg whites very stiffly. Add the
gelatine, steaming hot, in a thin
stream to the egg mixture, and stir
in. Fold in the cream and the
stiffly-whipped whites. Fold the
mixture very lightly until setting
is imminent—the mixture pulls
against the spoon. Pour into the

soufflé dish and leave to set. Remove the paper band by coaxing it away from the mixture with a knife dipped in hot water. Decorate the sides with chopped, blanched pistachio nuts, and the top with piped cream, if liked.

6 helpings
Setting time—2 hr.

Variations
APRICOT SOUFFLE

½ pt. apricot purée   4 eggs   2–3 oz. castor sugar (according to sweetness of apricots)   lemon juice   carmine
½ oz. gelatine   4 tablesp. water
¼ pt. double cream

Use the purée in place of rind and juice of lemons in Milanaise soufflé. Taste and sweeten as liked. Add lemon juice to sharpen. When thick and creamy, colour carefully with one or two drops of carmine. Finish as for Milanaise soufflé.

Decorate with chopped, blanched pistachio nuts.

6 helpings
Setting time—2 hr.

ORANGE SOUFFLE

3–4 eggs according to size   4 oz. castor sugar   3 oranges   rind of ½ lemon   orange colouring
½ oz. gelatine   4 tablesp. water
½ pt. double cream

Proceed as for Milanaise Soufflé, using oranges in place of lemons. A little orange colouring may be necessary.

Decorate with chopped, blanched pistachio nuts.

6 helpings
Setting time—2 hr.

CHOCOLATE SOUFFLE

2 eggs   2 oz. sugar   12 tablesp. evaporated milk   2 oz. milk chocolate   ½ oz. gelatine
4 tablesp. warm water

Put the yolks of the eggs and sugar in a double saucepan, and whisk until thick and creamy. Whip the evaporated milk until thick, and add to the eggs and sugar. Melt the chocolate over very gentle heat, add to the egg and sugar mixture. Put the gelatine in the warm water and heat to dissolve; then stir it into the chocolate mixture. Whip up the egg whites stiffly and stir into the chocolate mixture. Put into the prepared soufflé case. When set, remove the paper carefully, and decorate the top with whipped cream.

6 helpings
Setting time—2 hr.

CUSTARDS
(see also Hot Sweets—Custards, pp. 250–5)

APPLE CUSTARD

2 lb. apples   1 tablesp. water   4 oz. sugar   3 eggs   2 oz. castor sugar
1 pt. milk   vanilla essence (optional)

Peel, core, slice and cook the apples in the water and sugar until pulped. Beat well, *or* sieve, and put in the bottom of an oven-glass dish. Separate the yolks and whites of the eggs and beat the yolks slightly with 1 oz. castor sugar. Stir in the milk and strain mixture into a saucepan which has been rinsed with cold water. Whisk over moderate heat to ensure even thickening, but do not let the custard boil or it will curdle. Cool quickly in a bowl, stirring occasionally to prevent a skin forming and flavour with a little vanilla essence, if liked. Whisk the egg whites to a stiff, dry foam and beat in 1 teasp. castor sugar to sweeten. Pour cooled custard over apple pulp and pile meringue lightly on the top. Dust surface with castor sugar and bake in a very cool oven (290° F., *Gas* 1) until the meringue is dry and crisp and is a pale, glossy, golden brown on top (20 min.).

6 helpings
Time—1½ hr.

ORANGE CUSTARD

4 oranges   1½ pt. boiling water
4 oz. granulated sugar   3 eggs
½ pt. cream   candied orange peel

Wash oranges and cut off thin strips of outer rind avoiding white pith. Put rind, water and sugar into a bowl and leave to stand, covered, for 2 hr. After 2 hr. strain into a saucepan, heat through and pour gradually over the well-beaten eggs, stirring all the time. Strain the mixture back into the rinsed pan and heat again to thicken and cook the eggs. Do not allow the custard to boil or curdling will occur. Whisk or stir during cooking. Allow to cool, stir in the strained juice of the oranges and pour into custard glasses. When quite cold (or chilled in refrigerator) pile whipped cream on top. Decorate with fine strips of candied orange peel.

6 helpings
Time—3 hr.

PINEAPPLE CUSTARD

1 large can pineapple   1½ oz.
cornflour   1 pt. milk   2 eggs
1 oz. castor sugar

DECORATION
Glacé cherries   angelica

Drain the juice from the fruit, chop the latter and put it in the bottom of an oven-glass dish. Blend the cornflour with 3 tablesp. of the milk, heat the remainder of the milk and pour over the blended cornflour, stirring all the time. Return to the pan and cook until thick, continuing after that for 3–4 min. to cook all the cornflour. Avoid excessive evaporation. Add ½ pt. of pineapple juice and stir in the egg yolks. Reheat almost to boiling to cook the eggs. Sweeten if necessary and pour over

the pineapple. Make a meringue with the egg whites and 1 oz. castor sugar (p. 39). Pile on the top and cook until crisp and dry in a very cool oven (290° F., Gas 1).

Decorate with small pieces of cherry and angelica. Serve hot or cold.

6 helpings
Time—1 hr.

FRUIT MOULD
APRICOT MOULD

1 lb. apricots   1½ pt. water   1 lemon
3 oz. sugar   ¾ oz. gelatine

Wash apricots, and soak overnight in the measured water. Cook with thinly-cut strips of lemon rind and sugar until quite soft. Remove lemon rind. Remove stones and chop apricots to a pulp. Soak the gelatine in 2 tablesp. cold water for a few minutes, then heat until dissolved. Add to the apricot mixture and flavour with lemon juice. If liked the kernels may be removed from the apricot stones, shredded and added. Stir thoroughly and pour into a wet mould. Turn out when set and serve with thin custard.

6 helpings
Setting time—2 hr.

TRIFLES
APPLE TRIFLE

2 lb. cooking apples   6 oz. sugar
grated rind of ½ lemon   6 individual
sponge cakes   ¾ pt. custard

DECORATION
⅓ pt. double cream   almonds—
blanched, shredded and lightly
browned (p. 315)

Peel, quarter and core the apples and cook gently with the sugar, lemon rind and about 2 tablesp. water until soft. Beat to a smooth pulp, or sieve. Slice the sponge cakes and place in individual dishes or in a large flat glass dish. Spread the apple purée over the cake. Pour sufficient custard over the top to run smooth and leave to go cold.

Decorate with whirls of whipped cream and golden shredded almonds.

6 helpings

NOTE: Gooseberries may be substituted for apples. Omit lemon rind and increase sugar if necessary.

APRICOT TRIFLE (1)

2 apricot halves per person   1 round of sponge cake ½ in. thick and slightly larger than the fruit, for each person   1 tablesp. sherry (optional)   fruit juice   1 oz. sugar to ¼ pt. juice   ¼ pt. cream   6 pistachio nuts, blanched and chopped

If fresh fruit is used, prepare as required, dust with castor sugar and allow to stand 1 hr. to sweeten and become juicy. If canned fruit is used, drain from juice on a sieve. Soak the rounds of sponge cake in the sherry (if used) and a little fruit juice. Place in individual dishes and chill. Arrange the fruit on the top and glaze with a thick syrup made by boiling together ¼ pt. fruit juice and 1 oz. sugar. Pipe whipped cream round the edge of the sponge and decorate with chopped pistachio nuts.

Peach or *Pineapple* trifle: substitute 1 peach half or slice of pineapple per person for apricots.

APRICOT TRIFLE (2)

**5–6 slices Swiss jam roll
1–2 macaroons   2–3 tablesp. sherry
1 can apricots   1 pt. custard
6-oz. can cream   1 teasp. gelatine
2 teasp. boiling water
1 oz. blanched almonds**

Cut the jam roll into small cubes and place with broken macaroons in the bottom of a shallow glass dish; pour the sherry and a little apricot juice over. Cut up some of the apricots and add to the dish; pour over the custard. Allow to set. Whip the cream, adding the gelatine melted in the water. Pile the cream roughly so that it is fairly high in the centre. Decorate with apricots spiked with almonds.

PEAR AND CHOCOLATE TRIFLE

**6 individual sponge cakes
6 halves of dessert or canned pears**

SAUCE
**1 oz. butter or margarine
¾ oz. cocoa   1 oz. flour   1 pt. milk
½ oz. gelatine   1 tablesp. water
1 oz. sugar**

DECORATION
Whipped cream   angelica

Place sponge cakes neatly in a glass dish *or* individual dishes. Drain pears and place, rounded side uppermost, on top of the sponge cakes. Make the sauce: melt the fat in a saucepan; add cocoa, and stir well in. Add flour, mix well, and gradually mix in the milk. Soak the gelatine in the water and heat to dissolve. Bring the milk mixture to the boil, stirring all the time to keep it smooth. Sweeten. Add the dissolved gelatine and remove from heat. Stand pan in a bowl of cold water to cool slightly to a coating consistency. Pour carefully over the pears and allow to run smoothly around the dish. Decorate when cold with piped whipped cream and angelica.

6 helpings

ST. HONORE TRIFLE

**1 round sponge cake (1 in. thick by 6 in. across)   2–3 egg whites   4 oz. castor sugar   ¼ lb. macaroons or ratafia biscuits   ¼ pt. sherry
½ pt. double cream**

DECORATION
Glacé cherries   angelica

Place sponge cake on a baking sheet. Make meringue with egg whites and sugar (p. 39). Pipe a border of meringue around the top edge of the sponge cake, and dry off in a very cool oven (265° F., Gas ½). Do not allow meringue to colour. Place a thick layer of macaroons or ratafias on top of the cake and soak well with the sherry for at least 1 hr. Avoid touching the meringue with sherry, otherwise it may crumble. Pile whipped cream on top and decorate with cherries and angelica.

6 helpings

TRIFLE—TRADITIONAL RECIPE

4 individual sponge cakes
raspberry or strawberry jam
6 macaroons   12 ratafia biscuits
¼ pt. sherry   grated rind of ½ lemon
1 oz. almonds (blanched and
shredded)   ½ pt. custard (p. 251)
using ½ pt. milk, 1 egg and 1 egg
yolk   ¼ pt. double cream   1 egg
white   1–2 oz. castor sugar
glacé cherries   angelica

Split the sponge cakes into two and spread the lower halves with jam. Replace tops. Arrange in a glass dish and cover with macaroons and ratafias. Soak with sherry, and sprinkle with lemon rind and almonds. Cover with the custard and leave to cool. Whisk the cream, egg white and sugar together until stiff and pile on top of the trifle. Decorate with glacé cherries and angelica.

6 helpings

MISCELLANEOUS

APPLE SNOW

4 large baking apples (1½ lb.)   rind
and juice of 1 lemon   ½ pt. milk
2–3 eggs   3 oz granulated sugar
(approx.)   4 individual sponge cakes
glacé cherries

Reduce the apples to a purée. The finest flavour is obtained by washing the apples and baking them, dry, in a moderate oven (350° F., Gas 4) until quite soft, when the skins and cores may easily be separated from the pulp. Otherwise, peel, core, slice and cook in the minimum amount of water.

Wash the lemon, remove the rind in thin strips, avoiding any white pith, and infuse slowly in the milk. Make a cup custard with this and the egg yolks (p. 251). Sweeten to taste. Place the sponge cakes, split if liked, in the bottom of a large glass dish and pour the custard over them. Rub the apple-pulp through a fine nylon sieve and sweeten to taste. Add lemon juice to flavour and leave to cool. Whisk the egg whites until quite stiff. Whisk in the apple purée, 1 tablesp. at a time, keeping the foam firm and light. Pile the apple foam on top of the soaked sponge cakes and decorate with glacé cherries.

6 helpings

BANANA WHIP or SNOW

6 bananas   2 tablesp. soft sugar
2 teasp. lemon juice   ½ pt. yoghourt
¼ pt. double cream   3 egg whites

DECORATION
Almonds

Mash bananas with sugar and lemon juice. Mix in the yoghourt and cream. Whisk egg whites to a stiff foam and fold lightly into the banana cream. Pile into dishes and sprinkle with chopped roasted almonds.

6 helpings

BLANCMANGE

See Powdered Grain Moulds (p. 281).

FLOATING ISLANDS

2 egg whites   2–3 tablesp.
raspberry jam or redcurrant jelly
1 pt. sweetened cream

Beat the egg whites until stiff, then lightly fold in the jam or jelly a teaspoonful at a time. Whip the cream until stiff and spread lightly in the bottom of a glass dish. Drop tablespoonfuls of the egg mixture on to the cream, making each small pile as rocky as possible.

FRESH FRUIT SALAD

1 pt. water or **fruit juice   3 oz. sugar selection of fruit as liked** (see below) **juice of 1 lemon   1 tablesp. brandy** or **kirsch** (optional) **2 tablesp. sherry** (optional)

Boil the water and sugar together until reduced to half quantity, but sufficient syrup should be made to cover fruit completely. Prepare the fruit according to kind:

Apples: Peel, core, quarter and slice thinly.

Oranges: Peel in a similar way to an apple, with a very sharp knife, cutting deeply enough to expose the flesh. Cupping the peeled fruit in the hand, cut the pulp cleanly from each section by loosening the thin skin from both sides. Work over a plate as juice is likely to escape.

Grapes: Remove seeds and skins from black grapes. If black colour is required for contrast, leave a few half-grapes unskinned.

Apricots, Peaches: Split around the natural groove, "unscrew" the two halves, skin, stone and cut each half in two or four.

Pineapple: Slice off the top cleanly, just below the leaves, using a sharp, thin knife, cut around the rim of the fruit, cutting down to the base, all round. Withdraw the inner "barrel" of fruit by means of a corkscrew. Cut fruit in slices.

Cherries: Remove stones neatly—a fine, sterilized hairpin may be kept for this purpose.

Strawberries, Raspberries: Hull carefully.

Plums: Halve and stone.

Bananas: Slice thinly. This fruit must never be chilled, unless covered, as such treatment causes discoloration.

Melon: Cut into slices and, if flesh alone is required, remove with a silver spoon. The melon may be used as a receptacle for fruit salad by cutting off the top, removing the seeds, and the flesh, with a spoon. The melon "cup" is then flavoured with kirsch and set on ice to become chilled, while the flesh is used as an ingredient of the mixed salad to be served in the melon case.

Pour the syrup over the prepared fruit and flavour with lemon juice. Cover the bowl and allow the salad to become quite cold. Stir in the liqueur and wine, if used, a few minutes before serving. Serve with cream, custard, ice cream, *or* chopped nuts.

FRUIT FOOL

1½ lb. fruit (approx.) (see below) **sugar according to taste and sweetness of fruit   1 pt. thick, pouring custard** (p. 250) or **1 pt. double cream** or **½ pt. custard and ½ pt. cream mixed   ratafia biscuits** or **tiny macaroons for decoration**

Prepare the fruit and cook if necessary:

Gooseberries and *Damsons* will require about 1 pt. water.

Pink, forced *Rhubarb* if cooked gently in a wet earthenware *or* oven-glass casserole requires *no* water. Sweeten with brown sugar to produce a rich juice.

Red- and *Black Currants* require about ¼ pt. water.

Strawberries, Loganberries and *Raspberries* should be crushed, sprinkled with castor sugar and left overnight.

Rub the softened fruit through a fine nylon sieve. Allow to cool, then blend with the cream *or* cold custard; taste and sharpen with a little lemon juice if necessary. Sweeten to taste with castor sugar. Chill and serve with ratafia biscuits arranged carefully on top.

6 helpings

JUNKET

2 pt. fresh milk   2 teasp. castor sugar   2 teasp. rennet
flavouring (see below)

Warm the milk to blood heat and stir in the sugar until dissolved. Add the rennet, stir and pour at once into serving dishes. Put in a warm place to set.

Serve with cream, if liked.

6 helpings

FLAVOURINGS

Coffee: Add to milk, coffee essence to flavour, and decorate finished junket with chopped nuts.

Chocolate: Add 2–3 oz. plain chocolate, grated and dissolved in a little of the measured milk.

Rum: Add rum to taste.

Vanilla, almond, raspberry, etc.: Add a few drops of essence.

NOTE: When using rennet in liquid or powder form, the manufacturer's instructions should be followed carefully to ensure the desired result.

STEWED FRUIT

Fresh fruit or dried fruit (see below)
sugar (see below)

FLAVOURING

Lemon or orange rind   ½ in. cinnamon stick   claret   cloves   sherry

NOTE: The amount of sugar required will depend on the sweetness of the fruit, e.g. dried fruits 1–2 oz. sugar per lb. of fruit; gooseberries 2–4 oz. sugar per lb. The amount of water will vary from ¼ pt. to ½ pt. per lb. of fruit, e.g. forced rhubarb requires very little water, whereas apples and pears should be covered in order to retain their white colour. Flavourings should be added to the water at the beginning and if rind is used it should be strained from the juice before reducing it after the fruit is cooked.

Dried Fruit should be washed and soaked overnight in cold water, allowing 1 pt. water per lb. fruit. If liked, freshly made cool tea may be used instead of water.

Fresh Fruit is prepared according to kind:

Apples, Pears: May be peeled, cored and left whole if small, or quartered if large. They should be placed immediately into the sugar and water syrup as each is prepared, otherwise the air causes a brown discoloration on the peeled surface. Apples may be stewed in oven-glass or earthenware dish in the oven, 2–3 cloves added to the syrup improve the flavour.

Rhubarb: Forced rhubarb is wiped with a damp cloth, cut into suitable lengths and covered with brown sugar. If cooked very gently in oven-glass or earthenware dish, no water is required and a rich red juice is obtained. If unforced rhubarb is old, the stringy outer skin should be stripped off.

Gooseberries, Plums, any sour Stone Fruit: Should be washed, the stalks removed, the stones may be left or removed as liked; gooseberries should be topped and tailed. Cook very slowly in the sugar and water until the skins crack, so that the sweet syrup can be absorbed by the flesh. If a little skin is removed from gooseberries during the topping and tailing their flavour will be much improved.

When the fruit is cooked, drain from the syrup and place in serving dish.

Boil the syrup to reduce it to a

thicker consistency, cool, and pour it over the fruit.

Time (Dried fruit)—1–2 hr.
   (Fresh fruit)—½ hr. approx.

SUMMER PUDDING

12 individual sponge cakes (approx.)
2–4 oz. sugar according to sweetness
of fruit   1½–2 lb. soft fruit: apples,
or rhubarb, gooseberries, strawberries, raspberries, redcurrants, or
blackcurrants, or a mixture, as liked

Choose a 1½ pt. pudding basin *or* charlotte *or* soufflé mould. Cut sponge cakes into inch-wide fingers for lining the sides, and triangles for lining the base. Cook the selected fruit, with the least pos-sible amount of water, until pulped; and sweeten to tast. Pour into the lined mould. Cover the top with slices of sponge cake, press down with a small weighted saucer, and leave pudding to be-come cold. Turn out on to a dish.

Coat with either custard or fruit juice thickened to coating consistency with 1 level teasp. arrowroot to ½ pt. juice. Decorate with choice pieces of fruit *or* shredded almonds.

6 helpings

GATEAUX

APRICOT GATEAU

1 round of Genoese pastry (p. 326)
or rich, light cake 6 in. diameter and
1 in. thick   2 tablesp. sherry or
fruit juice   2 doz. savoy fingers
(p. 327) soft textured   2 tablesp.
sieved apricot jam   a length of 1-in.
wide, pale coloured ribbon to tie
round the sponge fingers (about
12 in.)   angelica

FILLING
1 large can apricots   ½ pt. lemon
jelly tablet   ¾ pt. double cream
castor sugar to taste

Place the round of cake on a serving plate and sprinkle with the sherry or juice. Trim the sponge fingers so that the sides are quite straight and all are equal in length, with one end trimmed straight across. Melt the ½ pt. jelly tablet in ¼ pt. of apricot juice and allow to cool, but not set. Brush inside of trimmed end of each sponge finger to 1 in. in depth with sieved apricot jam; dip one edge only in cool jelly, and press firmly against the side of the round of cake. As each finger is so treated, the jellied edge will be in contact with the dry edge of the adjacent finger, and a firm case may be made without danger of the fingers becoming sodden and crumbling. The rounded, sugary surface of the finger faces out-wards. Tie the ribbon round the finished case so that the sponge fingers are held firmly upright, and leave to set.

FILLING: Drain apricots well, and reserve 6 halves for decoration. Cut the remainder into quarters. Whip the cream until the fork leaves a trail; sweeten to taste with castor sugar. Put ¼ of the cream into a forcing bag with rose pipe, for decorating (optional). Stir the quartered apricots into the re-mainder of the cream. Lastly stir in ⅛ pt. of the liquid jelly, steam-ing hot. Pour immediately into the sponge-finger case. Arrange the 6 apricot halves (either whole *or* cut as liked) on the top, and pipe cream roses between and around to cover the surface of the cream. Decorate with angelica.

VARIATIONS: Use fresh *or* canned strawberries, *or* chopped pineapple, *or* fruit-flavoured ice cream, *or* custard cream fillings.

MERINGUE GATEAU

6 egg whites   12 oz. castor sugar
1½ lb. strawberries   juice of 1 lemon
castor sugar   ¼–½ pt. double cream

Make the meringue (p. 39). Put into a plain forcing pipe ($\frac{1}{2}$ in.) and pipe a round base, working from the centre outwards, 6 in. in diameter. Build up the sides to a height of $1\frac{1}{2}$ in. Pipe the remaining meringue into small shell shapes. Bake in a very cool oven (265° F., Gas $\frac{1}{2}$); then cool.

Prepare strawberries, sprinkle with lemon juice and castor sugar and allow to stand until meringue case is ready. Reserve a few choice fruits for decoration; place the rest in the merigue case. Cover with the whipped cream. Decorate with meringue shells and strawberries.

NOTE: The meringue case, if completely dried by gentle cooking, will remain firm if kept in an airtight tin. It cannot retain its crispness for long after the inclusion of fruit and cream. Do not put in a refrigerator.

6 helpings

VARIATIONS: Use ice cream or fresh fruits or custard creams (pp. 288–9) for the filling.

SPONGE GATEAU

2 sponge cakes (p. 327) **7 in. in diameter   3 tablesp. sherry or fruit juice   1 family block ice cream, flavoured as required** (see below) **$\frac{1}{2}$ pt. double cream, whipped and sweetened approx. 1 lb. fruit for garnish**

Place one round of sponge on the serving dish and sprinkle with sherry or juice. Cut out the centre of the other round, leaving a 1-in. border all round. Place the border on the prepared base. Cut the ice cream quickly into chunks and pile into the hollow. Decorate the border and sides of the sponge with stars of whipped cream and suitable pieces of fruit. Serve at once.

NOTE: All canned and fresh fruits such as strawberries, raspberries, loganberries, apricots, peaches, are suitable, with vanilla or strawberry ice cream. Coffee ice cream can be sprinkled with chopped roasted almonds or grated chocolate.

6 helpings

ICES

ICES may be broadly divided into two classes: water ices and ice creams.

Water Ices and Sherbets (Sorbets): Water ices are made from the juice of fresh fruit or fruit purée mixed with syrup or fruit syrup. Sherbets (Sorbets) are half-frozen water ices containing egg white or gelatine.

Ice Creams: These are sometimes composed almost entirely of cream—sweetened, flavoured, and decorated in many ways; but more frequently consist principally of custard with the addition of fruit pulp, almonds, chocolate, coffee, liqueurs and other flavourings.

Making Ice Cream in a Refrigerator: To obtain a smooth, evenly-textured ice cream in a refrigerator, the mixture must be frozen quickly and whisked well. The quicker the freezing the less likelihood there is of ice crystals forming, so set the refrigerator to the coldest point ½ hr. before putting the mixture to freeze, unless instructed otherwise in the recipe. Chill all ingredients and utensils before use.

Prepare the mixture, place it in the ice tray or drawer, and replace the tray in the freezing compartment.

Air acts as a deterrent to crystal formation, so remove the mixture after ½ hr. and whisk well in a chilled bowl. Replace in the tray and put back into the freezing compartment.

Making Ice Cream in a Freezer: An ice cream freezer consists of a metal container, in which the ice cream mixture is placed—and an outer container, usually a wooden bucket; the space between the two being packed with alternate layers of crushed ice and salt. Air is incorporated into the mixture by churning.

The recipes are based on a one-quart, bucket-type mixture: this bucket needs 7 lb. of ice and 2 lb. freezing salt (common salt may be substituted). Broken ice alone is insufficient to freeze or mould the ices.

1. Add sugar carefully, too much sugar will prevent the ice mixture from freezing successfully, and insufficient sugar will cause the mixture to freeze hard and rocky.
2. Do not put warm mixtures into the container, and do not fill the container, as freezing increases the bulk of the mixture.
3. Raise the lid from time to time and scrape down, with a wooden spatula or spoon, the thin coating of ice which will have formed on the side and mix well.
4. Wipe the lid of the container carefully before raising it, so that no salt or salt water is allowed to get into the mixture.
5. If the ice cream is to be served unmoulded it must be frozen quite stiffly.

Moulding Ices: If the mixture is to be moulded it should be removed from the freezer or refrigerator in a semi-solid condition, and then packed into a dry mould or bomb, well shaken, and pressed down into the shape of the mould. The mould should have a tightly-fitting lid, which must be sealed with a thick layer of lard. The mould or bomb is then wrapped in greaseproof paper and buried in broken ice and freezing salt for

1½–2 hr. To unmould, remove the paper and lard, wipe the mould carefully, dip it into cold water, and turn the ice on to a dish in the same way as a jelly or cream.

SYRUP (for Water Ices) (1)

2 lb. loaf sugar   1 pt. water

Place the sugar and water in a strong saucepan. Allow the sugar to dissolve over gentle heat. Do not stir. When the sugar has dissolved, gently boil the mixture for 10 min., or, if a saccharometer is available, it should register 220° F. Remove scum as it rises. Strain, cool and store.

1 pt. syrup
Time—½ hr.

SYRUP (2)

8 oz. loaf sugar   1 pt. water

Proceed as for Syrup (1).

APPLE WATER ICE

1 pt. apple pulp   1 pt. syrup
2 tablesp. lemon juice   carmine

Stew the apples with a minimum amount of water. Pass through a nylon sieve and stir the pulp into the hot syrup. When cold, add the lemon juice and carmine. Chill and freeze.

10–12 helpings
Time—2–2½ hr.

CIDER ICE

1 large Bramley apple   ½ pt. cider
½ pt. syrup (1)   juice of 1 large lemon

Peel, core and slice the apple. Cook in a covered saucepan with 1 tablesp. of water. Pass the cooked apple through a fine hair or nylon sieve and add all other ingredients. Chill and freeze.

6 helpings
Time—2–2½ hr.

LEMON WATER ICE

6 lemons   2 oranges   1½ pt. syrup

Thinly peel the fruit and place the rind in a basin. Add the hot syrup, cover and cool. Add the juice of the lemons and oranges. Strain, chill and freeze.

6 helpings
Time—1½ hr.

PINEAPPLE WATER ICE

½ pt. canned pineapple juice   1 pt. syrup (1)   2 tablesp. lemon juice

Thoroughly mix all ingredients. Chill and freeze.

6 helpings
Time—1½–2 hr.

RASPBERRY or STRAWBERRY WATER ICE

1 lb. ripe strawberries or raspberries   juice of 2 lemons
1 pt. syrup

Rub the fruit through a nylon sieve and add the lemon juice. Add the syrup and a little colouring if necessary. Chill and freeze.

6 helpings
Time—1 hr.

LEMON SHERBET (SORBET)

1 pt. water   8 oz. loaf sugar
½ pt. lemon juice   2 egg whites

Dissolve the sugar in the water. Boil it for 10 min., strain and cool. Add the lemon juice and the stiffly beaten egg whites. Freeze and serve at once.

6 helpings
Time—1½ hr.

PINEAPPLE SHERBET (SORBET)

1 pt. water   8 oz. loaf sugar
½ pt. canned pineapple juice
2 egg whites

Dissolve the sugar in the water. Boil it for 10 min.; strain and cool. Add the pineapple juice and the stiffly beaten egg whites. Freeze and serve at once.

6 helpings
Time—1½ hr.

CUSTARD (for Ice Cream) (1)
—Economical

1 oz. custard powder 1 pt. milk
4 oz. castor sugar

Blend the custard powder with a little of the milk. Boil remaining milk and pour on to the blended mixture. Return to pan and simmer—stirring continuously. Add sugar; cover, and allow to cool.

CUSTARD (2)

1 pt. milk 3 eggs
4 oz. castor sugar

Heat the milk. Beat together eggs and sugar. Add the hot milk, stirring continuously. Return to pan and cook without boiling until custard coats the back of a wooden spoon. Strain, cover and cool.

BANANA ICE CREAM

3 bananas 2 tablesp. lemon juice
½ pt. cream or ¼ pt. cream and
¼ pt. custard (1) or (2)
3–4 oz. castor sugar

Peel and slice the bananas, cover with lemon juice. Pass fruit through a nylon sieve. Add the half-whipped cream, cold custard if used, and sugar. Chill and freeze.

6 helpings

CARAMEL ICE CREAM

2 oz. loaf sugar ¾ gill cream
1½ pt. custard (2)

Put the sugar into a small saucepan with a few drops of water and boil until it acquires a deep golden colour. Add the cream and when boiling, stir into the custard. Chill and freeze.

6–7 helpings
Time—1½–2 hr.

CHOCOLATE ICE CREAM

4 oz. plain chocolate ½ gill water
½ pt. custard (2) 1 gill cream
1–2 teasp. vanilla essence

Break chocolate roughly, place in pan, add water. Dissolve over low heat. Add melted chocolate to the custard. Cool. Add the half-whipped cream and vanilla to taste. Chill and freeze.

6–8 helpings

COFFEE ICE CREAM (1)

½ pt. cream ½ pt. custard (1) or (2)
2 tablesp. liquid coffee
2 oz. castor sugar

Half whip the cream. Add the custard, coffee and sugar. Mix well. Chill and freeze.

6 helpings

COFFEE ICE CREAM (2)

3 teasp. instant coffee
½ gill hot water ½ pt. cream
3 oz. castor sugar

Dissolve the coffee in the hot water. Cool. Half whip the cream and add castor sugar. Fold in the dissolved coffee. Chill and freeze.

6 helpings
Time—2½ hr.

STRAWBERRY ICE CREAM

½ pt. milk ½ pt. cream 1–2 egg yolks 6 oz. castor sugar 1 lb. strawberries 1 dessertsp. granulated sugar 1 teasp. lemon juice carmine

Put milk and cream in a saucepan and bring nearly to boiling-point. Beat together the egg yolks and castor sugar, add to the milk and cream and stir over a low heat until they thicken. Pass the strawberries through a sieve, together with the granulated sugar. Mix with the custard, add the lemon juice and carmine to colour. Chill and freeze.

6–8 helpings
Time—about 1–1½ hr.

VANILLA ICE CREAM

¾ pt. cream or prepared evaporated milk (see p. 287) 1 pt. cold custard (1) 1 teasp. vanilla essence

Half whip the cream or evaporated milk. Add the custard and vanilla. Chill and freeze.

6 helpings
Time—2½ hr.

REFRIGERATOR ICE CREAMS

LEMON ICE CREAM

**8 egg yolks ½ lb. castor sugar
juice of 2 lemons ½ pt. cream**

Set the refrigerator at coldest temperature. Beat the egg yolks until very thick. Add the sugar and beat again. Stir in the lemon juice. Add the half-whipped cream carefully. Pour into the tray and freeze ½ hr. Remove, stir and continue freezing for another 1½ hr.

6–8 helpings

MARSHMALLOW ICE CREAM

14 marshmallows ¼ pt. evaporated milk ¼ pt. fruit purée 3 oz. castor sugar ¼ pt. cream

Melt the marshmallows in the evaporated milk over hot water. Cool. Add the fruit purée and sugar. Lastly fold in the half-whipped cream. Pour into the tray and freeze at medium. Stir once after the first ½ hr. and continue to freeze for a further 1½ hr.

6 helpings

VANILLA ICE CREAM

2 level tablesp. icing sugar 1 gill cream 2 egg whites 1 oz. glacé cherries vanilla essence

Sieve the icing sugar. Whip the cream and add 1 tablesp. of the sugar. Stiffly whip the egg whites and fold in the other tablesp. of sugar. Carefully mix together the cream, egg whites, quartered cherries and vanilla. Turn into a tray of the ice chamber and freeze.

SUNDAES, ETC.
BANANA SPLIT

**6 bananas 1 pt. vanilla ice cream
(p. 302) or 1 family brick**

½ pt. melba sauce ¼ pt. whipped sweetened cream 2 oz. chopped walnuts 8 maraschino cherries

Peel bananas, split in half lengthways and place in small oval dishes. Place two small scoops or slices of ice cream between the halves of bananas. Coat the ice cream with melba sauce; sprinkle with chopped nuts. Decorate with piped cream and cherries.

CHOCOLATE SUNDAE

**¼ pt. chocolate ice cream (p. 302) or 1 small brick ¼ pt. chocolate sauce ¼ pt. vanilla ice cream (p. 302) or 1 small brick
2 oz. chopped walnuts
¼ pt. sweetened whipped cream
8 maraschino cherries**

Place a scoop of chocolate ice cream in 6–8 sundae glasses; coat with chocolate sauce. Place a scoop of vanilla ice cream on top; coat with chocolate sauce. Sprinkle with chopped nuts. Pipe with cream. Decorate with cherries.

OMELETTE SOUFFLEE EN SURPRISE

**1 round Genoese pastry or sponge cake 1 tablesp. liqueur 1 egg yolk
2 oz. castor sugar 3 egg whites
a few drops of vanilla essence
1 pt. vanilla ice cream (p. 302)**

DECORATION
Glacé cherries angelica

Place the cake on a silver or fireproof dish and soak with liqueur. Whip the egg yolk and sugar until thick and fold in the stiffly-beaten egg whites. Add vanilla essence and place the soufflé mixture in a piping bag with a large rose pipe. Place the ice cream on top of the cake. Completely cover with piped soufflé mixture. Dredge with icing sugar and place in a very hot oven for 3 min. Decorate and serve immediately.

6–8 helpings

PEACH MELBA

1 pt. vanilla ice cream (p. 302)
6 canned peach halves
½ pt. melba sauce (opposite)
¼ pt. whipped sweetened cream

Place a scoop or slice of ice cream in 6 sundae glasses. Cover with a peach half. Coat with melba sauce. Pipe a large rose of cream on top of each.

6 individual glasses

PEAR DELICE

8 pear halves   1 pt. strawberry ice cream (p. 302)   ½ pt. chocolate sauce (p. 106)   2 oz. grated chocolate

Arrange a half of pear in 8 small, flat, glass dishes, hollow side up. Place a scoop of ice cream in the hollow of the pears. Coat with hot chocolate sauce. Sprinkle with grated chocolate.

8 individual dishes

STRAWBERRY BASKET

1 sponge cake (p. 327) cut to size of ice cream brick   1 wineglass of sherry, liqueur or fruit juice
1 family brick ice cream
½ pt. sweetened whipped cream
12 ice cream wafer biscuits
½ lb. strawberries   1 strip angelica

Place the sponge cake on a silver dish and soak with sherry, liqueur or juice. Place the family brick ice cream on top of the sponge. Pipe a band of cream round the sides of the ice cream. Stand the wafers overlapping round the four sides and press them to the block. Pipe cream on top. Arrange the strawberries on top of the cream. Make a handle with the strip of angelica. Serve at once.

6–8 helpings

STRAWBERRY LAYER GATEAU

1 family brick ice cream   ½ lb. strawberries   ¼ pt. sweetened whipped cream   castor sugar

Cut the family brick, which must be firm, in half horizontally. Cover the lower half with halves of strawberries. Sprinkle with castor sugar and replace the top half. Pipe with rosettes of cream and place small strawberries all over the top. Dredge with castor sugar and serve immediately.

6 helpings

TUTTI FRUTTI ICE CREAM

1 pt. ice cream mixture, any flavour
4 oz. mixed candied fruits
pistachio nuts

Chop the fruits and nuts into small pieces. Half freeze the ice cream mixture, mix in the chopped fruits and nuts. Complete the freezing. Serve with Melba sauce.

SAUCES FOR ICE CREAM

COFFEE SAUCE

6 tablesp. freshly ground coffee
¾ pt. water   ¼ oz. gelatine
3 egg yolks   3 oz. castor sugar

Boil the water and pour over the coffee. Strain when cool. Dissolve the gelatine in 1 tablesp. water. Beat together the egg yolks and sugar. Place all the ingredients in a saucepan. Cook slowly, without boiling, until the mixture thickens. Strain and chill. Use as required.

MELBA SAUCE

To make Melba sauce pass the required quantity of fresh raspberries through a nylon sieve and sweeten with icing sugar. The sauce is not cooked.
Use as required.

MOCK MELBA SAUCE

½ oz. arrowroot   ½ pt. water   ½ gill raspberry jam   juice of ½ lemon

Blend the arrowroot with a little of the water. Boil remaining water with the jam and lemon juice. Strain it on to the blended mixture, return to the pan and boil up, stirring all the time.

Cool before using.

ICED DRINKS

ICED COFFEE

½ pt. milk   6 oz. castor sugar   2 pt. strong, clear, hot coffee a few drops of vanilla essence ½ pt. cream

Place the milk and sugar in a saucepan. Bring almost to the boil, add the coffee and vanilla essence, allow to cool. Strain, stir in the cream, and chill until it has the consistency of thick cream. Serve very cold, in tall glasses, and hand castor sugar separately.

MILK PUNCH

2 pt. milk   4 oz. loaf sugar
2 tablesp. brandy or rum
¼ pt. cream

Boil the milk, dissolve the sugar in it, strain and chill. Add the brandy or rum and the whipped cream. Mix well and half freeze. Serve in a half-frozen condition in small china sorbet cups and, if liked, grate a little nutmeg or cinnamon on top before serving.

6–8 helpings

DESSERT

AT formal dinners the last course to be served is the dessert, which is composed principally of fruits in season, nuts (with or without raisins) and often ices, petits fours or dessert biscuits, dainty sweets and bonbons. Salted almonds are much appreciated after a sweet course.

The chief fruits served are grapes, peaches, nectarines, plums, cherries, pineapple, apples, pears, oranges, dates and figs. The fruit looks most attractive served on a dish lined with green leaves (preferably vine leaves, if available), which can form part of the table décor. If to be handed round separately, the fruit is served after the table has been cleared and dessert plates, knives and forks have been placed before each person. The fruit should of course be first washed or wiped with a damp cloth, and afterwards polished with a soft, dry cloth.

On the Continent fruit is often served instead of a sweet course, whilst in America the pudding course is referred to as the dessert.

BAKING

BAKING is a most interesting and fascinating branch of cookery, giving satisfaction to the producer no less than the consumer.

BREAD-MAKING

Bread is obtained by baking a mixture of flour, water and salt, which is made light and porous by the use of yeast or some other means of aeration. Bread which has not been aerated is known as unleavened bread and is eaten by the Jews in commemoration at their special religious feasts.

Flour used for break-making is primarily that obtained from the wheat grain, a white flour being obtained when all the outer husk has been removed before grinding. *Wholemeal* is the entire grain ground down. In the case of the latter, the keeping quality may be less good because of the fat content of the flour, but on the other hand a more nutritionally valuable food is obtained.

Yeast: The fermentation method of raising dough involves the use of yeast. The yeast which is probably used most in the home is compressed yeast. When in good condition it should have a beery smell and be a fresh putty colour. To keep it fresh, store in a screw-top jar in a cold place. It will keep 3–4 days.

Another form of yeast commonly used is described as "Dry granular". This yeast keeps without refrigeration. It can be bought in tins or packets and instructions for use are stated on the package.

The term "Quick Breads" is used to describe breads which are made with a raising agent which is quick in action, e.g. baking-powder bread raised with baking-powder, soda bread raised with bicarbonate of soda and cream of tartar or other acid, e.g. sour milk, and bread leavened with the latter and cooked by steam.

Baking-powder is a leavening or raising agent. The baking-powder should leave a tasteless and harmless residue in the bread, etc., and it should not deteriorate in the tin with keeping. Baking-powder is used in the proportion of one to three teaspoonfuls to each pound of flour, depending on the richness of the mixture—usually the plainer the mixture (fewer eggs, less fat) the more baking-powder is required.

Egg powders are just coloured baking-powders and must not be confused with dried egg.

Eggs (fresh) act as raising agents because when beaten they possess the property of holding air which expands on heating.

Bicarbonate of Soda and Cream of Tartar (without starchy material as in baking-powders) are used in the making of scones, etc. The proportion used in scones is one teaspoonful bicarbonate of soda and two and a quarter teaspoonfuls cream of tartar to one pound of flour, or equal quantities if sour milk (acid) is used.

Self-raising Flour may be used for some things; in this case the raising agent has been added to the flour and *generally* no more is required.

YEAST BREADS
WHOLEMEAL BREAD

3 lb. wholemeal flour   3 teasp. salt
1 teasp. sugar   1–2 oz. yeast
2 oz. lard   1¾ pt. warm water

Mix salt, sugar and flour in a large basin. Dissolve the yeast in the warm water, add the melted fat, and mix with the flour to an elastic dough. Knead well until smooth, cover with a cloth, to prevent surface evaporation, and set in a warm place to rise to double its size—about 1 hr. When the dough is sufficiently risen it has a honeycombed appearance. The first kneading distributes the yeast and strengthens the gluten. Knead the dough a second time to distribute the carbon dioxide gas which has formed. Continue kneading until, when the dough is cut, there are no large holes in it, but do not knead too heavily. Divide into the number of loaves required. Place in warmed greased tins, making the top round. Allow to prove or recover for 20 min. or until the dough is well up to the top of the tin. If the dough is over-proved it will collapse and give heavy bread. Bake in top middle of a very hot oven (450° F., Gas 8) (to kill the yeast), for 10–15 min., then reduce heat to fairly hot (375° F., Gas 5) baking in all about 1 hr. When ready the loaf should have a hollow sound when knocked on the bottom, and should be well risen and nicely browned with a crisp crust.

4 loaves
Cooking time—1 hr.

WHITE BREAD
Basic Recipe

3 lb. white flour   4 teasp. salt
1 oz. yeast   1 teasp. sugar
1¾ pt. warm water

Grease 4 loaf tins and put them to warm. Mix salt, sugar and flour well together, mix in yeast and add to warm water. Make a well in the centre of the flour, pour the liquid into the well and sprinkle on or mix in a little of the flour to form a pool of batter and allow to stand in a warm place for 20 min. Mix to an elastic dough, using more water if required; knead well till the dough leaves the basin clean, and put to rise in a warm place until the dough his doubled its size. Then turn on to a floured board, knead again not too heavily but until there are only small holes in the dough, and put into the prepared tins. Put to prove until the dough is well up the sides of the tin, then bake in a hot oven.

3–4 loaves
Cooking time—1 hr.

MILK BREAD
Basic Recipe

1 lb. plain flour   1 teasp. salt
½ oz. yeast   ¼ teasp. sugar   2 oz. lard or margarine   ½ pt. warm milk (approx.)   1 egg (optional)

Mix the salt with the warmed flour, cream the yeast with the sugar. Rub fat into flour and mix with the yeast, milk and egg if used, to a fairly soft, light dough. Beat until mixture is smooth and leaves the sides of the basin clean. Allow to stand in a warm place till twice its original size. Proceed as for White Bread (opposite), or see following recipes.

Variations

Bridge Rolls or Sandwich Buns

1 lb. flour, etc., as for Milk Bread, using 1–2 eggs in mixing the dough

Make the dough as for Milk Bread and divide raised dough into required number of pieces; roll each piece into long finger-shaped buns about 3–3½ in. long. Place on warmed greased baking-sheets and pat down a little to make a good shape. Put the rolls touching one another so that they bake with soft edges. Prove for 10 min., brush with egg and milk and bake in a hot oven (425° F., Gas 7).

45–50 rolls
Cooking time—8–10 min.

Cheese Bread Plait

As for Milk Bread, adding 3-4 oz. finely grated cheese with the dry ingredients. Place in a hot oven (450° F., Gas 8). Prove for 10-15 min. Bake for 20-30 min., reducing heat after first 10 min. to 400° F., Gas 6 or 375° F., Gas 5.

French Shapes

1 lb. plain flour, etc., as for Milk Bread

Make the dough as for Milk Bread, then divide risen dough into required number of pieces, knead lightly and form into shapes, e.g.:

Small plait: Divide the dough into 3 and shape each into a long roll, plait together, sealing ends securely.

Small Twists: Divide dough into 2, shape into long rolls, twist together and secure ends.

Cottage Loaf: Cut off ⅔ of dough and make into bun shape, treat ⅓ in the same way. Place smaller one on top of larger one and secure by putting little finger through centre or pierce with a wooden skewer.

"S" Shape: Make a long roll with the dough and twist into an "S" shape.

Horseshoe Shape: Roll out dough thinly and cut into triangular shapes. Roll up from the base and twist into a horseshoe shape. Pierce with skewer to represent nails.

Allow buns to prove 10-15 min., brush with egg and milk and bake in a hot oven (425° F., Gas 7) until cooked through and a rich golden brown.

24-28 shapes
Cooking time—10-15 min.

CROISSANTS

1 lb. plain flour   ½ teasp. salt   ½ oz. yeast   1 teasp. sugar   ½ pt. warm milk and water   3 oz. margarine

Make as for Milk Bread (p. 307), omitting margarine. When the dough has risen to double its size, roll out on a floured board three times its width and spread with ⅓ of the margarine, in small pieces. Dredge lightly with flour, fold up ⅓ and down ⅓ (as for flaky pastry) and seal the edges. Repeat with the other ⅔ of margarine. Put the dough in a warm place again to rise for 30 min. Roll the dough out like pastry ⅛ in. thick, and cut into 12 pieces 5 in. square. Turn the squares over so that the smooth side comes outside and damp the surface very lightly with warm water. Beginning at one corner, roll up the square, pressing the opposite corner over to make it stick to the roll. Bend the two ends towards each other to form a crescent. Place on greased trays and allow to prove 15 min. Bake in a fairly hot oven (425° F., Gas 7). Brush with egg yolk and milk when almost ready, then dry them off.

12 croissants
Cooking time—15-20 min.

GRISINI BREAD or SALT STICKS

1 lb. plain flour   1 teasp. salt
1 oz. margarine or lard   enough warm water to make a fairly stiff dough   ½ oz. yeast   ½ teasp. sugar
3-4 tablesp. warm milk

Make as for Milk Bread (p. 307), allow to rise for 1-1½ hr. Form into long sticks 6-8 in. in length and when proved brush with egg white, bake in a hot oven (425° F., Gas 7) until crisp.

If liked, they may be brushed with milk and sprinkled with a little coarse salt before baking.

12 sticks
Cooking time—20-30 min.

YEAST BUNS
BATH BUNS

1 lb. plain flour   ½ teasp. salt

3 oz. fat—margarine and lard
good ½ oz. yeast   3 oz. sugar
2 eggs   1½–2 gills warm milk

GLAZE

1 tablesp. water   1 dessertsp. sugar

Mix salt with warmed flour and
rub in fat. Mix in most of the
sugar. Mix to a light dough with
yeast creamed with remainder of
sugar, egg and milk. Put to rise
till double its size, then knead
lightly. Divide into 24 pieces and
shape each 3½–4 in. long and 1 in.
wide. Place fairly close together
(so that they join up in baking) on
greased baking-sheets and prove
15 min. Bake in a hot oven (425°
F., Gas 7) 10–15 min.

To make the glaze—boil together the water and sugar until
slightly syrupy. Brush the buns
immediately they come from the
oven so that the syrup dries on.

Dredge thickly with castor
sugar. Break buns apart before
serving.

NOTE: 2 oz. sultanas and 1 oz.
chopped peel may be worked into
the dough after it has risen.

24 buns
Cooking time—10–15 min.

CHELSEA BUNS

½ lb. plain flour   ¼ teasp. salt   1 oz.
lard or margarine   ½ oz. yeast
1 gill warm milk   ½ oz. currants or
sultanas   ½ oz. chopped candied
peel   1 oz. sugar

Mix flour and salt; rub in fat,
cream yeast and add to flour, with
warm milk. Beat well and put to
rise to double its size. Knead risen
dough lightly and roll out in a
square of about 10 in. Sprinkle
with the fruit and sugar and roll
up like a Swiss roll. Cut roll into
7 pieces and put cut side uppermost. Place buns in a greased 8-
in. sandwich cake tin so that they
will join together when cooked,
and allow to prove till up to the
top of the tin. Brush with milk or
egg, bake in a hot oven (425° F.,
Gas 7) 20–25 min. Make sure they
are cooked well in the bottom.
When buns are ready, brush over
with glaze as for Bath Buns (opposite), and dust with castor sugar.
Break buns apart when cool.

7 buns
Cooking time—20–25 min.

DOUGHNUTS

½ lb. plain flour   ¼ teasp. salt   2 oz.
margarine (or ¾ oz. lard and 1 oz.
margarine)   1 oz. castor sugar
½ oz. yeast   ¼–⅜ gill warm milk
1 egg   cinnamon sugar for coating
fat for deep frying

Rub the fat into the warmed
flour and salt; add sugar, having
taken out ½ teasp. to cream the
yeast. Add the warm milk and
egg to the creamed yeast and pour
into the flour. Mix well (do not
make too soft as the dough is to
be cut out), and put to rise to
double its size. Knead lightly and
roll out ½ in. thick. Cut into rings,
using 2½–2¾-in cutter for outside
and 1½–1¾-in for inner ring, and
prove on warm tray for 5 min.
Drop into very faintly smoking fat
and cook 5 min.; drain well and
toss in castor sugar *or* sugar mixed
with ground cinnamon to taste.

NOTE: Proving may be un-
necessary, the first doughnuts may
be ready to fry by the time the last
are cut out.

14–16 doughnuts

HOT CROSS BUNS

1 lb. plain flour   ½ teasp. salt   2 oz.
margarine or margarine and lard
4 oz. sugar   1 teasp. mixed spice or
cinnamon   ½ oz. yeast   1–2 eggs
1½–2 gill milk   2 oz. currants or 2 oz.
raisins and peel   short crust pastry

Mix salt with warmed flour. Rub
in fat. Add sugar, spice, creamed
yeast, and eggs with the warm
milk. Mix to a soft, light dough,

beat well and put to rise. When
well risen, knead the dough lightly,
working in the fruit, and divide
into 20–24 pieces. Form into
round shapes, flatten slightly and
put to prove for 15 min. Cut
narrow strips of pastry 1½–2 in.
long, brush tops of buns with egg
wash or milk, place pastry crosses
on top and bake in a hot oven
(425° F., Gas 7).

NOTE: If there is no pastry
available cut a deep cross on each
bun.

20–24 buns
Cooking time—15–20 min.

LUXEMBURG BUNS

Make as for Bath Buns (p. 308).
Do not glaze, but when cold,
spread tops with glacé icing (p.
333). The buns look attractive if
made round in shape.

PIKELETS
(or Crumpets)

½ lb. plain flour   ½ teasp. salt   ½ oz.
yeast   ¼ teasp. sugar   ½ pt. milk and
water   pinch of bicarbonate of soda

Warm the flour and mix with
the salt. Cream yeast with sugar,
add to the warmed milk and water
and mix with flour to consistency
of a soft batter. Cover and leave to
rise 30–45 min. Dissolve the soda
in 1 tablesp. warm water, add to
the mixture, beating well, and put
to rise again for 30 min. Grease
a girdle, thick frying-pan or electric hotplate and heat until fairly
hot. Grease pikelet rings or large
plain cutters (3½–4 in), place on
the girdle and pour in enough
batter to cover the bottom of ring
to a depth of ¼ in. When top is set
and bubbles burst, turn and cook
underside. Serve hot with butter.

8–10 pikelets

TEA CAKES

1 lb. plain flour   ¼ teasp. salt   2 oz.
lard and margarine   ½ oz. yeast

1 oz. sugar   ½ pt. warm milk
2–3 oz. currants (if liked)

Sift warm flour and salt and rub
in the fat. Cream the yeast with
the sugar, add the warm milk to it
and mix with the flour and fruit
to a light elastic dough. Put to rise
to double its size. Divide risen
dough into 4–6 pieces, knead each
into a round and roll out to the
size of a tea plate. Place on greased
baking sheets, prick the top neatly, and allow to prove for 15 min.
Bake in a hot oven (425° F., Gas 7)
for 20–25 min.

If liked, the cakes may be
brushed with egg and water before baking or rubbed over with
margarine after baking.

4–6 cakes

WAFFLES

8 oz. plain flour   ¼ teasp. salt   ¾ oz.
yeast   ½ teasp. sugar   1 pt. milk
2 oz. margarine   2–3 eggs

Sift flour and salt into a bowl.
Cream the yeast with the sugar and
add to it the warm milk and margarine; beat the eggs. Add the
yeast, milk and egg to the flour,
using more milk if required to
make a pouring batter. Set aside
to rise for 30–45 min. Heat and
grease the waffle iron and pour in
enough batter to fill the iron sections—the lid must press on the
batter. The waffles are ready when
nicely browned.

Serve hot with maple or ordinary syrup.

30–40 waffles

QUICK BREADS
BAKING-POWDER BREAD

1 lb. plain flour   1 teasp. salt   2 oz.
lard or margarine   2 round or
4 level tablesp. baking-powder
milk to mix to light spongy dough—
average ½ pt.

Sift the flour and salt and rub
in the fat until quite fine. Add the

baking-powder and mix very lightly with the milk. Shape into small loaves or bake in two greased 6-in. cake-tins. Put into a hot oven 450°–425° F., Gas 8–7).

Cooking time (small loaves)—
   10–15 min   (large)—25–30 min.

DATE AND WALNUT LOAF

14 oz. plain flour   ¼ teasp. salt
½ lb. chopped dates   4 oz. sugar
2 oz. margarine   2 level teasp.
bicarbonate of soda   1½ gill boiling
water   1 egg   2 oz. chopped walnuts
1 teasp. vanilla essence

Sift together the flour and salt. Put chopped dates (weigh after stoning), sugar, margarine and soda in a mixing bowl and pour the boiling water over, stir thoroughly. Add the egg, flour, walnuts and essence and beat well. Bake in a greased cake-tin or large loaf-tin in a fairly hot oven (400°–350° F., Gas 6–4).

1 loaf
Cooking time—1–1½ hr.

MALT BREAD

1 lb. self-raising flour   2 level teasp.

bicarbonate of soda   4 tablesp.
golden syrup   4 tablesp. malt
extract   ½ pt. milk   2 eggs
2 teacups sultanas or raisins

Sift the flour and soda into a bowl. Melt syrup and malt in a pan with the milk and add with beaten eggs to the flour; lastly add the fruit. Pour into greased tins (cake- or bread-tins) and bake in a fairly hot oven (400°–375° F., Gas 6–5).

2 medium loaves
Cooking time—40–50 min.

NUT AND RAISIN BREAD

¾ lb. wholemeal flour   ¼ teasp. salt
2 oz. lard or dripping or margarine
2 round teasp. baking-powder   2 oz.
sugar   2 oz. sultanas   4 oz.
chopped nuts   1 egg   ½ pt. milk

Rub the fat into the sifted flour and salt. Add remaining dry ingredients and mix to a fairly soft dough with egg and milk. Put into a well-greased tin (bread- or cake-tin) and bake in a fairly hot oven (400°–375° F., Gas 6–5).

1 loaf
Cooking time—1 hr.

SCONES

IT is not economically sound to heat an oven solely for making a few scones for tea, and this is where the girdle will be found a good cooking substitute. Even a strong frying-pan will do, and, of course, many people use the electric hot-plate.

The plain oven scone recipe can be used for girdle cookery, but it is important to remember that the dough must be rolled out more thinly than for oven scones.

A good method of greasing a girdle is to tie a piece of suet (hard fat) in muslin and rub the heated surface with this; it lasts for a considerable time, as suet has

a high melting-point. When a girdle is hot the greased surface should show a *faint* haze rising from it. Another method of testing a hot girdle is to sprinkle on a little flour—if the flour browns within a few seconds the girdle is ready for use.

IMPORTANT POINTS
1. It is most essential to be accurate with proportions.
2. Whereas yeast mixtures are kept warm, scones, etc., made with other raising agents should be kept as *cool* as possible.
3. The most important rule is to add *all* the liquid *at once* and

mix lightly to a spongy dough.
4. The scones should be handled as little as possible.
5. Scones should be cooked quickly.
6. Cool oven scones on a cooling tray to keep the outside crisp. Girdle scones are best cooled in a tea towel to keep the skin soft.

NOTE: From experiment it has been found that better results are obtained if the scones are allowed to stand (after cutting out) for 10 minutes before cooking. This applies to scones raised with bicarbonate of soda and cream of tartar.

PLAIN SCONES

1 lb. plain flour   ½ teasp. salt
2–3 oz. lard or margarine

and

2 level teasp. bicarbonate of soda and 4½ level teasp. cream of tartar with ½ pt. fresh milk

or

2 level teasp. bicarbonate of soda and 4½ level teasp. cream of tartar with ½ pt. fresh milk

or

4–6 level teasp. baking-powder with ½ pt. fresh milk

Sift flour and salt and lightly rub in the fat; sift in the raising agents and mix well. Add *all the milk at once* and mix *lightly* to a *spongy* dough. Knead very lightly to make the dough smooth and roll out ⅓–½ in. thick. Cut out with a 2-in. cutter, brush with egg *or* milk, if desired, and bake in a hot oven (425°–450° F., Gas 7–8). The dough may be divided into 4 and each piece formed into a round cake and marked into 6.

24–30 scones
Cooking time—about 10 min.

Variations

Cheese Scones: Add 4–6 oz. grated cheese to above proportions.

Cut out in finger shapes or squares.
Cheese Whirls: Add 4–6 oz. grated cheese to the basic recipe. Roll out dough into oblong shape. Spread with cheese and roll up like a Swiss Roll. Cut into slices and lay on greased baking-sheets with the cut side uppermost. Brush with milk or egg. If any cheese is left over, sprinkle it on and bake the whirls in a hot oven (425°–450° F., Gas 7–8).

20–24 scones
Cooking time—10–15 min.

Fruit Scones: Add 2 oz. sugar and 2–4 oz. fruit (currants, sultanas, etc.) to the basic recipe.
Girdle Scones: Add 2–3 oz. currants; roll out ¼ in. thick, cut into 2½-in. rounds or triangles; cook on both sides on a moderately hot girdle about 5 min. till nicely brown and edges dry. Cool in a towel.
Nut Scones: Add 2–4 oz. chopped nuts to the basic recipe.
Sweet Scones: Add 2 oz. sugar and, if liked, 1 egg.
Treacle Scones: Add 1 oz. sugar, 1 teasp. ground cinnamon, 1 teasp. mixed spice, 2 tablesp. black treacle. Put the treacle in with ⅔ of the milk, then add the rest as required.
Wholemeal Nut Scones: Use half wholemeal flour and half plain flour, add 2–4 oz. chopped nuts.

POTATO SCONES

½ lb. cold cooked potatoes
½ oz. margarine   salt
3 oz. plain flour (approx.)

Sift or mash potatoes very smoothly and mix with the melted margarine and salt—the amount of the latter depends on how much salt has been used in cooking the potatoes. The scones are very tasteless unless there is some salt in the mixture. Work in as much flour as the paste will take up and roll out very thinly. Cut into rounds with a 3½-in. cutter, or triangles, and prick well. Place on a moderately hot girdle and cook for 3 min. on each side. Cool in a towel. If desired, scones may be buttered and served hot.

8-10 scones

TEA SCONES

8 oz. plain flour   ¼ teasp. salt   2 oz. margarine   2 oz. castor sugar
2 level teasp. cream of tartar   1 level teasp. bicarbonate of soda   2 eggs water or milk to make a light spongy mixture (average ½–¾ gill)

Sift the flour and salt and lightly rub in the fat. Add the other dry ingredients and mix with the beaten eggs and water to make a light spongy dough. Roll out ¼ in. thick and cut into rounds. Bake on a greased, fairly hot girdle or in a hot oven (450°–425° F., Gas 8–7). If the scones are to be baked in the oven, roll the dough ½ in. thick.

12-15 scones
Cooking time—10 min.

CAKE-MAKING

ONE way of classifying cakes is as follows:

(a) Plain cakes and buns—where the fat is rubbed in and the proportion of fat to flour is small, e.g. rock buns. (b) Plain cakes—where the fat is melted, e.g. gingerbread. (c) Rich cakes— where the fat and sugar are creamed because there is a larger proportion of fat to flour, e.g. queen cakes, sandwich cakes, Dundee cake, etc.—the proportion of sugar, fruit and eggs to the pound of flour is also increased. (d) Sponge cakes—where there is a large proportion of egg, with or without fat, e.g. Swiss roll. (e) Miscellaneous—belonging to no definite class, e.g. jap cakes, brandy snaps.

Preparation of Tins: (a) For small cakes, e.g. queen cakes—grease with clarified fat. (b) For sponge cakes (not Swiss roll)—grease with clarified fat and dust greased tins with equal quantities of castor sugar and flour mixed together—this gives a crisp outside to the cake. (c) Large cake-tins—line with greaseproof paper. Even for plain cakes line the bottom with paper. Treat sandwich tins in the same way. The richer the cake and the longer the baking, the thicker the paper lining should be to protect the cake during cooking.

Round and Square Tins: A square tin takes approximately the same amount of mixture as a round tin which measures 1 in. more in diameter than the length of one side of the square tin. If there is a difference in the depth of the tins this should, of course, be taken into account.

Flour: For large solid rich cakes where a close texture is desired, it is always advisable to use plain flour plus baking-powder or bicarbonate of soda, as required. The richer the cake and the more eggs used, the less baking-powder will be needed, probably none at all. *Self-raising flour:* This may be utilized for some of the smaller cakes, and cakes of the sandwich and spongy types, where the texture of the finished article is more "open" than for large fruit cakes. *Rice-flour:* Is used, e.g. in the making of shortbread, macaroons, etc. *Cornflour:* Sometimes called cornstarch, is another type of flour used generally in conjunction with plain flour. Its addition tends to produce a cake which is rather short and dry, crumbles easily and "melts" in the mouth. *For cake-making, flour should always be sifted.*

Fats: Butter gives the best flavour. Its cost, however, may make it prohibitive, and *margarine* proves a very good substitute; it is easily creamed. *Lard* is flavourless and should only be used alone where there are highly flavoured ingredients introduced, e.g. spices and black treacle. Lard is 100% fat and this must be taken into account when considering proportions. A point to note is that it does not hold air well when creamed, and, for this reason also, is unsuitable for the making of many cakes. Lard is particularly good, combined with margarine, in the making of pastry. There are on the market fats which are sometimes described as "all-purpose" fats. When using these "all-purpose" fats the "fork mix" method is advocated by the manufacturers.

Sugar: Castor sugar is best for most cakes; *granulated sugar* is apt to give a speckled appearance. *Moist brown sugar* is satisfactory for gingerbread and cakes where a good dark brown colour is required. *Loaf sugar* crushed down to suitable small-sized pieces is effective when sprinkled on the top of yeast mixtures such as bath buns, etc. *Icing sugar*, being very fine, is used mostly for icings—glacé, royal, almond paste, etc.; it can be introduced successfully into short crust pastry and some mixtures.

Eggs: All eggs should be very fresh or an unpleasant flavour will be imparted to the cake. New-laid eggs are best for sponge cakes and meringues. In making large cakes the eggs may be added whole, one at a time, each being beaten in very thoroughly to the creamed fat and sugar.

Fruits: It is best to buy *dried fruit* when the grocer gets in his fresh stock. Dry-cleaning of fruit with flour is not to be advocated. No adverse results should arise from washing the fruit immediately before use, so long as it is very thoroughly dried on a clean cloth to remove as much moisture as possible, otherwise it will be heavy and will tend to sink to the bottom of the cake. Stones must always be removed from *raisins*; the sugar is removed from *peel* before shredding and chopping. Citron peel is best for putting on top of a Madeira cake. *Glacé cherries* are very heavy and for most cakes it is advisable to cut them into pieces. *Angelica* (a candied stem) is used more as decoration but it can be chopped as peel and used in the cake.

Caraway Seeds: These should be used with care; they make a delicious cake but are not universally popular.

Nuts: Almonds require to be blanched to remove the skins. Put the nuts into cold water and bring almost to boiling-point; pour away the water and run plenty of cold water over them. Pinch off the skins and rub the nuts dry in a soft cloth. They are usually either chopped or shredded, but if for the top of a Dundee cake, etc., they are generally split into halves and distributed over the top of the cake with the rounded side up. *To brown almonds:* Blanch, skin, shred and place on an oven tray, put in a moderate oven till a good golden colour. Turn frequently, allow to cool and store in a jar. *To make almonds shine:* Brush them over with egg white and dry off in the oven.

Coconut—desiccated or shredded. Desiccated coconut may be included in cake mixtures or used to coat a cake already brushed with jam or spread with butter or glacé icing. Shredded, it may be used for decoration.

Pistachio nuts: Skin by immersing in hot water for a minute or two, then cut or chop. Thin cross sections, three together, can be used as shamrock in decoration, or the finely chopped nuts can be sprinkled for green decoration.

Walnuts are not blanched; they may be chopped up to go into the mixture or left whole for decorating an iced cake. In their chopped state they are used, e.g. to coat the sides of an iced sandwich cake, sieved apricot jam being used to make the nuts adhere to the sides.

POINTS TO REMEMBER

1. Have correct proportions. Fat and sugar are liquefying ingredients, therefore the richer the cake, the less liquid, such as milk, is required; in some cases, none. It is better to add water instead of milk in the sandwich cake type of mixture.

2. For cakes of the sponge variety,

e.g. sandwich cake, as much as possible of the egg should be added to the creamed fat without the addition of flour, unless the mixture appears to be curdling. For fruit cakes, where a close texture is required, add egg and flour alternately.

3. For rich cakes add the fruit at the end, mixed with some of the flour to help to keep the fruit suspended in the cake.

4. Generally speaking the plainer the cake, the hotter the oven; the richer the cake, the cooler the oven. Bake small cakes in the top or the hottest part of the oven, larger cakes in the middle, and very large cakes in the lower part of the oven. Cakes must not be placed over the flame at the sides of a gas oven or too near the element in an electric oven. Never bake a cake on a browning sheet.

5. Avoid opening the oven door before a cake has begun to set. Do not slam the door.

TESTS FOR READINESS

The time given for baking cakes is approximate. Open door carefully and just enough to test cake quickly. The cake should be well risen and evenly browned. Touch the surface lightly and, if it seems firm to the touch, the cake is done. If the impression of the finger remains the cake is not ready. Insert a warm skewer into the cake; if it comes out dry the cake is ready. If the cake is shrinking from the sides of the tin it is probably over-baked.

MEASURING RAISING AGENTS AND SPICES

1 teasp. bicarbonate of soda=
                    1 rounded teasp.
1 teasp. cream of tartar=
                    1 rounded teasp.
1 teasp. baking powder=
                    1 rounded teasp.

For accuracy it is wise to measure in level teaspoons so that 1 rounded teaspoonful of bicarbonate of soda will be 2 level ones. The addition of too much soda gives an unpleasant taste, smell and colour.

PLAIN BUNS or COOKIES
Basic Recipe

(Self-raising flour can be used for any of the following, in which case omit the raising agent.)

1 lb. plain flour   ½ teasp. salt
2–6 oz. margarine or lard or
dripping   4–6 oz. sugar   3 teasp.
baking-powder   2 eggs   1–1½ gill
milk or enough to make a stiff
consistency

Sift flour and salt into bowl, cut in fat with round-bladed knife, then rub with fingertips till quite fine. Add sugar and baking-powder. Mix with egg and milk to a stiff consistency. (The fork with which the buns are mixed should stand up in the mixture.) Divide into pieces and form into rocky heaps on a greased baking-sheet. Bake in a hot oven (450°–425° F., Gas 8–7).

24–32 buns
Cooking time—10–15 min.

Variations

Chocolate Buns: Add 1–1½ oz. cocoa to the flour and 1 teasp. vanilla essence with the milk.

Coconut Buns: Mix in 4 oz. desiccated coconut with the sugar.

Ginger Buns: Add 2 small teasp. ground ginger to the flour and add 4 oz. chopped or grated crystallized ginger with the sugar.

Lemon Buns: Add 1 teasp. lemon essence with the milk. Turn mixture on to floured board and make into a roll. Divide into 24 pieces, form into balls, brush with egg or milk and sprinkle with coarse sugar.

London Buns: Add 2 oz.

chopped peel and 2 teasp. grated lemon rind when adding the sugar and form mixture into balls as for lemon buns. Glaze and sprinkle with coarse sugar. Place 2 pieces of lemon *or* orange peel on top of each bun.

Nut Buns: Add 4 oz. chopped nuts when adding the sugar.

Raspberry Buns: Form basic mixture into 24 balls, make a hole in each bun and place a little raspberry jam in the hole. Close the opening, brush with milk *or* egg and sprinkle with coarse sugar.

Rock Buns: Add 4–6 oz. currants and 2 oz. chopped peel when adding the sugar.

Seed Buns: Add 2 dessertsp. caraway seeds with the sugar.

DOUGHNUTS WITHOUT YEAST

8 oz. plain flour   ⅛ teasp. salt
1½ oz. butter *or* margarine   1½ oz. sugar   a little grated lemon rind
1½ teasp. baking-powder   1 egg
⅔ gill milk or enough to make a light dough

Mix flour and salt, rub in fat. Add other dry ingredients and mix to a light dough with egg and milk. Roll out on a floured board ½ in. thick, cut out and fry as for yeast doughnuts (p. 309).

NOTE: 2 small level teasp. cream of tartar may be used and 1 small level teasp. bicarbonate of soda instead of baking-powder.

12–16 doughnuts

VICTORIA BUNS

10 oz. plain flour   ¼ teasp. salt
3–4 oz. sugar   2 small teasp. ground cinnamon   ¼ teasp. grated nutmeg
1 level teasp. bicarbonate of soda
2 teasp. golden syrup   2 teasp. treacle   4 oz. butter *or* margarine
2 eggs   enough warm milk to make a pouring consistency

DECORATION
Blanched almonds

Grease queen cake or deep patty tins and place half a blanched almond in the bottom of each. Mix all dry ingredients in a bowl, heat the fat, syrup and treacle and add to dry ingredients with the beaten eggs. Add enough warm milk to make a pouring consistency. Half-fill the prepared tins and bake in a moderate oven (350° *F., Gas* 4).

26–30 buns
Cooking time—20–30 min.

PLAIN CAKES

Line the bottom of all cake-tins with greaseproof paper.

DATE AND WALNUT CAKE

¾ lb. plain flour   ¼ teasp. salt
4½ oz. butter *or* margarine   5 oz. sugar   a little grated nutmeg
1½ level teasp. bicarbonate of soda
2 level teasp. cream of tartar   4 oz. chopped dates   1½ oz. chopped walnuts   2 eggs
1½–2 gill milk (approx.)

Sift flour and salt and rub in the fat. Add the other dry ingredients and mix with the eggs and milk to a dropping consistency. Put into a greased 8-in. tin and bake in a fairly hot oven (375° *F., Gas* 5). Reduce heat to moderate (350° *F., Gas* 4) after 15 min.

Cooking time—1¼–1½ hr.

ECONOMICAL SULTANA CAKE

8 oz. plain flour   ⅛ teasp. salt
3 oz. beef dripping   2 level teasp. cream of tartar   1 level teasp. bicarbonate of soda   4 oz. moist sugar   ½ lb. sultanas   2 oz. mixed shredded peel   1 egg
1¼ gill milk (approx.)

Sift flour and salt and rub in the fat. Mix raising agents thoroughly with the flour and add other dry ingredients. Beat egg and add with milk to make a soft dropping consistency. Place in a greased 7-in. cake-tin and bake in a fairly hot oven (375° *F., Gas* 5). Reduce heat after 15 min. to moderate (350° F., *Gas* 4).

Cooking time—1½ hr.

SPICE CAKE

8 oz. plain flour   ½ teasp. salt
3 oz. margarine   1 teasp. mixed
spice   3 oz. sugar   1½ teasp. baking-
powder   1 egg   1–1½ gill milk or
enough to make a soft dropping
consistency

Grease a 6-in. cake-tin and line the bottom with greaseproof paper.

Sift flour, salt and spice into a bowl, cut in fat with a round-bladed knife, then rub with finger-tips till quite fine. Add sugar and baking-powder. Mix with egg and milk to a soft dropping consistency. Put into the cake-tin and bake in a fairly hot oven (375° F., *Gas* 5).

NOTE: Self-raising flour may be used with advantage in the above recipe, in which case omit the baking-powder.

Cooking time—1¼ hr.

GINGERBREAD

GINGERBREAD

¾ lb. plain flour   ½ teasp. salt
¼ oz. ground ginger   3 oz. sugar
3 oz. lard   ½ lb. black treacle
4–6 tablesp. milk   1 level teasp.
bicarbonate of soda   1 egg

Sift the flour, salt and ginger into a bowl, add the sugar. Put the fat, treacle and most of the milk into a pan and warm them. Dissolve the soda in the rest of the milk. Pour the warm liquid into the flour, add the beaten egg and the dissolved soda and beat well—the mixture should be soft enough to run easily from the spoon. Pour into a greased 7–8-in. tin, or into a bread-tin and bake in a moderate oven (350°–335° F., *Gas* 4–3), reduce heat to the lower temperature after 20 min.

Cooking time—about 1¼–1½ hr.

GOOD GINGERBREAD

8 oz. plain flour   ½ teasp. salt
1–2 level teasp. ground cinnamon
1–2 level teasp. mixed spice   2 level
teasp. ground ginger   2 oz. dates or
raisins, or sultanas   1 level teasp.
bicarbonate of soda   2–4 oz.
crystallized ginger   2 oz. blanched
and chopped almonds   4 oz. butter
or margarine   4 oz. sugar
4 oz. treacle   2 eggs
a little warm milk, if required

Grease a 7-in. tin and line the bottom with greased greaseproof paper.

Mix flour and salt and other dry ingredients with prepared fruit, crystallized ginger—cut into pieces, and almonds—chopped roughly. Melt fat, sugar and treacle, add to dry ingredients with beaten eggs. If the mixture seems stiff, add a little warm milk but do not make it too soft. Pour into the tin, and bake in a warm to cool oven (335°–310° F., *Gas* 3–2).

Cooking time—1¾–2 hr.

MOIST GINGERBREAD

10 oz. plain flour   ½ level teasp.
bicarbonate of soda   ¼ teasp. salt
4 oz. brown sugar   2 level teasp.
ground cinnamon   2 level teasp.
ground ginger   4 oz. sultanas
1–2 oz. shredded almonds   2 oz.
treacle   2 oz. golden syrup
6 oz. butter or margarine   2 eggs
warm milk to mix

Grease a 7-in. tin and line the bottom with greased greaseproof paper.

Mix sifted flour and soda with other dry ingredients. Cream treacle, syrup and fat together. Add dry ingredients, beaten eggs and enough warm milk to make a stiff consistency. Put into the tin and bake in a moderate oven (350°–335° F., *Gas* 4–3), reduce heat to the lower temperature after 20 min.

Cooking time—1¼–1½ hr.

STEAMED GINGERBREAD

8 oz. plain flour $\frac{1}{4}$ teasp. salt
1 teacup medium oatmeal   3 oz.
butter or margarine   1 level teasp.
mixed spice   2 level teasp. ground
ginger   2 level teasp. bicarbonate of
soda   2 oz. moist sugar   2 oz.
sultanas or raisins   2 tablesp. black
treacle   1 egg
buttermilk or sour milk

Grease a 7-in. cake-tin and line the bottom with greased greaseproof paper.

Sift flour and salt, add oatmeal, rub in the fat and mix with other dry ingredients. Add treacle, mixed with beaten egg, and enough milk to make a dropping consistency. Put into the tin, cover with paper and steam 1$\frac{1}{2}$ hr. Place in a moderate to slow oven (350°–335° F., Gas 4–3) to dry for 15–20 min.

Cooking time—about 1$\frac{3}{4}$ hr.

RICH CAKES—LARGE
RICH CAKE
Basic Recipe

6 oz. butter or margarine   6 oz.
sugar   3 eggs   8 oz. plain flour
$\frac{1}{4}$ teasp. salt   1$\frac{1}{2}$–2 level teasp.
baking powder
milk or water to mix

Line a 7-in. cake-tin with greaseproof paper. Cream the fat and sugar till white, whisk eggs and add to the fat, a little at a time, beating well between each addition. If mixture shows signs of curdling, add a little flour. Sift the flour and salt. Add the flour to the mixture, stirring in lightly with the baking-powder. (The eggs may be added whole and the egg and flour may be added alternately for a close-textured cake, e.g. fruit cake.) Add milk or water to make a fairly soft consistency. Turn into the cake-tin and bake in a moderate oven (350° F., Gas 4).

Cooking time—1$\frac{1}{4}$–1$\frac{1}{2}$ hr.

Variations of Basic Recipe

Cherry Cake: Add 4 oz. chopped glacé cherries when adding the flour.

Cornflour Cake: Use 6 oz. cornflour and 2 oz. flour in the basic mixture. Dredge top of the cake with castor sugar before baking. The tin may be prepared by greasing and dusting with equal quantities of sugar and flour.

Fruit Cake: Add 6–8 oz. sultanas, currants, raisins or dates to basic mixture. For fruit cake add eggs and flour alternately. Stir in fruit mixed with some of the flour *after* eggs have been added.

Ginger Cake: Sift $\frac{1}{2}$ teasp. ground ginger with the flour, add 2–4 oz. coarsely chopped crystallized ginger with the flour

Ground Rice Cake: Use 6 oz. flour and 2 oz. ground rice in basic mixture.

Lemon Cake: Add the grated rind of 2 lemons with the flour. The cake may be iced when cold with lemon glacé icing (p. 334).

Madeira Cake: Add the grated rind of 1 lemon with the flour. Place 2 strips of citron peel on top of the cake when mixture has begun to set (after about 30 min.).

Seed Cake: Add 2 teasp. caraway seeds with the flour.

AMERICAN WALNUT CAKE

2$\frac{1}{2}$ oz. butter or margarine   3 oz.
castor sugar   2 eggs   1 oz.
roughly-chopped walnuts $\frac{1}{2}$ teasp.
vanilla essence   5 oz. plain flour
2 level teasp. baking-powder
pinch of salt   American frosting
(p. 333) using 8 oz. sugar, etc.
some walnut halves

Line a 6-in. cake-tin with greaseproof paper. Cream the fat and sugar till light and white, add the beaten eggs gradually, beating well between each addition. Add the walnuts, essence and the sifted flour, baking-powder and salt. Put the mixture into the cake-tin and bake in a moderate oven (350° F., Gas 4).

When cold cut the cake through the middle, spread with a small amount of American frosting and sandwich together again. Coat with American frosting and decorate immediately with the walnuts.

Cooking time—1–1¼ hr.

BIRTHDAY CAKE

4 oz. butter or margarine   4 oz. moist brown sugar   1½ oz. golden syrup   2 eggs   6 oz. plain flour ⅛ teasp. salt   1 level teasp. baking-powder   1 level teasp. mixed spice 11 oz. mixed fruit—sultanas, currants, glacé cherries 2 oz. candied peel or marmalade ½ gill milk (approx.)

Line a 6–7-in. cake-tin with greaseproof paper. Cream fat, sugar and syrup thoroughly. Whisk eggs and add alternately with the sifted flour, salt and baking-powder, beating well with each addition. Add remaining ingredients and fruit, which has been mixed with a little of the flour. Mix to a fairly soft consistency with milk and place in the cake-tin. Bake for ½ hr. in a moderate oven (350° F., Gas 4) and a further 2–2½ hr. in a cool oven (310°–290° F., Gas 2–1).

NOTE: This cake can be coated with almond paste (p. 334) and decorated with royal icing (p. 335).

Cooking time—about 3 hr.

CHRISTMAS CAKE (1)

8 oz. butter or margarine   8 oz. castor sugar   ½ teasp. gravy browning   8 oz. plain flour ¼ teasp. salt   1 level teasp. mixed spice   ½ level teasp. baking-powder 5–6 eggs   1 lb. currants   8 oz. raisins   4 oz. glacé cherries   2 oz. chopped peel   4 oz. blanched, chopped almonds   milk, if necessary 4–5 tablesp. brandy (optional)

Line an 8-in. cake-tin with greaseproof paper.

Cream fat and sugar until white; add gravy browning. Sift together flour, salt, mixed spice and baking-powder. Add egg and flour alternately to the creamed fat, beating well between each addition. Stir in the prepared fruit, almonds and, if necessary, add a little milk to make a heavy dropping consistency. Place the mixture in the cake-tin and tie a piece of paper round the outside of the tin. Smooth the mixture and make a depression in the centre. Bake in a warm oven (335° F., Gas 3) for ½ hr., then reduce heat to 290° F., Gas 1 for a further 3–3½ hr. Allow to firm before removing from tin and when cold remove paper. Prick bottom of cake well and sprinkle brandy over. Leave for a few days before icing (see p. 333).

Cooking time—4 hr.

CHRISTMAS CAKE (2)

4 oz. butter   12 oz. plain flour 6 oz. moist sugar   ½ oz. ground ginger   ½ lb. raisins   ½ pt. cream 5 tablesp. treacle   2 eggs 1 tablesp. vinegar 2 level teasp. bicarbonate of soda

Grease and line a 7-in. cake-tin.

Warm the butter but do not allow it to oil. Sift the flour into a bowl, add the sugar, ginger and chopped raisins. Mix well, then stir in the butter, cream, treacle and well-beaten eggs. Beat for a few minutes. Pour the vinegar on to the soda and stir into the mixture. Put into the prepared cake-tin and place immediately in a warm oven (335° F., Gas 3). Reduce heat to 310° F., Gas 2.

Cooking time—2¼ hr.

DUNDEE CAKE

6 oz. butter or margarine   6 oz. castor sugar   3 eggs   ½ gill brandy (optional)   8 oz. plain flour

⅛ teasp. salt   1 level teasp. baking-powder   ½ teasp. ground cinnamon   ⅛ teasp. grated nutmeg   grated rind of 1 lemon   6 oz. currants   3 oz. stone, chopped raisins   4 oz. sultanas   2 oz. chopped, mixed peel   2 oz. chopped and blanched almonds   milk, if necessary

Line a 7-in. cake-tin with greaseproof paper. Cream the fat and sugar; add the well-beaten eggs, one at a time, beating between each addition (add a little flour if any sign of curdling), and stir in the brandy, if used. Sift flour, salt and baking-powder, mix prepared fruit with a small amount of the flour. Mix in the flour, fruit and lemon rind and half of the chopped almonds. If necessary add a little milk but do not make too moist. Place the mixture in the cake-tin; sprinkle over the remainder of the almonds and bake in a moderate oven (350° F., Gas 4), reduce heat after ¾ hr. to warm to cool (335°–310° F., Gas 3–2).

Cooking time—2–2¼ hr.

ICED COCONUT CAKE

4 oz. self-raising flour   pinch of salt   3 oz. butter or margarine   3 oz. castor sugar   2 eggs   1 oz. desiccated coconut   pink glacé icing, using 4 oz. icing sugar

Grease and line a 7½ in. × 3¾ in. and 2¼ in. deep loaf tin.

Sift the flour and salt. Cream the fat until soft, add the sugar and beat until light in colour and soft in texture. Add the eggs one at a time, together with 1 tablesp. sifted flour. Stir, then beat well. Fold in the coconut and the rest of the flour carefully but thoroughly. Put the mixture into the prepared tin, smooth level and bake for 40 min. on the middle shelf of a moderate oven (350° F., Gas 4). When cold pour the glacé icing over the top of the loaf.

Sprinkle a little coconut over the top and leave to set.

MOCHA CAKE

1½ tablesp. cocoa   2 tablesp. hot water   4 oz. margarine   5 oz. castor sugar   2 eggs   4 oz. self-raising flour   1 tablesp. milk

For the icing:
3 oz. margarine   8 oz. icing sugar (sieved)   1 tablesp. milk   1 dessertsp. coffee essence   ½ lb. almond paste   1 oz. chopped walnuts   5 walnut halves to decorate

Grease an 8-in. sandwich tin, line the bottom with greaseproof paper. Blend the cocoa and hot water together and leave to cool. Cream the margarine and sugar till very light; add the blended cocoa mixture. Beat in the eggs one at a time, adding a little sifted flour with the second. Fold in the flour, then the milk. Place in the tin, bake on the middle shelf of a pre-heated moderate oven (350° F., Gas 4) for 30–40 min. To make the icing: Cream the margarine with ½ the icing sugar until very light. Add remaining icing sugar with the milk and coffee essence. Beat until smooth and creamy. Roll out the almond paste thinly, cut into 10 triangles (1 in. wide and 3 in. long approx.). Make the remaining paste into balls. Leave to dry for 2–3 hr.

Spread the cake sides with icing and roll in chopped walnuts. Cover the top with icing and make a pattern with a fork. Decorate the top with the almond paste triangles and balls, the walnuts and remaining icing piped into stars.

ORANGE CAKE

6 oz. butter or margarine   6 oz. castor sugar   3 eggs   8 oz. plain flour   ¼ teasp. salt   1½ level teasp. baking-powder   1 orange

Line a 7-in. cake-tin with greaseproof paper. Cream the fat

and sugar till white; add the
beaten eggs gradually, beating
well between each addition. Sift
flour, salt and baking-powder and
add, with the grated rind and juice
of the orange, to the creamed fat;
mix well. Place in the cake-tin
and bake in a moderate oven (350°
F., Gas 4) for 1–1¼ hr.

SAND CAKE

4 oz. butter or margarine grated
rind of 1 lemon 4 oz. castor sugar
2 large eggs 4 oz. cornflour
½ oz. ground rice pinch of salt
¼ level teasp. baking-powder
ratafia crumbs (optional)

Grease a border mould or 6-in.
cake-tin and, if liked, coat with
ratafia biscuit crumbs or with
equal quantities of castor sugar and
flour.

Cream the fat with the lemon
rind; add the sugar and cream
again. Beat the eggs and add them
gradually, beating well between
each addition. Sift together the
cornflour, ground rice, salt and
baking-powder. Add the flour
lightly to the creamed fat, ⅓ at a
time, and put the mixture into
the mould. Bake in a moderate
oven (350°–335° F., Gas 4–3).
Cooking time—about 1 hr.

SIMNEL CAKE

Mixture: as for Birthday Cake
(p. 320) or any other fruit cake.
Almond paste: 6 oz. ground almonds, etc. (p. 334).
Glacé icing: 2 oz. icing sugar, etc.
(p. 333).
Line a 6–7-in. cake-tin with
greaseproof paper. Cut off about
⅓ of the almond paste and roll out
into a round slightly less than the
diameter of the tin to be used.
Place half the cake mixture in the
tin, cover with a round of almond
paste and place the remaining
cake mixture on top. Bake in a
moderate oven (350° F., Gas 4)
for ½ hr., reduce heat to cool (310°

–290° F., Gas 2–1) for 2–2½ hr.
Leave for 24 hr. Using about half
the remaining almond paste, cover
the top of the cake. With the
remainder, make small balls and
place these at even intervals round
top edge of the cake. Brush them
over with egg wash. Tie a band
of greaseproof paper tightly round
the top of the cake. Place in a hot
oven until balls are nicely
browned. When cool, pour glacé
icing into the centre of the cake
and decorate as required with almond paste eggs, small chicks, etc.
Cooking time—about 3 hr.

Note: This cake used to be
served only on Mother's Day but
is now often served on Easter
Sunday.

WALNUT LAYER CAKE

6 oz. butter or margarine 6 oz.
castor sugar 3 eggs 6 oz. plain
flour pinch of salt
2 teasp. coffee essence
1 level teasp. baking-powder

FILLING

2 oz. butter or margarine 4 oz.
icing sugar 1–2 teasp. coffee
essence 2 oz. chopped walnuts

DECORATION

American frosting, using 8 oz.
sugar, etc.

Cream fat and sugar; beat in
the eggs, one at a time. Fold in
the sifted flour, baking-powder
and salt and add coffee essence.
Put mixture into a 6-in. lined
cake-tin (or it may be baked in 2
or 3 sandwich cake-tins) and bake
in a moderate oven (350° F., Gas
4) for 1 hr. Cut the cake into
three sections when cold. Make
the filling: cream together the fat
and sugar, and add the coffee
essence and chopped walnuts.
Spread each section with filling
and sandwich together again.
Make the American frosting and
quickly pour over the cake to cover

it completely.

To finish the cake put a few half-walnuts on top before the icing has set.

WEDDING CAKE

NOTE: These quantities are sufficient for a 3-tier cake.

3–3½ lb. flour   ¼ teasp. salt   3 level teasp. ground cinnamon   3 level teasp. ground mace   1 nutmeg (grated)   1½ teasp. baking-powder 3 lb. butter   3 lb. castor sugar 1½ teasp. parisian essence or other gravy browning   24 large eggs 5½ lb. currants   2 lb. sultanas 1–1½ lb. glacé cherries   1–1¼ lb. mixed chopped peel   rind and juice of 1 lemon   ½–1 lb. blanched, chopped almonds   1½ gill rum or brandy or rum and brandy

Prepare and line 3 cake-tins, one 12 in. diameter, one 8 in., and one 4 in. diameter.

Sift together flour, salt, spices and baking-powder. Mix together all the fruit with a little of the measured flour. Cream the butter and sugar very well, add browning. Add egg and flour alternately to the creamed fat, beating well between each addition. Stir in the prepared fruit, almonds and brandy. Divide half of the mixture between the 2 smaller tins, and put the remaining half of the mixture in the biggest tin. Tie a thick band of brown paper round the outside of each tin. Smooth the mixture and make a depression in the centre of each cake. Bake the 4-in. cake for 2–3 hr., the 8-in. cake for 3½–4 hr., and the 12-in. cake for 5–6 hr. Put in a cool oven (310° F., Gas 2) for the first ½ hr., then reduce heat to very cool (290°–240° F., Gas 1-½) for the remainder of the time.

To finish the cakes see pp. 334–6.

To cover the 4-in. cake with almond paste 1 lb. ground al-

monds, etc., will be required; 2 lb. ground almonds, etc., for the 8-in. cake and 3 lb. ground almonds, etc., for the 12-in. cake.

For the royal icing use 1 lb. icing sugar, etc., for the 4-in. cake, 2 lb. for the 8-in. cake and 3 lb. sugar, etc., for the 12-in. cake.

Decoration of each cake is then completed upon silver boards (of correct size) covered with a lace d'oyley. The cake is then assembled by placing one cake on top of the other with pillars supporting them. The pillars for the bottom tier should be 3 in. in height and for the top the pillars should be 4 in. high. Place a silver vase containing white flowers and smilax on top.

SANDWICH CAKES

In each case the tin is greased and the bottom lined with paper.

Basic Recipes
SANDWICH CAKE

3 oz. butter or margarine   4 oz. sugar   2 eggs   5 oz. plain flour 1 level teasp. baking-powder pinch of salt

Cream fat and sugar well; add egg yolks and continue beating. Sift flour, baking-powder and salt and stir into the mixture. Fold in the stiffly-whisked egg whites; add a little tepid water if necessary to make the mixture "easy". Place in a prepared 7-in. sandwich cake-tin and bake in a moderate oven (350° F., Gas 4).

NOTE: Self-raising flour may be used with satisfactory results, in which case no baking-powder is required.

Cooking time—30–40 min.

LARGE SANDWICH CAKE

3 oz. butter or margarine   4½ oz. sugar   3 eggs   4½ oz. plain flour pinch of salt 2 level teasp. baking-powder

As for Victoria sandwich cake (below), using an 8-in. sandwich cake-tin. Bake in a moderate oven (350° F., Gas 4).
Cooking time—50–60 min.

SMALL SANDWICH CAKE
(useful for icing variations)

2 oz. butter or margarine 3 oz. castor sugar 2 eggs 3 oz. self-raising flour pinch of salt
½ level teasp. baking-powder
cold water as required—
1–2 dessertsp.

As for Victoria sandwich (below), using a 6-in. sandwich tin. Bake in a moderate oven (350° F., Gas 4).
Cooking time—40 min.

VICTORIA SANDWICH

4 oz. butter or margarine 4 oz. castor sugar 2 eggs 4 oz. plain flour pinch of salt
1½ level teasp. baking-powder

Cream fat and sugar very thoroughly. Add well-whisked eggs gradually, beating well between each addition—if sign of curdling, add some flour. Sift flour, salt and baking-powder and stir lightly into the creamed fat and eggs. Mix to a soft dropping consistency, adding a little water if necessary. Place the mixture in a prepared 7-in. sandwich tin and bake in a moderate oven (350° F., Gas 4).
Cooking time—40–45 min.

Variations
BATTENBURG CAKE

2 Victoria sandwich cakes made in oblong tins, one white and the other coloured pink 1 tablesp. apricot glaze (p. 333) almond paste (p. 334) using 3 oz. ground almonds, etc.

DECORATION
Glacé cherries angelica

Cut the cakes into strips 8–9 in. long and 1½ in. square at ends—

2 pink and 2 white pieces will be needed. Join these together with apricot glaze to make a square end having pink and white pieces alternately. Roll almond paste into an oblong, wide enough and long enough to wrap round the cake, leaving the ends open. Trim edges of almond paste. Spread top of cake with apricot glaze and invert on to almond paste. Spread the remaining three sides with glaze, roll up firmly and join almond paste neatly. To decorate, pinch the two top edges between thumb and forefinger. Mark the top of the cake lattice-fashion with a knife and decorate with cherries and angelica.

ICED SANDWICH CAKE
1 small sandwich cake

FILLING
Butter icing (p. 336) using 2 oz. butter, etc.

DECORATION
Glacé icing (p. 333) using 7 oz. icing sugar

Colour and flavour the butter icing as desired. Cut the sandwich cake through the middle and spread with just over half of the butter icing. Sandwich together again and remove any loose crumbs with a clean pastry brush. Place cake on a cooling tray over a plate. Mix glacé icing to coating consistency, colour and flavour carefully. Pour icing on to centre of cake and allow to run over top and down sides. Try to avoid touching the top with a knife—a knife will be necessary for completing the sides. Allow to set.

Decorate, if desired, by piping with remaining butter icing.

ORANGE SANDWICH CAKE

1 large sandwich cake
orange-flavoured butter icing
crystallized orange slices

Cut cake through centre and spread with orange-flavoured butter icing; sandwich together again. Spread the top of the cake with icing, smooth with a knife and decorate with slices of crystallized orange.

NOTE: A more pronounced flavour may be obtained by adding the finely-grated rind of 1 orange when mixing the cake.

Lemon may be substituted for orange if liked.

CHOCOLATE SANDWICH

3½ oz. self-raising flour   ½ oz. cocoa
pinch of salt   4 oz. butter or
margarine   4 oz. castor sugar
2 eggs   chocolate butter icing
(p. 336), using 4 oz. butter, etc.

Grease and line an 8-in. sandwich tin. Sift the flour, cocoa and salt. Cream the fat until soft, add sugar, and beat until the mixture is light in colour and fluffy in texture. Add the eggs one at a time with 1 tablesp. of the sifted dry ingredients, beat well between each addition. Stir in remainder of dry ingredients lightly but thoroughly. Put the mixture into the tin, smooth level. Bake for 30–35 min. on the middle shelf of a fairly hot oven (375° F., Gas 5). When the sandwich is cold, cut in half horizontally. Spread ½ the butter icing in the centre of the cake; put the rest on the top. Decorate with the end of a round-bladed knife and finish with chocolate drops, walnuts, etc.

COFFEE LAYER CAKE

4 oz. butter or margarine   4 oz.
castor sugar   2 eggs   8 oz. plain
flour   1 teasp. baking-powder
2 teasp. soluble coffee powder
3 tablesp. milk

MOCHA ICING
2 teasp. soluble coffee powder
2 oz. chocolate   4 tablesp. water

3 oz. butter or margarine
1 lb. icing sugar

DECORATION
Almonds

Cream the fat and sugar until very light and add the eggs one at a time with a dessertsp. of flour—beat well. Sift the flour, baking-powder and coffee powder and fold lightly into the mixture with the milk. Pour into 2 greased sandwich tins and spread evenly. Bake in a fairly hot oven (375° F., Gas 5) for 35–40 min. until firm. Cool.

To make the mocha icing: dissolve coffee powder and grated chocolate in the almost boiling water. Cream the fat and 2 tablesp. of the sugar. Beat well. Add the rest of the sugar and liquid alternately, beating until it is smooth and easy to spread.

Cut the two cakes across in half, and sandwich the halves together with some of the icing, spreading the rest of the icing on the top and sides and frost or "rough up" with a fork. Decorate with blanched almonds.

RICH CAKES—SMALL

The following is a suitable mixture for small cakes; it can be varied in many ways.

Basic Recipe

2 oz. butter or margarine   2 oz.
castor sugar   3 oz. self-
raising flour or 3 oz. plain flour and
1 level teasp. baking-powder
pinch of salt
water or milk as required

Beat the fat and sugar until creamy and white. Whisk the egg and add gradually; beat well between each addition. Sift together the flour, salt and baking-powder. Gently stir flour, etc., into creamed fat; add milk or water to make a soft dropping consistency (water is considered best). Half-fill greased bun tins with the mixture and bake in a fairly hot to moderate oven (375°–350° F., Gas 5–4).

NOTE: This mixture may be baked in paper cases and decorated with glacé icing or cherries.

10–12 cakes

Cooking time—15–20 min.

Variations

Cherry Cakes: Add 1–2 oz. coarsely chopped glacé cherries with the flour.

Chocolate Cakes: Sift ½ oz. cocoa with the flour, and add a few drops of vanilla essence with the water or milk. The cakes may be iced with chocolate glacé icing (p. 334).

Coconut Cakes: Add ½ oz. coconut with the flour and add ¼ teasp. vanilla essence with the milk or water.

Lemon Cakes: Add the grated rind of 1 lemon with the flour, and ice with lemon glacé icing (p. 334).

Madeleines: Bake the basic mixture in greased dariole moulds. Turn out when baked; cool. Spread all round top and side with warmed apricot jam. Roll in desiccated coconut, decorate with ½ glacé cherry.

Nut Cakes: Add 1–2 oz. coarsely chopped walnuts, almonds, etc., with the flour.

Queen Cakes: Add 1–2 oz. currants *or* sultanas with the flour, or a few currants may be placed in the bottom of each queen cake tin and the mixture placed on top.

APRICOT BASKETS

The basic mixture baked in small bun tins   1 small can apricots
¼ pt. packet lemon jelly   a little whipped, sweetened cream
piece of angelica 6 in. long

Whilst the buns are cooling, drain the apricots from the syrup. Make up the syrup to just under ¼ pt. with water, bring to the boil and pour on to the jelly. Stir until

dissolved and leave to cool until it is just starting to thicken. *To make the baskets:* Put an apricot, round side uppermost, on each bun, coat with the jelly, which must be just starting to thicken. Pipe small stars of whipped cream around the apricot. Soak the angelica in warm water, cut into strips ¼ in. wide and long enough to arch over the buns to form a "handle". Make two small holes in each bun with a skewer to keep the handle in place.

BUTTERFLY CAKES

The basic mixture (p. 325) cooked in greased bouché (small) tins
1 gill sweetened and flavoured cream   a little jam

Cut a thin slice from the top of each cake, cut each slice in two to make wings; dredge with icing sugar. Spread cut top of cake with a little red jam, pipe a large rosette of beaten cream on this and place wings in position.

GENOESE PASTRY (Base for small cakes)

Basic Recipe

4 oz. flour   pinch of salt   4 eggs
4 oz. castor sugar
3 oz. butter or margarine

Sift our and salt. Beat eggs and sugar in a basin over a pan of hot water till thick. Clarify the fat and fold lightly into egg mixture, then fold in salted flour. Pour into lined Swiss roll tin and bake in a moderate oven (350° F., Gas 4). When cold (after 24 hr.) cut and use as desired for small iced cakes, etc.

Cooking time—30–40 min.

Variations

CONTINENTAL CAKES

Genoese pastry   butter icing (p. 336), using 1½ oz. butter, etc., flavoured with vanilla and coloured pink   glacé icing (p. 333), using 12 oz. icing sugar

Cut Genoese pastry into rounds $1\frac{1}{2}$ in. in diameter or into diamond shapes 1 in. by $1\frac{3}{4}$ in. Pile some butter icing on to the top of each cake and smooth off with a knife to shape of cake. Allow icing to harden and stand cakes on wire cooling tray over a large dish. Make glacé icing and coat cakes; the butter icing should just show through. When set decorate by piping lines or spirals of coloured glacé icing on cakes.

20–26 cakes

MOCHA FINGERS

Genoese pastry shredded browned almonds (p. 315) coffee butter icing (p. 336), using 2–3 oz. butter, etc.

When Genoese pastry is cold, spread top with coffee butter icing, rather roughly. Press shredded browned almonds over and dredge with icing sugar. Cut into fingers 3 in. by 1 in.

SPONGES
SAVOY FINGERS

5 oz. plain flour 1 oz. cornflour
pinch of salt 4 eggs 5 oz. sugar

Sift together flour, cornflour and salt. Beat the whites of the eggs stiffly, add the sugar and beat well again. Stir in the beaten yolks and fold in the sifted flour. Place the mixture into a bag with a plain $\frac{1}{2}$-in. pipe and pipe on to a greased baking-sheet in 3-in. lengths. Dust the biscuits with castor sugar. Bake in a moderate oven (350° F., Gas 4).

NOTE: These biscuits are particularly useful for making such sweets as Charlotte Russe (p. 290).
28 fingers
Cooking time—10–20 min.

SPONGE CAKE

4 oz. plain flour pinch of salt
3 eggs $4\frac{1}{2}$ oz. castor sugar
grated lemon rind jam

Grease and dust a 6-in. tin with 1 teasp. flour and 1 teasp. castor sugar, mixed together. Sift the flour and salt. Beat the eggs and sugar over a pan of hot water till thick and creamy. Fold flour, salt and lemon lightly into the egg and turn the mixture into the tin. Bake in a warm oven (335° F., Gas 3). When cold, split the sponge and spread with jam. Dust with icing sugar.

This may be cooked in a border or other mould if to be used as the base of a sweet.

Cooking time—45 min.

SPONGE CAKES—SMALL

3 oz. plain flour pinch of salt
3 eggs 3 oz. sugar
1 level teasp. baking-powder
$\frac{1}{4}$ teasp. vanilla essence

As for Sponge Cake. Put the mixture into oblong sponge cake-tins prepared by greasing and dusting with equal quantities of flour and castor sugar. Half-fill the tins and dredge the tops with castor sugar. Bake in a moderate oven (350°–335° F., Gas 4–3) until well risen, firm and a pale fawn colour.

10–12 cakes
Cooking time—20 min.

SPONGE DROPS

4 oz. plain flour pinch of salt
1 level teasp. baking-powder
2 eggs 4 oz. castor sugar jam
$\frac{1}{4}$ pt. sweetened and flavoured, whipped cream or mock cream

Sift together flour, salt and baking-powder. Whisk eggs and sugar together over hot water till thick and creamy; fold the flour in lightly. Force out into drops or put teaspoonfuls on a greased, floured baking-sheet. Dredge thickly with castor sugar and bake in a moderate oven (375°–350° F., Gas 5–4).

When cold, spread half of the drops with jam, and force a rose

of cream on the remaining half.
Sandwich them together.

6–7 doubles
Cooking time—10–15 min.

SWISS ROLL

3 oz. plain flour   pinch of salt
1 level teasp. baking-powder
3 fresh eggs   3 oz. castor sugar
¼ teasp. vanilla essence
2 tablesp. raspberry jam

Line and grease a Swiss roll tin.
Sift flour, salt and baking-powder. Beat eggs and sugar in a bowl over a pan of hot water till thick and pale in colour. Do not let the bottom of the bowl touch the water. Lightly fold in flour, etc., and add the vanilla essence. Spread on the tin and bake in a hot oven (425° F., Gas 7). Quick cooking is essential to keep the roll moist. Sprinkle castor sugar on to a sheet of kitchen paper, turn the roll on to this and cut half-way through the roll, about 1 in. from bottom end. Spread the roll with the warm jam to within ½ in. of edge. Turn in the 1 in. at the bottom to make the initial roll and continue to roll up firmly with the aid of the kitchen paper. Press gently to keep in place. Remove paper and dust with castor sugar. (A very *lightly* damped clean tea-cloth may be used instead of paper.)
NOTE: If the edges are very crisp it is advisable to trim them before rolling or the roll may crack.

Cooking time—7 min.

CHOCOLATE SWISS ROLL

As for Swiss Roll, with the addition of 2–3 teasp. cocoa sifted with the flour.

When the roll is cooked, turn on to sugared paper, place a piece of greaseproof paper on top and roll up. When the roll has cooled, unroll it gently and spread with vanilla butter icing (p. 336). Roll up again. Dust with castor sugar.

MISCELLANEOUS CAKES

ALMOND FINGERS

PASTRY
6 oz. margarine   8 oz. plain flour
pinch of salt   4 oz. sugar   2 oz.
cakecrumbs   2 oz. ground almonds
1 egg yolk   raspberry jam

TOPPING
3 egg whites   8 oz. castor sugar
3 oz. blanched, chopped almonds
¼–½ teasp. almond essence

Make the pastry: rub fat into sifted flour and salt; add sugar, crumbs and ground almonds. Mix with egg yolk and enough water to make a stiff consistency. Roll out to ¼ in. thickness and line a shallow baking-tin 13 in. by 9 in. Bake lightly in a moderate oven (350° F., Gas 4). When nearly cooked spread with raspberry jam.
Make the topping: whisk egg whites stiffly, fold in sugar, chopped almonds and essence, put into a saucepan and stir lightly till mixture boils. Spread on to pastry, return to oven and bake in a moderate-warm oven at 350°–335° F., Gas 4–3, until set and lightly browned. When cold cut into fingers about 3 in. long and 1 in. wide.

18 fingers
Cooking time—about 30–40 min.

ANGEL CAKE

2 oz. flour   4½ oz. castor sugar
½ pt. egg whites   pinch of salt
½ teasp. cream of tartar
½ teasp. vanilla essence

Use a 6-in. sandwich cake-tin or a funnel tin which is not greased. Sift the flour and sugar separately three times, then sift the flour with ¼ of the sugar. Put the egg white and salt in a large, clean, dry bowl and whisk until frothy. Sprinkle on the cream of tartar and continue whisking till the white stands up in peaks. Avoid over-whisking so that the white has lost its glossiness. Lightly beat in the sugar and flavouring, then, using a tablespoon, fold in the sifted flour and sugar carefully and gradually. Pour into tin and gently cut through mixture with a knife to release air bubbles. Bake for 40–45 min. in a very cool oven (290° F., Gas 1), increasing the heat to 335° F., Gas 3) for the last 10–15 min. Allow the cake to stand in the inverted tin for 30 min., then turn out on to a cooling tray.

NOTE: When top springs back on finger pressure the cake is considered ready.

COCONUT CONES

2 egg whites   5 oz. castor sugar
5–6 oz. desiccated coconut
1 teasp. ground rice or semolina

Beat the egg whites stiffly, stir in the other ingredients. Make into small cone shapes or, if desired, pack the mixture into wet egg-cups and turn out on to a greased baking-sheet. Bake in a cool oven (310° F., Gas 2) until fawn colour.

NOTE: If desired, cones may be coloured pink by adding carmine to egg whites while whisking.

12–14 cones

JAP CAKES

2 egg whites   4 oz. castor sugar
4 oz. ground almonds   a few drops
almond essence   glacé icing (p. 333)
butter icing (p. 336) using 1½ oz.
butter, etc., flavoured with coffee

Grease and flour a small baking-tray. Whisk egg whites—not too stiffly. Whisk in half of the castor sugar, then fold in ground almonds, essence and remaining sugar, lightly. Spread the mixture evenly over the prepared tray. Bake in a moderate oven (350° F., Gas 4) until almost set, then cut at once into rounds 1½ in. in diameter, return them to the oven

with the trimmings, until quite firm, and place on a cooling tray. Allow trimmings to continue cooking till a good golden colour, and when cold crush with a rolling-pin and pass through a fine sieve. Sandwich rounds together in pairs with butter icing, spread top and sides smoothly with butter icing and coat with the sieved crumbs.

Re-shape the cakes, using a knife, and decorate the top of each with a little pink glacé icing dropped in the centre.

12–14 cakes
Cooking time—20–30 min.

MERINGUES

2 egg whites   pinch of salt   4 oz.
castor sugar   ½ pt. sweetened and
flavoured cream

Place egg whites and salt in a clean dry bowl and whisk until whites stand up in points. Beat in 2–3 teasp. of sugar, then lightly fold in remainder. Using a bag and plain vegetable pipe, force the mixture in shell shapes on to greaseproof paper on a baking-sheet. Alternatively, use 2 dessertsp. to shape oval meringues, dip the spoons in cold water. Dredge with castor sugar and bake in a very cool oven (265° F., Gas ½). When meringues are firm, loosen from paper and press in the soft centre; return to oven till dry and crisp. When cool, sandwich 2 meringue shells together with whipped cream. Decorate with glacé cherries and angelica.

12 shells or 6 doubles
Cooking time—3–4 hr.

PRINCESS CAKES

7 oz. butter or margarine   1–2 oz.
castor sugar   8 oz. self-raising flour
pinch of salt   grated rind of
½ orange   orange butter icing
(p. 336)
chocolate glacé icing (p. 334)

Beat fat and sugar till very creamy and soft, stir in the sifted flour and salt. Stir in the orange rind. Using a vegetable star pipe, pipe out the mixture in 3½–4-in. lengths on greased baking-sheets. Bake in a moderate oven (375°–350° F., Gas 5–4), then sandwich 2 together with butter icing and dip the ends in chocolate glacé icing.

NOTE: Half an egg may be added to the creamed fat and sugar.

16–20 cakes
Cooking time—15–20 min.

SHORTBREAD (SCOTTISH)

8 oz. flour   2 oz. castor sugar
4 oz. butter

Put the flour and sugar in a pile on a pastry-board. Gradually knead the sugared flour into the butter with the hand. It is important not to let the butter become broken up. When a firm dough is formed, roll out and shape into a cake about 1 in. high. Decorate the edges by marking with a fork or fluting with finger and thumb, or make in a shortbread mould, and prick a pattern on top with a fork or skewer. Fasten a narrow band of paper round to keep the cake in shape. Bake in a warm to cool oven (335°–310° F., Gas 3–2). Dredge with castor sugar when cooked.

Cooking time—about 1 hr.

ALMOND SHORTCAKE

4 oz. butter or margarine   2 oz. Barbados sugar   ½ egg yolk   8 oz. wholemeal flour   pinch of salt
1 oz. ground almonds

Cream fat and sugar; add egg yolk, sifted flour and salt. Add the almonds. Knead all together to a stiff dough. Make into a cake as for Shortbread (Scottish) and bake in a warm to cool oven (335°–310° F., Gas 3–2).

The dough may be cut into fin-gers or other fancy shapes and baked as biscuits.

Cooking time—50–60 min.

STRAWBERRY SHORTCAKE

8 oz. plain flour   ⅛ teasp. salt
pinch of baking-powder   ½ oz. ground almonds   4½ oz. margarine
2 oz. sugar   1 egg yolk

FILLING
1 pt. strawberries   sugar to taste
1–2 gill whipped cream

Sift flour, salt and baking-powder and mix with the ground almonds. Cream the fat and sugar and add egg yolk. Work in the flour mixture as for a cake of shortbread. Divide into three pieces and roll into rounds a good ¼ in. thick. Bake in a moderate oven (350° F., Gas 4) until golden brown, then allow to become cold. Crush strawberries slightly with sugar to taste and add a little whipped cream. Spread this on to the first round of shortcake, cover with the second round and so on, finishing with a layer of straw-berries. Pipe whipped cream on top and round edges. Decorate as desired.

Cooking time—30–40 min.

NOTE: Self-raising flour may be used if liked.

BISCUITS
BRANDY SNAPS

2½ oz. sugar   1 oz. butter or margarine   1 oz. golden syrup
1 oz. plain flour
1 level teasp. ground ginger

Cream sugar, fat and syrup, and stir in the sifted flour and ginger. Make into 12–16 small balls and place well apart on greased baking-sheets. Bake in a cool oven (310° F., Gas 2) until rich brown colour. Allow to cool slightly, remove from sheet with a knife and, while soft enough, roll round the handle of a wooden spoon; remove when set.

The snaps may be filled with sweetened and flavoured cream.

12–16 brandy snaps
Cooking time—10–15 min.

CREAM BISCUITS

2 oz. margarine   2 oz. sugar
½ teasp. vanilla essence   2½ oz. plain flour   1½ oz. custard powder or cornflour   ½ egg (approx.)
vanilla butter icing (p. 336) using 3 oz. icing sugar, etc.

Cream the margarine, sugar and flavouring. Sift flour and custard powder, and add to the creamed margarine. Mix with enough egg to make a stiff but pliable dough. Roll out thinly on a floured board and cut into fingers 1 in. by 3 in. Bake in a moderate oven (350° F., Gas 4) until crisp but still cream in colour. When cold, sandwich pairs together with vanilla butter icing.

NOTE: The use of a ridged roller gives an attractive and more unusual surface to the biscuits.

12–16 doubles
Cooking time—20 min.

GINGER SNAPS

6 oz. self-raising flour   pinch of salt   1 level teasp. bicarbonate of soda   2 level teasp. ground ginger
3–4 oz. sugar   2 oz. lard or shortening   1½ oz. golden syrup
1 egg

NOTE: Take small measure of bicarbonate and ginger.

Sift flour, salt, soda and ginger; add sugar. Melt lard and syrup, cool slightly, then add to dry ingredients; add the egg. Divide into 24 pieces and make into balls, place well apart on greased baking-sheets. Bake in a fairly hot to moderate oven (375°–350° F., Gas 5–4) till a good rich brown colour.

24 ginger snaps
Cooking time—20 min.

MACAROONS

2 egg whites   4 oz. castor sugar
3 oz. ground almonds   1 teasp. rice flour   ½ teasp. vanilla essence
rice paper or greaseproof paper
shredded almonds for top

Beat egg whites stiffly in a large bowl. Mix the sugar, almonds and rice flour together and fold into the beaten whites; add vanilla essence. Place the rice paper or greaseproof paper on a baking-sheet. Put the mixture into a large bag with a ½–1-in. plain pipe and pipe on to the rice paper in rounds about 1½ in. diameter. Decorate with the shredded almonds and bake in a moderate oven (350° F., Gas 4).

20 macaroons
Cooking time—20–30 min.

OATCAKES—Rich

3 oz. plain flour   ½ teasp. salt
2 level teasp. bicarbonate soda
2 level teasp. cream of tartar
1 lb. oatmeal   1 oz. sugar
4 oz. butter and lard or margarine and lard   milk

Sift the flour, salt, soda and cream of tartar; add the oatmeal and sugar and rub in the fat. Add the milk, and mix to a stiff but not hard dough. Dust the baking-board with a mixture of flour and oatmeal, and roll out thinly. Rub the surface with oatmeal and cut out with a 3½–4-in. cutter or cut into triangles. Place on a baking-sheet and cook in a warm to cool oven (335°–310° F., Gas 3–2).

About 40 oatcakes—depending on size
Cooking time—20–30 min.

PARKIN BISCUITS

2 oz. plain flour   2 oz. oatmeal
1½ oz. sugar   ½ level teasp. ground ginger   ½ level teasp. powdered cinnamon   ¼ level teasp. mixed spice   1 oz. lard or all-purpose shortening   1 level teasp.

bicarbonate of soda 1½ oz. golden
syrup ½ egg blanched almonds

Sift and mix flour, oatmeal,
sugar and spices, and rub in the
fat. Add soda, syrup and egg. Mix
well to a fairly stiff consistency.
Form into balls and place a little
apart on greased baking-sheets;
put ½ a blanched almond on top of
each. Bake in a moderate to warm
oven (350°–335° F., Gas 4–3).
Allow to cool slightly before removing from sheet.

12–14 biscuits
Cooking time—15–20 min.

PETITS FOURS (1)

2 egg whites 4 oz. ground almonds
2 oz. castor sugar a few drops
almond essence rice paper

DECORATION
Glacé cherries angelica

Whisk egg whites very stiffly
and fold in mixed almonds and
sugar very lightly, with the almond
essence. Place the mixture in a
forcing bag fitted with a large rose
vegetable pipe and force it on to
rice paper in rosettes or oblongs.
Decorate with small pieces of
cherry and angelica and bake in a
moderate to warm oven (350°–
335° F., Gas 4–3) till golden
brown.

20–30 petits fours
Cooking time—20–30 min.

PETITS FOURS (2)

Genoese pastry (p. 326) apricot
marmalade or glaze butter icing
(p. 336) and cakecrumbs almond
paste (p. 334) glacé icing or
royal icing (p. 335)

Cut neat shapes of Genoese pastry squares, rings, triangles, etc.
Using apricot marmalade, fasten a
small piece of almond paste or
some butter icing mixed with cake-
crumbs and flavoured with vanilla,
kirsch, rum, etc., neatly on top of
each piece of Genoese. Coat with

glacé or royal icing and decorate
with fine piping, scrolls, etc.

RATAFIA BISCUITS

1½ egg whites 1 oz. butter 6 oz.
castor sugar 4 oz. ground almonds
rice paper or greaseproof paper

Beat the egg whites stiffly in a
large bowl. Cream the butter and
sugar. Add the ground almonds
and mix well together. Fold into
the egg whites and mix to a smooth
paste. When the mixture begins to
get stiff put it into a large bag
with a plain pipe. Place the rice
paper or greaseproof paper on a
baking-sheet and pipe small drops
about 2 in. apart. Bake in a
moderate oven (350° F., Gas 4).

24–30 ratafias
Cooking time—about 15 min.

SCOTTISH OATCAKES

8 oz. medium oatmeal ½ teasp. salt
pinch of bicarbonate of soda
1 tablesp. melted dripping
boiling water

Mix oatmeal, salt and bicarbonate of soda in a bowl; add melted
fat and enough boiling water to
make a pliable but not wet dough.
Knead well. Sprinkle board with
oatmeal and roll mixture out thinly. Cut into 3½-in. rounds or alternatively cut into 6-in. rounds
and divide into 4 triangles. Rub
with oatmeal to whiten. Cook on
one side on a moderately hot
girdle, then place in oven or before
fire to crisp through and till ends
curl up.

12 oatcakes, depending on size

SHREWSBURY BISCUITS

4 oz. butter or margarine 4 oz.
castor sugar 1 small egg 8 oz.
plain flour ½ level teasp. ground
cinnamon or 1 teasp. grated lemon
rind milk as required

Cream the fat and sugar and
beat in the egg. Sift flour with
cinnamon, or add grated rind, and

add to the creamed fat mixture. Mix to a stiff consistency, using milk if required. Roll out fairly thinly and cut out with a 2½-in. cutter. Place on a greased baking-sheet and bake in a moderate oven (350° F., Gas 4) till light fawn colour.

30–32 biscuits
Cooking time—15–20 min.

ICINGS AND CAKE DECORATION

AMERICAN FROSTING

8 oz. granulated sugar   4 tablesp. water   1 egg white

Put the sugar and water into a pan, dissolve the sugar slowly in the water and when quite dissolved bring to boiling-point. Boil to 240° F. without stirring. Brush down the sides of the pan with a brush dipped in cold water and remove scum as it rises. Pour on to the stiffly beaten egg white, beating all the time. Continue beating until the icing begins to thicken and coats the back of a spoon thickly. Pour quickly over the cake, spread with a palette knife and work up the icing in swirls.

NOTE: ½ teasp. vanilla essence or lemon juice and a pinch of cream of tartar may be added if liked. The frosting may be used either as a covering or as a filling.

APRICOT GLAZE

**2 tablesp. apricot jam
1 tablesp. water**

Sieve apricot jam and water and bring to boiling-point. Use to glaze the top of small cakes, and to stick almond paste to Christmas cakes, etc.

FONDANT ICING

**1 lb. loaf or granulated sugar
¼ pt. water   1½ teasp. glucose or a good pinch of cream of tartar**

Dissolve the sugar in the water over a low heat, add the glucose or cream of tartar, bring to the boil quickly, and boil to a temperature of 237° F. Pour on to an oiled or wetted slab, let it cool slightly (if worked when too hot it will grain), and work well with a palette knife, keeping the mass together as much as possible. When the paste is sufficiently cool, knead well with the hands. Wrap in paper and store in an airtight tin.

When required put into a basin over a saucepan containing sufficient hot water to come half-way up the sides of the basin. Stir over a very low heat until icing has the consistency of thick cream. Flavour and colour as required. Allow to cool slightly before using.

FLAVOURINGS

Chocolate: Add 3 dessertsp. grated chocolate, *or* 2 dessertsp. cocoa, or to taste.

Coffee: Stir in 2 dessertsp. coffee essence or to taste.

GLACE ICING

Basic Recipe

4 oz. icing sugar   1 tablesp. warm water   flavouring   colouring

If the sugar is lumpy, break up the lumps by rolling the sugar with a rolling-pin before sieving. Sieve the icing sugar and put into a small bowl over hot water. Add the 1 tablesp. warm water gradually. Stir until all the sugar is dissolved and the icing is smooth and warm. Do not allow to get too hot or the icing will lose its gloss. Add the flavouring and the colouring a drop at a time until the required shade is obtained. The icing should be thick enough to coat the back of the spoon; if too thin add more sugar, if too thick add more water.

When of the correct consistency, cool slightly, then use at once.

This quantity will coat the top of a 6–8-in. cake.

Coffee icing: Add ½ teasp. coffee essence to the basic recipe, omitting ½ teasp. of the water.

Lemon icing: Substitute strained lemon juice for all or part of the water in the basic recipe. Add a few drops of colouring.

Orange icing: Substitute strained orange juice for all or part of the water in the basic recipe. Add a few drops of colouring.

CHOCOLATE GLACÉ ICING

3 oz. chocolate (preferably couverture or plain chocolate)
8 oz. icing sugar   ½ gill water

Break the chocolate into small pieces, put into a small bowl over a bowl of warm water and allow to dissolve. Add the sieved icing sugar and water, stir until well mixed and smooth. Use as required.

To Apply Glacé Icing

Place cakes on a wire cooling tray over a large flat dish or clean table-top. Petits fours and other small cakes that have to be coated all over are best dipped into the icing on a fork or skewer, then drained. For large cakes the cake top should be fairly level. Brush off any loose crumbs. When the icing is of the desired consistency pour quickly into the centre of the cake and allow to run down the sides. Avoid using a knife if possible, but if this is necessary use a palette knife dipped in hot water and dried.

Put any ready-made decorations on to the icing while it is still soft, but piped icing should be added after the surface is dry and firm.

TRANSPARENT ICING

1 lb. loaf sugar   ½ gill warm water
lemon juice to flavour

Put the sugar and water into a strong saucepan, let it dissolve, then bring to the boil and simmer for about 5 min., or until a thick syrup is formed (230° F. on a saccharometer), brushing down the sides of the pan with a damp brush to remove the sugar. Stir in the lemon juice, and beat until the icing thickens and becomes opaque, then use as required.

ALMOND PASTE (ICING)

6 oz. icing sugar and 6 oz. castor sugar or 12 oz. icing sugar   12 oz. ground almonds   juice of ½ lemon
¾ teasp. orange flower water
¾ teasp vanilla essence   1–2 egg yolks

Sieve the icing sugar into a bowl and mix with the ground almonds and castor sugar. Add the lemon juice, essences and enough egg yolk to bind the ingredients into a pliable but dry paste. Knead thoroughly with the hand until smooth.

NOTE: A whole egg or egg whites may be used instead of egg yolks. Egg yolk gives a richer and yellower paste, whilst egg white gives a whiter, more brittle paste. (Economically the yolks can be used for almond paste and the whites used for royal icing.)

This quantity of paste is sufficient to cover the top and sides of an 8-in. cake.

To Apply Almond Paste (see Plate 14)

Brush the top and sides of the cake with warm apricot glaze, using a pastry brush. Dredge a little castor sugar on to a clean board and roll out the almond paste to a round which is 4 in. wider than the diameter of the cake. Place the cake in the centre of this with its glazed top downwards and work the paste upwards round the sides of the cake with the hands until it is within ¼ in. of the top edge, i.e. the cake bottom. Using a straight-sided jar or thick tumbler, roll firmly round the sides, pressing slightly with the other hand on the upturned bottom of the cake and turning the cake round on the sugared board when necessary.

Continue rolling and turning until the sides are straight and smoothly covered and the top edges of the cake are sharp and smooth.

NOTE: Allow a few days for the almond paste to dry, before putting on the royal icing, or the oil from the almond paste will discolour it. Cover with a clean cloth to protect from dust whilst drying.

ROYAL ICING

1 lb. icing sugar (approx.)
2 egg whites   1 teasp. lemon juice

If the sugar is lumpy, roll with a rolling-pin before sieving. Put the egg whites into a bowl, beat slightly with a wooden spoon. Add 2 tablesp. sieved sugar and beat again. Gradually add the remainder of the sugar, beating well until a thick, smooth consistency and a good white colour are obtained. Add the lemon juice and beat again.

NOTE: If a softer icing is required 1 teasp. glycerine may be stirred in after the sugar.

If the icing is not to be used immediately, cover the bowl with a damp cloth to keep the icing soft.

Some cooks add 1 or 2 drops of confectioner's blue to make the icing white, but if the eggs are fresh and the icing is sufficiently well beaten, no blue colouring is necessary.

To Ice a Cake with Royal Icing (Plate 14)

NOTE: These quantities are sufficient to coat a cake of 8 in. diameter.

Place the cake already covered with almond paste on a cake-board or inverted plate. Place the cake-board on a turntable if available.

AMOUNTS REQUIRED

First coating: Royal icing, using 1¼ lb. icing sugar, etc., mixed to a stiff consistency.

Second coating: ¾–1 lb. icing sugar, etc., consistency to coat the back of a spoon.

Decorative piping: ½ lb. icing sugar, etc., mixed to a stiff consistency, i.e. that will stand up in points when the back of the spoon is drawn away from the side of the bowl.

To apply first coating: With a tablespoon take enough icing to cover the top, and place it in the centre of the cake. Spread evenly over top, smoothing the surface with a hot, wet palette knife (shake or dry the knife after dipping it in hot water as too much water softens the icing). Take up small portions of the icing with the end of the palette knife blade, spread it smoothly round the side until the cake is completely covered and the surface smooth.

Allow to set for a few days before applying the second coat. Whilst the icing is drying, and as soon as it is hard enough, place a thin sheet of paper lightly over the top to protect it from dust.

To apply second coating: Mix icing to a thin coating consistency and pour over the cake. Prick any bubbles with a fine skewer or pin; allow to firm before decorating.

To decorate the cake with piped icing: Cut pieces of greaseproof paper the same sizes as the top and sides of the cake. Sketch on to these the patterns to be used for the decoration. Pin papers firmly into position on cake and prick pattern through. Mix icing to a stiff consistency and pipe design on to cake, starting at centre and working outwards, and finishing with the sides and the base.

Using a forcing bag: Decorative icing can be piped from a forcing bag and pipe. Form a triangular piece of greaseproof paper into a cone-shaped bag. Cut off the point and slip a forcing pipe into the bag. Make a bag for each pipe to be used. Fill the bags ⅔ full with icing and fold over the top edges. Holding the pipe between the first and second fingers, force the icing through the pipe by exerting pressure with the thumbs on the top of the bag.

Icing syringes are made of metal or plastic and can be bought in sets complete with decorative pipes and a turntable. If coloured icings are being used the syringe must be washed before filling with another colour.

All pipes must be kept clean. Always keep the bowl containing the icing covered with a damp cloth whilst decorating, to prevent the icing drying out.

For Christmas cakes other decorations may be made with coloured marzipan, e.g. holly, mistletoe, etc., and the smooth icing surface roughened into points with a palette knife to form "snowdrifts". For this one coat only is needed.

CAKE FILLINGS

ALMOND AND WALNUT FILLING

3 tablesp. ground almonds
1 teasp. vanilla essence
1 tablesp. chopped walnuts
2–3 tablesp. sieved apricot jam

Work all the ingredients well together.

BUTTER ICING (BUTTER CREAM)

2 oz. butter or margarine   3 oz. icing sugar   flavouring   colouring

Cream the butter or margarine. Add the sugar gradually and cream together. Beat until smooth, creamy and pale. Add flavouring and colouring to taste.

NOTE: In cold weather the butter may be warmed slightly to facilitate creaming, but do not allow it to oil.

FLAVOURINGS

Almond: Beat in ¼ teasp. almond essence.

Chocolate: Dissolve 1 oz. chocolate in 1 tablesp. water and beat in, or beat in 1 dessertsp. cocoa and a few drops of vanilla essence.

Coffee: Beat in 1 dessertsp. coffee essence.

Jam: Add 1 tablesp. strong-flavoured jam, e.g. plum, raspberry.

Lemon: Beat in 1 dessertsp. strained lemon juice.

Orange: Beat in 1 teasp. strained orange juice.

Vanilla: Beat in ½ teasp. vanilla essence.

Walnut: Add 2 oz. chopped walnuts and 1–2 teasp. coffee essence.

CHOCOLATE FILLING

2 oz. butter or margarine   2 oz. grated plain chocolate   2 oz. ground almonds   2 oz. castor sugar

Cream the fat, work in the grated chocolate, add ground almonds and sugar.

COCONUT FILLING

2 oz. icing sugar   1 egg yolk
1 tablesp. lemon juice
1 oz. desiccated coconut

Sift the sugar into a basin and mix to a smooth paste with the egg yolk and lemon juice. Place the basin over a pan of hot water over a low heat and cook until thick—about 5 min.—stirring all the time. Remove from heat and stir in coconut; allow to cool before using.

COFFEE FILLING

2 oz. butter or margarine 1 tablesp.
castor sugar 1 tablesp. cold water
1 tablesp. hot water
few drops of coffee essence

Cream together the fat and
sugar. Gradually beat in the cold
water, then the hot (not boiling)
water. Add coffee essence to taste.

CONFECTIONERS' CUSTARD

½ pt. milk ¾ oz. cornflour 2 yolks
or 1 whole egg 1 oz. sugar
¼ teasp. vanilla essence

Blend the cornflour with the
milk, stir in the egg yolks and
sugar, and cook over a gentle heat
until thick. Beat in the vanilla.
Allow to cool.

MINCEMEAT (1)

1 lb. cooking apples (prepared
weight), finely chopped 1 lb.
currants, cleaned and picked 1 lb.
beef suet, finely chopped 1 lb. large
raisins, stoned and quartered ½ lb.
sultanas, halved 1 lb. demerara
sugar 2 oz. almonds, blanched and
finely chopped ½ gill rum 2 oz.
each candied lemon, orange and
citron peel, all finely chopped
grated rind and juice of 2 large
lemons ½ nutmeg, finely grated
¼ level teasp. each ground cloves and
cinnamon ⅛ teasp. each ground
mace and ginger ½ level teasp. salt
¼ pt. brandy

Mix all the prepared ingredients
together, stirring well and cover
closely in clean dry jars. Keep for
2 or 3 weeks to allow to mellow
before using.

MINCEMEAT (2)

1½ lb. cooking apples (prepared
weight) 1 lb. currants 1 lb. seedless
raisins ½ lb. sultanas ½ lb. candied
peel 1 lb. beef suet 1 lb. sugar
grated rind and juice of 2 lemons
1 level teasp. ground nutmeg ¼ level
teasp. ground cloves ¼ level teasp.

ground cinnamon ½ level teasp. salt
⅛ pt. brandy (see note below)

Peel and core the apples. Put
these, with the fruit, candied peel
and suet, through the mincer. Add
the other ingredients and mix
well. Cover in jars and use as
required.

NOTE: If the mincemeat is to be
used within a few days the brandy
may be omitted.

MOCHA FILLING

½ oz. cornflour 1 gill milk 1 oz.
loaf sugar ½ oz. butter 1 teasp.
coffee essence a few drops of
vanilla essence 1 egg

Blend the cornflour in a little
cold milk. Put the remaining milk
and sugar in a saucepan and bring
to boiling-point. Pour the boiling
milk on to the blended cornflour,
stirring all the time, return the
mixture to the saucepan and boil
for 3 min. Add the butter and
flavourings and lastly the beaten
egg. Stir till the mixture thickens,
then allow to cool.

MOCK CREAM

½ oz. cornflour ½ pt. milk
1 oz. margarine 1 oz. sugar
a few drops of vanilla essence

Blend the cornflour with a little
of the milk, and put the rest of the
milk on to boil. Pour the boiling
milk on to the blended cornflour,
stirring well. Return mixture to
pan and cook for 2–3 min. Cool.
Cream together the margarine
and sugar. Gradually beat the
cornflour mixture into the creamed
fat, a little at a time, beat well.
Stir in the vanilla essence.

RUM AND WALNUT FILLING

2 oz. butter 3 oz. brown sugar
1–2 dessertsp. rum
2 oz. chopped walnuts

Cream together the butter and
sugar. Add the rum a few drops
at a time, beating well between
each addition. Beat in the walnuts.

PASTRY-MAKING

THE aim in pastry-making is to make the pastry as light as possible and this depends on the amount of cold air incorporated in the mixture during the making. The cold air expands on heating, thus making the pastry light.

When making puff, flaky or rough puff pastry, the air is incorporated in the pastry in thin layers, while in short crust and suet pastry the air fills the cavities all through the pastry. Self-raising flour is suitable only for suet crust pastry and plain short crust pastry, and should not be used for rich pastries.

Butter, or butter and lard in equal quantities, should be used for pastry-making if possible, but in all the following recipes margarine may be substituted for butter.

When the amount of fat is less than $\frac{1}{2}$ the amount of flour a little baking-powder (1 level teasp. to $\frac{1}{2}$ lb. flour) may be added.

GENERAL HINTS

1. Keep everything for pastry-making cool.
2. Work in a cool place, if possible on a marble slab or enamelled surface.
3. Always sift the flour.
4. When rubbing the fat into the flour use the fingertips.
5. Use freshly drawn cold water for mixing.
6. Allow the pastry to stand for a short time in a cool place after making, particularly in hot weather.
7. Roll the pastry lightly, quickly and evenly with short strokes, lifting the rolling-pin between each stroke.
8. Use very little flour for rolling out and remove any surplus flour with a pastry brush.
9. Most pastries are baked in a fairly hot oven, but the richer the pastry the hotter the oven required for cooking.

NOTE: Hot Water Crust, Choux Pastry and Genoese Pastry are exceptions to these rules.

To glaze pastry: Meat pies, patties, sausage-rolls, etc., are usually brushed over with well-beaten egg before or during baking.

Fruit tarts, puffs, etc., may be brushed lightly with cold water, and dredged with castor sugar before baking.

To keep pastry: Pastry not intended for immediate use should be folded in greaseproof paper and kept in a refrigerator or cool place.

BUTTER CRUST

For boiled puddings

1 lb. plain flour   pinch of salt
6 oz. butter   cold water to mix

Sift the flour and salt and, using a knife, mix to a smooth paste with cold water, adding the water gradually. Roll out thinly. Place the butter over it in small pieces and dredge lightly with flour. Fold the pastry over, roll out again.

Use as required.

CHEESE PASTRY

For savoury pies and canapés

4 oz. flour   pinch of dry mustard
pinch of salt   cayenne pepper
3 oz. butter   3 oz. Parmesan cheese
1 egg yolk   2 teasp. cold water

Sift flour, mustard and seasonings. Cream butter till very soft and white. Add flour, grated cheese and enough egg yolk and water to mix to a stiff dough. Bake in a fairly hot oven (400° F., *Gas* 6).

CHOUX PASTRY

For Cream buns, Cream puffs and Eclairs

4 oz. plain flour   ½ pt. water
⅛ teasp. salt   2 oz. butter or margarine   ½ teasp. vanilla essence
1 egg yolk   2 eggs

Sift and warm the flour. Place water, salt and fat in a pan, and bring to boiling-point. Remove from heat, add flour all at once and beat well (using a wooden spoon) over the heat again, until it becomes a smooth soft paste and leaves the sides of the pan clean. Remove from the heat, add vanilla and egg yolk immediately and beat well. Add the other two eggs one at a time, beating thoroughly between each addition. (It is important to get the first of the egg in while the mixture is hot enough to cook it slightly, otherwise it becomes too soft.) Use as required.

Bake in a fairly hot oven (400°–425° F., *Gas* 6–7).

FLAKY PASTRY

For Pies, Tarts and Tartlets

1 lb. plain flour   pinch of salt
10 oz. butter or butter and lard
cold water to mix
½ teasp. lemon juice

Sift the flour and salt into a basin. Divide the butter into 4 equal portions and lightly rub ¼ of the butter into the flour. (If a mixture of butter and lard is used, blend them together with a round-bladed knife to get an even consistency, before dividing into 4.) Mix to a soft dough with cold water and lemon juice.

Roll out into an oblong strip, keeping the ends square and place ¼ of the butter in small pieces on the top ⅔ of the pastry. Dredge lightly with flour, fold up the bottom third of pastry on to the fat and fold down the top third. Using the rolling-pin, press the edges lightly together to prevent the air escaping. Half-turn the pastry so that the folded edges are left and right when rolling. With the rolling-pin press ridges in the pastry to distribute the air evenly. Roll out as before. If possible, allow the pastry to relax in a cool place.

Repeat the process with the other two portions of butter and again allow the pastry to relax. Roll out once more and use as required.

Flaky pastry should be put into a very hot oven (450° F., *Gas* 8) until set, then the heat should be reduced to fairly hot (375° F., *Gas* 5).

FRENCH CRUST

1 lb. plain flour   ½ teasp. salt   6 oz. butter   2 eggs   cold water to mix

Sift the flour and salt. Lightly rub in the butter. Mix to a smooth firm paste with the eggs and cold water added gradually. Use as required.

OATMEAL PASTRY

½ lb. plain flour   ¼ lb. oatmeal
pinch of salt   ¼ lb. butter and lard
cold water to mix

Mix the flour, oatmeal and salt together. Rub in the butter and lard. Mix to a stiff dough with cold water.

Use as required.

PATE SUCREE

8 oz. plain flour   pinch of salt
5 oz. butter   2 oz. sugar   1 egg yolk
cold water to mix

Sift together the flour and salt. Cut the butter into small pieces and rub it lightly into the flour, using the fingertips. Add the sugar and mix with egg yolk and sufficient cold water to make a stiff paste.

Use as required.

NOTE: In warm weather only a very small quantity of water will be required.

POTATO PASTRY

For covering meat or vegetable pies

1 lb. dry floury potatoes   1 lb. plain flour   2 oz. lard   2 oz. dripping pinch of salt   2 teasp. baking-powder   1 egg   warm milk to mix

Bake sufficient potatoes (in their skins) to give 1 lb. potatoes. Remove skins and either mash the potatoes or rub them through a fine wire sieve. Rub the fat lightly into the flour and add the potatoes, salt and baking-powder. Add the beaten egg and enough milk to mix to a smooth paste.

Use as required.

PUFF PASTRY

For Pies, Tarts, Tartlets, Bouchées, Vol-au-Vents, Patties, etc.

1 lb. plain flour   pinch of salt
1 lb. butter   1 teasp. lemon juice
$\frac{1}{3}$ pt. cold water (approx.)

Sift the flour and salt and rub in about 2 oz. of butter. Press the remaining butter firmly in a floured cloth to remove moisture, and shape into a flat cake. Add the lemon juice to the flour and mix to a smooth dough with cold water. The consistency of the dough must be the same as that of the butter. Knead the dough well and roll it out into a strip a little wider than the butter and rather more than twice its length. Place the butter on one $\frac{1}{2}$ of the pastry, and fold the other $\frac{1}{2}$ over. Leave in a cool place for 15 min. to allow the butter to harden.

Roll out into a long strip 3 times the original length but the original width. Fold the bottom $\frac{1}{3}$ up and the top $\frac{1}{3}$ down, half turn the pastry so that the folded edges are on the right and left. Roll and fold again and lay aside in a cool place for 15 min. Repeat this process until the pastry has been rolled out 6 times. The rolling should be done as evenly as possible and the pastry kept in a long narrow shape which, when folded, forms a square. Roll out as required and leave in a cool place before cooking.

Bake in a very hot oven (450° F., Gas 8)—the oven door should not be opened until the pastry has risen and become partially baked, as a current of cold air may cause the pastry to collapse.

To Make a Vol-au-Vent Case: Roll out the puff pastry to about $\frac{3}{4}$ in. thickness, and, with a cutter previously dipped in flour, cut into a round or oval shape as desired. Place on a baking-sheet, brush over the top of the pastry with beaten egg. With a smaller, floured cutter cut an inner ring, cutting the pastry to about $\frac{1}{2}$ its depth. Bake in a very hot oven (450° F., Gas 8). When baked, remove the lid and scoop out the soft inside.

To Make Patty Cases: Roll out the puff or flaky pastry to a thickness of $\frac{1}{8}$ in. and cut into rounds with a 2$\frac{1}{2}$-in. or 3-in. cutter. Remove the centres from half of these rounds with a 1$\frac{1}{4}$-in. or 1$\frac{1}{2}$-in. cutter. Turn the pastry upside down after cutting. Moisten the plain halves and place the ringed halves evenly on top. Prick the centres. Place on a baking-tray and allow to stand for at least 10 min. in a cold place. Glaze the ringed halves and the small lids and bake in a very hot oven (450° F., Gas 8). When baked, remove and scoop out any soft inside part. If liked, the cases can be made as vol-au-vent cases, using smaller cutters.

To Make Horn or Cornet Cases:
Roll out pastry thinly, then cut into strips ½ in. wide and 12–14 in. long. Moisten strips with water and wind round cornet mould from the point upwards with moist surface on outside. Finish final overlap on underside of tin and trim neatly. Brush with milk and bake in the middle of a very hot oven (450° F., *Gas* 8).
Cooking time—10–15 min.

RAISED PIE CRUST or HOT WATER CRUST PASTRY

For Pork, Veal and Ham or Raised Game Pies
**10 oz. plain flour   ½ teasp. salt
3 oz. lard   ¼ pt. milk or water**

Sift the flour and salt into a warm bowl, make a well in the centre, and keep in a warm place. Heat the lard and milk *or* water together gently until boiling, then add them to the flour, mixing well with a wooden spoon, until cool enough to knead with the hands. Knead thoroughly, use as required.

Bake in a hot oven (425° F., *Gas* 7), reduce heat to moderate (350° F., *Gas* 4) as soon as pastry is set.

To Raise a Pie: The pastry must be raised or moulded whilst still warm. Reserve ¼ for the lid and leave in the bowl in a warm place covered with a cloth. Roll out the remainder to about ¼ in. thickness in a round or oval shape. Gently mould the pie with the hands; if this proves too difficult mould it over a jam-jar. Grease and flour the jar, invert it, place the pastry over and mould the pastry round the sides, taking care not to stretch the pastry and ensuring that the sides and base are of an even thickness. Leave to cool.

When cold, remove the pastry case from the jar, put in the filling. Roll the ¼ of pastry reserved for the lid, damp the rim of the case, put on the lid and press edges firmly together.

Three or four folds of greased paper should be pinned round the pie to preserve its shape during baking and to prevent it becoming too brown.

RICH SHORT CRUST PASTRY

For Pies, Tarts, etc.
**1 lb. plain flour   pinch of salt
10–12 oz. butter   2 teasp. castor
sugar   2 egg yolks   cold water to mix**

Sift the flour and salt together. Cut the butter into small pieces and rub it lightly into the flour, using the fingertips. Add the sugar and mix to a stiff paste with the egg yolks and 1 tablesp. cold water, using more water if necessary. Use as required.

ROUGH PUFF PASTRY

½ lb. plain flour   pinch of salt   6 oz. butter or butter and lard   ½ teasp. lemon juice   cold water to mix

Sift the flour and salt. Add the butter cut up into pieces the size of a walnut and mix lightly with the flour. Make a well in the centre, put in the lemon juice and gradually add sufficient water to mix to an elastic dough. Roll into a long strip, keeping the corners square, fold into three. With the rolling-pin seal the edges and give the pastry a half-turn, so that the folded edges are on the right and left. Repeat until the pastry has been rolled and folded 4 times, if possible leaving for 15 min. in a cool place between the second and third rollings.

Use as required. Bake in a very hot oven (450° F., *Gas* 8).

SHORT CRUST PASTRY

For Pies, Tarts, etc.
½ lb. plain flour   pinch of salt   2 oz. butter   2 oz. lard   cold water to mix

Sift together the flour and salt. Rub the butter and lard lightly into the flour, using the fingertips. Mix to a stiff paste with cold water.

Use as required.

SUET CRUST PASTRY

For Meat puddings, Fruit puddings, Jam Roly Poly, Suet puddings, etc.

3–4 oz. suet   ½ lb. plain flour
¼ teasp. salt   1 teasp. baking-powder
cold water to mix

Chop the suet finely with a little flour or use shredded suet. Sift the flour, salt and baking-powder, and mix in the suet. Mix to a firm dough with cold water. Use as required.

SWEET PASTRY FOR TARTLETS

1 lb. plain flour   pinch of salt
5 oz. butter   rind of ½ lemon
8 oz. castor sugar   1 egg
cold water, if necessary

Sift the flour and salt. Rub in the butter, add the sugar and finely grated lemon rind and mix to a stiff dough with beaten egg and a little cold water, if necessary.

Use as required.

TRANSPARENT PASTRY

For certain pies

¾ lb. butter   1 lb. plain flour
pinch of salt   1 egg

Remove as much moisture as possible from the butter, using a dry cloth. Melt the butter over a very low heat; allow to cool. When almost cold stir in the sifted flour, salt and beaten egg. Knead lightly until smooth and use as required.

FLANS

To line a 7-in. flan ring about 4 oz. pastry (i.e. 4 oz. flour plus the other ingredients made into pastry) will be required. Grease a baking-sheet and the flan ring; place the flan ring on the baking-sheet. Roll the pastry into a circle about 1 in. larger than the flan ring and ⅛ in.

thick. Lift the pastry with the rolling-pin to prevent stretching and line the ring carefully. Press to fit the bottom and sides so that no air bubbles form underneath the crust. Trim off the surplus pastry with a sharp knife or roll across the top of the ring with the rolling-pin.

If a flan is to be cooked without filling it must be baked "blind". Prick the bottom of the flan, cover with a piece of greaseproof paper and fill with rice, beans, etc. (this prevents the flan from losing its shape during cooking). Bake according to the kind of pastry. When the pastry is cooked remove the paper and rice, beans, etc., and replace the flan case in the oven for 5 min. to dry the bottom. The rice or beans can be used over and over again—cool, store in a tin and keep them for this purpose. See Plate 15.

OPEN TARTS

Open tarts are usually baked on fireproof glass plates. For a 7-in. plate about 4 oz. of pastry will be required. Knead the dough into a round shape, then roll into a round about ⅛ in. thick and a little larger than the plate. Fold the pastry over the rolling-pin and gently lift it on to the plate. Smooth it over carefully with the fingers so that no air is trapped between the pastry and the plate—but take care that the pastry is not stretched in the process, as it will only shrink back later.

If the tart is being baked without a filling prick the base well or bake it "blind". When baking stand the plate on a baking-sheet.

The tart may be given a lattice top or the edge may be decorated with fancy shapes, see Plate 16.

BAKEWELL TART

Short crust pastry (p. 341), using
4 oz. flour, etc.   raspberry jam

2 oz. butter   2 oz. sugar   1 egg
2 oz. ground almonds   2 oz. cake-
crumbs   almond essence   icing sugar

Line a 7-in. flan ring or a pie-
plate with the pastry. Place a
good layer of raspberry jam on the
bottom. Cream together the butter
and sugar till thick and white.
Beat in the egg and add the ground
almonds and cake-crumbs and a
few drops of almond essence.
Spread the mixture on top of the
jam and bake in a fairly hot oven
(400° F., Gas 6) for about ½ hr.

Sprinkle icing sugar on top and
serve hot or cold.

5–6 helpings

BANANA FLAN

Short crust pastry (p. 341), using
4 oz. flour, etc.   ½ pt. confectioner's
custard (p. 337)   3 bananas
apricot glaze (p. 333)

Line a 7-in. flan ring with
the pastry and bake it "blind".
When cool, pour in the confectioner's custard and cover the
custard with overlapping rings
of banana arranged neatly on top.
Glaze immediately with hot apricot glaze, allow to set and serve
cold.

CUSTARD FLAN

Short crust pastry (p. 341), using
4 oz. flour, etc.   1 egg   1 egg yolk
¾ oz. sugar   ½ pt. milk
grated nutmeg

Line a 7-in. flan ring with short
crust pastry. Bake "blind". Beat
the eggs and add to them the
sugar and warmed milk. Strain
into the flan case, sprinkle with
grated nutmeg and bake in a warm
oven till set (335° F., Gas 3).

5–6 helpings
Cooking time—30–40 min.

FRANGIPANE TART

Rich short crust pastry (p. 341),
using 4 oz. flour, etc.   2 oz. sugar

2 oz. butter   1 egg   2 oz. ground
almonds   1 teasp. flour

Line a 7-in. flan ring or pie-
plate with the pastry. Cream the
butter and sugar till thick and
white. Add the egg, beating well,
and then mix in the ground almonds and flour. Place the mixture in the pastry case and bake in
a moderate oven (350° F., Gas 4)
for 25–30 min. When cool, dredge
with icing sugar.

6 helpings

FRUIT FLAN

Rich short crust pastry (p. 341),
using 4 oz. flour, etc.

FILLING
1 medium-sized can of fruit or ¾ lb.
fresh fruit, e.g. strawberries, pears,
pineapple, cherries, apricots,
peaches, etc.

COATING GLAZE
¼ pt. syrup from canned fruit, or
fruit juice or water   sugar (if
necessary)   1 teasp. arrowroot
lemon juice to taste

DECORATION (optional)
Whipped sweetened cream

Line a 7-in. flan ring with the
pastry. Prick the bottom of the
flan, and bake it "blind". Bake
for about 30 min., first in a fairly
hot oven (400° F., Gas 6) reducing the heat, as the pastry sets, to
moderate (350° F., Gas 4). When
the pastry is cooked remove the
paper and dummy used for blind
baking and replace the case in the
oven for 5 min. to dry the bottom.
Allow to cool.

If fresh fruit is used, stew gently
till tender, if necessary. Drain the
fruit. Place the sugar if used and
liquid in a pan and boil for 10 min.
Blend the arrowroot with some
lemon juice and add it to the
syrup, stirring all the time. Continue stirring, cook for 3 min.,

then cool slightly. Arrange the fruit attractively in the flan case and coat it with fruit syrup.

If liked, the flan may be decorated with piped, whipped, sweetened cream.

JAM TART

Trimmings of puff pastry
any kind of jam

Grease a fireproof plate or tart pan. Roll out the pastry to a thickness of $\frac{1}{8}$ in. and line the plate with it. Spread with jam and decorate the edges. Bake the tart in a hot oven (425° F., Gas 7) for 10–15 min.

LEMON MERINGUE FLAN

Short crust pastry (p. 341), using
4 oz. flour, etc.   1 oz. cornflour
rind and juice of 2 lemons   1–2 oz.
granulated sugar   1 oz. butter
2 eggs   3 oz. castor sugar

Line a 7-in. flan ring with the pastry and bake it "blind" (see p. 342). Make the lemon juice up to ½ pt. with water. Blend the cornflour in a little of the lemon liquid, boil the remaining liquid and pour it over the blended cornflour, stirring all the time. Put the mixture back in the pan, boil for 3 min. and add the granulated sugar, grated lemon rind and butter. Allow to cool slightly, add the egg yolks and pour the mixture into the flan case. Bake in a moderate oven (350° F., Gas 4) till set. Whisk the egg whites stiffly, fold in the castor sugar and pile on top of the flan. Dredge with castor sugar and return to the oven (290° F., Gas 1) till the meringue is set and lightly browned.

6 helpings
Cooking time—45–50 min.

TREACLE TART

Short crust pastry (p. 341), using
6 oz. flour, etc.   3 tablesp. golden
syrup   lemon juice or ginger
2 oz. fresh breadcrumbs

Slightly warm the syrup, flavour with a pinch of ginger or a little lemon juice, then stir in the breadcrumbs.

Line a 9-in fireproof plate with the pastry, trim and decorate the edge. Spread over the syrup mixture, decorate with cross strips of pastry, and bake in a fairly hot oven (400° F., Gas 6) for about 30 min.

NOTE: If preferred the tart may be baked as a double crust tart; increase the amount of pastry and bake for 50 min. Crushed cornflakes may be substituted for the breadcrumbs, if liked.

6 helpings

PUDDINGS USING PASTRY

To Line the Sides of a Pie-dish: For a 1½-pt. pie-dish 4 oz. pastry will be required (i.e. 4 oz. flour, etc.).

Wet the pie-dish with cold water. Roll out the pastry thinly, cut a strip 3–4 in. wide and lay it round the sides of the dish so that it lies slightly over the outer rim (to allow for shrinkage during baking). Press the pastry well on to the pie-dish, joining the strip neatly by wetting the edges with cold water and pressing firmly together. Wet the rim of pastry and decorate the edge with small fancy shapes of pastry laid round.

ALMOND PUDDING

Short crust pastry (p. 341), using
4 oz. flour, etc.   3 oz. butter   2 oz.
castor sugar   2 eggs   2 oz. cake- or
white breadcrumbs   ½ lemon   4 oz.
ground almonds   1 pt. milk

Line the sides of a 1½-pt. pie-dish with pastry. Cream the butter and sugar together; beat in the eggs gradually. Add the crumbs, lemon rind, juice and almonds. Boil the milk, pour it over the rest

of the ingredients, stirring all the
time. Pour the mixture into the
lined pie-dish. Bake in a moderate
to fairly hot oven (350°–375° F.,
Gas 4–5) until the pastry is cooked
and the filling is golden brown and
set, about 20–30 min.

6–7 helpings

APPLE AMBER

**Short crust pastry (p. 341), using
4 oz. flour, etc. 1½ lb. cooking
apples 2 tablesp. water rind of
1 lemon 2 oz. butter or margarine
3 oz. brown sugar 2 eggs
2–3 oz. castor sugar for the meringue**

Line the sides of a 1½-pt. pie-
dish with the pastry and decorate
the edge.

Peel, core and slice the apples;
put them in a saucepan and stew
with the water and the lemon rind.
When soft, pass through a nylon
sieve. Return the apple pulp to
the pan and reheat slightly, add
the butter, brown sugar and egg
yolks. Put the mixture into the
lined pie-dish and bake gently in a
moderate oven (350° F., Gas 4)
for about 30 min., until the apple
mixture is set. Stiffly whisk the
egg whites and fold in 2–3 oz. of
castor sugar. Pile on top of the
apple mixture, dredge lightly with
castor sugar and decorate, if liked,
with pieces of angelica and glacé
cherry. Bake in a very cool oven
(290° F., Gas 1) until the meringue is golden brown; about 30–40
min. Serve hot or cold.

NOTE: A good pinch of ground
cinnamon and ground cloves can
be added to the apples before the
butter, sugar and egg yolks, if
liked.

6–7 helpings

APRICOT PUDDING

**¾ pt. milk ¾ pt. fresh breadcrumbs
or cake-crumbs short crust pastry
(p. 341), using 5–6 oz. flour, etc.
one 12-oz. can or 1 bottle of**

apricots 2 oz. castor sugar
**2 eggs 1 glass sherry
2–4 oz. castor sugar for the meringue**

Boil the milk, pour it over the
breadcrumbs and let them soak for
½ hr. Line the sides of a 2-pt. pie-
dish with the pastry.

Strain the apricots, pass them
through a fine sieve and add to
them 2 oz. sugar, egg yolks,
sherry and soaked crumbs. Pour
into the pie-dish. Bake in a fairly
hot oven (400° F., Gas 6) until
the pastry is cooked and the filling
is set—25–30 min. Whisk the
egg whites stiffly, stir in lightly
the 2–4 oz. castor sugar and spread
this meringue over the top of the
pudding. Dredge well with castor
sugar and decorate with strips of
angelica and cut glacé cherry, if
liked. Bake in a very cool oven
(290° F., Gas 1) until the
meritngue is crisp and golden
—about 30 min.

6 helpings

COCONUT PUDDING

**Short crust pastry (p. 341), using
5–6 oz. flour, etc. 6 oz. desiccated
coconut ¾ pt. milk 1½ oz. butter
1½ oz. sugar 3 eggs 1½ oz. cake-
crumbs ¼ pt. cream or milk
vanilla essence 2 oz. castor sugar**

Line the sides of a 2-pt. pie-dish
with the pastry. Simmer the coconut in the ¾ pt. milk until tender
—about 10–15 min.; allow to cool.
Cream together the butter and the
1½ oz. sugar until soft, work in the
egg yolks one at a time and add
the cake-crumbs, cream or milk,
the prepared coconut and the
vanilla essence. Pour the mixture
into the pie-dish and bake in a
fairly hot oven (375° F., Gas 5)
until the pastry is cooked and the
mixture set—about ½ hr. Stiffly
whisk the egg whites and fold in
the 2 oz. castor sugar; pile on top
of the pudding. Reduce oven heat
to very cool (290° F., Gas 1) and

put the pudding back into oven until the meringue is golden—30–40 min.

6 helpings

GOOSEBERRY PUDDING

1 lb. gooseberries   1 gill water
short crust pastry (p. 341), using
5–6 oz. flour, etc.   3–4 oz. castor
sugar   ½ pt. breadcrumbs   2 oz.
butter or margarine   2 eggs

Top and tail the gooseberries and cook them in the water until tender. Line the sides of a 2-pt. pie-dish with the pastry. Rub the gooseberries through a fine sieve and add sugar to sweeten. This should give about 1 pt. of purée. Add to the purée the breadcrumbs, butter and well-beaten eggs. Pour the mixture into the lined pie-dish. Bake in a moderate oven (350° F., Gas 4) for about 40 min., until set.

4 helpings

ORANGE PUDDING

Short crust pastry (p. 341), using
5–6 oz. flour, etc.   4 oranges   ½ pt.
milk   3 oz. sugar   3 oz. cake-
crumbs or sponge cakes   pinch of
grated nutmeg   2 eggs

Line the sides of a 2-pt. pie-dish with the pastry. Thinly cut the rind from one orange and infuse this in the milk for about 20 min., then remove it. Add to the milk, the sugar, cake-crumbs, nutmeg and well-beaten eggs and lastly the juice of all the oranges. Pour into the lined pie-dish and bake in a fairly hot oven (375° F., Gas 5) until the pastry is cooked and the mixture is set—about 30–35 min.

WEST RIDING PUDDING

Short crust pastry (p. 341), using
5–6 oz. flour, etc.   4 oz. butter or
margarine   4 oz. castor sugar
2 eggs   6 oz. plain flour   1 teasp.
baking-powder   milk to mix
2 tablesp. jam

Line and decorate the sides of a 2-pt. pie-dish with the pastry.

Cream the fat and sugar together until white and creamy. Beat in the eggs gradually. Beat thoroughly. Sift in the flour and baking-powder. Stir in lightly, adding milk until the mixture drops easily from the spoon. Cover the bottom of the pie-dish with the jam; then spread on the mixture. Bake in a fairly hot oven (375° F., Gas 5) for about 1 hr., until the pudding is cooked and brown.

PIES OR TARTS

TO MAKE A FRUIT PIE OR TART

A 1½-pt. pie-dish will require about 6 oz. pastry (i.e. 6 oz. flour plus the other ingredients made into pastry) and 1½–2 lb. fruit.

Place ½ the amount of fruit in the dish, sprinkle over the sugar and flavouring (if used) and pile the remaining fruit on top. The sugar should not be sprinkled on top as it would go into the pastry and make it soggy. Roll out the pastry a little larger than the pie-dish. Cut off a strip of pastry, wet the edge of the pie-dish with cold water and place the strip on the pie-dish cut edge inwards, without stretching it. Join the strip by wetting the cut ends and pressing them firmly together. Wet the strip of pastry; lift the remaining pastry with the rolling-pin and place it gently over the dish, taking care not to stretch it. Press the strip and the cover together and trim off the surplus with a sharp knife. Knock up the edge of the pastry with the back of a knife and decorate as desired (see Plate 16).

To allow the steam to escape either cut a slit in the centre of the crust before placing pie in the oven; or leave a few gaps under the pastry cover at the edge; or raise the pastry slightly at one corner immediately after cooking.

DOUBLE CRUST PIES OR TARTS

About 8 oz. pastry (i.e. 8 oz. flour plus the other ingredients made up into pastry) will be required for an 8–9-in. plate. Divide the dough into 2 portions, form each into a round shape and roll one portion into a round about $\frac{1}{8}$ in. thick and a little larger than the plate. Fold over the rolling-pin and lift on to the plate; smooth to fit the plate without stretching the pastry. Cut off the surplus pastry with a sharp knife or scissors. Put in a layer of filling, sprinkle with sugar, if required, and cover with another layer of filling. Roll the remaining pastry into a round a little larger than the plate. Wet with cold water the edge of the pastry lining the plate; lift on the cover and ease into position without stretching. Press the 2 edges together firmly, knock up the edge and decorate.

Bake according to the type of pastry, and to ensure that the bottom crust cooks through stand the plate on a baking-sheet.

APPLE PIE or TART

Short crust pastry (p. 341), using
6 oz. flour, etc.   1½–2 lb. apples
4 oz. moist sugar   6 cloves or
½ teasp. grated lemon rind

Peel, quarter and core the apples and cut in thick slices. Place half the apples in a 1½-pt pie-dish, add the sugar and flavouring and pile the remaining fruit on top. Line the edge of the pie-dish with pastry and cover the pie with pastry. Knock up the edges of the pastry with the back of a knife. Bake for 40 min., first in a fairly hot oven (400° F., Gas 6), reducing the heat to moderate (350° F., Gas 4) when the pastry is set. Dredge with castor sugar and serve

hot or cold. If liked, the pastry may by brushed with egg white and sprinkled with sugar before cooking.

6 helpings

APRICOT TART

Short crust pastry (p. 341), using
6 oz. flour, etc.   1 large can of
apricots   sugar to taste

Place the apricots in a 1½-pt. pie-dish; sprinkle with sugar and half fill the dish with the syrup from the can. Line the edge of the dish with pastry, cover with the remaining pastry and bake in a fairly hot oven (400° F., Gas 6) for 30–40 min. When the pastry has set brush it over lightly with water and dredge well with castor sugar. Return to oven quickly and finish cooking.

6 helpings

GOOSEBERRY TART

Short crust pastry (p. 341), using
6 oz. flour, etc.   1½ lb. gooseberries
2 tablesp. water
4 oz. demerara sugar

Top and tail the gooseberries with a pair of scissors, wash the gooseberries well. Place half of them in a 1½-pt. pie-dish, add the sugar and water and then the remaining gooseberries. Line the edge of the dish with pastry, cover with the remaining pastry. Bake in a fairly hot oven (400° F., Gas 6) reducing the heat to moderate (350° F., Gas 4) when the pastry is set. Continue cooking till the fruit is tender—about 45 min. altogether.

Dredge with castor sugar and serve.

6 helpings

REDCURRANT AND RASPBERRY TART

Short crust pastry (p. 341), using
6 oz. flour, etc.   1½ lb. redcurrants
½ lb. raspberries   2–3 tablesp. sugar

Strip the currants from the stalks, rinse and place half of the currants in a 1½-pt. pie-dish. Add the sugar, the hulled raspberries, then the remaining redcurrants. Line the edge of the dish with pastry. Cover with pastry, brush lightly with water and dredge well with castor sugar. Bake in a fairly hot oven (400° F., Gas 6) for about ¾ hr.

6 helpings
Cooking time—about 45 min.

TARTLETS AND PASTRY BASE CAKES

ALMOND CHEESECAKES

Short crust pastry (p. 341), using
6 oz. flour, etc.   1–2 dessertsp. jam
4 oz. castor sugar   2 oz. ground
almonds   ¼ teasp. almond essence
2 egg whites   1 dessertsp. water

Roll pastry out thinly, cut into rounds and line patty or bouché tins. Place a little jam in the bottom of each. Mix castor sugar and ground almonds, add essence to egg whites and whisk stiffly. Fold almond mixture into egg white and add water. Half-fill pastry cases with mixture. If desired, place pastry crosses on top of the mixture. Bake in a fairly hot to moderate oven (375°–350° F., Gas 5–4 for 15–20 min.).

16–18 cheesecakes

APRICOT BOUCHEES

Puff pastry (p. 340), using 8 oz.
flour, etc.   1 can apricots   ¼ pt.
double cream   sugar to sweeten

Roll out the pastry to rather less than ½ in. thickness. Cut into rounds 2½ in. diameter with a cutter dipped in hot water. Make an incision half-way through the rounds with a smaller cutter. Bake in a hot oven (450° F., Gas 8) for about 12 min. When cool, scoop out the paste within the ring. Drain the apricots from the syrup, and place ½ an apricot, rounded

side down, in each case. Pipe a rosette of stiffly-whipped sweetened cream in each hollow.

12–14 bouchées

BEATRICE TARTLETS

Pâte sucrée (p. 339), usng 6 oz.
flour, etc.   3 bananas   juice of
1 lemon   ½ oz. castor sugar   1 oz.
chopped walnuts   ¼ pt. double
cream   1 oz. finely-grated chocolate

Line 12 patty tins with pâte sucrée and bake them "blind" in a moderate oven (350° F., Gas 4). Allow to cool. Chop the bananas with the lemon juice and add sugar and walnuts. Pile the mixture into the tartlet cases. Pipe a large rosette of whipped sweetened cream on top and dredge with grated chocolate.

12 tartlets
Cooking time—15 min.

CHERRY TARTLETS

Rich short crust pastry (p. 341)
using 6 oz. flour, etc.   1 can bright
red cherries   ¼ pt. fruit syrup
1½ oz. loaf sugar   lemon juice to
flavour   1 teasp. arrowroot   carmine
sweetened, whipped cream

Line 15 patty tins or boat-shaped moulds with the pastry. Bake them "blind" in a fairly hot oven (400° F., Gas 6) until set. Remove the weighted paper and return the tartlet cases to the oven for 2–3 min. to dry the pastry. Drain the juice from the cherries and remove the stones. Place a layer of cherries in the tartlet cases. Dissolve the sugar in the fruit syrup and boil for 5 min. Blend the arrowroot with the lemon juice, add to the syrup, stirring all the time, and boil for 2 min. till the syrup is clear. Add a few drops of carmine to colour. Pour a little syrup over the cherries and allow to set. Decorate with piped, sweetened, whipped cream.

NOTE: The syrup must be stirred and boiled gently.

15 tartlets

CHOCOLATE TARTLETS

Short crust pastry (p. 341), using
6 oz. flour, etc.   3 oz. castor sugar
2 eggs   4 oz. cake-crumbs
2 oz. grated chocolate
½ oz. cornflour   2 oz. butter
chocolate glacé icing (p. 334)

Line 15 patty tins with the pastry. Cream the sugar and egg yolks well together till thick and white, and add the cake-crumbs, chocolate, cornflour and melted butter. Whisk the egg whites till stiff and fold them carefully into the mixture. Fill the patty tins and bake in a fairly hot oven (400° F., Gas 6) for 20–25 min. When cold spread with chocolate glacé icing.

15 tartlets

CREAM BUNS

Choux pastry (p. 339), using 4 oz. flour, etc.   icing sugar

FILLING
½ pt. sweetened double cream flavoured with vanilla essence or confectioner's custard or mock cream may be used

Put the pastry into a forcing bag and pipe balls on to a greased baking-sheet, using a 1-in. vegetable pipe, or shape the mixture with a spoon into piles and bake in a fairly hot oven (425°–400° F., Gas 7–6) for 30 min. (do not open the door), then move to a cooler part of the oven for about 10 min. until dried inside. Split the buns and remove any damp mixture. When cold fill with whipped cream and dust with icing sugar.

12 buns
Cooking time—40 min.

CREAM HORNS

Puff or flaky pastry (p. 339), using

4 oz. flour, etc.   raspberry jam
1 gill sweetened and flavoured cream
chopped pistachio nuts

Roll pastry out ⅛ in. thick and cut into strips ½ in. wide and 12–14 in. long. Moisten strip with water and wind round the cornet mould from the point upwards, keeping moist surface on the outside. Finish final overlap on under side of tin and trim neatly. Allow to stand for 1 hr. Place horns on baking-sheet, brush over with egg and milk and place in a hot oven (425° F., Gas 7) until nicely browned and cooked through. Remove tins and return horns to oven to dry for a few minutes. When cool, place a little jam in each horn, pipe a rosette of cream on top and sprinkle with nuts.

7–8 horns
Cooking time—15–20 min.

CREAM SLICES

Puff pastry (p. 340), using 3 oz. flour, etc., a little royal icing (p. 335)
½ pt. sweetened, flavoured cream

Roll pastry ½ in. thick and cut into fingers 4 in. by 1 in. Spread top thinly with royal icing. Bake in a hot oven (425°–450° F., Gas 7–8) until pastry is well risen and icing lightly browned. Allow to cool. Slit carefully through the centre, spread bottom half with jam. Pipe or spread whipped cream over the jam and sandwich the two halves together again.

NOTE: If liked, glacé icing may be spread on top *after* the slices have been baked.

8 slices
Cooking time—20 min.

CUSTARD TARTLETS

Short crust pastry (p. 341), using
6 oz. flour, etc.   2 eggs   ¾ pt. milk
1 tablesp. granulated sugar   2 egg whites   3 oz. castor sugar

Line 12 deep patty tins with pastry and partially bake. Beat the

2 eggs and add the granulated
sugar and warm milk. Strain into
the pastry-lined patty tins and bake
in a warm oven (335° F., Gas 3)
for 15–20 min. until the custard
sets. Whisk the egg whites stiffly
and fold in the castor sugar. Pile
lightly on the tarts and bake in a
very cool oven (290° F., Gas 1)
until the meringue hardens and
becomes lightly coloured. Serve
cold.

12 tartlets
Cooking time—45–55 min.

ECCLES CAKES

Flaky or rough puff pastry (p. 341),
using 6 oz. flour, etc. or trimmings
may be used   ½ oz. butter or margarine   ¼ oz. sugar   2 oz. currants
¾ oz. chopped peel   ¼ teasp. mixed
spice   a little grated nutmeg

Roll out pastry ¼ in. thick, cut
into 4-in. rounds. Cream fat and
sugar, add currants, peel and spice
and place a good teasp. of the mixture in the centre of each round of
pastry. Gather the edges together, pinch firmly, and form into
a flat cake; reverse the cake and
roll gently till the fruit begins to
show through. Make two cuts on
top of each, brush with water and
dust with castor sugar. Bake in a
hot oven (425° F., Gas 7).

12–14 cakes
Cooking time—20 min.

ECLAIRS

Choux pastry (p. 339)   ½ pt. double
cream or confectioner's custard or
mock cream   sugar to sweeten
vanilla essence   chocolate or
coffee glacé icing (p. 334)

Grease a baking-sheet. Place the
pastry in a forcing bag with a large
plain pipe (¾ in. to 1 in.), and pipe
mixture out on to the greased sheet
in 4-in. lengths, cutting off each
length with a knife dipped in hot
water. Bake in a hot oven (425°–
400° F., Gas 7–6) until risen and
crisp (do not open the door during
this time). Reduce heat and move
to a cooler part of the oven, until
éclairs are light and dry inside,
about 30 min. altogether. Place on
a cooling tray and slit open. When
cold fill the cavities with stiffly-
whipped, sweetened cream flavoured with vanilla. Spread tops
with chocolate or coffee glacé icing
(p. 334). Put the icing on in a
straight line, using a teaspoon—
hold the éclair in a slanting position when doing so.

9–10 éclairs
Cooking time—30 min.

FRUIT or JAM TURNOVERS

Short crust, flaky, rough puff or puff
pastry (pp. 339–41)   stewed fruit or
jam   castor sugar

Roll the pastry thinly and cut
into rounds of about 4 in. diameter.
Place some jam or fruit in the
centre of each round and moisten
the edges with cold water. Fold
the pastry over and press the edges
together. Knock up the edges with
the back of a knife and place on a
baking-sheet. Brush the top with
water, sprinkle with sugar and
bake in a fairly hot or hot oven
(400°–425° F., Gas 6–7)—depending on the type of pastry—for 20
min.

FRUIT TARTLETS

Short crust pastry (p. 341), using
3–4 oz. flour, etc.

FILLING

Fresh fruit, e.g. strawberries, raspberries, etc., or canned fruit, e.g.
cherries, peaches, etc.

COATING GLAZE

1 teasp. arrowroot   a few drops of
colouring   ½ pt. fruit syrup

or if no fruit syrup

1 teasp. arrowroot   ½–1 oz. sugar
½ pt. water   a few drops of
colouring   lemon juice to taste

DECORATION

1 gill whipped, sweetened and flavoured cream

Roll pastry thinly, cut out with fluted cutter and line small tartlet tins. Bake them "blind" in a fairly hot oven (425°–400° F., Gas 7–6) for 15 min. Remove weighted paper and return cases to oven for 2–3 min. or till dry. When cool arrange fruit neatly in the cases. Blend the arrowroot with a little syrup, boil remainder of syrup and pour on to blended mixture, stirring gently. Return to pan and bring to boil again, stirring *very* gently, otherwise the mixture loses its clear colour because of bubbles of air introduced in stirring or boiling syrup. Pour the glaze gently over the fruit and allow to cool. Pipe the cream neatly round the edge.

8–10 tartlets

JAM TARTLETS

Short crust or rich short crust, flaky or rough puff pastry (pp. 339–41) using 4 oz. flour, etc.
3–4 tablesp. jam

Roll out pastry thinly, cut into rounds with fluted cutter (a little larger than patty tin to allow for depth of tin). Line the tins with the pastry and press in well with the fingers. About half-fill with jam and bake in a hot oven (425° F., Gas 7).

10–12 tartlets
Cooking time—15 min.

LEMON CHEESECAKES

Short crust pastry (p. 341), using 12 oz. flour, etc.   1 lb. loaf sugar 4 oz. butter   3 lemons   3 eggs finely-shredded candied peel

Line about 30 patty tins with the pastry. Put the sugar, butter, juice of 3 lemons and the grated rind of 2 lemons in a pan and stir till the sugar is dissolved. Add the beaten eggs and stir over a gentle heat until the mixture becomes thick. Allow to cool, then ¾ fill the patty tins with the mixture. Place a few strips of candied peel on top and bake in a fairly hot oven (400° F., Gas 6) for about 20 min.

30 cheesecakes

MAIDS OF HONOUR

Puff pastry (p. 340), using 4 oz. flour, etc.   4 oz. ground almonds 2 oz. castor sugar   1 egg ½ oz. flour   2 tablesp. cream 1 tablesp. orange-flower water

Roll out the pastry thinly and line 12 patty tins. Mix the ground almonds and sugar together, add the beaten egg and mix in the flour, cream and orange-flower water. Put a little mixture in each patty tin and bake in a fairly hot oven (400° F., Gas 6) till set and golden brown.

10–12 tartlets
Cooking time—25–30 min.

MINCE PIES

Short crust, rich short crust, flaky, rough puff or puff pastry (pp. 339–41), using 6 oz. flour, etc.   10–12 oz. mincemeat   castor or icing sugar

Roll the pastry out to about ⅛ in. thickness. Cut half of it into rounds of about 2½ in. diameter and reserve these for lids. (Use a plain cutter for flaky, rough puff or puff pastry.) Cut the remaining pastry into rounds of about 3 in. diameter and line some patty tins. Place some mincemeat in the tins. brush the edge of the pastry with water and place a lid on top of each. Press the edges well together; if a plain cutter has been used knock up the edges. Brush the tops with water and sprinkle with sugar. Make a hole or 2 small cuts in the top of each. Bake in a hot oven (450°–425° F., Gas 8–7) depending on the type of pastry, for 25–30 min. Dredge tops with castor sugar.

8–10 pies

VANILLA SLICES

Puff pastry (p. 340), using 3 oz.
flour, etc.   a little glacé icing

FILLING

½ pt. milk   ¾ oz. cornflour   2 egg
yolks or 1 whole egg   1 oz. sugar
¼ teasp. vanilla essence

Roll pastly ½ in. thick and cut
into fingers 4 in. by 1 in. Bake
in a fairly hot oven (425° F., Gas
7) until pastry is well risen.
Allow to cool. Blend the cornflour
with the milk, beat in the egg
yolks and sugar, and cook over a
gentle heat until thick. Beat in
the vanilla. Allow to cool. Slit
carefully through the centre of
the pastry fingers, spread the custard over one half and sandwich
the halves together again. Spread
tops thinly with glacé icing.

8 slices
Cooking time—20 min.

WELSH CHEESECAKES

Short crust pastry (p. 341), using
4 oz. flour   2 oz. butter or margarine   2 oz. sugar   3 oz. plain flour
½ level teasp. baking-powder
grated rind of ½ lemon   1 egg
milk or water, if necessary
raspberry jam

Roll out pastry thinly, cut into
rounds, using a cutter a little larger
than the tins, and line 12 patty
tins. Cream the fat and sugar.
Sift flour and baking-powder, add
the grated lemon rind. Whisk the
egg, and add a little at a time to
the creamed fat. Stir in the flour
and add milk or water to make a
soft dropping consistency. Half-
fill the pastry cases with the mixture, after putting a small amount
of jam in the bottom of each.
Place on top 2 strips of pastry in
the form of a cross and bake in a
fairly hot oven (400° F., Gas 6).

12 cheesecakes
Cooking time—15–20 min.

SAVOURIES AND APPETIZERS

In this section are included a number of different kinds of savoury dishes. Some easy-to-make recipes that form a fitting end to a good lunch or dinner—some people omit the sweet, preferring a savoury to a sweet at the end of the meal. On the other hand these recipes will be found very useful for a light lunch or supper dish—served in a somewhat larger quantity. Also savouries for cocktail parties, for buffet parties, and for the evenings when the family and friends are watching television. Some of the recipes for hors d'œuvre—if put on rounds of toast, etc.—are very suitable for these occasions.

A selection of interesting, easy-to-make, yet delicious-tasting snacks will be appreciated in these days of informal entertaining.

ANCHOVY ECLAIRS

Puff pastry (p. 340), using 4 oz. flour, etc. 12–15 anchovy fillets milk 3 tablesp. grated Parmesan cheese

The éclairs should have the appearance of miniature sausage rolls.

Roll out the pastry thinly, cut it into oblong pieces, slightly longer than the anchovy fillets. Enclose an anchovy fillet in each piece, seal the edge folded over with a little milk, sprinkle with cheese, and bake in a hot oven (425°–450° F., Gas 7–8) until nicely browned and crisp.

NOTE: If liked, sardines may be substituted for anchovies.

12–15 savouries
Cooking time—10–15 min.

ANCHOVY FINGERS

Buttered toast 1 shallot chopped parsley 8–10 anchovy fillets lemon juice cayenne pepper or paprika pepper ½ oz. butter

Cut the toast into fingers, sprinkle them with finely-chopped shallot and parsley, and place on each an anchovy fillet. Add a few drops of lemon juice and a seasoning of pepper. Sprinkle on a little paprika or cayenne pepper, place a little butter on each. Heat for a few minutes in a fairly hot oven (400° F., Gas 6).

8–10 savouries
Cooking time—5–10 min.

ANCHOVY TOAST

1 small can of anchovies 1 small shallot or onion 1 oz. butter ½ teasp. chopped parsley 4 eggs cayenne pepper 4 slices buttered toast

Drain the anchovy fillets, chop them coarsely. Chop the shallot or onion. Heat the butter in a small saucepan, fry the shallot or onion until lightly browned, then add the anchovies, parsley and eggs and season with cayenne pepper. Stir over low heat until the mixture thickens, then pour it on the buttered toast.

4 helpings or 8–10 small savouries
Cooking time—3–4 min.

"ANGELS ON HORSEBACK"

12 oysters 12 small thin slices of bacon paprika or cayenne pepper ½ teasp. chopped shallot or onion ½ teasp. chopped parsley lemon juice 12 small rounds of fried bread or 4 slices of toast

Beard the oysters, trim the bacon, cutting each piece just large enough to roll round an oyster, season with paprika or cayenne pepper, sprinkle on a little shallot and parsley. Lay an oyster on each, add a few drops of lemon juice, roll up tightly and secure the bacon in position with a fine skewer. Cook in a frying-pan, under the grill or in a hot oven ($425°$ F., Gas 7), *just long enough* to crisp the bacon (further cooking would harden the oysters), remove the skewers and serve on the croûtes.

4 helpings or 12 small savouries
Cooking time—5–10 min.

ASPIC FINGERS

To about 6 slices of bread allow
½ pt. aspic jelly

SELECTION OF TOPPINGS
FOR THE BREAD
Sardines anchovies tiny pieces of smoked salmon prawns shrimps cooked peas and diced carrots asparagus tips

GARNISH
Savoury butter (p. 401)

Making aspic fingers is a troublesome rather than difficult task. Either butter the bread, or toast and spread with butter or one of the flavoured butters used for piping.

Arrange the topping on the toast or bread. Make the aspic jelly and allow it to become quite cold and just beginning to thicken, then either spread this over the topping with a knife dipped in hot water or brush it over. It is better to have several thin coatings—allowing each one to set before adding the next—than to try and give too thick a coating.

The piping in the flavoured butter can either be put on top of the set aspic jelly or put on the topping and then coated with a thin layer of aspic jelly. The latter method is best since it prevents the butter from drying. When the jelly is quite set, cut the slices of bread into tiny fingers with a sharp knife dipped in hot water.

It is advisable to stand the slices of bread on a tray or pastry-board when coating with jelly, so that any jelly that drips off the bread can be picked up and used again.

BLOATER TOAST

2 bloaters with soft roes   1½ oz.
butter   1 egg   salt   cayenne pepper
8 squares of buttered toast or
2 large pieces of toast

Remove the roes, grill the bloaters, free them from skin and bone, then chop or rub them through a fine sieve. Heat 1 oz. of butter in a small saucepan, add the fish, and when hot put in the egg, season to taste, and stir over a low heat until the mixture thickens. Meanwhile divide the roes into 8 pieces, and fry them in the remainder of the butter. Spread the fish mixture on the toast, place the roe on the top, and serve as hot as possible.

2 helpings or 8 small savouries
Cooking time—5 min.

CANAPES

Canapés for savouries can be neat shapes of bread and butter, toast or fried bread; or crisp biscuits of cheese, short or flaky pastry. Tiny, round, firm pancakes are a good base for savoury mixtures too.

Toast is the most usual, but it does become soft if prepared too far ahead. Fried bread should be very well drained on kitchen or crumpled tissue paper so that it is dry and no longer greasy.

CHEESE MERINGUES

2 egg whites   pinch of cayenne
pepper   pinch of salt   2 oz. grated

Parmesan cheese   deep fat for frying
a little Parmesan cheese for garnish

Whisk the egg whites to a very
stiff froth. Add a good seasoning of
cayenne and a little salt to the
cheese, then stir it lightly into the
whisked egg whites. Have ready
a deep pan of hot fat, drop in the
mixture in small teaspoonfuls, and
fry until nicely browned. Drain
well, and serve sprinkled with
Parmesan cheese and more
cayenne pepper.

About 14 savouries
Cooking time—5 min.

CHEESE PUDDING

2 eggs   4 oz. grated cheese   1 teasp.
mixed mustard   pinch of salt
pinch of pepper   ½ pt. milk
1 oz. breadcrumbs

Beat the eggs slightly, add to
them the cheese, mustard, salt and
pepper. Boil the milk, pour over
the eggs, then add the breadcrumbs.
Pour into a pie-dish or soufflé-dish
and bake for 25–30 min. in the
centre of a fairly hot oven (375°
F., Gas 5). Serve at once. If baked
in 4 or 5 individual dishes allow
approximately 15 min.

4–5 helpings

CHEESE SOUFFLE

A little butter for greasing   1 oz.
butter   1 oz. flour   ¼ pt. milk
2 eggs   3 oz. grated cheese   pinch
of salt   pinch of cayenne pepper
1–2 egg whites

Coat a soufflé dish well with
butter and tie round it a well-
buttered, thickly folded piece of
paper to support the soufflé when
it rises above the level of the dish.
Melt the 1 oz. butter in a pan, stir
in the flour, add the milk, and boil
well. Remove from heat, and mix
in the 2 egg yolks, beat well, then
stir in the cheese and add seasoning to taste. Whisk all the egg
whites to a stiff froth, add them
lightly to the rest of the ingre-

dients, pour the mixture into the
soufflé dish, and bake in a moderate oven (350° F., Gas 4) for 30–
35 min. Serve in the dish in which
it is baked. Serve immediately.

5–6 helpings
Cooking time—35 min.

CROUTES OF HERRING ROES

Toast   butter   anchovy paste
8 fresh herring roes   1 lemon
cayenne pepper   lemon   parsley

Cut the toast into rounds or
triangles and butter, then spread
liberally with anchovy paste. Melt
about 1 oz. butter in a pan and fry
the roes until lightly browned.
Drain well, then put on to the prepared toast, sprinkle with lemon
juice and cayenne pepper. Garnish
with slices of lemon and parsley.

NOTE: Frozen or canned roes
can be used instead of fresh roes.
Frozen roes should be defrosted,
then fried, but since canned roes
are already cooked they need to be
just browned in the butter.

2 helpings or 8 small savouries
Cooking time—5 min.

"DEVILS ON HORSEBACK"

1–2 chicken livers or equivalent of
calf's liver   butter   salt and pepper
cayenne pepper   8 well-drained
canned prunes   8 short, thin,
rindless rashers streaky bacon
4 small bread squares
olives stuffed with pimento

Gently cook the liver in a little
butter, then cut it into 8 pieces.
Season well and dust with a few
grains of cayenne pepper. Stone
the prunes and stuff with the
liver. Stretch the bacon to double
its size with the flat of a knife. Encircle each prune in a piece of
bacon and secure with a cocktail
stick. Grill all over or bake in a
very hot oven. Fry the bread in
shallow bacon fat and drain well.
Remove sticks and place the

"devils" on the bread. Garnish with a pimento-stuffed olive.

4 helpings

FOIE GRAS CROUTES

Foie gras   cream or white sauce
salt and pepper   croûtes of fried or
toasted bread

Pound the foie gras, adding a little cream or white sauce until the right consistency is obtained. Pass through a fine sieve, season to taste, and arrange on the croûtes, using a piping bag if available.

GOLDEN BUCK

4 oz. Cheshire or Cheddar cheese
¼ oz. butter   3 tablesp. ale   ½ teasp.
Worcester sauce   ½ teasp. lemon
juice or vinegar   2 eggs   pinch of
celery salt   pinch of cayenne pepper
2 large slices buttered toast

Grate the cheese finely. Put it into a pan with the butter and ale and stir vigorously until creamy. Then add the Worcester sauce, lemon juice or vinegar and the eggs, previously beaten. Season to taste with celery salt and cayenne pepper, and continue stirring briskly until the mixture thickens. Trim the toast, and cover with cheese mixture. Garnish with parsley. Serve as hot as possible.

4 small or 2 large helpings
Cooking time—10 min.

HAM ROLLS

4 thin slices of cooked ham   2 oz.
cream cheese   1–2 tablesp. sweet
chutney   crisp lettuce

Spread each slice of ham on a board, trim off surplus fat. Mix the cream cheese and chutney together, spread over the ham and roll. Put on to lettuce leaves. If wished cut the slices into 1-in. lengths and instead of putting on to lettuce leaves put on small buttered biscuits and garnish with watercress leaves.

4 helpings or 12 small savouries

HELFORD ANGELS

Thin slices of brown bread   butter
oysters   pepper   nutmeg

Thickly spread the slices of brown bread with butter and trim into neat 2-in. squares. Place a raw oyster on each, sprinkle with a shake of pepper and grated nutmeg, and roll up cornerwise. Place in a greased fireproof dish and bake in a fairly hot oven (375° F., Gas 5) about 10 min. until the bread is crisp. Spear with cocktail sticks and serve immediately.

Serve as a savoury, allowing 2 per helping; or as "hot" individual savouries for a cocktail party.

HERRING ROE TIT-BITS

6 large soft herring roes   salt and
pepper   6 rashers of bacon   a little
lemon juice   12 small rounds of
toast or fried bread   anchovy paste
2–3 small gherkins

Cut the roes into halves, season lightly with salt and pepper. Divide the rashers of bacon into halves, remove the rinds and wrap each piece of roe in the bacon. Sprinkle lemon juice on the bacon and secure the rolls on a skewer. Cook for about 15 min. in a fairly hot oven (375° F., Gas 5) or under a moderately hot grill—reducing the heat after crisping the bacon, to make sure the roes are cooked. Spread the rounds of toast or fried bread with anchovy paste and thin slices of gherkin. Put the roes on top—serve hot or cold.

12 savouries
Cooking time—15 min. in the oven ;
   6 min. (approx.) under the grill

IRISH RABBIT or RAREBIT

3 tablesp. milk   1 oz. margarine or
butter   4 oz. grated Cheddar or
Cheshire cheese   1 teasp. vinegar
1 teasp. mixed mustard   salt and
pepper   1 dessertsp. chopped
gherkin   buttered toast

Put the milk, butter and cheese into a saucepan, and stir over a *low* heat until the cheese melts and the mixture becomes creamy. Add the vinegar, mustard, a good pinch of salt and pepper and lastly the gherkin. Put on to hot buttered toast and either serve at once, or brown for a few minutes under a hot grill.

2 helpings or **4–5 small savouries**
Cooking time—8 min. (approx.)

OYSTER TIT-BITS

9 small oysters   1 oz. butter
9 round croûtes of bread   anchovy paste   3 small rashers of bacon
lemon juice   cayenne pepper
watercress

Beard the oysters and place between 2 plates with their own liquid and the butter. Warm thoroughly in the oven, or over a saucepan of boiling water. Spread the croûtes of bread—which can be toasted or fried if wished—with anchovy paste. Cut each rasher of bacon into 3 pieces, grill or fry, put on the croûtes of bread and top with a hot oyster. Sprinkle with lemon juice and cayenne pepper, and garnish with watercress.

Can be served cold, but nicer hot.

9 small savouries
Cooking time—12–15 min. (approx.)

OYSTERS ON TOAST

White or brown bread   butter for toast   2–3 oz. cooked ham, cut very thinly   12 small oysters   seasoning
1 oz. butter for coating oysters
lemon

Toast slices of white or brown bread, and cut into small rounds—1½–2 in. diameter. Cover with butter, and small rounds of ham. Beard the oysters and put on the ham, season well, put a small knob of butter on each and bake in a hot oven (425° *F.*, *Gas* 7) for about 3 min. until the butter has melted. Garnish with wedges of lemon.

12 small savouries
Cooking time—3 min. (approx.)

PASTRY CASES

Vol-au-vent shapes or cornet shapes—filled with savoury mixtures—are excellent for buffet parties. They can be served hot or cold. If the mixture is being put into the cold pastry cases make sure it is quite cold. If, on the other hand, it is being put into hot pastry cases heat the filling and the pastry separately, and put together at the last minute, so that the filling does not make the pastry soft.

Directions for making vol-au-vent shapes and cornet shapes are given in the Pastry section (pp. 340–1).

SUGGESTED FILLINGS: Quantities given are enough to fill 12 medium-sized vol-au-vent cases or about 16 cornet cases (allowing a liberal amount of filling).

Chicken

½ pt. thick sauce made with ½ milk and ½ chicken stock   ¾–1 lb. diced cooked chicken (approx.)   seasoning

Mix together well, and if possible, add just 1 tablesp. cream.

Mushroom

¾ lb. mushrooms   2 oz. butter or margarine   2½ gill milk   1½ oz. flour
seasoning   cayenne pepper

Chop the mushrooms into small pieces and toss in the hot butter for a few minutes. Add ½ pt. of milk and cook gently for about 10 min. Blend the flour with the other ½ gill milk, add to the mushroom mixture. Season well and boil until smooth and thick. Stir as the mixture cools. If wished add 1 tablesp. thick cream. Dust with cayenne pepper when the cases are filled.

Sardine

1 small can of sardines   1 tablesp.

white or tomato sauce   salt and
pepper   a few drops of lemon juice
2 teasp. grated Parmesan cheese or
1 tablesp. grated Cheddar cheese

Remove the bones and mash the
sardines. Mix with the white or
tomato sauce (if using white sauce,
add a few drops of anchovy essence). Season, blend with a few
drops of lemon juice and the
cheese.

Savoury Egg

5 eggs   3 tablesp. cream or mayonnaise   1 oz. butter   seasoning
2 oz. finely-diced lean tongue

Beat the eggs and cream or
mayonnaise together. Heat the
butter, add the eggs, season well
and cook gently until commencing
to thicken. If serving the mixture
hot add the diced tongue—but if
serving cold do not add this until
the eggs are cold. Take care the
mixture does not become too stiff
—if it appears rather dry beat in
more cream or mayonnaise.

Shellfish

½ pt. thick sauce—made with ½ milk
and ½ stock made by simmering
prawn or lobster shells   1 large
flaked lobster or about 1½ pt. picked
prawns   2 tablesp. thick mayonnaise
seasoning

Mix well together, and if wished
add 1–2 chopped gherkins and
capers. Garnish with whole
prawns.

SCOTCH WOODCOCK

4 slices of toast   butter   4 eggs
2 tablesp. milk   good pinch of salt
good pinch of pepper
1 small can anchovy fillets

Cover the hot toast with butter
and keep warm. Beat the eggs with
the milk and seasoning. Put a good
knob of butter (about 1 oz.) into a
saucepan, heat gently, then add the
eggs and milk. Cook gently until
the mixture thickens. Spread on

toast and garnish with anchovy
fillets—arranged in a lattice design.

4 helpings or 8 small savouries
Cooking time—6 min. (approx.)

SWISS EGGS

1½ oz. butter or margarine
2 tablesp. grated cheese   4 eggs
good pinch of salt   pinch of pepper
cayenne or paprika pepper

Well grease 4 small dishes. Put
½ the cheese at the bottom of the
dishes. Carefully break the eggs
and put one into each dish on top
of the cheese. Cover with seasoning, cheese and butter. Bake for
about 10 min. in a fairly hot oven
(400° F., Gas 6). Garnish with
pepper and serve at once with hot
rolls or crisp toast.

4 helpings

TOMATO JUICE COCKTAIL

1 pt. tomato juice (canned or
bottled)   2 teasp. lemon juice
1–2 teasp. Worcester sauce
good pinch of celery salt
good pinch of paprika pepper

Mix all the ingredients together. Serve very cold.

Sufficient for 4–5 people

UGLI COCKTAIL

2 uglis   juice of 1 lemon
few drops of Maraschino

Cut the uglis in half and remove
the pulp. Sprinkle the pulp with
lemon juice and add Maraschino
to taste. Put into cocktail glasses
or return to the skins, and serve
very cold.

6 helpings

WELSH RAREBIT

1 oz. butter or margarine   1 level
tablesp. flour   5 tablesp. milk; or
3 tablesp. milk and 2 tablesp. ale or
beer   1 teasp. mixed mustard
few drops of Worcester sauce
4–6 oz. grated Cheddar cheese   salt
and pepper   4 slices of buttered toast

Heat the fat in a pan and stir in the flour. Cook for several minutes, stirring well. Add the milk and stir well over the heat until a smooth thick mixture, then add the ale, mustard, Worcester sauce, cheese and a good pinch of salt and pepper. Do not overcook the mixture otherwise the cheese will become oily. Spread on the slices of buttered toast and put under a hot grill until golden brown. Serve at once.

NOTE: A larger quantity of Welsh Rarebit mixture can be made and stored in the refrigerator, being used as required.

4 helpings or 8 small savouries
Cooking time—10 min. (approx.)

BUCK RAREBIT

As for Welsh Rarebit, but top each slice of cooked Welsh Rarebit with a poached egg and serve at once.

YORKSHIRE RAREBIT

As for Welsh Rarebit, but add 2 oz. cooked ham. The ham can either be cut into 4 thin slices, put on the toast and warmed for a minute under the grill before putting the cheese mixture on top *or* it can be diced and mixed with the cheese, etc.

BREAKFAST AND SUPPER DISHES

WE give here a selection of dishes suitable for serving at breakfast, high teas, suppers and supper parties. Recipes for other dishes which may be served at such meals will be found in the sections on Savouries, p. 353; Vegetables, p. 209; Cereals, p. 366; Eggs, p. 403; Cheese, p. 402; Réchauffés, p. 369; and for cold supper dishes *see also* Salads, p. 237.

All such familiar standard breakfast dishes as bacon, eggs, sausages, kidneys, cutlets, rissoles, etc., are fully dealt with under their respective headings of Beef, Lamb, Mutton, Pork and Eggs. Those who prefer cereals to more solid food should refer to the section on Cereals.

BACON AND EGG PIE

6 oz. short crust pastry   ½ lb.
smoked streaky bacon   3 eggs
pepper   a little beaten egg

Grease a 7-in. sandwich tin or flan ring. If the latter is used, place it on a piece of greased paper on a baking-sheet. Divide the pastry into 2 uneven pieces. Roll out the larger piece into a round about 9 in. in diameter, and line the tin. Cut off the bacon rinds, cut the bacon into small pieces (or put through a mincer) and season with pepper. Arrange the bacon in the pastry case, leaving 3 spaces for the eggs. Drop an egg into each space and sprinkle with pepper. Brush the edge of the pastry with beaten egg or water. Roll out the remainder of the pastry and cover the pie. Trim and decorate the edges. Brush the top

with beaten egg and decorate with pastry leaves. Make a hole in the centre. Bake for 40 min. on the middle shelf of a fairly hot oven (400° F., Gas 6), covering with greaseproof paper when the top is sufficiently brown. Serve cold.

BLOATERS—GRILLED

Split the bloaters open and remove the backbone, then either fold each bloater back into shape, or leave them opened out flat and place 2 together with their insides facing. Rub over with a little oil or fat and grill as for kippers.

CHEESE AND ONION PIE

short crust pastry (p. 341), using
8 oz. flour, etc.   3 small onions
½ oz. flour   salt and pepper
4 oz. cheese   2 tablesp. milk

Parboil the onions whilst making the pastry. Line an 8-in. fireproof plate with half the pastry. Mix the salt and pepper with the flour. Slice the onions and dip in the seasoned flour, spread them over the bottom of the lined plate. Grate the cheese and sprinkle it over the onion, add the milk. Wet the edge of the pastry, put on the cover and press the edges firmly together. Knock up the edges, decorate as desired and brush over with milk. Bake in a hot oven (425° F., Gas 7) for about 40 min.

NOTE: This can be made as an open tart if liked; use 4 oz. pastry.

6–8 helpings

CORNISH PASTIES

½ lb. raw meat   ½ lb. potatoes
½ teasp. finely-chopped onion

mixed herbs to taste   salt and pepper
2 tablesp. gravy or water   short
crust pastry, using 8 oz. flour, etc.

Mince the meat finely. Dice the
potatoes. Add the onion, herbs,
salt, pepper and gravy to the meat
and potatoes, and mix well together.
Divide the pastry into 8 equal portions and roll them out ¼ in. thick,
keeping the portions as round as
possible. Pile the mixture in the
centre of each piece of pastry, wet
the edges and join them together
on the top to form an upstanding
frill, prick them with a fork. Bake
in a hot oven (425° F., Gas 7) for
10 min., then reduce heat to
moderate (350° F., Gas 4) and
cook for about 50 min. longer.

5–6 helpings

CREAMED HAM ON TOAST

6 oz. cooked ham   ½ pt. white sauce
(p. 91)   3 hard-boiled eggs
¼ teasp. dry mustard   salt and
pepper   6 slices buttered toast

Dice the ham. Add to the white
sauce, the chopped ham, sliced
eggs, mustard and seasoning to
taste. Serve hot on toast with
stuffed olives.

6 helpings

GRILLED KIPPERS

1–2 kippers per person
butter or margarine

Remove the heads and lay the
kippers flat, skin side up, on the
grid. Cook for about 3 min. each
side, adding a dab of butter or
margarine when they are turned
over.

Serve alone or on a slice of toast.
Anternatively, place a pair of
kippers, flesh sides together, and
grill under medium heat, first on
one side then on the other; to
serve, separate and top each with
a nut of butter.

HAM AND EGG PIE

4 oz. mushrooms   4 tablesp. milk

salt and pepper   6–8 oz. cooked
ham   3 oz. cooked peas   2 hard-
boiled eggs   1 teasp. mixed mustard
flaky pastry (p. 339), using 8 oz.
flour, etc.   egg or milk

Prepare the mushrooms and
simmer them for 10 min. in milk
seasoned with salt and pepper.
Chop the ham roughly and mix
with the peas, hard-boiled eggs,
mushrooms, mustard and seasoning. Divide the pastry into 2 un-
equal portions. Roll out the larger
piece and cover a fireproof dish
or plate and trim the edges. Put
in the prepared filling. Roll out the
remaining pastry and cover the pie.
Flake and scallop the edges and
decorate as desired. Glaze top with
beaten egg or milk. Bake in a very
hot oven (450° F., Gas 8) until
set and then reduce heat to warm
(335° F., Gas 3) for the remainder
of the time. Cook for about 45 min.
in all.

HAM AND TONGUE SOUFFLE

3 oz. cooked ham   3 oz. cooked
tongue   1½ gill tomato purée
1½ oz. butter or fat   1½ oz. flour
1½ gill stock   2 teasp. chopped
parsley   salt and pepper   3 eggs

Remove all the skin and bone,
then mince the meat. Rub either
fresh or canned tomatoes through
a sieve to make the purée. Melt the
fat in a saucepan, add the flour
and cook a little, then add the
stock, tomato purée and parsley
and cook until boiling. Lightly
sprinkle in the meat, season to
taste and cook together for a few
minutes. Cool slightly, then add
the egg yolks one at a time. Whisk
the egg whites to a stiff froth and
fold them lightly in. Pour the mixture into a well-greased soufflé
dish, leaving room for it to rise.
Bake in a moderate oven (350° F.,
Gas 4) for about 30–45 min. until
well risen and firm.

HAM MOUSSE

½ lb. cooked ham   salt and pepper
grated nutmeg   ½ pt. Espagnole
sauce   ½ oz. gelatine   ¼ pt. aspic
jelly   2 tablesp. white stock   1 drop
of carmine   1½ gill cream or milk
1 tablesp. chopped truffles
½ gill pale aspic jelly

Tie a band of stiff paper round
a china soufflé dish of about 5 in.
diameter so that it stands about 2
in. higher than the dish.

Pass the ham twice through a
mincer and sieve it. Season with
salt, pepper and nutmeg. Add the
Espagnole sauce, which is well
coloured and flavoured with
tomato. Dissolve the gelatine in
the aspic, together with the stock;
colour with carmine and add to the
ham. Whip the cream very lightly
and fold lightly into the mixture.
When it is beginning to set cream-
ily, pour into the prepared
soufflé case and allow to set. Add
the chopped truffle to the pale
aspic and pour on the top of the
mould, when the jelly is cold, but
not set. When set remove paper
and serve with green salad.

JUGGED KIPPERS

Simply place the kippers in a
tall jug and cover with boiling
water. Cover the jug and stand it
in a warm place for 5-10 min.
Drain, and serve with a knob of
butter or margarine on each
kipper.

NOTE: This method produces
plump, juicy kippers, though some
say a little flavour is lost.

KEBOBS

1 lb. canned meat   1 medium-sized
onion   1 dessertsp. curry powder
salt and pepper   1 egg   flour
dripping

Mince the meat finely; chop the
onion finely. Stir the onion into
the meat with the curry powder,
salt and pepper to taste and the
egg. Form into small balls or flat
cakes, roll lightly in flour and fry
in hot dripping until nicely
browned.

NOTE: Plainly boiled rice and
chutney usually accompany this.

5-6 helpings

LOBSTER CROQUETTES

1 medium-sized lobster or 1 can of
lobster   1 oz. butter   1 tablesp. flour
1 tablesp. cream or milk   cayenne
pepper   salt and pepper   1 egg yolk
egg and breadcrumbs   frying fat

Chop the flesh of the lobster
finely. Melt the butter in a saucepan, stir in the flour, add just
under 1 gill cold water and boil
well. Add the lobster, cream or
milk, pinch of cayenne, salt and
pepper to taste. Stir over the heat
until thoroughly hot, then add the
egg yolk. When the mixture begins
to thicken, spread it on a plate
to cool and, when ready to use,
shape into croquettes. Coat with
egg and breadcrumbs and fry in
hot fat until golden brown.

5-6 helpings

PORK CHEESE

1 lb. cold roast pork   1 dessertsp.
finely-chopped parsley   ¼ teasp.
powdered sage   ¼ teasp. mixed herbs
½ teasp. grated lemon rind   ⅛ teasp.
grated nutmeg   salt and pepper
½ pt. good jellied stock

Cut the pork into neat dice, removing the fat according to taste.
Add the parsley, sage, herbs, lemon
rind, nutmeg, salt and pepper to
the meat and mix well together.
Press tightly into a mould and fill
up with hot jellied stock. Bake for
about 1½ hr. in a moderate oven
(350° F., Gas 4). Leave until cold
and then unmould.

6 helpings

POTATO PASTY

4 oz. lean beef   1 oz. finely-chopped
onion   4 oz. raw diced potato
salt and pepper   a little gravy or

stock   short crust pastry, using
8 oz. flour, etc.

Dice the meat and mix with the onion and potato. Season well, moisten with 2–3 tablesp. of gravy or stock. Roll out the pastry ¼ in. thick, keeping it as round as possible. Place the mixture on one half of the pastry round and wet the edges. Then fold over the other half, forming a semicircle, press and crimp the edges. Bake in a hot oven (425° F., Gas 7) and reduce after 10 min. to moderate (350° F., Gas 4). Bake for about 45 min., testing with a skewer to see if the filling is cooked. If preferred, after rolling out the pastry, it can be cut into rounds about the size of a saucer and individual pasties made.

4 helpings

ROES ON TOAST

¾ lb. herring roes   seasoned flour
1 bacon rasher   4 rounds of toast

Wash and dry the roes, dip in seasoned flour and fry in a little hot fat. Chop the bacon and add it to the roes when they are almost cooked.

Serve piled on rounds of buttered toast.

4 helpings

SAUSAGE CROQUETTES

1 lb. pork sausages   ½ oz. butter
½ lb. mashed potatoes   1 dessertsp.
cream or milk   salt and pepper
nutmeg   1 egg yolk   egg and
breadcrumbs   frying fat

Prick the sausages, put them into boiling water, cook them for 10 min. and when cold remove the skins and cut them across in half. Melt the butter in a saucepan, add the potatoes and cream, season well with salt, pepper and nutmeg. Stir until hot, then add the egg yolk and continue the cooking and stirring for about 5 min. longer. Let the potato cool, then spread a thin layer over each piece of sausage. Coat with egg and breadcrumbs and fry in hot fat until golden brown.

Garnish with fried parsley.

4 helpings

SAUSAGE ROLLS

Rough puff pastry (p. 341), using
4 oz. flour, etc.   ½ lb. sausages
egg yolk to glaze

Roll out the pastry and cut into 8 even-sized squares. Skin the sausages. Divide the sausage meat into 8 portions and make each piece into a roll the same length as the pastry. Place the sausage meat on the pastry, wet the edge and fold over, leaving the ends open. Knock up the edges with the back of a knife. Make three incisions on top. Brush over with beaten egg and place on a baking-sheet. Bake in a hot oven (425° F., Gas 7) until the pastry is well risen and brown. Reduce the heat and continue baking till the pastry is cooked.

NOTE: Small sausage rolls can be quickly made by rolling the pastry into an oblong. Form the sausage meat into long rolls the length of the pastry, place the meat on the pastry, then divide the pastry into strips wide enough to encircle the meat. Damp one edge of each strip, fold over and press together firmly. Cut into rolls of the desired length, finish as above.

8 sausage rolls
Cooking time—about ½ hr.

SAUTED KIDNEYS

2 sheep's or 1 pork kidney   1 shallot
or small onion   1 oz. butter
¼ teasp. finely-chopped parsley
salt and pepper
3–4 tablesp. good brown sauce

Skin the kidneys, cut them across into very thin slices and remove the core. Chop the shallot or onion finely. Heat the butter and fry the shallot until golden brown, then put in the kidney and parsley. Season with salt and pepper, and toss over heat for 5–6 min. Add the brown sauce, mix it well with the kidneys and, when thoroughly hot, serve.

2 helpings

SAVOURY MACARONI

4 oz. macaroni ¼ pt. white sauce (p. 91) 1 tablesp. grated cheese 2–3 tablesp. cream or milk 1 teasp. anchovy essence cayenne pepper salt and pepper

Break the macaroni into short pieces, throw them into rapidly-boiling salted water, boil for 20 min. or until tender, then drain well. Add the macaroni to the sauce, with the cheese, cream or milk, anchovy essence, cayenne, salt and pepper to taste. Mix well, then turn into ramakin cases. Bake in a fairly hot oven (375° F., Gas 5) until well browned, serve hot.

SAVOURY PANCAKES

Batter as for Batter pudding (p. 255) 4 bacon rashers dripping

Whilst the batter is standing for ½ hr., remove the rind from the bacon, cut the bacon into small pieces and fry gently. Remove from frying-pan and stir into the batter. Put a little dripping into the frying-pan and heat until smoking hot. Quickly pour in enough batter to coat the bottom of the pan evenly. Cook until brown underneath, turn and brown on the other side. Serve immediately.

4 helpings

SAVOURY SANDWICH LOAF

1 day-old loaf butter or margarine 6 tablesp. lean cooked ham (minced) mayonnaise 6–8 oz. cream cheese 2 hard-boiled eggs salt and pepper 6 tablesp. crushed sardines

1 small tomato 2 green olives green colouring (optional)

Remove crusts from loaf and cut loaf lengthwise in five equal slices. Butter each slice and spread the lower one with the ham mixed with enough mayonnaise to make an easy spreading consistency. Spread the next slice with 2 oz. cream cheese and place on top of the ham slice. Spread the third slice with crushed eggs, seasoned and mixed to a spreading consistency with mayonnaise; place on top of the cheese slice. Spread the fourth slice with sardines, place on top of the egg slice. Put the fifth slice on top, so that it has the form of the original loaf. Soften the remaining cream cheese with a little milk if necessary, colour if liked, and coat the top and sides of the loaf.

Decorate with slices of tomato and olives. The loaf can be wrapped in damp, greaseproof paper and a cloth and stored in the refrigerator until required.

STUFFED ONIONS IN BATTER

8 large peeled onions 8 oz. cold roast pork, finely-chopped 1 small apple, peeled and chopped finely 1 oz. dripping 1 teasp. dried sage salt and pepper 1 oz. self-raising flour 6 tablesp. milk batter (½ quantity for Batter pudding p. 255)

Boil the onions in salted water for 15–20 min. Scoop out the centre of each onion. Chop the onion from the centre, and mix with the chopped pork and apple. Fry the mixture in the dripping for a few minutes. Add sage, pepper, salt, flour and milk, cook for a few moments longer, stirring all the time. Fill the onions with the mixture, piling up on top of each onion. Grease a shallow fireproof dish or tin (11 in. by 8 in.), place the onions in the dish. Cover and bake for 2 hr. on the middle shelf

of a warm oven (335° F., *Gas* 3).
While the onions are cooking make
the batter and leave to stand for $\frac{1}{2}$
hr. When the onions are cooked,
stir the batter thoroughly, pour
into the dish and bake for 30 min.
on the middle shelf of a hot oven
(425° F., *Gas* 7).

TOAD IN THE HOLE

4 oz. plain flour $\frac{1}{4}$ teasp. salt
1 egg $\frac{1}{2}$ pt. milk or milk and water
1 lb. sausages   1 tablesp. cooking fat

Make a batter with the flour,
salt, egg and milk, and leave to
stand for $\frac{1}{2}$ hr. Heat the fat in a
Yorkshire pudding-tin, skin the
sausages, put the sausages in the
hot fat, pour the batter over and
bake in a hot oven (425° F., *Gas*
7) for about 30 min.

VEAL AND HAM PATTIES

8 oz. cold cooked veal   2–4 oz. ham
salt and pepper   pinch of mixed
herbs   pinch of nutmeg   stock or
water   puff, rough puff or flaky
pastry, using about 8 oz. flour, etc.
egg or milk   parsley

Cut the veal and ham into small
dice, season and add the herbs and
nutmeg. Moisten with stock or
water. Roll out the pastry thinly.
Stamp out with a cutter a little
larger than the patty pans as many
rounds as possible. Put 12 aside
for the covers. Roll out the trimmings and stamp out as before.
Use these for lining the patty pans.
Fill each pan with seasoned meat,
damp the edges and put on the
covers. Press the edges together
and decorate to taste. Make a small
hole in the centre, brush over with
egg or milk and bake in very hot
oven (450° F., *Gas* 8) until the
pastry is set and brown, then reduce the heat. Cook for about 20
min. altogether. Garnish with
parsley.

6 helpings

CEREALS, RISOTTOS AND PASTA

THE success of this type of cooking depends largely upon giving the cereal, which is normally rather tasteless, a pleasant texture and a full, appetizing flavour when cooked. The dishes can be used for economical meals and are most useful for providing filling meals cheaply, where these are required. They are also easily varied in flavour and can provide a wide range of dishes from the same basic method.

Dishes containing starchy substances should be made fresh as required and not kept hot or reheated where it can be avoided, as this spoils the flavour and the texture; and they are easily contaminated by bacteria if left uncovered.

Macaroni is best cooked until it is just tender, but can still be felt between the teeth when bitten, i.e. not too soft.

Colourful garnishing is important as these dishes may tend to be colourless. For garnishing, choose foods for their colour and shape to add interest, e.g. shrimps, croûtons, parsley, paprika, cayenne, browned onion rings, etc., and where the dish is browned before serving, cook to an appetizing golden brown and serve very hot indeed.

GNOCCHI AU GRATIN

½ pt. water 2 oz. butter salt 3 oz. flour or 2 oz. semolina 2 eggs 3 oz. chopped ham 3 oz. grated cheese ½ pt. Béchamel sauce paprika pepper

Put the water, butter and a good pinch of salt into a saucepan over heat. When boiling stir in the flour or semolina, and work vigorously over the heat until the dough leaves the sides of the pan clear. Allow to cool slightly, then beat in the eggs separately, and add the ham and 2 oz. of the cheese. Shape the mixture into quenelles, poach them for about 10 min. in salted boiling water, and drain well. When cool, arrange in a buttered fireproof dish, pour over the Béchamel sauce, sprinkle on the remainder of the cheese, and season well with paprika pepper. Bake in a hot oven (425° F., Gas 7) for about 10 min., and serve.

4–5 helpings

MACARONI AND TOMATOES

4 oz. macaroni ½ pt. tomato purée 1 oz. butter 1 oz. flour good pinch of sugar salt and pepper

Break the macaroni into short lengths, put it into rapidly-boiling salted water and cook until tender. Melt the butter in a saucepan, add the flour and cook for a few minutes. Put in the tomato purée, sugar and season to taste. Let it boil for a few minutes, then add the macaroni, and when thoroughly hot turn on to a dish and serve.

2–3 helpings

MACARONI AU GRATIN

4 oz. macaroni 1 pt. white sauce 4 oz. grated cheese salt and pepper brown breadcrumbs butter

Break the macaroni into pieces about 1½ in. long, put them into rapidly-boiling salted water and boil for about 20 min., or until the macaroni is tender. (If not required for immediate use, cover the macaroni with cold water to prevent the pieces sticking together.) Cover the bottom of a well-buttered baking-dish with white sauce, sprinkle liberally with cheese, seasoning to taste, and add a layer of macaroni. Repeat the layers, cover the last layer of macaroni thickly with sauce, sprinkle the surface lightly with breadcrumbs and add a few small pieces of butter. Bake in a hot oven (425° F., Gas 7) for about 20 min., then serve in the dish in which it is cooked.

6–7 helpings

NOUILLE or NOODLE PASTE
(also called Ribbon Macaroni)

1 lb. flour   1½ oz. butter   3 egg yolks or 2 small whole eggs   salt a little milk or water

Sift the flour into a basin, make a well in the centre, and put in the butter, eggs and a good pinch of salt. Mix thoroughly and add a little milk or water if necessary, but the paste should be rather stiff. Knead well for about 15 min., or until the paste is perfectly smooth and elastic, then use as required.

8 helpings

RAVIOLI

½ lb. nouille paste (above)   ½ pt. tomato sauce   brown breadcrumbs butter

FILLING

4 oz. cooked chicken   1 oz. cooked ham   2½ oz. grated Parmesan cheese 1 egg yolk   1 tablesp. thick cream ½ teasp. finely-chopped parsley salt and pepper   nutmeg

Mince the chicken and ham finely, pound with the other filling ingredients until smooth, seasoning

to taste, then rub through a fine sieve. Roll out the nouille paste as thinly as possible, cut out some rounds of about 1½ in. diameter. Place a small teaspoonful of the filling in the centre of half of the rounds, wet the edges. Cover with the remaining rounds, and press the edges well together. Put into rapidly-boiling salted water, boil for about 20 min. from the time the water re-boils, then drain well. Place in layers in a well-buttered dish, coating each layer with tomato sauce and a good sprinkling of cheese. Cover the top layer thickly with sauce, sprinkle well with brown breadcrumbs, and add a few small pieces of butter. Bake in a hot oven (425° F., Gas 7) or put under the grill for about 10 min., then serve hot.

5–6 helpings

RICE

To boil rice for curry and savoury dishes, see p. 38.

RICE—CURRIED

4 oz. Patna rice   2 shallots, finely chopped   1½ oz. butter   1 teasp. curry powder   1 tomato   1 gill stock 1 tablesp. cream   1 gill brown sauce salt and pepper   mace   nutmeg 1 hard-boiled egg   watercress

Pick over, wash, drain and dry the rice thoroughly. Fry the shallots slightly in hot butter, sprinkle in the curry powder, cook for a few minutes, then add the rice and cook and shake well over the heat. Now add the tomato skinned and cut into dice, the stock, cream and sauce, season to taste with salt, pepper, mace and nutmeg, and cook gently until the rice is tender, adding more stock or sauce, if necessary, to prevent the rice becoming too dry. When ready, pile on a hot dish, garnish with slices of hard-boiled egg and tufts of watercress.

RISOTTO

½ lb. Patna rice   2 oz. butter
1 small onion, finely chopped
¼ teasp. saffron   nutmeg   1 teasp.
salt   ½ teasp. pepper   stock
1 pt. tomato sauce
2 oz. grated Parmesan cheese

Wash, drain and dry the rice thoroughly in a clean cloth. Heat the butter in a saucepan, put in the onion, and when lightly browned add the rice, and shake the pan over the heat for about 10 min. Then sprinkle in the saffron, a good pinch of nutmeg, salt and pepper. Cover with stock, and cook gently for about 1 hr., adding meanwhile the tomato sauce and as much stock as the rice will absorb, the sauce being added when the rice is about half cooked. Just before serving stir in the cheese.

NOTE: This is frequently used for borders instead of plainly-boiled rice or mashed potatoes.

SPAGHETTI

½ lb. spaghetti   1 oz. butter   2 oz. grated cheese   ½ pt. white or tomato sauce   nutmeg   cayenne pepper   salt and pepper

Put the spaghetti into boiling salted water, cook rapidly for about 20 min. or until tender, and drain well. Stir in the butter, cheese and sauce, add nutmeg, cayenne, salt and pepper to taste, and mix well. The spaghetti may be served in this state, or, if white sauce has been used, it may be browned in the oven or under the grill in a shallow baking-dish.

3–4 helpings

RECHAUFFES

EVERY housewife at some time is faced with left-over food, and, with a little skill and ingenuity, the economical wife will turn this into tempting, palatable dishes to be served at another meal. We suggest here some ways in which left-over food may be used; *see also* cold meats in the Meat section, p. 186, and also Breakfast and Supper Dishes, p. 360.

FISH CAKES

1 lb. cooked fish   1 oz. butter or margarine   ½ lb. mashed potatoes
2 eggs   salt and pepper
breadcrumbs

Remove skin and bones and chop fish coarsely. Heat the butter in a saucepan, add the fish, potatoes, yolk of 1 egg, salt and pepper. Stir over heat for a few minutes, then turn on to a plate and allow to cool. When cold, shape into round flat cakes, brush over with beaten egg, coat with breadcrumbs and fry in hot fat. The fish may be made into one large cake instead of several small ones, in which case grease a fish mould or flat tin and shape the mixture as much like a fish as possible. Brush over with egg, cover with slightly browned breadcrumbs and bake for 20 min. in a fairly hot oven (375° F., Gas 5).

3–7 helpings

KEDGEREE

1 lb. cold fish (smoked haddock is generally preferred)   ½ lb. rice
2 hard-boiled eggs   2 oz. butter
salt and pepper   cayenne pepper

Boil and dry the rice. Divide the fish into small flakes. Cut the whites of the eggs into slices and sieve the yolks. Melt the butter in a saucepan, add to it the fish, rice, egg whites, salt, pepper and cayenne and stir until hot. Turn the mixture on to a hot dish. Press into the shape of a pyramid with a fork, decorate with egg yolk and serve as hot as possible.

5–6 helpings
Cooking time—40–50 min.

BUBBLE AND SQUEAK

Thin slices of cold roast or boiled meat   dripping   1 shredded onion
cold mashed potatoes   cold greens of any kind   salt and pepper
vinegar (optional)

Heat some fat in a frying-pan and put in the meat and fry quickly on both sides until lightly browned. Remove and keep hot. Fry the onion until browned, add the potatoes and greens, which have been mixed together and well seasoned. Stir until thoroughly hot, add a little vinegar if liked, and turn on to a hot dish. Place the meat on top and serve.

NOTE: The name Bubble and Squeak is now often given to a dish of reheated vegetables without meat.

Cooking time—about 20 min.

MEAT CROQUETTES

½ lb. cold, cooked beef or mutton
½ oz. fat   ½ oz. flour   1 gill stock or gravy   salt and pepper   1 teasp. chopped parsley   1 teasp. of any savoury sauce   egg and breadcrumbs
deep fat   fresh or fried parsley

Remove all the fat, skin and gristle from the meat and mince or chop the meat finely. Melt the ½ oz. fat in a saucepan, add the flour and cook for a few minutes. Add the stock, stir and bring to the boil; cook for 3 min. Add the meat, salt, pepper, chopped parsley and sauce, and stir over heat for 2–3 min. Then turn the mixture on to a plate, smooth over and mark into 6–8 equal-sized sections. Allow to become quite cold and firm before forming into 6–8 croquettes. Coat well with egg and breadcrumbs and press the coating firmly on. Fry in hot, deep fat until crisp and a good brown colour, then drain well. Serve piled on a hot dish garnished with fresh or fried parsley

6 helpings

SHEPHERD'S PIE

1 lb. cold, cooked beef or mutton
1 small onion   ½ pt. gravy   2 lb. cooked, mashed potatoes   egg or milk   salt and pepper

Remove any skin, gristle or bone and cut the meat into small dice. Parboil and finely chop the onion and place in a pie-dish with the meat and the gravy. Season well. Cover with mashed potatoes and smooth and decorate the top to look like pie-crust. Glaze with beaten egg or milk if liked. Bake in a moderate oven (350° F., Gas 4) for about ½ hr. until thoroughly warmed and the surface is well browned.

6 helpings

BEEF AU GRATIN

1½ lb. cold, cooked beef   1 oz. butter or fat   1 small Spanish onion
1 oz. flour   ¾ pt. well-flavoured stock
salt and pepper   breadcrumbs

Mince the beef very finely. Melt the fat in a saucepan and fry the sliced onion until lightly browned. Add the flour and cook, stirring, until nut-brown. Then add the stock and stir until boiling. Season to taste and simmer gently for 20 min. Strain and add to the meat. Fill well-greased scallop shells with the mixture, cover

thickly with breadcrumbs and dot with butter or fat. Put in a fairly hot oven (375° F., Gas 5) until browned. Garnish with sprigs of parsley and serve immediately.

6 helpings
Cooking time—about 35 min.

BEEF HASH

1 lb. cold roast beef   2–3 streaky bacon   2 onions   1 oz. butter or fat   ¾ pt. mixed Espagnole and tomato sauce

GARNISH
Croûtes of fried or toasted bread
parsley

Trim and cut the meat into thin slices. Dice the bacon, slice the onions; melt the fat and fry them until light brown. Add the sliced meat and pour the mixed sauces over. Heat thoroughly without boiling for about ½ hr. If liked this dish can be prepared and served in a casserole and heated in the oven. Serve neatly garnished with croûtes and parsley.

6 helpings

CURRY OF COLD BEEF

1½ lb. cold, cooked beef   1 oz. butter or fat   1 onion   1 sour apple
1–2 teasp. curry powder   1 oz. flour
1 pt. stock or coconut infusion
1 teasp. curry paste   salt and pepper
4–6 oz. Patna rice   2 teasp. lemon juice   1 teasp. jam or jelly

GARNISH
Parsley   paprika   gherkins

Trim the meat and cut into small, neat pieces. Heat the fat and fry the finely-chopped onion and apple for about 7 min. without browning too much. Add the curry powder and flour and cook for at least 5 min. Add the stock or coconut infusion, curry paste and salt, and, whilst stirring, bring slowly to the boil. Put in the meat and simmer very gently for 20–30 min. until the meat is thoroughly heated and blended with the curry. Cook the rice and arrange as a border on a hot dish and keep hot. Add the lemon juice and jelly to the curry, season if required. Pour into the centre of the rice border, garnish with chopped parsley, paprika and slices of gherkin.

6 helpings
Cooking time—45 min. (approx.)

MINCED BEEF AND POACHED EGGS

½ lb. under-done roast beef   ½ oz. butter   1 small onion   ½ oz. flour   ¼ pt. gravy or stock   ½ teasp. mushroom ketchup, Worcester sauce or vinegar   salt and pepper   2 eggs   toast

Mince or cut the meat into dice. Melt the butter in a saucepan and fry the finely-chopped onion until lightly browned. Sprinkle in the flour and brown slightly, then add the gravy or stock and boil for 2–3 min. Add the meat, ketchup, sauce or vinegar, season with salt and pepper, and keep hot without boiling for 10–15 min. Meanwhile poach the eggs and cut the toast into small triangles. Turn the mince on to a hot dish, place the eggs on top and place the pieces of toast round the base.

2 helpings

RAGOUT OF BEEF

1½ lb. cold under-done roast beef   2 onions   2 oz. fat   1½ oz. flour   1 pt. stock   salt and pepper   1 tablesp. mushroom ketchup or vinegar

GARNISH
2 diced carrots   2 diced turnips   parsley

Cut the meat into neat slices. Chop the onions coarsely. Melt the fat in a saucepan, add the onions and fry until brown. Sprinkle in the flour, stir and cook slowly until well browned. Add the stock, stir

and bring to the boil. Season to taste, add the carrot and turnip trimmings from the garnish, mushroom ketchup or vinegar, and simmer for 15 min. Put in the slices of meat and heat thoroughly without boiling for about 1 hr. When nearly ready, cook the diced vegetables. Place the meat on a hot dish and pour the strained sauce over it. Garnish with the diced vegetables and chopped parsley.

6 helpings

NEST OF MINCED LAMB

1¼ lb. cold cooked lamb   2 lb. potatoes   ½ oz. butter   1 egg yolk   salt and pepper   brown breadcrumbs   egg or milk   ¼ pt. gravy or stock   1 tablesp. ketchup   2 tablesp. finely-chopped parsley   ½ pt. brown gravy

Cook the potatoes and drain well. Mash them with the butter, egg yolk, pepper and salt. Well grease a loose-bottomed cake-tin and cover well with fine brown breadcrumbs. Carefully and evenly line the sides and the bottom with the mashed potato, leaving a hole in the centre (the nest). Smooth the top edge of the potato with a knife, then rough up with a fork and brush with egg or milk. Bake in a hot oven (425° F., Gas 7) until set and brown on top. Meanwhile, mince the lamb and heat with the ¼ pt. gravy or stock and ketchup, seasonings and parsley. Season well. When the potato nest is set, stand the tin on a jam-jar and push off the side of the cake-tin, leaving the nest intact on the loose bottom. Place the nest on a hot dish, fill with hot mince and serve with brown gravy.

6 helpings

MUTTON AND POTATO PIE

2 lb. cold cooked lean mutton   2 lb. potatoes   2 onions   salt and pepper   ¾ pt. gravy

Cut the meat into neat, thin pieces. Make the gravy from the meat trimmings. Parboil and slice the potatoes and onions. Line a pie-dish with slices of potato and cover with layers of meat, onions and potatoes, seasoning each layer. Repeat in layers, until all the ingredients are used; the top layer should consist of potato. Add the gravy, cover with greaseproof paper and bake in a moderate oven (350° F., Gas 4) for 1 hr. For the last 15 min. remove the greaseproof paper to allow the potatoes to brown.

6 helpings

RECHAUFFE OF MUTTON

1½ lb. slices of cold mutton   1 turnip
1 small carrot   salt and pepper
1 onion   1½ oz. butter or good
dripping   1½ oz. flour
1 tablesp. mushroom ketchup

To make stock: put the bones, meat trimmings, sliced turnip and carrot in a saucepan and just cover with water. Simmer for at least 1 hr. Strain and season to taste.

Finely chop the onion. Heat the fat in a saucepan and fry the onion until lightly browned. Then add the flour, stir and cook slowly until brown. Add ¾ pt. stock and stir until boiling. Season to taste and add the mushroom ketchup. Place the slices of meat in the prepared sauce and simmer for at least ½ hr. Then arrange the meat neatly on a hot dish and strain the sauce over.

6 helpings

HAM CROQUETTES

½ lb. cooked ham   4 oz. fresh
breadcrumbs   2 tablesp. mashed
potatoes   ½ egg   4 tablesp. white
sauce   salt and pepper   1 egg
breadcrumbs   deep fat   paprika
pepper   parsley

Mince the ham and mix with the breadcrumbs and potatoes.

Place in a small pan and, heating gently, bind with the beaten egg and white sauce. Season well and spread on a plate. Divide into 12 equal portions and leave until cool. Shape into croquettes, coat with egg and breadcrumbs, and fry until golden brown in deep fat. Drain, sprinkle with paprika pepper and garnish with parsley.

Serve with tomato sauce.

6 helpings

MINCED PORK

1¼ lb. cold roast pork   2 onions
2 apples   2 oz. butter or fat
1 dessertsp. flour   a pinch of dry
mustard   ¼ pt. stock   salt and
pepper   1 teasp. lemon juice

Cut the meat into neat dice— any bones and trimmings may be boiled (for at least 1 hr.) to make the stock. Finely chop the onions and coarsely chop the apples. Melt the fat in a saucepan and fry the onions until lightly browned. Add the apple and cook with lid on until tender but not pulped. Sprinkle in the flour and mustard and stir and cook gently for 3-4 min. Add the strained stock, bring to the boil and correct the seasoning. Put in the meat and lemon juice and simmer for about ½ hr. Do not allow to boil. The meat may be served on a border of rice or mashed potato, or garnished with sippets of toast.

6 helpings

PORK CROQUETTES

½ lb. cold, cooked lean pork   ½ oz.
butter or fat   ½ teasp. finely-
chopped onion   ¾ oz. flour   ½ pt.
good stock   a pinch of marjoram
¼ teasp. powdered sage   salt and
pepper   egg and breadcrumbs
deep fat

Finely chop the pork. Melt the butter in a saucepan and fry the onion lightly. Stir in the flour, add the stock, and boil gently for 10–

12 min., stirring continually. Add the meat, marjoram, sage and seasoning. Stir until well mixed, then turn out on to a plate to cool. Form into croquettes and coat with egg and breadcrumbs. Fry in hot deep fat until golden brown.

6 helpings

PORK HASH

1½ lb. cold roast or boiled pork salt cayenne pepper 2 oz. butter or dripping 1 dessertsp. Worcester sauce 1 level teasp. mixed mustard 1 teasp. lemon juice

Cut the meat into small neat pieces and sprinkle with salt and a little cayenne. Melt the fat in a pan and add the sauce, mustard and lemon juice. When hot, add the meat and toss over the heat for about 15–20 min. until thoroughly hot and impregnated with the flavours.

6 helpings
Cooking time—about 20 min.

MINCED VEAL WITH MACARONI

4 oz. macaroni ¾ lb. cold roast veal 3 oz. minced ham 4 oz. bread-crumbs salt and pepper pinch of nutmeg 1 egg 2 tablesp. gravy or good stock ½–¾ pt. gravy

Put the macaroni in boiling salted water and cook until just tender. Finely mince the veal and ham. Mix together the veal, ham, breadcrumbs, salt, pepper, and grated nutmeg and mix with the beaten egg and as much gravy or stock as is necessary to bind the mixture together. Strain, and re-fresh with cold water the macaroni, and arrange some of it at the bot-tom and on the sides of a well-greased basin or mould in trellis form. Cut the remainder in short lengths and mix with the meat mixture. Press the whole mixture lightly into the mould. Cover with greased paper and steam gently

for 1 hr. Unmould carefully on to a hot dish and serve the gravy separately.

4 helpings

VEAL LOAF

1 lb. cold roast veal ½ lb. sausage meat 1 oz. breadcrumbs salt and pepper 1 egg gravy or stock flour or egg and breadcrumbs fat for basting sauce or gravy or salad

Finely chop the veal and mix with the sausage meat and bread-crumbs. Season well and add the beaten egg. Mix thoroughly, add-ing gravy or stock until the whole mixture is well moistened, but not wet. Form into a short thick roll and coat lightly with flour or egg and breadcrumbs. Heat some fat in a saucepan, put in the meat roll and baste. Bake in a fairly hot oven (400° F., Gas 6) for about 1 hr., basting occasionally.

Serve either hot with a good gravy or sauce, or cold with salad.

6 helpings

VEAL PATTIES

8 oz. lean, cooked veal 2 oz. lean, cooked ham salt and pepper pinch of nutmeg finely-grated rind of ½ lemon 1 teasp. lemon juice 1 tablesp. stock 4–5 tablesp. good white sauce 8 patty cases parsley

Chop the veal and ham very finely, and if liked rub through a sieve. Add the salt, pepper, nut-meg, lemon rind, lemon juice and a little stock to moisten. Add the white sauce and more seasoning if necessary. Fill the cases with the mixture, replace the lids and garn-ish with sprigs of parsley.

Serve hot or cold.

CHICKEN RISSOLES

4 oz. cooked chicken 2 oz. cooked ham or tongue 4 small mush-rooms 1 truffle (optional) ½ oz. butter ½ oz. flour ¼ pt. white stock 1 tablesp. cream or milk salt and pepper rough puff pastry

(p. 341), **using 4 oz. flour, etc.
egg and breadcrumbs frying-fat**

Chop chicken and ham finely, dice mushrooms and truffle. Melt the butter in a saucepan, stir in flour, add stock gradually, stir and boil until cooked. Add chicken mixture to sauce, reheat, season, then add mushrooms and truffle, stir in cream or milk and allow to cool. Roll pastry very thinly, cut into rounds about 2 in. in diameter. Place 1 teasp. of mixture on to half the rounds, dampen the edges, put other pastry rounds on top, and seal well. (Alternatively, cut 4-in. rounds, put mixture on each and fold in half.) Coat rissoles with egg and breadcrumbs, fry in hot deep fat until golden brown, then drain well.

**4–6 helpings
Cooking time—about 25 min. to
cook sauce and to fry**

MINCED CHICKEN

**1 lb. cold, cooked chicken   1 pt.
white coating sauce   salt and pepper
4 poached eggs**

Boil chicken bones and trimmings about 1½ hr., use this stock to make the sauce. When sauce is cooked, add minced chicken, season well, and heat thoroughly. Serve in a shallow dish, very hot, with poached eggs on top.

NOTE: The sauce may be made with ½ pt. stock and ½ pt milk.

4 helpings

DUCK AND RED CABBAGE

**Trimmings of 2 cold, roast ducks
½ red cabbage   2 oz. butter   good
gravy or stock   salt and pepper
1 tablesp. vinegar**

Wash and drain cabbage, shred it finely and cook gently for 1 hr. with the butter, in a tightly-covered pan, adding gravy or stock if necessary to prevent burning; season well. Divide duck into neat joints and heat the pieces in a little

gravy. Add vinegar to the cabbage —turn on to hot dish. Arrange the duck on top, and serve with good gravy.

FRIED FOWL—WITH PEAS

**Trimmings of 2 cold, roast fowls
2 oz. butter   1 oz. flour   ¾ pt. stock
salt and pepper**

GARNISH
Boiled garden peas

Cut fowl into pieces convenient for serving. Boil fowl bones for stock. Heat the butter in a saucepan. Fry pieces of fowl in butter until brown. Remove fowl from butter, add flour to butter and brown lightly; stir in stock, simmer 5 min. and season. Replace fowl in sauce, cover and cook gently until thoroughly hot.

Serve with sauce strained over and garnish with peas.

Cooking time—about 40 min.

HASHED FOWL

**Trimmings of 2 cold, roast fowls
1 bay leaf   1 blade mace   1 carrot
1 onion   a little celery   piece of
turnip   salt and pepper   1½ oz.
butter   1½ oz. flour   1 pt. stock**

Divide fowl into neat pieces. Boil fowl bones, bay leaf, mace and sliced vegetables in 1 pt. water for good stock. Melt butter in a saucepan, stir in flour, and lightly brown the roux; stir in the stock, boil well and season to taste. Add the trimmed pieces of fowl to sauce and heat thoroughly.

Dish the fowl, and strain the sauce over.

**Cooking time—1½ hr., including
making stock**

BLANQUETTE OF TURKEY

**¾–1 lb. cold turkey   1 small onion
1 blade of mace   salt and pepper
1½ oz. butter   1 oz. flour   ¾ pt.
stock or water   pinch of nutmeg
2 tablesp. cream or milk   1 egg yolk**

Cut turkey into neat pieces. Place some turkey bones, the sliced onion, mace and seasoning in a pan, cover with stock or water, simmer at least 1 hr. Melt butter in a saucepan, stir in flour, cook 3 min. without browning, stir in hot, strained stock. Simmer 10 min., season to taste, add nutmeg and pieces of turkey, allow to heat thoroughly—about 20 min. Mix cream or milk with egg yolk, stir in a little of the hot liquid, return all to pan, heat gently without boiling for about 5 min.

Serve hot.

4 helpings

HASHED TURKEY
¾–1 lb. cold, roast turkey

¾ pt. turkey stock   1½ oz. butter
1½ oz. flour   salt and pepper
toasted bread or mashed potato

Cut the turkey into neat pieces. Make turkey stock with water, turkey bones, vegetables, bouquet garni, seasoning. Melt butter in a saucepan, stir in flour, cook without browning for 3 min., stir in strained stock, boil 10 min., correct seasoning. Add pieces of turkey, allow to heat thoroughly—15–20 min.

Serve on hot buttered toast, or in a border of mashed potato.

4–6 helpings
Cooking time—about 2 hr., including stock

PRESERVES

JAM MAKING

THE fruits from which jams are made vary in their content of sugar, acid and pectin (a natural gum-like substance). All three of these make an essential contribution to the set and finished result. Generally speaking, fruits can be divided into three main categories:

1. Fruits which are easy to make into a well set jam, e.g. apples, blackcurrants, damsons, gooseberries, plums, redcurrants.
2. Fruits of medium setting quality, e.g. apricots, blackberries, raspberries and loganberries.
3. Fruits of poor setting quality, e.g. cherries and strawberries.

If there is any doubt about the pectin content of the fruit in any particular season the housewife can perform a simple test on the juice (*see* Pectin Test, p. 380).

Fruit for Jams: Choose firm ripe fruit. Never use over-ripe fruit or the jam will not set. One exception to the above: gooseberries should be hard and under-ripe.

Choice of a Preserving-Pan for Jams: Choose a pan which is large enough. It should not be more than half-full when the fruit and sugar are in because they must boil together rapidly without risk of boiling over. A pressure pan must never be more than half filled when ready for pressure cooking jams.*

Use a preserving-pan, or a large pan of aluminium, stainless steel or unchipped enamel. Copper or brass preserving-pans can be used —so long as any metal polish used for cleaning is thoroughly removed —but jam made in these pans may contain less vitamin C. Do not use iron or zinc pans.

To prevent the jam sticking and to help to avoid scum, the inside of the pan can be rubbed before use with glycerine or a small piece of butter or margarine.

TEST FOR SETTING POINT

There are several tests for setting point. Unless otherwise stated in the recipe, jams are usually tested when high frothing ceases and boiling becomes noisy, with heavy plopping bubbles. If the jam is not set then, continue testing at frequent intervals.

1. *Cold Plate Test:* Remove the pan from the heat (otherwise setting point may be missed while this test is being made). Spoon a little jam on to a cold plate or saucer, and allow it to cool. If the setting point has been reached, the surface will set and will wrinkle when pushed with the finger.

2. *Temperature Test:* For this an accurate thermometer marked in degrees up to and above 220° F. is required. Put the thermometer in hot water before and after use. Stir the jam thoroughly so that it is all of an even temperature. Transfer the thermometer into the jam, holding it well in. Provided a reliable recipe which gives sufficient acid and sugar is being used, a good set should be obtained when the jam reaches 220° F. Occasionally a temperature of 221° F. or 222° F. will give better results. Use this test in conjunction with the Flake Test.

3. *Flake Test:* Dip a clean wooden spoon into the jam, remove it and twirl it around until the jam on it has cooled slightly. Then tilt the spoon to allow the

jam to drop from it; if it has been boiled sufficiently, the jam will partially set on the spoon and the drops will run together to form flakes which will fall cleanly and sharply.

4. *Volume Test:* In a good recipe it is generally reckoned that 5 lb. of jam should be obtained for every 3 lb. of sugar used. To test the volume of the jam:

(*a*) Fill a 1-lb. jam-jar with water five times, pouring the water into the preserving-pan. See that the pan is perfectly level. (*b*) Carefully hold the handle of a wooden spoon upright in the centre of the pan, and mark on it the level of the water. Then empty the pan and make the jam. (*c*) When the jam is to be tested, remove it from the heat so that the bubbling will subside, then hold upright in it the handle of the wooden spoon. A good setting jam should be obtained when the level has been boiled down to the mark on the spoon handle.

NOTE: It is an excellent plan to have another wooden spoon marked off in this way permanently, to give the level in the centre of your pan *for each pt.* of liquid it contains. This means that if, for example, a recipe calls for the addition of 1 lb. sugar to every 1 pt. jam or marmalade, you do not have to pour the preserve out to measure it. Use a pt. measure in place of the jam-jar, to pour the water in.

APRICOT JAM (Fresh Fruit)

3 lb. fresh apricots   ½ pt. water
3 lb. sugar

Wash, halve and stone the fruit and put into the preserving-pan with the water. If desired, crack a few of the stones, remove the kernels and blanch them by dipping in boiling water. Add the halved kernels to the pan. Simmer till tender and the contents of the pan are reduced. Add the sugar and stir over a low heat till dissolved. Bring to the boil and boil rapidly until setting point is reached. Skim, pot and cover.

Yield—5 lb.

APRICOT or PEACH JAM
(Dried Fruit)

This is a popular jam for making in the winter when most other fruits are scarce.

1 lb. dried apricots or peaches
2–3 pt. water (2 pt. for peaches,
3 pt. for apricots)   juice of 1 lemon
3 lb. sugar   2–3 oz. blanched and
finely-shredded almonds (optional)

Wash the fruit and put in a basin with the water. Soak for 24–48 hr. Transfer the fruit and water to the preserving-pan and simmer for 30 min., stirring occasionally. Add the sugar, lemon juice and the shredded almonds. Stir over a low heat until the sugar is dissolved. Boil rapidly until setting point is reached. Skim, pot and cover.

Yield—approx. 5 lb.

BLACKBERRY JAM

3 lb. blackberries   2 tablesp. lemon
juice   3 lb. sugar

Pick over the blackberries, wash gently but thoroughly. Place the berries in the pan with the lemon juice and simmer gently until the fruit is cooked and well softened. Add the sugar and stir over a low heat till dissolved. Bring to the boil and boil rapidly until setting point is reached. Skim. Pour into hot, dry jars. Cover.

Yield—5 lb.

BLACKBERRY AND APPLE JAM

¾ lb. sour apples (weighed when
peeled and cored)   ½ pt. water
2 lb. blackberries   3 lb. sugar

Slice the apples and stew them till soft in ½ pt. of the water. Pick

over the blackberries, add the
other ¼ pt. of water and stew
slowly in another pan till tender.
Mix the 2 cooked fruits together.
Add the sugar, heat gently until
dissolved, then boil rapidly until
setting point is reached. Skim,
pour into warm, dry jars and
cover.

Yield—5 lb.

BLACKCURRANT JAM

2 lb. blackcurrants   1½ pt. water
3 lb. sugar

Remove currants from the stalks.
If the fruit is dirty, wash it thoroughly and drain. Put into the
preserving-pan with the water, and
stew slowly till the skins are soft.
*This will take at least ½ hr., prob-
ably more.* As the pulp thickens,
stir frequently to prevent burning.
Add the sugar, stir over a low
heat until dissolved, then boil
rapidly till setting point is
reached. (Test for set at intervals
after about 10 min. rapid boiling.)
Skim, pour into dry, warm jars and
cover.

NOTE: This is a good jam for
beginners—it sets very easily. But
beware of adding the sugar too
soon, otherwise hard, "boot-
button" currants will result. Try
adding I tablesp. blackcurrant jam
when cooking curry; it helps to
darken the curry and gives a good
flavour.

Yield—5 lb.

CHERRY (BLACK) JAM
(with added pectin)

2½ lb. black cherries (after stoning)
¼ pt. water   6 tablesp. lemon juice
3 lb. sugar   1 bottle pectin

Place the washed and stoned
cherries in a preserving-pan with
the water and lemon juice. Cook
gently with the lid on for 15 min.
Remove lid. Add the sugar and
stir over gentle heat until it has
dissolved. Bring to a full rolling

boil and boil rapidly for 3 min.
Remove from heat, stir in the
pectin, return to heat, bring to
boil and boil 1 min. only. Cool for
15 min. to prevent fruit rising.
Pot and put on waxed discs immediately. Cover and label.

Yield—5 lb.

DAMSON JAM

2½ lb. damsons   ¾–1 pt. water
3 lb. sugar

Remove the stalks, wash the
damsons and put into the pan with
the water. Stew slowly until the
damsons are well broken down.
Add the sugar, stir over a low heat
till dissolved, bring to the boil,
then boil rapidly. Remove stones
as they rise to the surface (a stone-
basket clipped to the side of the
pan is useful for holding the
stones, and allows any liquid to
drip back into the pan). Continue
boiling rapidly until setting point
is reached. (Test for set after
about 10 min. boiling.) Skim,
pour into dry, warm jars and
cover.

Yield—5 lb.

GOOSEBERRY JAM—GREEN
or RED

2¼ lb. gooseberries   ¾–1 pt. water
3 lb. sugar

Pick or buy the gooseberries at
the green stage, before they have
ripened or turned colour. Top and
tail and wash them, and put in a
pan with the water. Simmer
gently until the fruit is soft (this
may take ½ hr. or longer). Then
add the sugar and stir over a low
heat until dissolved. Bring to the
boil and boil rapidly until setting
point is reached (remove from the
heat after 10 min. rapid boiling to
test for the set). Skim, pour into
dry, warm jars and cover.

NOTE: This is a good jam for
beginners, because it is a notori-
ously good setter. It is specially

good served on scones with whipped cream.

GREENGAGE JAM

3 lb. greengages   ½–¾ pt. water
3 lb. sugar

Remove stalks and put the washed greengages into the pan with the water. Stew slowly until the fruit is well broken down. Ripe fruit or very juicy varieties will need only a small quantity of water and will be cooked in a few minutes. Firmer varieties may take about 20 min. to break down, and will need the larger quantity of water. Add the sugar, stir over a low heat till dissolved, then boil rapidly, removing the stones as they rise to the surface (a stone basket clipped to the side of the pan is useful for holding the stones, and allows any liquid to drip back into the pan). Keep testing for setting point after about 10 min. rapid boiling. Skim, pot and cover.

Yield—5 lb.

LEMON CURD

3 eggs   3 oz. butter   8 oz. sugar
rind and juice of 2 lemons

Whisk the eggs and put into a basin with the butter, sugar, finely-grated lemon rind and the juice. Place the basin over a pan of boiling water, stir until the mixture is thick and smooth. Pour into clean, warm jars and cover.

MELON AND LEMON JAM

4 lb. melon (weighed when prepared)
4 lemons   3 lb. sugar

Peel the melon and remove the centre pith, reserving the pips. Cut the flesh into cubes. Wash the lemons, wipe dry and peel with a vegetable peeler to remove only the yellow rind. Cut the fruit in halves and squeeze out the juice. Strain off the juice into a small bowl. Put the lemon peel (yellow part only) and the pips and pulp from the squeezer and the pips from the melon into a loose muslin bag and add this to the melon in the preserving-pan. Heat gently until the juice runs and then cook gently until the melon is tender and transparent (30–45 min.). Remove the muslin bag. Add the lemon juice and sugar and stir without further heating until the sugar is completely dissolved. Bring to the boil and boil as rapidly as possible until a set is obtained. Pour into hot, dry jars and cover.

Yield—approx. 5 lb.

ORANGE CURD

Rind and juice of 2 oranges   juice
of 1 lemon   4 eggs   2 oz. butter
8 oz. loaf sugar

Finely grate the orange rind. Squeeze the juice from the oranges and lemon and remove the pips. Thoroughly whisk the eggs. Place the butter in a double saucepan, or in a basin over boiling water, and when the butter has melted add the orange rind, juices, sugar and eggs. Cook gently until the curd thickens, stirring frequently to obtain an even consistency.

Yield—1½ lb. (approx.)

PECTIN STOCK

(To add to fruit deficient in pectin when making jams.)

Prepare apples, redcurrants or gooseberries, cook and strain through a scalded jelly bag as for jelly making. Bring the juice to the boil but do not add any sugar. Pour into hot preserving jars, sterilize in a pan of hot water, raised to boiling-point and boiled for 5 min. (*See* Fruit Pulps, p. 391.)

PLUM JAM

3 lb. plums   3 lb. sugar   ½–¾ pt.

water ($\frac{1}{4}$ pt. for ripe, juicy dessert
plums, $\frac{3}{4}$ pt. for cooking varieties)

Proceed as for Greengage Jam
(p. 379). If desired, a few of the
raw plums may be stoned; crack
the stones, remove the kernels,
blanch them by dipping in boiling
water and add the halved kernels
to the pan.

Yield—approx. 5 lb.

PLUM AND APPLE JAM

1$\frac{1}{2}$ lb. plums   1$\frac{1}{2}$ lb. apples
(prepared weight) $\frac{3}{4}$ pt. water
3 lb. sugar

Wash the plums. Peel and core
the apples. Stew the fruit slowly
in the water until the skins of the
plums are softened. Add the
sugar, stir over a low heat till dissolved, bring to the boil and boil
rapidly till setting point is reached.

Pour into warm, dry jars and
cover.

NOTE: As many stones as
possible should be removed during
cooking. Alternatively, the plums
may be stoned before cooking.

Yield—5 lb.

RASPBERRY JAM—
Quick Method

This jam does not set very
firmly, but it has a delicious fresh
flavour. Do not wash the raspberries unless absolutely necessary;
if they have to be washed, drain
very thoroughly.

2$\frac{1}{2}$ lb. raspberries
3 lb. granulated sugar

Bring the fruit gently to the
boil, then boil rapidly for 5 min.
Remove from the heat, add the
warmed sugar and stir well over a
low heat until all the sugar has
dissolved. Bring to the boil and
boil rapidly for 1 min. Skim
quickly, pour the jam at once into
dry, warm jars and cover.

Yield—5 lb.

STRAWBERRY JAM

3$\frac{1}{2}$ lb. hulled strawberries   juice of
1 large lemon   3 lb. sugar

Heat the strawberries and
lemon juice gently in the pan,
stirring constantly to reduce the
volume. Add the sugar, stir till
dissolved and boil until setting
point is reached. Remove the
scum. Leave the jam undisturbed
to cool until a skin forms on the
surface and the fruit sinks (about
20 min.). Stir gently to distribute
the strawberries. Pour into warm,
dry jars and cover immediately
with waxed discs. Tie down when
cold.

Yield—5 lb.

JELLY-MAKING

IMPORTANT POINTS

1. Use fresh fruit, not over-
ripe.

2. Simmer gently in water till
the fruit is tender and thoroughly
broken down (usually about $\frac{3}{4}$–1
hour). *If in any doubt about its
setting properties, test for pectin at
this stage*, as a good set depends
upon the amount of acid, pectin
and sugar present.

Test for pectin: After the fruit
has cooked till tender, squeeze
from it 1 teasp. of juice. Place to
cool in a cup or glass. Then add
3 teasp. methylated spirits. Shake
gently and leave 1 min. If there
is plenty of pectin in the fruit, a
transparent jelly-like lump will
form. If there is only a moderate
amount of pectin there may be
two or three lumps, not very firm.
If there is insufficient pectin, the
lump will break into many small
pieces and the fruit should be
simmered for a little longer before
another pectin test is made. It is
a waste of effort to strain the juice
and attempt to make jelly if there
is only a poor amount of pectin.
It is preferable to mix with an-

other fruit which is known to be a good setter (e.g. apple—*see* Blackberry and Apple Jelly, below).

3. After cooking, strain the fruit through a jelly bag, first scalding the bag by pouring boiling water through it. Hang the bag on a special frame, or suspend it from the legs of an upturned stool *or* chair with a basin below to catch the drips.

4. Never hurry the straining of the juice by squeezing the bag —this might make the jelly cloudy, but do not leave the juice too long before completing the jelly—certainly not more than 24 hours.

5. Measure the juice into a preserving-pan, bring to the boil. Add the sugar. Strained juice rich in pectin needs 1 lb. sugar to each pint of juice. Juice with only a fair pectin content needs only ¾ lb. sugar to each pint.

6. After dissolving the sugar, boil rapidly till setting point is reached (about 10 min.—test by any of the methods for Jam on p. 376).

7. Skim, removing the last traces of scum from the surface with the torn edge of a piece of kitchen paper. Pour into warm jars at once, before it has time to begin setting in the pan. Put on waxed circles (waxed side down) immediately. Cover when hot or cold. Do not tilt the jars until the jelly has set. Store in a cool, dry, dark place.

NOTE: *Exact yield of jelly from each recipe cannot be given because of varying losses in straining the juice, but usually 10 lb. of jelly should be made from each 6 lb. sugar used.*

APPLE JELLY

4 lb. well-flavoured crabapples, or cooking apples (windfalls can be used) flavouring: lemon peel or root ginger sugar

Wash the apples and cut up without peeling or coring—just remove any bad portions. Barely cover with water (about 2–3 pt.) and simmer with the chosen flavouring till tender and well mashed (about 1 hr.). Strain through a scalded jelly bag. Bring the strained juice to the boil and test for pectin. Add the sugar (usually 1 lb. sugar to every pint of juice). Stir to dissolve. Boil briskly till setting point is reached.

BLACKBERRY AND APPLE JELLY

4 lb. blackberries 4 lb. cooking apples 2 pt. water sugar

Rinse the fruit. Cut up the apples without peeling or coring. Simmer the blackberries and apples separately with the water for about 1 hr., until the fruits are tender. Mash well and allow to drip through a jelly bag. Measure the juice. Bring to the boil, then stir in the sugar (usually 1 lb. to each 1 pt. of juice). Boil briskly till set.

BLACKCURRANT JELLY

**4 lb. ripe blackcurrants
2½ pt. water sugar**

Remove the leaves and only the larger stems and wash the blackcurrants. Place in the preserving-pan, add 1½ pt. water, and simmer gently until thoroughly tender. Mash well, then strain the pulp through a scalded jelly bag, leaving it to drip undisturbed for at least 15 min. Return the pulp left in the jelly bag to the pan, add another pint of water and simmer for ½ hr. Tip this pulp back into the bag and allow to drip for 1 hr. Mix the first and second extracts together. Measure the juice into the cleaned pan, bring to the boil. Then add 1 lb. sugar to each pint of juice and stir till dissolved. Boil briskly, without stirring, until setting point is reached. Remove the scum, then immediately pour the jelly into warm jars.

CRANBERRY AND APPLE JELLY

3 lb. apples   2 lb. cranberries
water   sugar

Rinse the fruit. Slice the apples, without peeling or coring, and place in a pan with the cranberries and sufficient water to cover. Simmer gently till thoroughly mashed. Test for pectin. Allow to drip through a jelly bag. Measure the juice. Allow usually 1 lb. sugar to each pint of juice, but this depends on the pectin test. Bring the juice to the boil. Add the sugar and stir till dissolved, then boil briskly till setting point is reached.

GOOSEBERRY JELLY

4 lb. green gooseberries   sugar
2–3 pt. water

Wash the gooseberries and place them in the pan without topping and tailing. Add the water, cook till thoroughly tender and broken. Test for pectin (*see* p. 380). Strain through a scalded jelly bag and add ¾–1 lb. of sugar to each pint of cold juice. (The amount depends on the results of the pectin test.) Bring to the boil, stirring to dissolve the sugar, and boil rapidly till setting point is reached.

NOTE: The addition of sugar to the cold juice allows it a longer boiling time and gives a darker, pleasanter colour to the jelly.

MINT JELLY

3 lb. green apples   1¼ pt. water
a small bunch of fresh mint
1¼ pt. vinegar   sugar
3 level tablesp. chopped mint
a few drops of green colouring

Wash the apples, cut in quarters and place in a preserving-pan with the water and the bunch of mint. Simmer until the apples are soft and pulpy, then add the vinegar and boil for 5 min. Strain overnight through a cloth, measure the juice, and to each pint allow 1 lb. sugar. Put the juice and sugar into the pan and bring to the boil, stirring until the sugar is dissolved. Boil rapidly until setting point is nearly reached, add the chopped mint and colouring, then boil until setting point is reached. Pour into hot jars and cover immediately with waxed discs. When quite cold, tie down with parchment or transparent covers, label and store.

RASPBERRY JELLY

8 lb. raspberries   sugar

Put the raspberries in the pan without any added water and heat gently until they are quite soft. Crush the fruit well. Strain through a scalded jelly bag. Return the measured juice to the clean pan, bring it to the boil and add 1 lb. sugar to each pint of juice. Stir until the sugar is dissolved, then boil rapidly till setting point is reached.

REDCURRANT JELLY—RICH

6 lb. large, juicy redcurrants or
redcurrants and whitecurrants
mixed   sugar

Remove the leaves and only the larger stems. Place the cleaned fruit in the preserving-pan, without any water, and heat very gently until the currants are softened and well cooked (about ¾ hr.). Mash, then strain the pulp through a scalded jelly bag, leaving it to drip undisturbed. Measure the juice into the cleaned pan. Add 1¼ lb. of sugar to each pint of juice. Bring to the boil, stirring constantly, and boil, without stirring, for 1 min. Swiftly skim the jelly and immediately pour it into the warmed jars, before it has a chance to set in the pan.

the contents of the pan are reduced by at least ⅓. Remove the muslin bag. Add the sugar, stir until dissolved, then bring to the boil and boil rapidly till setting point is reached (approx. 15–20 min.).

Yield—5 lb. approx.

LEMON JELLY MARMALADE

2 lb. lemons   3½ pt. water
3 lb. sugar

Scrub the lemons and wipe dry. Peel off the outer yellow skin, using a vegetable peeler or sharp knife, and cut the peelings into fine shreds. Tie these in a muslin bag. (N.B. If a marmalade with fewer shreds is preferred, add the shredded peel from only half the lemons.) Cook the shreds in 1½ pt. of water, in a covered pan, until tender. Meanwhile, roughly cut up the fruit and cook with the remaining water in a preserving-pan for 2 hr., with the lid on the pan. Pour off the liquid from the shreds, add it to the cooked fruit and strain it all through a scalded jelly bag. Pour the strained liquid into the rinsed preserving pan, simmer a little if it seems rather thin, then add the sugar and stir over a low heat till dissolved. Add the shreds and boil hard until setting point is reached.

ORANGE JELLY MARMALADE

2 lb. Seville oranges   4½ pt. water
juice of 2 lemons   3 lb. sugar

Peel the oranges, remove the thick pith and shred finely 4 oz. of the rind. Cook the shreds in 1 pt. water, in a covered pan, until tender (approx. 1½ hr.). Meanwhile, roughly cut up the fruit and put it with the lemon juice and 2½ pt. water in a pan. Simmer for 2 hr., with the lid on the pan. Drain the liquid from the shreds, add it to the cooked fruit and strain it all through a scalded jelly bag.

After it has dripped for ¼ hr., return the pulp to the preserving-pan and add 1 pt. water. Simmer for 20 min., then strain again through the jelly bag, allowing it to drip undisturbed. Pour the strained liquid into the rinsed preserving-pan, simmer a little if it seems rather thin, then add the sugar and stir over a low heat till dissolved. Add the shreds and boil hard until setting point is reached.

Yield—5 lb.

SEVILLE ORANGE MARMALADE (1)

1½ lb. Seville oranges   4 pt. water
juice of 1 lemon   sugar

Wash the fruit and cut it in half. Squeeze out the juice and the pips. Cut the peel into shreds. Tie the pips in a muslin bag and put into a bowl with the orange and lemon juice, water and peel. Soak for 24–48 hr., covered to keep it clean. Transfer to the pan and cook gently until the peel is soft (approx. 1½ hr.). Remove the bag of pips, squeezing it gently. Take the pan from the heat, add 1 lb. sugar to each pint (*see* volume test, p. 377) and stir till dissolved. Return pan to heat, bring to the boil, and boil rapidly until setting point is reached.

Yield—about 6½ lb.

SEVILLE ORANGE MARMALADE (2)

1½ lb. Seville oranges   2 pt. water
juice of 1 lemon   3 lb. sugar

Wash the fruit and put it whole and unpeeled into a saucepan. Pour on 2 pt. boiling water and simmer gently *with the lid on the pan* until the fruit is tender enough to be pierced easily with a fork (approx. 2 hr.). (*Alternatively, the whole fruit and water can be baked in a covered casserole in a cool oven until the fruit is soft; this will take about 4–5 hr.*) When the fruit is tender, cut it in half and remove pips, then cut up the fruit with a knife and fork, carefully retaining all the juice. Return the pips to the water in which the fruit was cooked, and boil for 5 min. to extract more pectin. Put the sliced fruit with the liquid (strained free from pips) and lemon juice in the preserving-pan. Reduce the heat, add the sugar and stir till dissolved. Bring to the boil and boil rapidly till setting point is reached.

NOTE: This method is simple to do and is recommended if a fairly coarse-cut marmalade is liked.

Yield—5 lb.

TANGERINE MARMALADE
(with added pectin)

3 lb. tangerines 2 pt. water
juice of 3 lemons 5 lb. sugar
1 bottle pectin

Wash the tangerines and put into a preserving-pan with the water. Simmer gently, covered, for 40 min. When cool enough to handle, remove peel and cut up fruit, taking out the pips and the very coarse tissue. Return the pips and tissue to the liquid and boil hard for 5 min. Shred half the peel, discard the rest. Strain the liquid, discarding the pips and tissue, and put back in the preserving-pan with the pulp, peel, lemon juice and sugar. Stir over gentle heat until the sugar has dissolved and then bring to a full rolling boil. Boil hard for 3 min. Remove from heat, stir in pectin, boil for 1 min. Skim if necessary. Cool slightly and pot in the usual way.

NOTE: Tangerine Marmalade is normally a difficult one to set; the addition of pectin gives an easy method.

Yield—about 7lb.

BOTTLING

FRUIT BOTTLING

Preparing and Testing the Jars:
There are two main types of preserving jar—one which fastens with a screw-band and the other fastening with clips or grips. Jam jars can also be used—fastened with special covers.

Always examine jars before use to see that they are unchipped. If the lid or the rim of the jar is chipped, discard it because it would prevent an air-tight seal.

Preparing the Syrup or Brine:
Fruit can be preserved in plain water, but a sugar syrup gives a better flavour and colour. The quantity of sugar used for a sugar syrup may be varied according to taste, but the usual quantity for most fruits is 8 *oz. granulated or loaf sugar to each* 1 *pt. of water.* Heat together and, when dissolved, bring to boiling-point and boil for 1 min. If it is to be kept hot for long, put the lid on the pan to prevent evaporation. If preferred, substitute equal weights of *golden syrup* or *honey* for sugar.

To prepare brine for bottling tomatoes—add ½ oz. salt to each 1 qt. of water. Bring to the boil and boil for 1 min.

Choosing, Preparing and Packing the Fruit: Choose fresh, firm, ripe fruit (except gooseberries, which should be green and hard). Grade according to size, so that fruit of the same size is packed into each jar. If necessary, use the handle of a wooden spoon to help to place firm fruit in position.

FRUIT

Apples: Peel, core, cut into slices, or rings ¼ in. thick. To prevent discoloration drop them into brine (1 oz. salt to 4 pt. water), keeping under surface with a plate. Drain, rinse and pack immediately.

Apples—(Solid Pack): After draining from brine (as above), scald in boiling water 2–3 min. A mixed pack of alternate layers of apples (solid pack) and blackberries (unscalded) is recommended.

Apricots: Choose fully ripe fruit, not too soft. Stalk and rinse. Pack whole, *or* halve by slitting and twisting the fruit; stone and pack quickly to avoid browning. A few cracked kernels can be added to each jar.

Blackberries: Choose large, juicy, fully ripe berries. Remove stalks, leaves and unsound fruit.

Cherries: Should have small stones and plump flesh (Morello, for choice). Stalk and rinse. Can be stoned, but take care not to lose the juice.

Damsons: Choose ripe, firm, purple fruit. Stalk and rinse.

Gooseberries: Top and tail and, if preserving in syrup, cut off a small slice at either end with a stainless steel knife (this prevents shrivelling and toughening, but is not necessary with preserving by pressure pan).

Greengages: Choose firm, ripe fruit. Remove stalks. After processing, the fruit will turn greenish-brown and the syrup may be cloudy. But if a pressure pan is used the fruit should keep a good colour, due to the short cooking time.

Peaches: Choose a free-stone variety (e.g. Hale) just fully ripe.

Halve and stone by slitting and twisting the fruit. Dip in a pan of boiling water for 1 min., then put into cold water: the skin should then peel off easily. Pack quickly.

Pears: Choose one of the best dessert varieties, e.g. Williams' Bon Chrétien, Conference, Doyenné du Comice, just fully ripened. Peel, halve and scoop out cores and fibres with a sharp-pointed teaspoon. Place in an acid brine (4 pt. water; 1 oz. salt; ½ oz. citric acid), keeping below surface with a plate. Rinse when ready for packing. Pack quickly.

Pears—cooking: Prepare like the dessert varieties. Then stew till tender in a sugar syrup (4–6 oz. sugar to 1 pt. water). Drain, pack and cover with the syrup in which they were cooked. Sterilize as for other pears.

Plums: Choose Victoria plums when they are fully grown but firm and just turning pink. Choose purple varieties before the colour has developed, when they are bright red. Choose yellow varieties when they are firm and lemon-yellow. Remove stalks, and rinse in cold water. Wipe to remove the bloom. Free-stone varieties can be halved, others must be packed whole. Prick whole plums before preserving by Pressure Pan method.

Rhubarb: Choose Champagne or Linnaeus rhubarb and bottle it in the spring when it is tender and needs no peeling. Wipe the stalks and cut in short lengths. Pack straight away (in water or syrup) *or* after soaking. *To soak* pour a hot syrup (8 oz. sugar to 1 pt. water) over the prepared rhubarb. Leave to soak and shrink for 8–12 hr. Pack, cover with the syrup.

Tight Pack for small soft fruit, e.g. elderberries, blackberries, raspberries, strawberries, mulberries: Roll the fruit in castor sugar, then pack into the jars tightly, without

any added liquid. Process as for Deep Pan methods.

Tomatoes: Tomatoes in their own juice: Dip into boiling water for up to 30 seconds (according to ripeness), then into cold water; the skins should then peel off easily. Leave whole, or pack in halves or quarters if large. Press tightly into the jars, sprinkling the layers with sugar and salt—use 1 teasp. sugar and 2 teasp. salt to each 2 lb. tomatoes. No aditional liquid is needed.

Whole, unskinned tomatoes (best for oven method). Remove stalks, rinse tomatoes and pack into jars. Use a brine (½ oz. salt to 1 qt. water) in place of syrup or water. *See* p. 391 for recipes for Tomato Purée and Tomato Juice.

METHODS OF BOTTLING

QUICK DEEP PAN

1. Pack prepared fruit tightly into tested jars. Put rubber rings to soak in warm water. 2. Fill jars to overflowing with HOT (about 140° F.) syrup or water. For tomatoes use hot brine. 3. Dip the rubber rings in boiling water and put them on the jars, with the lids. Fasten with screwbands, clips or other grips. 4. If using screwbands, tighten them, *then unscrew ¼ turn to allow for expansion.* 5. Stand jars in the pan on wooden slats or on a thick piece of towelling or cardboard. See that they do not touch each other or the side of the pan. Cover completely with WARM (about 100° F.) water. Put on the lid of the pan. 6. Bring up to SIMMERING POINT (190° F.) in 25–30 min. Simmer for time indicated on p. 389. Then remove jars one at a time on to a wooden surface (use tongs to lift jars *or,* using a cup, empty out sufficient water to enable jars to be lifted with a cloth). 7. Tighten screw-

bands. Cool 24 hr., tightening screwbands further if necessary. Clips should hold properly without attention. 8. Next day, remove screwband or clip. Lift each jar by lid. If properly sealed the lid will stay on securely. Label with date and other details and store in a cool, dark, dry place. Wash, dry and grease screwbands and clips and store till next year.

Processing Times for Quick Deep Pan Method: Simmer for time indicated below:

2 *min.* Apple rings, Blackberries, Gooseberries (for pies), Rhubarb (for pies).

10 *min.* Apricots, Cherries, Damsons, Gooseberries (for dessert), Greengages, Plums (whole), Rhubarb (for dessert), Tight pack of soft Fruit (except Strawberries).

20 *min.* Apples (solid pack), Peaches, Plums (halved), Tight pack of Strawberries.

40 *min.* Pears, Tomatoes (whole).

50 *min.* Tomatoes (in own juice).

SLOW DEEP PAN

This is the same as the quick deep pan method, with the following exceptions: At step 2, the jars are filled with COLD syrup, water or brine. At step 5, the fastened jars are covered with COLD water. At step 6, the water is raised gradually (i.e. in 90 min.) to the temperature indicated below, and is maintained at that temperature for the time stated below.

Processing Times: Raise to 165° F. and maintain at that temperature for 10 min.

Apple rings, Blackberries, Gooseberries (for pies), Rhubarb (for pies), Strawberries.

Raise to 180° F. and maintain at that temperature for 15 min.

Apples (solid pack), Apricots, Cherries, Damsons, Gooseberries (for dessert), Greengages, Plums

(whole or halved), Peaches, Rhubarb (for dessert), Tight pack of soft Fruit.

Raise to 190° F. and maintain at that temperature for 30 min.

Pears, Tomatoes (whole).

Raise to 190° F. and maintain at that temperature for 40 min.

Tomatoes (in own juice).

PRESSURE PAN

(These instructions apply to most suitable-sized pressure pans with a gauge or weight control to maintain a steady pressure. But as different makes of pressure pan vary, consult also the manufacturer's handbook for your particular make.)

1. Place clean, warm, tested preserving jars (*see* p. 387) into a large bowl of very hot water. 2. Remove jars one at a time and pack tightly to the top with prepared fruit (*see* pp. 387-8). Fill with BOILING syrup or water to within $\frac{1}{4}$ in. of the top. 3. Dip the rubber rings in boiling water and put them on the jars with the lids. Fasten with screwbands, clips or grips. *If using screwbands, tighten them, then unscrew them $\frac{1}{4}$ turn to allow for expansion.* Put jars back into the bowl of hot water until all are packed and fastened. 4. Meanwhile, put the trivet (inverted) and about $1\frac{1}{2}$ pt. water into the pressure pan (water should be 1 in. deep in the pan). Add 1 tablesp. of vinegar or a little lemon juice to prevent the pan from staining. Bring to the boil. 5. Lift the prepared jars of fruit on to the trivet, making sure they do not touch each other or the sides of the pan. 6. Fix on the lid. Allow steam to escape from the centre vent until it will form drops of moisture on a knife blade passed through it. 7. BRING UP TO 5 LB. PRESSURE, adjusting the heat so that it takes about 3 min. to bring to pressure (i.e. on a MEDIUM heat if using an

electric cooker). 8. Process according to the times given below. Lower the heat sufficiently at this stage to maintain a steady pressure. Fluctuations in pressure must be avoided because they cause loss of liquid from the jars and the fruit may be underprocessed. 9. Remove the pan gently away from the heat. *Allow the pressure to drop at room temperature for* 10 *min.* 10. Lift out the jars one at a time on to a wooden surface, tightening screwbands immediately. Cool 24 hr., tightening screwbands further if necessary. Clips should hold properly without attention. 11. Test, label and store—*see* Step 8, "Quick Deep Pan Method".

Processing Times

Process at 5 *lb. pressure for* 1 *min.*

Apples (quarters), Apricots, Cherries, Damsons, Fruit Pulp, Gooseberries, Plums, Rhubarb (not soaked).

Process at 5 *lb. pressure for* 3 *min.*

Blackberries, Greengages, Loganberries, Raspberries, Strawberries.

Process at 5 *lb. pressure for* 3–4 *min.*

Peaches.

Process at 5 *lb. pressure for* 5 *min.*

Pears, Tomatoes (whole or halved).

Process at 5 *lb. pressure for* 15 *min.*

Tomatoes (solid pack).

SPECIAL PREPARATIONS FOR BOTTLING BY PRESSURE PAN

(*a*) SOFT FRUIT, e.g. blackberries, loganberries, raspberries, strawberries.

1. Lay the prepared fruit in a single layer in the bottom of a large enamel, glass or china bowl (not metal). 2. Prepare a syrup with 6 oz. sugar to 1 pt. water and pour, boiling, over the fruit. Leave to soak overnight. 3. Next morning, drain off the syrup (using this syrup to cover the fruit in the jars). Continue as from No. 1 of the directions on p. 390. The pressure cooking time for a solid pack of soft fruit like this is 3 *min. at* 5 *lb. pressure.*

(*b*) FRUIT PULP, e.g. apples, cranberries, tomatoes.

1. Wash and cut up, without coring or peeling. 2. Remove the trivet from the pressure pan, and pressure cook the fruit or tomatoes in $\frac{1}{4}$ pt. water at 15 lb. pressure for 2–3 min. (NOTE: The pan must not be more than half full.) 3. Reduce pressure at room temperature. Sieve. 4. *While still hot* (reheat if necessary), pour into the prepared warm jars, leaving 1 in. headspace. 5. Continue from nos. 3–7 of the directions on p. 461. 6. Process at 5 *lb. pressure for* 1 *min.* and continue with the directions.

OVEN METHOD

1. Fill the warmed jars tightly with the prepared fruit (*see* pp. 387–8). 2. Fill to within 1 in. of the top with boiling syrup or water. 3. Put on the rubber rings and lids (both first dipped in boiling water). Both clips and screwbands should not be put on until after the processing. 4. Line a baking-sheet with newspaper, to catch any liquid should it boil over during heating. Stand the jars, 2 in. apart, on the paper. 5. Put in the central part of the oven, preheated for 15 min., to 300° F. Process for the times given below. 6. Remove on to a wooden surface. Fasten clips and screwbands and tighten screwbands further as the jars cool. Next day, test for seal (see Step 8, "Quick Deep Pan Method"), label and store.

NOTE: Four 1-lb. jars require the same processing time as two 2-lb. jars.

Processing Times

30–40 min. (*if processing* 1 lb.– 4 lb.)

45–60 min. (*if processing* 5 lb.– 10 lb.)

Apple rings, Blackberries, Gooseberries (for pies), Loganberries, Rhubarb (for pies).

40–50 min. (*if processing* 1 lb.– 4 lb.)

55–70 min. (*if processing* 5 lb.– 10 lb.)

Apricots, Cherries, Damsons, Gooseberries (for dessert), Greengages, Plums (whole), Rhubarb (for dessert).

50–60 min. (*if processing* 1 lb.– 4 lb.)

65–80 min. (*if processing* 5 lb.– 10 lb.)

Apples (solid pack), Peaches, Plums (halved).

60–70 min. (*if processing* 1 lb.– 4 lb.)

75–90 min. (*if processing* 5 lb.– 10 lb.)

Pears, Tomatoes (whole).

70–80 min. (*if processing* 1 lb.– 4 lb.)

85–100 min. (*if processing* 5 lb.– 10 lb.)

Tomatoes (in own juice).

SPECIAL RECIPES

Fruit: Pulped soft and stone fruit, e.g. blackcurrants, apples, tomatoes, plums. (*See* p. 390 for bottling fruit pulp by Pressure Pan Method.) Avoid copper or iron utensils. Remove skins if necessary, stems and diseased or bruised portions. Peel and core apples. Stone plums. Stew with just suffi-cient water to prevent burning. When cooked right through, pour quickly (while still boiling) into hot, clean preserving jars. Seal *immediately* with hot lids and rubber rings dipped in boiling water. Process, using a pan with a false bottom.

To Process: Cover the jars with hot water, raise to boiling-point and boil for 5 min. Remove from water. Test for seal next day.

Apple purée: Cut unpeeled apples into slices, removing bruised or diseased portions. Stew apples till soft in just sufficient water to prevent burning. Rub through a sieve. Add a paring of lemon rind and sugar to taste. Immediately return the pulp and rind to the pan, bring to the boil, stirring to dissolve the sugar, pour into hot preserving jars and seal at once. Process as for pulp above.

Tomato purée: Rinse the ripe tomatoes. Heat in a covered pan with a little salt and water. When soft, rub through a hair or nylon sieve. Reheat, and fill quickly into hot preserving jars. Fasten and process, using a pan with a false bottom.

To process: Cover the jars with hot water, raise to boiling-point, and boil for 10 min. Remove from water. Test for seal next day.

Tomato juice: Rinse and heat the ripe tomatoes in a covered pan till they are soft. Sieve through a hair or nylon sieve. To each quart of pulp add: ½ pt. water, 1 teasp. salt, 1 oz. sugar and a pinch of pepper. Reheat, fasten and process as for Tomato Purée above.

PICKLES, CHUTNEYS AND SAUCES

POINTS TO WATCH

1. When making vegetable pickles, it is usual either to soak the vegetables in brine or to cover them with layers of salt. This draws some of the water from the vegetables. When they are covered with the spiced vinegar, they should be covered by at least $\frac{1}{2}$ in. and the jars should be covered tightly so that none of the vegetables are left out of the vinegar by subsequent evaporation.

2. Use aluminium, unchipped enamel-lined or monel metal pans, NOT brass, copper or iron.

3. If sieving is necessary, use a hair, nylon or fine-meshed monel metal sieve—other metals may give an unpleasant taste.

4. Cover the jars with one of the following:

(*a*) A cork, boiled to be thoroughly clean, and covered with greaseproof paper. (*b*) Synthetic skin. (*c*) A well-lacquered metal cap, lined with a layer of cork, waxed cardboard or vinegar-proof paper. The vinegar must not come in contact with the metal otherwise it may cause corrosion and rusting. (*d*) Greaseproof paper, covered with a circle of cotton material dipped in melted paraffin wax.

Spiced Vinegar: Buy only the best bottled vinegar for pickling; this should have an acetic acid content of at least 5 per cent.

To make spiced vinegar, add to 1 qt. of vinegar: $\frac{1}{2}$ oz. cloves, $\frac{1}{2}$ oz. allspice, $\frac{1}{2}$ oz. ginger, $\frac{1}{2}$ oz. cinnamon, $\frac{1}{2}$ oz. white pepper.

NOTE: All the above spices should be whole, not ground. Buy them fresh. If you find this spice too strong, the quantities can be reduced—even halved.

Steep the spices in the unheated vinegar for 1–2 months. Shake the bottle occasionally. Then strain and re-cork until needed.

Tarragon Vinegar: This can be bought ready-made, but if you grow tarragon it is cheaper to make the vinegar at home. Pick the leaves just before the herb flowers. Half-fill a wide-mouthed jar or bottle with the freshly gathered leaves (bang them lightly to bruise them). Fill the jar with best-quality malt vinegar and cover. Leave for 2 weeks or longer before removing the leaves. Put a cork or stopper on the jar before storing.

PICKLES

MIXED PICKLE

Make a selection of available vegetables. Any of the following are suitable: small cucumbers, cauliflower, small onions, French beans. Prepare the vegetables: only the onions need be peeled, the rest should merely be cut into suitably-sized pieces.

Put all into a large bowl, sprinkle with salt, and leave for 24 hr. Drain thoroughly and pack into jars. Cover with cold spiced vinegar, seal, and leave for at least a month before using.

PICCALILLI

2 lb. mixed vegetables (see over)
2 oz. cooking salt   1 pt. vinegar
15 chillies $\frac{1}{2}$ lb. granulated sugar

2 oz. mustard   ½ oz. turmeric
2 level tablesp. cornflour

Cut into small pieces a variety of vegetables such as cauliflower, cucumber, shallots and young kidney beans, weighing about 2 lb. in all when prepared. Place in a large earthenware bowl and sprinkle with the cooking salt. Leave to stand for 24 hr. and then drain well. Boil the vinegar and chillies for 2 min., allow to stand for ½ hr. and then strain the vinegar.

Mix together the sugar, mustard, turmeric and cornflour. Blend with a little of the cooled vinegar, bring the remainder of the vinegar back to the boil, pour over the blend, return to the saucepan and boil for 3 min. Remove from the heat and fold in the strained vegetables. Pack into prepared jars and cover at once with vinegar-proof covers.

PICKLED BEETROOT

Beetroots are obtainable most of the year and, like all the root crops, require cooking before pickling. Wash off any soil still clinging to the roots, taking care not to break the skin, for beetroot bleeds easily. If pickling for immediate use, simmer for 1½–2 hr. When cold, skin and cut into squares or slices, and cover with unspiced or spiced vinegar, whichever is preferred.

If pickling for storage, bake the roots in a moderate oven (350° F., Gas 4) until tender and, when cold, skin and cut into squares—it packs better that way for keeping; cover with spiced vinegar to which has been added ½ oz. salt to each pint.

Beetroot contains a good deal of sugar, and fermentation is more likely than with other vegetables, so seal thoroughly well to exclude air.

PICKLED CUCUMBER

The easiest way to pickle cucumbers is to quarter them lengthwise, cut into smaller pieces, brine with dry salt for 24 hr., then pack and cover with spiced vinegar. Like most of the vegetables they are best mixed with others.

PICKLED GHERKINS

The small immature cucumbers that are known as dills or gherkins require a longer process, especially if their deep green colour is to be fixed, and they need partial cooking.

Select gherkins of a uniform size, place in a saucepan and cover with standard brine (½ lb. salt to 3 pt. water). Bring to nearly boiling-point, do not actually boil, but simmer for 10 min.

Drain until cold, then pack into jars and cover with spiced vinegar, preferably aromatic.

A great many people prefer gherkins sweet; they are particularly popular at cocktail parties. These are quite easy to prepare from the ordinary pickled fruit.

A spoonful of sugar added to the jar and shaken up, then allowed to stand for 24 hr., is all that is necessary. It is not advisable to do this too long in advance as sugar added to a cold pickle in this way may very easily start to ferment. Another way is to turn the gherkins out on to a shallow dish, the one in which they will be served, and sprinkle with sugar. They can be done this way with a few hours' notice.

PICKLED ONIONS

Use small, even-sized pickling onions. Peel with a stainless knife and drop them into a basin of salted water until all have been peeled. Remove from water and allow to drain thoroughly before packing into jars or bottles. Cover with cold spiced vinegar and keep for at least 1 month before using.

PICKLED RED CABBAGE

Choose a firm, fresh cabbage. After removing any discoloured outer leaves, cut the cabbage into quarters and then into shreds. Put layers of the shreds into a large basin or dish, sprinkling each layer with salt. Leave overnight. Next day, drain very thoroughly in a colander, pressing out all the surplus liquor.

Pack layers of the shreds into large jars; pack about 3 in. of cabbage, cover with a layer of very thinly sliced onion, and sprinkle with 1 teasp. brown sugar. Then add another 3 in. of cabbage, another layer of onion and another teaspoon of sugar. Continue until the jars are filled, ending with the onion and sugar.

Cover with cold spiced vinegar, tie down and leave for at least 5 days to a week before opening jar.

NOTE: Do not make too much of this pickle at a time, because it will lose its essential crispness after 2 or 3 months' storage.

PICKLED SHALLOTS

Use even-sized shallots. Do not skin, place straight in a brine (1 lb. salt to 1 gall. water), leave for 12 hr.

Remove from brine and peel, using a stainless knife. Cover with fresh brine, making sure that all are kept below surface, and leave for a further 24–36 hr. Drain thoroughly. Pack tightly in the jars. Cover with cold spiced vinegar so that the vinegar comes $\frac{1}{2}$ in. above onions and keep for 3 months before use.

PICKLED WALNUTS

Use walnuts whose shells have not begun to form. Prick well with a silver fork; if the shell can be felt, do not use the walnut. The shell begins to form opposite the stalk, about $\frac{1}{4}$ in. from the end.

Cover with a brine (1 lb. salt to 1 gall. water) and leave to soak for about 6 days. Drain, make fresh brine, and leave to soak for a further 7 days.

Drain, and spread in a single layer on dishes, leaving them exposed to the air, preferably in sunshine, until they blacken (1–2 days). Pack into jars and cover with hot spiced vinegar. Tie down when cold and leave for at least a month before using.

NOTE: To help to prevent stained hands, wear gloves when handling the walnuts.

CHUTNEYS AND KETCHUPS

APPLE CHUTNEY

6 lb. apples 2 lb. sultanas $\frac{3}{4}$ lb. preserved ginger 3 pt. vinegar
$3\frac{1}{2}$ lb. sugar 1 oz. salt
1 teasp. allspice

Peel, core and chop the apples into small pieces and chop up the sultanas and ginger. Mix the vinegar, sugar, salt and spice together and bring to the boil, then add the apples and simmer for 10 min. before adding the ginger and sultanas. Simmer until the mixture becomes fairly thick, then pour into the jars.

GOOSEBERRY CHUTNEY

4 lb. gooseberries $\frac{1}{2}$ lb. mustard seed 1 lb. moist sugar 1 qt. vinegar 1 lb. onions $1\frac{1}{2}$ lb. stoned raisins 2 oz. allspice $\frac{1}{2}$ lb. salt

Bruise the mustard seed gently. Mix the sugar with 1 pt. of the vinegar and boil until a syrup forms, then add the finely-chopped onions, raisins and spice.

Boil the gooseberries in the rest of the vinegar until tender, then mix both lots together and cook until it thickens. Bottle and tie down tightly.

NOTE: The longer kept the better.

GREEN TOMATO CHUTNEY

5 lb. green tomatoes   1 lb. onions
½ oz. peppercorns   1 oz. salt
1 lb. sugar   1 qt. vinegar
½ lb. raisins   ½ lb. sultanas

Slice the tomatoes and chop the onions and mix together in a basin with the peppercorns and salt. Allow this to stand overnight. Next day boil up the sugar in the vinegar, then add the raisins (which may be chopped) and the sultanas. Simmer for 5 min., then add the tomatoes and onions, and simmer till thick.

PLUM CHUTNEY (in a pressure cooker)

3 lb. plums   2 medium onions
2 medium apples   4 tablesp. ground ginger   4 tablesp. cinnamon
4 tablesp. allspice   1½ tablesp. salt
1 pt. vinegar (approx.)   ¾ lb. sugar

Peel and chop the onions; peel, core and chop the apples; stone the plums and cut the plums in quarters. Remove the trivet from the pressure cooker. Put into the cooker the plums, onions and apples, the spices and salt and half the vinegar. Bring to the boil slowly in the open cooker, then cover, bring to 15 lb. pressure in the usual way, and cook for 10 min. Reduce pressure at room temperature. Return the cooker to the heat and, stirring all the time, add some of the vinegar gradually until the mixture is thick and smooth. Add the sugar and if necessary a little more of the vinegar, then boil rapidly until the chutney is the consistency of thick jam. Pour into hot jars and seal immediately.

TOMATO KETCHUP

6 lb. ripe tomatoes   1 pt. vinegar
½ lb. sugar   1 oz. salt   ½ teasp.

allspice   ½ teasp. cloves   ½ teasp.
cinnamon   ½ teasp. cayenne pepper

Cut the tomatoes into quarters, place them in a preserving-pan with the salt and vinegar and simmer until the tomatoes are quite soft and broken up. Strain the mixture through coarse muslin or a nylon sieve, then return the purée to the preserving-pan and add the sugar. Continue to simmer till the ketchup starts to thicken, and then add the spices a little at a time, stirring thoroughly until the flavour is to taste.

When the ketchup is reasonably thick, fill into hot bottles and seal immediately, or allow it to cool slightly, then fill the bottles and sterilize at 170° F. for 30 min.

Remember it will be thicker when cold than hot, so don't reduce it too far.

RED TOMATO CHUTNEY (in a pressure cooker)

2 lb. tomatoes   1 apple   1 onion
6 oz. sultanas   3 oz. dates
3 teasp. mixed whole spice
1 oz. salt   ½ pt. vinegar
½ lb. brown sugar

Skin the tomatoes. Peel, core and slice the apple. Peel and slice the onion. Wash the sultanas and dates in hot water before chopping. Remove the trivet from the pressure cooker, then put in these ingredients. Add the spices, tied in a muslin bag, the salt and ¼ pt. of the vinegar. Bring to 15 lb. pressure and cook for 10 min. Allow pressure to reduce at room temperature. Add the rest of the vinegar and the sugar and stir until the sugar is dissolved. Bring to the boil and simmer gently, in the open cooker, until thick. Pour into hot jars and seal immediately.

TOMATO SAUCE

6 lb. tomatoes   ½ pt. water
½ teasp. ground ginger.   ½ teasp.

ground mace ½ teasp. ground
cloves   pinch of cayenne pepper
1 oz. salt   ½ lb. sugar   1 gill vinegar

Slice the tomatoes; remove the
trivet from the pressure cooker and
put the tomatoes in the cooker together with the water. Bring to
15 lb. pressure over a medium
heat, and pressure cook for 3 min.
Reduce pressure immediately with
cold water, and rub the pulp
through a hair or nylon sieve.
Dissolve the spices, salt and sugar
in the vinegar and return, together with the sieved tomatoes, to
the open cooker. Stir over a
medium heat until the consistency
of thick cream—this takes ½ hr. or
longer.

With a pressure cooker, it is easy
to sterilize this sauce so that it can
be kept.

(a) Pour the sauce immediately
into hot, prepared bottling jars,
leaving 1 in. head space; adjust
rings and lids; if using screw-top
jars, screw bands tight, unscrewing
¼ turn.

(b) Rinse out the cooker and return it to the stove with 1½ pt.
boiling water, to which 1 tablesp.
vinegar has been added, and put in
the inverted trivet.

(c) Lift in the prepared jars and
bring cooker to 5 lb. pressure over
a medium heat. This process
should take approximately 5 min.

(d) Pressure cook for 2 min.

(e) Remove the cooker from the
heat and reduce pressure at room
temperature for 10 min.

(f) Lift out jars; tighten screwbands and leave for 24 hr.

(g) Test, seal and store in a cool,
dark place.

Yield—2 pt. of sauce

DAIRY PRODUCE

MILK

MILK as a food needs no introduction to either the housewife or the nutrition scientist.

Not all milk comes from a cow but, because it is the kind most widely known and used in this country, it is the one considered here.

Because milk is the principal source of calcium in the diet, medical authorities recommend certain daily quantities for various age groups—1 pt. for adults, 1–1½ pt. for young children, while for teenagers, whose needs are greatest, 1½ pt. or more.

CARE OF MILK

Milk should be kept "cool, clean and covered". Never let milk stay outside. Put it in a refrigerator, or a cool part of the larder, as soon as possible after it is delivered. If you have no refrigerator, it is a good idea to stand the bottles in a basin of cold water, covered with a damp piece of muslin. Milk should be kept in the dark because sunlight destroys some of the important vitamins and will tend to spoil the flavour. It should also be kept covered, because an open bottle or jug will soon pick up dust and germs and because milk has a tendency to absorb flavours and odours from other food.

CREAM

Cream is a concentration of the fat globules in milk and the standards of butterfat content are laid down as follows: *Single Cream* (sometimes known as pouring or coffee cream): not less than 18% (usually homogenized); *Double Cream* (sometimes known as thick or whipping cream): not less than 48%; and *Canned Cream:* 23% (usually sterilized). *Clotted Cream* has been heat-treated so that the liquid in it is reduced and the butterfat content is a minimum of 48%—though it is often nearer 60%.

Single cream will not whip unless helped by the addition of a stiffly-whisked egg white. Really fresh cream will not whip as well as that which is 24 hours old. It is best to use it straight from a refrigerator for whipping, although it should not be too cold when served.

BUTTER

Butter is a conglomeration of fat globules in large clusters and is made from the cream of milk. It usually consists of 80% fat but also contains some protein and milk sugar adhering in the buttermilk together with minerals and Vitamins A and D. Its main purpose in the diet is to provide energy.

Storing Butter: Butter is best kept in its wrapper in a cool, dark place, away from strong flavours or odours. If you have no refrigerator, an earthenware dish or butter cooler is useful.

MARGARINE

In many ways, margarine today is vastly superior to that of earlier days. The manufacturing processes have improved and the product is clean and wholesome. The proportion of fat is the same as the average specimen of butter and the keeping quality is superior.

In recent years, the flavour of most margarines has been greatly improved and prejudice against it has almost completely disappeared. Some manufacturers add about 10% butter to improve the flavour and texture still further.

CHEESE

Nutritional Value of Cheese: All classes of cheese contain a high proportion of protein. An ordinary fat cheese consists of one-third protein, one-third fat and one-third water with large amounts of calcium and riboflavin (one of the B vitamins) and worthwhile quantities of Vitamins A and D. Cheese, therefore, has an extremely high nutritional value.

Digestibility: There has been much discussion as to the digestibility of cheese and this has led to differences of opinion. However, it is generally agreed that if certain rules are followed in the preparation and cooking, cheese will be easily digested. Owing to its high nutritive value, it is most important that it should be included in the diet. Before cooking, cheese should be finely divided by grating or chopping. It should be very well chewed if eaten raw. The eating of some form of starch will aid the digestion and, as starch is usually accompanied by some vegetable protein, it is particularly recommended by nutritionists. (If animal and vegetable protein are eaten together, more value is obtained from both than if they are taken separately.)

Hard and Soft Cheeses: Generally speaking, the cheeses made from skimmed milk are hard and those made from full-cream are soft. There is one notable exception to this—Cottage Cheese (made from soured skimmed milk) is soft.

To Choose Cheese: The taste and smell are the best indications of quality and there is so much difference of taste that the old saying "taste and try before you buy" is still to be recommended where

possible. However, the opportunity does not often arise and the next wisest course is to consult your grocer. He can usually give helpful advice.

Storage Hints: Cheese will keep well if wrapped in a polythene bag to prevent drying and then stored in a cool larder (50°–60° F.) or in a refrigerator. In the latter case the cheese should be tightly wrapped and brought to room temperature half an hour before serving.

Serving Cheese: Cheese is often served as a separate course and, where possible, a variety of types should be offered. They should be attractively arranged on a cheeseboard or large plate and accompanied by bread rolls or a choice of biscuits. Vegetables such as watercress, radishes, small onions or celery go very well with cheese and make an attractive addition to the course. Many people like a little butter with cheese. Stilton Cheese deserves special mention because it is so often incorrectly served. It should be cut horizontally—not scooped from the centre. Port may be served *with* it but should not be poured *into* it.

KINDS OF CHEESE

There are well over 400 different kinds of cheese but those in the following list are among the best known.

English cheeses

Caerphilly Cheese is the small white cheese which originated in a small Glamorgan village but is now made in the West of England. It has a mild, creamy taste and a smooth, springy texture. *Cheddar Cheese:* A good Cheddar is solid and firm, pale yellow in colour with a succulent, nutty taste. *Cheshire Cheese* has a keen, tangy flavour and an open texture. There are red, white and blue varieties,

"Old Blue" being the richest and rarest. *Cream Cheese* is always very mild in flavour. It must be eaten fresh as it will not keep for very long and is therefore normally made up in small quantities. *Derby Cheese* is another mild, creamy cheese with a smooth texture. If allowed to mature for 4–6 months, it develops a fuller flavour. The rare *Sage Derby* is given extra flavour with layers of finely-chopped sage leaves. *Dorset Blue* or *Blue Vinny* is an unusual strong-tasting cheese. It is straw-coloured with deep blue veins and a stiff, crumbly texture. It is the only English cheese made from partly skimmed milk. *Double Gloucester Cheese* is a pungent, smooth-textured cheese somewhat similar to Cheddar, but fuller in flavour. *Lancashire Cheese* is especially famous for its toasting qualities. It has a crumbly and fairly soft texture which makes it easy to spread, while its flavour is clean and mild. *Leicester Cheese* is a fine dessert cheese with a mild flavour which becomes more piquant with maturity. It is rich red in colour and has a soft, crumbly texture. *Stilton Cheese:* The rich, mellow, strong-flavoured Blue Stilton is creamy white in colour with plenty of blue veins and a wrinkled brown coat. The texture should be open and flaky and the body soft and slightly moist. A creamy, young White Stilton has a mild flavour and is popular in the North. *Wensleydale Cheese* has a unique lingering, sweet flavour. Its texture is velvety and, when mature, is creamy enough to spread. The White Wensleydale is most common, but small quantities of Blue Wensleydale are also made.

Scottish cheese

Dunlop Cheese is the principal Scottish cheese. Its flavour is not unlike that of Cheddar, but it has a closer texture and is more moist.

Danish cheeses

Danish Blue Cheese is a semi-hard cheese made from whole milk. It is ripened by blue-green mould which gives it a mottled appearance. The texture is creamy and the flavour mellow. *Samsoe Cheese* is another Danish cheese made from whole milk. It is mild and creamy with a nutty flavour. Like some Swiss cheese, it has a number of holes, or eyes.

French cheeses

Camembert Cheese is a rich cream cheese from Normandy. It is small and flat, pale yellow in colour and has a dark rind. *Roquefort Cheese* is another very rich French cheese. Strictly speaking it should be made from ewe's milk but similar types are made in other countries from other kinds of milk. The flavour is sharp and peppery, while the appearance is of white curd with mottled blue veins. It has to be kept a considerable time before ripening and is similar in size to Stilton or Dorset Blue. *Tôme au Raisin Cheese* is a rich cream cheese which also comes from France. The outside is coated with grape pips which impart a unique flavour to the cheese.

Italian cheeses

Bel Paese is the name given to the best known of a group of Italian table cheeses. They are uncooked, soft, sweet and mild. Bel Paese is made from whole milk and the finished product is wrapped in tinfoil. *Gorgonzola Cheese* is the principal blue-veined cheese from Italy. It now has counterparts in many other countries. The interior has blue-green veins mottling the creamy cheese and its coat resembles a form of clay. *Mozzarella Cheese* is a soft, plastic-curd cheese that was originally made from buffalo's milk. Made mainly in Southern Italy, it is now produced from cow's milk as well. *Parmesan Cheese* is the name given to a group of very hard cheeses which originated in Italy but are now made in some other countries. Made entirely from skimmed cow's milk, their high flavour is largely due to the pasturage but also to the long maturing period—from 6 months to 4 years. This cheese is very hard and therefore grates easily. It is often sold in the powder form and keeps almost indefinitely. *Provolone Cheese* is made in many parts of Italy as well as in the United States. It is light in colour, mellow and smooth, cuts without crumbling and has a delightful flavour. This cheese is made in many shapes and sizes—each one having a special name.

Dutch cheeses

Edam Cheese originated in the Netherlands and is a semi-soft to hard, sweet-curd cheese made from cow's milk in which the fat content has been slightly reduced. It has a mild, clean flavour with a rather firm but crumbly texture. Those which are exported have a bright red coat but when consumed in their home country this is omitted. *Gouda Cheese* is very similar to Edam but contains more fat. Its shape is almost spherical. Like Edam, it has a bright red coating when exported from the Netherlands.

Swiss cheeses

Emmenthaler Cheese is a famous Swiss cheese similar to Gruyère in that it has an elastic body in which holes develop. However, its nut-like, sweetish flavour is more mild. *Gruyère Cheese* takes its name from a Swiss village although much of it is, in fact, produced in

France. Made from whole milk, it has a sharp flavour. The body is elastic in texture and as the cheese ripens, holes, or eyes, develop in it.

Processed Cheeses are usually sold in tinfoil or plastic wrapping, in separate portions or slices. The cheese has been specially treated to avoid any further ripening or deterioration during storage.

CREAM

DEVONSHIRE CREAM

Before starting to make Devonshire Cream at home, fresh milk should be allowed to stand for some hours. In very cold weather, this period should be 12 hours, but about half that time is sufficient if the weather is warm.

The milk should be heated, in a milk pan, until it is quite hot but not boiling. Boiling coagulates the protein and a skin will form on the surface. The more slowly the milk is heated, the better will be the result. The time required depends upon the size and shape of the pan and the amount of heat applied but slight movement on the surface of the milk indicates that it is sufficiently scalded.

When scalding is completed, the pan should at once be transferred to a cold place and left there until the following day. The cream can then be skimmed off the surface.

BUTTERS

CREAMED BUTTER
(for sandwiches)

8 oz. butter   1 gill double cream
mustard   salt and pepper
cayenne pepper

Beat the butter to a cream. Whip the cream stiffly and add it lightly to the butter. Season to taste with mustard, salt and pepper or cayenne.

Savoury Butters

General Method:

Roughly chop the ingredients to be mixed with butter. Crush and pound the additions. Pound the butter and additions together. Usually the compound butter is sieved and chilled.

NOTE: Herbs are best scalded in boiling water and dried in a cloth before being chopped and pounded.

"BLACK" BUTTER

Butter   vinegar

Heat the required amount of butter till brown but not burnt, strain, add a dash of vinegar. Use hot.

CURRY BUTTER

4 oz. butter   1 heaped teasp. curry powder   2 teasp. lemon juice salt to taste

Cream the butter, then stir in the curry powder and lemon juice. Beat well and add salt to taste.

DEVILLED BUTTER

2 oz. butter   ¼ teasp. cayenne ⅛ teasp. pepper   ½ teasp. curry powder   ¼ teasp. ground ginger

Pound all the ingredients together, rub through a fine sieve.

GREEN BUTTER

4 oz. butter   1½ tablesp. finely chopped, washed parsley anchovy essence or paste 1 tablesp. lemon juice   seasoning

Cream the butter, add the parsley, lemon juice, and anchovy essence or paste to taste. Season with salt and pepper and, when thoroughly mixed, use as required.

LOBSTER BUTTER

Coral and spawn of lobster double this quantity of butter salt and pepper

Dry coral thoroughly, then pound until smooth. Season to taste, add butter gradually until twice as much butter as coral has been added. Pass through a sieve.

NOTE: If this butter is to be used in Cardinal Sauce, the *raw* spawn should be pounded, then creamed with butter.

MAITRE D'HOTEL BUTTER

2 teasp. finely-chopped parsley ¼ teasp. chopped chervil and tarragon (optional)   2 oz. butter 1 teasp. lemon juice salt and pepper

Scald the parsley, chervil and tarragon, if used, in boiling water and dry in a cloth before chopping. Cream the butter, mix in the herbs gradually, add the lemon juice a drop at a time, season to taste. Do not sieve but spread on a plate and chill until firm.

MEUNIERE BUTTER or NOISETTE BUTTER

Butter   lemon juice

Heat the required amount of butter till it just turns golden-fawn, add a dash of lemon juice. Use hot.

MUSTARD BUTTER

2 oz. butter 1–2 teasp. French mustard

Cream the butter, then mix in the mustard.

Sweet Butters

BRANDY BUTTER (Hard sauce)

3 oz. butter   6 oz. icing sugar or 4½ oz. icing sugar and 1 oz. ground almonds   1 teasp.–1 tablesp. brandy 1 whipped egg white (optional)

Cream the butter till soft. Sift the icing sugar and cream it with the butter till white and light in texture. Mix in the almonds if used. Work the brandy carefully into the mixture. Fold the stiffly-whipped egg white into the sauce.

NOTE: This sauce may be stored for several weeks in an airtight jar.

RUM BUTTER

4 oz. butter   8 oz. soft brown sugar
1 sherryglass rum

Beat the butter to a cream and
beat in the sugar. When light and
creamy, add the rum gradually.
Transfer to a serving dish and chill
thoroughly before using.

SHERRY BUTTER

As for Rum Butter, using sherry
in place of rum and castor sugar in
place of soft brown sugar.

Cheese Dishes

CHEESE BUTTERFLIES

Cheese pastry (p. 338), using 3 oz.
flour, etc.   3 oz. cream cheese
few drops anchovy essence or
cochineal

Roll out the pastry thinly, and
cut into rounds about 1½ in. in
diameter. Cut ½ the rounds across
the centre—the "butterfly wings".
Bake for about 10 min. in a fairly
hot oven (400° F., Gas 6), then
cool on the baking-sheets. When
quite cold lift off. Colour the
cream cheese a delicate pink. Pipe
a line of this across each biscuit
circle and press the wing-shaped
biscuits on top.

15–16 savouries
Cooking time—10 min.

CHEESE FONDUE

4 oz. grated Gruyère or Swiss
cheese   1 oz. butter   1 oz. flour
¼ pt. milk   a pinch of salt
a small pinch white pepper   2 eggs

Melt the butter in a saucepan
and mix in the flour. Stir in the
milk and simmer gently until
smooth and thick. Add the cheese,
salt and pepper. When well mixed,
pour the mixture on to the well-
beaten egg yolks. Whisk the egg
whites and stir them lightly into
the mixture. Grease a fondue dish
or tin which is large enough for
the mixture to ½ fill it. Pour in
the mixture and bake in a fairly

hot oven (375° F., Gas 5) for about
20 min. This dish should be served
the moment it is ready.

4 helpings
Cooking time—20 min.

CHEESE RAMAKINS

1 tablesp. breadcrumbs   milk
1 oz. grated Parmesan cheese   1 oz.
grated Cheshire cheese   1 oz.
butter   1 egg   salt and pepper
mace

Barely cover the breadcrumbs
with boiling milk and leave to
stand for 10 min. Stir well. Add
cheeses, butter, egg yolk and seasoning to taste. Beat until the mixture is quite smooth. Whisk the egg
white to a stiff froth and fold it
into the mixture. Pour into well-
greased ramakin dishes and bake
in a hot oven (425° F., Gas 7) until
set.

4–6 helpings
Cooking time—15 min.

CHEESE STRAWS

Cheese pastry (p. 338), using 3 oz.
flour, etc.

Roll out pastry thinly, cut into
strips about 4 in. long and about
⅛ in. wide, and from the trimmings cut out some rings of about
1¼ in. diameter. Bake in a fairly
hot oven (400° F., Gas 6) until
crisp. Cool on the baking-sheet.
Fill each ring with straws and
arrange neatly on a dish.

18 straws
Cooking time—10 min.

CREAM CHEESE

Although not regarded as a true
cheese, cream cheese is often made
at home. It is usually ready to eat
after 2 days, but it should be made
only in small quantities, as it will
not keep as long as other types of
cheese.

Double Cream Cheese. The fat
content of the cream should be
high—between 50% and 60%—

and, after cooling to 50° F., add 1½ oz. salt for every 4 pt. double cream. The cream may then be left to sour naturally or starter may be added to hasten this process. Leave to stand in a cool place for 12 hr. Place a strong linen cloth over a large basin and pour the cream into the cloth. Gather the four corners and tie a piece of string round them (using a slip knot) to form a bag. Hang the bag over the basin in a cool place (*not* a refrigerator) with a good draught. Every 4 or 5 hr., open the bag and scrape the sides. When drainage is complete, the cheese may be shaped into small portions (usually about 1-2 oz.), wrapped and stored in a refrigerator.

Single Cream Cheese. The fat content of the cream should be between 20% and 40%. Heat the cream to 80° F. and add ¼ teasp. cheese-making rennet (to which 1 teasp. cold water has been added) to every 4 pt. single cream. Leave for about 3 hr. until a curd has formed. Transfer the mixture to a strong linen cloth placed over a basin and hang it up to drain, keeping it at a temperature of about 60° F. Leave for 24 hr. and then scrape the sides of the cloth. Transfer the bag and basin to a cool place (*not* a refrigerator) and leave to hang until drainage is complete. Make up in small portions, wrap and store in a refrigerator.

For more recipes for Cheese Dishes *see* the Savouries Section, p. 353.

EGGS

Food Value: Eggs are rich in protein, including the ten amino acids considered indispensable for growth and tissue repair; they contain Vitamins A, B, D and E, as well as the minerals iron and calcium.

Buying and Keeping Eggs: In buying eggs, avoid those that have been kept for days in sunny shop windows: glass attracts heat, and heat is bad for eggs. Avoid, too, buying dirty eggs: an eggshell is porous and dirt and germs are quickly absorbed. For the same reason, do not keep eggs next to onions, cheese, fish or other strong-smelling foods.

Keeps eggs pointed end downwards, in an egg box, in the cool. In a refrigerator, well away from the ice-box or freezer is ideal; but do take them out some time before use to give them time to reach room temperature, otherwise they often crack on being boiled, and are difficult to whip.

Ducks' eggs are larger and richer than hens' eggs. They can be used for most egg dishes, but it is advisable always to cook them well.

Cooking and Serving Eggs: There are limitless ways in which eggs can be used. Served alone they can be fried, boiled, baked, poached and scrambled. They are the essentials of omelettes and soufflés. As cooking aids, they have a leavening effect on cakes, they help to prevent the formation of ice-crystals in ice-cream, they thicken sauces and custards; their fat properties are essential to good mayonnaise; they serve as a binding agent in meat loaves; with breadcrumbs, they make a coating for fish and meat to be fried.

Preserving Eggs: Hens' eggs only should be preserved; it is unwise to preserve ducks' eggs even when newly laid. When buying eggs for preserving, tell your shopkeeper why you want them and make sure he sells you those from his latest delivery. Preserve them straight away. Even if you have the opportunity of doing so, do *not* preserve eggs taken straight from the nest. Time must be allowed (say 24-48 hr.) for the internal temperature and air pressure to drop.

Do not preserve dirty eggs, or those with rough or mis-shapen shells. If the eggs are soiled, dry-clean them with a stiff brush or wipe clean with a damp cloth. Make sure the eggs are cool before you start; the material used in pre-serving must be cool, and the eggs must be stored in a cool place. Whichever method of preserving is used, follow the manufacturer's instructions implicitly.

The Waterglass Method: Use a pail, galvanized iron bath or stone jar, and sufficient waterglass (sodium silicate) to fill it about ¾ full.

Place the eggs, if possible pointed end downwards, in the solution. More eggs can be placed in the solution as they become available, but always be sure they are completely covered by the liquid. Keep the receptacle covered to avoid dust and evaporation. Should evaporation take place, leaving the top layer of eggs ex-posed, add cold water until the original level is reached. A fall in the level due to removal of eggs should not be made good except by the addition of more solution of the same strength.

Dry Preserving: This consists of applying a protective coating of fat on the shell; there are two ways of doing this:

(a) The eggs may be treated with a special liquid preparation, con-sisting of fat dissolved in a suit-able solvent. This evaporates, leaving a coating of fat over the egg.

(b) The eggs may be rubbed over with white vaseline or other odourless, greasy preparation, us-ing the palms of the hands. Care must be taken to cover the shell completely.

Pickling Eggs: For every 6 eggs allow 1 pt. of white wine or cider vinegar, 6 cloves of garlic, 1 oz. pickling spice, a small piece of orange peel and a piece of whole mace. Boil together all the ingredi-ents (except the eggs) for ½ hr. When the liquid is cool, strain into a wide-mouthed earthen or glass jar with a screw lid, or tight cork. Put the whole, shelled eggs that have been hard boiled, into the liquid. They can be added to as convenient, but must always be covered by the liquid. The eggs should be left for 6 weeks before eating.

ALPINE EGGS

4 eggs   2 oz. butter   6 oz. cheese
finely-chopped parsley
salt and pepper

Butter a fireproof baking-dish thickly, line it with most of the cheese cut into thin slices and break the eggs over this, keeping the yolks whole. Grate the re-mainder of the cheese and mix it with the parsley. Season the eggs liberally, sprinkle the grated cheese on top and add the re-mainder of the butter broken into small pieces. Bake till set.

4 helpings
Cooking time—10 min. (approx.)

BOILED EGGS

Boiling eggs is a simple job, but not everyone does it perfectly. There are three ways of doing it; a good cook finds the method that suits her best, and sticks to it.

Method 1. Bring to the boil sufficient water to cover the eggs. Gently place the eggs in the water, set the egg-timer, or make a note of the time, and cook from 3–4½ min., according to taste. Take out the eggs, tap each lightly, once, with the back of a spoon, and serve.

Method 2. Put the eggs into a pan containing cold water and bring to the boil. When boiling-point is reached, start timing.

Cooking will take a little less time than with Method 1.

Method 3. This method is, in effect, coddling, and it produces an egg with a softer white than if actually boiled. Have a pan of boiling water ready, put in the eggs, cover the pan and turn off the heat. Let the pan stand for 6–8 min., according to the degree of softness required.

Hard-Boiled Eggs

For a really hard-boiled egg, cook by either Method 1 or 2, boiling for about 12 min. Then take out the eggs and put them under cold running water to cool them as quickly as possible. This prevents discoloration around the yolk.

BUTTERED EGGS—INDIAN STYLE

3 hard-boiled eggs   ½ oz. butter
½ teasp. curry powder   cayenne
pepper   2 raw eggs   salt and pepper
browned breadcrumbs

Cut the hard-boiled eggs, cross-wise, in rather thick slices. Place them in a well-buttered gratin dish or baking-dish, in which they may be served, and sprinkle the curry powder and a few grains of cayenne over them. Slightly beat the raw eggs, season with salt and pepper, and pour them into the dish. Cover the surface lightly with browned breadcrumbs, add a few pieces of butter, then bake in a moderate oven (350° *F.*, *Gas* 4) for about 10 min. Serve very hot.

4–5 helpings

CURRIED EGGS

4 hard-boiled eggs   4 oz. cooked
rice   1 small onion   1 oz. butter
1 teasp. flour   1 teasp. curry powder
⅓ pt. stock or milk   salt
lemon juice

Prepare the rice (*see* p. 38), shell the eggs and cut them into quarters. Chop the onion finely

and fry lightly in the butter, sprinkle in the flour and curry powder, and cook slowly for 5–6 min. Add the stock or milk, season with salt and lemon juice and simmer gently for ½ hr. Then add the eggs and let them remain until thoroughly heated and serve. The rice may be arranged as a border, or served separately.

Cooking time—45 min. (approx.)

CURRIED SCRAMBLED EGGS

4 eggs   1 small onion   ½ oz. butter
1 teasp. curry powder   salt   ¼ pt.
milk   buttered toast   lemon juice

Chop the onion finely. Melt the butter in a stewpan, add the onion and fry for 2–3 min.; sprinkle in the curry powder, let this cook for a few minutes, stirring meanwhile. Beat the eggs slightly, season with salt, add the milk, pour the mixture into the stewpan and stir until the eggs begin to set. Have ready squares of well-buttered toast, pile the egg mixture lightly on them, sprinkle with lemon juice and serve at once.

4 helpings
Cooking time—15 min. (approx.)

EGG FRITTERS—MILANAISE STYLE

4 hard-boiled eggs   ½ oz. butter
½ oz. flour   ⅛ pt. milk   1 oz. finely-
chopped ham or tongue   1 teasp.
finely-chopped parsley   1 small
shallot, chopped and fried in butter
lemon juice   salt and pepper
egg and breadcrumbs   frying fat
parsley

Halve the eggs lengthwise, and remove the yolks. Melt butter in a saucepan, stir in the flour, add the milk and boil gently for 2–3 min. Add chopped ham or tongue, parsley, shallot, chopped yolks, a little lemon juice and seasonings. Mix well. Fill egg whites with the mixture, coat carefully with egg and breadcrumbs, and fry in hot fat until nicely browned. Drain well and serve garnished with parsley.

4 helpings

Cooking time—30 min.

EGG MORNAY

4–5 hard-boiled eggs   1 oz. butter
nutmeg   salt and pepper   1½ oz.
grated cheese
¼ pt. white sauce (see p. 91)

Cut the eggs into thick slices, place them on a well-buttered fire-proof dish, sprinkle them lightly with nutmeg and more liberally with salt and pepper. Add 1 oz. cheese to the sauce and pour it over the eggs. Sprinkle thickly with cheese, and add a few tiny pieces of butter. Brown the surface in a hot oven or under the grill and serve.

4–5 helpings

Cooking time—5 min. (approx.)

EGGS A LA DREUX

4 eggs   ¼ lb. lean cooked ham
1 dessertsp. finely-chopped parsley
½ oz. butter   cayenne pepper   salt
4 small rounds buttered toast

Chop the ham finely, add the parsley and mix. Coat 4 deep patty tins thickly with butter, and cover them completely with a thin layer of ham mixture. Break an egg into each tin, taking care to keep the yolk whole. Sprinkle with a little cayenne pepper and salt, and add a small piece of butter. Place the patty tins in a deep baking-tin, surround them to half their depth with boiling water, and cook in a moderate oven (350° F., Gas 4) until the whites are set. Cut the rounds of toast to the size of the patty tins, dish the eggs on them.

4 helpings

Cooking time—10 min. (approx.)

EGGS IN ASPIC

3 hard-boiled eggs   1 pt. aspic
jelly (see p. 40)   chervil   cress

Coat the bottom of 6 dariole moulds with jelly, decorate them with chervil; when set, put in slices of egg and aspic jelly alternately, taking care that each layer of jelly is firmly set before adding the egg. When the whole is firmly set, unmould and decorate with chopped aspic and cress.

6 helpings

Time (including setting)—2 hr. (approx.)

FRICASSEE OF EGGS

4 hard-boiled eggs   ½ pt. white
sauce (see p. 91)   salt and pepper
chopped parsley
fried or toasted croûtons of bread

Reserve 1 egg yolk for garnishing; slice the other eggs. Well season the sauce, put in the sliced eggs and heat through thoroughly. Arrange on a hot dish, sprinkle with parsley and the egg yolk passed through a sieve, garnish with croûtons and serve.

2–3 helpings

Cooking time—30 min. (approx.)

ŒUFS A LA POELE

These are eggs fried on one side only. Melt a little bacon fat or butter in a frying-pan, break the eggs and slip them carefully into the pan. Cook over a gentle heat, basting the eggs with some of the hot fat, until the white is no longer transparent and the yolk is set. Season with pepper and salt.

ŒUFS EN COCOTTE

Heat one cocotte (a special little dish manufactured for this purpose) for each person. Add a little butter or cream, break an egg into each, season to taste, and place the cocottes in a pan of boiling water to come half-way up their sides. Cover the pan and place in a moderate oven (350° F., Gas 4). Cooking time when the eggs are in thin china dishes will be 6–7 min.; allow 8–9 min. with thicker dishes.

ŒUFS FRITS

Only one egg can be cooked at a time, but each takes less than one minute. Put a teacupful of oil into a small pan so that the egg will actually swim in the oil. Heat until the oil begins to smoke lightly, then maintain this temperature. Break the egg into a cup or saucer and season the yolk with salt and pepper. Slip it quickly into the oil, putting the edge of the cup to the surface of the oil. Dip a smooth wooden spoon into the hot oil, then pull the white over the yolk so as to cover it completely. Then turn the egg over in the oil and leave for a second only. It will then be done.

ŒUFS SUR LE PLAT

These are usually cooked in small dishes, one for each person, but the dish can be larger provided that the egg whites do not spread out too much when broken in, otherwise they will cook before the yolks. Heat the dish, add butter, eggs and seasonings as for Œufs en Cocotte. Place the dish in a moderate oven (350° F., Gas 4) and cook until the white is set but soft, and the yolk shows through a film of white. This will take about 5 min.; time will vary according to the thickness of the eggs and dish.

PIPERADE BASQUE

6 eggs   2 red peppers   2 green peppers   1½ lb. tomatoes   1 clove garlic   salt   olive oil   pinch of sugar   black pepper   croûtons

Cut the peppers in half, remove the seeds and pith, chop finely and plunge into boiling, salted water. Simmer for about 10 min. Reserve 3 tomatoes, skin and quarter the rest. Crush garlic with a pinch of salt and add to 4 tablesp. olive oil in a sauté pan. Heat, add the strained peppers and cook slowly for 3–4 min. Then add the quar-

tered tomatoes, salt and pepper, and sugar. Cover pan and simmer for 15 min. Skin and slice the 3 tomatoes and fry gently in oil. When the pepper mixture is mushy, beat the eggs lightly and add to the pan. Cook, stirring constantly, over a low heat, then pile on a dish and serve with the sliced tomatoes and croûtons arranged around.

8 helpings
Cooking time—40 min. (approx.)

POACHED EGGS

To poach well, eggs must be fresh. They should be broken into a cup or saucer and then slipped into boiling, salted water to which 1 tablesp. vinegar has been added. The water will cease to boil when the eggs are added: do not let it boil again. An average egg will take about 3 min. to poach: it is ready when the white has enveloped the yolk and may be touched without breaking. Remove with a perforated spoon.

POACHED EGGS WITH SPINACH

6 eggs   1 pt. spinach purée (fresh or canned)   1 oz. butter   nutmeg   salt and pepper   1 tablesp. brown sauce (see p. 94)   croûtons of toast

Prepare the spinach purée (*see* p. 232), place it in a saucepan, add the butter, a good pinch of nutmeg, salt and pepper, and the brown sauce. Heat through thoroughly. Meanwhile, poach the eggs and trim them neatly. Turn the spinach on to a hot dish, flatten the surface slightly and on it place the eggs. Garnish with croûtons and serve a good gravy or brown sauce separately.

6 helpings
Cooking time—30 min. (approx.)

SCOTCH EGGS

3 hard-boiled eggs   ½ lb. sausage

**meat   egg and breadcrumbs
frying fat**

Shell the eggs and cover each
egg with sausage meat. If liked, a
little finely-chopped onion can be
mixed with the sausage meat
before using. Coat carefully with
beaten egg and breadcrumbs, fry
in hot fat until nicely browned.
Cut each egg in half. Scotch eggs
can be served either hot or cold.

**3 helpings
Cooking time—40 min. (approx.)**

SCRAMBLED EGGS

The secret of serving good
scrambled eggs lies in slow cooking
over a very low heat (a double
saucepan is useful for this), continuous stirring, and immediate
service as the eggs go on cooking
in their own heat. It is helpful to
add a little butter, or cream, when
the scrambling is almost finished :
this stops the cooking and improves the flavour.

**4 eggs   salt and pepper
1 tablesp. butter
½ tablesp. butter or cream**

Break the eggs into a bowl, add
seasonings and beat eggs lightly.
Meanwhile melt the 1 tablesp.
butter in the bottom of a pan and
roll it around. Before it begins to
sizzle pour the eggs into the pan.
Reduce the heat to very low, and
stir the mixture evenly and constantly with a wooden spoon.
When almost ready add about ½
tablesp. butter or cream. Remove
from the heat as soon as the eggs
are set to a soft creamy consistency. Serve immediately.

**2 helpings
Cooking time—10 min. (approx.)**

SCRAMBLED EGGS AND HAM

**2 eggs   1 oz. butter   2 tablesp.
finely-chopped ham   1 tablesp.
milk   salt and pepper
2 rounds buttered toast**

Melt the butter in a pan, add
the ham and let it heat gradually in
the butter. Beat the eggs, add the
milk and season to taste, pour into
the pan and stir until the eggs
begin to set. Have the toast ready
and pile the egg mixture on it.
Serve at once. Tongue or other
cold meat may be substituted for
ham.

**2 helpings
Cooking time—15 min. (approx.)**

SEPARATED EGGS

Recipes often call for the use of
egg yolks or whites alone, resulting in one or the other remaining
unused.

Egg Yolks. Whole yolks will
keep for 2–3 days if covered with
cold water and placed in a screw-
top jar in a refrigerator.

To use them: add an extra egg
yolk or two to scrambled eggs and
custards, it will make them more
creamy. Or add them to a cream
sauce or soup, but do not let the
liquid boil after adding the yolks.
Or poach them hard and put
through a sieve, then use the
"mimosa balls" to garnish salads,
rice dishes and soups.

Egg Whites. Place in a covered
bowl in a refrigerator (well away
from the ice-box), and they will
keep for 5–6 days.

To use them: add an extra egg
white to a mousse, meringue or
soufflé. Or whisk the white and
fold it into a jelly just before it
sets. Or give a meringue top to
plain milk puddings or tarts; a few
minutes in a hot oven, just long
enough to set the meringue, is
sufficient.

MOUSSES

CHICKEN MOUSSE

**3 egg yolks   1 tablesp. gelatine
1 teacup chicken broth   salt and
pepper   1 teacup cooked chicken,
minced finely   1 teacup double**

cream, lightly whipped
¼ teacup mayonnaise

Soak the gelatine for 5 min. in
½ cup broth. Beat the egg yolks
and stir lightly in the remaining
broth, add salt and pepper, cook in
top of a double boiler, stirring constantly until thickened to custard
consistency. Stir in the dissolved
gelatine. Pour this over the chicken
until the mousse begins to set.
(This operation is speeded up if
the chicken is put in a basin
stood in cold water or cracked ice.)
Then fold in the cream and
mayonnaise. Turn into a mould
which has been moistened with
cold water. Chill until set.

To serve, turn out and garnish
with watercress and lettuce.

4 helpings
Cooking time—45 min. (approx.)

CHOCOLATE MOUSSE

4 eggs   4 oz. plain or vanilla
chocolate (sweetened)

Melt the chocolate with 1
tablesp. water (or black coffee) in
a pan over a very low heat. Stir
until smooth. Meanwhile separate
the eggs and beat the yolks. Stir
the melted chocolate into the
yolks. Whip the whites very stiff
and fold them into the chocolate.
Make sure they are perfectly
blended. Turn into a serving dish,
or 4 individual dishes and leave to
cool. Unless in a hurry, it is best
not to put chocolate mousse in a
refrigerator.

4 helpings
Cooking time—15 min. (approx.)

EGG MOUSSE

4–5 hard-boiled eggs   1 dash
Worcester or anchovy sauce
4 tablesp. aspic jelly   ½ pt. (bare)
double cream   salt and pepper
½ teasp. paprika

Chop the egg whites finely and
sieve the yolks. Mix the yolks
with the sauce and aspic, let the
mixture start to set, then add the
lightly whipped cream and seasonings; fold together. Add the
chopped whites and leave to set,
preferably in a refrigerator. Turn
out to serve.

4 helpings
Cooking time—45 min. (approx.)

FISH MOUSSE

2 eggs   1 lb. canned or cooked fish
(canned salmon is excellent)
½ teacup milk   1 teacup
breadcrumbs   salt and pepper
1 dessertsp. lemon juice
1 tablesp. chopped parsley

Drain the fish, remove the skin
and bone; and flake. Put the milk
and breadcrumbs into a pan and
add the juice from the canned fish
(or ½ teacup liquid in which the
fish was cooked). Put this over a
low heat for 5 min., stirring occasionally. Then add the fish, salt
and pepper, lemon juice and parsley. Mix, leave to cool slightly.

Separate the eggs; add the
lightly beaten yolks to the fish
mixture and stir well, beat the
whites until stiff and fold them in
thoroughly. Pour into a well-
greased mould, cover with greaseproof paper and place in a tin of
hot water reaching quarter-way up
the side of the mould. Bake in a
cool oven (310° F., Gas 2) for
40–45 min. During the last 10
minutes' cooking have the mould
uncovered.

4 generous helpings
Cooking time—1 hr. (approx.)

SAVOURY OMELETS

There are two types of omelet:
the French, which is flat and
generally served folded into three;
and the English, which is fluffy and
more like a soufflé.

FRENCH OMELETTE

2–3 eggs   salt and pepper
½ oz. butter

Break the eggs into a basin. Add salt and pepper to taste. Beat the eggs with a fork until they are lightly mixed. Heat the butter in the pan and slowly let it get hot, but not so hot that the butter browns. Without drawing the pan off the heat, pour in the egg mixture. It will cover the pan and start cooking at once.

Shake the pan and stir the eggs with a fork away from the side to the middle. Shake again. In about 1 min. the omelette will be soft but no longer runny. Let it stand for 4 or 5 seconds for the bottom to brown slightly. Then remove from the heat.

Using a palette knife, fold the omelette from two sides over the middle. Then slip on to a hot dish, or turn it upside down on to the dish.

This omelette can be eaten plain, or it can be filled. There are two methods of filling: flavouring such as herbs; cheese can be added to the eggs after they are beaten, or added to the omelette just before it is folded.

Suggested savoury fillings (quantities given are for 2 egg omelettes)

Cheese: Grate 2 oz. hard cheese finely. Add most of it to the mixed eggs, saving a little to top the finished omelette.

Fines Herbes: Finely chop 1 tablesp. parsley and a few chives, and add this to the mixed eggs before cooking.

Onion: Sauté a large onion in a little butter but do not get it too greasy. When cool, add to the egg mixture, saving a few hot morsels for garnishing the omelette.

Kidney: Peel, core and cut 2 lamb's kidneys into smallish pieces and sauté them in a little butter with a small chopped onion or shallot. Pile this mixture along the centre of the omelette after cooking but before folding.

Mushroom: Wash and chop 2 oz. mushrooms, sauté them in a little butter until tender. Put them along the centre of the cooked omelette.

Shellfish: Shrimps, prawns, crayfish, lobster or crab, fresh or canned, can be used. Chop if necessary and warm slowly through in a little white sauce (*see* p. 91) so they are hot when the omelette is cooked. Then pile the mixture along the centre.

Spanish: Make a mixture of chopped ham, tomato, sweet pepper, a few raisins, 1 or 2 mushrooms, and sauté in a little butter or olive oil. Add this to the egg before cooking; serve omelette flat.

ENGLISH OMELET

Separate the eggs. Add half an eggshell of water for each egg, to the yolks: beat them with a wooden spoon until creamy. Whisk the whites until they stay in the basin when turned upside down. Gently fold the whites into the yolks. Have the butter ready in the pan as for the French Omelette. Pour in the egg mixture, and cook until it is golden brown on the underside. Then put the pan under the grill and lightly brown the top. Fillings are usually spread over the cooked omelet. Now run a palette knife round the edge of the pan. Fold the omelet over and slip on to a hot dish.

PRESSURE COOKERY

As cooking in a pressure cooker means that the food is cooked in steam it is essential always to have in the cooker a liquid which, when it boils, will give steam. This may be water, stock, gravy, fruit juice, milk or cooking wine, but can never be fat, of any kind, on its own.

As pressure-cooking times are very much shorter than ordinary ones and as evaporation is almost completely eliminated, only a very small quantity of liquid is necessary and, wherever possible, this should be kept to the minimum. This amount must nevertheless be sufficient completely to cover the bottom of the cooker and to last the required cooking time. The actual quantities for each recipe will be shown in the manufacturer's booklet. When cooking soups, stews, milk puddings, etc., the amount of liquid is increased, however, to that required per person, regardless of the cooking time.

When cooking solids, a pressure cooker should be not more than two-thirds full. There must be room for the steam to circulate and do its work and there should always be sufficient space between the food and the cover to prevent the steam vent getting blocked. With a flat cover this is two-thirds of the base; with a domed cover the base can be filled to the top. When cooking liquids, the maximum quantity is one-half of the base. In this case, space must be left to allow for the liquid boiling up. Stock, milk, soup could easily fill the pan, and boil over or block the steam outlet.

To adjust recipes to cook for varying numbers of people a simple guide is to remember that, where the food is being timed by the pound, e.g. a joint of meat, the cooking time increases with the weight and so does the amount of liquid required. If only the quantity of food is being increased, e.g. 4 lb. potatoes, instead of 1 lb., no addition need be made to the cooking time or the liquid.

There is really no hard-and-fast rule for changing one's own favourite dishes over to pressure cooking, but usually a basic recipe containing similar ingredients can be found in the instruction booklet. Working from this, a method —together with the necessary amount of liquid and time required—can often be worked out. Otherwise, it is best to make one's first experiment, taking one-third of the normal cooking time, and then an adjustment of more or less time can be made as necessary.

BEVERAGES

COCOA AND CHOCOLATE

To Make Cocoa: Allow 1½ teasp. cocoa to ¼ pt. milk and ¼ pt. water. Mix the cocoa smoothly with a little cold water, boil the remainder of the water and the milk, and pour these on to the blended cocoa, stirring well meanwhile.

To Make Drinking Chocolate: Various proprietary brands of powdered chocolate are now on the market, which when mixed with hot milk or milk and water provide a nourishing drink. Alternatively, grated block chocolate may be substituted for powdered chocolate; sweeten to taste.

COFFEE

To Make Coffee: To make perfect coffee the beans should be roasted and ground just before they are to be used. As this is impracticable, it is better to buy the beans and grind only as many as are required for immediate use. The beans should be stored in an airtight container. If a coffee mill is not available, it is better to buy only a small quantity of ground coffee at a time to avoid loss of flavour, and to store it in an airtight container.

Allow 2 heaped dessertsp. coffee (or 2 of the coffee measuring spoons sponsored by the Coffee Publicity Association) and ½ pt. freshly boiled water for each person. Some people also add a pinch of salt.

Method 1: Warm an ordinary china jug, put in the coarsely-ground coffee, pour on to it the boiling water, and stir vigorously. Allow the jug to stand for 1 min., then skim off any floating coffee grains, stand for a further 4 min., closely covered, where the contents will remain just below boiling-point. The coffee can then be poured slowly or strained into another warmed china jug and used at once.

Method 2: Put the coffee (coarsely-ground) with the water into an enamel saucepan and bring almost to the boil. Reduce the heat and simmer very gently for 3 min. Dash in 1 teasp. cold water to help the grounds to settle. Strain into a warmed coffee-pot or jug.

Method 3: Use a percolator and fine- or medium-ground coffee. Into the percolator put as much fresh cold water as is required and bring to the boil. Put the coffee into the basket and insert it in the percolator, cover, and return to heat. Allow to percolate *gently* for 6–8 min.

Method 4: The vacuum method. The equipment for this method consists of 2 bowls plus a source of heat. Put the required amount of cold water into the lower bowl and place on the heat. Put the filter in the upper bowl and the required amount of fine- or medium-ground coffee in the upper bowl. Allow the water in the lower bowl to boil, then reduce heat—if electric switch off, then insert upper bowl with a slight twist to ensure a tight fit. Some vacuum models can be assembled completely before placing on the heat. When the water has risen into the upper bowl (some water will always remain in the lower bowl) stir well. In 1–3 min. (fine-ground coffee will require the shorter time) turn off heat; remove electric models from unit. When all the coffee has been drawn into the lower bowl, remove upper bowl and serve.

Method 5: Café filtre. Heat a coffee-pot or individual cups, place the finely-ground coffee in the strainer over the coffee-pot and slowly pour over freshly-boiled water and allow to drip through. When the water has dripped through remove strainer—if the coffee is not strong enough filter again.

Equipment for making coffee should always be kept scrupulously clean.

Coffee may be served black (*Café Noir*) or with milk (*Café au Lait*) or with cream (*Café Crème*). When serving *Café au Lait* it is usual to pour the 2 liquids into the cup at the same time, *the milk should be hot but not boiled.*

Liqueurs such as Kirsch, Cognac or liqueur brandy, as well as one or two of the following: Bénédictine, Chartreuse, Kümmel, Curaçao, Cherry Brandy or other sweet liqueur, are usually served with coffee.

There are several patent coffee powders on the market with which one can make a quick cup of coffee, full instructions for their use are printed on the tin. Coffee is also sold in liquid form.

TEA

To make good tea it is necessary that the water should be quite boiling and freshly boiled. It is a good plan to empty the kettle and refill it with fresh cold water, and make the tea the moment the water reaches boiling-point.

The tea-pot should be thoroughly warmed before making the tea. The boiling water should be poured on the tea, then left to stand for 3–4 min., it should never be allowed to stand for longer. Some people like to stir the tea before pouring it out.

TABLE WINES

How to Store Wine: The ideal, of course, is to have a proper cellar, but in these days of flats and small houses the word cellar is receding from the vocabulary of wine.

Wine should always be kept lying on its side; otherwise the cork will become dry and possibly allow the entry of air. The contrary, however, prevails in the case of spirits, where the action of the spirit may eat into the cork. Therefore spirits must be kept upright, the ethers arising from the bottle's contents having the effect of keeping the cork moist. If a proper place is available for keeping wine, even though it may be only under the stairs, it is well to have a simple wine-rack placed there.

Wine should be kept in the dark, or as nearly as possible. Otherwise, a cloth covering or even a sheet of brown paper may be found effective.

Temperature: Wherever wine is kept one should keep an eye on the temperature. The accepted temperature for wine is from 55° to 60° F.

It is advisable to store wine with the label uppermost so that, if the bottles must necessarily be moved, they can be relaid in the same position, thus avoiding any serious disturbance of the sediment, if any.

WINE AND FOOD

MEALS	WINES BEST SUITED TO ACCOMPANY THEM			
Apéritifs, to stimulate the appetite	Sherry Fino *or* Amontillado	Vermouth French *or* Italian (chilled)	White Port	Dry Madeira
Soup, hors d'œuvres	Sherry Fino *or* Amontillado	Dry Madeira		
Shellfish, oysters, fish, cold chicken	A dry white wine such as Hock, Moselle, White Burgundy *or* Dry Graves. Dry white Portuguese *or* Spanish wines are also very drinkable.			
Meat dishes, roast chicken, goose, duck, game	A red wine, usually a light claret, with white meats and a heavier wine, like a Burgundy, with the stronger flavours. The lovers of German *or* Alsatian wine will cheerfully drink a stout dry Hock *or* Traminer here.			
Sweets, ices	Sweets with the sweet is the rule. Here a sweet white wine, a Sauterne, a sweet Graves, Barsac, Cerons, from Bordeaux; a rich sweet Hock *or* any sweet white wine from Spain, Portugal, Cyprus, Australia, South Africa.			
Nuts, coffee	A fine old Tawny Port *or* a Vintage Port.			

COMMONWEALTH COOKERY

Hors d'œuvre

PATE DE FOIS GRAS

2 lb. pork or calf liver   2 lb. green
bacon   salt and pepper   ½ teasp.
ground cinnamon or grated nutmeg
1 small onion   ½ lb. mushrooms
¼ cup butter or margarine   2 eggs
1 bay leaf   pinch of thyme

Cut up liver and bacon, discarding membrane of liver. Mince the
meat finely, add seasoning and
spice. Peel and chop onion; peel
(if necessary) and chop mushrooms. Melt fat and fry onion and
mushrooms, mix with minced
meat. Add the eggs and beat well.
Put mixture into a fireproof dish,
put the bay leaf on top, sprinkle
with thyme. Cover dish and place
in a steamer or pan containing
sufficient hot water to come half-
way up the side of the dish. Put
lid on steamer and steam in a cool
oven (310° F., Gas 2) for about
3 hr. Allow paté to cool (still
covered). When cool rub through
a strainer, correct the seasoning.
Put into individual moulds; chill.

Fish Dishes

BAKED BARRACOUTA

6 cutlets off a medium-sized
barracouta   1 oz. plain flour   salt
and pepper   juice of ½ lemon
2 oz. butter
1 tablesp. chopped parsley

Wash and dry the fish and place
the slices side by side in a fireproof
dish. Mix the flour and seasonings
together and sprinkle lemon juice
over fish. Mix the butter and
parsley and place in small pieces
on the fish. Bake in a moderate
oven (350° F., Gas 4) for 20 min.,
basting occasionally. Serve on a
hot dish with the liquor strained
over.

6 helpings

FISH A LA TASMANIA

6 portions striped trumpeter
3 oz. fat bacon   ½ small onion
3 oz. soft white breadcrumbs
¼ pt. thick white sauce
salt and pepper   flour   1 egg
fat for deep frying

Cook the fish in the oven, remove the skin and bone and flake
the flesh. Mix it with the finely-
choped bacon and onion and 1 oz.
of breadcrumbs. Stir into the
sauce and season well. Shape into
cones; coat in flour, brush over
with beaten egg, then toss in
breadcrumbs. Deep fry a golden
brown. Pile high on a dish and
serve with melted butter sauce or
anchovy sauce.

6 helpings
Time—1 hr.

PAUA ROE PATTIES

2-3 paua roes   ½ pt. white sauce
12 pastry cases

Carefully remove the roes from
the muscle part of the fish. Simmer the roes very gently for about
10 min. in a little milk and water,
strain and use the liquid for the
white sauce. Cut the roes into
small pieces and add them to the
white sauce. Put 1 teasp. of the
mixture into each pastry case, replace the tops of the cases, and

heat the patties thoroughly in the oven.

Meat Dishes

BREDIE—TOMATO

2 onions   1½ oz. butter or fat
2 lb. thick rib of mutton
12 ripe tomatoes   a small piece of
red chilli   a little sugar
salt and pepper

Chop the onions finely. Melt the fat in a broad shallow saucepan. Add onions, and brown lightly. Cut meat in small pieces, and add to onions. Stir well until all pieces are thoroughly seared. Remove skins from tomatoes by pouring boiling water over them, the skins can then be easily removed, chop up the flesh into small pieces and add to meat. Add the skin of the red chilli finely chopped, cover and simmer on the side of the stove for about 2 hr. Just before serving, add sugar, salt and pepper.

NOTE: No water is required if tomatoes are used, as they are sufficiently watery. A little boiling water is added to the meat if a bredie of any of the other vegetables, e.g. cabbage, cauliflower, potatoes, French beans, is desired. The meat is simmered in the same way, but the other vegetables are not added until ½ hr. before serving. They should be cut up into small pieces, added to the meat and allowed to cook gently, with frequent stirrings. More boiling water may be added, a little at a time, if the bredie becomes too dry, but it should never be allowed to become watery.

CARPET-BAG STEAK

4-lb. piece of topside, pocketed for stuffing

STUFFING

1½ oz. butter   12–18 oysters
¼ lb. fresh mushrooms   6 oz.
white breadcrumbs   1 tablesp.
chopped parsley   grated rind of
½ lemon   salt and paprika   1 egg

Heat the butter and into it toss the oysters and roughly-chopped mushrooms; cook for 5 min. Transfer to a basin and mix in the breadcrumbs, parsley, lemon rind and seasoning. Stir in the beaten egg. Press the mixture into pocket in steak and sew or skewer edges together. Roast in a warm oven (335° F., Gas 3) to prevent shrinkage for 2 hr. Serve with roast potatoes and pumpkin.

6 helpings

COOLGARDIE STEW

1½ lb. topside steak   2 hard-boiled
eggs   1 onion   1 heaped tablesp.
flour   salt   cayenne pepper or
curry powder   1 egg   ½ lb. bacon
rashers   flour   1 lb. tomatoes
juice of 1 lemon
1 pt. stock or water

Cut the steak into thin 5-in. lengths. Chop the hard-boiled eggs and onion and mix them with the 1 tablesp. flour, seasonings and beaten egg. Remove rind from bacon and cut bacon into 3-in. lengths. Roll a teaspoonful of egg mixture in each strip of bacon, and then in one of the pieces of steak. Secure with a toothpick. Toss in flour and sear in hot fat. Transfer from pan to casserole, add the tomatoes, skinned and sliced, lemon juice and stock or water. Place in a moderate oven (350° F., Gas 4) and allow to cook for 2 hr. Remove toothpicks. Serve with macédoine of vegetables and creamed potatoes.

4 helpings

Salad

FEIJOA SALAD

6 ripe feijoas   2 tablesp. chopped
walnuts   4 tablesp. mayonnaise
lettuce leaves

Peel and slice the feijoas. Add the chopped walnuts and the

mayonnaise and mix them lightly with a fork. Pile spoonfuls of the mixture into crisp lettuce leaves. Garnish with grated cheese or a small dab of vegetable extract.

Dessert
BLUEBERRY GRUNT

**2 cups blueberries   ½ cup sugar
2 tablesp. lemon juice   2 cups plain
flour   4 teasp. baking-powder
½ teasp. salt   2 tablesp. sugar
¼ cup shortening
¾ cup milk (approx.)**

Put the blueberries, ½ cup of sugar, lemon juice and 1 cup of water into a pan and bring to boil, stirring continuously. Boil for 3 min. Sift together the flour, baking-powder and salt, add the 2 tablesp. sugar. Cut in the fat and mix with milk to make a soft dough. Drop the dough over the boiling fruit, cover and simmer for 10 min. without raising the lid.

PASSION FRUIT FLUMMERY

**1 tablesp. gelatine   2 cups cold
water   ½ cup sugar   1 tablesp. plain
flour   juice of 2 oranges   juice of
1 lemon   ½ doz. passion fruit
custard or whipped cream**

Soak gelatine in 1 cup of the cold water for 2 hr. Add sugar. Blend flour with the remaining cup of cold water; add juice from oranges and lemon. Put all into a large saucepan and bring to the boil. Remove from heat, and when nearly cold add passion fruit pulp. Beat thoroughly till thick and white. Serve very cold with custard or whipped cream.

SPICED PINEAPPLE
UPSIDE-DOWN CAKE

**4 oz. butter   12 oz. brown sugar
1 large can pineapple slices
10 maraschino cherries   1 lb. self-
raising flour   1 teasp. cinnamon
1 teasp. nutmeg   2 eggs   ½ cup milk**

Melt half of butter in baking-tin; add half of sugar; stir until dissolved. Drain the pineapple slices and arrange in a neat pattern on the caramel coating. Place a cherry in the centre hole of each pineapple slice. Sift together the flour and spices. Beat eggs with remaining brown sugar; add milk and remaining butter, melted; stir into spiced flour. Pour over pineapple in tin. Bake in a moderate oven (350° F., Gas 4) for 45–50 min. Remove tin from oven and invert on to serving plate, leave the tin on for a few minutes so that caramel will run down over cake and not stick to tin. Remove tin and serve cake warm with cream.

Apricot or Peach Upside-Down Cake. Use drained, canned apricot or peach halves instead of pineapple slices, flavour with vanilla, omit spices.

PAVLOVA CAKE

**3 egg whites   6 oz. castor sugar
½ teasp. vanilla essence   ½ teasp.
cornflour   ½ teasp. vinegar**

Beat the egg whites until stiff. Continue beating, gradually adding the sugar. Beat until sugar is dissolved and at this stage the mixture should be very stiff and standing well in peaks. Fold in vanilla, cornflour and vinegar. Spread mixture in a 6–8-in. circle on greaseproof paper on a baking-sheet, making the sides higher than the centre to form a shell to hold filling. Or pipe small shapes for the sides. Place in a cool oven (310° F., Gas 2) for 1–1¼ hr.

The pavlova should be crisp and very lightly tinted on the surface yet remain soft and of the consistency of marshmallow in the centre. Cool and remove very carefully on to a flat cake-tray or board. Fill and serve.

FILLING

1. Pile ½ pt. whipped and flavoured cream into the pavlova shell and on top of this arrange a selection of fruit: pineapple; strawberries or other berry fruits; cherries; apricots; mandarins, passion fruit; grapes; fresh or canned peaches, etc., according to taste and season. Finally decorate with angelica, cherries or almonds.

2. Mash or slice 4–6 bananas. Mix a few tablespoonfuls of sherry or brandy into the mashed bananas or place the slices in a basin and cover with sherry or brandy. Allow to stand for 1 hr.

Strain off liquid if bananas are sliced, then fold fruit into ½ pt. whipped and sweetened cream, with a cupful of halved fresh or maraschino cherries. (If the sherry or brandy is inclined to liquefy the cream add 1 teasp. dissolved gelatine.) Pile into shell and sprinkle with shredded chocolate, chopped nuts or toasted coconut.

INDEX

Abbreviations, list of	53	fritters	258
Agro-dolce	95	gâteau	298
Aïoli	95	glaze	333
Almond and walnut filling	336	jam	377
castles	371	mould	293
cheesecakes	348	pudding	345
fingers	328	sauce	105
fritters	258	soufflé	261, 292
icing	334	tart	347
paste	334	trifle	294
pudding	344	upside-down cake	417
shortcake	330	Arrowroot pudding	250
Alpine eggs	404	sauce	105
Amber jelly	283	Artichoke bottoms	211
Ambrosia mould	281	Artichokes, globe, boiled	210
American cabbage salad	237	Jerusalem, boiled	211
frosting	333	Jerusalem, fried	211
okra soup	85	Jerusalem, mashed	211
walnut cake	319	Asparagus, boiled	211
Anchovies	60	points	212
Anchovy éclairs	353	Aspic cream	41
fingers	353	fingers	354
rolls	64	jelly	41
sauce	92	mayonnaise	104
toast	353	Aubergine, baked with cheese	212
Andalusian sauce	104	fried	212
Angel cake	328	Avocado pears	60
"Angels on Horseback"	353	pears and prawns	60
Appetizers	353–9		
Apple amber	345	Babas with rum syrup	276
and celery stuffing	110	Bachelor's pudding	266, 273
and cucumber salad	237	Bacon	174
and walnut stuffing	110	and egg pie	360
charlotte	272	boiled	176
chutney	394	Baked, see subject, e.g. Beef,	
crumble	272	Mutton, Potatoes, etc.	
custard	292	Bakewell tart	342
dumplings	265, 272	Baking	35, 306–37
fritters	258	Baking-powder bread	310
Apple jelly	381	Banana and tapioca sponge	280
pie	347	flan	343
pudding	265, 272	fritters	259
sauce	97, 105	ice cream	302
sauce with horseradish	97	jelly with cream	283
snow	295	salad	237
snowballs	247	snow	295
tart	347	split	303
trifle	293	whip	295
water ice	301	Barbel	116
Apples and rice	247	Barley pudding	249
baked	273	soup	77
Apricot baskets	326	Baroness pudding	266
bouchées	348	Barracouta, baked	415

Bath buns   308
Battenburg cake   324
Batter pudding   255
Batters   255-7
Bean, broad, purée   83
    butter, purée   87
    haricot and tomato soup   87
    haricot, soup   87
Beans, broad, with parsley sauce   213
    French, boiled   213
    haricot, and minced onions   213
    haricot, boiled   213
    runner, boiled   213
Béarnaise sauce   100
Beatrice tartlets   348
Béchamel sauce   100
Beef   147-61
    à la mode   149
    au gratin   370
    boiled   150
    braised   151
    brisket of   151
    broth   70
    curried   151
    curry of cold   470
    fillets of, Portuguese style   152
    fillets of, with fried bananas   152
    galantine of   186
    hash   370
    mignons of, Bourgeoise style   153
    minced, and poached eggs   371
    miniature round of   153
    noisettes of, with mushrooms   153
    olives   149
    potted   186
    pressed   186
    ragoût of   371
    roast   154
    roast fillet of   154
    sausages   157
    shin of, soup   78
    tenderloin of   156
    to buy   147-9
Beefsteak, fried   152
    grilled   152
    pie   149
    pudding   150
    smothered   155
Beetroot and celery salad   238
    baked   214
    boiled   214
    cassolettes   64
    pickled   393
    salad   238
Beverages   412-14
Birthday cake   320
Biscuits   330-3
Bisque   80
Bisque aux huîtres   80
    de crevettes   80
    d'homard   80

"Black" butter   401
Blackberry and apple jam   377
    and apple jelly   381
    jam   377
Blackcurrant jam   378
    jelly   381
    whip   286
Blancmange   295
Bloater toast   354
Bloaters—grilled   116, 360
Blueberry grunt   417
Boar's head sauce   95
Boiled, see subject, e.g., Beef,
    Mutton, etc.
Boiling   31-2
Bone stock   69
Bonne femme soup   88
Border of pears   251
Bortsch soup   88
Bottling   387-91
Bouillabaisse   81
Bouillon en tasses   70
Bouquet garni   68
Brain and tongue pudding   169
    sauce   92
Braising   33
Brandy butter   401
    sauce   106
    snaps   330
Brawn   188
Bread and butter fritters   259
    and butter pudding   252
    fritters   259
    -making   306
    pudding   273
    sauce   95
Breakfast dishes   360-5
Bredie—tomato   416
Bridge rolls   307
Brill   117
    à la Conti   117
Broad bean, see Bean, Broad
Broccoli   214
Broiling   33
Broths   70-3
Brown caper sauce   102
    chaudfroid sauce   96
    sauce   94
    stew   156
Browning   68
Brussels sprouts, boiled   215
    sprouts, fried   215
Bubble and squeak   369
Buck rarebit   359
Bullock's heart—stuffed and
    baked   158
Buns   316-17
Butter   397
    bean, see Bean, Butter
    cream   336
    crust pastry   338

icing 336
Buttered eggs—Indian style 405
Butterfly cakes 326
Butterscotch sauce 106

Cabbage, beetroot and carrot
    salad 238
  boiled 215
  red, pickled 394
  stewed 216
  stuffed 216
Cabinet pudding 252
Cake decoration 333–7
  fillings 336–7
  icings 333–6
  -making 314–16
Cakes 316–30
Calf's liver and savoury rice 184
Calves' brain cakes 183
  kidneys—stewed 183
Canadian pudding 252
Canapés 354
Canary pudding 266
Caper sauce 92
Capsicums 226
Caramel custard 252
  ice cream 302
  mould 280
  sauce 106
Cardinal sauce 100
Cardoons, boiled 216
Carp, baked 117
  stewed 118
Carpet-bag steak 416
Carrot salad 238
  soup 84
Carrots—conservatively cooked 216
  glazed 217
Carving 55–9
Castle pudding 273
Catfish 118
Cauliflower, boiled with white
    sauce 217
  with cheese 217
Celeriac with white sauce 217
Celery à la Grecque 65
  and chestnut salad 238
  braised 218
  cream soup 84
  soup 84
  vinegar 108
  with white sauce 218
Cereal moulds 278–82
Cereals 366–8
Chantilly sauce 106
Charlotte Russe 290
Chartreuse of bananas 290
Chaudfroid sauces 96
Cheese 398–400
  and onion pie 360
  bread plait 308

butterflies 402
fondue 402
meringues 354
omelette 410
pastry 338
pudding 355
ramakins 402
sauce 92
Cheese scones 312
  soufflé 355
  straws 402
  whirls 312
Chelsea buns 309
Cherry cake 319
  cakes 326
  jam 378
  pudding 274
  salad 238
  sauce 97
  tartlets 348
Chestnut pudding 274
  purée 84, 219
  sauce 96
  stuffing 110
Chestnuts au jus 218
Chicken à la Marengo 193
  boiled 193
  broth 71
  cannelons of 193
  cream 193
  curried 196
  en casserole 194
  escalopes 194
  fondue of 197
  forcemeat 194
  fricassée of 197
  grilled with mushroom sauce 197
  mayonnaise 194
  minced 374
  mousse 408
  patties 357
  pilaff 195
  potted 197
  purée 76
  ramakins 195
  réchauffé of 197
  rissoles 373
  roast 197
  roast, stuffed with herbs 198
  salad 239
  sauté 195
  soufflé 195
Chicken spatchcock 196
  stock 70
  timbales of 198
  with macaroni 196
  with rice and tomatoes 196
Chicory and white sauce 219
  salad 239
  soup 84
Chilli vinegar 109

Chocolate buns   316
  cakes   326
  cream   288
  drinking   412
  filling   336
  ice cream   302
  icing   333
  mousse   409
  pudding   266, 274
  sandwich   325
  sauce   106
  soufflé   261, 292
  sundae   303
  Swiss roll   328
  tartlets   349
Choux pastry   339
Christmas cakes   320
  pudding sauce   106
  puddings   266-7
Chutneys   392-6
Cider ice   301
  sauce   94
"Cleared" jellies   284-6
Coalfish   118
Coating batter   258
Cock-a-Leekie or Cockie-Leekie 71
Cockles   136
Cocoa   412
Coconut buns   316
  cakes   326
  cones   329
  filling   336
  mould   281
  pudding   267, 345
Cod à la Provençale   118
Cod, curried   119
  golden grilled   119
  hashed   119
  soup   82
  steaks   118
Cod's roe   119
Coffee   412
  cream   288
  filling   337
  ice cream   302
  layer cake   325
  sauce   106, 304
  whip   286
Cold green mousseline sauce   104
College pudding   275
Commonwealth cookery   415-18
Confectioners' custard   337
Conger eel   120
  eel, baked   120
  eel pie   120
Consommés   73-6
  à la Celestine   74
  à la Julienne   74
  à la mulligatawny   75
  à l'Indienne   75
  à l'Italienne   75

  aux nouilles   75
  aux patés Italiennes   75
  de queue de boeuf   75
  de torque fausse   75
  frappé   74
  Royale   76
Continental cakes   326
Cookies   316
Coolgardie stew   416
Corn on the cob, baked   219
  boiled   220
Cornflour cake   319
  custard   107
  mould   281
  sauce   107
Cornish pasties   360
Cottage pudding   275
Cow heel, boiled   158
  heel, fried   158
Crab   136
  dressed   137
  potted   137
  salad   239
  to prepare   137
Cranberry and apple jelly   382
  sauce   97
Crayfish   61, 137
  potted   138
Cream   397, 400
  biscuits   331
  buns   349
  cheese   402
  horns   349
  salad dressing   244
  slices   349
Creamed butter   400
  rice   279
Creams   287-91
Crême brûlée   253
  de Riz   280
  Vichyssoise   84
Crêpes suzette   256
Cress vinegar   109
Croissants   308
Croûtes of herring roes   355
Crumpets   310
Cucumber   65
  cream soup   84
  pickled   393
  salad   239
  stuffed, salads   243
  vinegar   109
  with sauce   220
Cucumbers, stuffed   220
Culinary hints   37-9
  terms   41-7
Cup custard   251
Currant pudding   267
Curry butter   401
  sauce   96
Custard, baked   251

flan 343
pie 253
sauce 107
Custard soufflé 261
steamed 251
tartlets 349
Custards for ice cream 302

Dabs 120
Dairy produce 397-410
Damson jam 378
Dandelion leaves, stewed 221
Danish salad 239
Dark coarse-cut marmalade 384
Date and walnut cake 317
and walnut loaf 311
roly poly pudding 268
Demi-glace sauce 102
Dessert 305
Devil sauce 96
Devilled butter 401
crab 60
"Devils on horseback" 355
Devonshire cream 400
Diet 14-15
Dogfish 120
Doughnuts 309
without yeast 317
Duck and red cabbage 374
braised with chestnuts 198
en casserole 199
hashed 199
roast 199
roast with orange 199
salmi of 200
stewed (whole) 200
Duckling, stuffed 200
Dundee cake 320
Dutch flummery 283
salad 239
stew 163

Eccles cakes 350
Eclairs 350
Eels, fried 120
jellied 121
stewed 121
Egg à la Dijon 65
fritters—Milanaise style 405
mornay 406
mousse 409
plant, see Aubergine
salad 240
sauce 92
soup 77
Eggs 403-8
à la Dreux 406
boiled 404
curried 405
scrambled 405
in aspic 406

poached 407
poached with spinach 407
scrambled 408
eggs and ham 408
separated 408
to pickle 404
to preserve 403
Electric cookers 18-19
Endive, braised 221
English omelet 410
salad 240
Escallops 138
baked 138
in shells 138
Escaveeke sauce 109
Escoffier sauce 105
Espagnole sauce 101
Essences 69
Evaporated milk dressing 244
Eve's pudding 275
Exeter pudding 275
stew 157

Faggot of herbs 68
Faggots 178
Fawn chaudfroid sauce 97
Feijoa salad 416
Fig pudding 268
Fines herbes omelette 410
Finger pudding 268
Finnan haddocks 123
First brown stock 69
Fish 113-43
à la Tasmania 415
cakes 369
chowder 81
forcemeat 111
mousse 409
pudding 135
salad 240
sauce 92
soup 82
soused 64
stock 70
to buy 113
to fillet 114
to skin 114
Five-fruit marmalade 384
Flake 121
Flaky pastry 339
Flans 342-4
Flavourings 47-8
Flemish salad 239
Floating islands 295
Flounders 121
fried 121
Foie gras as hors d'oeuvre 61
Foie gras croûtes 356
Fondant icing 333
Food values 13
Forcemeats 110-12

Forest pudding 253
Fowl, boiled 200
  curried 201
  fried with peas 374
  galantine of 201
  hashed 374
  ragôut of 201
  roast—stuffed 201
  stewed with rice 202
Frangipane tart 343
French bean, see Bean, French
  carrot salad 240
  crust pastry 339
  dressing 245
  omelette 409
French onion soup 89
  pancakes 256
  salads 240
  shapes 308
Fricassée of eggs 406
  of fish 136
Fritters 257–60
Frothy sauce 107
Fruit and yoghourt sauce 107
  bottling 387–91
  cake 319
  cream 289
  flan 343
  fool 296
  (fresh) salad 296
  in jelly 286
  mould 281, 293
  pudding with suet crust 268
  sauces 96–7, 105, 107–8
  scones 312
  sponge 276
  stewed 297
  tartlets 350
  turnovers 350
Frying 33
Fumets 69

Game purée 76
  purée with chestnuts 76
  salad 241
  sauce 102
  soup 78
  stock 70
Garfish, stewed 121
Garnishes 39–41
Gas cookers 19–20
Geneva pudding 247
Genoese pastry 326
Gherkins, pickled 393
Giblet gravy 98
  pie 202
  soup 78
  stuffing 111
Giblets, stewed 202
Ginger buns 316
Ginger cake 319

cream 288
pudding 269
sauce 108
snaps 331
Gingerbread 318–19
Girdle scones 312
Glacé icing 333
Gnocchi au gratin 366
Golden buck 356
Golden mousse praline 282
  pudding 269
Goose, roast 202
  roast green 203
Gooseberry charlotte 290
  chutney 394
  fritters 259
  jam 378
  jelly 382
  pudding 346
  sauce 97
  tart 347
Gosling, roast 203
Goulash or beef 157
  soup 89
Grape salad 241
Grapefruit 61
  baskets 61
  marmalade 384
  spiced 61
Gravy 97–8
  soup 78
Grayling, baked 122
  fried 122
Green butter 401
  chaudfroid sauce 97
  pea soup 85
  tomato chutney 395
Greengage jam 379
Grilling 33
Grisini bread 308
Ground rice cake 319
Gudgeon 122
Guinea fowl, roast 203
Gumbo soup 85
Gurnard 122
Gurnet, baked 122

Haddock, baked and orange 123
  soup 82
Haddocks, smoked 123
Haggis 171
Hake steaks, baked 123
Halibut, baked 123
  boiled 123
  Bristol 123
Ham 174
  and egg pie 361
  and tongue soufflé 361
  baked 176
  boiled 176
  creamed, on toast 361

croquettes   372
loaf, baked   176
mousse   362
potted   188
rolls   356
salad with pineapple   241
stuffing   111
Hare   205-7
en casserole   206
grilled   205
jugged   206
roast   206
soup   78
stock   70
to skin   205
to truss   205
Haricot bean, see Bean, haricot
Hasty pudding   249
Helford angels   356
Herb vinegar   109
Herbs   49
Herring-roe tit-bits   356
rolls   61
Herrings, baked stuffed fresh   124
red   124
soused   124
Hollandaise sauce   98, 101
Hollandaise soup   88
Honey pudding   249
Honeycomb mould   283
Hors d'oeuvres   60-6
Horseradish cream   98
sauce   92
vinegar   109
Hot cross buns   309
pot   152
water crust pastry   341
Hotch potch   71
Household stock   69
Hunter's soup   78
Hygiene   12

Iced coconut cake   321
coffee   305
drinks   305
sandwich cake   324
Ices   300-4
refrigerator   303
Indian corn   219
Irish Rabbit or Rarebit   356
stew   168
Italian pudding   253
salad   241
sauce   102

Jam-making   376-7
omelet   263
roll, baked   273
sauce   108
tart   344

tartlets   351
turnovers   350
Jap cakes   329
Jellies   282-7
Jelly-making   380-1
to clear   284
Jenny Lind pudding   253
John Dory   124
Junket   297

Kebabs   163
Kebobs   362
Kedgeree   369
Kidney and bacon croûtes   171
hot pot   158
omelette   410
purée   77
stewed   159
Kidneys, devilled   170
sautéd   171, 363
Kippers—grilled   361
jugged   362
Kitchen   16-30
equipment   24-7
Kohl-Rabi   221

Lamb   162-6
blanquette of   162
chops and spaghetti   163
cutlets, cold   187
cutlets—Malmaison style   164
fricassée of   163
leg of—French style   164
Navarin of   165
nest of minced   371
noisettes of   165
Shashlik   164
stewed   165
Lancashire hot pot   168
Large grain puddings   247-8
grain puddings—with eggs   247
Leek soup   85
Leeks, boiled   221
Lemon buns   316
cake   319
cakes   326
cheesecakes   351
curd   379
curd jelly   283
ice cream   303
jelly   285
jelly marmalade   385
marmalade   384
meringue flan   344
pudding   269, 276
sauce   92, 108
Lemon sherbet (sorbet)   301
water ice   301
whip   287
Lentil soup   87
Lentils, boiled

Lettuce salad   241
    stewed   222
Leveret, roast   207
Lima beans   222
Ling, baked   125
    fried   125
Liver à la Provençale   171
    and bacon   171
    farce   111
    hot pot   159
    pâté   61
    purée   77
    roast   160
    savoury   159
    stuffed   165
Lobster   138
    baked   139
    butter   401
    cocktail   62
    coquilles of   139
    creamed   62
    croquettes   362
    devilled   140
    mayonnaise   140
    mornay   140
    salad   241
    thermidor   140
    to prepare   139
London buns   316
Luxemburg buns   310

Macaroni and tomatoes   366
    au gratin   366
    pudding   248
Macaroons   331
Mackerel, baked   125
    boiled, with parsley sauce   125
    grilled with gooseberry sauce   126
Madeira cake   319
Madeira pudding   254
    sauce   102
Madeleines   326
Maids of honour   351
Maître d'Hôtel butter   401
    sauce   93
Maize   219
Malt bread   311
Margarine   397
Marmalade-making   383
    pudding   254, 269
    sauce   108
Marrow toast   160
Marshmallow ice cream   303
Mayonnaise   104, 245
Measures   50–3
M   144–89
                                       369
                  uddings   248
                                       126
                                       304

Melon   62
    and lemon jam   379
    Cantaloup au marasquin   62
Melted butter sauce   93
Menu suggestions   11
Meringue gâteau   298
Meringues   329
Meunière butter   401
Milanaise soufflé   291
Milk   397
    bread   307
    jelly (invalid)   283
    puddings   246–77
    punch   305
    soup with onion   88
Mince pies   351
Minced collops   153
Mincemeat   337
Minestrone   89
Mint jelly   382
    sauce   99
    sauce, bottled   109
    vinegar   109
Mixed pickle   392
Mocha cake   321
    filling   337
    fingers   327
Mock cream   337
Moist gingerbread   318
Mornay sauce   101
Moules marinières   141
Mousseline sauce   99
Mousses   408–9
Mullet, fried à la meunière   126
    grey   126
    red, grilled   126
Mulligatawny soup   79
Mushroom cream soup   85
    omelette   410
    patties   357
    sauce   93, 94, 102
Mushrooms, baked   222
    grilled   222
    preserved, with brown sauce   222
    stewed   223
    stewed with wine   222
Mussels   141
Mustard butter   401
    sauce   93
Mutton   166–72
    and potato pie   371
    breast of, boiled   166
    broth   72
    casserole of   167
    cutlets, braised   167
    cutlets, chaudfroid of   187
    grilled   167
    haricot   167
    knuckle of, boiled   166
    leg of, braised   166
    loin of, stuffed and roast   169

pies—Cumberland style 168
  pudding 169
  réchauffé of 372
  scrag of 169
  shoulder of, stuffed and roast 169

Nettle soup 86
Nettles 223
Noisette butter 401
Noisettes à la jardinière 165
Noodle paste 367
Norfolk dumplings 277
Nouille 367
Nut and raisin bread 311
  buns 317
  cakes 326
  scones 312
Nutrition 11–15

Oatcakes 331, 332
Oatmeal pastry 339
Oeufs à la poêle 406
  en cocotte 406
  frits 407
  sur le plat 407
Offals 144–6
Oil cooker 22
Okra, boiled 223
  soup 85
Okras, canned 223
Olive sauce 102
Olives 65
  à la Madras 66
Omelets, savoury 409–10
  sweet 262–3
Omelette soufflé en surprise 303
Onion omelette 410
  sauce 93, 94
  soup 86
Onions, baked 223
  boiled 224
  fried 224
  pickled 393
  stewed 224
  stuffed 224
  stuffed, in batter 364
Open tarts 342–4
Orange cake 321
  (clear shred) marmalade 383
  cream 289–90
Orange curd 379
  custard 293
  jelly 284
  jelly marmalade 385
  pudding 346
  salad 242
  sandwich cake 324
  sauce 102, 108
  soufflé 261, 292
  whip 287
Oven chart 54

Ox Tail, grilled 160
  soup 79
  stewed 160
Ox Tongue, potted 186
  savoury rolled 187
Oyster fritters 142
  sauce 93
  tit-bits 357
Oysters 62, 141
  à la marinière 142
  devilled 142
  on toast 357

Pacific prawns 62
Pancakes 256
Paprika sauce 103
Parkin biscuits 331
Parsley, fried 225
  sauce 93
Parsnips—conservatively
  cooked 225
  mashed 225
Passion fruit flummery 417
Pasta 366–8
Pastry base cakes 348–52
  cases 357
  -making 338–42
Pâté de foie gras 415
  sucrée 339
Paua roe patties 415
Pavlova cake 417
Pea soup 88
Peach condé 279
  jam 377
Peach Melba 304
  upside-down cake 417
Pear and chocolate trifle 294
  delice 304
Pears filled with nut and
  date salad 242
Peas, bottled, to dress 226
  canned, to dress 226
  dried 226
  green 225
Pease pudding 226
Pectin stock 379
Pepper sauce 103
Peppers, fried 226
Perch, boiled 126
Petits fours 332
Piccalilli 392
Pickles 392–6
Pies 346–8
Pig's cheek 177
  feet, stuffed 177
  fry 177
  head, boiled 177
Pike, baked 127
  stewed 127
Pikelets 310
Pilchards 127

Pineapple cream   290
    custard   293
    ham slices   177
    sherbet (sorbet)   301
    soufflé   262
    water ice   301
    whip   287
Piperade Basque   407
Piquant sauce   94
Pistachio cream   288
Plaice baked, stuffed   127
    fillets of, with lemon dressing   127
    fried   128
    mornay   128
Plum and apple jam   380
    chutney   395
    jam   379
Plum pudding   269
Poaching   32
Poivrade sauce   103
Polish soup   88
Pork   173-9
    braised—country style   174
    cheese   362
    chops   174
    croquettes   372
    cutlets   174
    galantine of   188
    hash   373
    minced   372
    pickled, boiled   174
    pie   175
    savoury loin of   175
    savoury tenderloin of   175
Port wine jelly   284
    wine sauce   99
Porterhouse steak   154
Pot-au-feu   72
Potato balls   229
    chips   229
    crisps   230
    croquettes   229
    pastry   340
    pasty   362
    puffs   230
    salad   242
    scones   312
    straws   229
Potatoes, Anna   227
    baked and stuffed   227
    baked in fat   229
    baked in their jackets   227
    boiled   227
    Duchess   228
    fried   229-30
    Lyonnaise   229
    mashed   228
    new—boiled   228
    Parisian   229
    sauté   230
    tossed   230

Poultry   190-204
    to bone   192
    to choose   190-1
    to pluck   191
    to truss   191-2
Pound pudding   270
Powdered grain moulds   281-2
    grain puddings   249
    grain puddings—with
        eggs   250
Prawn cocktail   63
Prawns   63, 142-3
    curried   142
    potted   143
Preparation terms   35-7
Preserves   376-86
Pressure cookery   23, 411
Princess cakes   329
Puddings   263-76
    using pastry   344-6
Puff pastry   340
Pumpkin, fried   230
    pie   231
Purées   76-7, 83-8

Queen cakes   326
    of puddings   254
Queen's pudding   254
Quick breads   310

Rabbit, curried   207
    en casserole   207
    pie   207
    ragoût of   207
    stock   70
Radishes   66, 231
Raised pie crust   341
Raisin pudding   276
Raspberry buns   317
    jam   380
    jelly   382
    vinegar   109
    water ice   301
Ratafia biscuits   332
Ravigote sauce   103
Ravioli   367
Réchauffés   369-75
Red cabbage, see Cabbage, red
    tomato chutney   395
Redcurrant and raspberry tart   347
    jelly   382
    sauce   97
Réform sauce   103
Refrigerators   23-4
Rémoulade sauce   105
Rice   367
    curried   367
    mould   278
    pudding   247, 248, 249
    stuffing   111
Rich cake   319

cakes (small) 325–7
  short crust pastry 341
Risotto 368
Roasting 32–3
Rock buns 317
  salmon 128
Rockfish 128
Roes on toast 363
Rollmop herrings 65
Roly poly pudding 270
Rough puff pastry 341
Royal icing 335
Rum and walnut filling 337
  butter 402
  cream 289
  omelet 263
Runner bean, see Bean,
  runner
Russian beetroot soup 88
  salad 243

Sabayon sauce 108
Sage and onion sauce 95
  and onion stuffing 111
Sago pudding 247, 248
St. Honoré trifle 294
Saithe 128
Salad dressings 244–5
Salads 237–44
Salads to serve in an hors
  d'œuvre 66
Salmi sauce 103
Salmon, baked 128
  boiled 128
  boiled in Court Bouillon 129
  cutlets en papillotes 129
  devilled smoked 129
  mousse 129
  potted 129
Salmon trout 130
  poached 130
Salsify (Salsafy) boiled 231
Salt cod and parsnips 120
  sticks 308
Sand cake 322
Sandwich buns 307
  cakes 323–5
Sardine patties 357
Sauces 91–110, 392–6
  for ice cream 304
Sauerkraut soup 86
Sausage croquettes 363
  rolls 363
  stuffing 111
Sausages—to boil 178
  to fry 178
  to make 178
Sautéing 34
Savarin 277
Savouries 353–9
Savoury butters 401

"ducks" 178
egg patties 358
macaroni 364
omelets 409–10
pancakes 364
sandwich loaf 364
vinegars 108–9
Savoy, see Cabbage
  fingers 327
  pudding 255
Scallops 138
Scampi 63
  fried 63
Scones 311–3
"Scotch" broth 72
  collops 155
  eggs 407
  woodcock 358
Scots broth 72
  kail brose 73
Scottish oatcakes 332
Sea Bream, baked 116
  baked, stuffed 116
Sea-food chowder 136
Sea pie 157
Seakale, boiled 231
Seed buns 317
  cake 319
Semolina mould 279
  pudding 248
Seville orange marmalade 385
Shad, baked 130
Shallots, pickled 395
Sharp sauce 99
Sheep's head 169
  head broth 73
  heart 170
  tongues, braised 172
Shellfish 136–43
  and tomato soup 82
  omelette 410
  patties 358
Shepherd's pie 370
Sherbets 301
Sherry butter 402
Short crust pastry 341
Shortbread (Scottish) 330
Shrewsbury biscuits 332
Shrimp moulds 64
  sauce 93
Shrimps 143
  potted 63, 143
Simnel cake 322
Skate, au beurre noir 130
  boiled 130
Small grain moulds 279
  grain puddings 248
Small grain puddings—with
  eggs 249
Smelts, baked 131
  fried 131

Smoked salmon	63	pudding	270
trout	64	Sultana cake	317
Snowdon pudding	270	Summer pudding	298
Sole	131	salad	240
au gratin	132	Sundaes, ice-cream	303–4
baked fillets of, with		Supper dishes	360–5
forcemeat	131	Suprême sauce	104
fillets of, aux fines herbes	131	Swede turnips	233
fillets of bonne femme	131	Swedish salad	244
fillets of meunière	132	Sweet butters	401–2
fried	132	corn	219
Solid fuel cookers	20–2	melted butter sauce	108
Sorbets	301	omelet	263
Sorrel purée	232	pastry for tartlets	342
Soubise sauce	101	potatoes	232
Soufflé fritters	260	potatoes, baked	232
Soufflés, cold	391–2	scones	312
hot	260–2	wine sauce	108
Soups	67–90	Sweetbreads, braised	184
Sour cherry soup	90	fried	166, 185
-sweet sauce	99	Sweets, cold	278–305
Soyer sauce	93	hot	246–77
Spaghetti	368	Swiss cream	282
pudding	248	eggs	358
Spanish omelette	410	pudding	276
Spice cake	318	Swiss roll	328
Spiced pineapple upside-		Syrup (for water ices)	301
down cake	417	sponge pudding	271
Spices	47–8		
Spinach, boiled	232		
soup	86	Table wines	413–4
Sponge cakes	327	Tangerine marmalade	386
drops	327	Tapioca cream	280
gâteau	299	cream pudding	248
Sprats	132	pudding	247–9
fried	133	Tarragon vinegar	109, 392
Spring Greens, see Cabbage		Tartare sauce	101, 105
Steak pudding	155	Tartlets	348–52
rolled	155	Tarts	346–8
stewed	156	Tea	413
see also Beefsteak		cakes	310
Steamed gingerbread	319	scones	313
Steamed, see subject, e.g.		Tench, baked	133
Fish, Chicken, etc.		Toad in the hole	365
Steaming	32	Tomato aspic	41
Stewing	32	chaudfroid sauce	97
Stock, recipes for	69–70	in salads	244
Store sauces	108–10	juice cocktail	358
cupboard	28–9	ketchup	395
Strawberry basket	304	mayonnaise	105
fritters	260	salad	244
ice cream	302	sauce	100, 395
jam	380	soup	86, 87
layer gâteau	304	stuffed, salad	243
shortcake	330	stuffing	112
soufflé	262	Tomatoes, baked	233
water ice	301	devilled	233
Stuffings	110–12	stuffed	233
Sturgeon, baked	133	Tongue, boiled	160
cutlets	133	Tournedos of beef à la	
Suet crust pastry	342	Béchamel	156

Transparent icing 334
  pastry 342
  pudding 271
Treacle layer pudding 271
  scones 312
  tart 344
Trifle 293–5
Tripe and onions 161
Trout, baked stuffed 133
Truites à la meunière 134
Truites au bleu 134
Turbot 134
  à la Dugléré 134
  poached 134
Turkey, blanquette of 374
  boiled 203
  fricassée of 204
  hashed 375
  legs, devilled 203
  roast 204
  roast, with chestnuts 204
  soup 79
Turnip greens 234
Turnips 233
  conservatively cooked 234
Tutti frutti ice cream 304

Ugli cocktail 358

Vanilla cream 289
  ice cream 303–4
  slices 352
  soufflé 262
Veal 179–85
  and ham patties 365
  and ham pie 189
  breast of, stewed 182
  cake 189
  curried 179
  cutlets 182
  escallops of—Viennese style 180
  fillets of 180
  fladgeon of 181
  knuckle of, stewed 182
  larded and roast 181
  loaf 373
  minced with macaroni 373
  mould 189
  neck of, braised 179
  olives 183
  Parisian 183
  patties 373
  pork and egg pie, raised 189
  pot pie of 181
  pressed 188
  ragoût of 181
  stuffing 112
Vegetable marrow 234–5
  marrow—conservatively
    cooked 235

marrow, stuffed 234
mixed, salad 242
oyster 231
purée 83
stock 70
Vegetables 209–36
  mixed—conservatively
    cooked 235
  mixed, for garnish 235
  to cook 209
Velouté sauce 103
Velvet cream 288
  soup 88
Vermicelli pudding 248
Victoria buns 317
  sandwich 324
Vinaigrette sauce 245
Vinegar, savoury 108–10
  spiced 392

Waffles 310
Walnut layer cake 322
  sauce 95
Walnuts, pickled 394
Washing up 29–30
Washington pudding 271
Water ices 301
  souchet 136
Wedding cake 323
Weights 50–3
Welsh cheesecakes 352
  rarebit 358
West Riding pudding 346
Whipped jellies 286–7
White bread 307
  chaudfroid sauce 96
  sauce 91
  stock 69
  wine sauce 94
Whitebait 135
Whiting 135
  baked 135
  baked aux fines herbes 135
  fried 135
Whole grain moulds 278
Wholemeal bread 306
  nut scones 312
Wine and food 414
  jelly 286
Witch 135
Worcester sauce 110

Yams 235
  baked 235
  boiled 235
Yeast breads 306–8
  buns 308–10
  mixtures 276–7
Yorkshire pudding 257
  rarebit 3

A SELECTION OF POPULAR PAN NON-FICTION

Harrison E. Salisbury
THE 900 DAYS: The Siege of Leningrad   95p
David Reuben, M.D.
EVERYTHING YOU ALWAYS WANTED TO
KNOW ABOUT SEX but were afraid to ask   45p
Peter F. Drucker
THE AGE OF DISCONTINUITY   60p
Norman Mailer
A FIRE ON THE MOON   40p
Leonard Mosley
ON BORROWED TIME (illus.)   65p
Robert K. Massie
NICHOLAS AND ALEXANDRA (illus.)   50p
C. Hamilton Ellis
THE TRAINS WE LOVED (illus. double format)   50p
edited by Bruce Campbell
THE COUNTRYMAN WILD LIFE BOOK (illus.)   30p
Andrew Duncan
THE REALITY OF MONARCHY   40p
Graham Hill
LIFE AT THE LIMIT (illus.)   35p
Ken Welsh
HITCH-HIKER'S GUIDE TO EUROPE (illus.)   35p
Miss Read
MISS READ'S COUNTRY COOKING   30p
Gavin Maxwell
RAVEN SEEK THY BROTHER (illus.)   30p